SUPERGIRL

VOLUME 1 THE GIRL OF STEEL

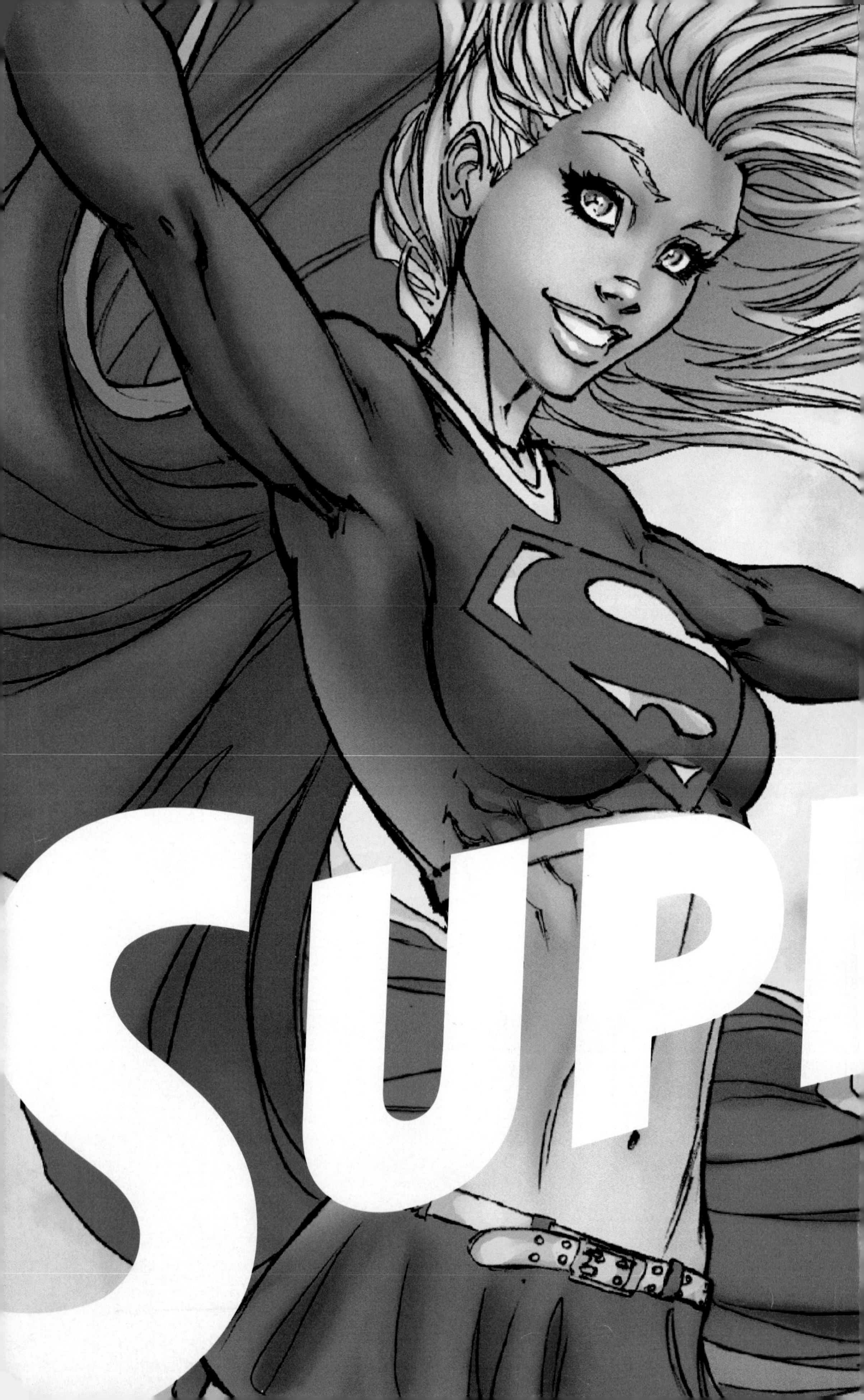
SUP

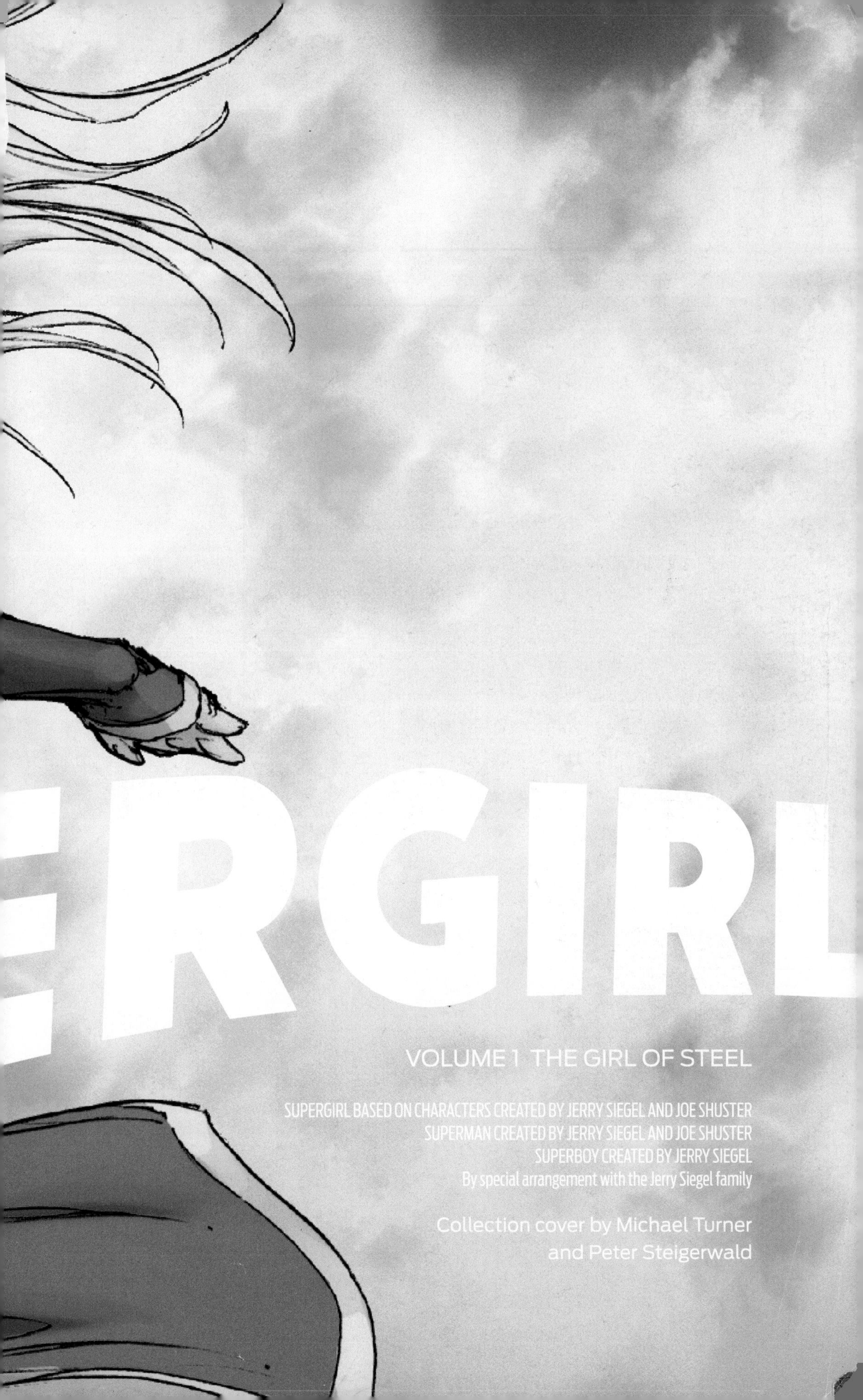
ERGIRL

VOLUME 1 THE GIRL OF STEEL

SUPERGIRL BASED ON CHARACTERS CREATED BY JERRY SIEGEL AND JOE SHUSTER
SUPERMAN CREATED BY JERRY SIEGEL AND JOE SHUSTER
SUPERBOY CREATED BY JERRY SIEGEL
By special arrangement with the Jerry Siegel family

Collection cover by Michael Turner
and Peter Steigerwald

Eddie Berganza Editor – Original Series
Jeanine Schaefer
Tom Palmer, Jr. Associate Editors – Original Series
Jeb Woodard Group Editor – Collected Editions
Robin Wildman Editor – Collected Edition
Steve Cook Design Director – Books
Louis Prandi Publication Design

Bob Harras Senior VP – Editor-in-Chief, DC Comics

Diane Nelson President
Dan DiDio and Jim Lee Co-Publishers
Geoff Johns Chief Creative Officer
Amit Desai Senior VP – Marketing & Global Franchise Management
Nairi Gardiner Senior VP – Finance
Sam Ades VP – Digital Marketing
Bobbie Chase VP – Talent Development
Mark Chiarello Senior VP – Art, Design & Collected Editions
John Cunningham VP – Content Strategy
Anne DePies VP – Strategy Planning & Reporting
Don Falletti VP – Manufacturing Operations
Lawrence Ganem VP – Editorial Administration & Talent Relations
Alison Gill Senior VP – Manufacturing & Operations
Hank Kanalz Senior VP – Editorial Strategy & Administration
Jay Kogan VP – Legal Affairs
Derek Maddalena Senior VP – Sales & Business Development
Jack Mahan VP – Business Affairs
Dan Miron VP – Sales Planning & Trade Development
Nick Napolitano VP – Manufacturing Administration
Carol Roeder VP – Marketing
Eddie Scannell VP – Mass Account & Digital Sales
Courtney Simmons Senior VP – Publicity & Communications
Jim (Ski) Sokolowski VP – Comic Book Specialty & Newsstand Sales
Sandy Yi Senior VP – Global Franchise Management

SUPERGIRL VOL. 1: THE GIRL OF STEEL

DC Comics, 2900 West Alameda Avenue, Burbank, CA 91505
Printed by RR Donnelley, Owensville, MO, USA, 12/18/15. First Printing.
ISBN: 978-1-4012-6093-4

Library of Congress Cataloging-in-Publication Data is Available.

PEFC Certified

Printed on paper from
sustainably managed
forests and controlled
sources

PEFC
PEFC/29-31-75   www.pefc.org

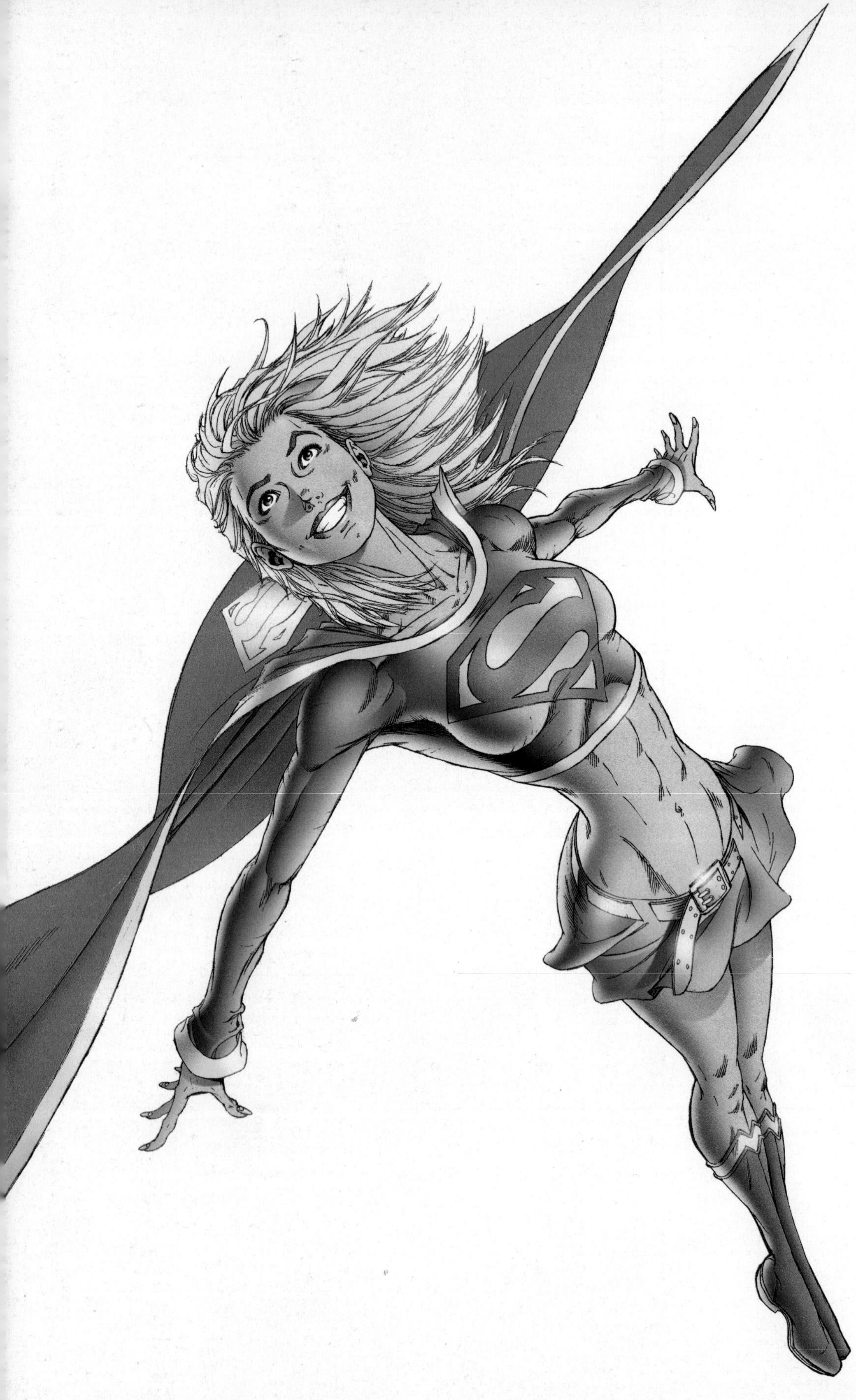

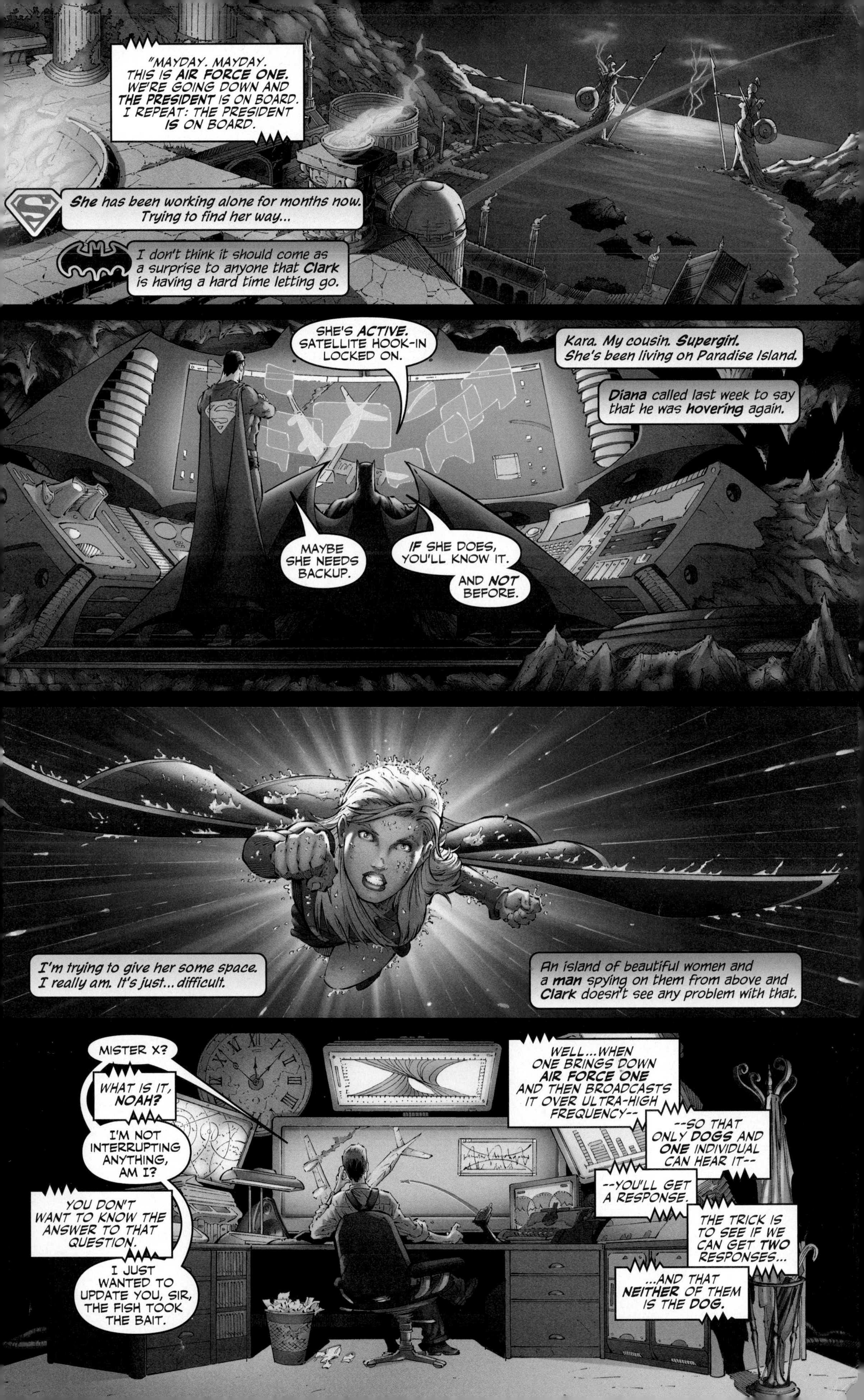
"MAYDAY. MAYDAY. THIS IS AIR FORCE ONE. WE'RE GOING DOWN AND THE PRESIDENT IS ON BOARD. I REPEAT: THE PRESIDENT IS ON BOARD.
She has been working alone for months now. Trying to find her way...
I don't think it should come as a surprise to anyone that Clark is having a hard time letting go.
SHE'S ACTIVE. SATELLITE HOOK-IN LOCKED ON.
Kara. My cousin. Supergirl. She's been living on Paradise Island.
Diana called last week to say that he was hovering again.
MAYBE SHE NEEDS BACKUP.
IF SHE DOES, YOU'LL KNOW IT.
AND NOT BEFORE.
I'm trying to give her some space. I really am. It's just... difficult.
An island of beautiful women and a man spying on them from above and Clark doesn't see any problem with that.
MISTER X?
WHAT IS IT, NOAH?
I'M NOT INTERRUPTING ANYTHING, AM I?
YOU DON'T WANT TO KNOW THE ANSWER TO THAT QUESTION.
I JUST WANTED TO UPDATE YOU, SIR, THE FISH TOOK THE BAIT.
WELL...WHEN ONE BRINGS DOWN AIR FORCE ONE AND THEN BROADCASTS IT OVER ULTRA-HIGH FREQUENCY--
--SO THAT ONLY DOGS AND ONE INDIVIDUAL CAN HEAR IT--
--YOU'LL GET A RESPONSE.
THE TRICK IS TO SEE IF WE CAN GET TWO RESPONSES...
...AND THAT NEITHER OF THEM IS THE DOG.

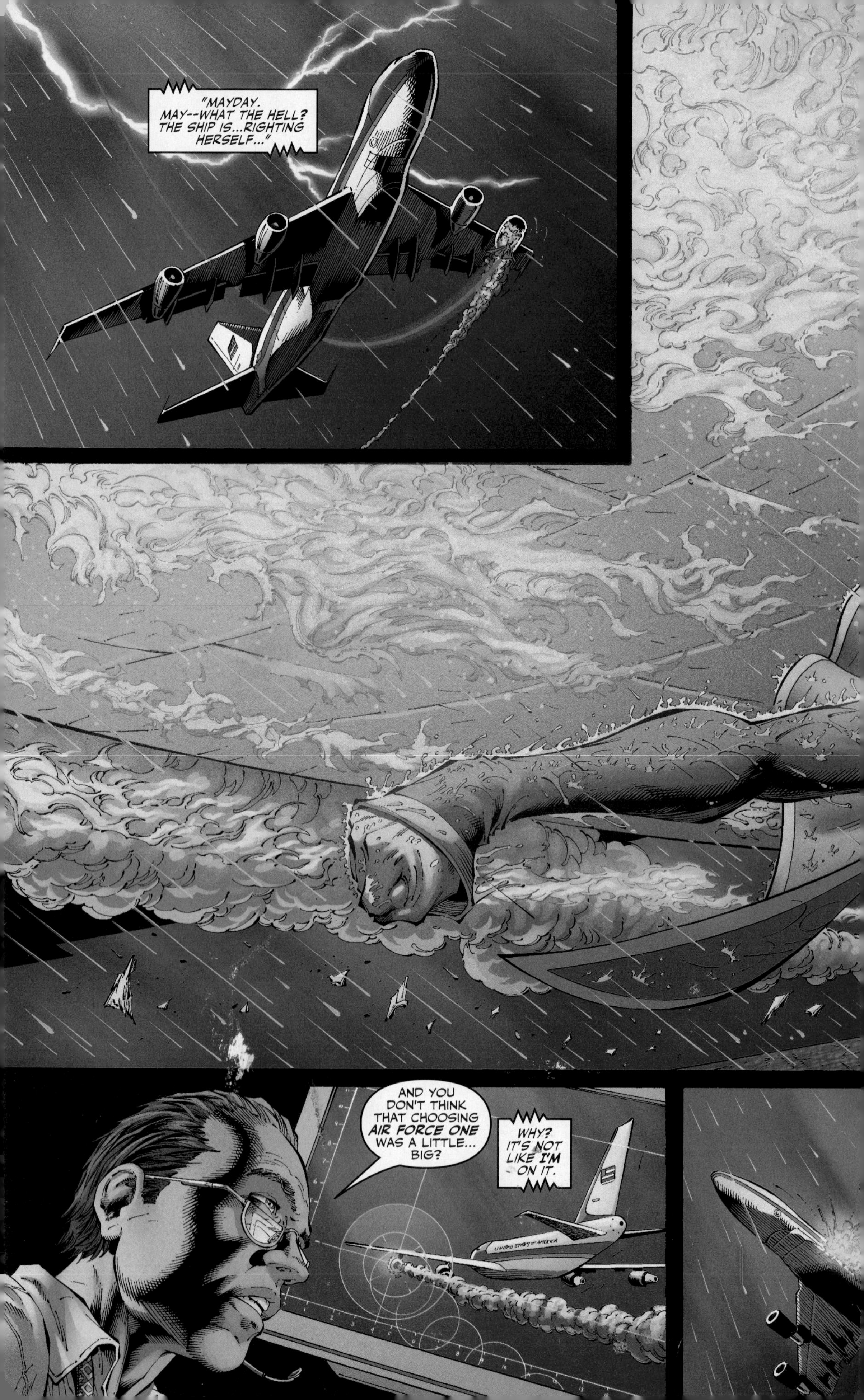
"MAYDAY. MAY--WHAT THE HELL? THE SHIP IS...RIGHTING HERSELF..."
AND YOU DON'T THINK THAT CHOOSING AIR FORCE ONE WAS A LITTLE... BIG?
WHY? IT'S NOT LIKE I'M ON IT.

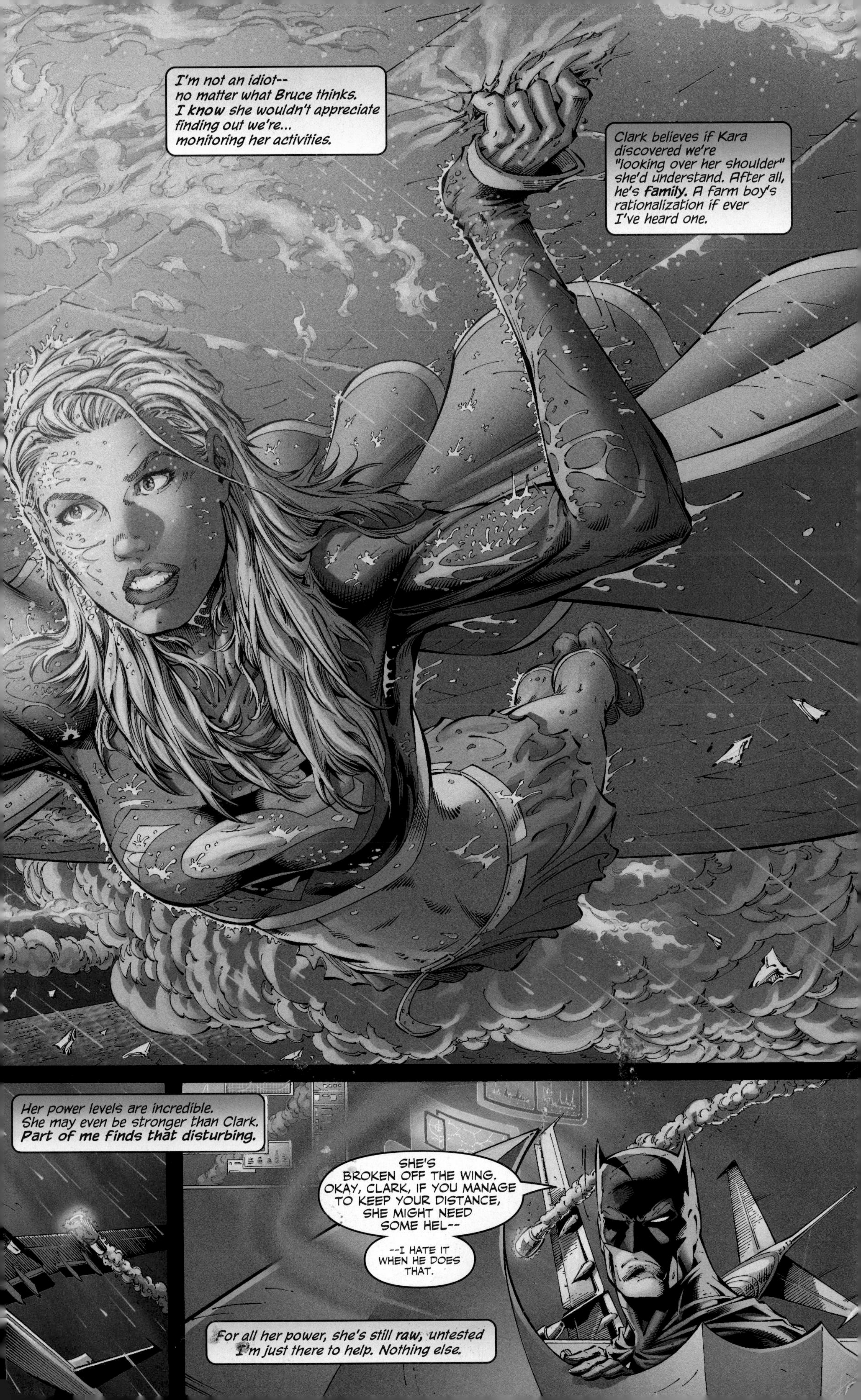
I'm not an idiot-- no matter what Bruce thinks. I know she wouldn't appreciate finding out we're... monitoring her activities.
Clark believes if Kara discovered we're "looking over her shoulder" she'd understand. After all, he's family. A farm boy's rationalization if ever I've heard one.
Her power levels are incredible. She may even be stronger than Clark. Part of me finds that disturbing.
SHE'S BROKEN OFF THE WING. OKAY, CLARK, IF YOU MANAGE TO KEEP YOUR DISTANCE, SHE MIGHT NEED SOME HEL--
--I HATE IT WHEN HE DOES THAT.
For all her power, she's still raw, untested I'm just there to help. Nothing else.

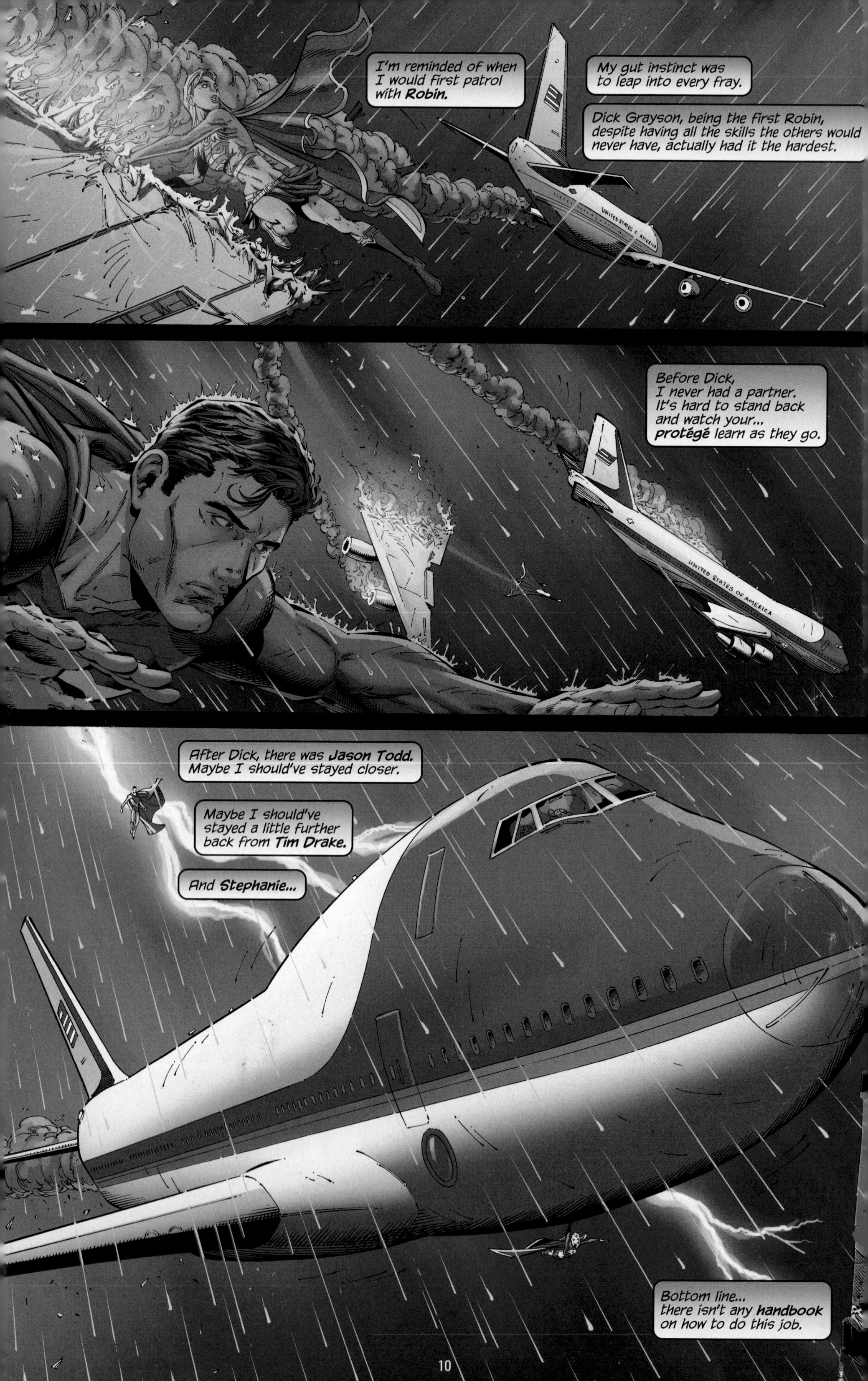

I'm reminded of when I would first patrol with Robin.
My gut instinct was to leap into every fray.
Dick Grayson, being the first Robin, despite having all the skills the others would never have, actually had it the hardest.
Before Dick, I never had a partner. It's hard to stand back and watch your... protégé learn as they go.
After Dick, there was Jason Todd. Maybe I should've stayed closer.
Maybe I should've stayed a little further back from Tim Drake.
And Stephanie...
Bottom line... there isn't any handbook on how to do this job.

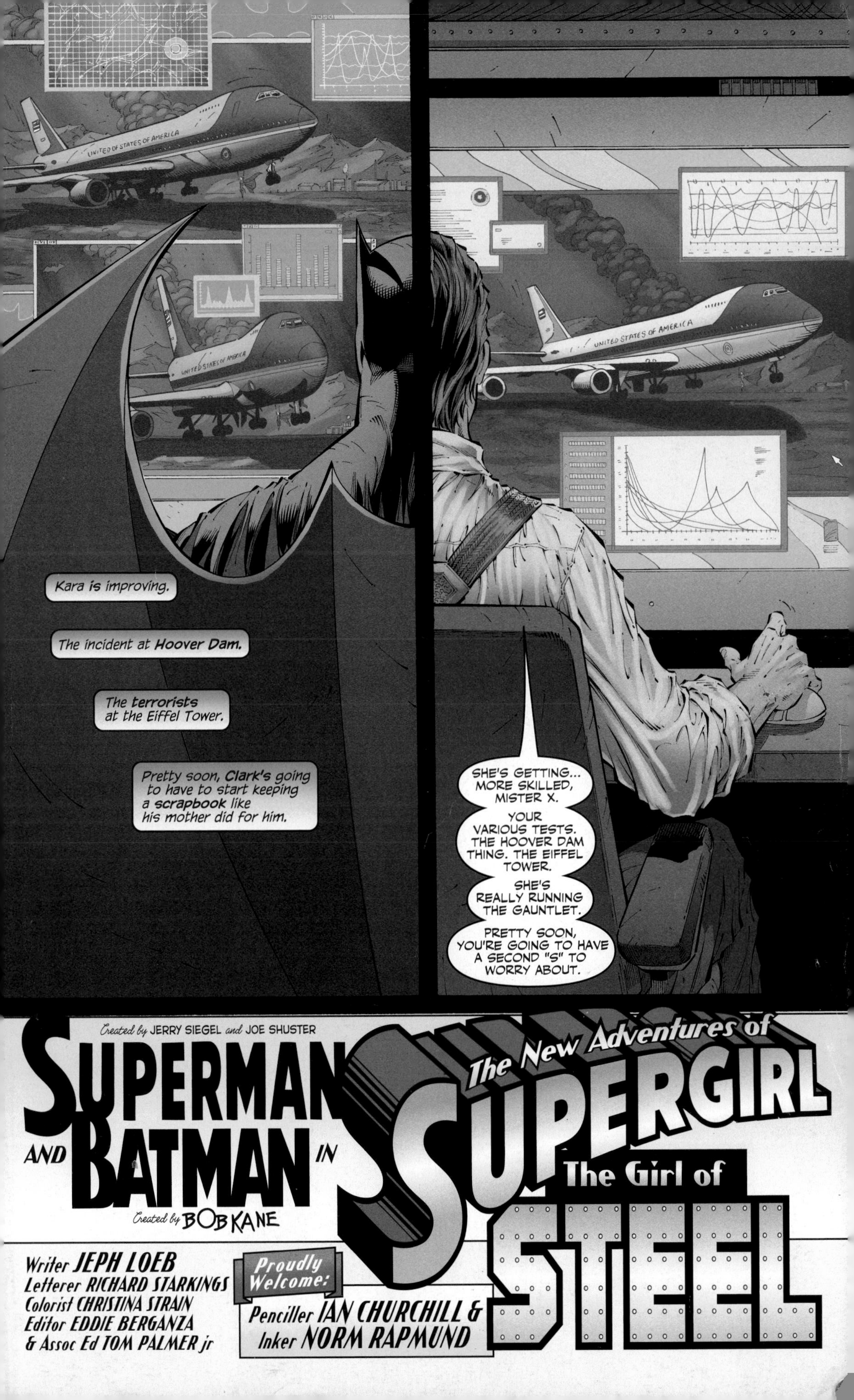

UNITED STATES OF AMERICA
Kara is improving.
The incident at Hoover Dam.
The terrorists at the Eiffel Tower.
Pretty soon, Clark's going to have to start keeping a scrapbook like his mother did for him.
SHE'S GETTING... MORE SKILLED, MISTER X.
YOUR VARIOUS TESTS. THE HOOVER DAM THING. THE EIFFEL TOWER.
SHE'S REALLY RUNNING THE GAUNTLET.
PRETTY SOON, YOU'RE GOING TO HAVE A SECOND "S" TO WORRY ABOUT.
Created by JERRY SIEGEL and JOE SHUSTER
SUPERMAN AND BATMAN Created by BOB KANE IN
The New Adventures of SUPERGIRL
The Girl of STEEL
Writer JEPH LOEB
Letterer RICHARD STARKINGS
Colorist CHRISTINA STRAIN
Editor EDDIE BERGANZA
& Assoc Ed TOM PALMER jr
Proudly Welcome:
Penciller IAN CHURCHILL &
Inker NORM RAPMUND

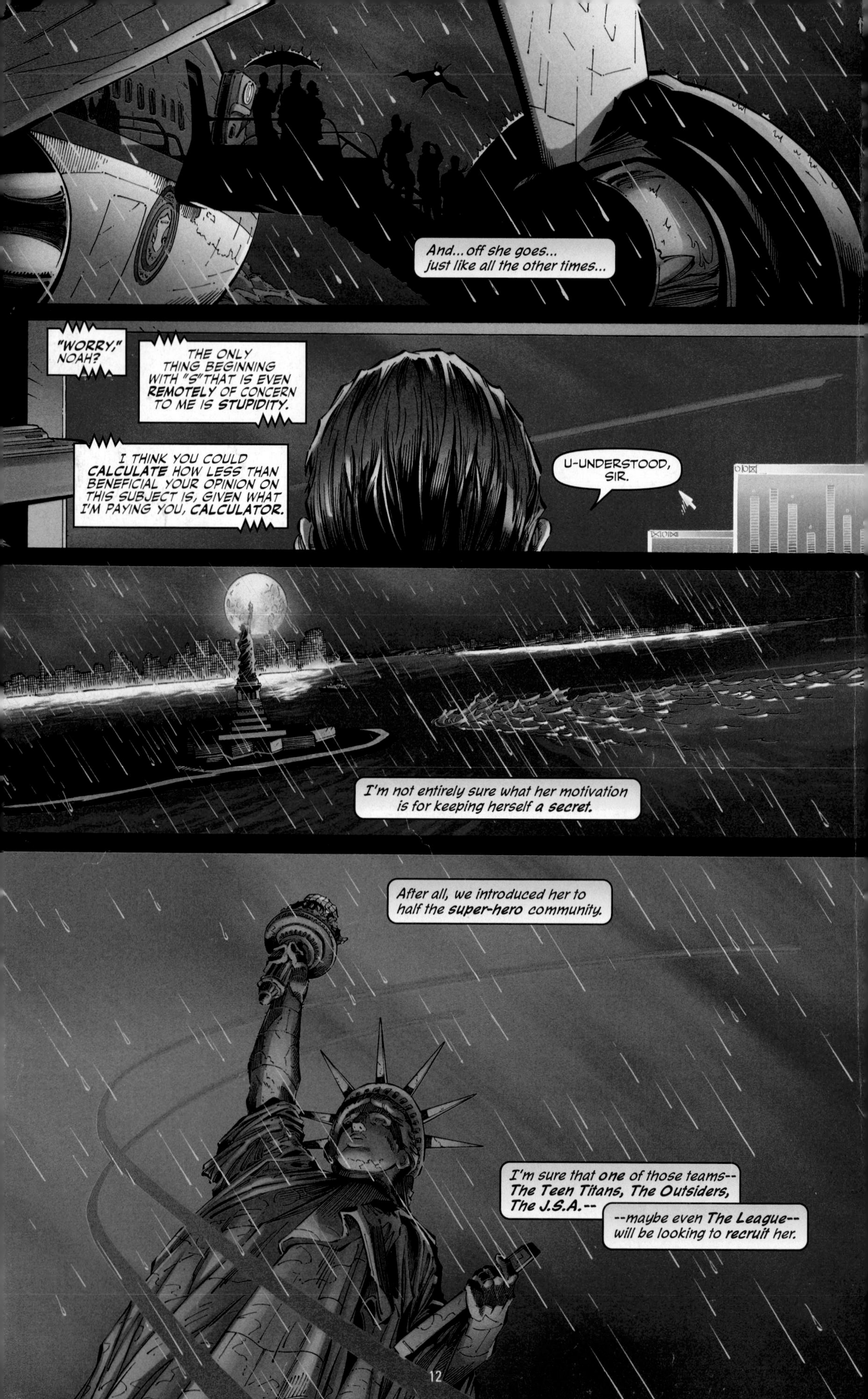
And... off she goes... just like all the other times...
"WORRY," NOAH?
THE ONLY THING BEGINNING WITH "S" THAT IS EVEN REMOTELY OF CONCERN TO ME IS STUPIDITY.
I THINK YOU COULD CALCULATE HOW LESS THAN BENEFICIAL YOUR OPINION ON THIS SUBJECT IS, GIVEN WHAT I'M PAYING YOU, CALCULATOR.
U-UNDERSTOOD, SIR.
I'm not entirely sure what her motivation is for keeping herself a secret.
After all, we introduced her to half the super-hero community.
I'm sure that one of those teams-- The Teen Titans, The Outsiders, The J.S.A.--
--maybe even The League-- will be looking to recruit her.

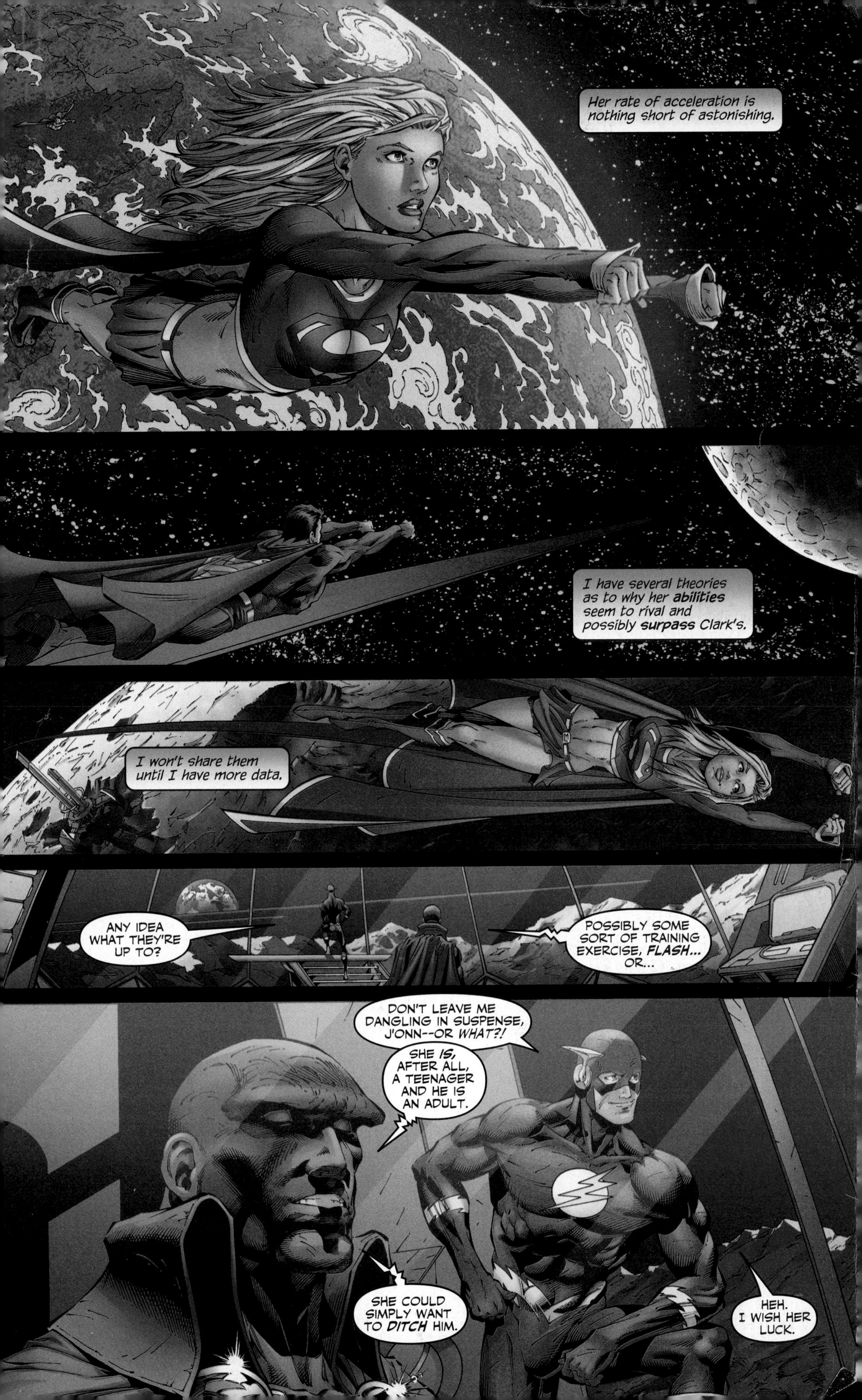
Her rate of acceleration is nothing short of astonishing.
I have several theories as to why her abilities seem to rival and possibly surpass Clark's.
I won't share them until I have more data.
ANY IDEA WHAT THEY'RE UP TO?
POSSIBLY SOME SORT OF TRAINING EXERCISE, FLASH... OR...
DON'T LEAVE ME DANGLING IN SUSPENSE, J'ONN--OR WHAT?!
SHE IS, AFTER ALL, A TEENAGER AND HE IS AN ADULT.
SHE COULD SIMPLY WANT TO DITCH HIM.
HEH. I WISH HER LUCK.

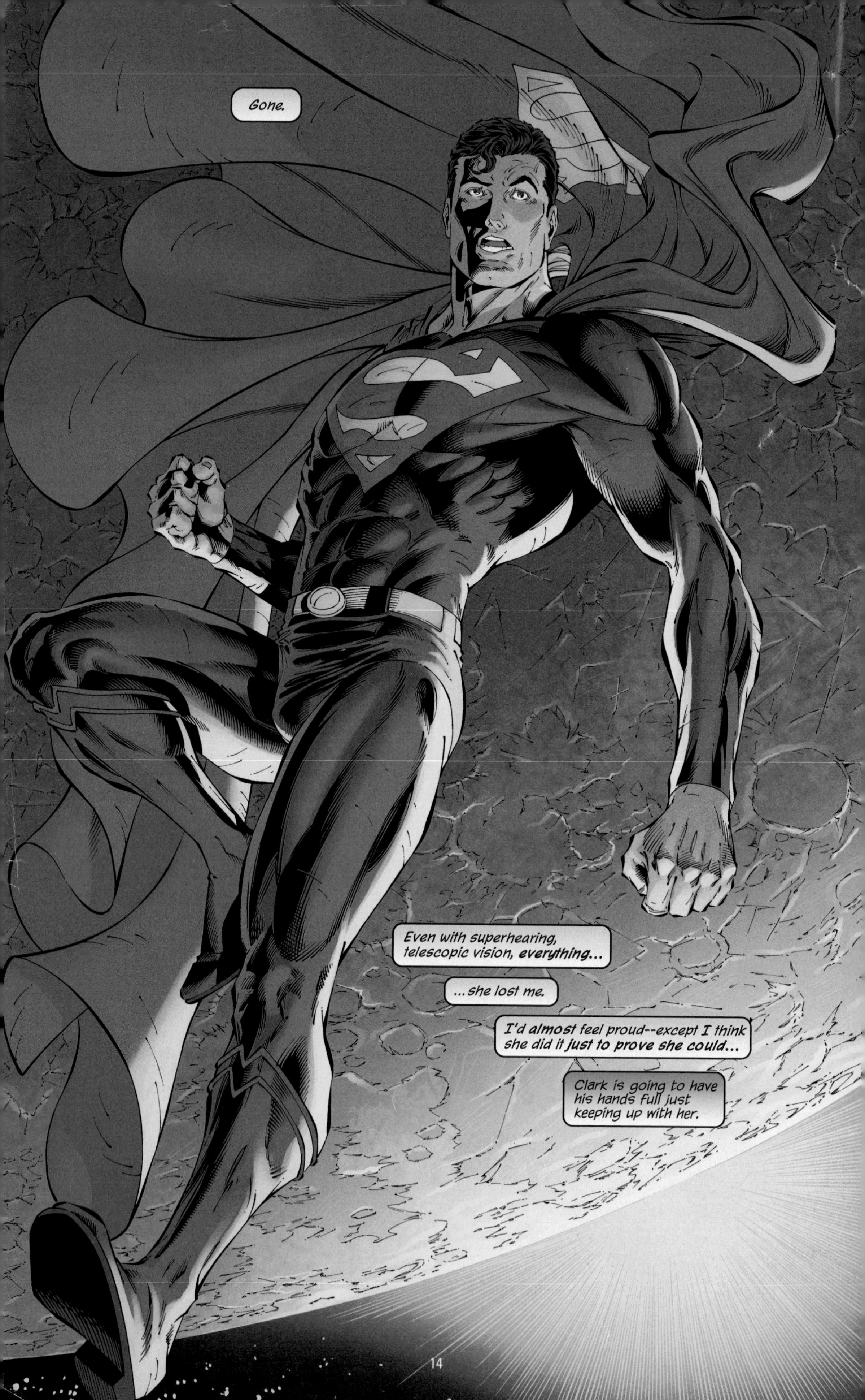
Gone.
Even with superhearing, telescopic vision, everything...
...she lost me.
I'd almost feel proud--except I think she did it just to prove she could...
Clark is going to have his hands full just keeping up with her.

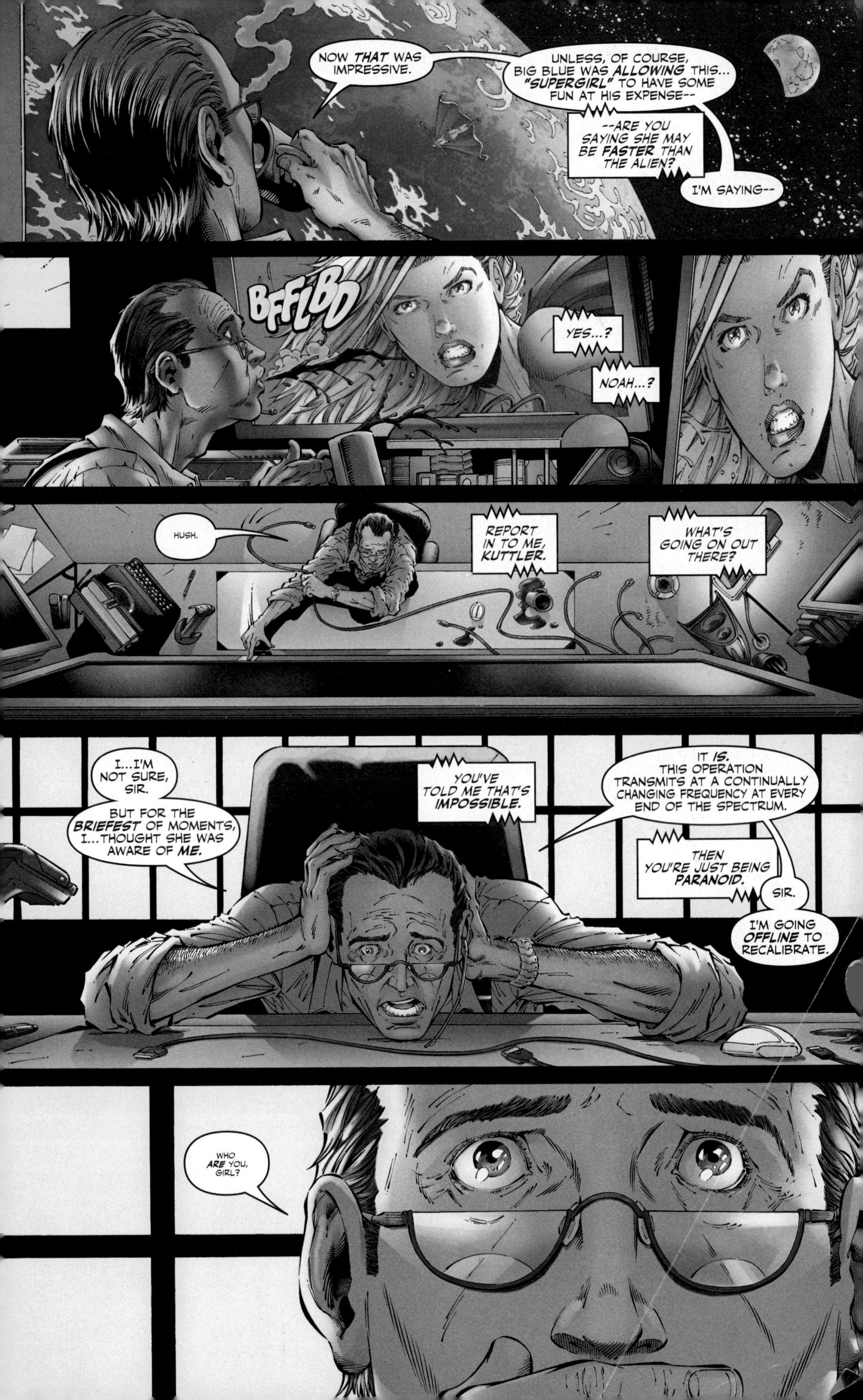
NOW THAT WAS IMPRESSIVE.
UNLESS, OF COURSE, BIG BLUE WAS ALLOWING THIS... "SUPERGIRL" TO HAVE SOME FUN AT HIS EXPENSE--
--ARE YOU SAYING SHE MAY BE FASTER THAN THE ALIEN?
I'M SAYING--
BFFLBD
YES...?
NOAH...?
HUSH.
REPORT IN TO ME, KUTTLER.
WHAT'S GOING ON OUT THERE?
I...I'M NOT SURE, SIR.
BUT FOR THE BRIEFEST OF MOMENTS, I...THOUGHT SHE WAS AWARE OF ME.
YOU'VE TOLD ME THAT'S IMPOSSIBLE.
IT IS. THIS OPERATION TRANSMITS AT A CONTINUALLY CHANGING FREQUENCY AT EVERY END OF THE SPECTRUM.
THEN YOU'RE JUST BEING PARANOID.
SIR.
I'M GOING OFFLINE TO RECALIBRATE.
WHO ARE YOU, GIRL?

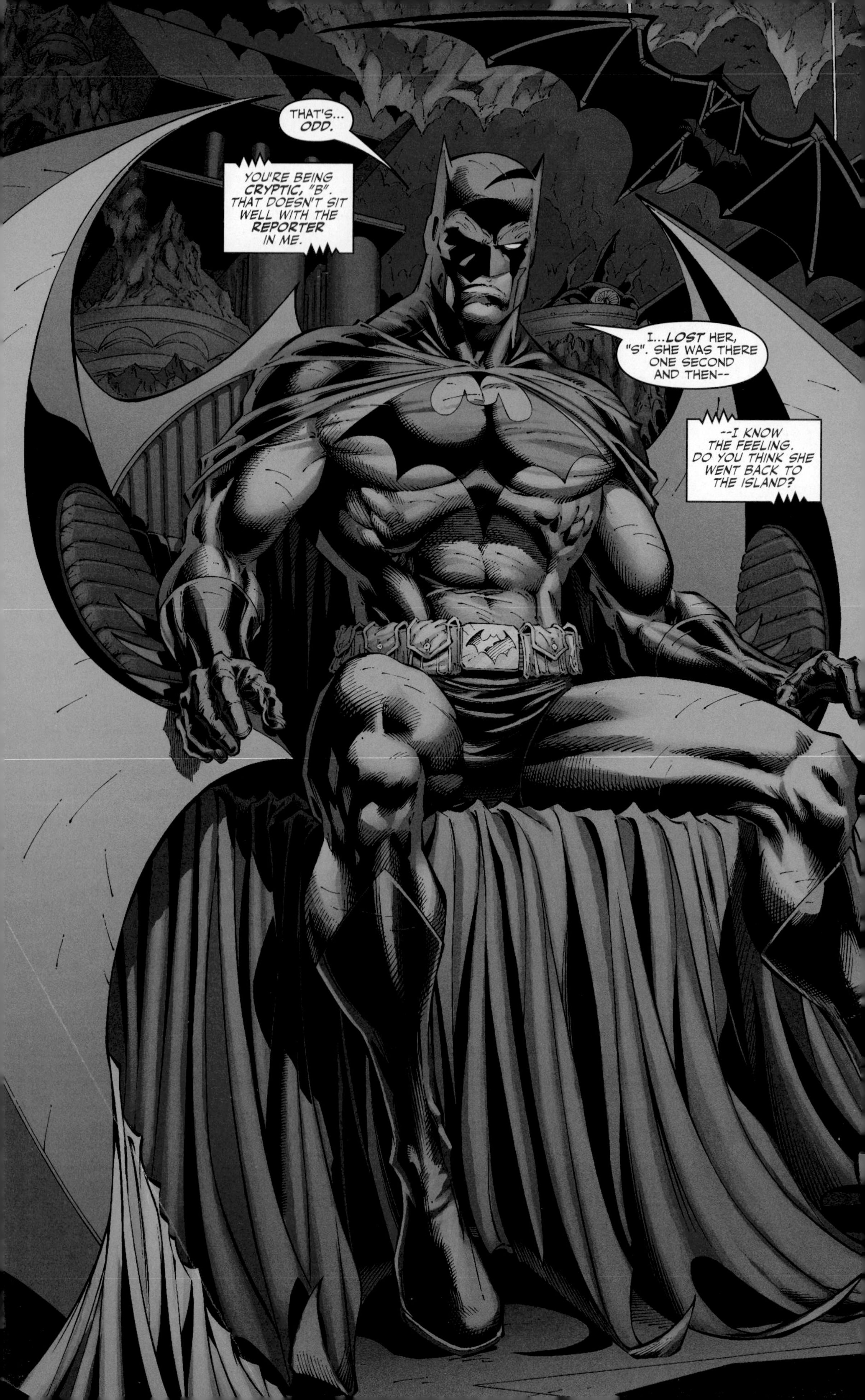
THAT'S... ODD.
YOU'RE BEING CRYPTIC, "B". THAT DOESN'T SIT WELL WITH THE REPORTER IN ME.
I...LOST HER, "S". SHE WAS THERE ONE SECOND AND THEN--
--I KNOW THE FEELING. DO YOU THINK SHE WENT BACK TO THE ISLAND?

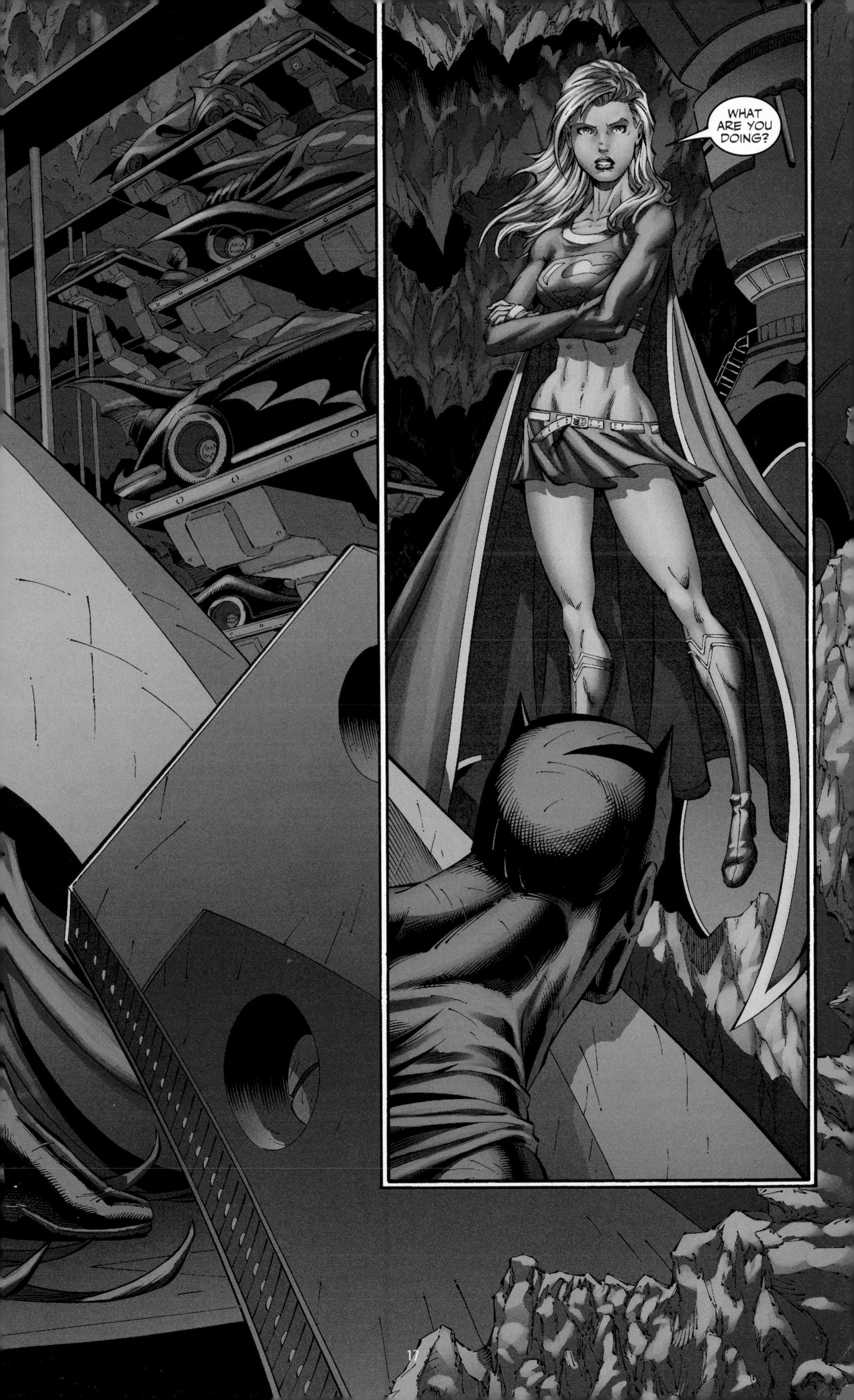
WHAT ARE YOU DOING?

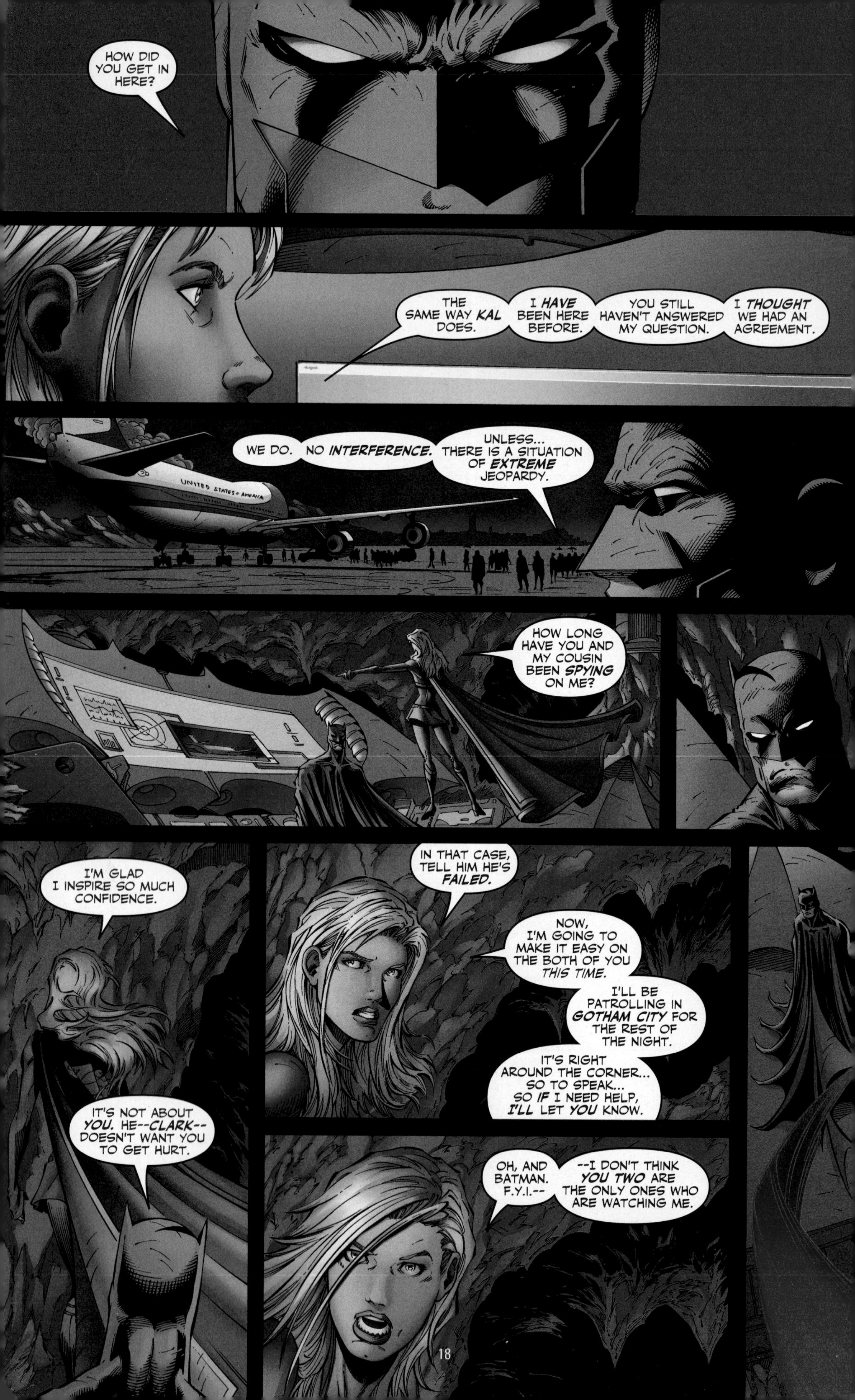
HOW DID YOU GET IN HERE?
THE SAME WAY KAL DOES.
I HAVE BEEN HERE BEFORE.
YOU STILL HAVEN'T ANSWERED MY QUESTION.
I THOUGHT WE HAD AN AGREEMENT.
WE DO.
NO INTERFERENCE.
UNLESS... THERE IS A SITUATION OF EXTREME JEOPARDY.
UNITED STATES OF AMERICA
HOW LONG HAVE YOU AND MY COUSIN BEEN SPYING ON ME?
I'M GLAD I INSPIRE SO MUCH CONFIDENCE.
IT'S NOT ABOUT YOU. HE--CLARK--DOESN'T WANT YOU TO GET HURT.
IN THAT CASE, TELL HIM HE'S FAILED.
NOW, I'M GOING TO MAKE IT EASY ON THE BOTH OF YOU THIS TIME.
I'LL BE PATROLLING IN GOTHAM CITY FOR THE REST OF THE NIGHT.
IT'S RIGHT AROUND THE CORNER... SO TO SPEAK... SO IF I NEED HELP, I'LL LET YOU KNOW.
OH, AND BATMAN. F.Y.I.--
--I DON'T THINK YOU TWO ARE THE ONLY ONES WHO ARE WATCHING ME.

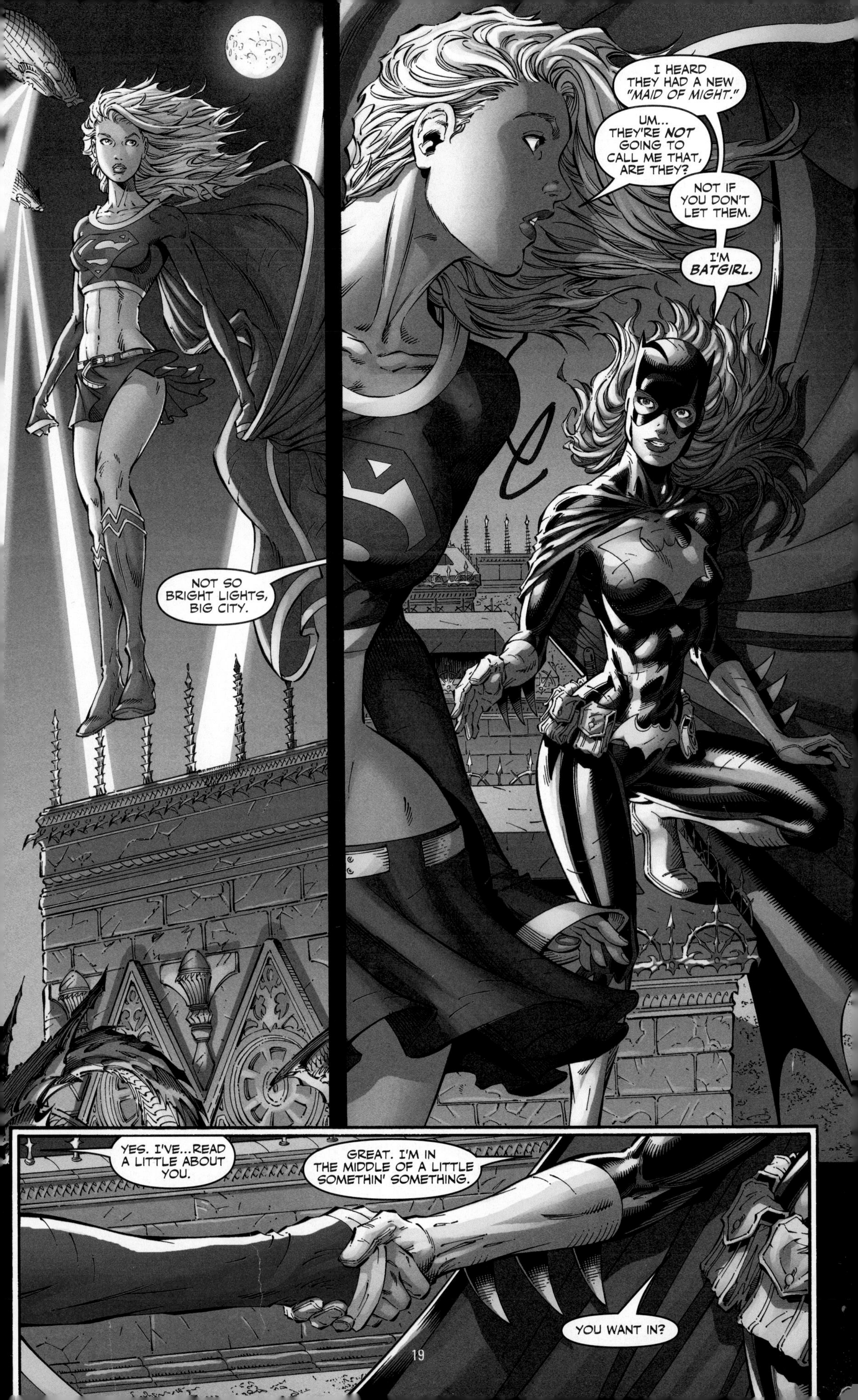
NOT SO BRIGHT LIGHTS, BIG CITY.
I HEARD THEY HAD A NEW "MAID OF MIGHT."
UM... THEY'RE NOT GOING TO CALL ME THAT, ARE THEY?
NOT IF YOU DON'T LET THEM.
I'M BATGIRL.
YES. I'VE...READ A LITTLE ABOUT YOU.
GREAT. I'M IN THE MIDDLE OF A LITTLE SOMETHIN' SOMETHING.
YOU WANT IN?

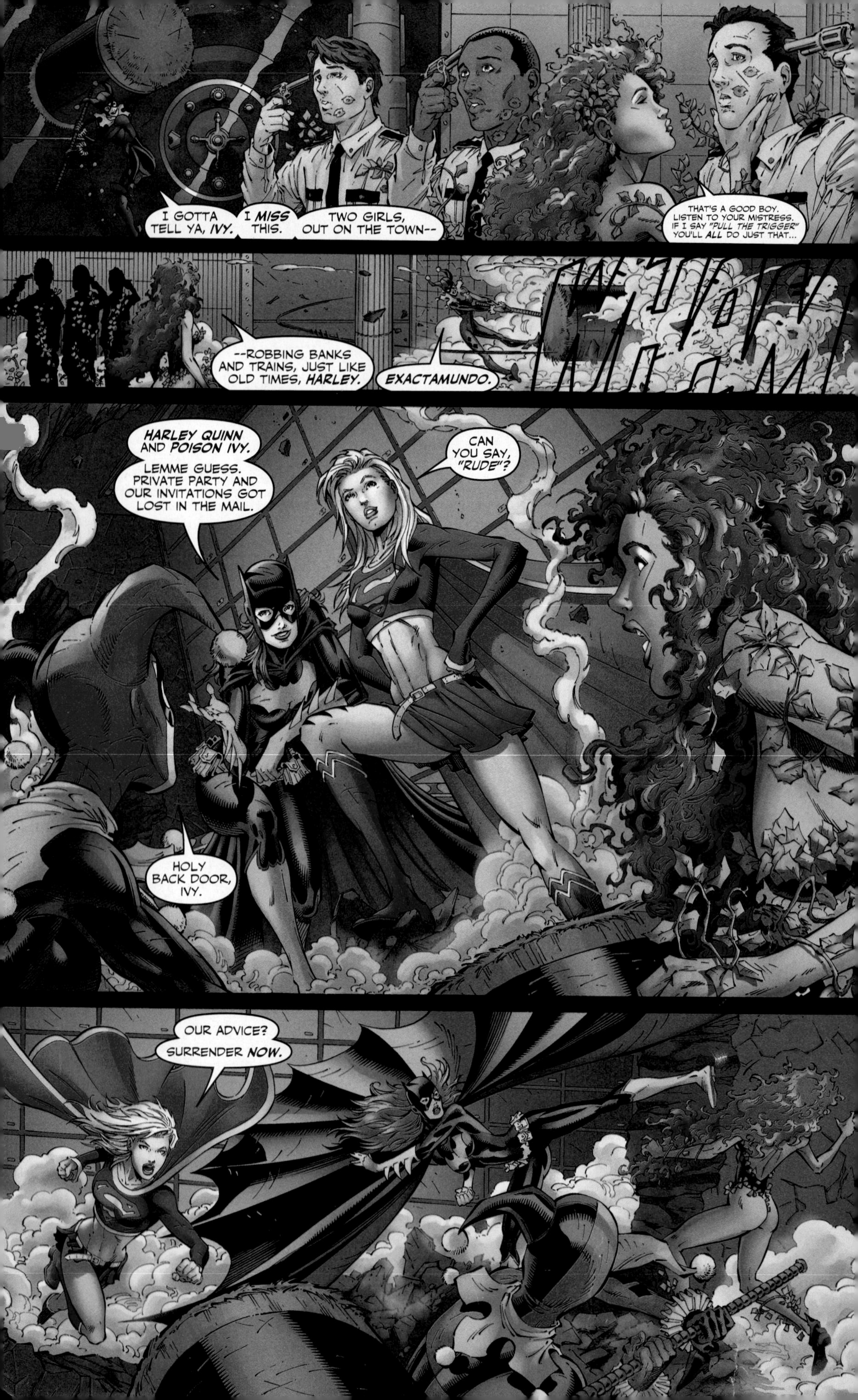
I GOTTA TELL YA, IVY.
I MISS THIS.
TWO GIRLS, OUT ON THE TOWN--
THAT'S A GOOD BOY. LISTEN TO YOUR MISTRESS. IF I SAY "PULL THE TRIGGER" YOU'LL ALL DO JUST THAT...
--ROBBING BANKS AND TRAINS, JUST LIKE OLD TIMES, HARLEY.
EXACTAMUNDO.
HARLEY QUINN AND POISON IVY. LEMME GUESS. PRIVATE PARTY AND OUR INVITATIONS GOT LOST IN THE MAIL.
CAN YOU SAY, "RUDE"?
HOLY BACK DOOR, IVY.
OUR ADVICE? SURRENDER NOW.

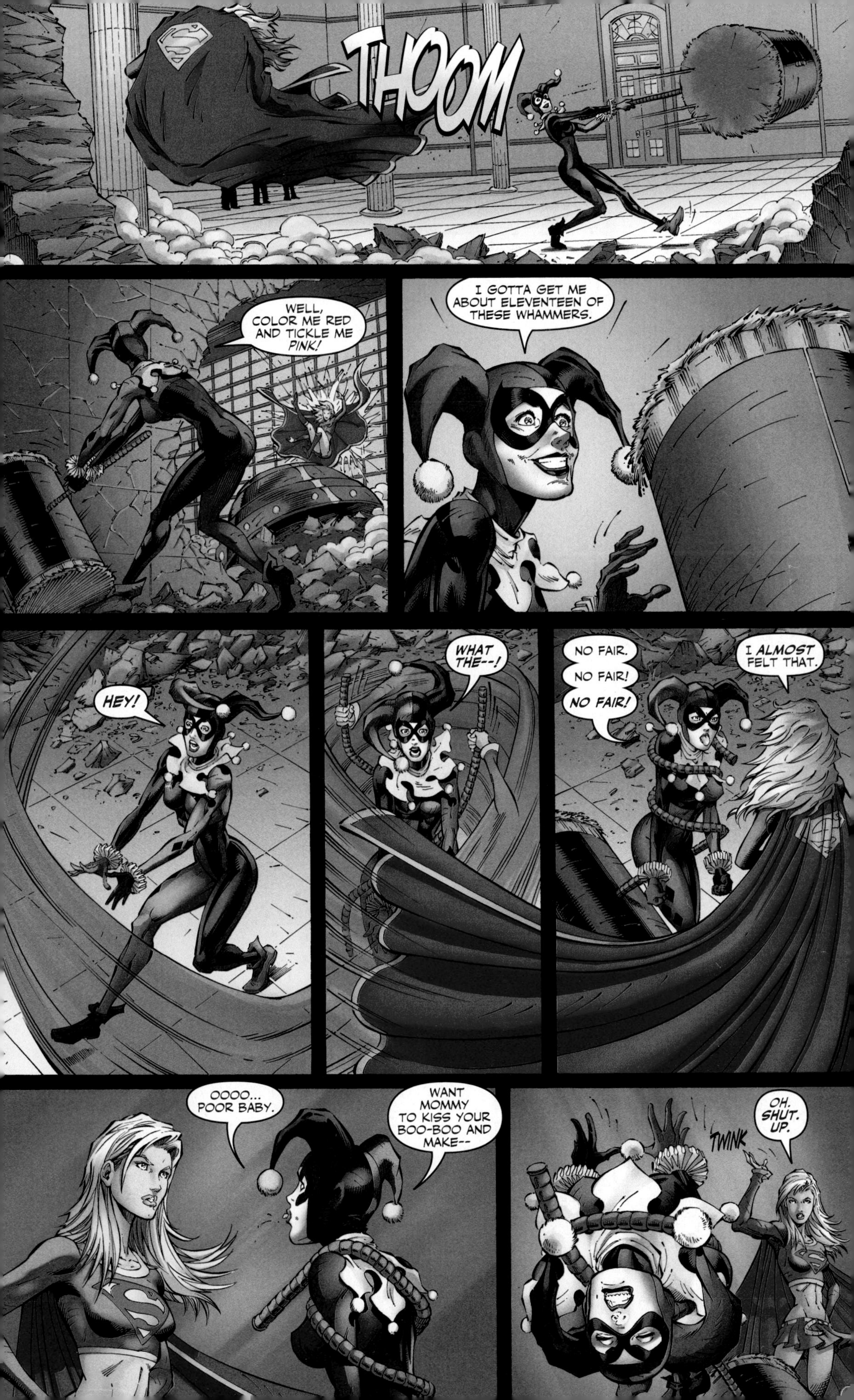
THOOM
WELL, COLOR ME RED AND TICKLE ME PINK!
I GOTTA GET ME ABOUT ELEVENTEEN OF THESE WHAMMERS.
HEY!
WHAT THE--!
NO FAIR.
NO FAIR!
NO FAIR!
I ALMOST FELT THAT.
OOOO... POOR BABY.
WANT MOMMY TO KISS YOUR BOO-BOO AND MAKE--
TWINK
OH. SHUT. UP.

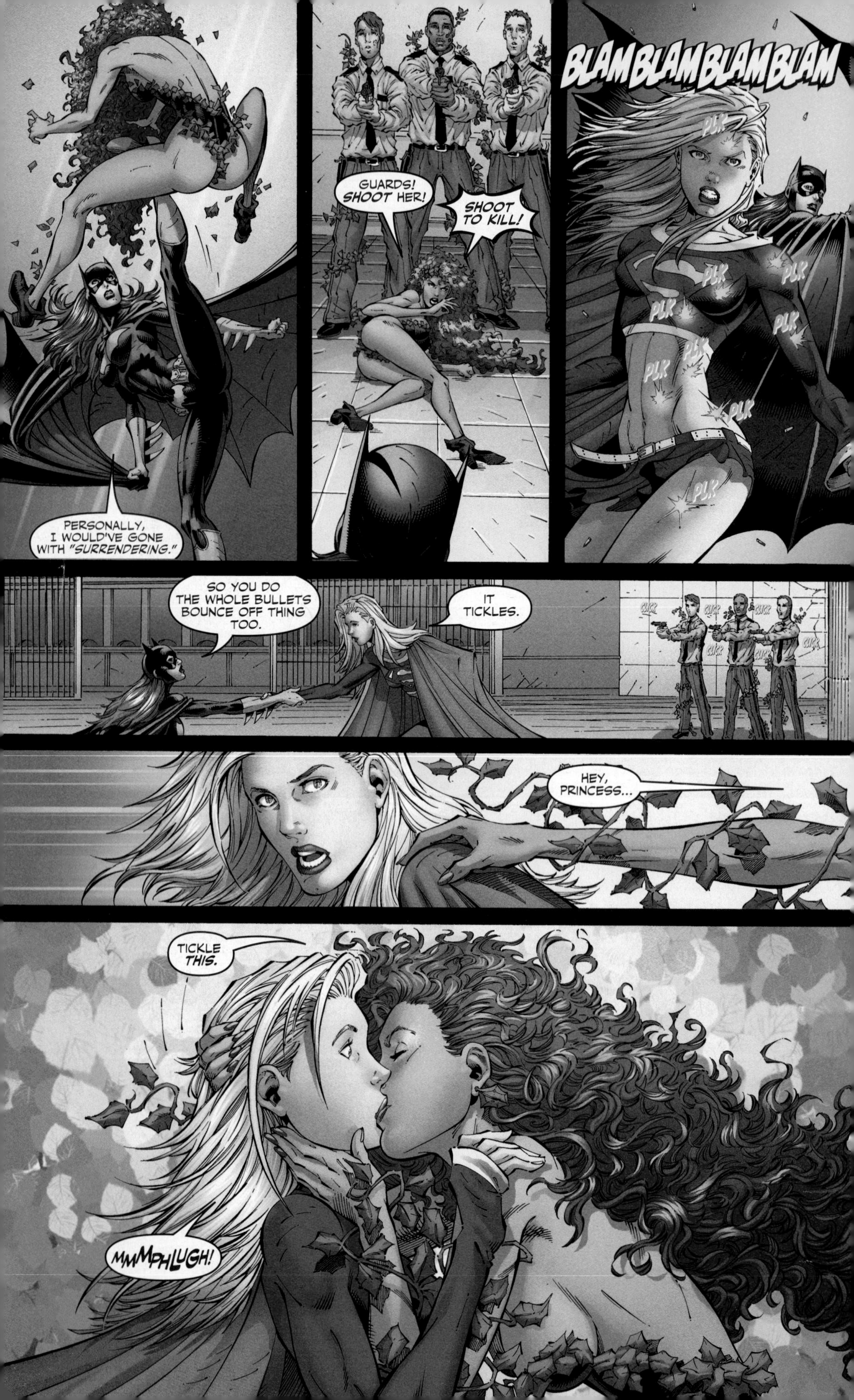
PERSONALLY, I WOULD'VE GONE WITH "SURRENDERING."
GUARDS! SHOOT HER!
SHOOT TO KILL!
BLAMBLAMBLAMBLAM
PLK
PLK
PLK
PLK
PLK
PLK
PLK
PLK
PLK
SO YOU DO THE WHOLE BULLETS BOUNCE OFF THING TOO.
IT TICKLES.
CLICK
CLICK
CLICK
CLICK
CLICK
CLICK
HEY, PRINCESS...
TICKLE THIS.
MMMPHLUGH!

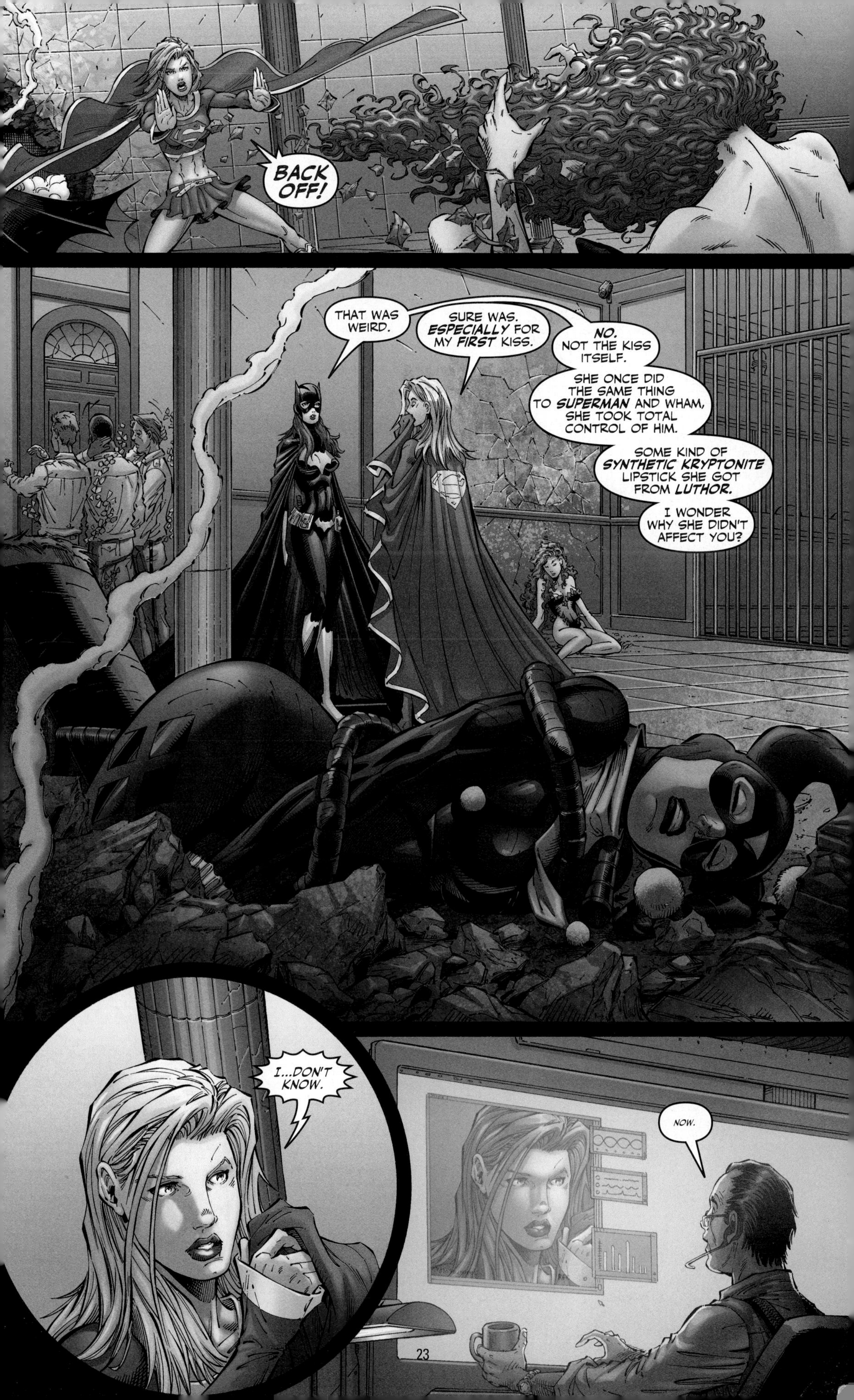

BACK OFF!
THAT WAS WEIRD.
SURE WAS. ESPECIALLY FOR MY FIRST KISS.
NO. NOT THE KISS ITSELF.
SHE ONCE DID THE SAME THING TO SUPERMAN AND WHAM, SHE TOOK TOTAL CONTROL OF HIM.
SOME KIND OF SYNTHETIC KRYPTONITE LIPSTICK SHE GOT FROM LUTHOR.
I WONDER WHY SHE DIDN'T AFFECT YOU?
I...DON'T KNOW.
NOW.

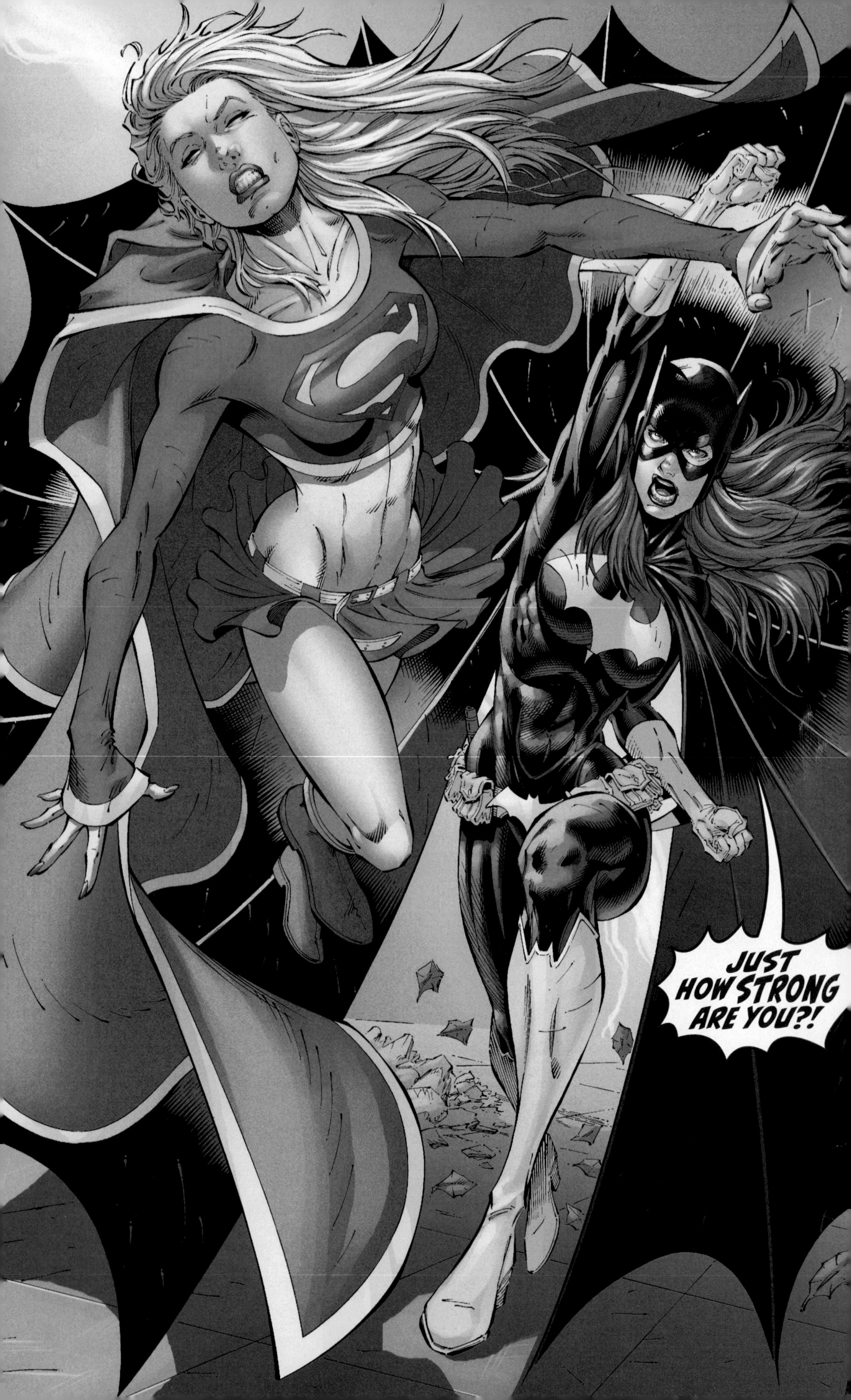
JUST HOW STRONG ARE YOU?!

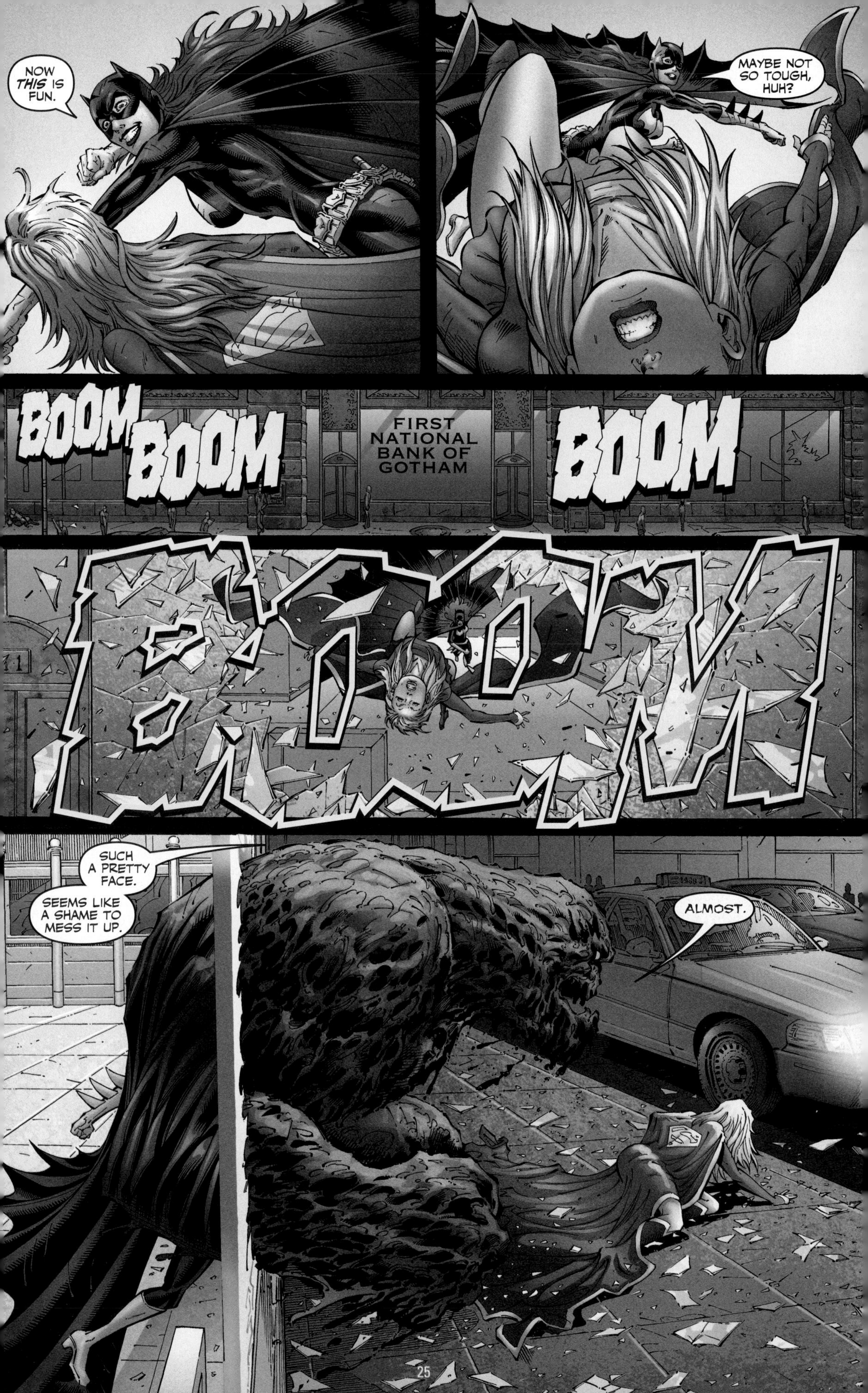
NOW THIS IS FUN.
MAYBE NOT SO TOUGH, HUH?
BOOM BOOM
FIRST NATIONAL BANK OF GOTHAM
BOOM
BOOM
SUCH A PRETTY FACE.
SEEMS LIKE A SHAME TO MESS IT UP.
ALMOST.

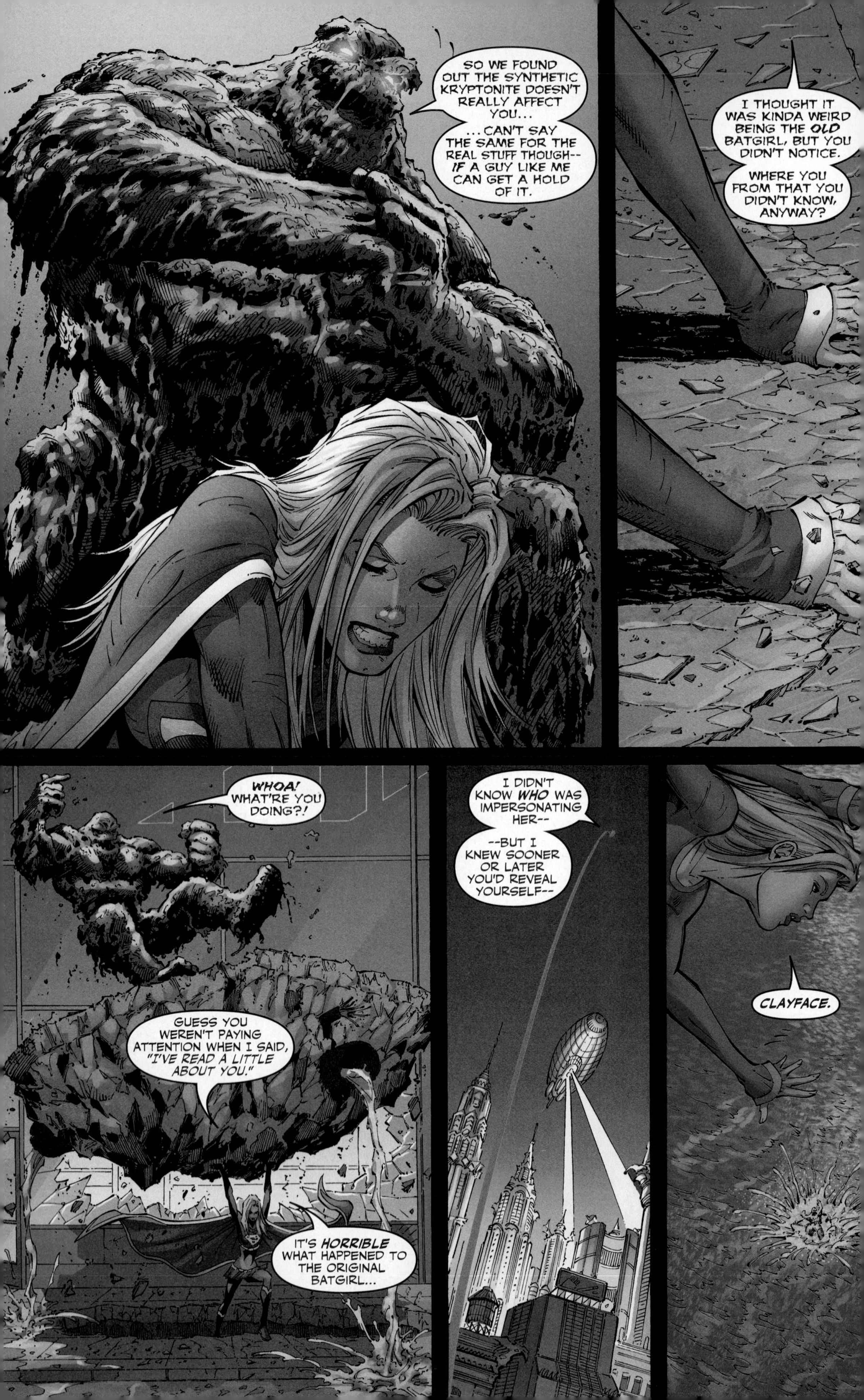
SO WE FOUND OUT THE SYNTHETIC KRYPTONITE DOESN'T REALLY AFFECT YOU...
...CAN'T SAY THE SAME FOR THE REAL STUFF THOUGH-- IF A GUY LIKE ME CAN GET A HOLD OF IT.
I THOUGHT IT WAS KINDA WEIRD BEING THE OLD BATGIRL, BUT YOU DIDN'T NOTICE.
WHERE YOU FROM THAT YOU DIDN'T KNOW, ANYWAY?
WHOA! WHAT'RE YOU DOING?!
GUESS YOU WEREN'T PAYING ATTENTION WHEN I SAID, "I'VE READ A LITTLE ABOUT YOU."
IT'S HORRIBLE WHAT HAPPENED TO THE ORIGINAL BATGIRL...
I DIDN'T KNOW WHO WAS IMPERSONATING HER--
--BUT I KNEW SOONER OR LATER YOU'D REVEAL YOURSELF--
CLAYFACE.

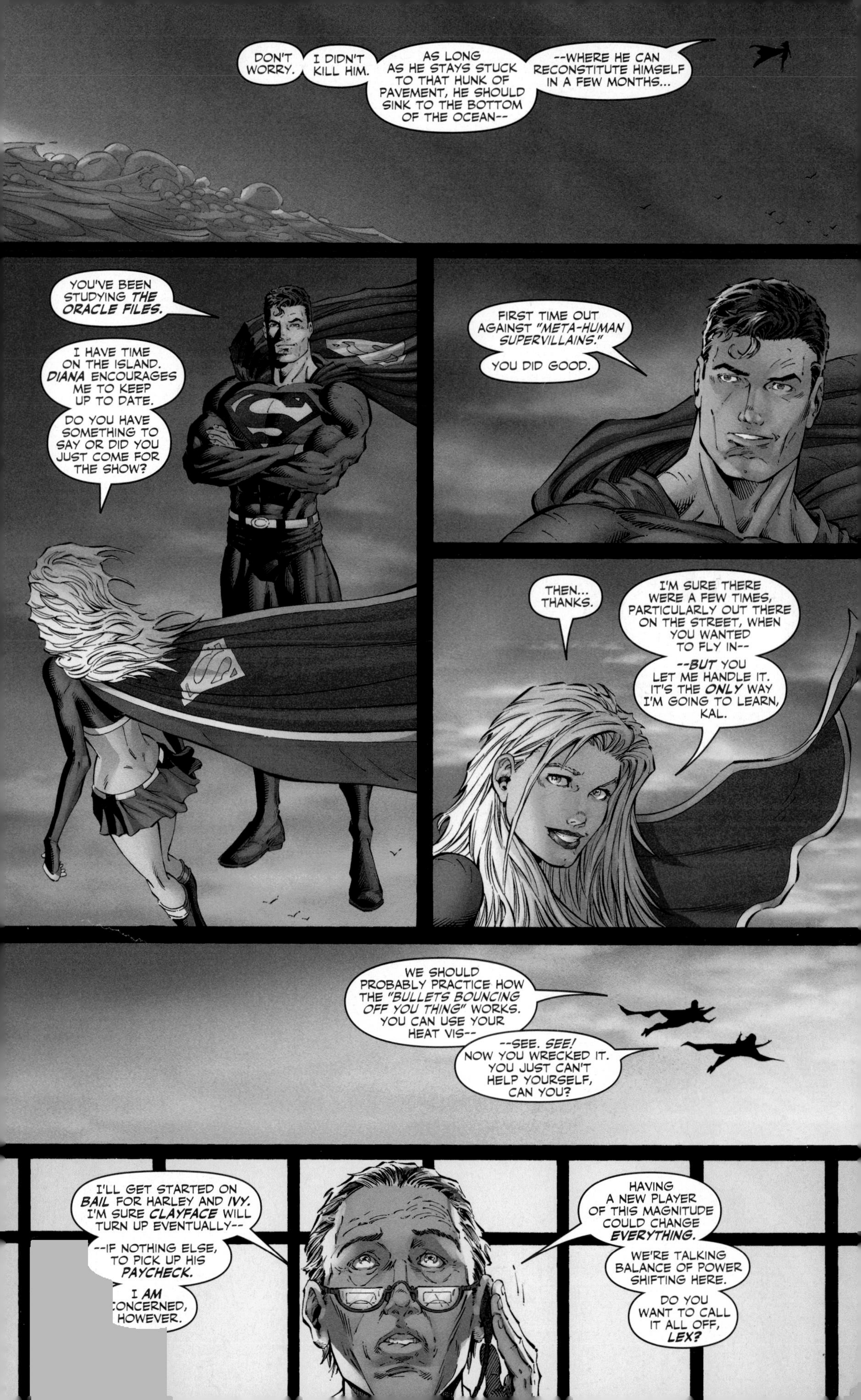
DON'T WORRY.
I DIDN'T KILL HIM.
AS LONG AS HE STAYS STUCK TO THAT HUNK OF PAVEMENT, HE SHOULD SINK TO THE BOTTOM OF THE OCEAN--
--WHERE HE CAN RECONSTITUTE HIMSELF IN A FEW MONTHS...
YOU'VE BEEN STUDYING *THE ORACLE FILES.*
I HAVE TIME ON THE ISLAND. *DIANA* ENCOURAGES ME TO KEEP UP TO DATE.
DO YOU HAVE SOMETHING TO SAY OR DID YOU JUST COME FOR THE SHOW?
FIRST TIME OUT AGAINST *"META-HUMAN SUPERVILLAINS."*
YOU DID GOOD.
THEN... THANKS.
I'M SURE THERE WERE A FEW TIMES, PARTICULARLY OUT THERE ON THE STREET, WHEN YOU WANTED TO FLY IN--
--BUT YOU LET ME HANDLE IT. IT'S THE *ONLY* WAY I'M GOING TO LEARN, KAL.
WE SHOULD PROBABLY PRACTICE HOW THE *"BULLETS BOUNCING OFF YOU THING"* WORKS. YOU CAN USE YOUR HEAT VIS--
--SEE. *SEE!* NOW YOU WRECKED IT. YOU JUST CAN'T HELP YOURSELF, CAN YOU?
I'LL GET STARTED ON *BAIL* FOR HARLEY AND *IVY.* I'M SURE *CLAYFACE* WILL TURN UP EVENTUALLY--
--IF NOTHING ELSE, TO PICK UP HIS *PAYCHECK.*
I *AM* CONCERNED, HOWEVER.
HAVING A NEW PLAYER OF THIS MAGNITUDE COULD CHANGE *EVERYTHING.*
WE'RE TALKING BALANCE OF POWER SHIFTING HERE.
DO YOU WANT TO CALL IT ALL OFF, *LEX?*

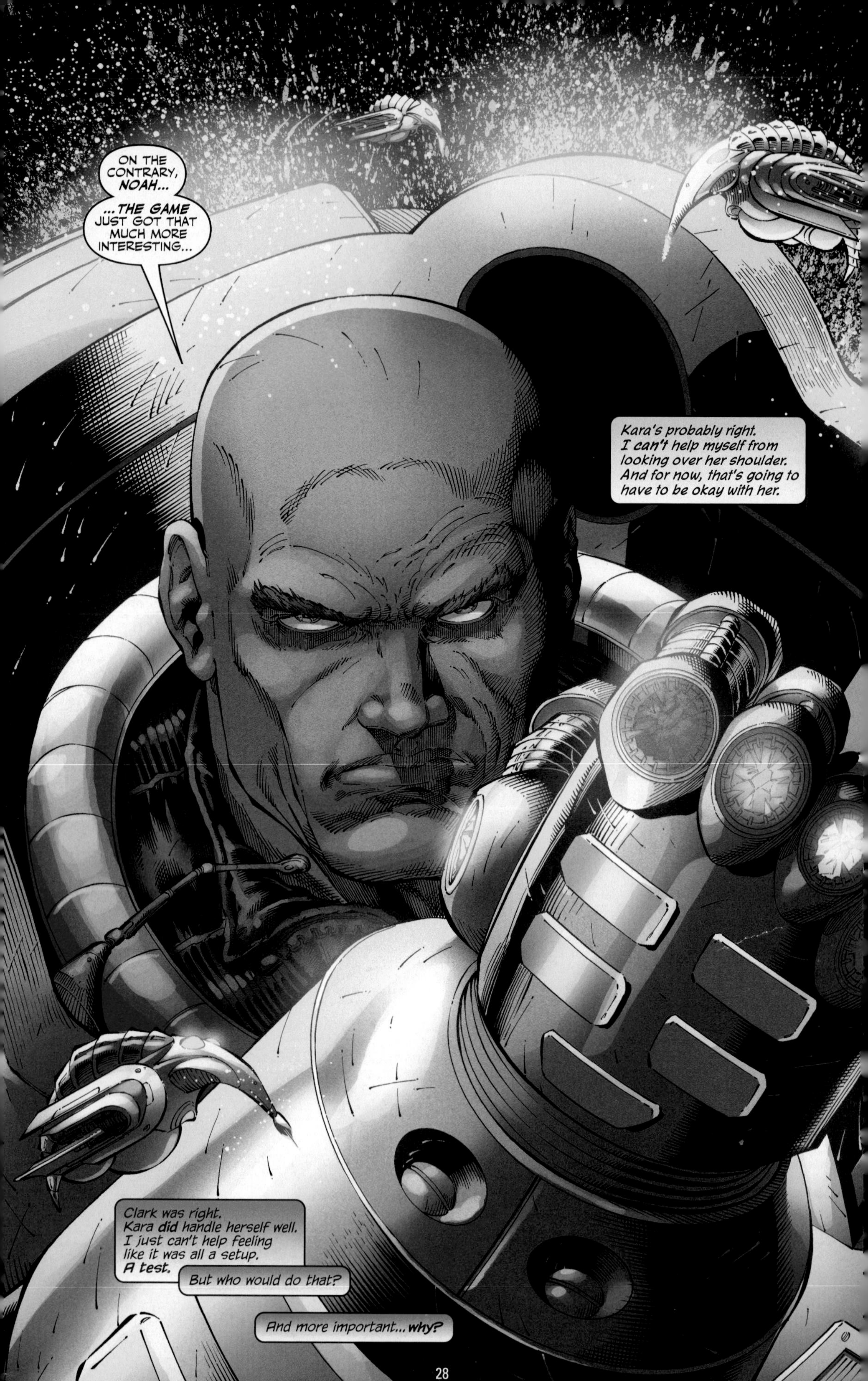
ON THE CONTRARY, NOAH...
...THE GAME JUST GOT THAT MUCH MORE INTERESTING...
Kara's probably right. I can't help myself from looking over her shoulder. And for now, that's going to have to be okay with her.
Clark was right. Kara did handle herself well. I just can't help feeling like it was all a setup. A test.
But who would do that?
And more important...why?

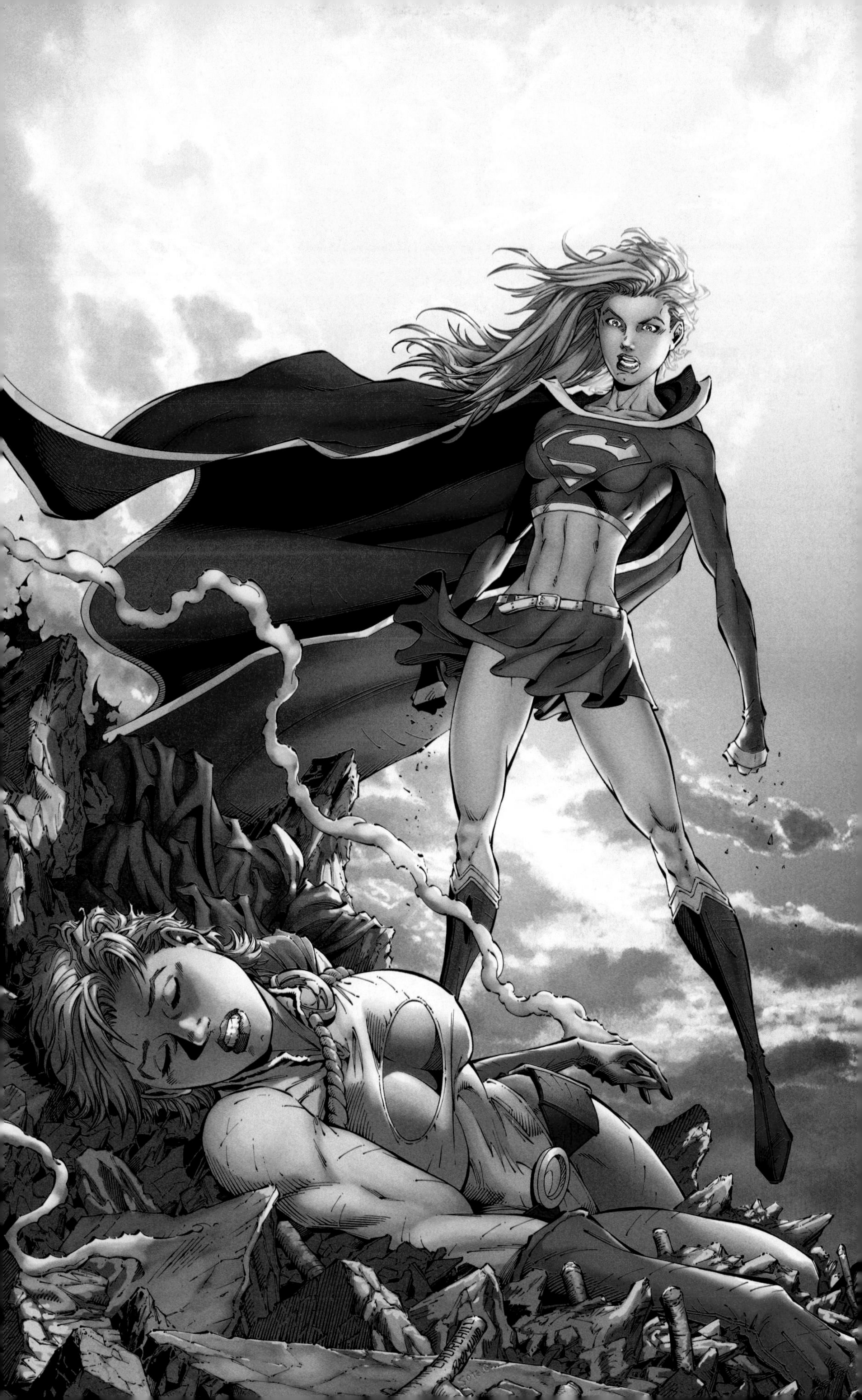

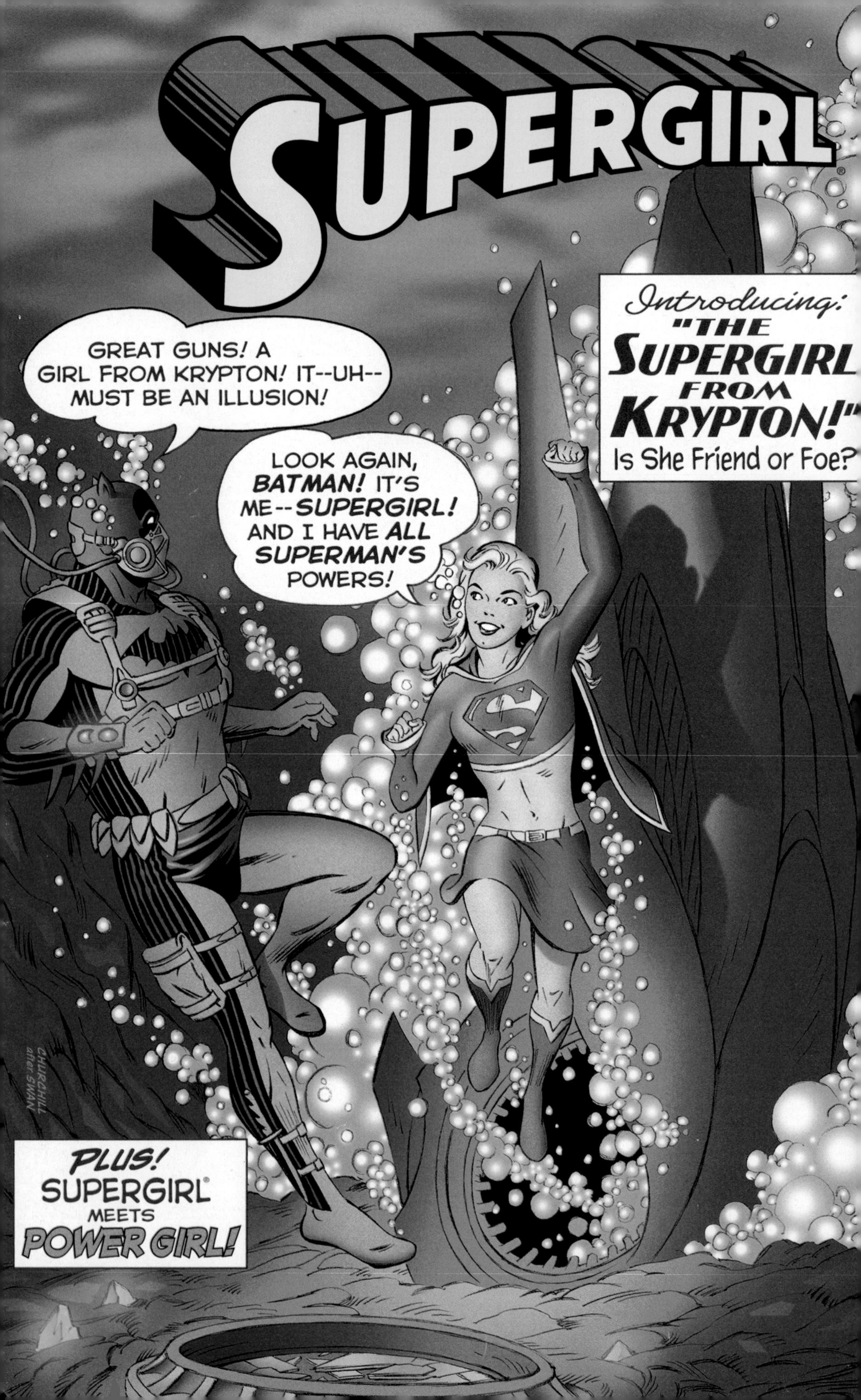
SUPERGIRL
GREAT GUNS! A GIRL FROM KRYPTON! IT--UH-- MUST BE AN ILLUSION!
LOOK AGAIN, BATMAN! IT'S ME--SUPERGIRL! AND I HAVE ALL SUPERMAN'S POWERS!
Introducing: "THE SUPERGIRL FROM KRYPTON!" Is She Friend or Foe?
CHURCHILL after SWAN
PLUS! SUPERGIRL MEETS POWER GIRL!

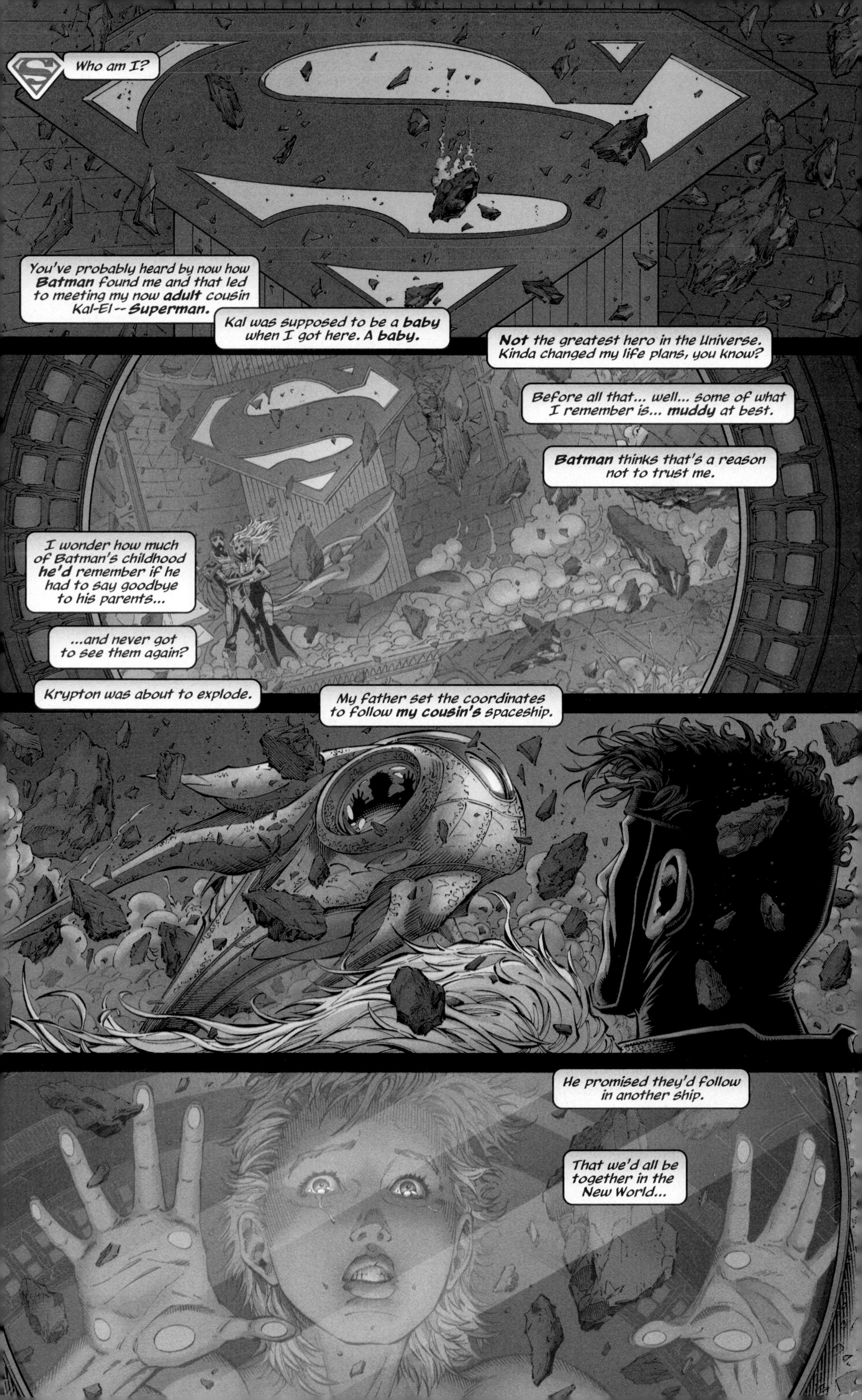
Who am I?
You've probably heard by now how Batman found me and that led to meeting my now adult cousin Kal-El -- Superman.
Kal was supposed to be a baby when I got here. A baby.
Not the greatest hero in the Universe. Kinda changed my life plans, you know?
Before all that... well... some of what I remember is... muddy at best.
Batman thinks that's a reason not to trust me.
I wonder how much of Batman's childhood he'd remember if he had to say goodbye to his parents...
...and never got to see them again?
Krypton was about to explode.
My father set the coordinates to follow my cousin's spaceship.
He promised they'd follow in another ship.
That we'd all be together in the New World...

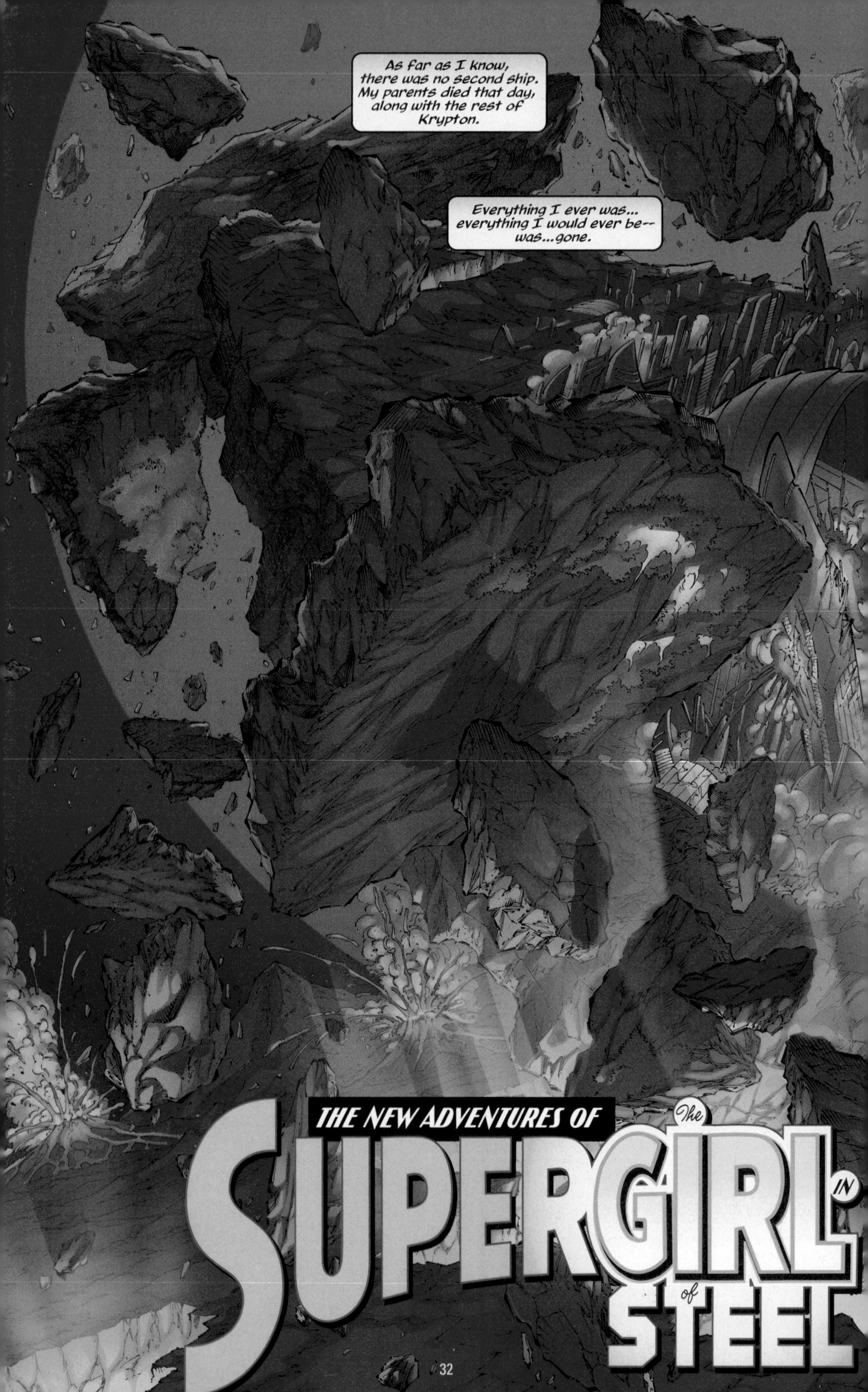
As far as I know, there was no second ship. My parents died that day, along with the rest of Krypton.
Everything I ever was... everything I would ever be-- was...gone.
THE NEW ADVENTURES OF
The SUPERGIRL IN of STEEL

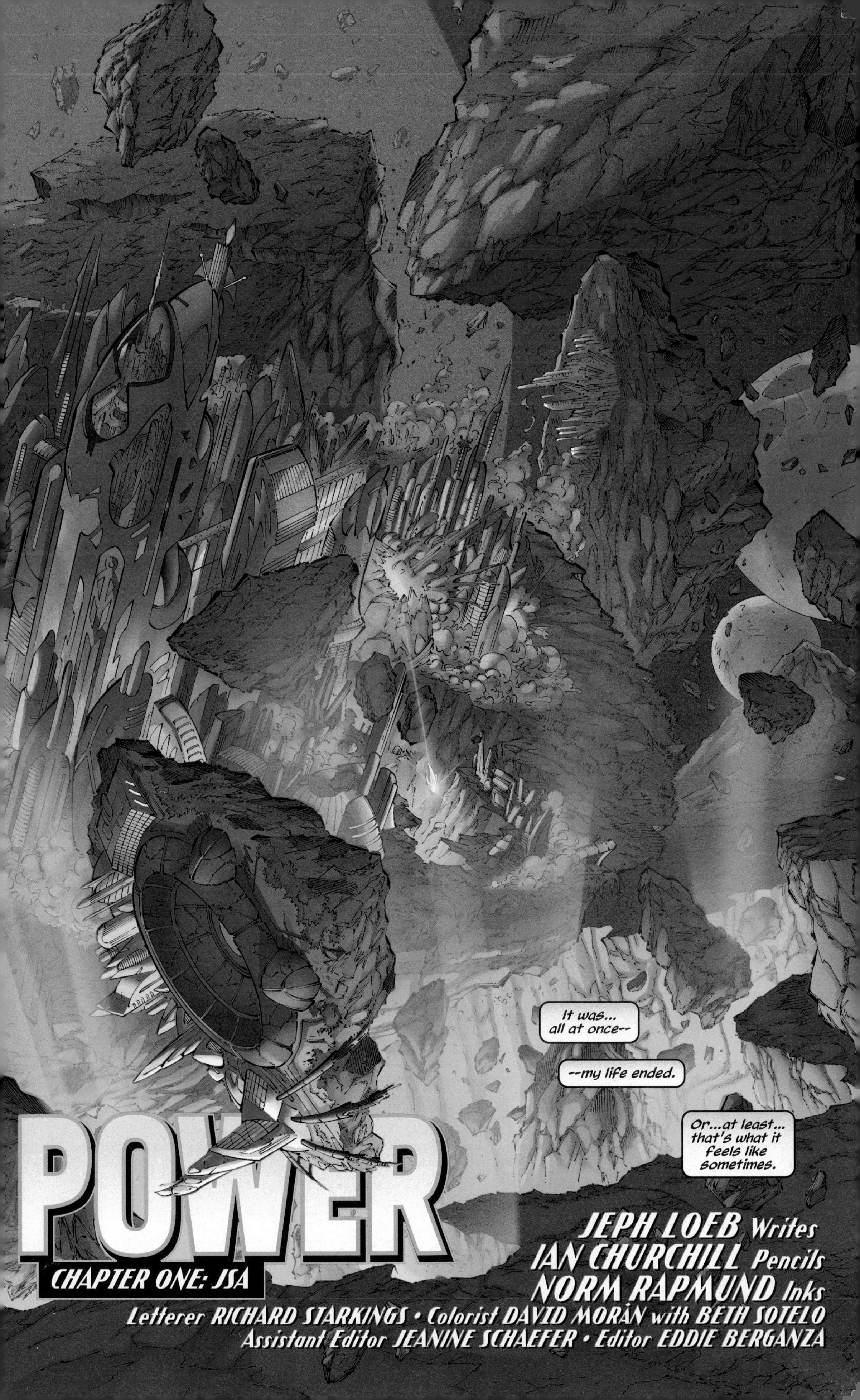
It was... all at once--
--my life ended.
Or...at least... that's what it feels like sometimes.
POWER
CHAPTER ONE: JSA
JEPH LOEB Writes
IAN CHURCHILL Pencils
NORM RAPMUND Inks
Letterer RICHARD STARKINGS • Colorist DAVID MORÁN with BETH SOTELO
Assistant Editor JEANINE SCHAEFER • Editor EDDIE BERGANZA

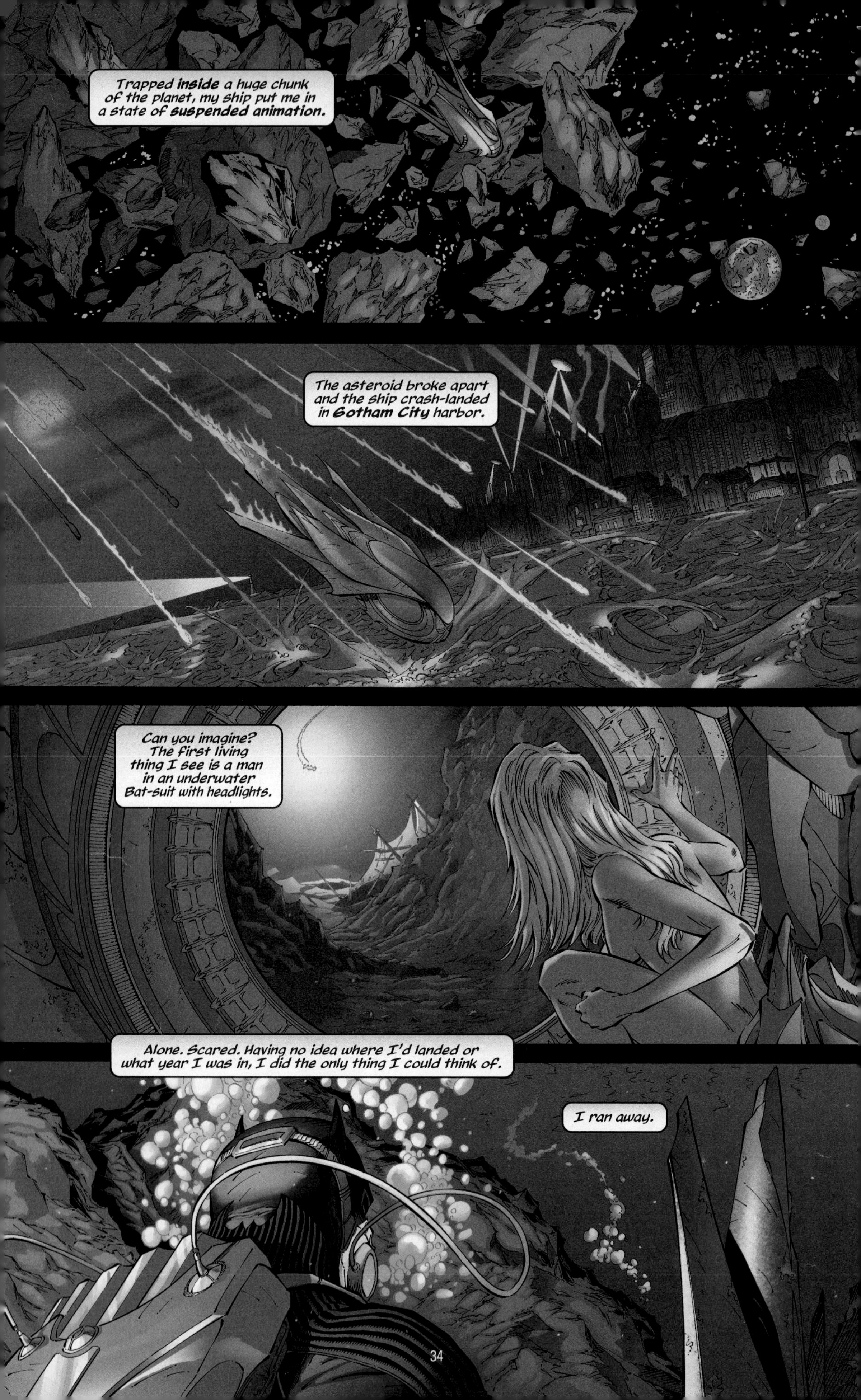
Trapped inside a huge chunk of the planet, my ship put me in a state of suspended animation.
The asteroid broke apart and the ship crash-landed in Gotham City harbor.
Can you imagine? The first living thing I see is a man in an underwater Bat-suit with headlights.
Alone. Scared. Having no idea where I'd landed or what year I was in, I did the only thing I could think of.
I ran away.

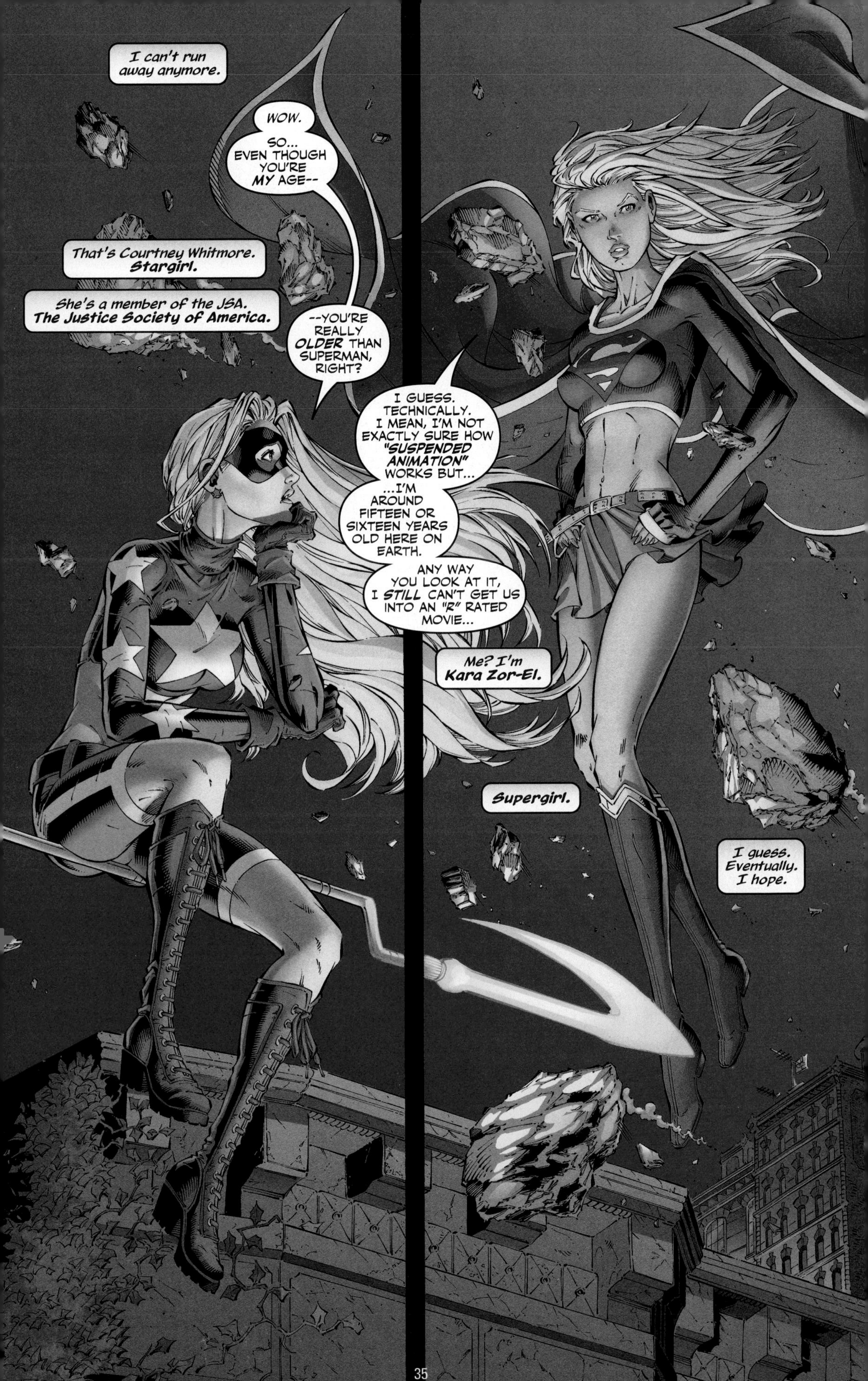
I can't run away anymore.
WOW.
SO... EVEN THOUGH YOU'RE MY AGE--
That's Courtney Whitmore. Stargirl.
She's a member of the JSA. The Justice Society of America.
--YOU'RE REALLY OLDER THAN SUPERMAN, RIGHT?
I GUESS. TECHNICALLY. I MEAN, I'M NOT EXACTLY SURE HOW "SUSPENDED ANIMATION" WORKS BUT...
...I'M AROUND FIFTEEN OR SIXTEEN YEARS OLD HERE ON EARTH.
ANY WAY YOU LOOK AT IT, I STILL CAN'T GET US INTO AN "R" RATED MOVIE...
Me? I'm Kara Zor-El.
Supergirl.
I guess. Eventually. I hope.

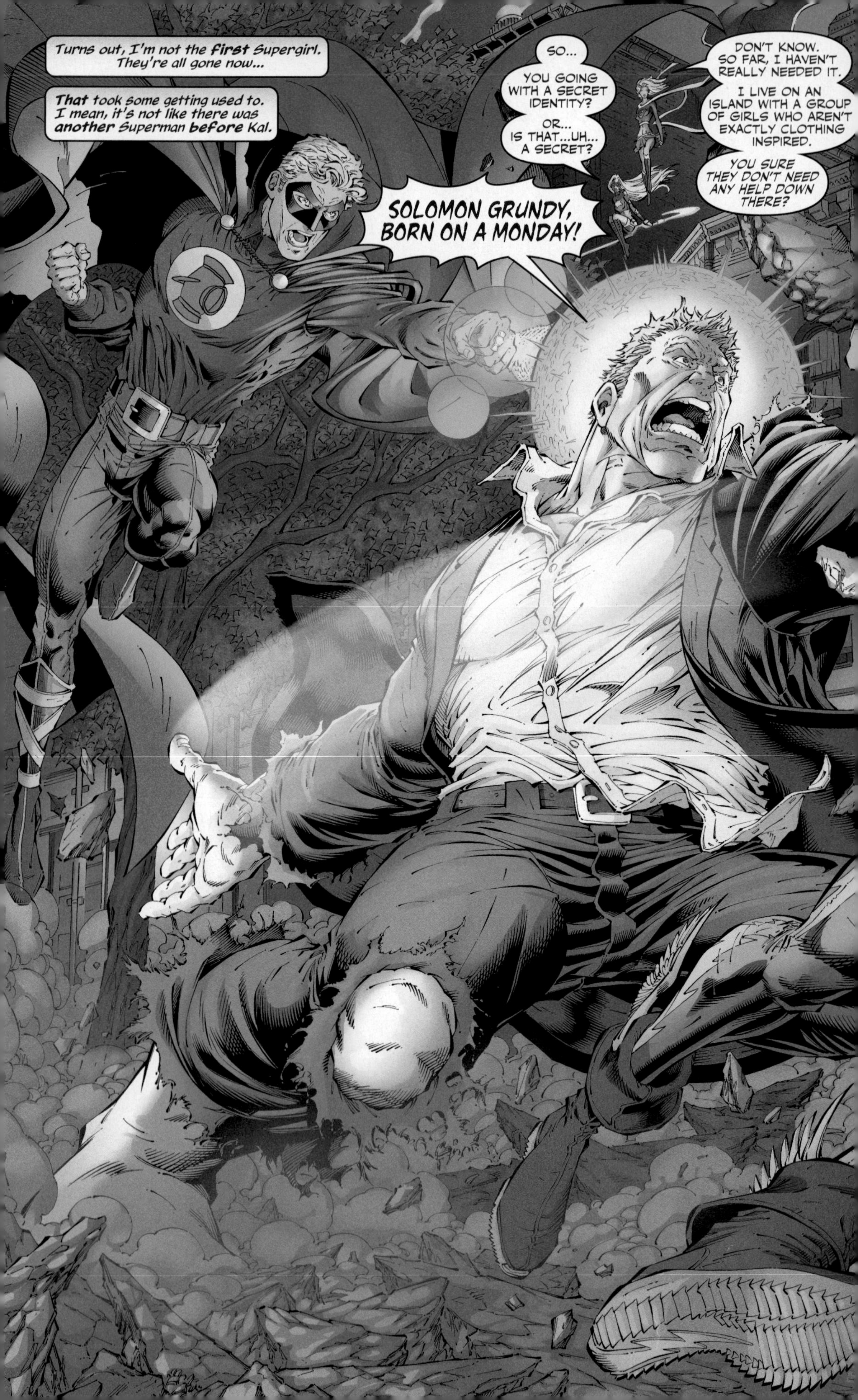
Turns out, I'm not the **first** Supergirl. They're all gone now...
That took some getting used to. I mean, it's not like there was **another** Superman **before** Kal.
SO...
YOU GOING WITH A SECRET IDENTITY?
OR... IS THAT...UH... A SECRET?
DON'T KNOW. SO FAR, I HAVEN'T REALLY NEEDED IT.
I LIVE ON AN ISLAND WITH A GROUP OF GIRLS WHO AREN'T EXACTLY CLOTHING INSPIRED.
YOU SURE THEY DON'T NEED ANY HELP DOWN THERE?
SOLOMON GRUNDY, BORN ON A MONDAY!

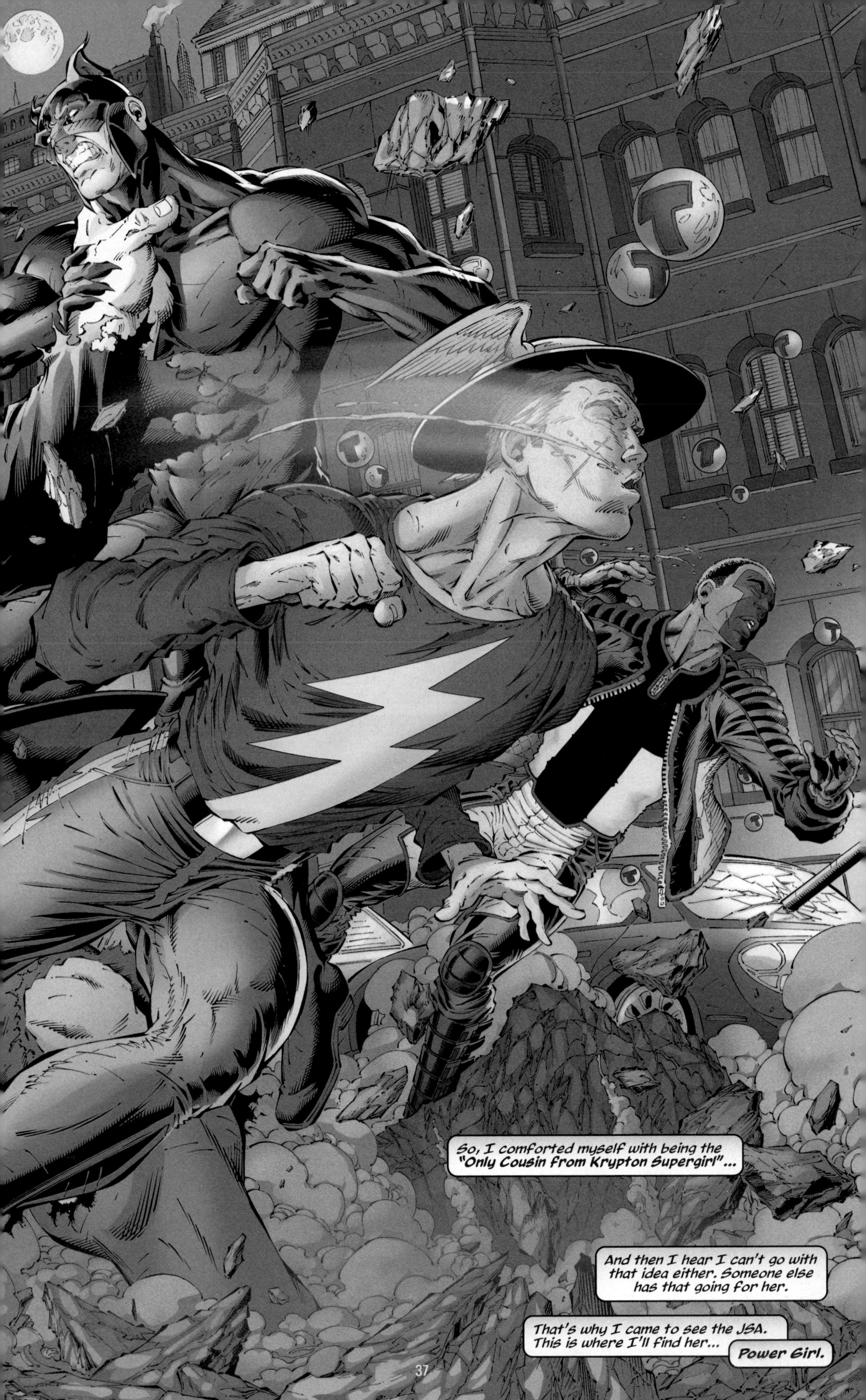
So, I comforted myself with being the "Only Cousin from Krypton Supergirl"...
And then I hear I can't go with that idea either. Someone else has that going for her.
That's why I came to see the JSA. This is where I'll find her...
Power Girl.

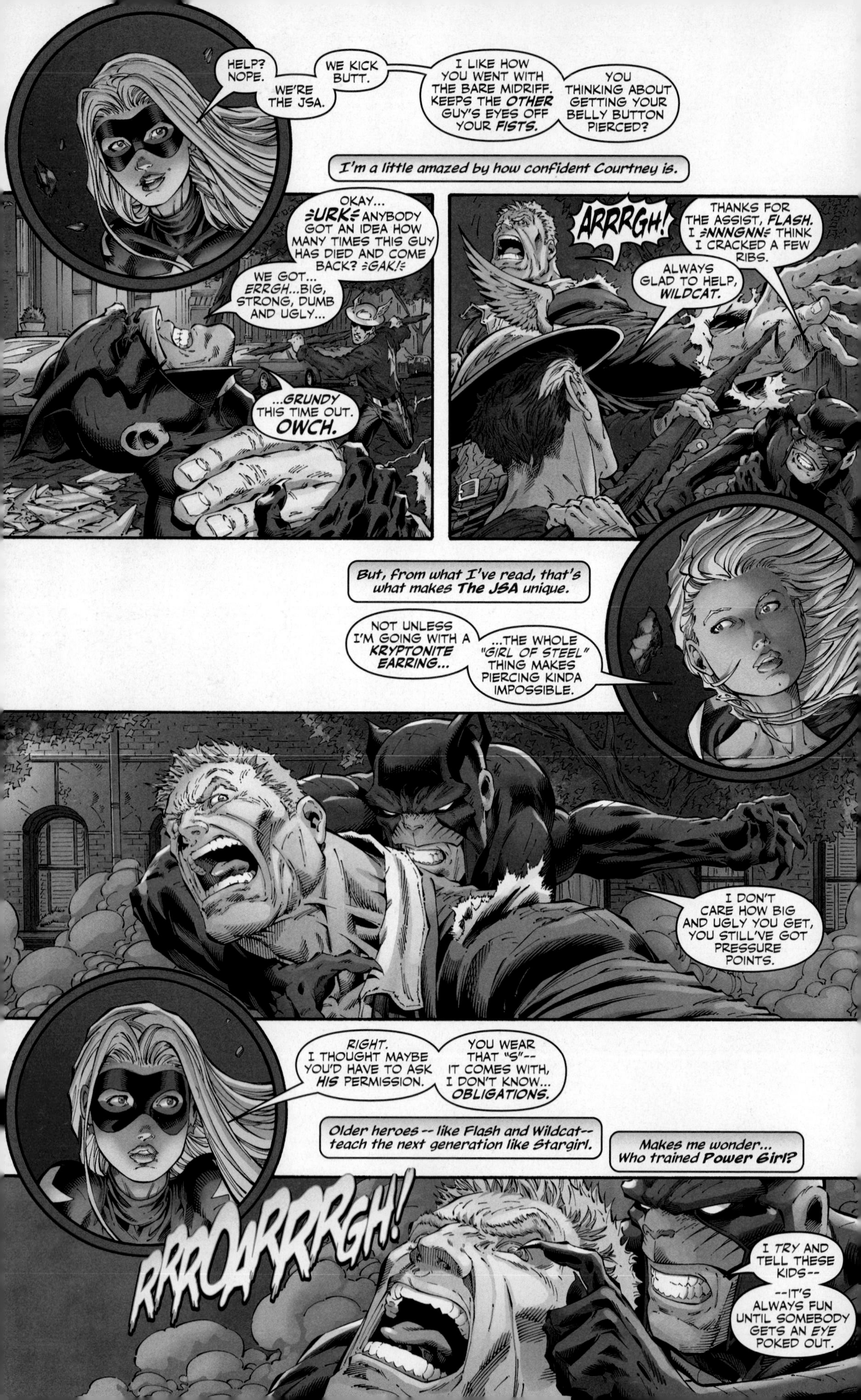
HELP? NOPE.
WE'RE THE JSA.
WE KICK BUTT.
I LIKE HOW YOU WENT WITH THE BARE MIDRIFF. KEEPS THE OTHER GUY'S EYES OFF YOUR FISTS.
YOU THINKING ABOUT GETTING YOUR BELLY BUTTON PIERCED?
I'm a little amazed by how confident Courtney is.
OKAY... URK ANYBODY GOT AN IDEA HOW MANY TIMES THIS GUY HAS DIED AND COME BACK? GAK!
WE GOT... ERRGH...BIG, STRONG, DUMB AND UGLY...
...GRUNDY THIS TIME OUT. OWCH.
ARRRGH!
THANKS FOR THE ASSIST, FLASH. I NNNGNN THINK I CRACKED A FEW RIBS.
ALWAYS GLAD TO HELP, WILDCAT.
But, from what I've read, that's what makes The JSA unique.
NOT UNLESS I'M GOING WITH A KRYPTONITE EARRING...
...THE WHOLE "GIRL OF STEEL" THING MAKES PIERCING KINDA IMPOSSIBLE.
I DON'T CARE HOW BIG AND UGLY YOU GET, YOU STILL'VE GOT PRESSURE POINTS.
RIGHT. I THOUGHT MAYBE YOU'D HAVE TO ASK HIS PERMISSION.
YOU WEAR THAT "S"-- IT COMES WITH, I DON'T KNOW... OBLIGATIONS.
Older heroes -- like Flash and Wildcat-- teach the next generation like Stargirl.
Makes me wonder... Who trained Power Girl?
RRROARRRGH!
I TRY AND TELL THESE KIDS--
--IT'S ALWAYS FUN UNTIL SOMEBODY GETS AN EYE POKED OUT.

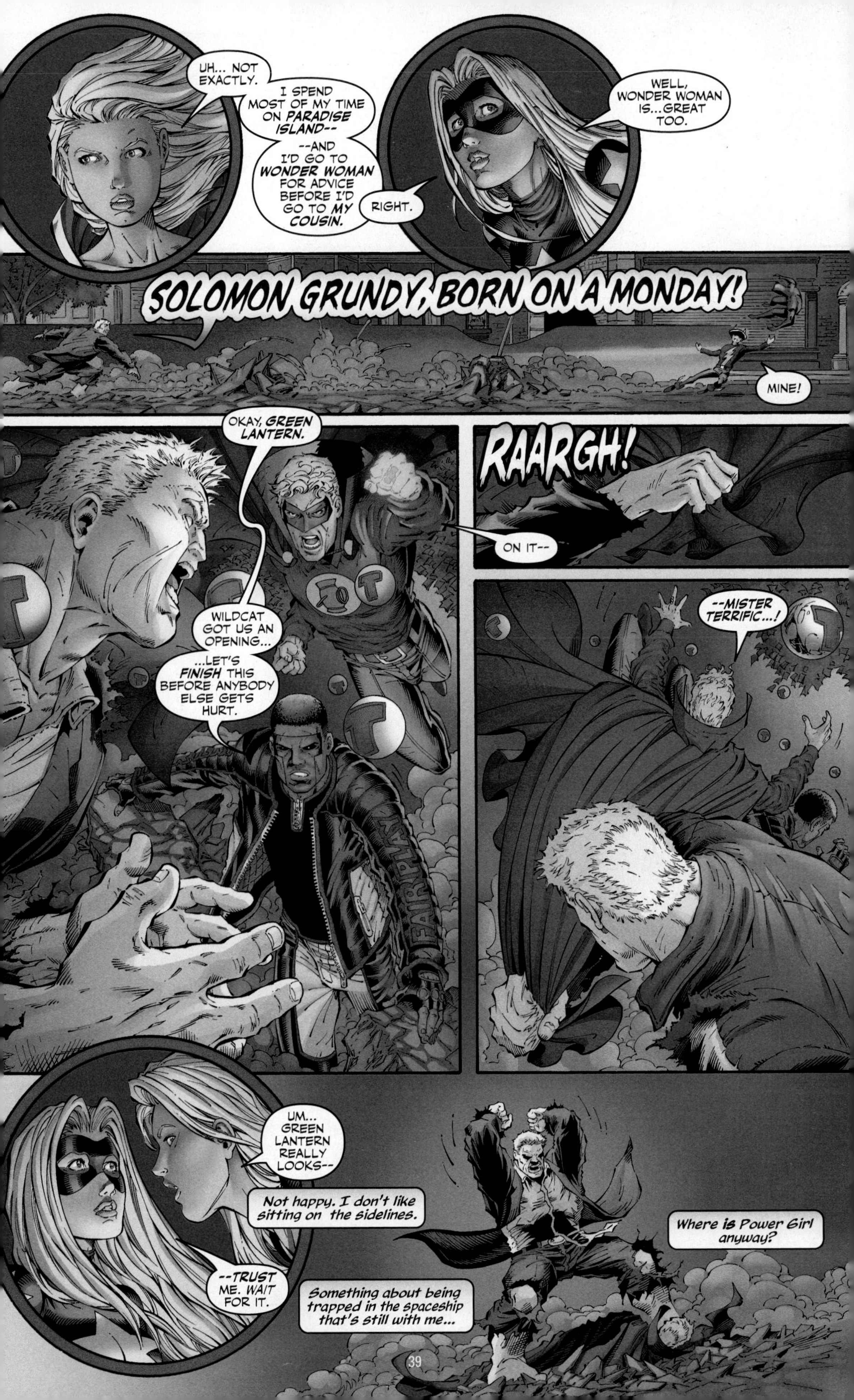

UH... NOT EXACTLY.
I SPEND MOST OF MY TIME ON *PARADISE ISLAND*--
--AND I'D GO TO *WONDER WOMAN* FOR ADVICE BEFORE I'D GO TO *MY COUSIN*.
RIGHT.
WELL, WONDER WOMAN IS...GREAT TOO.
SOLOMON GRUNDY, BORN ON A MONDAY!
MINE!
OKAY, *GREEN LANTERN*.
ON IT--
WILDCAT GOT US AN OPENING...
...LET'S *FINISH* THIS BEFORE ANYBODY ELSE GETS HURT.
RAARGH!
--MISTER TERRIFIC...!
UM... GREEN LANTERN REALLY LOOKS--
Not happy. I don't like sitting on the sidelines.
--*TRUST* ME. *WAIT* FOR IT.
Something about being trapped in the spaceship that's still with me...
Where *is* Power Girl anyway?

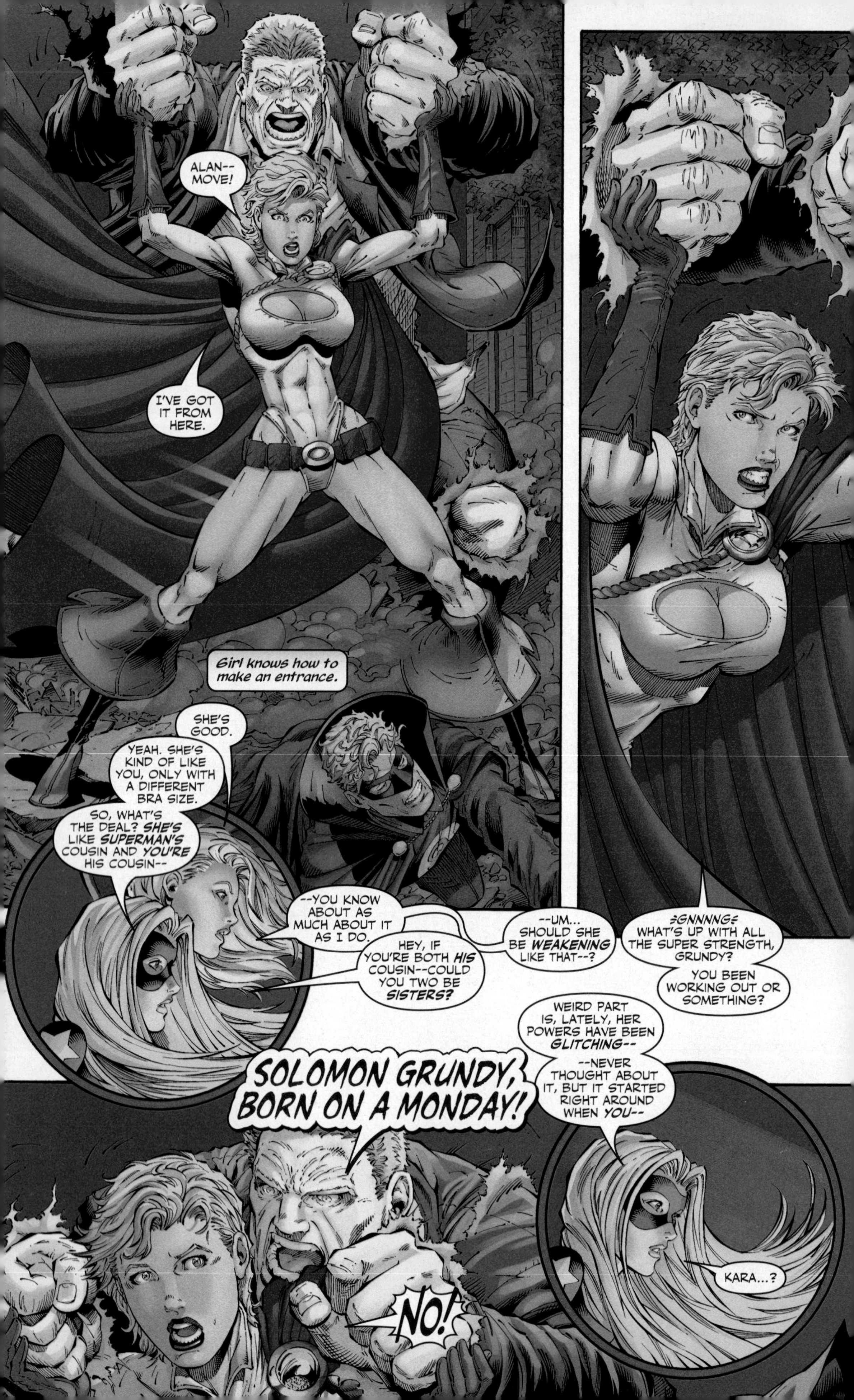
ALAN--
MOVE!
I'VE GOT IT FROM HERE.
Girl knows how to make an entrance.
SHE'S GOOD.
YEAH. SHE'S KIND OF LIKE YOU, ONLY WITH A DIFFERENT BRA SIZE.
SO, WHAT'S THE DEAL? SHE'S LIKE SUPERMAN'S COUSIN AND YOU'RE HIS COUSIN--
--YOU KNOW ABOUT AS MUCH ABOUT IT AS I DO.
HEY, IF YOU'RE BOTH HIS COUSIN--COULD YOU TWO BE SISTERS?
--UM... SHOULD SHE BE WEAKENING LIKE THAT--?
GNNNNG
WHAT'S UP WITH ALL THE SUPER STRENGTH, GRUNDY?
YOU BEEN WORKING OUT OR SOMETHING?
WEIRD PART IS, LATELY, HER POWERS HAVE BEEN GLITCHING--
--NEVER THOUGHT ABOUT IT, BUT IT STARTED RIGHT AROUND WHEN YOU--
SOLOMON GRUNDY, BORN ON A MONDAY!
KARA...?
NO!

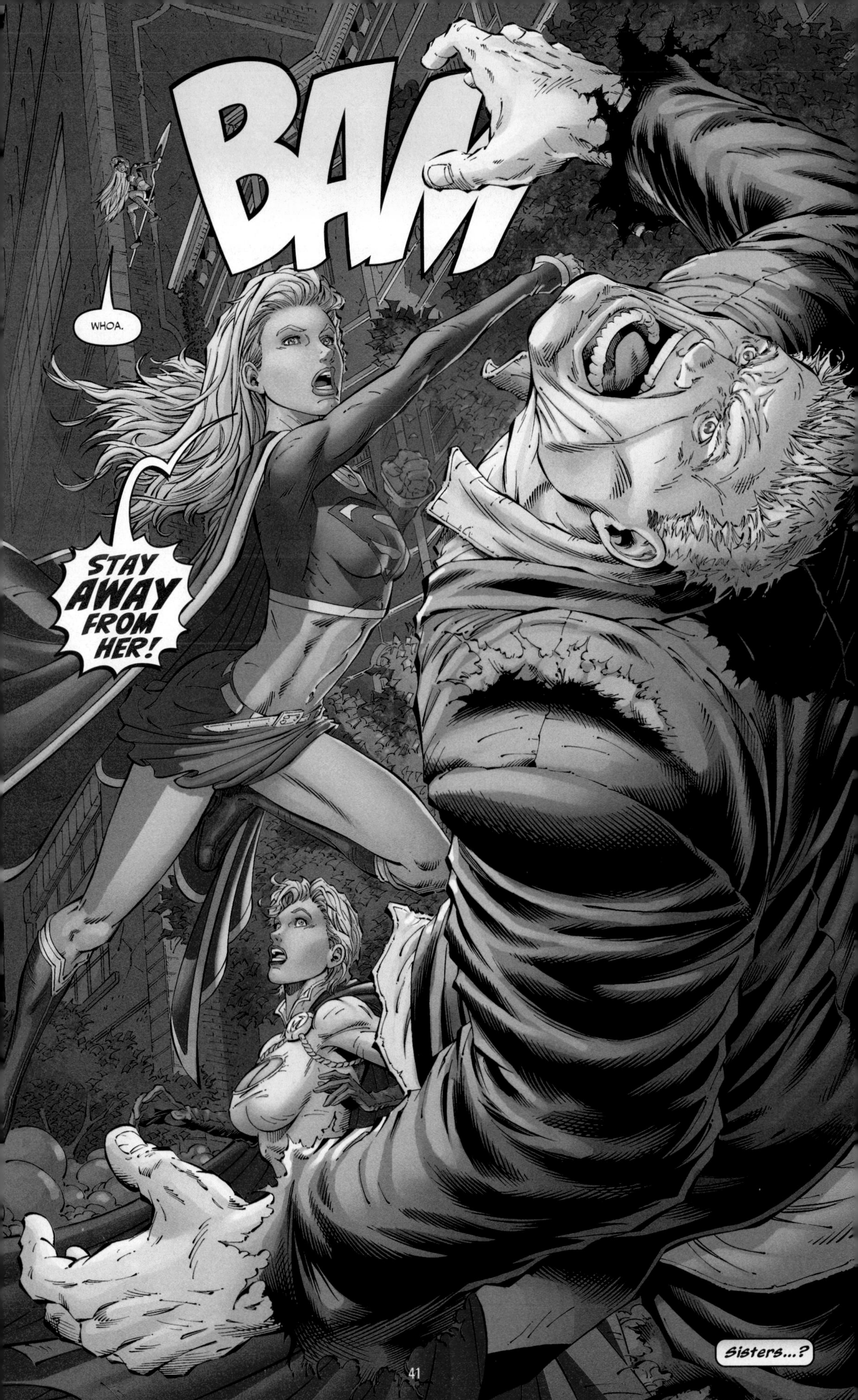
BAM
WHOA.
STAY AWAY FROM HER!
Sisters...?

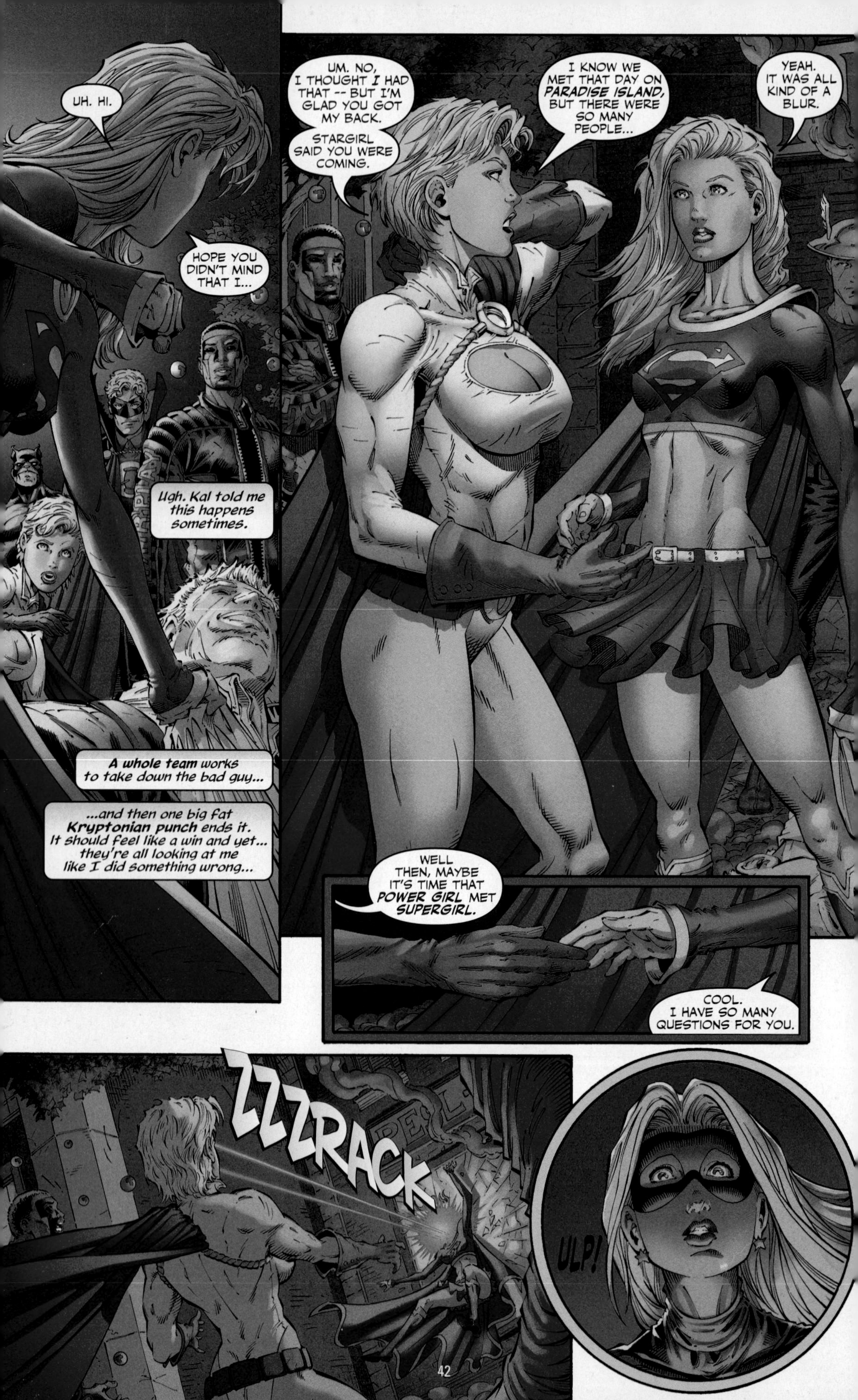
UH. HI.
HOPE YOU DIDN'T MIND THAT I...
Ugh. Kal told me this happens sometimes.
A whole team works to take down the bad guy...
...and then one big fat Kryptonian punch ends it. It should feel like a win and yet... they're all looking at me like I did something wrong...
UM. NO, I THOUGHT I HAD THAT -- BUT I'M GLAD YOU GOT MY BACK.
STARGIRL SAID YOU WERE COMING.
I KNOW WE MET THAT DAY ON PARADISE ISLAND, BUT THERE WERE SO MANY PEOPLE...
YEAH. IT WAS ALL KIND OF A BLUR.
WELL THEN, MAYBE IT'S TIME THAT POWER GIRL MET SUPERGIRL.
COOL. I HAVE SO MANY QUESTIONS FOR YOU.
ZZZRACK
ULP!

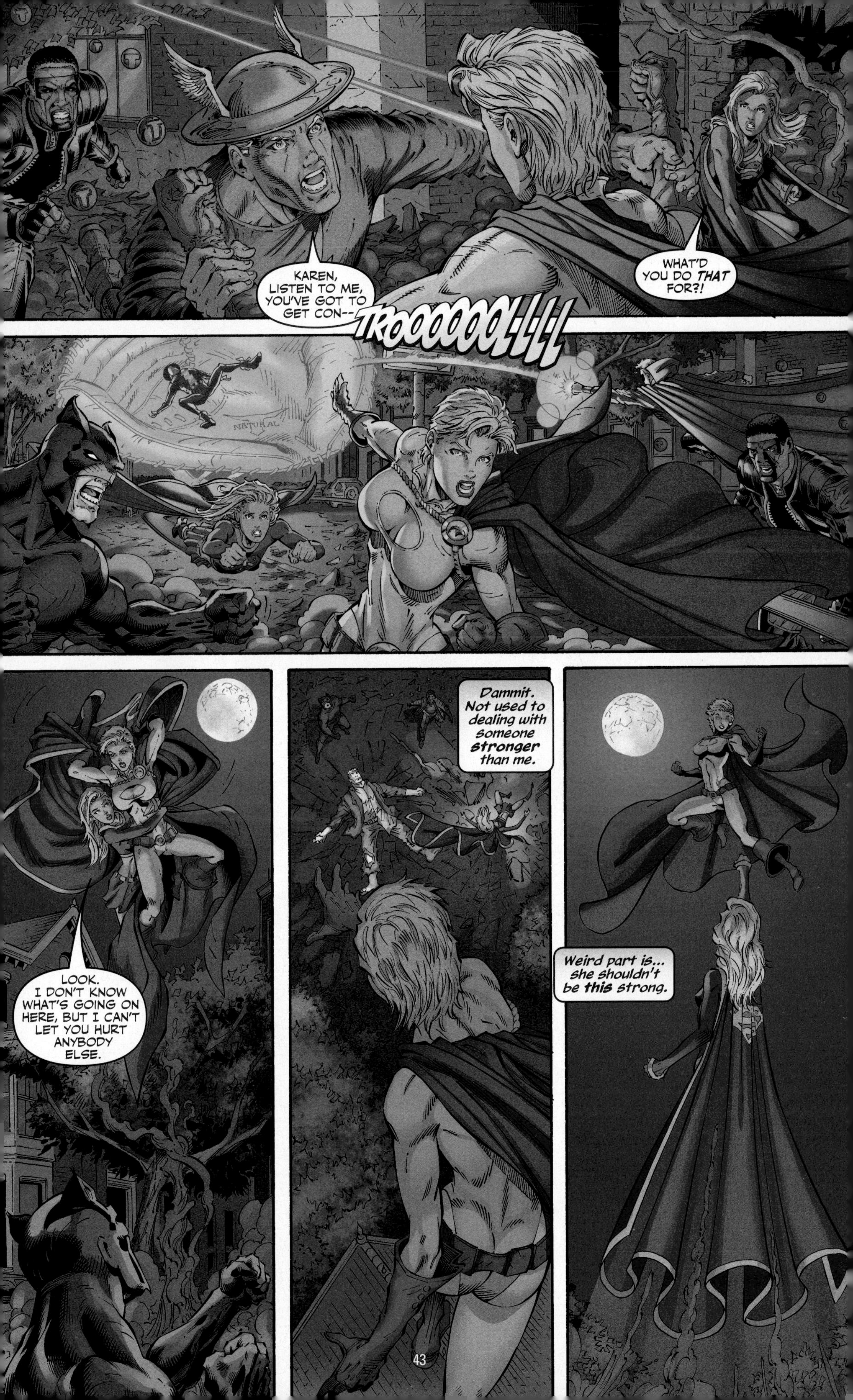
KAREN, LISTEN TO ME, YOU'VE GOT TO GET CON--
TROOOOOOLLLL
WHAT'D YOU DO THAT FOR?!
NATURAL
LOOK. I DON'T KNOW WHAT'S GOING ON HERE, BUT I CAN'T LET YOU HURT ANYBODY ELSE.
Dammit. Not used to dealing with someone stronger than me.
Weird part is... she shouldn't be this strong.

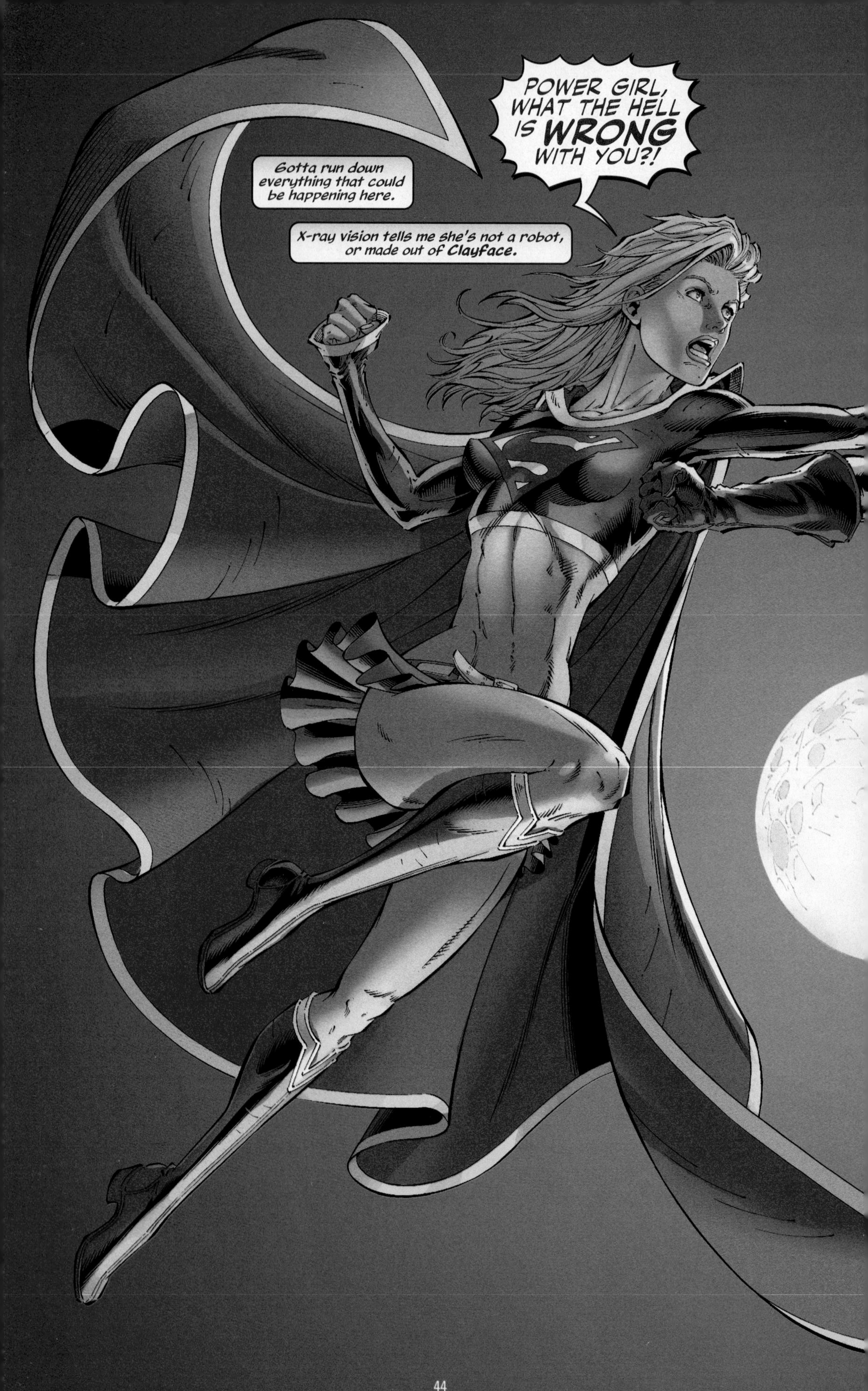
Gotta run down everything that could be happening here.
X-ray vision tells me she's not a robot, or made out of Clayface.
POWER GIRL, WHAT THE HELL IS WRONG WITH YOU?!

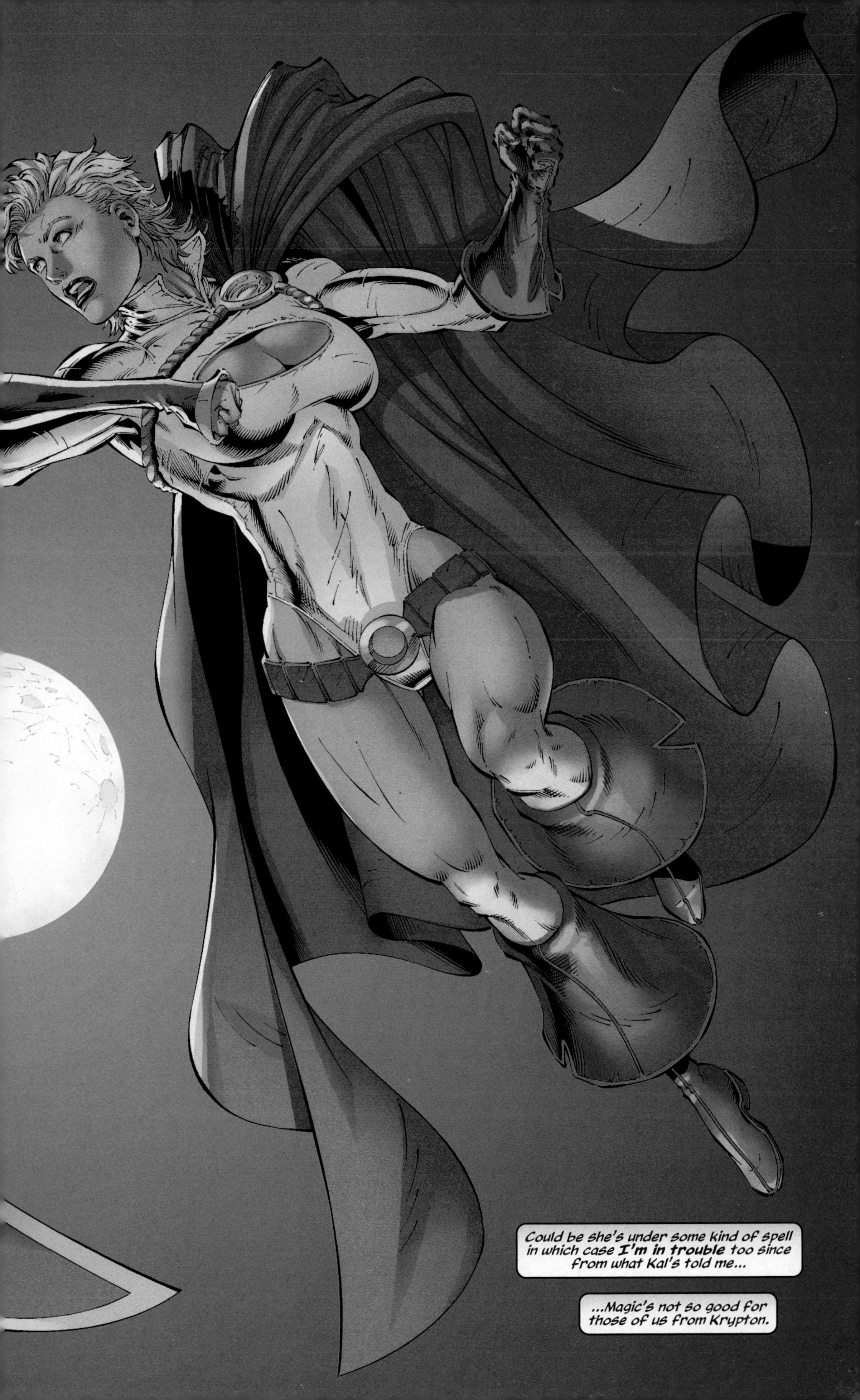
Could be she's under some kind of spell in which case **I'm in trouble** too since from what Kal's told me...
...Magic's not so good for those of us from Krypton.

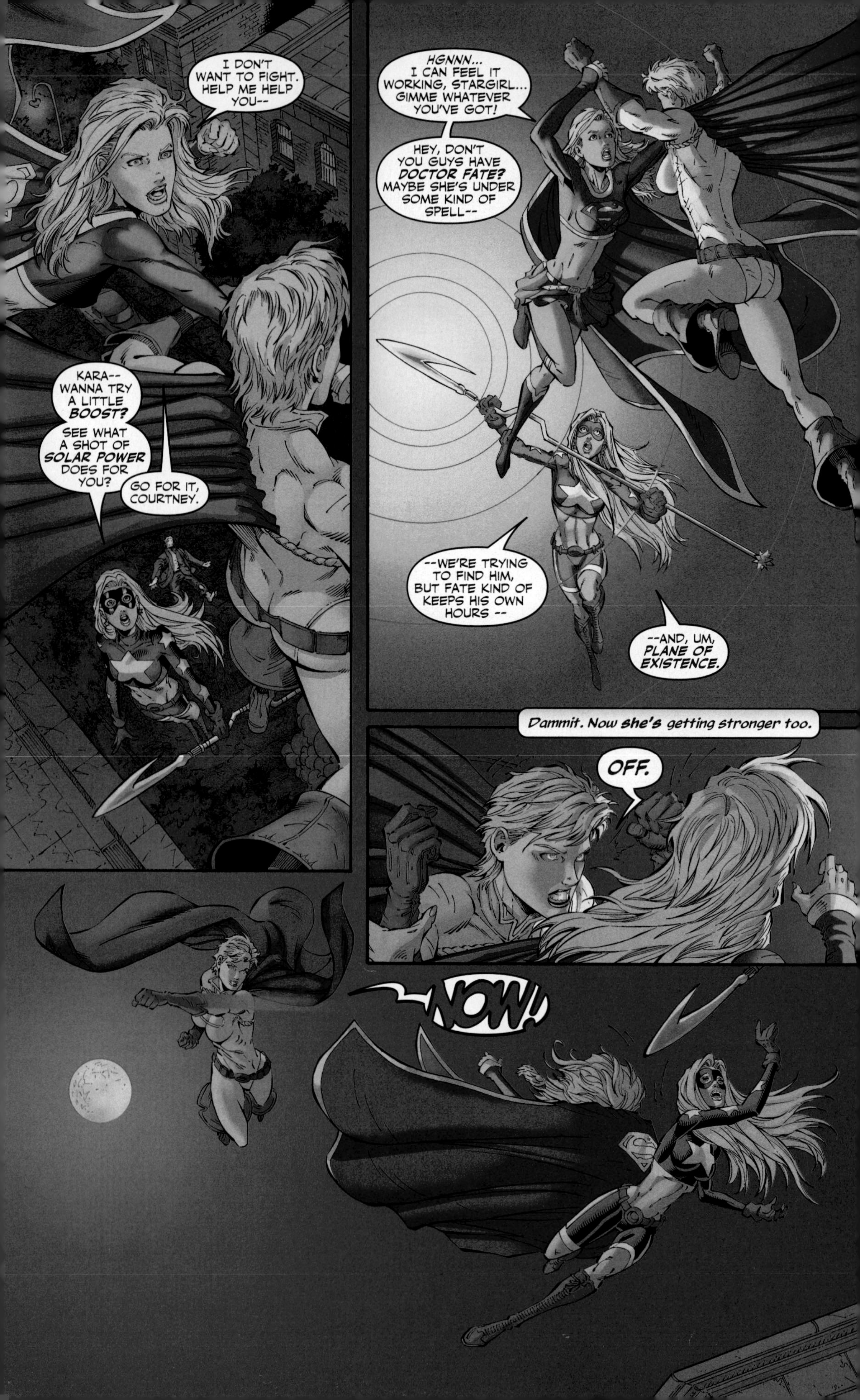
I DON'T WANT TO FIGHT. HELP ME HELP YOU--
KARA-- WANNA TRY A LITTLE BOOST? SEE WHAT A SHOT OF SOLAR POWER DOES FOR YOU?
GO FOR IT, COURTNEY.
HGNNN... I CAN FEEL IT WORKING, STARGIRL... GIMME WHATEVER YOU'VE GOT!
HEY, DON'T YOU GUYS HAVE DOCTOR FATE? MAYBE SHE'S UNDER SOME KIND OF SPELL--
--WE'RE TRYING TO FIND HIM, BUT FATE KIND OF KEEPS HIS OWN HOURS --
--AND, UM, PLANE OF EXISTENCE.
Dammit. Now she's getting stronger too.
OFF.
NOW!

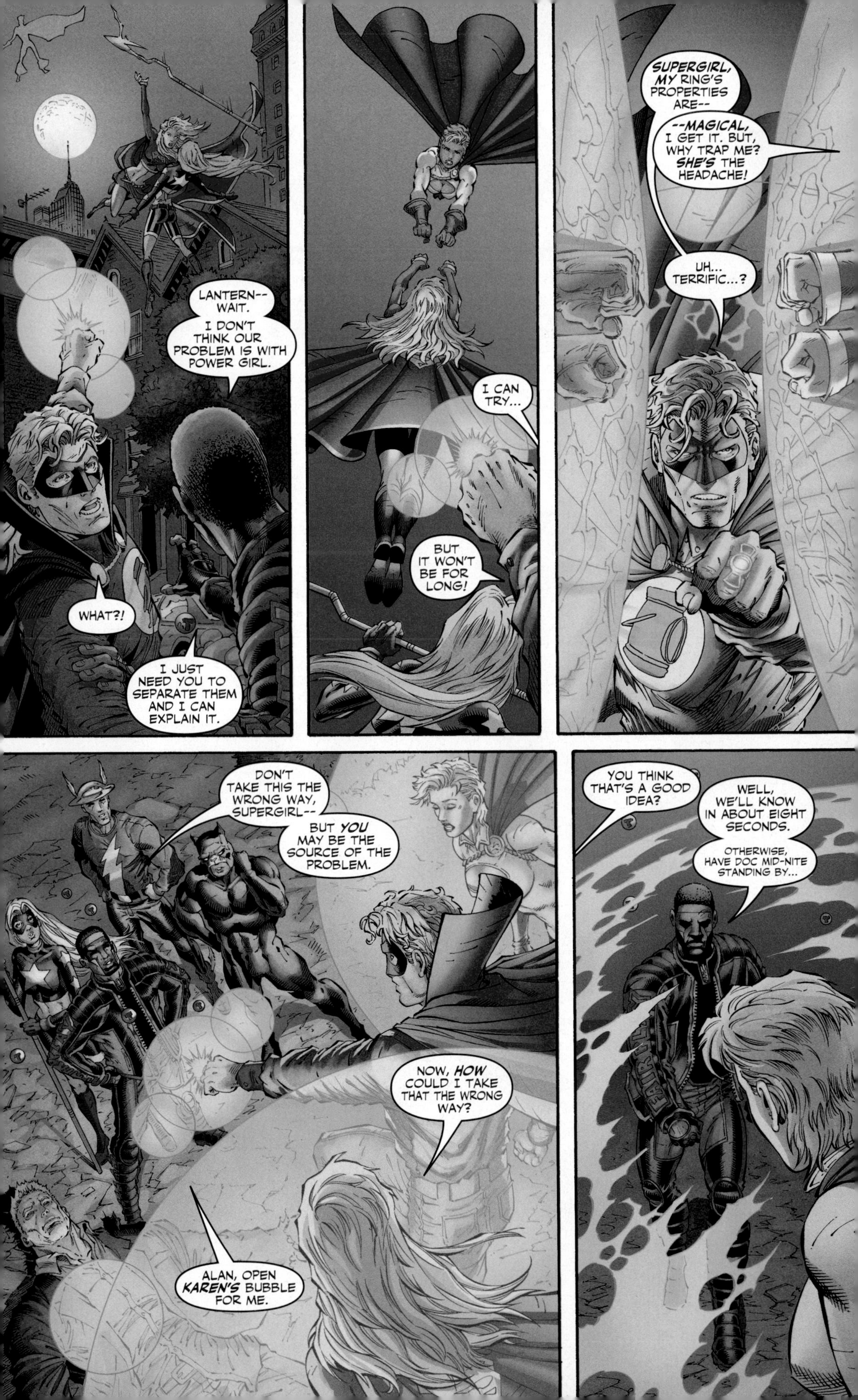
LANTERN-- WAIT. I DON'T THINK OUR PROBLEM IS WITH POWER GIRL.
WHAT?!
I JUST NEED YOU TO SEPARATE THEM AND I CAN EXPLAIN IT.
I CAN TRY...
BUT IT WON'T BE FOR LONG!
SUPERGIRL, MY RING'S PROPERTIES ARE--
--MAGICAL, I GET IT. BUT, WHY TRAP ME? SHE'S THE HEADACHE!
UH... TERRIFIC...?
DON'T TAKE THIS THE WRONG WAY, SUPERGIRL--
BUT YOU MAY BE THE SOURCE OF THE PROBLEM.
NOW, HOW COULD I TAKE THAT THE WRONG WAY?
ALAN, OPEN KAREN'S BUBBLE FOR ME.
YOU THINK THAT'S A GOOD IDEA?
WELL, WE'LL KNOW IN ABOUT EIGHT SECONDS.
OTHERWISE, HAVE DOC MID-NITE STANDING BY...

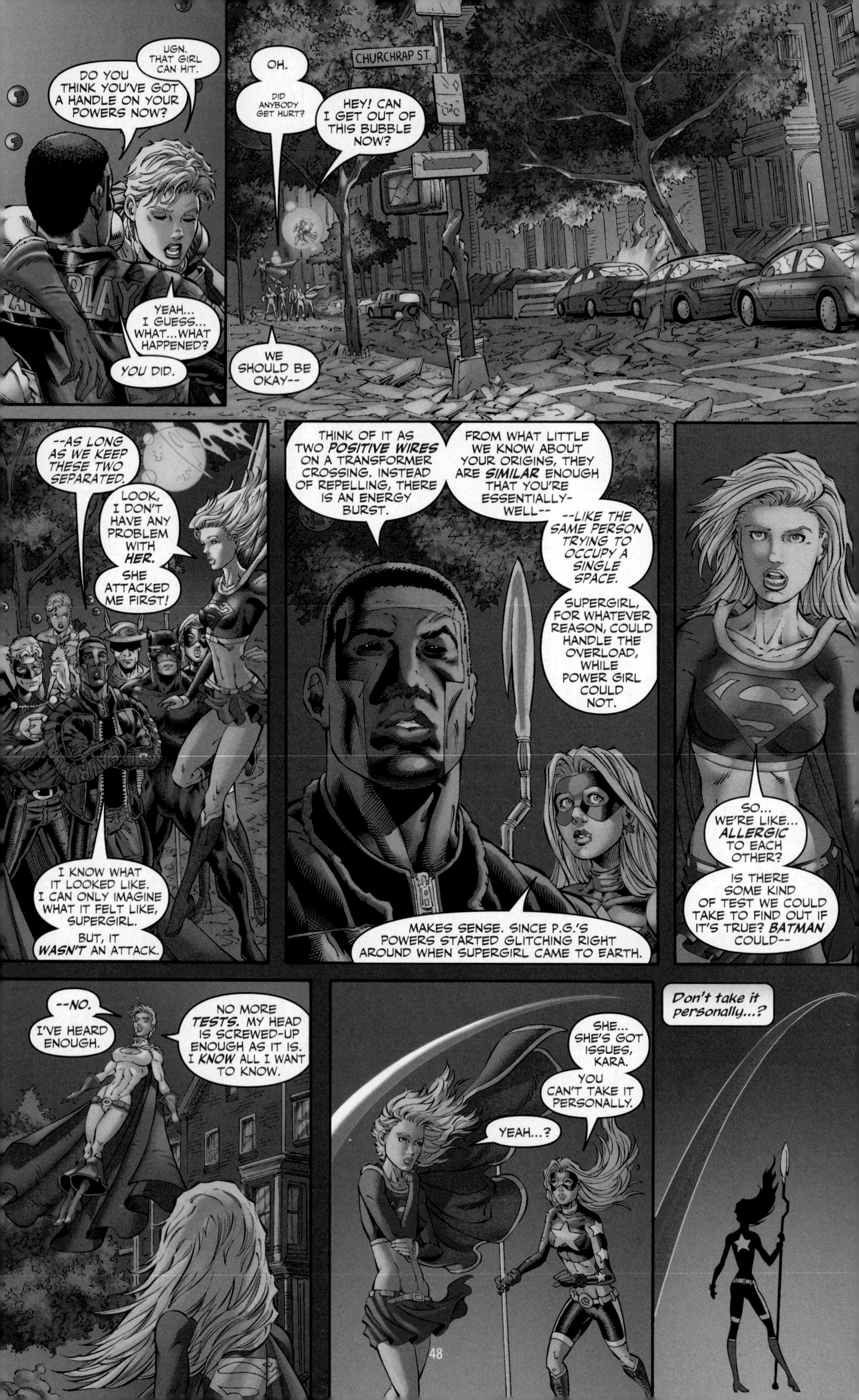
UGN. THAT GIRL CAN HIT.
DO YOU THINK YOU'VE GOT A HANDLE ON YOUR POWERS NOW?
YEAH... I GUESS... WHAT...WHAT HAPPENED?
YOU DID.
OH.
DID ANYBODY GET HURT?
CHURCHRAP ST.
HEY! CAN I GET OUT OF THIS BUBBLE NOW?
WE SHOULD BE OKAY--
--AS LONG AS WE KEEP THESE TWO SEPARATED.
LOOK, I DON'T HAVE ANY PROBLEM WITH HER.
SHE ATTACKED ME FIRST!
I KNOW WHAT IT LOOKED LIKE. I CAN ONLY IMAGINE WHAT IT FELT LIKE, SUPERGIRL.
BUT, IT WASN'T AN ATTACK.
THINK OF IT AS TWO POSITIVE WIRES ON A TRANSFORMER CROSSING. INSTEAD OF REPELLING, THERE IS AN ENERGY BURST.
FROM WHAT LITTLE WE KNOW ABOUT YOUR ORIGINS, THEY ARE SIMILAR ENOUGH THAT YOU'RE ESSENTIALLY- WELL--
--LIKE THE SAME PERSON TRYING TO OCCUPY A SINGLE SPACE.
SUPERGIRL, FOR WHATEVER REASON, COULD HANDLE THE OVERLOAD, WHILE POWER GIRL COULD NOT.
MAKES SENSE. SINCE P.G.'S POWERS STARTED GLITCHING RIGHT AROUND WHEN SUPERGIRL CAME TO EARTH.
SO... WE'RE LIKE... ALLERGIC TO EACH OTHER?
IS THERE SOME KIND OF TEST WE COULD TAKE TO FIND OUT IF IT'S TRUE? BATMAN COULD--
--NO.
I'VE HEARD ENOUGH.
NO MORE TESTS. MY HEAD IS SCREWED-UP ENOUGH AS IT IS. I KNOW ALL I WANT TO KNOW.
SHE... SHE'S GOT ISSUES, KARA.
YOU CAN'T TAKE IT PERSONALLY.
YEAH...?
Don't take it personally...?

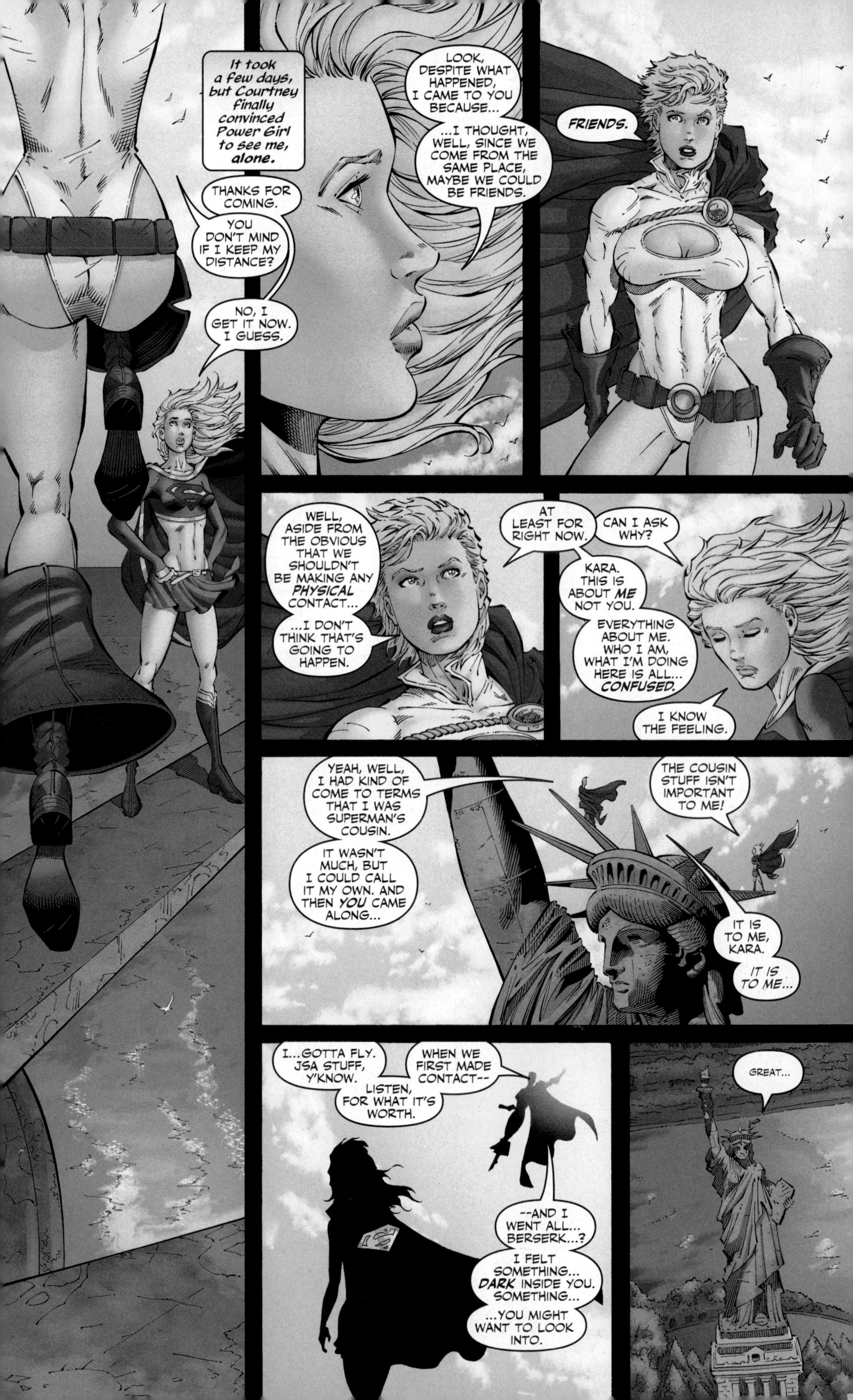
It took a few days, but Courtney finally convinced Power Girl to see me, alone.
THANKS FOR COMING.
YOU DON'T MIND IF I KEEP MY DISTANCE?
NO, I GET IT NOW. I GUESS.
LOOK, DESPITE WHAT HAPPENED, I CAME TO YOU BECAUSE...
...I THOUGHT, WELL, SINCE WE COME FROM THE SAME PLACE, MAYBE WE COULD BE FRIENDS.
FRIENDS.
WELL, ASIDE FROM THE OBVIOUS THAT WE SHOULDN'T BE MAKING ANY PHYSICAL CONTACT...
...I DON'T THINK THAT'S GOING TO HAPPEN.
AT LEAST FOR RIGHT NOW.
CAN I ASK WHY?
KARA. THIS IS ABOUT ME NOT YOU.
EVERYTHING ABOUT ME. WHO I AM, WHAT I'M DOING HERE IS ALL... CONFUSED.
I KNOW THE FEELING.
YEAH, WELL, I HAD KIND OF COME TO TERMS THAT I WAS SUPERMAN'S COUSIN.
IT WASN'T MUCH, BUT I COULD CALL IT MY OWN. AND THEN YOU CAME ALONG...
THE COUSIN STUFF ISN'T IMPORTANT TO ME!
IT IS TO ME, KARA.
IT IS TO ME...
I...GOTTA FLY. JSA STUFF, Y'KNOW.
LISTEN, FOR WHAT IT'S WORTH.
WHEN WE FIRST MADE CONTACT--
--AND I WENT ALL... BERSERK...?
I FELT SOMETHING... DARK INSIDE YOU. SOMETHING...
...YOU MIGHT WANT TO LOOK INTO.
GREAT...

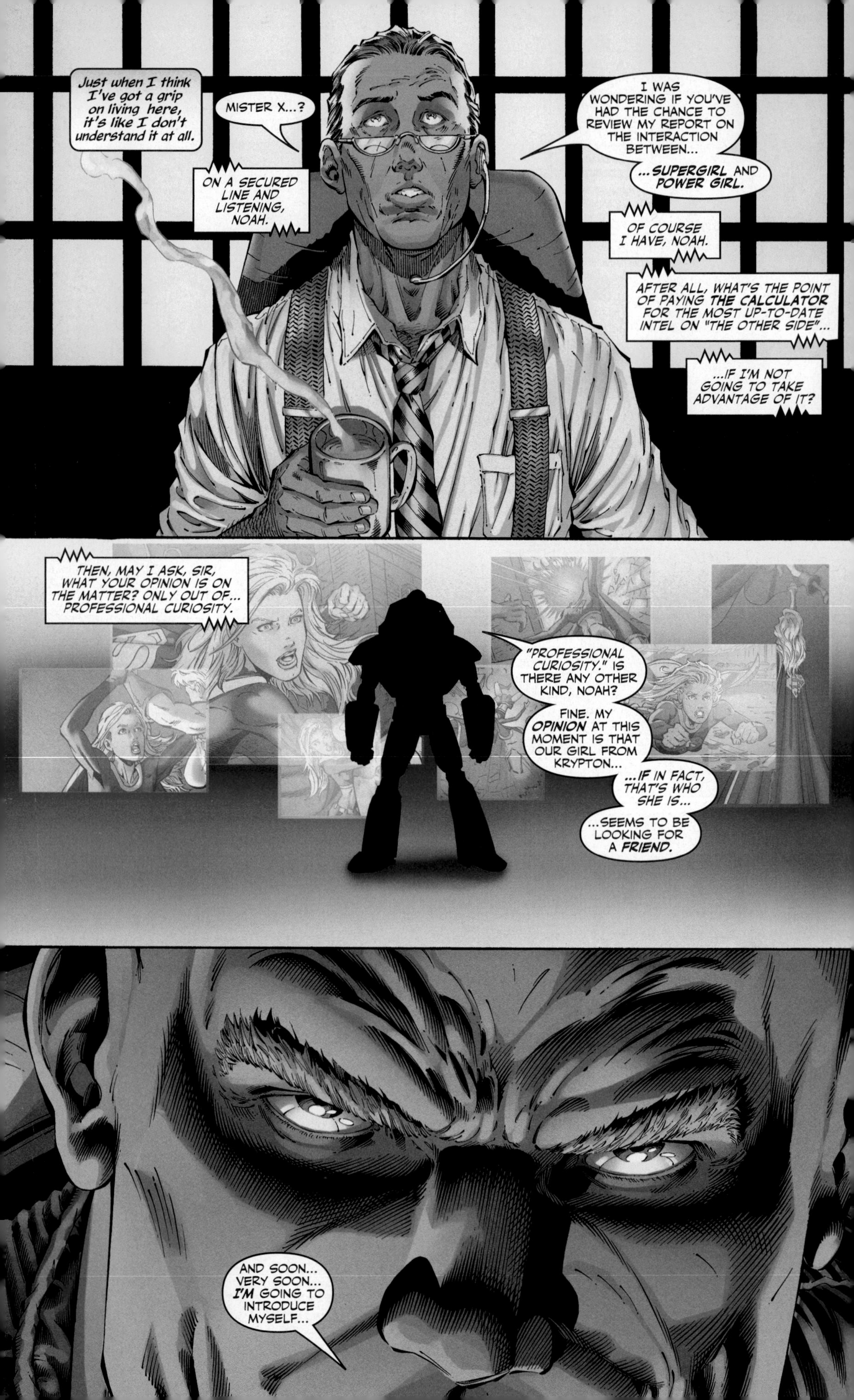
Just when I think I've got a grip on living here, it's like I don't understand it at all.
MISTER X...?
I WAS WONDERING IF YOU'VE HAD THE CHANCE TO REVIEW MY REPORT ON THE INTERACTION BETWEEN...
...SUPERGIRL AND POWER GIRL.
ON A SECURED LINE AND LISTENING, NOAH.
OF COURSE I HAVE, NOAH.
AFTER ALL, WHAT'S THE POINT OF PAYING THE CALCULATOR FOR THE MOST UP-TO-DATE INTEL ON "THE OTHER SIDE"...
...IF I'M NOT GOING TO TAKE ADVANTAGE OF IT?
THEN, MAY I ASK, SIR, WHAT YOUR OPINION IS ON THE MATTER? ONLY OUT OF... PROFESSIONAL CURIOSITY.
"PROFESSIONAL CURIOSITY." IS THERE ANY OTHER KIND, NOAH?
FINE. MY OPINION AT THIS MOMENT IS THAT OUR GIRL FROM KRYPTON...
...IF IN FACT, THAT'S WHO SHE IS...
...SEEMS TO BE LOOKING FOR A FRIEND.
AND SOON... VERY SOON... I'M GOING TO INTRODUCE MYSELF...

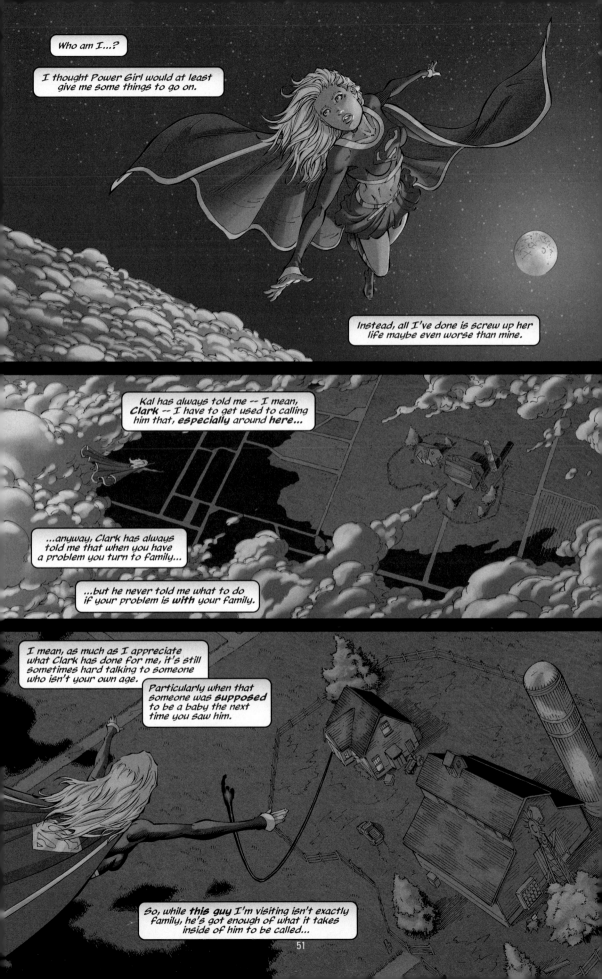

Who am I...?

I thought Power Girl would at least give me some things to go on.

Instead, all I've done is screw up her life maybe even worse than mine.

Kal has always told me -- I mean, **Clark** -- I have to get used to calling him that, **especially** around **here**...

...anyway, Clark has always told me that when you have a problem you turn to family...

...but he never told me what to do if your problem is **with** your family.

I mean, as much as I appreciate what Clark has done for me, it's still sometimes hard talking to someone who isn't your own age.

Particularly when that someone was **supposed** to be a baby the next time you saw him.

So, while **this guy** I'm visiting isn't exactly family, he's got enough of what it takes inside of him to be called...

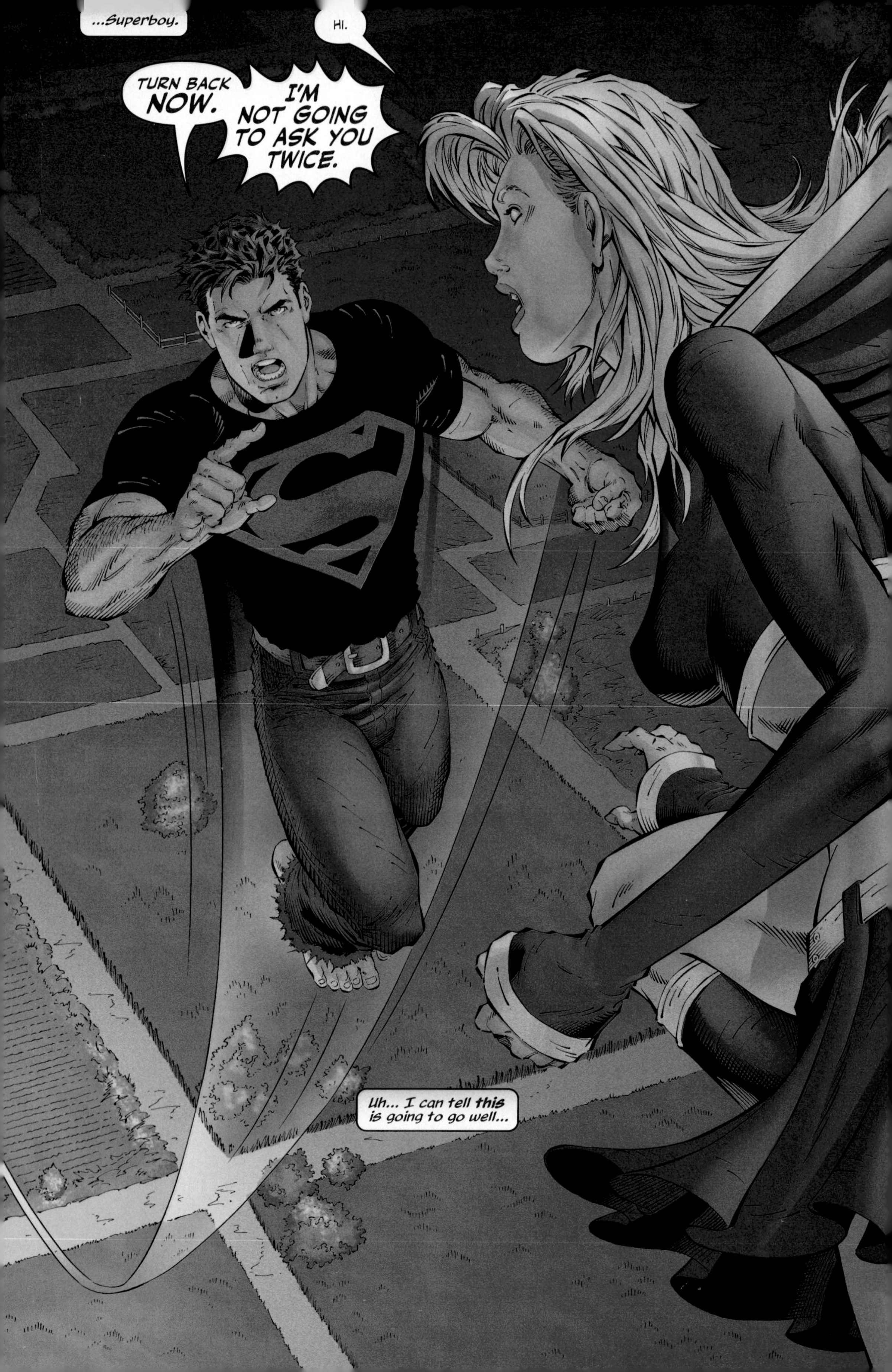

...Superboy.
HI.
TURN BACK NOW.
I'M NOT GOING TO ASK YOU TWICE.
Uh... I can tell this is going to go well...

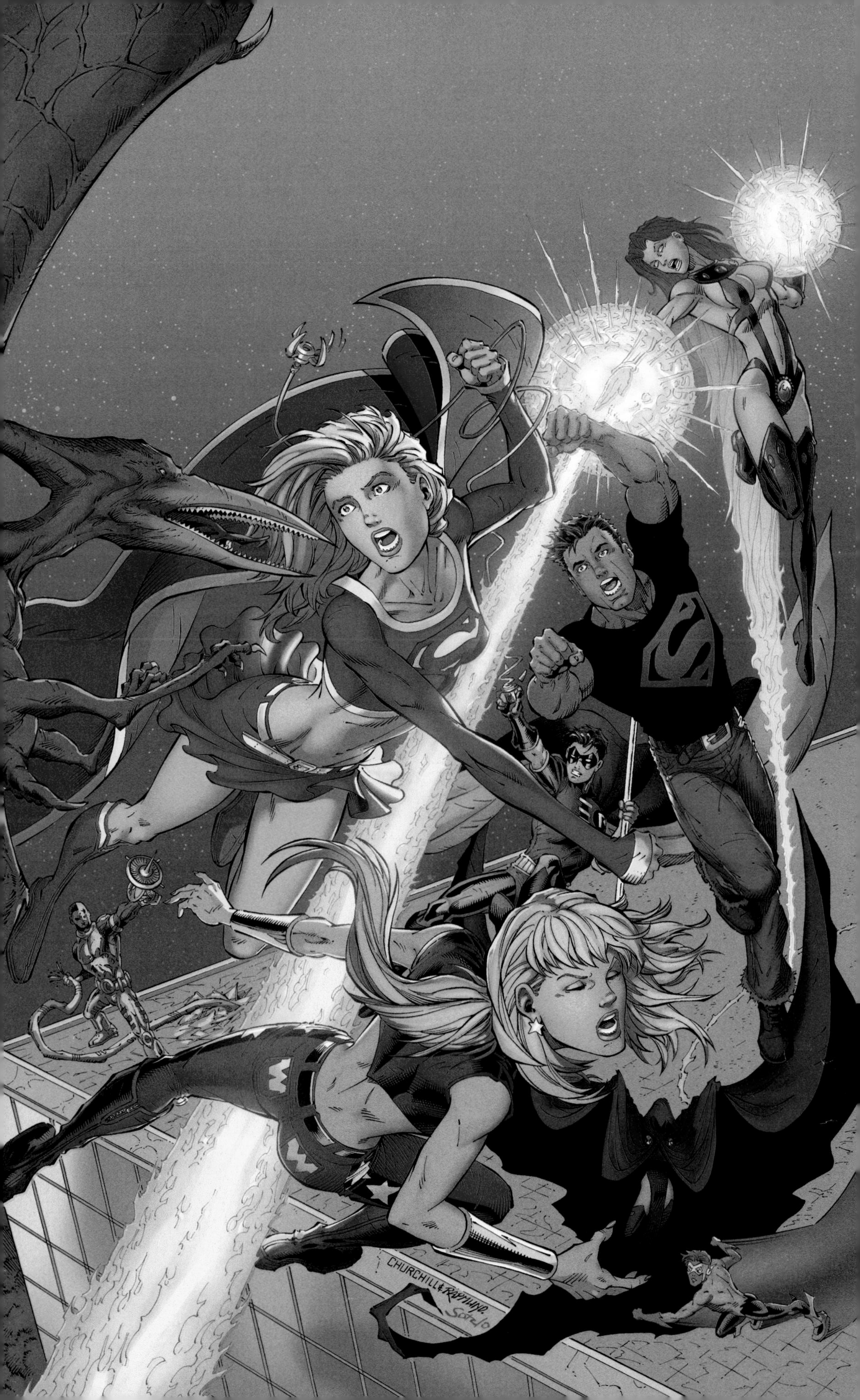
CHURCHILL&RAPMUND.

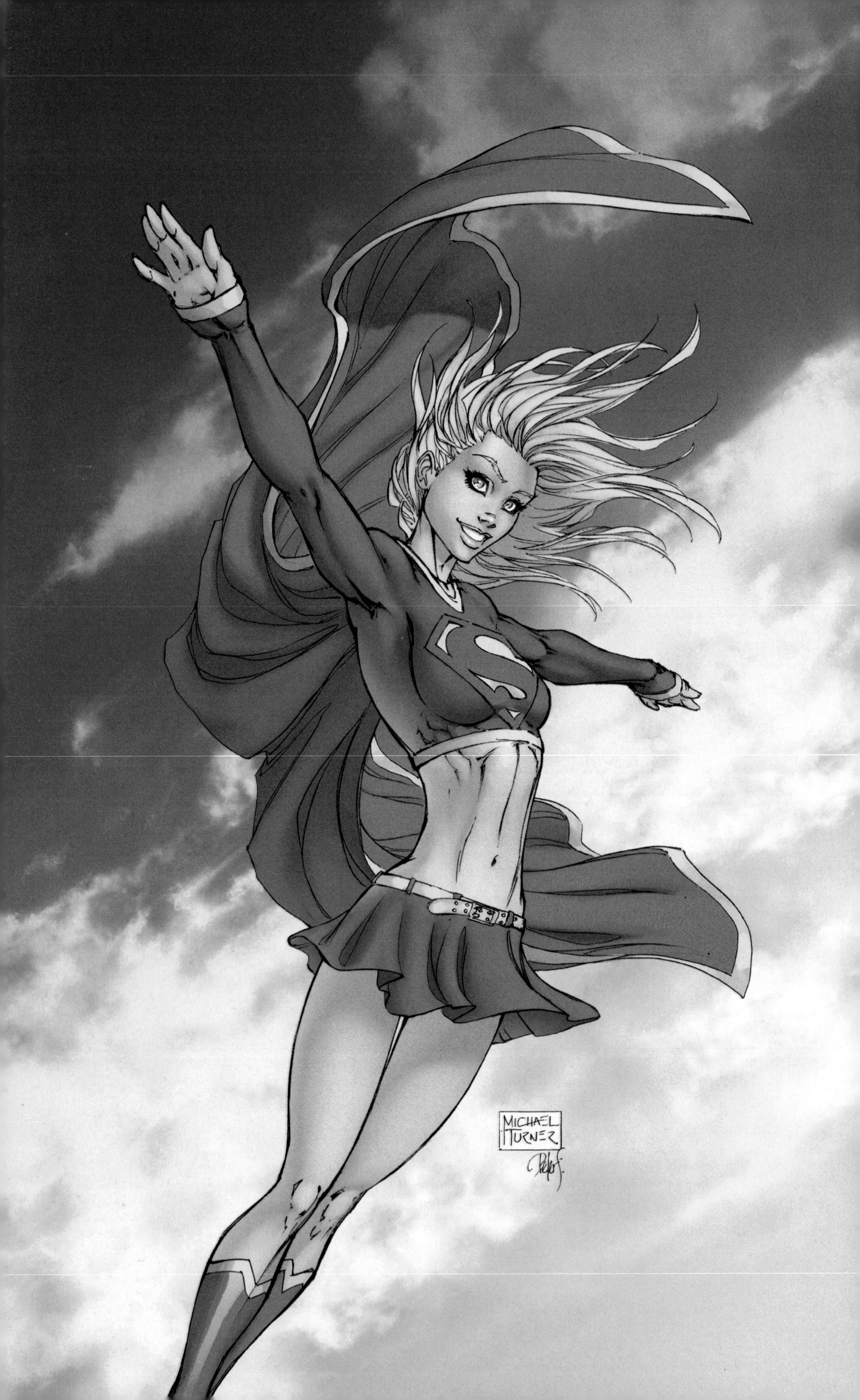
MICHAEL TURNER

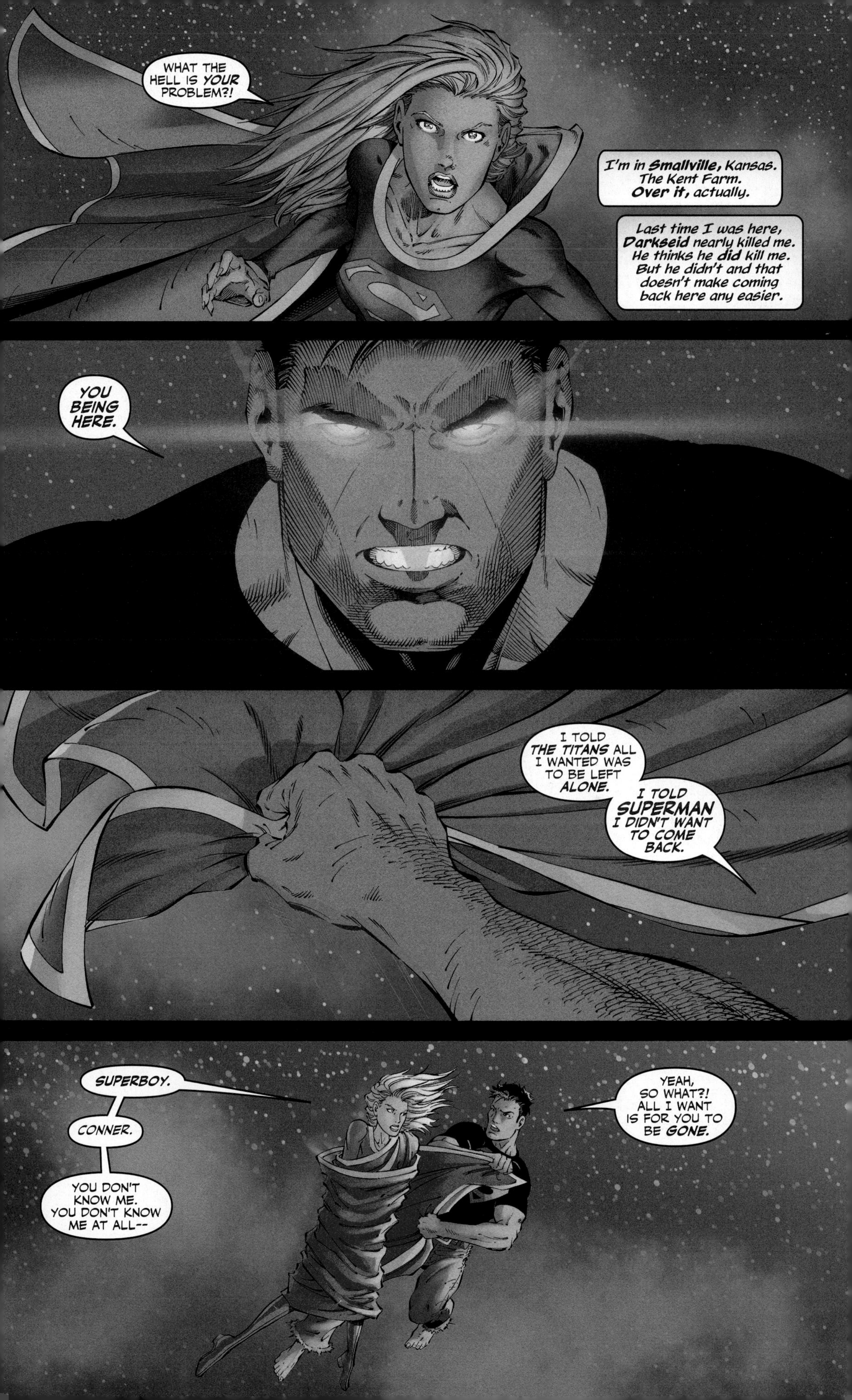
WHAT THE HELL IS YOUR PROBLEM?!
I'm in Smallville, Kansas. The Kent Farm. Over it, actually.
Last time I was here, Darkseid nearly killed me. He thinks he did kill me. But he didn't and that doesn't make coming back here any easier.
YOU BEING HERE.
I TOLD THE TITANS ALL I WANTED WAS TO BE LEFT ALONE.
I TOLD SUPERMAN I DIDN'T WANT TO COME BACK.
SUPERBOY.
CONNER.
YOU DON'T KNOW ME. YOU DON'T KNOW ME AT ALL--
YEAH, SO WHAT?! ALL I WANT IS FOR YOU TO BE GONE.

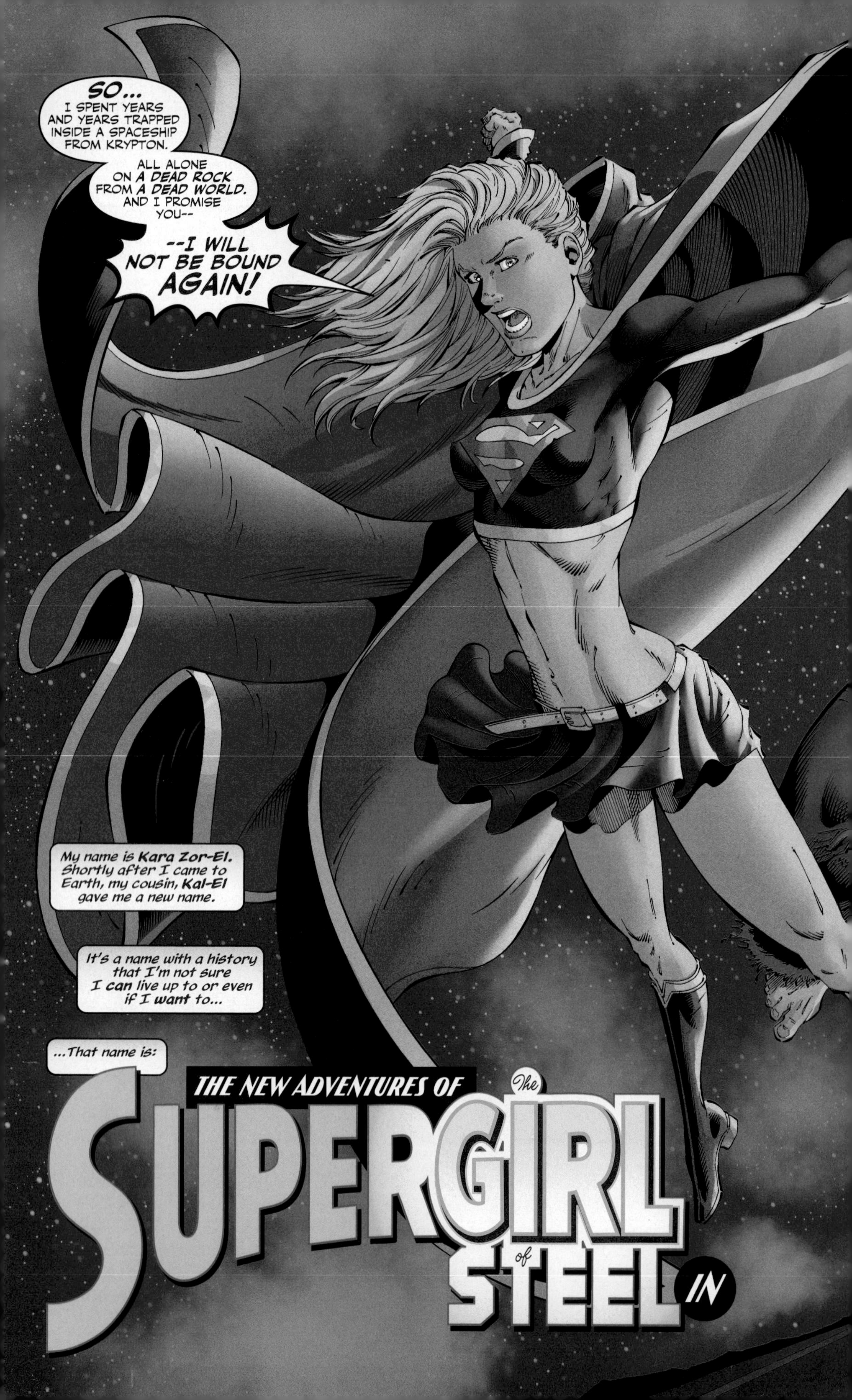
SO...
I SPENT YEARS AND YEARS TRAPPED INSIDE A SPACESHIP FROM KRYPTON.
ALL ALONE ON A DEAD ROCK FROM A DEAD WORLD. AND I PROMISE YOU--
--I WILL NOT BE BOUND AGAIN!
My name is Kara Zor-El. Shortly after I came to Earth, my cousin, Kal-El gave me a new name.
It's a name with a history that I'm not sure I can live up to or even if I want to...
...That name is:
THE NEW ADVENTURES OF
The SUPERGIRL of STEEL IN

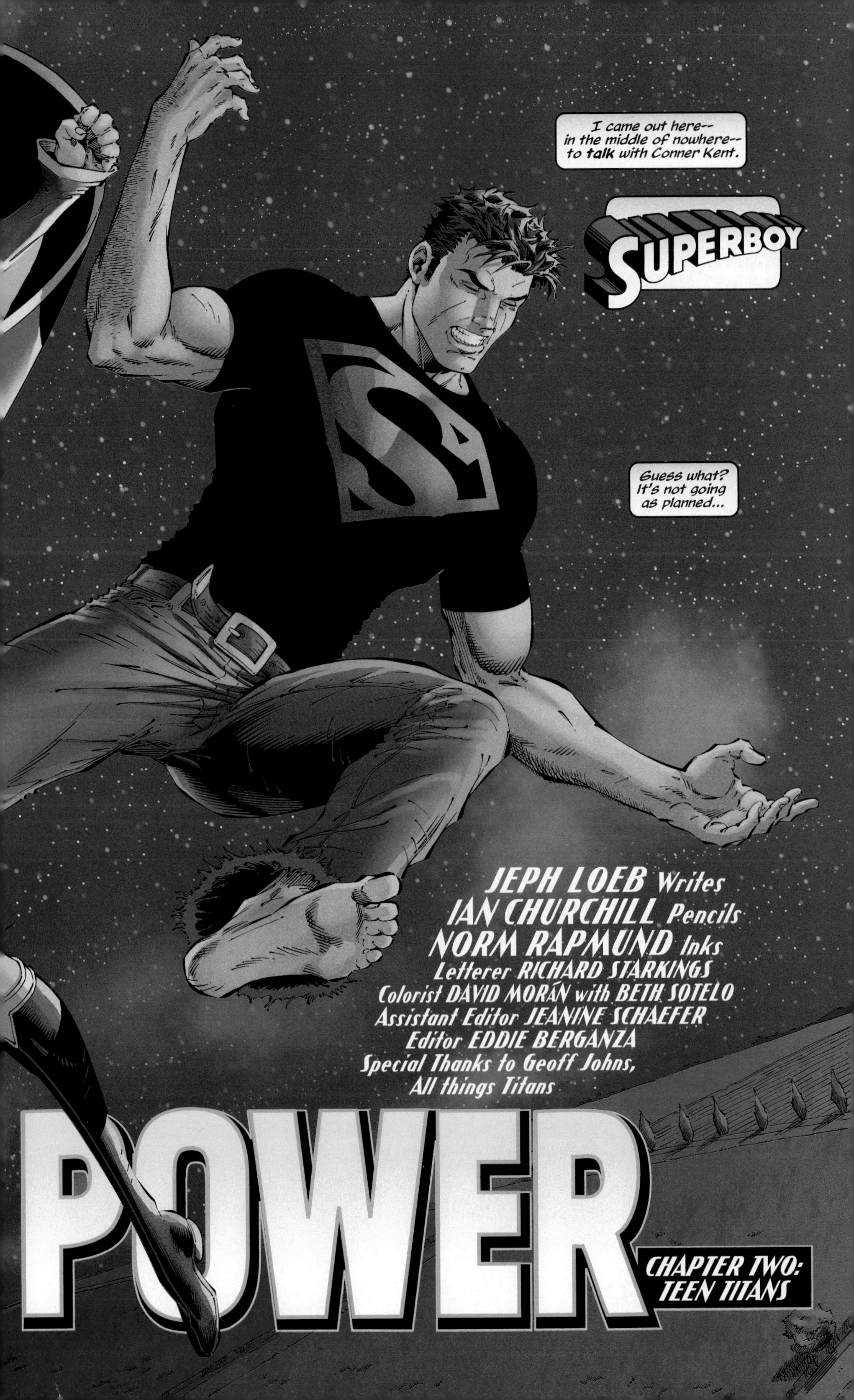

I came out here-- in the middle of nowhere-- to talk with Conner Kent.
SUPERBOY
Guess what? It's not going as planned...
JEPH LOEB Writes
IAN CHURCHILL Pencils
NORM RAPMUND Inks
Letterer RICHARD STARKINGS
Colorist DAVID MORÁN with BETH SOTELO
Assistant Editor JEANINE SCHAEFER
Editor EDDIE BERGANZA
Special Thanks to Geoff Johns, All things Titans
POWER
CHAPTER TWO: TEEN TITANS

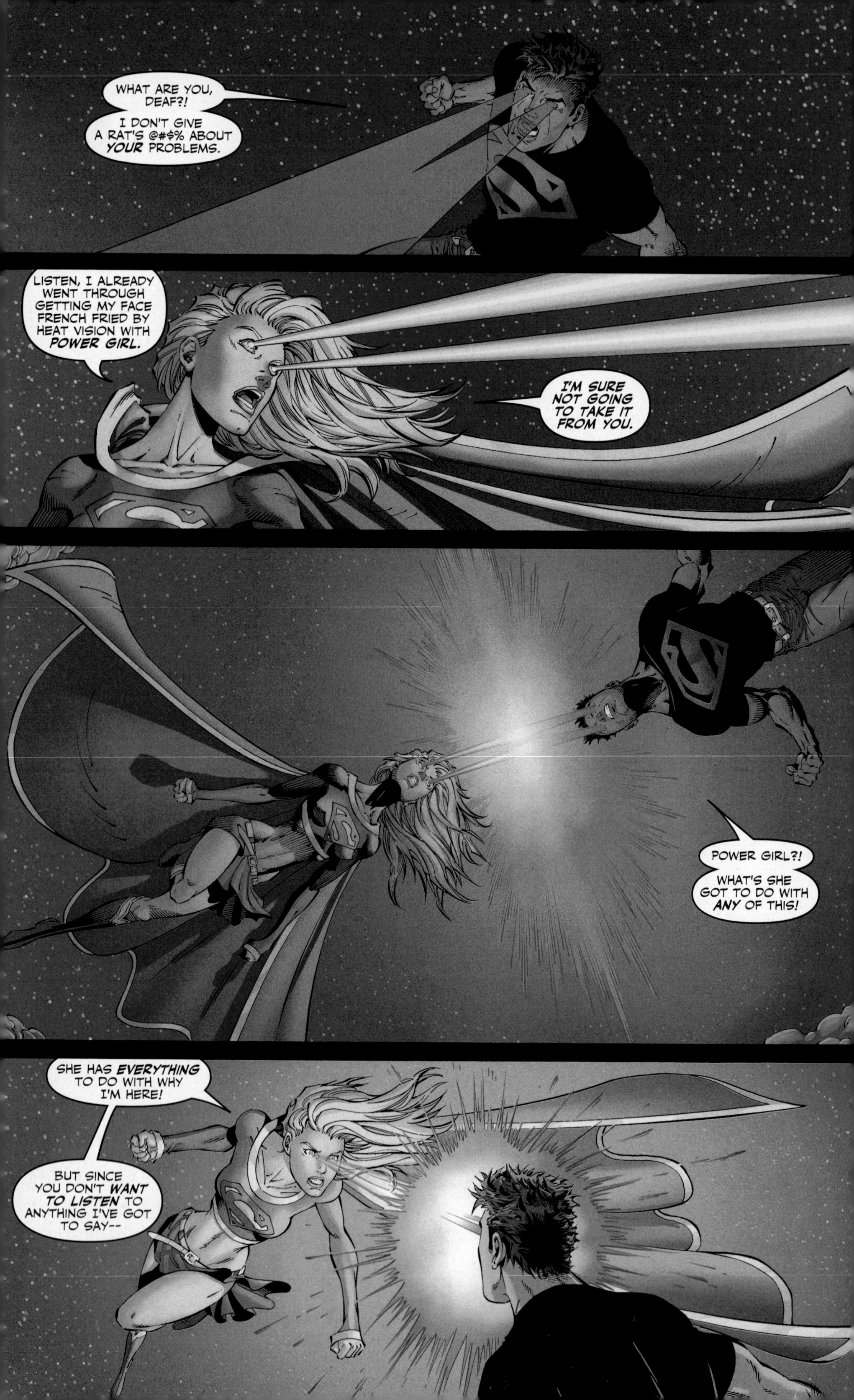
WHAT ARE YOU, DEAF?!
I DON'T GIVE A RAT'S @#$% ABOUT *YOUR* PROBLEMS.
LISTEN, I ALREADY WENT THROUGH GETTING MY FACE FRENCH FRIED BY HEAT VISION WITH *POWER GIRL.*
I'M SURE NOT GOING TO TAKE IT FROM YOU.
POWER GIRL?!
WHAT'S SHE GOT TO DO WITH *ANY* OF THIS!
SHE HAS *EVERYTHING* TO DO WITH WHY I'M HERE!
BUT SINCE YOU DON'T *WANT TO LISTEN* TO ANYTHING I'VE GOT TO SAY--

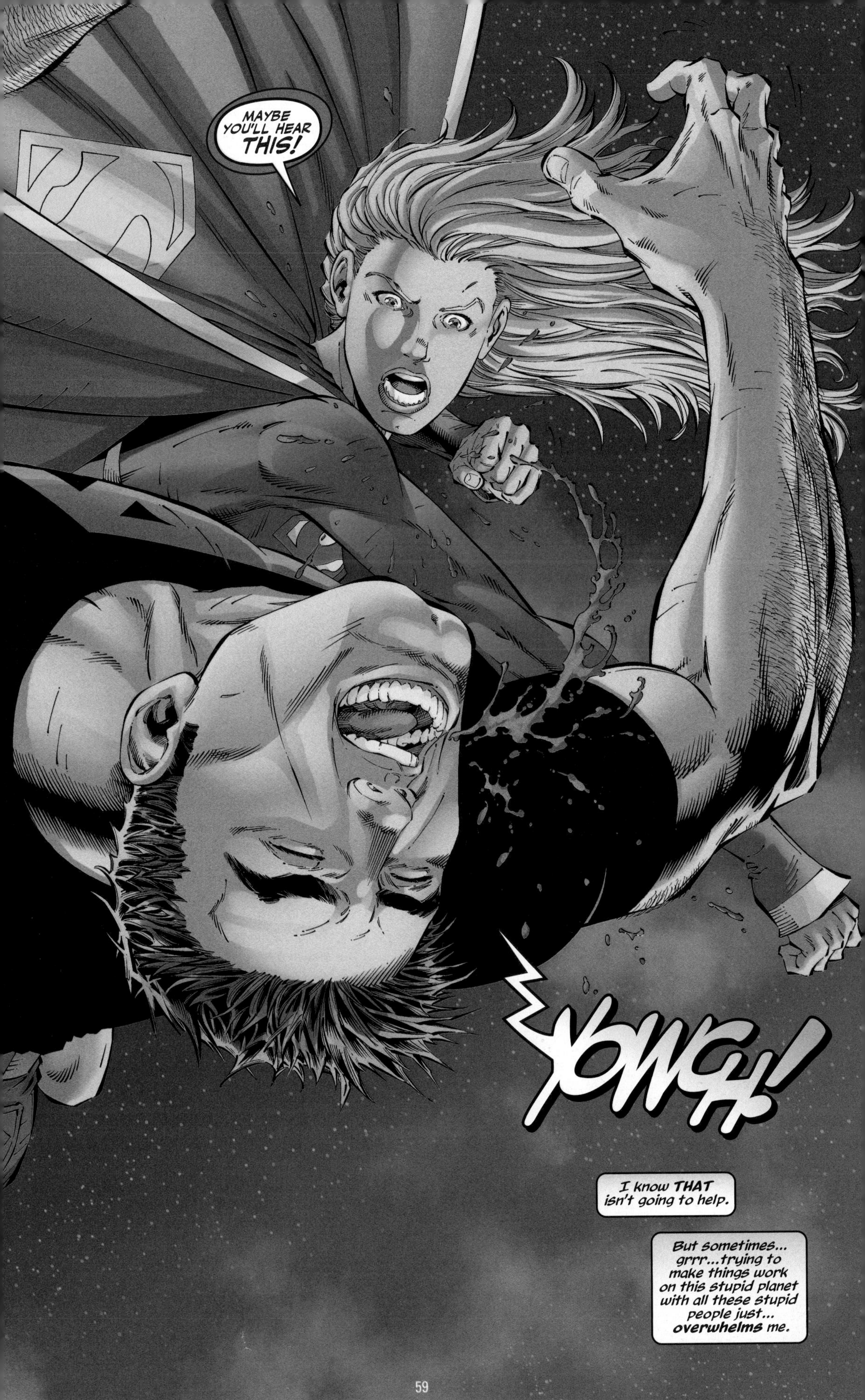

MAYBE YOU'LL HEAR THIS!
YOWCH!
I know THAT isn't going to help.
But sometimes... grrr...trying to make things work on this stupid planet with all these stupid people just... overwhelms me.

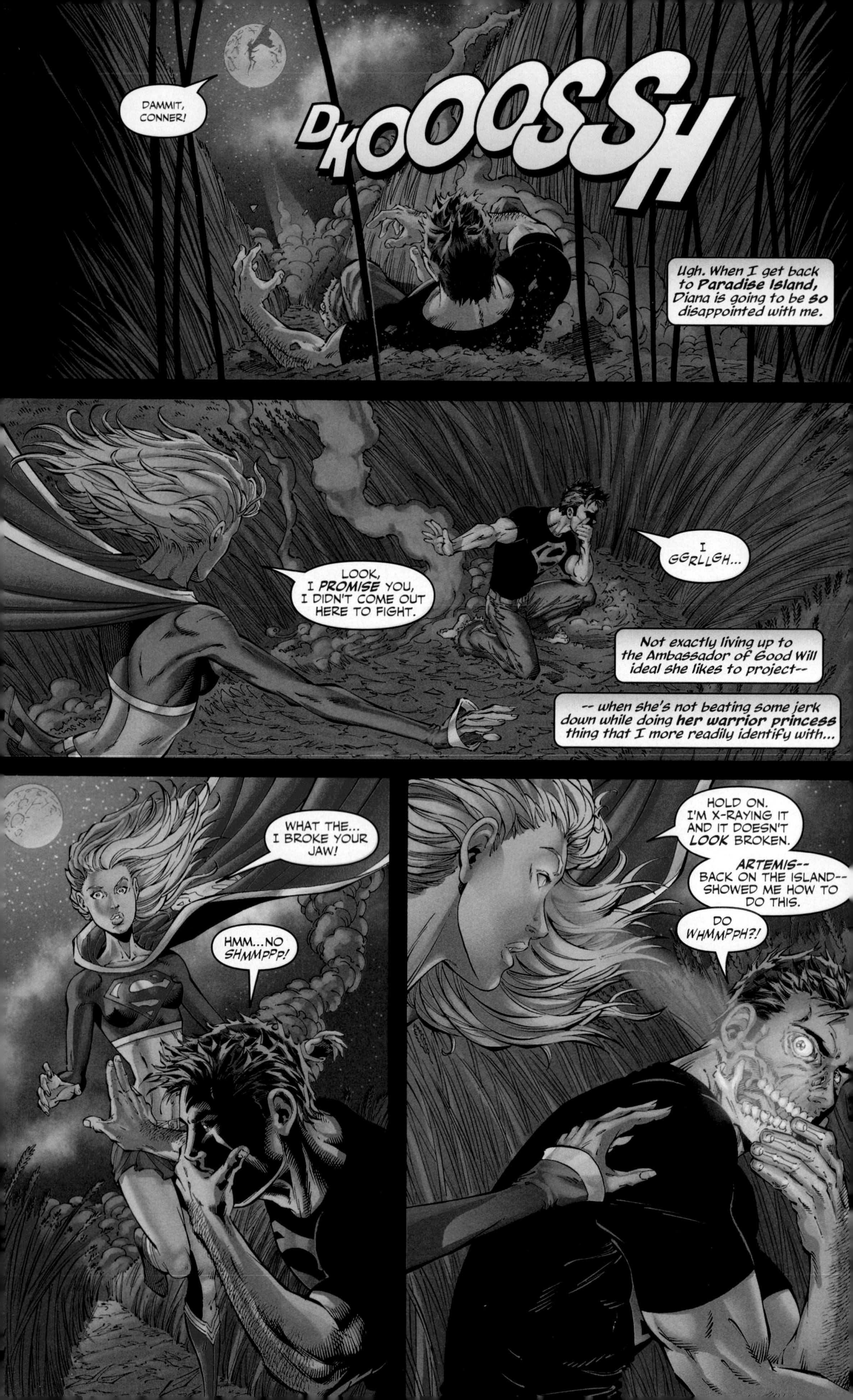
DAMMIT, CONNER!
DKOOOOSSH
Ugh. When I get back to Paradise Island, Diana is going to be so disappointed with me.
LOOK, I PROMISE YOU, I DIDN'T COME OUT HERE TO FIGHT.
I GGRLLGH...
Not exactly living up to the Ambassador of Good Will ideal she likes to project--
-- when she's not beating some jerk down while doing her warrior princess thing that I more readily identify with...
WHAT THE... I BROKE YOUR JAW!
HMM...NO SHMMPPP!
HOLD ON. I'M X-RAYING IT AND IT DOESN'T LOOK BROKEN.
ARTEMIS-- BACK ON THE ISLAND-- SHOWED ME HOW TO DO THIS.
DO WHMMPPH?!

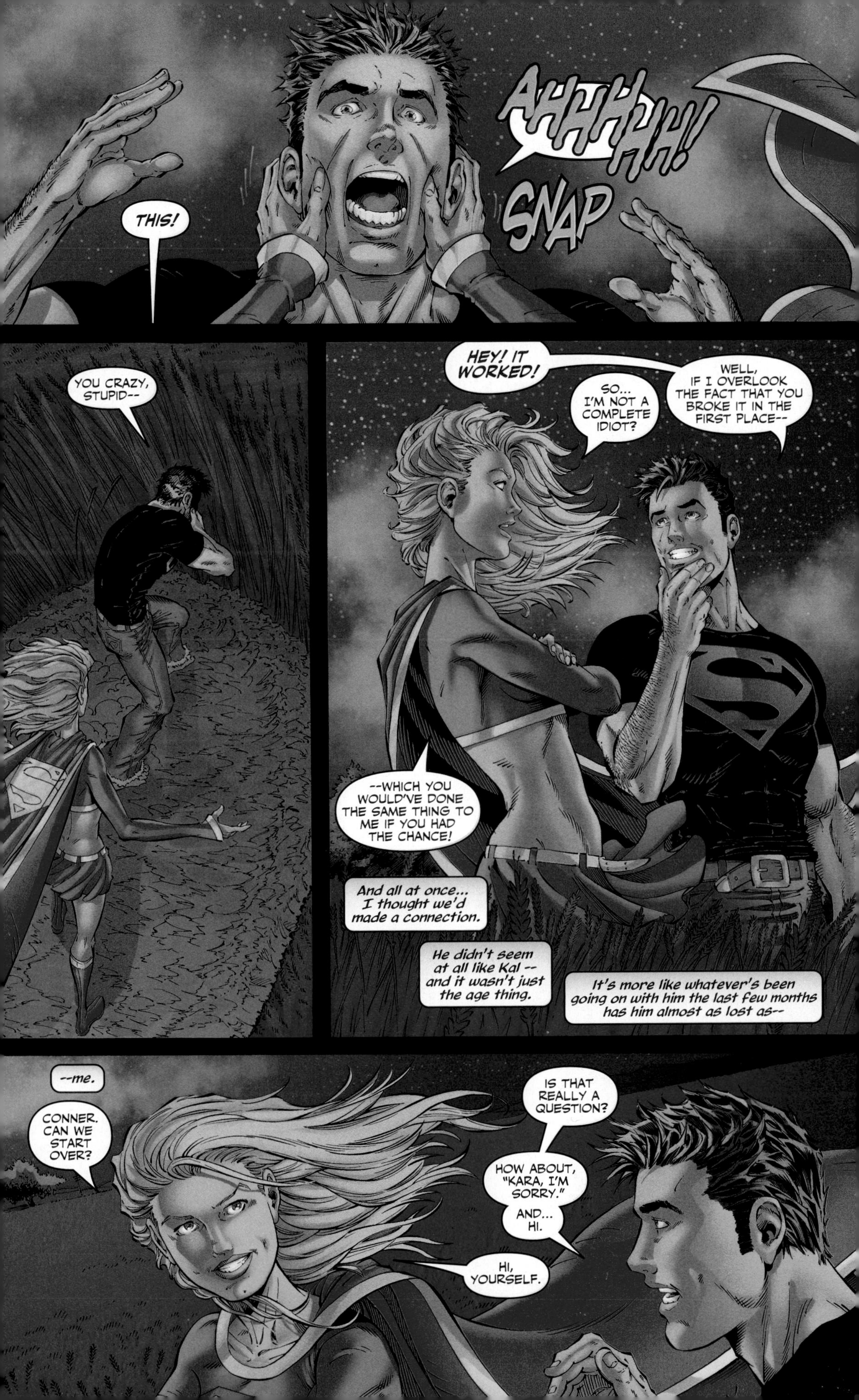
THIS!
AHHHHHH!
SNAP
YOU CRAZY, STUPID--
HEY! IT WORKED!
SO... I'M NOT A COMPLETE IDIOT?
WELL, IF I OVERLOOK THE FACT THAT YOU BROKE IT IN THE FIRST PLACE--
--WHICH YOU WOULD'VE DONE THE SAME THING TO ME IF YOU HAD THE CHANCE!
And all at once... I thought we'd made a connection.
He didn't seem at all like Kal -- and it wasn't just the age thing.
It's more like whatever's been going on with him the last few months has him almost as lost as--
--me.
CONNER. CAN WE START OVER?
IS THAT REALLY A QUESTION?
HOW ABOUT, "KARA, I'M SORRY."
AND... HI.
HI, YOURSELF.

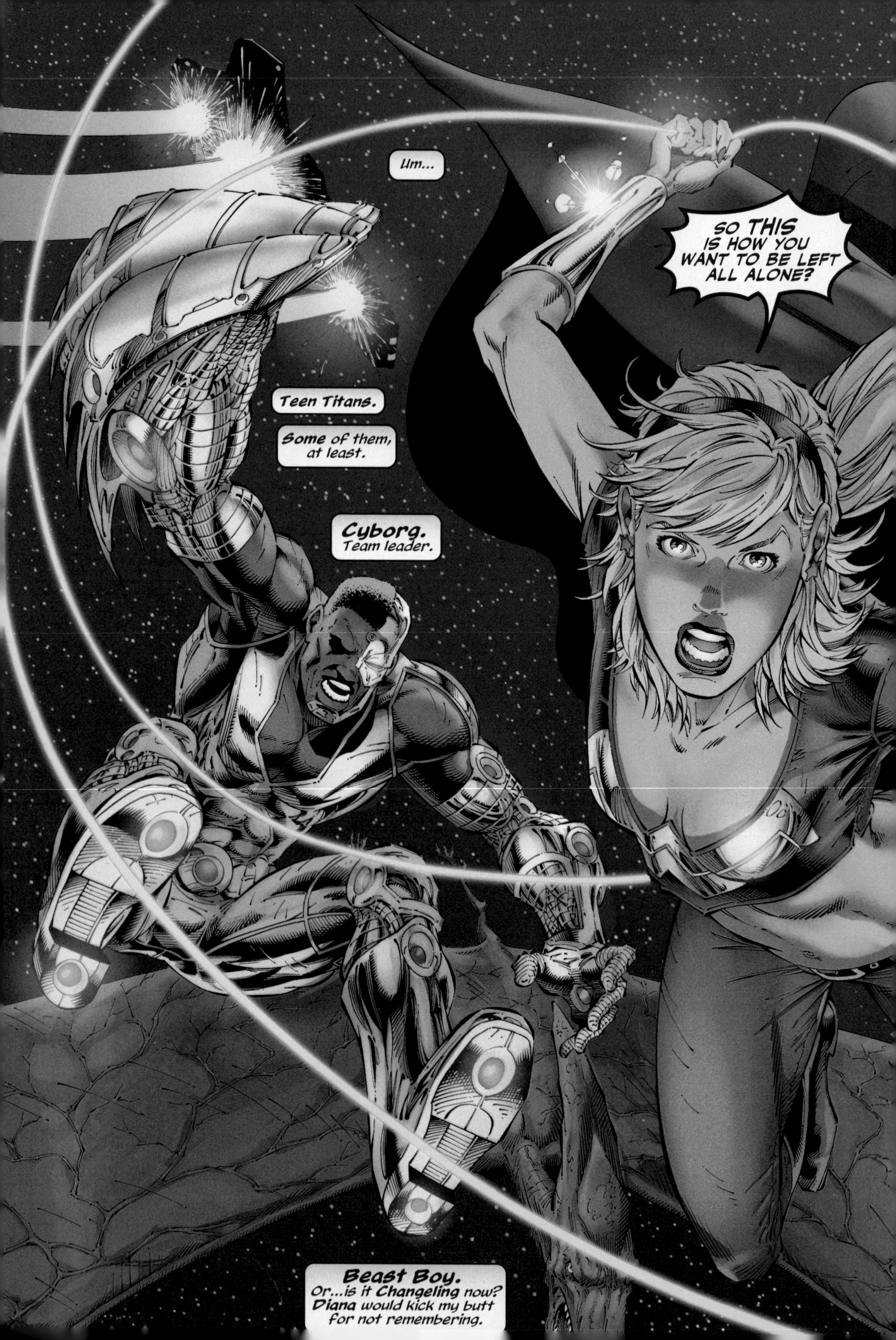
Um...
SO THIS IS HOW YOU WANT TO BE LEFT ALL ALONE?
Teen Titans.
Some of them, at least.
Cyborg. Team leader.
Beast Boy. Or...is it Changeling now? Diana would kick my butt for not remembering.

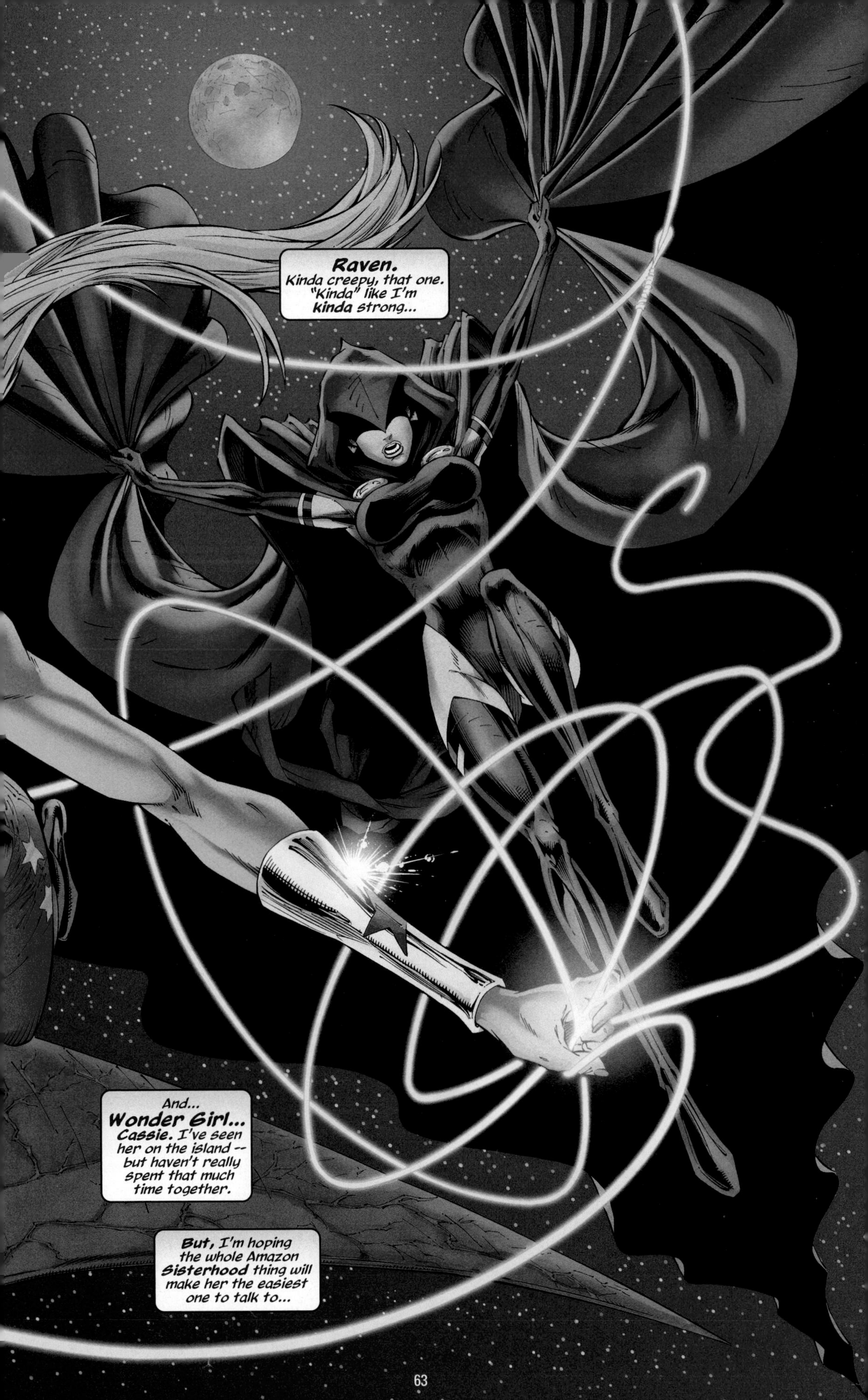
Raven. Kinda creepy, that one. "Kinda" like I'm kinda strong...
And... Wonder Girl... Cassie. I've seen her on the island -- but haven't really spent that much time together.
But, I'm hoping the whole Amazon Sisterhood thing will make her the easiest one to talk to...

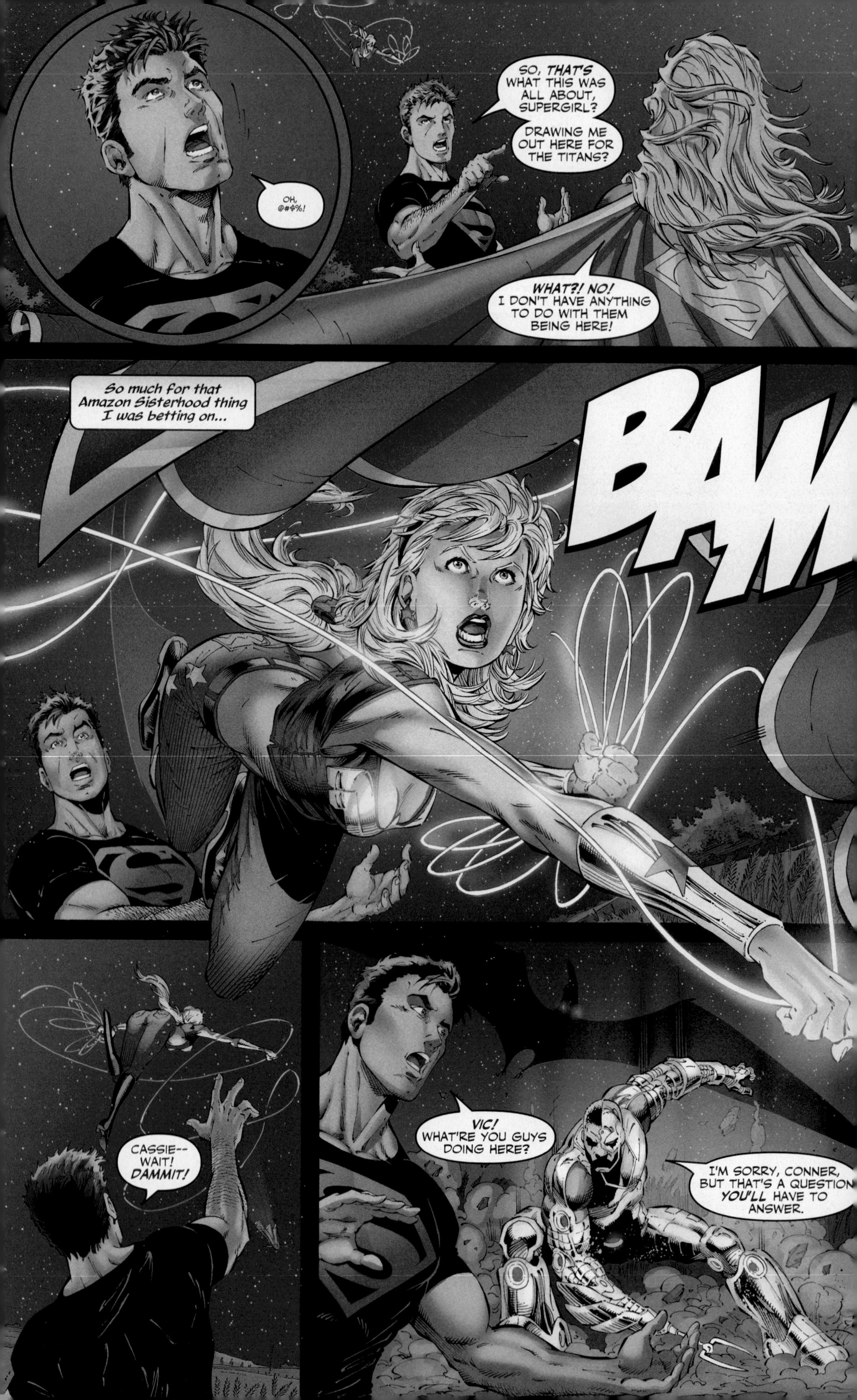
OH, @#$%!
SO, THAT'S WHAT THIS WAS ALL ABOUT, SUPERGIRL?
DRAWING ME OUT HERE FOR THE TITANS?
WHAT?! NO! I DON'T HAVE ANYTHING TO DO WITH THEM BEING HERE!
So much for that Amazon Sisterhood thing I was betting on...
BAM
CASSIE-- WAIT! DAMMIT!
VIC! WHAT'RE YOU GUYS DOING HERE?
I'M SORRY, CONNER, BUT THAT'S A QUESTION YOU'LL HAVE TO ANSWER.

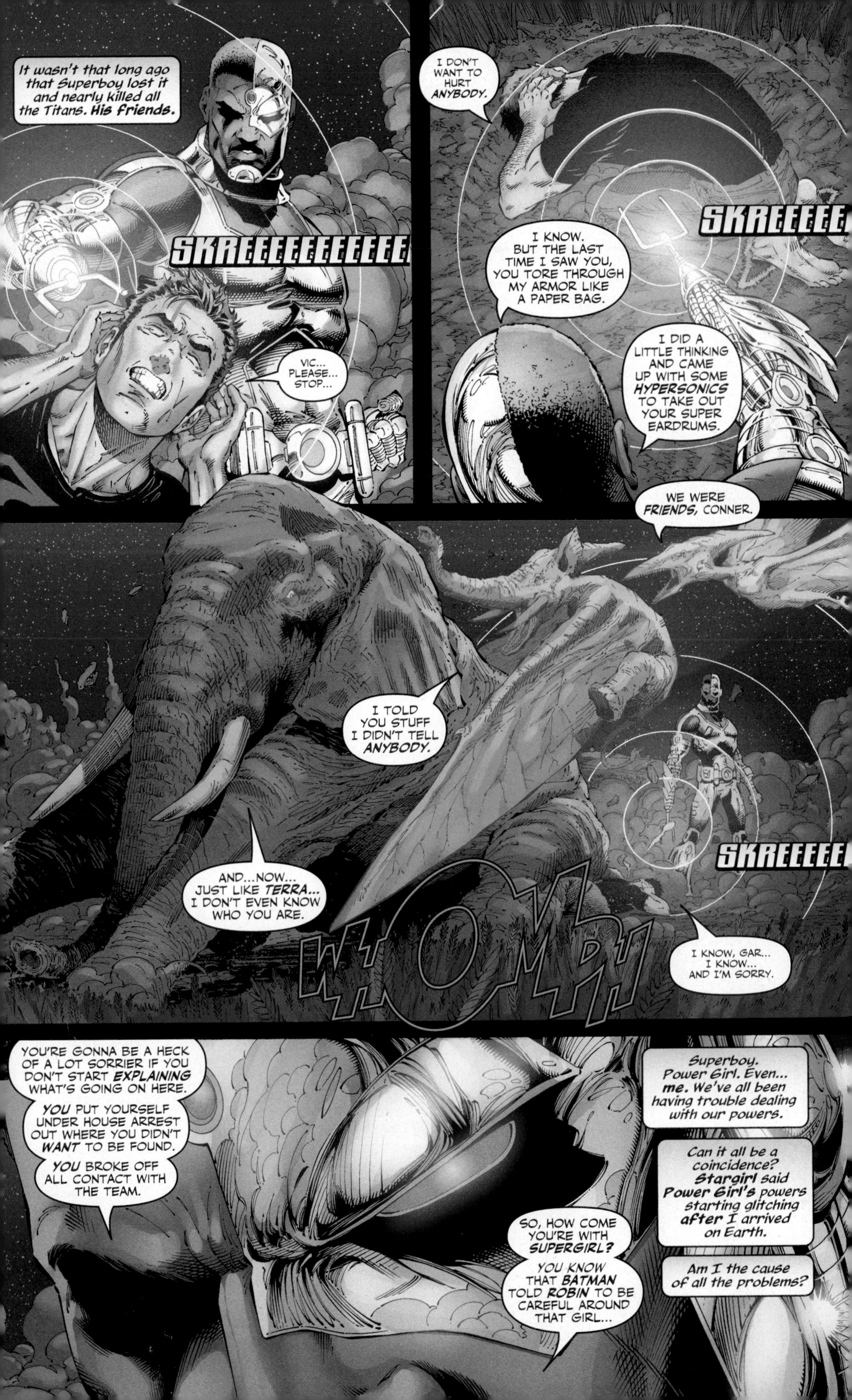

It wasn't that long ago that Superboy lost it and nearly killed all the Titans. His friends.
SKREEEEEEEEEEEE
VIC... PLEASE... STOP...
I DON'T WANT TO HURT ANYBODY.
SKREEEEEE
I KNOW. BUT THE LAST TIME I SAW YOU, YOU TORE THROUGH MY ARMOR LIKE A PAPER BAG.
I DID A LITTLE THINKING AND CAME UP WITH SOME HYPERSONICS TO TAKE OUT YOUR SUPER EARDRUMS.
WE WERE FRIENDS, CONNER.
I TOLD YOU STUFF I DIDN'T TELL ANYBODY.
AND...NOW... JUST LIKE TERRA... I DON'T EVEN KNOW WHO YOU ARE.
SKREEEEEE
WHOMPH
I KNOW, GAR... I KNOW... AND I'M SORRY.
YOU'RE GONNA BE A HECK OF A LOT SORRIER IF YOU DON'T START EXPLAINING WHAT'S GOING ON HERE.
YOU PUT YOURSELF UNDER HOUSE ARREST OUT WHERE YOU DIDN'T WANT TO BE FOUND.
YOU BROKE OFF ALL CONTACT WITH THE TEAM.
SO, HOW COME YOU'RE WITH SUPERGIRL?
YOU KNOW THAT BATMAN TOLD ROBIN TO BE CAREFUL AROUND THAT GIRL...
Superboy. Power Girl. Even... me. We've all been having trouble dealing with our powers.
Can it all be a coincidence? Stargirl said Power Girl's powers starting glitching after I arrived on Earth.
Am I the cause of all the problems?

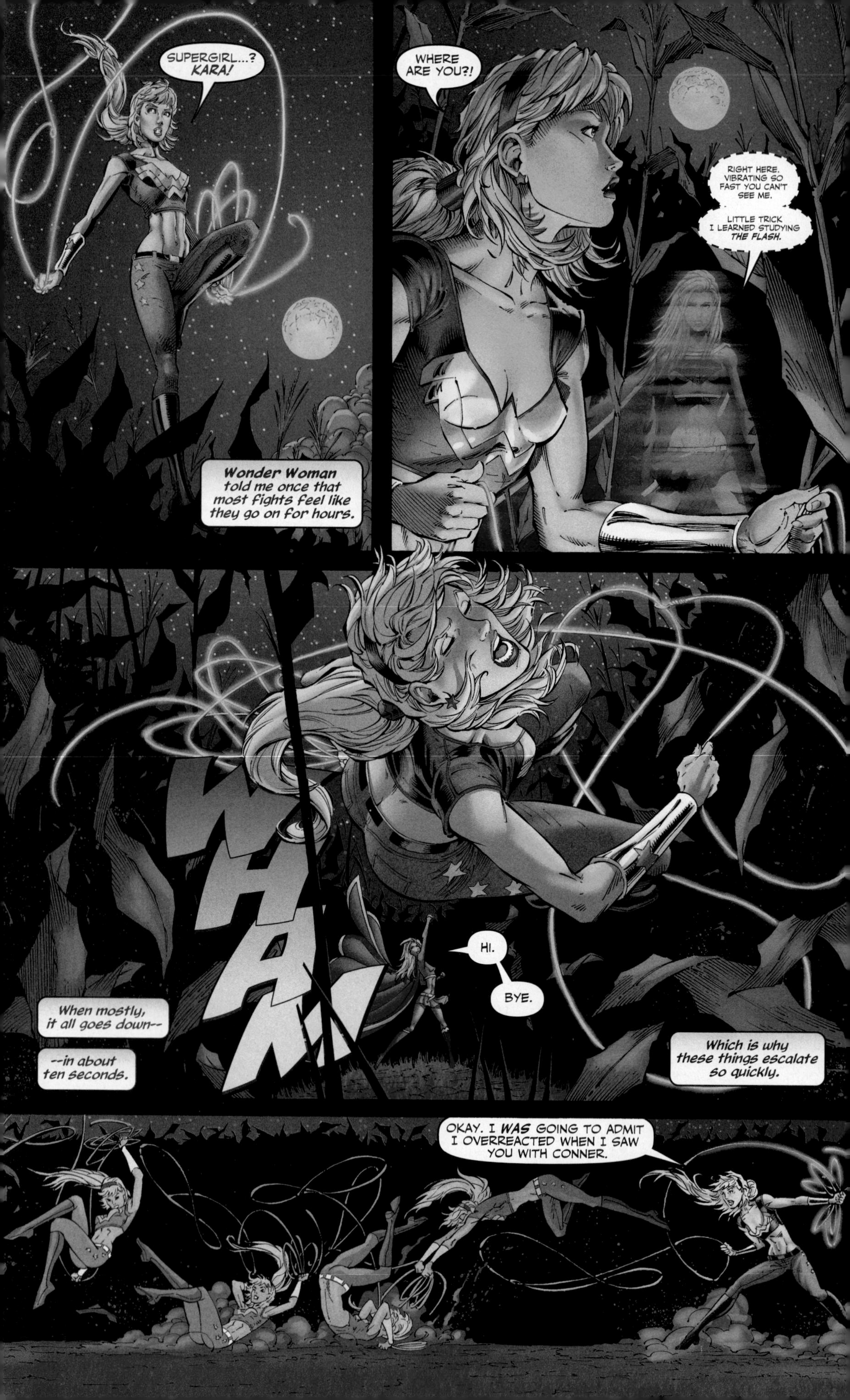
SUPERGIRL...? KARA!
Wonder Woman told me once that most fights feel like they go on for hours.
WHERE ARE YOU?!
RIGHT HERE. VIBRATING SO FAST YOU CAN'T SEE ME.
LITTLE TRICK I LEARNED STUDYING THE FLASH.
When mostly, it all goes down--
--in about ten seconds.
WHAM!!
HI.
BYE.
Which is why these things escalate so quickly.
OKAY. I WAS GOING TO ADMIT I OVERREACTED WHEN I SAW YOU WITH CONNER.

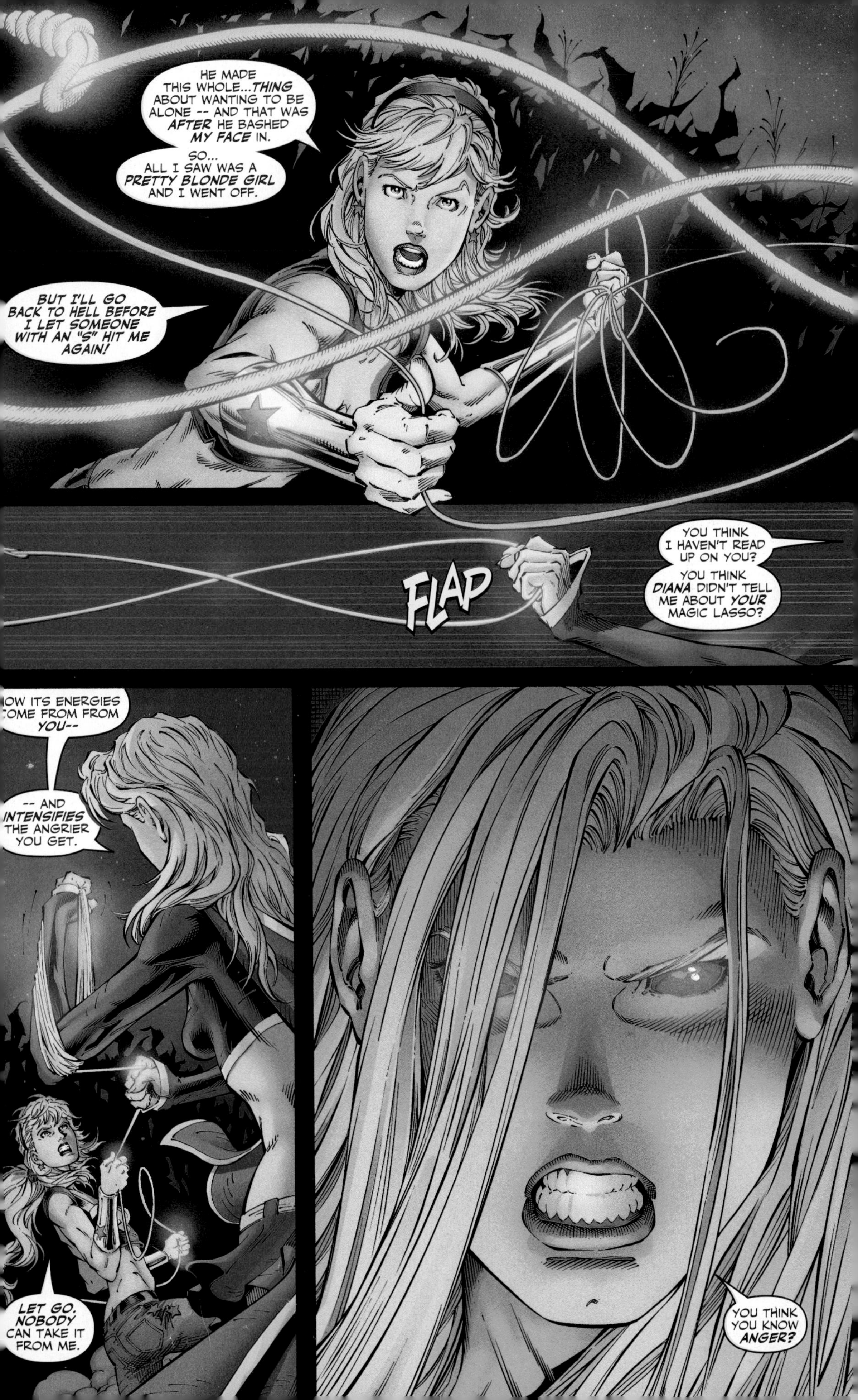
HE MADE THIS WHOLE...THING ABOUT WANTING TO BE ALONE -- AND THAT WAS AFTER HE BASHED MY FACE IN.
SO... ALL I SAW WAS A PRETTY BLONDE GIRL AND I WENT OFF.
BUT I'LL GO BACK TO HELL BEFORE I LET SOMEONE WITH AN "S" HIT ME AGAIN!
FLAP
YOU THINK I HAVEN'T READ UP ON YOU?
YOU THINK DIANA DIDN'T TELL ME ABOUT YOUR MAGIC LASSO?
OW ITS ENERGIES COME FROM FROM YOU--
-- AND INTENSIFIES THE ANGRIER YOU GET.
LET GO. NOBODY CAN TAKE IT FROM ME.
YOU THINK YOU KNOW ANGER?

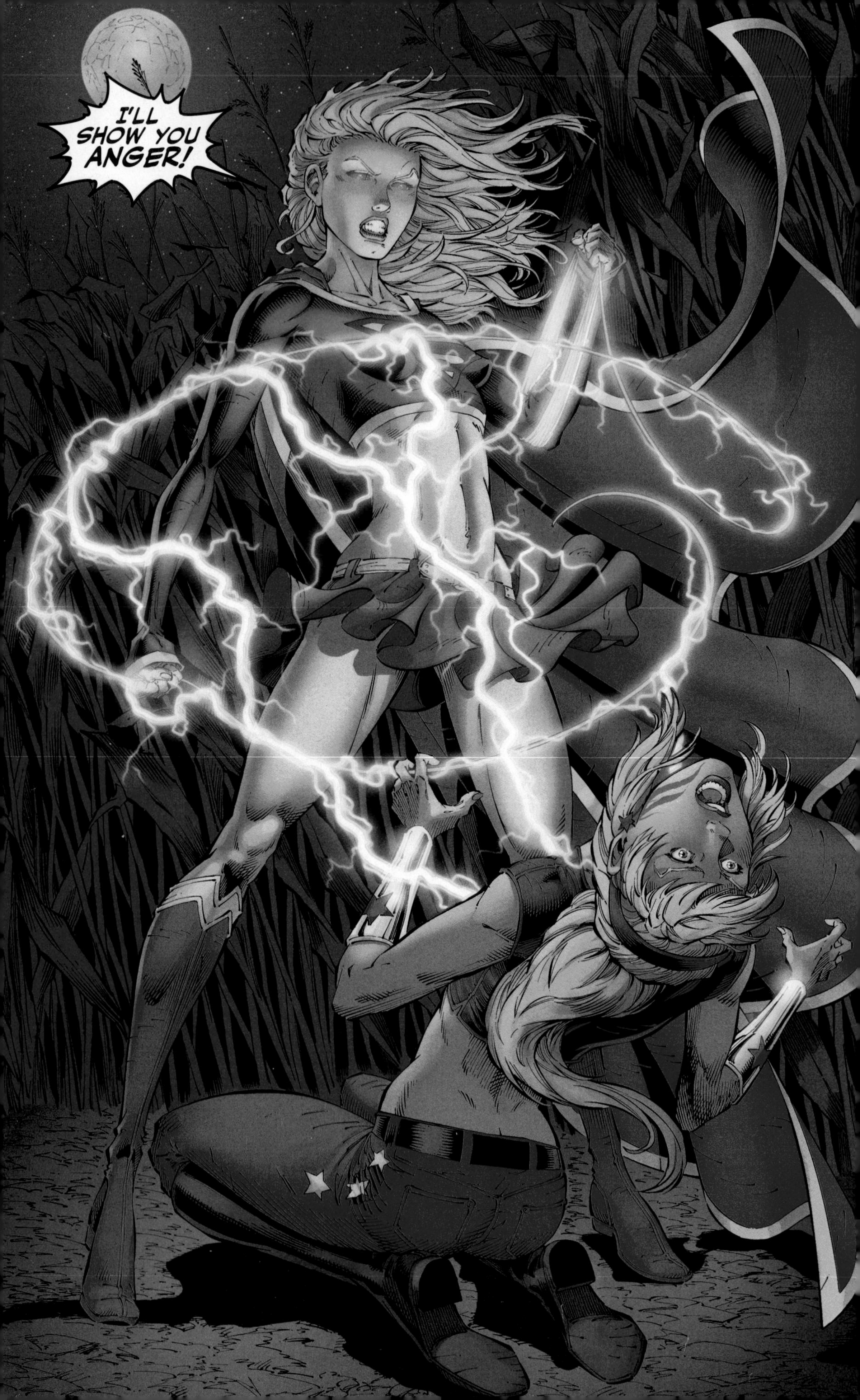
I'LL SHOW YOU ANGER!

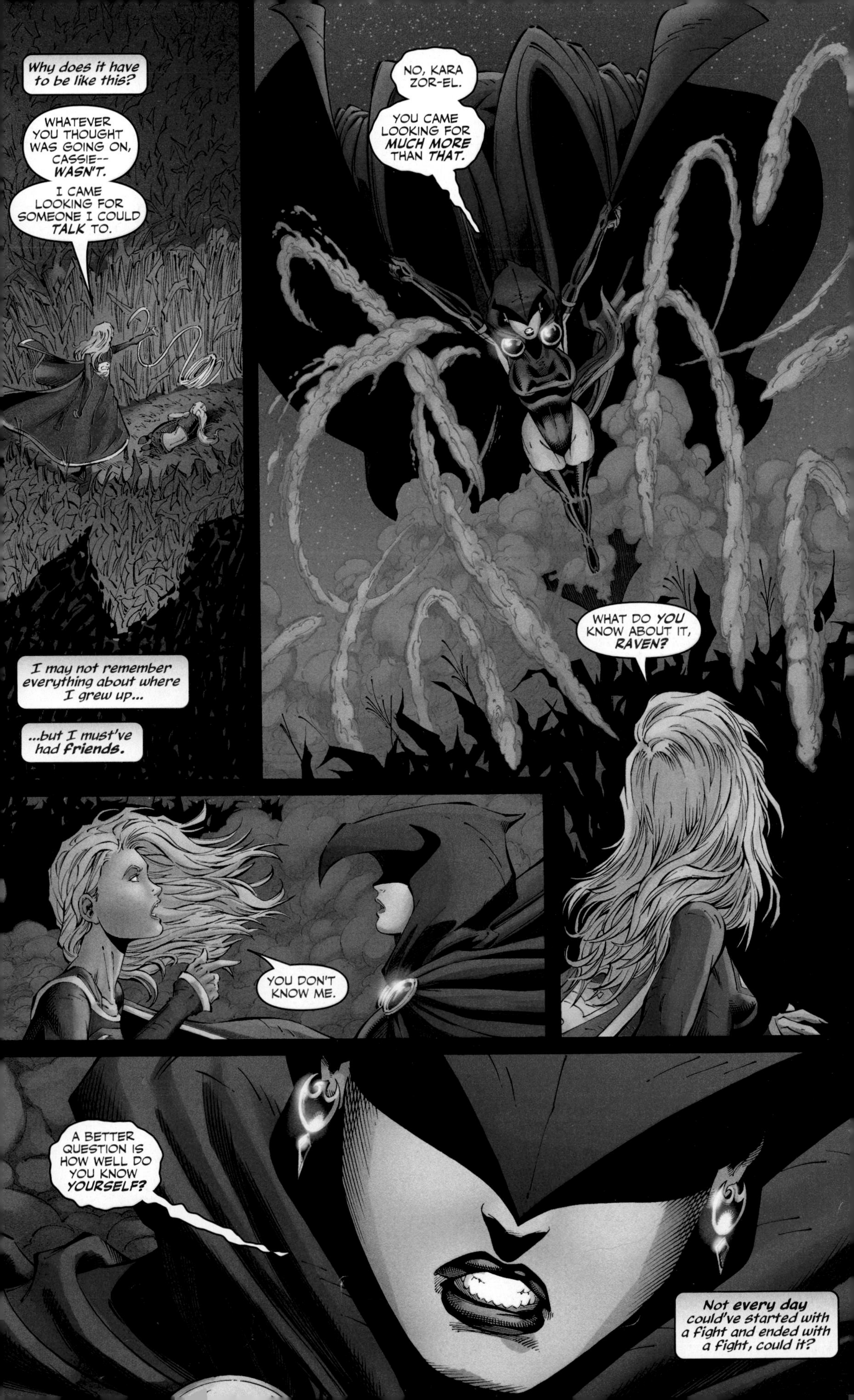

Why does it have to be like this?
WHATEVER YOU THOUGHT WAS GOING ON, CASSIE-- WASN'T.
I CAME LOOKING FOR SOMEONE I COULD TALK TO.
NO, KARA ZOR-EL.
YOU CAME LOOKING FOR MUCH MORE THAN THAT.
WHAT DO YOU KNOW ABOUT IT, RAVEN?
I may not remember everything about where I grew up...
...but I must've had friends.
YOU DON'T KNOW ME.
A BETTER QUESTION IS HOW WELL DO YOU KNOW YOURSELF?
Not every day could've started with a fight and ended with a fight, could it?

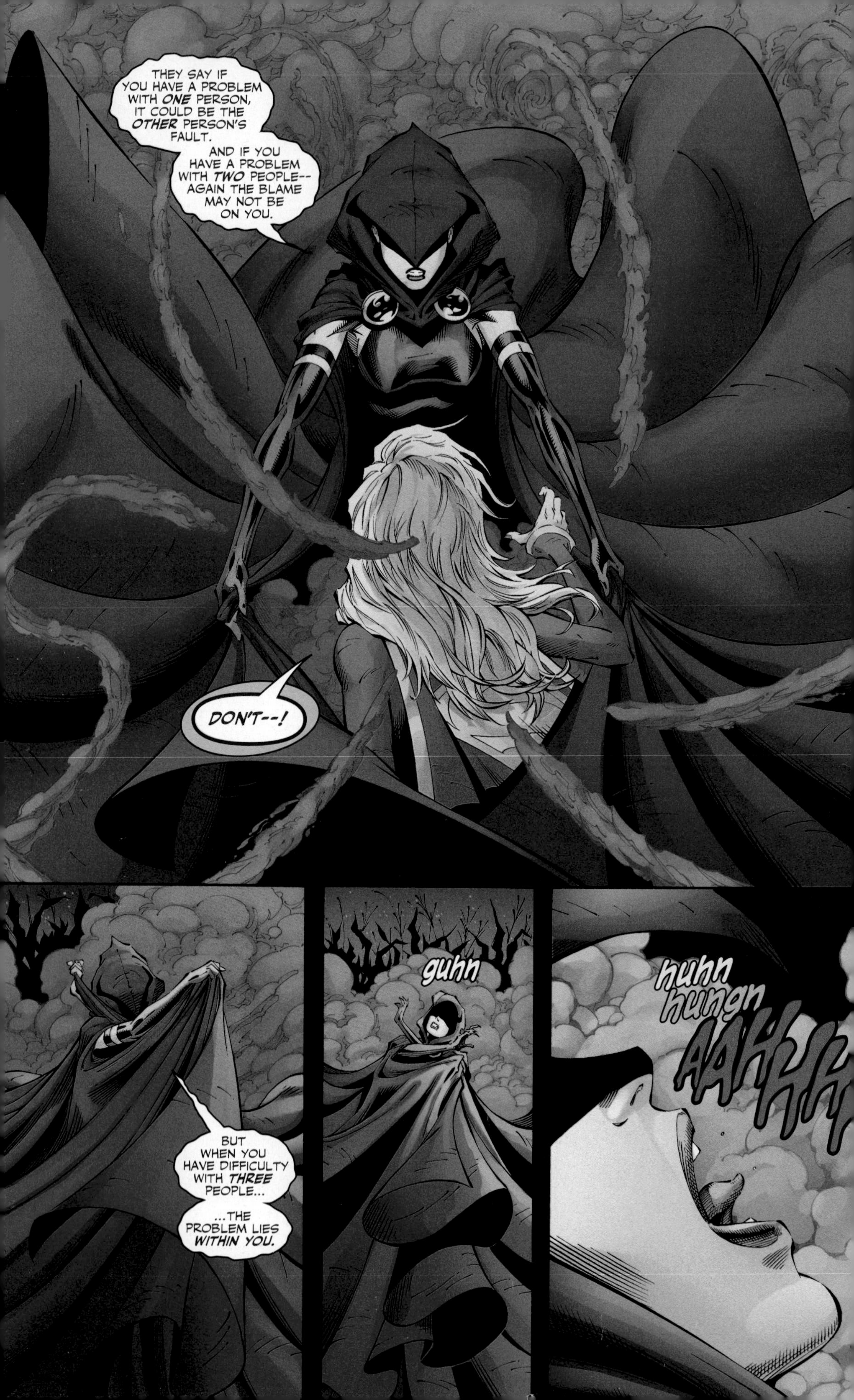

THEY SAY IF YOU HAVE A PROBLEM WITH *ONE* PERSON, IT COULD BE THE *OTHER* PERSON'S FAULT.
AND IF YOU HAVE A PROBLEM WITH *TWO* PEOPLE-- AGAIN THE BLAME MAY NOT BE ON YOU.
DON'T--!
BUT WHEN YOU HAVE DIFFICULTY WITH *THREE* PEOPLE...
...THE PROBLEM LIES *WITHIN YOU.*
guhn
huhn
hungn

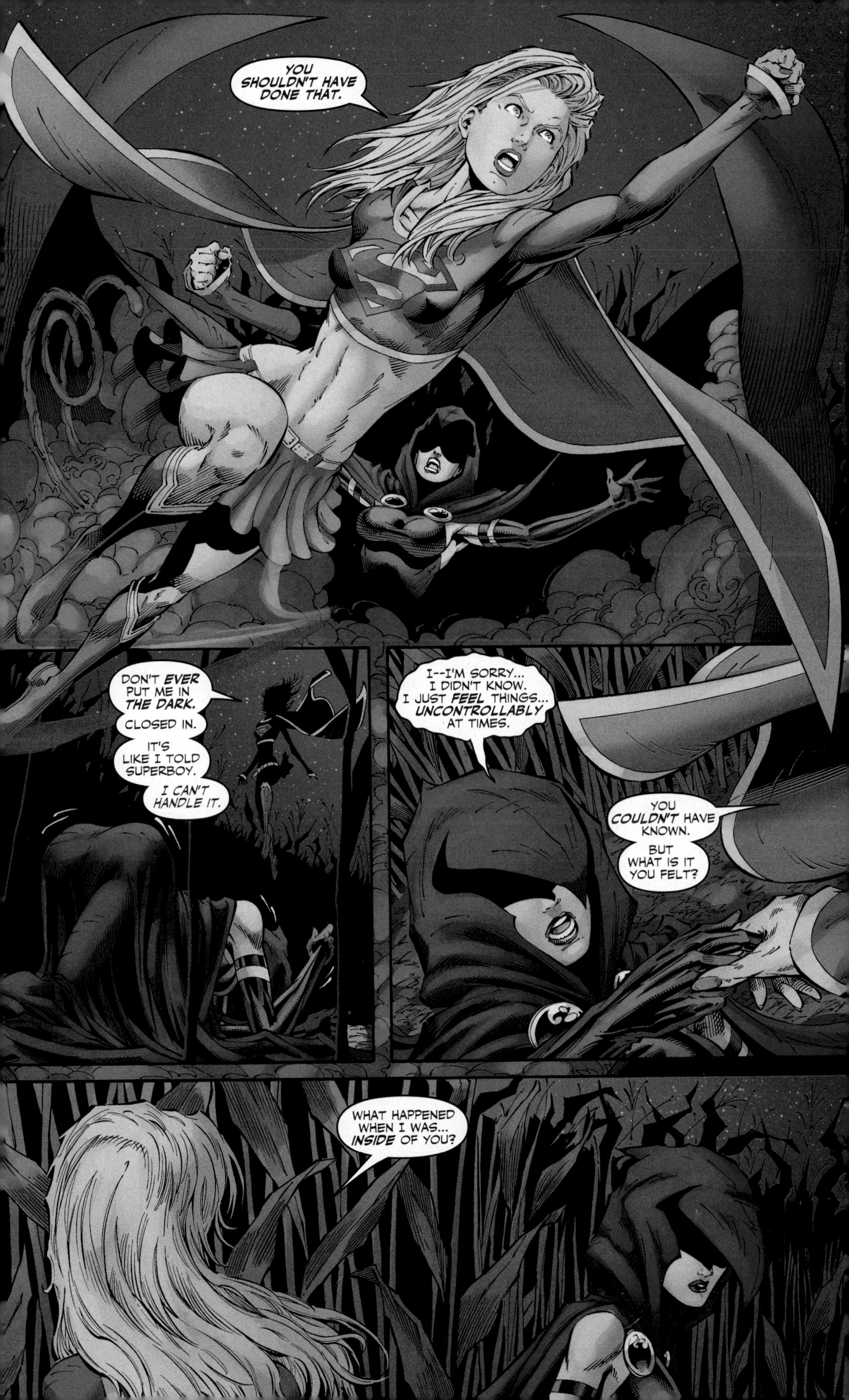
YOU SHOULDN'T HAVE DONE THAT.
DON'T EVER PUT ME IN THE DARK.
CLOSED IN.
IT'S LIKE I TOLD SUPERBOY.
I CAN'T HANDLE IT.
I--I'M SORRY... I DIDN'T KNOW. I JUST FEEL THINGS... UNCONTROLLABLY AT TIMES.
YOU COULDN'T HAVE KNOWN.
BUT WHAT IS IT YOU FELT?
WHAT HAPPENED WHEN I WAS... INSIDE OF YOU?

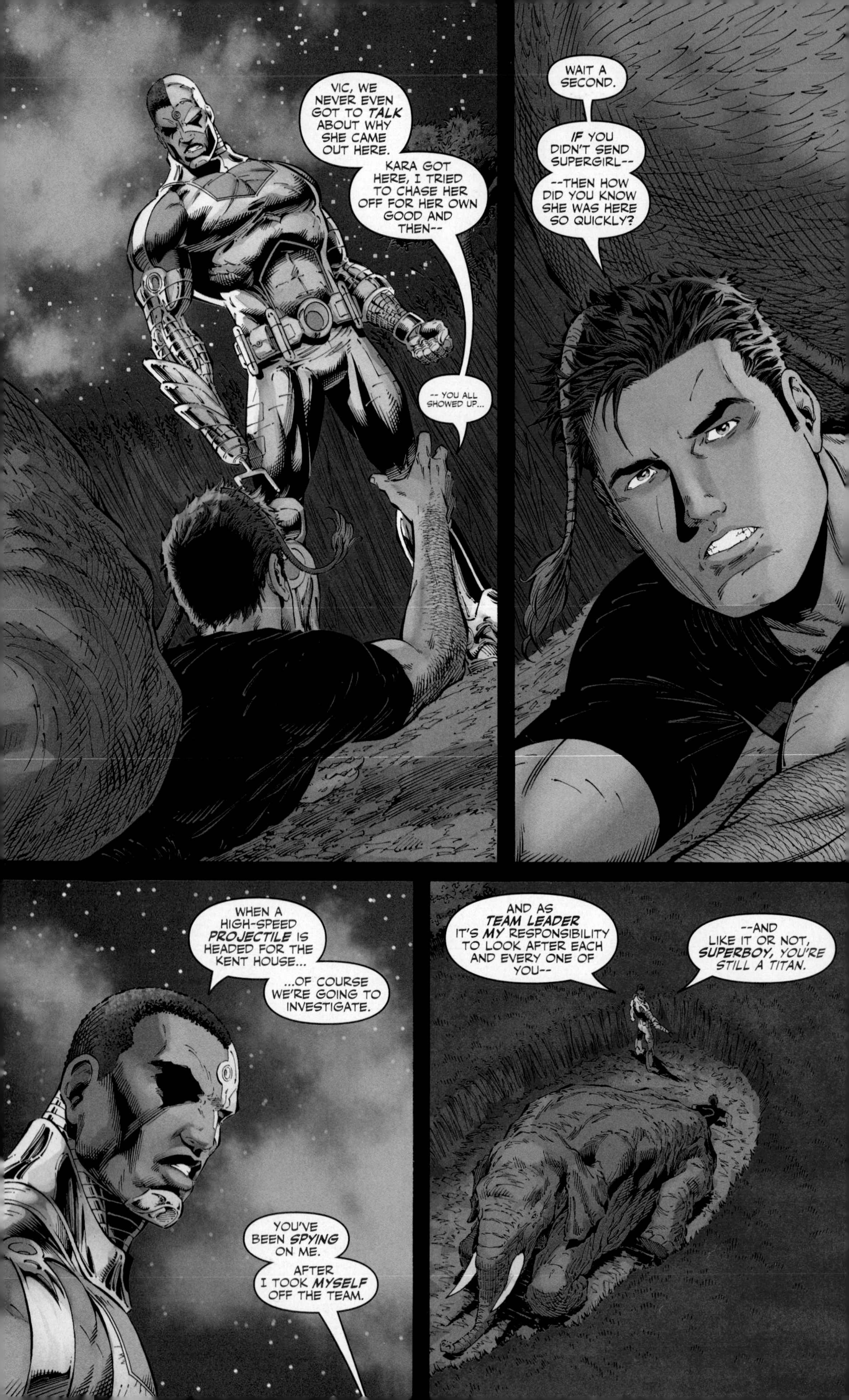
VIC, WE NEVER EVEN GOT TO TALK ABOUT WHY SHE CAME OUT HERE.
KARA GOT HERE, I TRIED TO CHASE HER OFF FOR HER OWN GOOD AND THEN--
-- YOU ALL SHOWED UP...
WAIT A SECOND.
IF YOU DIDN'T SEND SUPERGIRL--
--THEN HOW DID YOU KNOW SHE WAS HERE SO QUICKLY?
WHEN A HIGH-SPEED PROJECTILE IS HEADED FOR THE KENT HOUSE...
...OF COURSE WE'RE GOING TO INVESTIGATE.
YOU'VE BEEN SPYING ON ME.
AFTER I TOOK MYSELF OFF THE TEAM.
AND AS TEAM LEADER IT'S MY RESPONSIBILITY TO LOOK AFTER EACH AND EVERY ONE OF YOU--
--AND LIKE IT OR NOT, SUPERBOY, YOU'RE STILL A TITAN.

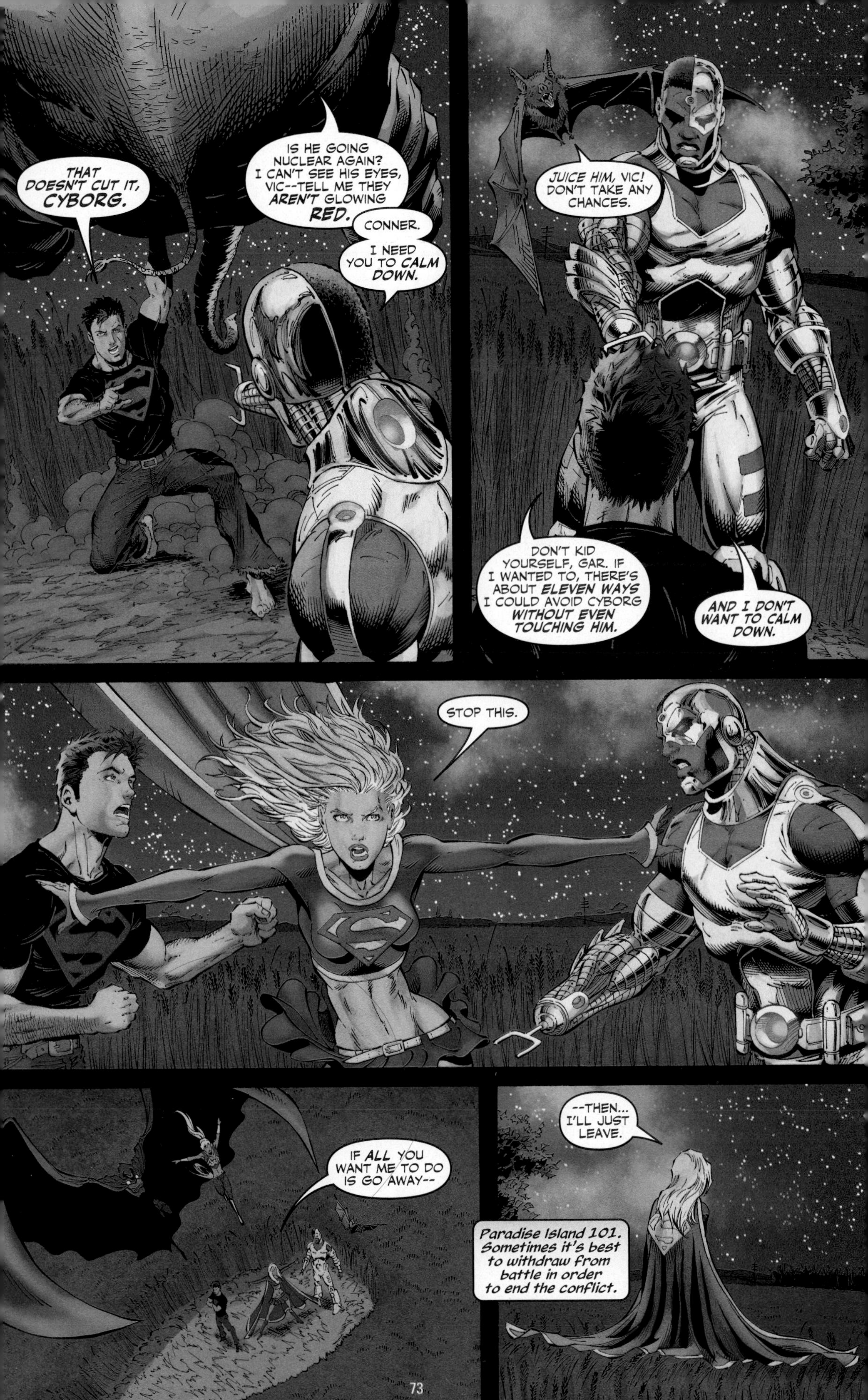
THAT DOESN'T CUT IT, CYBORG.
IS HE GOING NUCLEAR AGAIN? I CAN'T SEE HIS EYES, VIC--TELL ME THEY AREN'T GLOWING RED.
CONNER.
I NEED YOU TO CALM DOWN.
JUICE HIM, VIC! DON'T TAKE ANY CHANCES.
DON'T KID YOURSELF, GAR. IF I WANTED TO, THERE'S ABOUT ELEVEN WAYS I COULD AVOID CYBORG WITHOUT EVEN TOUCHING HIM.
AND I DON'T WANT TO CALM DOWN.
STOP THIS.
IF ALL YOU WANT ME TO DO IS GO AWAY--
--THEN... I'LL JUST LEAVE.
Paradise Island 101. Sometimes it's best to withdraw from battle in order to end the conflict.

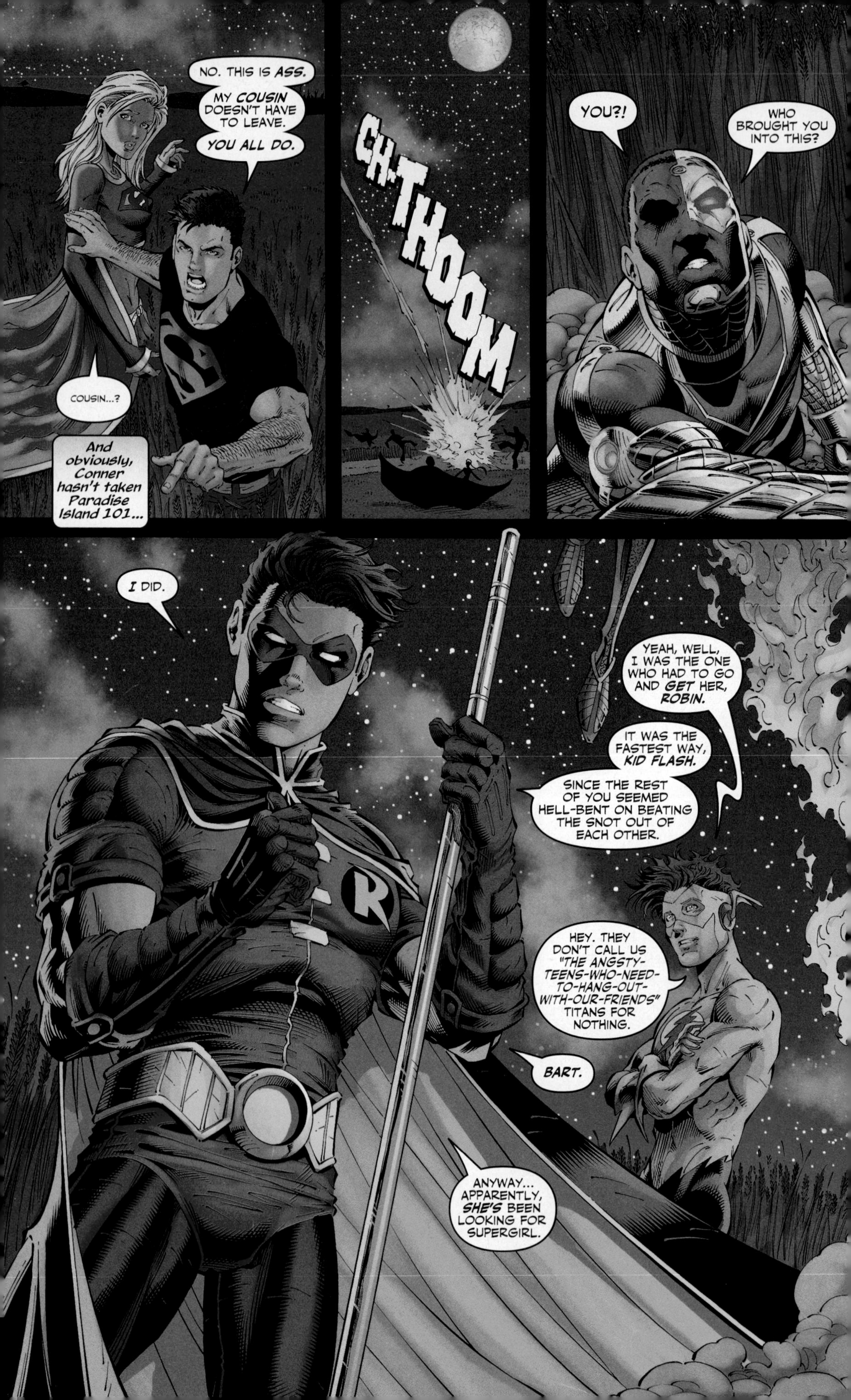
NO. THIS IS ASS.
MY COUSIN DOESN'T HAVE TO LEAVE.
YOU ALL DO.
COUSIN...?
And obviously, Conner hasn't taken Paradise Island 101...
CH-THOOM
YOU?!
WHO BROUGHT YOU INTO THIS?
I DID.
YEAH, WELL, I WAS THE ONE WHO HAD TO GO AND GET HER, ROBIN.
IT WAS THE FASTEST WAY, KID FLASH.
SINCE THE REST OF YOU SEEMED HELL-BENT ON BEATING THE SNOT OUT OF EACH OTHER.
HEY. THEY DON'T CALL US "THE ANGSTY-TEENS-WHO-NEED-TO-HANG-OUT-WITH-OUR-FRIENDS" TITANS FOR NOTHING.
BART.
ANYWAY... APPARENTLY, SHE'S BEEN LOOKING FOR SUPERGIRL.

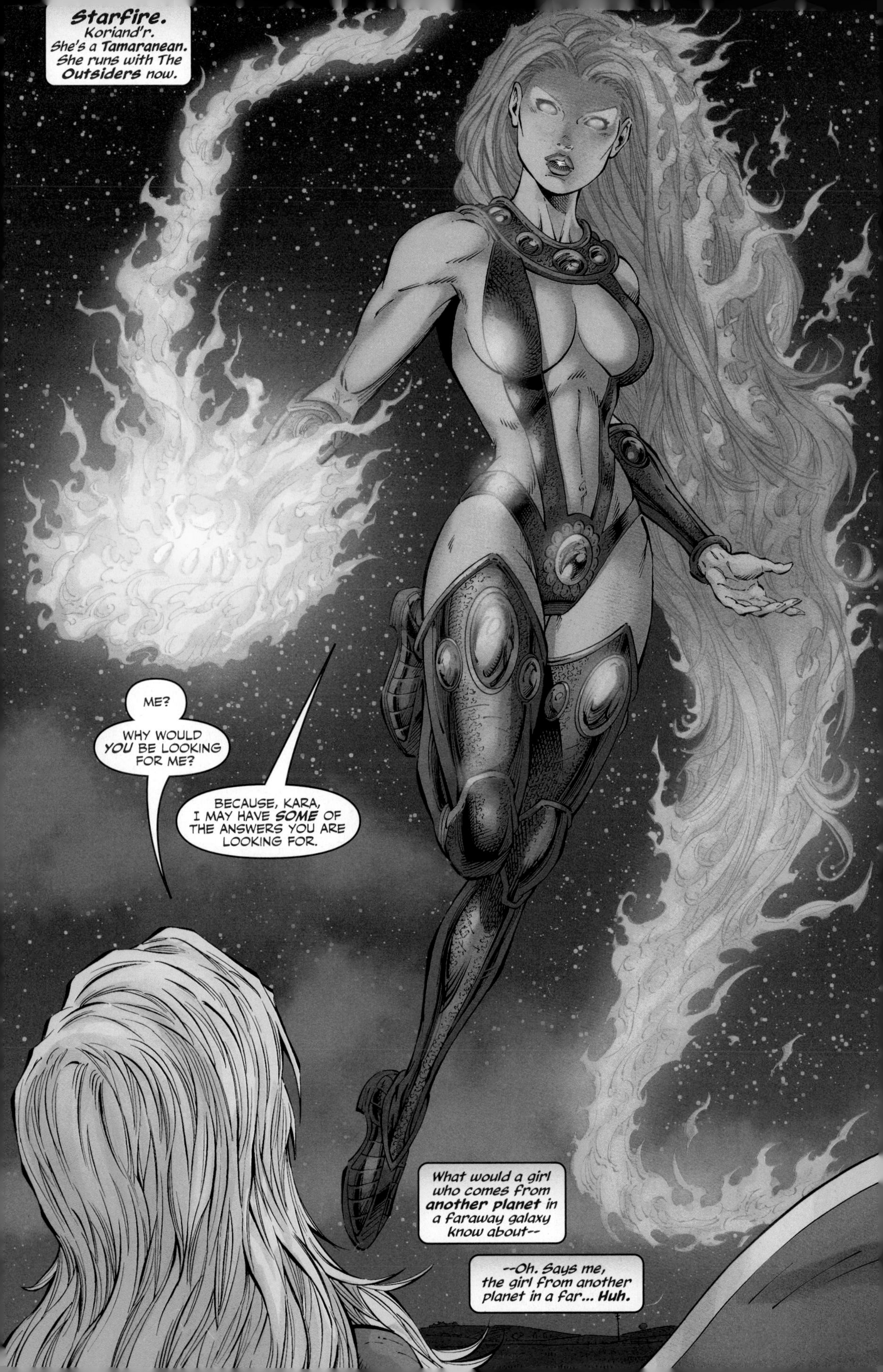
Starfire. Koriand'r. She's a Tamaranean. She runs with The Outsiders now.
ME?
WHY WOULD YOU BE LOOKING FOR ME?
BECAUSE, KARA, I MAY HAVE SOME OF THE ANSWERS YOU ARE LOOKING FOR.
What would a girl who comes from another planet in a faraway galaxy know about--
--Oh. Says me, the girl from another planet in a far... Huh.

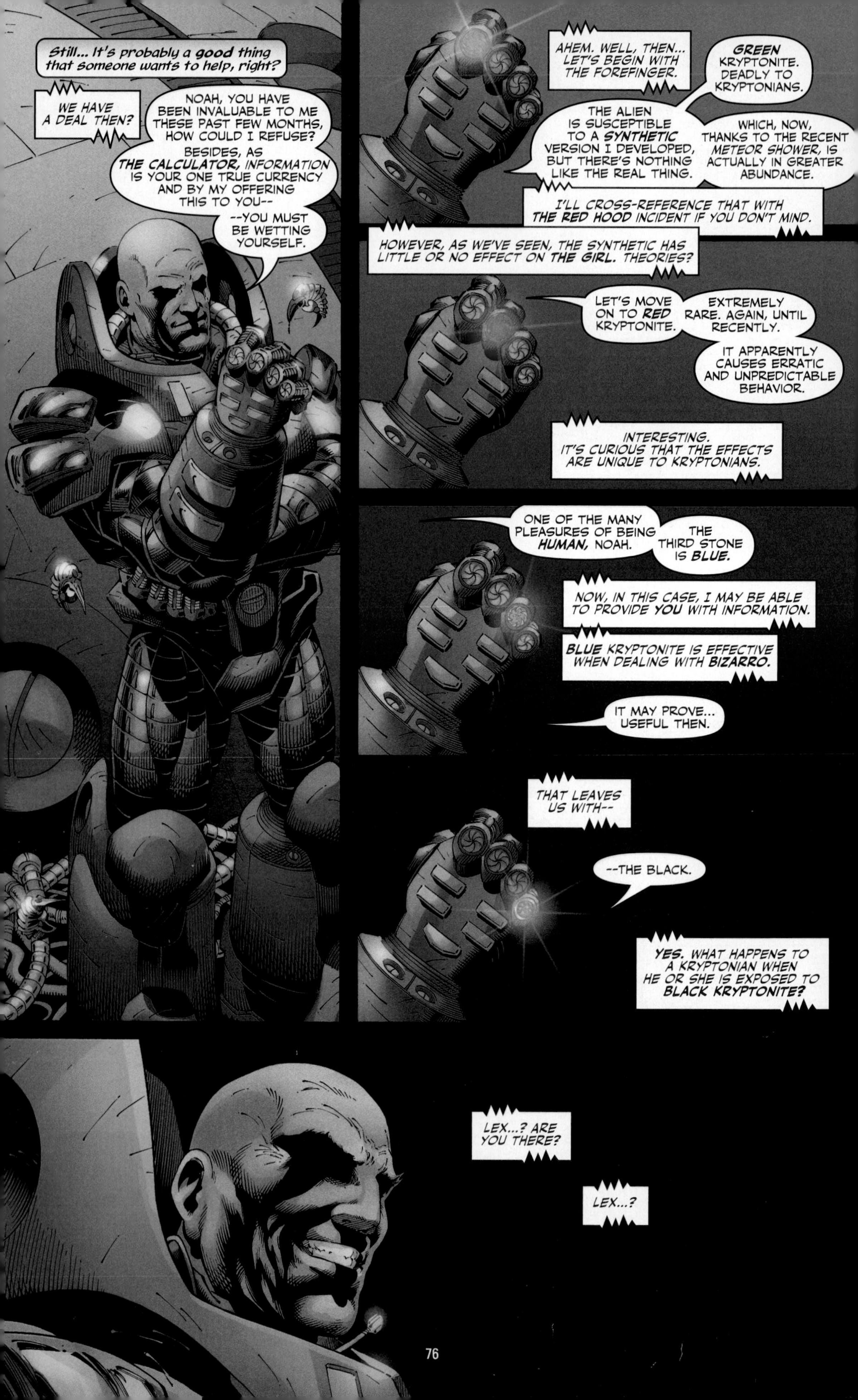
Still... It's probably a good thing that someone wants to help, right?
WE HAVE A DEAL THEN?
NOAH, YOU HAVE BEEN INVALUABLE TO ME THESE PAST FEW MONTHS, HOW COULD I REFUSE?
BESIDES, AS THE CALCULATOR, INFORMATION IS YOUR ONE TRUE CURRENCY AND BY MY OFFERING THIS TO YOU--
--YOU MUST BE WETTING YOURSELF.
AHEM. WELL, THEN... LET'S BEGIN WITH THE FOREFINGER.
GREEN KRYPTONITE. DEADLY TO KRYPTONIANS.
THE ALIEN IS SUSCEPTIBLE TO A SYNTHETIC VERSION I DEVELOPED, BUT THERE'S NOTHING LIKE THE REAL THING.
WHICH, NOW, THANKS TO THE RECENT METEOR SHOWER, IS ACTUALLY IN GREATER ABUNDANCE.
I'LL CROSS-REFERENCE THAT WITH THE RED HOOD INCIDENT IF YOU DON'T MIND.
HOWEVER, AS WE'VE SEEN, THE SYNTHETIC HAS LITTLE OR NO EFFECT ON THE GIRL. THEORIES?
LET'S MOVE ON TO RED KRYPTONITE.
EXTREMELY RARE. AGAIN, UNTIL RECENTLY.
IT APPARENTLY CAUSES ERRATIC AND UNPREDICTABLE BEHAVIOR.
INTERESTING. IT'S CURIOUS THAT THE EFFECTS ARE UNIQUE TO KRYPTONIANS.
ONE OF THE MANY PLEASURES OF BEING HUMAN, NOAH.
THE THIRD STONE IS BLUE.
NOW, IN THIS CASE, I MAY BE ABLE TO PROVIDE YOU WITH INFORMATION.
BLUE KRYPTONITE IS EFFECTIVE WHEN DEALING WITH BIZARRO.
IT MAY PROVE... USEFUL THEN.
THAT LEAVES US WITH--
--THE BLACK.
YES. WHAT HAPPENS TO A KRYPTONIAN WHEN HE OR SHE IS EXPOSED TO BLACK KRYPTONITE?
LEX...? ARE YOU THERE?
LEX...?

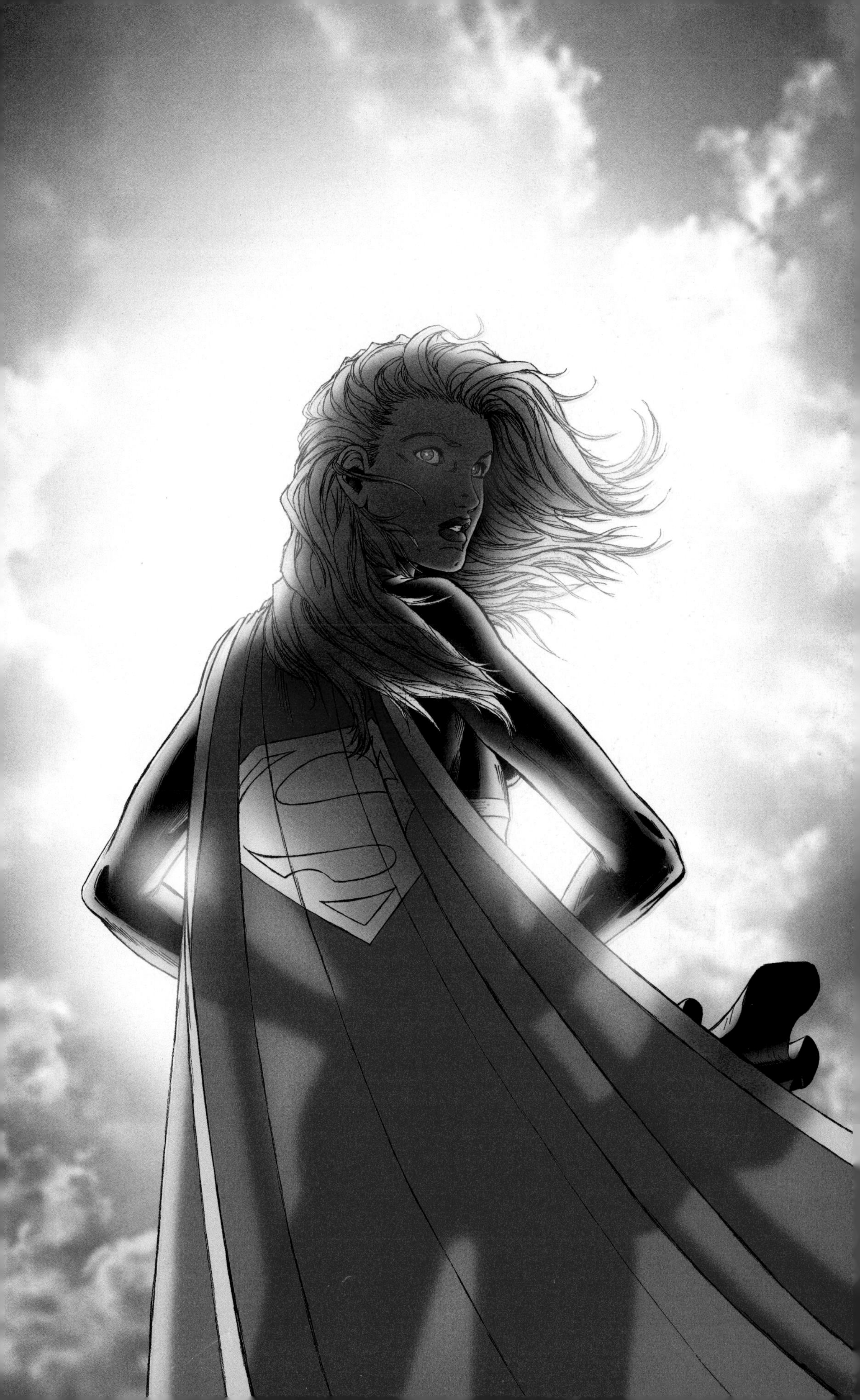

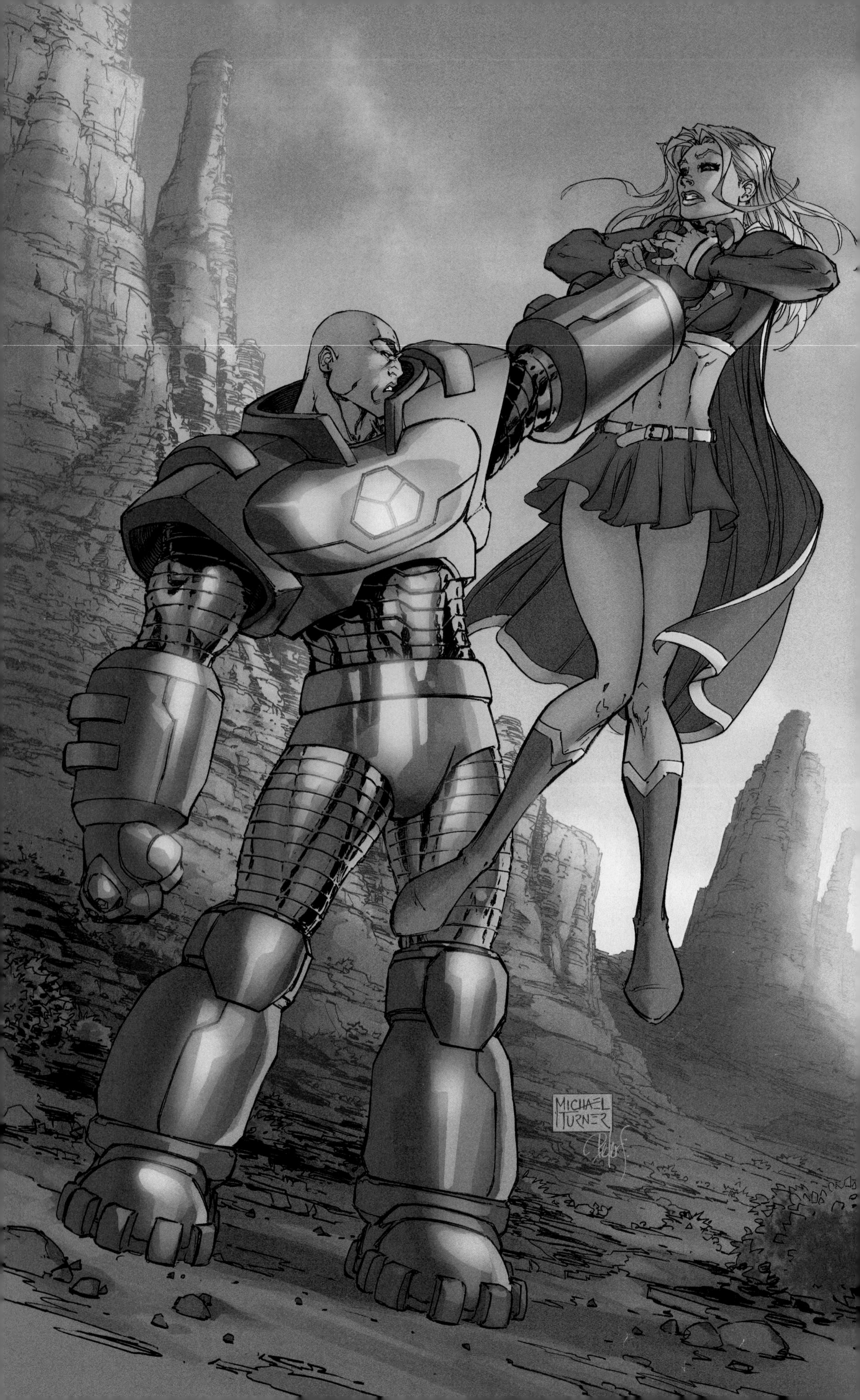
MICHAEL TURNER

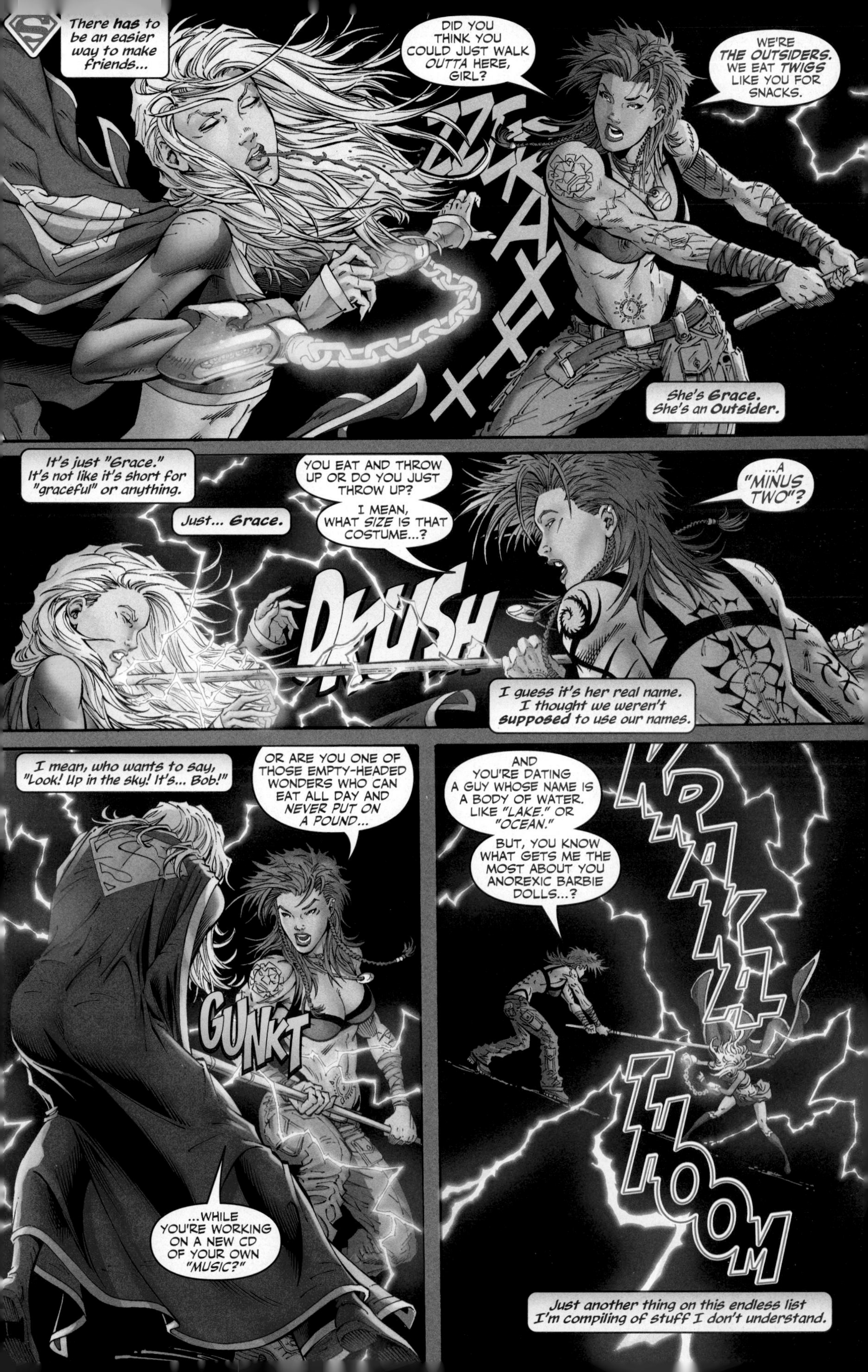
There **has** to be an easier way to make friends...
DID YOU THINK YOU COULD JUST WALK *OUTTA* HERE, GIRL?
WE'RE *THE OUTSIDERS.* WE EAT *TWIGS* LIKE YOU FOR SNACKS.
She's Grace. She's an **Outsider**.
It's just "Grace." It's not like it's short for "graceful" or anything.
Just... Grace.
YOU EAT AND THROW UP OR DO YOU JUST THROW UP?
I MEAN, WHAT *SIZE* IS THAT COSTUME...?
...A "MINUS TWO"?
DKRUSH
I guess it's her real name. I thought we weren't **supposed** to use our names.
I mean, who wants to say, "Look! Up in the sky! It's... Bob!"
OR ARE YOU ONE OF THOSE EMPTY-HEADED WONDERS WHO CAN EAT ALL DAY AND *NEVER PUT ON* A POUND...
GUNKT
...WHILE YOU'RE WORKING ON A NEW CD OF YOUR OWN "MUSIC?"
AND YOU'RE DATING A GUY WHOSE NAME IS A BODY OF WATER. LIKE "LAKE." OR "OCEAN."
BUT, YOU KNOW WHAT GETS ME THE MOST ABOUT YOU ANOREXIC BARBIE DOLLS...?
KRAKKA THOOM
Just another thing on this endless list I'm compiling of stuff I don't understand.

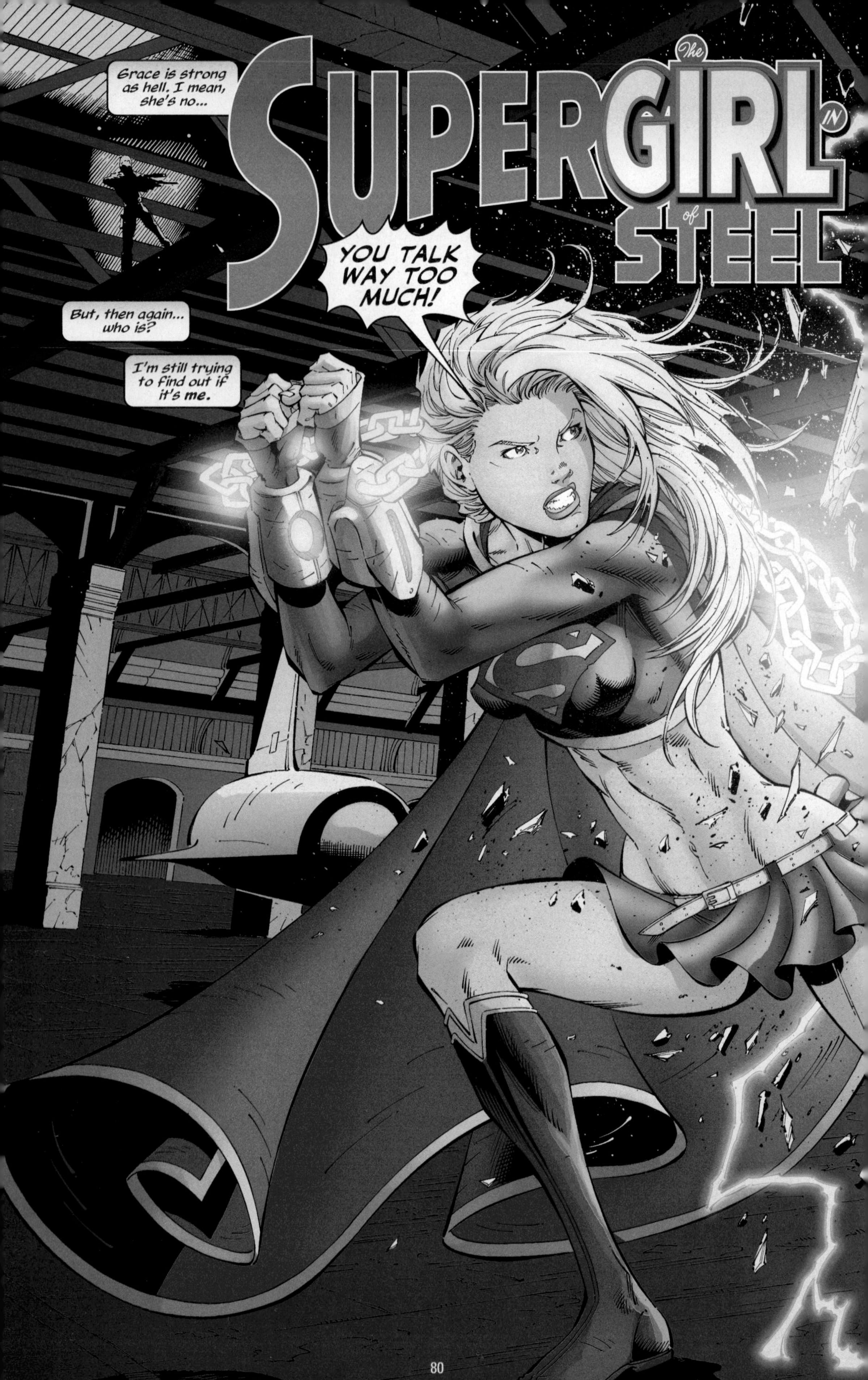
Grace is strong as hell. I mean, she's no...
The SUPERGIRL in STEEL of
YOU TALK WAY TOO MUCH!
But, then again... who is?
I'm still trying to find out if it's me.

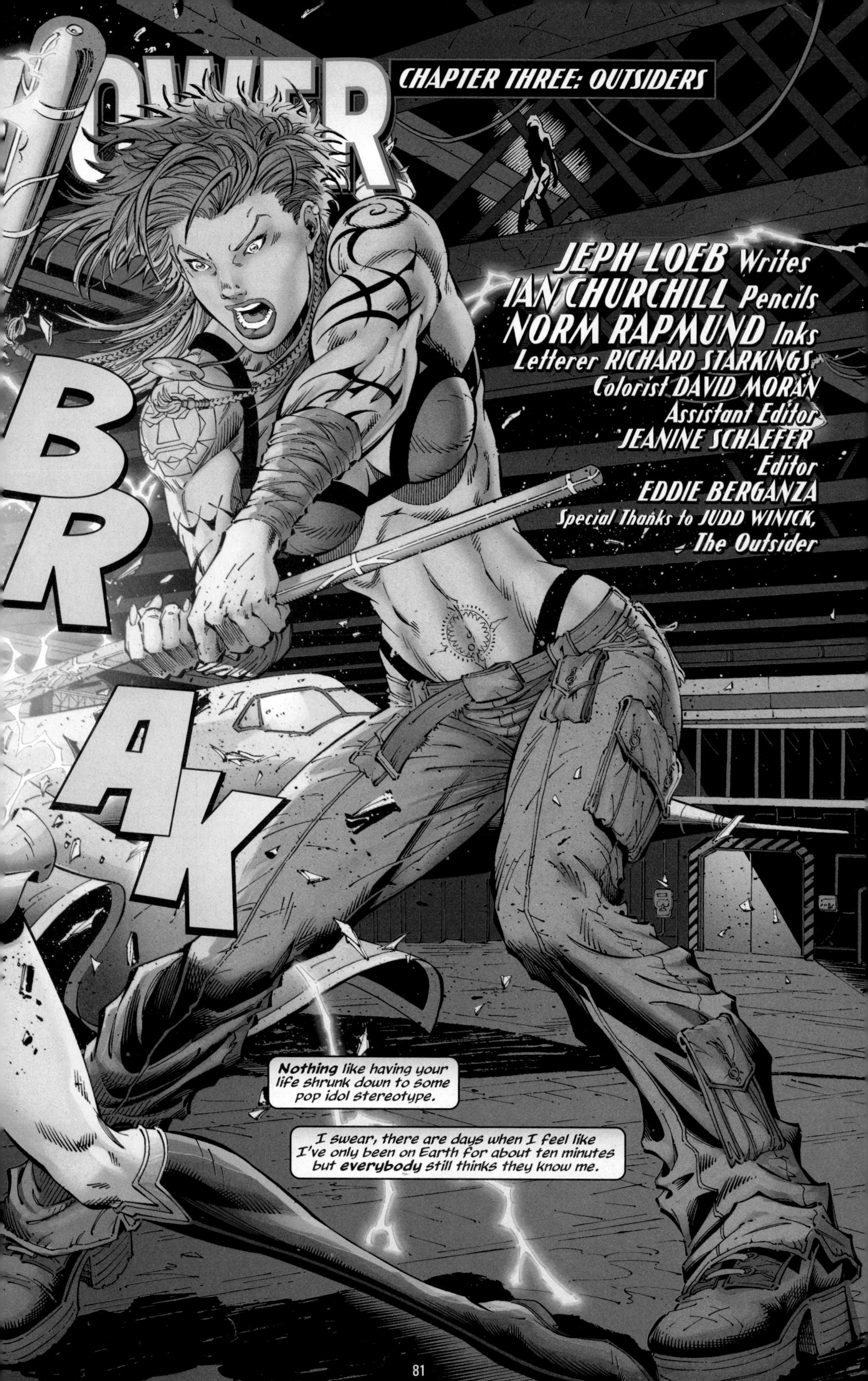

CHAPTER THREE: OUTSIDERS
JEPH LOEB Writes
IAN CHURCHILL Pencils
NORM RAPMUND Inks
Letterer RICHARD STARKINGS
Colorist DAVID MORÁN
Assistant Editor
JEANINE SCHAEFER
Editor
EDDIE BERGANZA
Special Thanks to JUDD WINICK,
The Outsider
BRRAK
Nothing like having your life shrunk down to some pop idol stereotype.
I swear, there are days when I feel like I've only been on Earth for about ten minutes but everybody still thinks they know me.

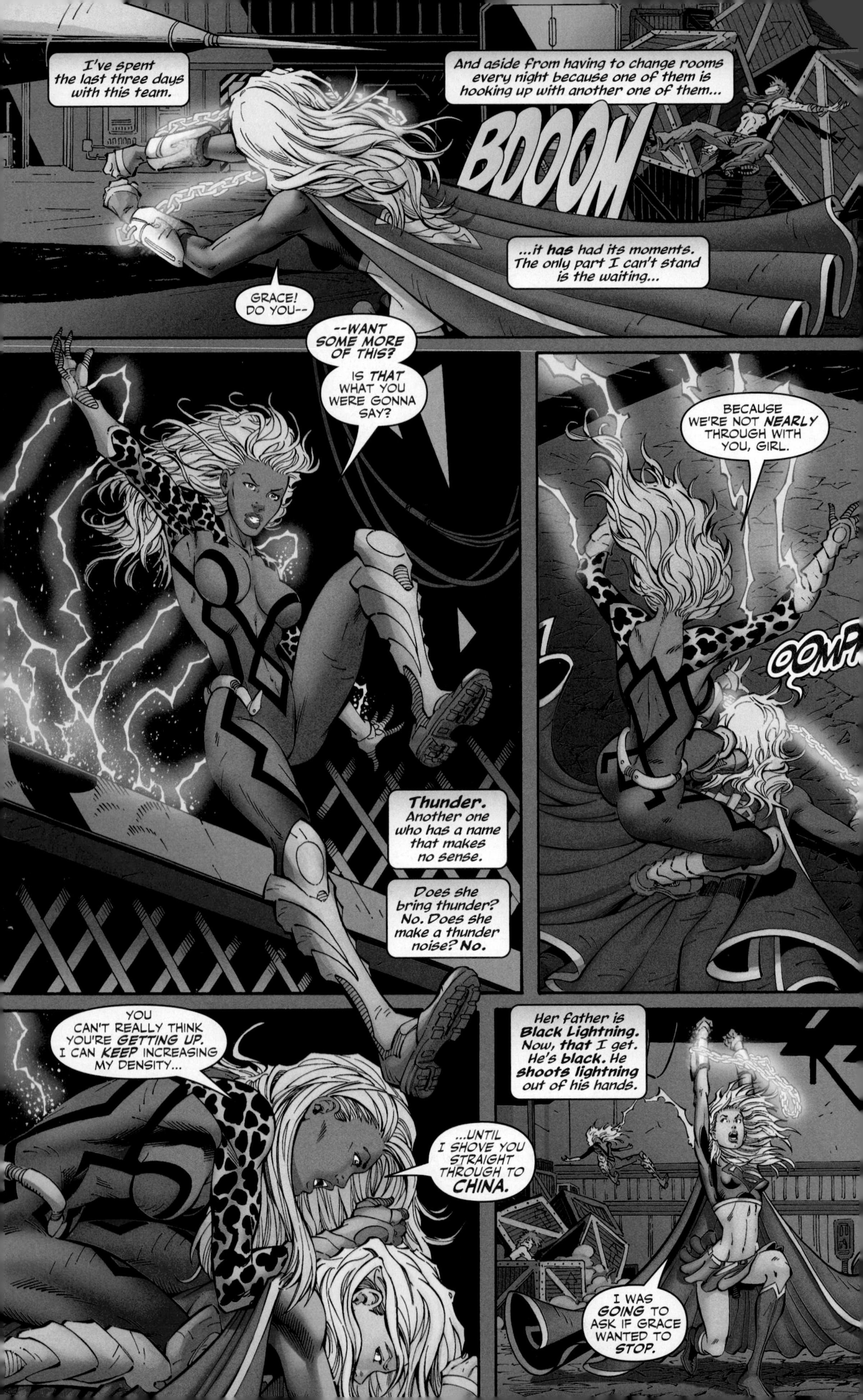
I've spent the last three days with this team.
And aside from having to change rooms every night because one of them is hooking up with another one of them...
BDOOM
...it has had its moments. The only part I can't stand is the waiting...
GRACE! DO YOU--
--WANT SOME MORE OF THIS?
IS THAT WHAT YOU WERE GONNA SAY?
Thunder. Another one who has a name that makes no sense.
Does she bring thunder? No. Does she make a thunder noise? No.
BECAUSE WE'RE NOT NEARLY THROUGH WITH YOU, GIRL.
YOU CAN'T REALLY THINK YOU'RE GETTING UP. I CAN KEEP INCREASING MY DENSITY...
...UNTIL I SHOVE YOU STRAIGHT THROUGH TO CHINA.
Her father is Black Lightning. Now, he's, that I get. He's black. He shoots lightning out of his hands.
I WAS GOING TO ASK IF GRACE WANTED TO STOP.

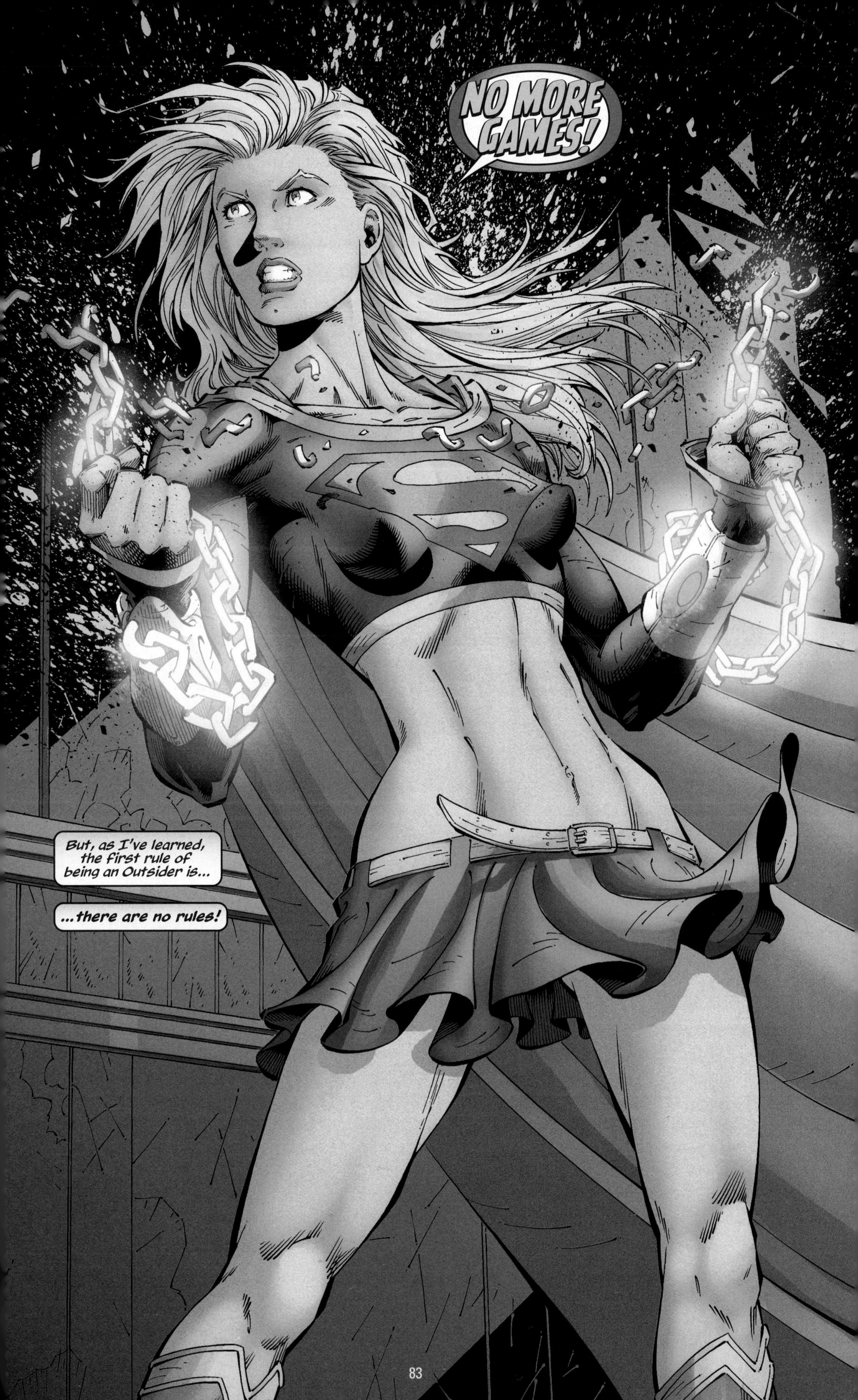
NO MORE GAMES!
But, as I've learned, the first rule of being an Outsider is...
...there are no rules!

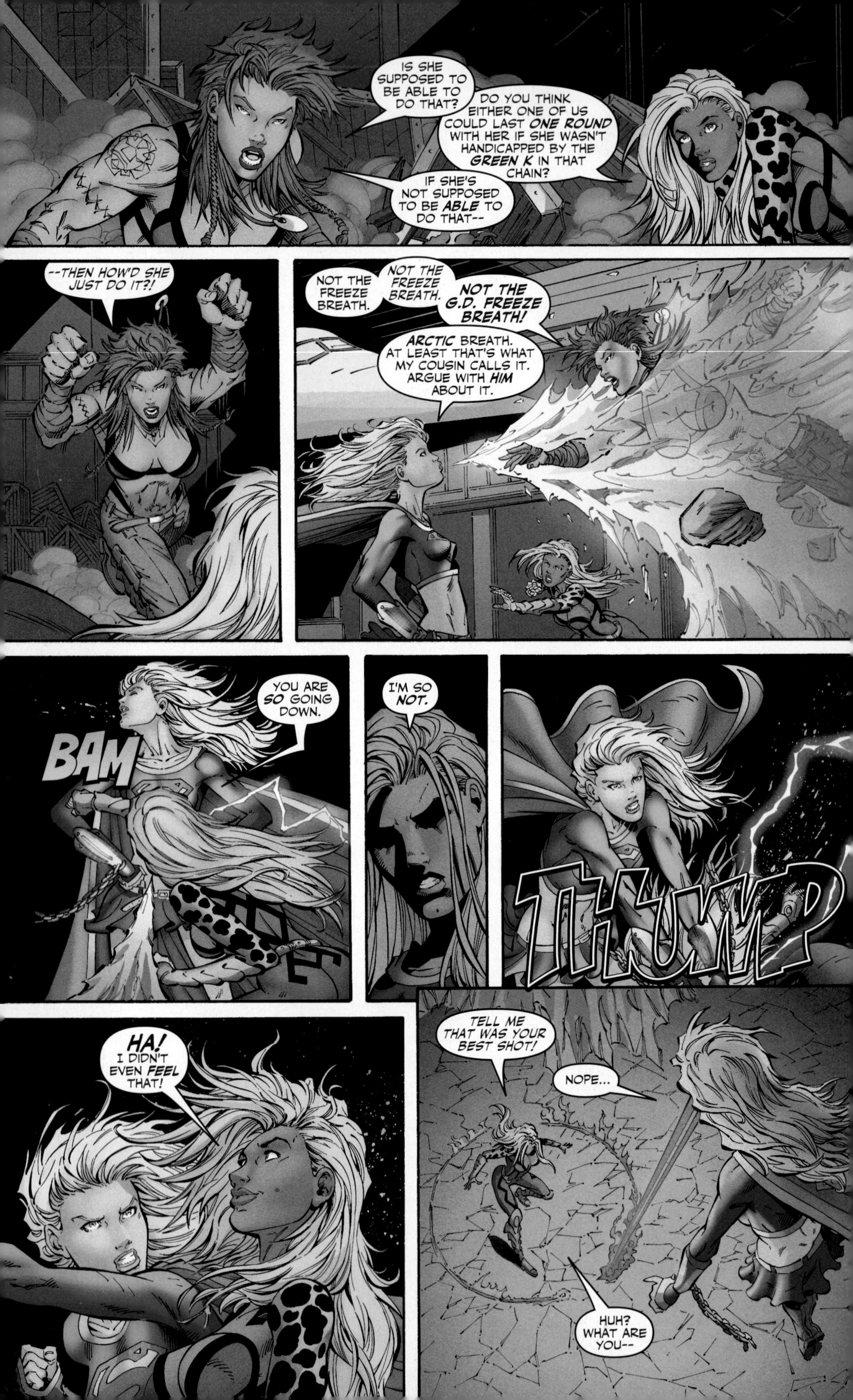
IS SHE SUPPOSED TO BE ABLE TO DO THAT?
DO YOU THINK EITHER ONE OF US COULD LAST ONE ROUND WITH HER IF SHE WASN'T HANDICAPPED BY THE GREEN K IN THAT CHAIN?
IF SHE'S NOT SUPPOSED TO BE ABLE TO DO THAT--
--THEN HOW'D SHE JUST DO IT?!
NOT THE FREEZE BREATH.
NOT THE FREEZE BREATH.
NOT THE G.D. FREEZE BREATH!
ARCTIC BREATH. AT LEAST THAT'S WHAT MY COUSIN CALLS IT. ARGUE WITH HIM ABOUT IT.
YOU ARE SO GOING DOWN.
BAM
I'M SO NOT.
THUMP
HA! I DIDN'T EVEN FEEL THAT!
TELL ME THAT WAS YOUR BEST SHOT!
NOPE...
HUH? WHAT ARE YOU--

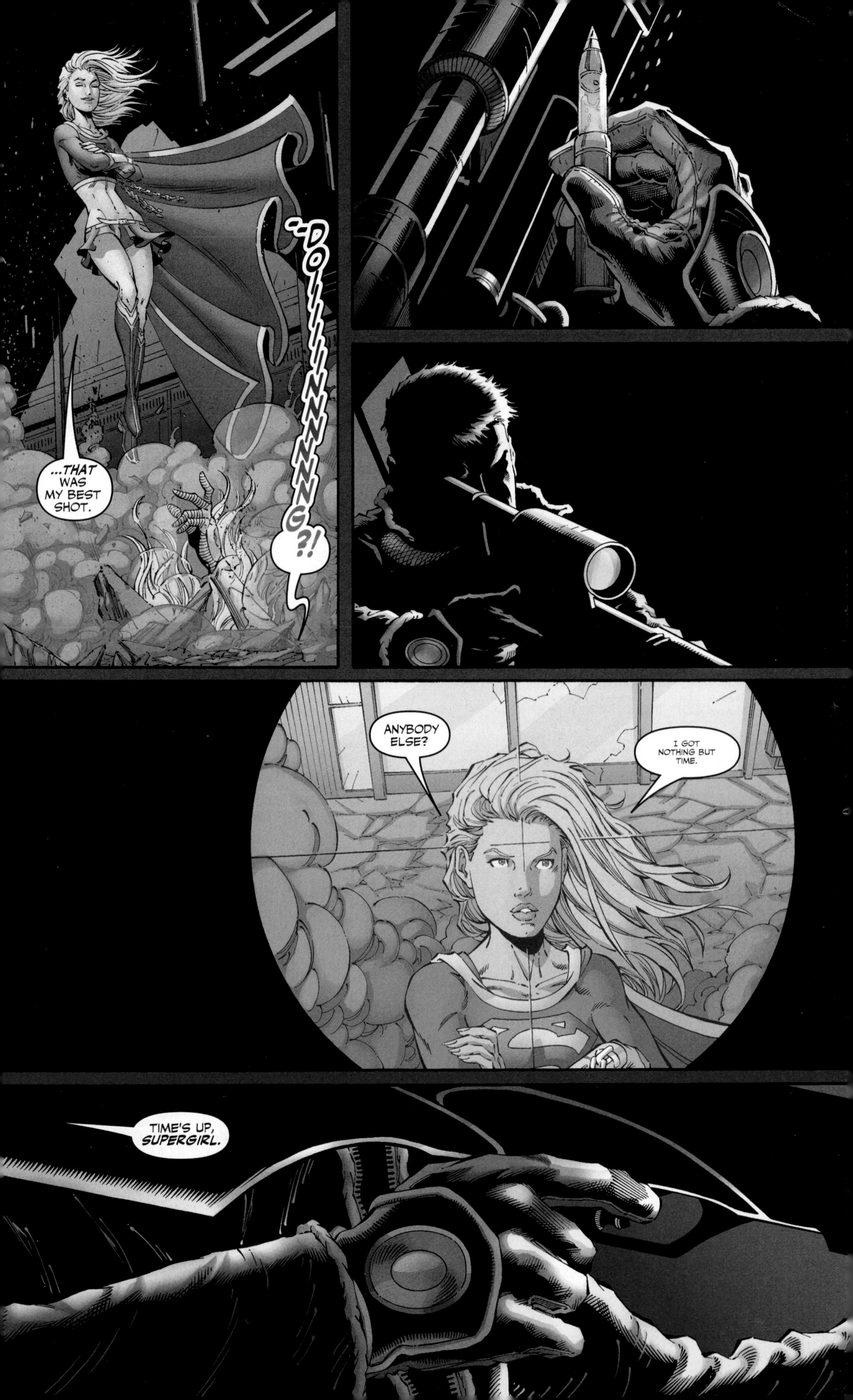
...THAT WAS MY BEST SHOT.
--DOIIIIIINNNNNNG?!
ANYBODY ELSE?
I GOT NOTHING BUT TIME.
TIME'S UP, SUPERGIRL.

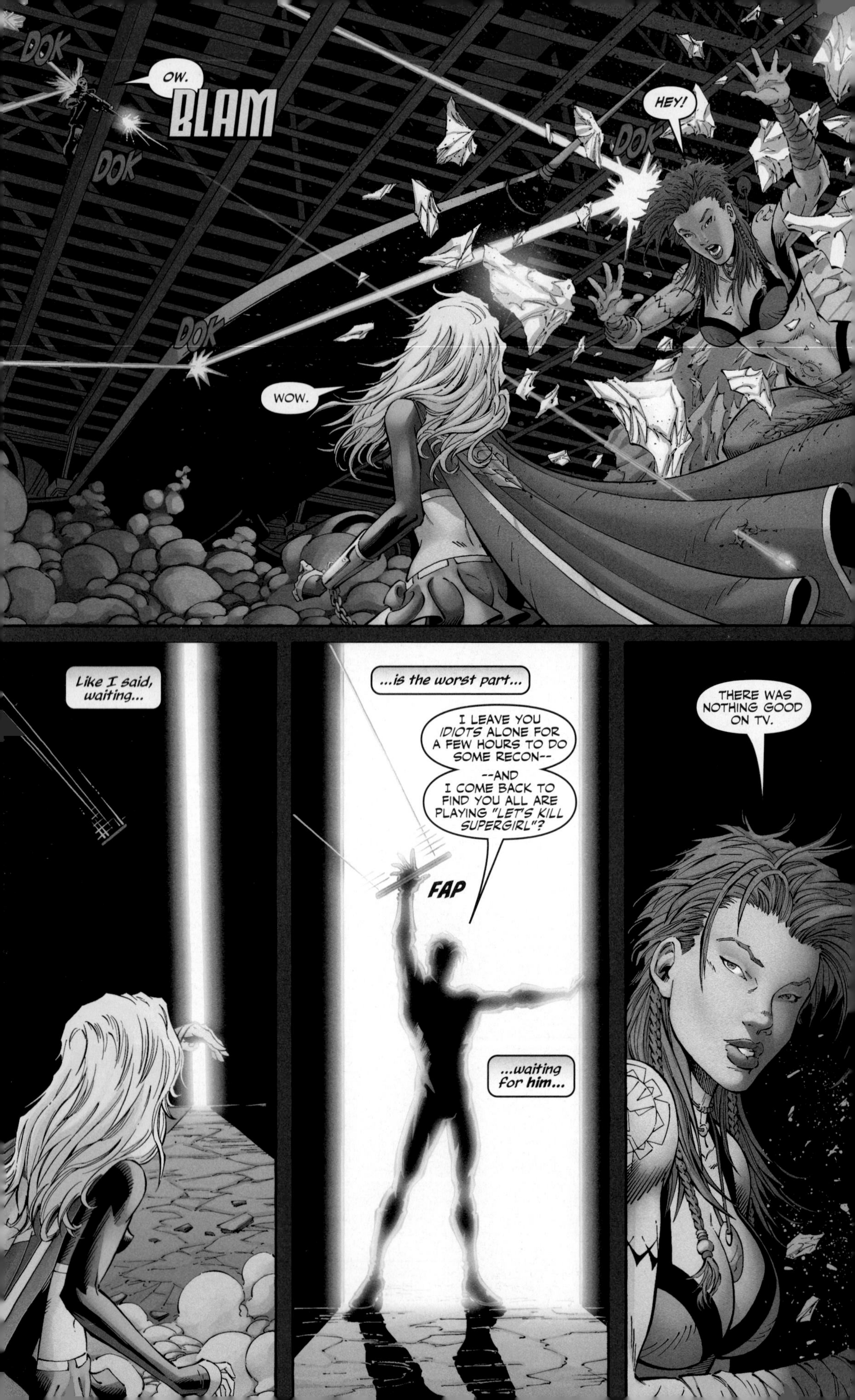
DOK
OW.
BLAM
DOK
HEY!
DOK
DOK
WOW.
Like I said, waiting...
...is the worst part...
I LEAVE YOU IDIOTS ALONE FOR A FEW HOURS TO DO SOME RECON--
--AND I COME BACK TO FIND YOU ALL ARE PLAYING "LET'S KILL SUPERGIRL"?
FAP
...waiting for him...
THERE WAS NOTHING GOOD ON TV.

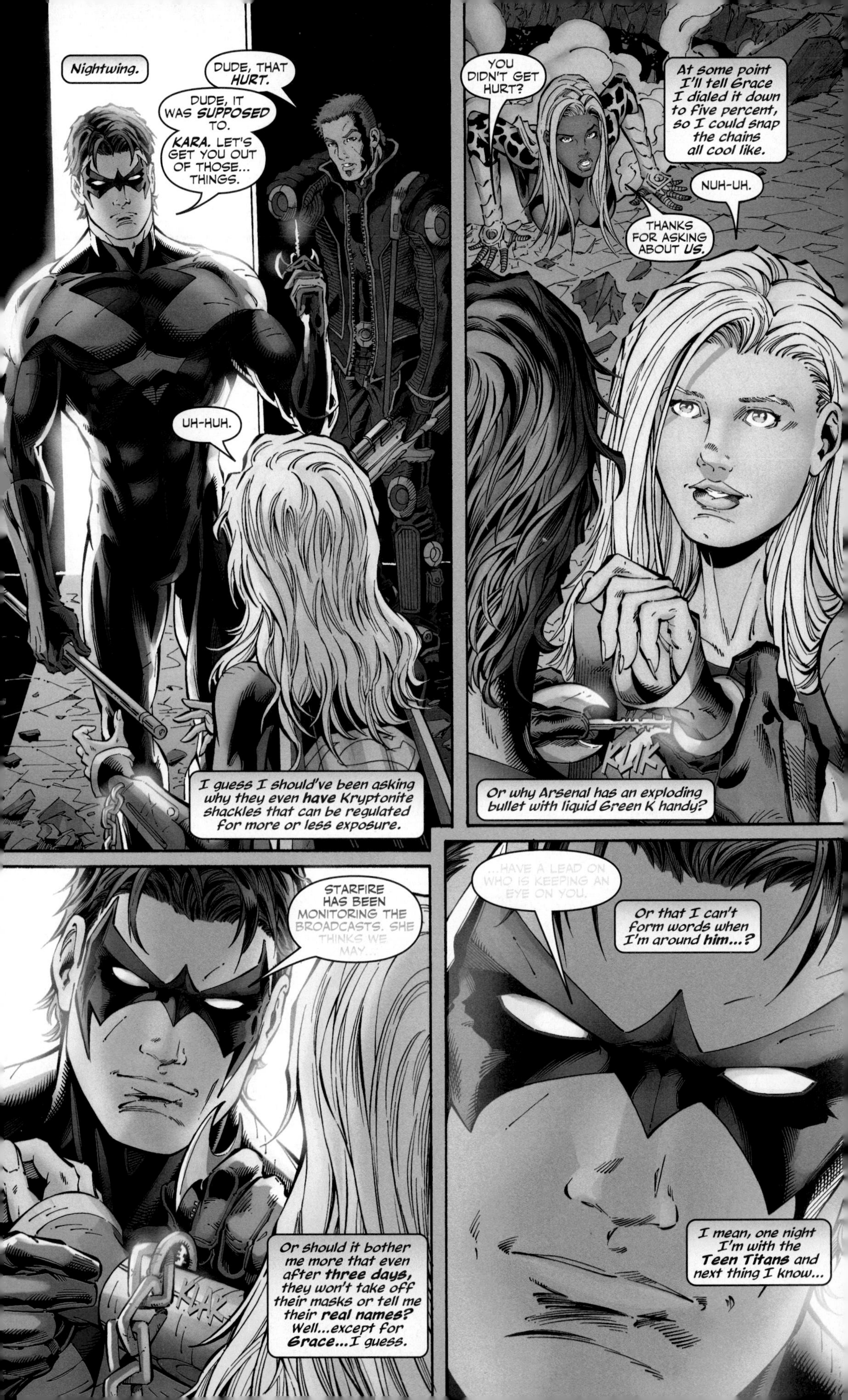

Nightwing.
DUDE, THAT HURT.
DUDE, IT WAS SUPPOSED TO.
KARA. LET'S GET YOU OUT OF THOSE... THINGS.
UH-HUH.
I guess I should've been asking why they even have Kryptonite shackles that can be regulated for more or less exposure.
YOU DIDN'T GET HURT?
At some point I'll tell Grace I dialed it down to five percent, so I could snap the chains all cool like.
NUH-UH.
THANKS FOR ASKING ABOUT US.
KLIK
Or why Arsenal has an exploding bullet with liquid Green K handy?
STARFIRE HAS BEEN MONITORING THE BROADCASTS. SHE THINKS WE MAY...
Or should it bother me more that even after three days, they won't take off their masks or tell me their real names? Well...except for Grace...I guess.
...HAVE A LEAD ON WHO IS KEEPING AN EYE ON YOU.
Or that I can't form words when I'm around him...?
I mean, one night I'm with the Teen Titans and next thing I know...

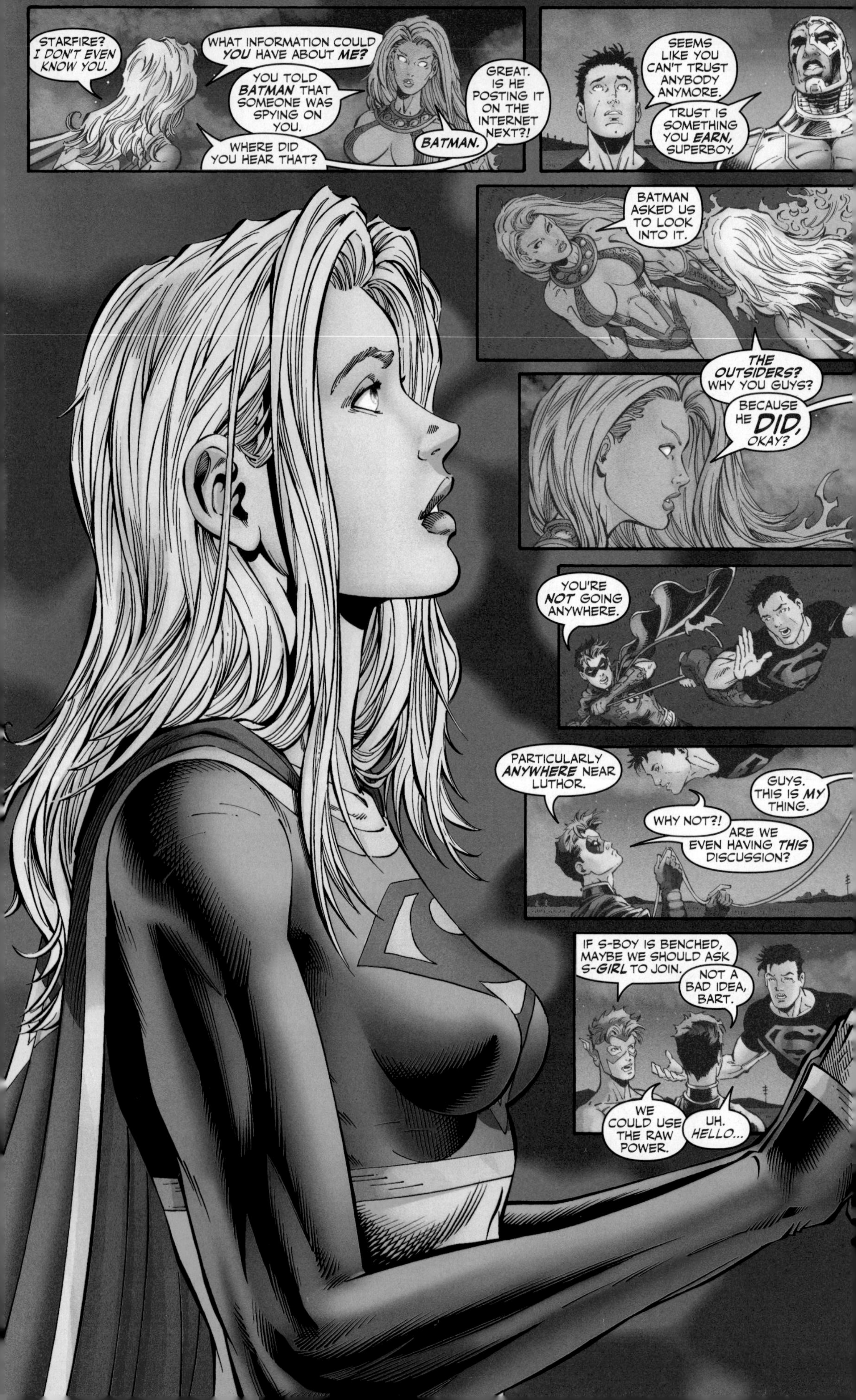
STARFIRE? I DON'T EVEN KNOW YOU.
WHAT INFORMATION COULD YOU HAVE ABOUT ME?
YOU TOLD BATMAN THAT SOMEONE WAS SPYING ON YOU.
WHERE DID YOU HEAR THAT?
BATMAN.
GREAT. IS HE POSTING IT ON THE INTERNET NEXT?!
SEEMS LIKE YOU CAN'T TRUST ANYBODY ANYMORE.
TRUST IS SOMETHING YOU EARN, SUPERBOY.
BATMAN ASKED US TO LOOK INTO IT.
THE OUTSIDERS? WHY YOU GUYS?
BECAUSE HE DID, OKAY?
YOU'RE NOT GOING ANYWHERE.
PARTICULARLY ANYWHERE NEAR LUTHOR.
GUYS. THIS IS MY THING.
WHY NOT?!
ARE WE EVEN HAVING THIS DISCUSSION?
IF S-BOY IS BENCHED, MAYBE WE SHOULD ASK S-GIRL TO JOIN.
NOT A BAD IDEA, BART.
WE COULD USE THE RAW POWER.
UH. HELLO...

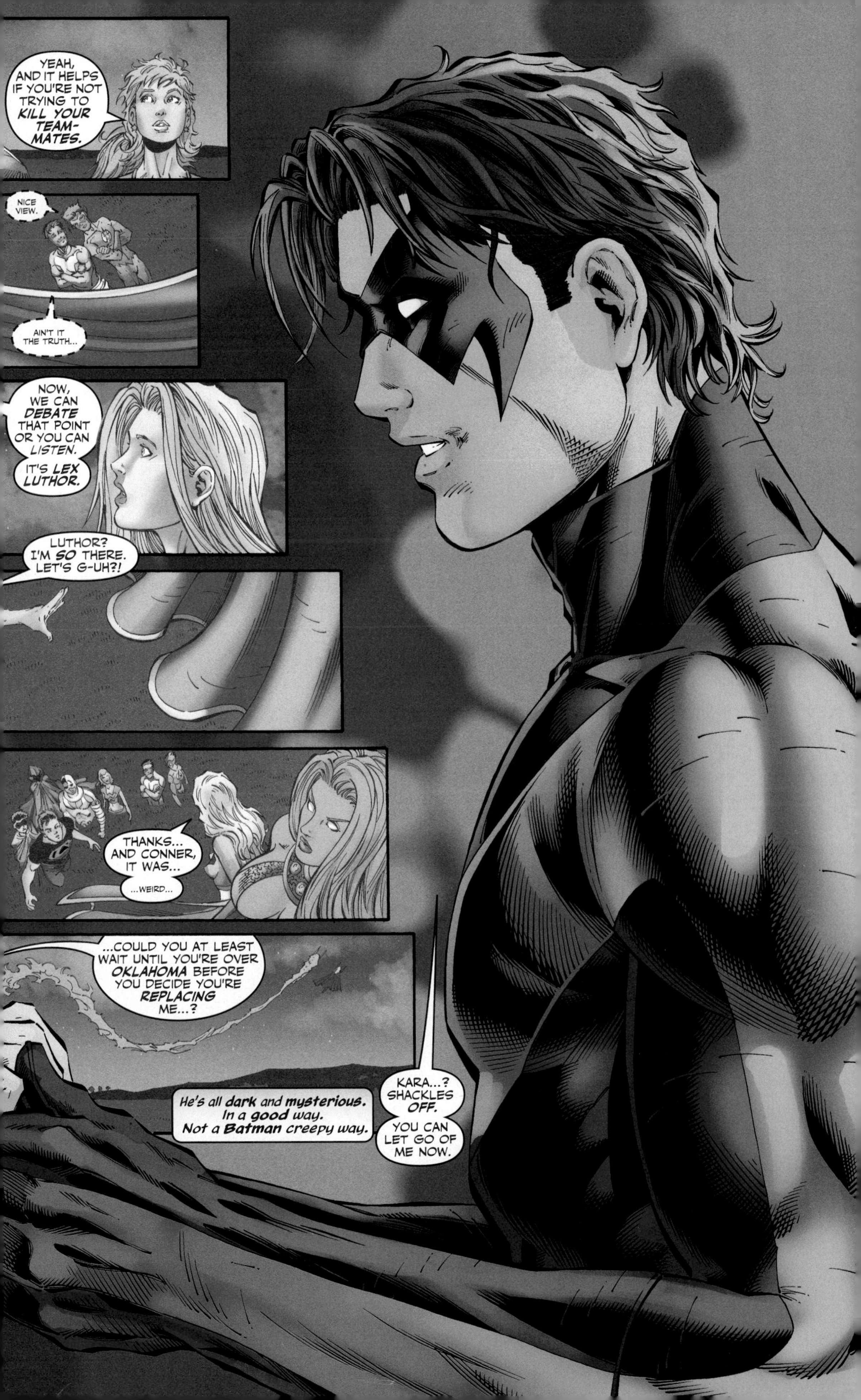

YEAH, AND IT HELPS IF YOU'RE NOT TRYING TO KILL YOUR TEAM-MATES.
NICE VIEW.
AIN'T IT THE TRUTH...
NOW, WE CAN DEBATE THAT POINT OR YOU CAN LISTEN.
IT'S LEX LUTHOR.
LUTHOR? I'M SO THERE. LET'S G-UH?!
THANKS... AND CONNER, IT WAS...
...WEIRD...
...COULD YOU AT LEAST WAIT UNTIL YOU'RE OVER OKLAHOMA BEFORE YOU DECIDE YOU'RE REPLACING ME...?
He's all dark and mysterious. In a good way. Not a Batman creepy way.
KARA...? SHACKLES OFF.
YOU CAN LET GO OF ME NOW.

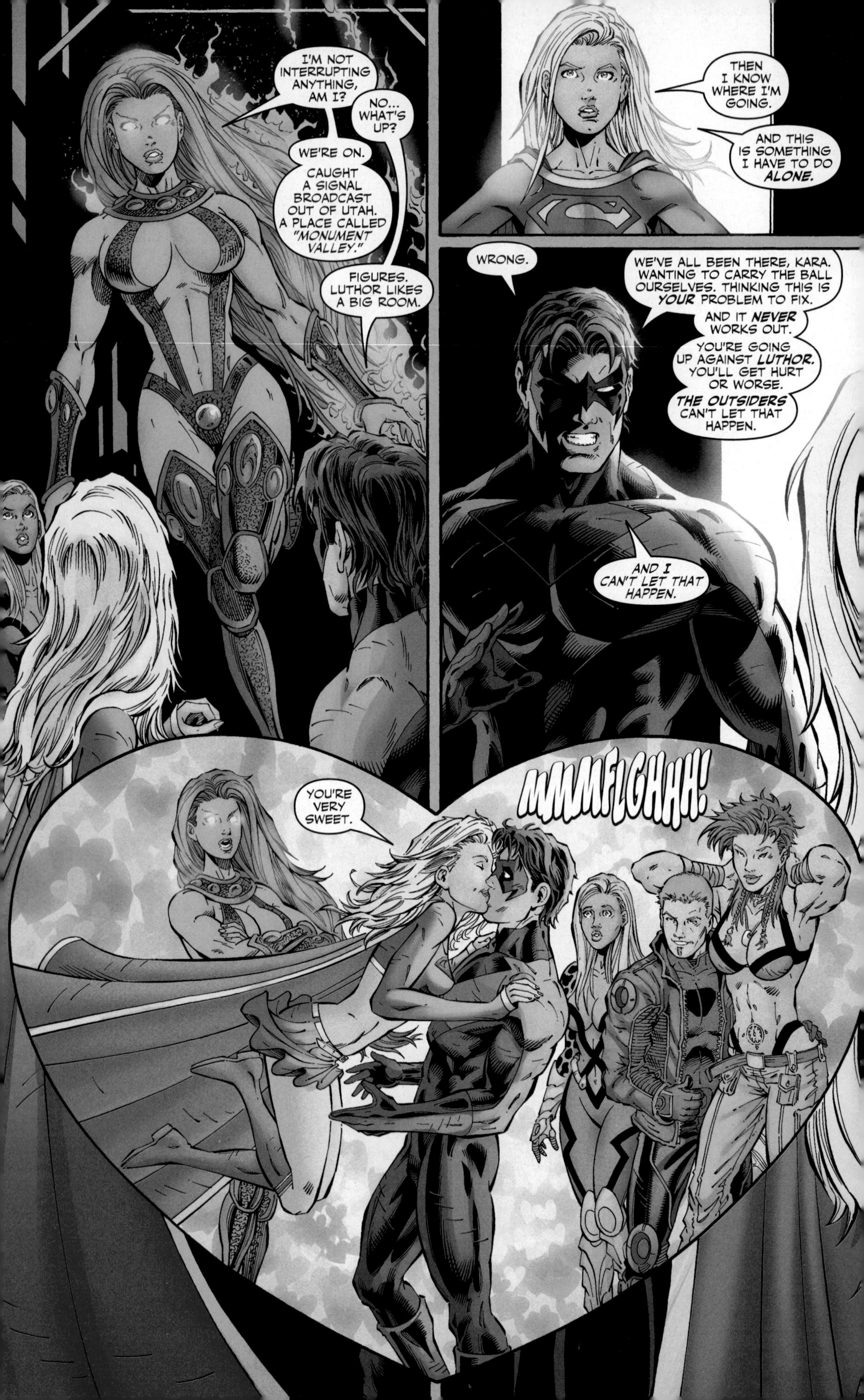
I'M NOT INTERRUPTING ANYTHING, AM I?
NO... WHAT'S UP?
WE'RE ON.
CAUGHT A SIGNAL BROADCAST OUT OF UTAH. A PLACE CALLED "MONUMENT VALLEY."
FIGURES. LUTHOR LIKES A BIG ROOM.
THEN I KNOW WHERE I'M GOING.
AND THIS IS SOMETHING I HAVE TO DO ALONE.
WRONG.
WE'VE ALL BEEN THERE, KARA. WANTING TO CARRY THE BALL OURSELVES. THINKING THIS IS YOUR PROBLEM TO FIX.
AND IT NEVER WORKS OUT.
YOU'RE GOING UP AGAINST LUTHOR. YOU'LL GET HURT OR WORSE.
THE OUTSIDERS CAN'T LET THAT HAPPEN.
AND I CAN'T LET THAT HAPPEN.
YOU'RE VERY SWEET.
MMMFLGHHH!

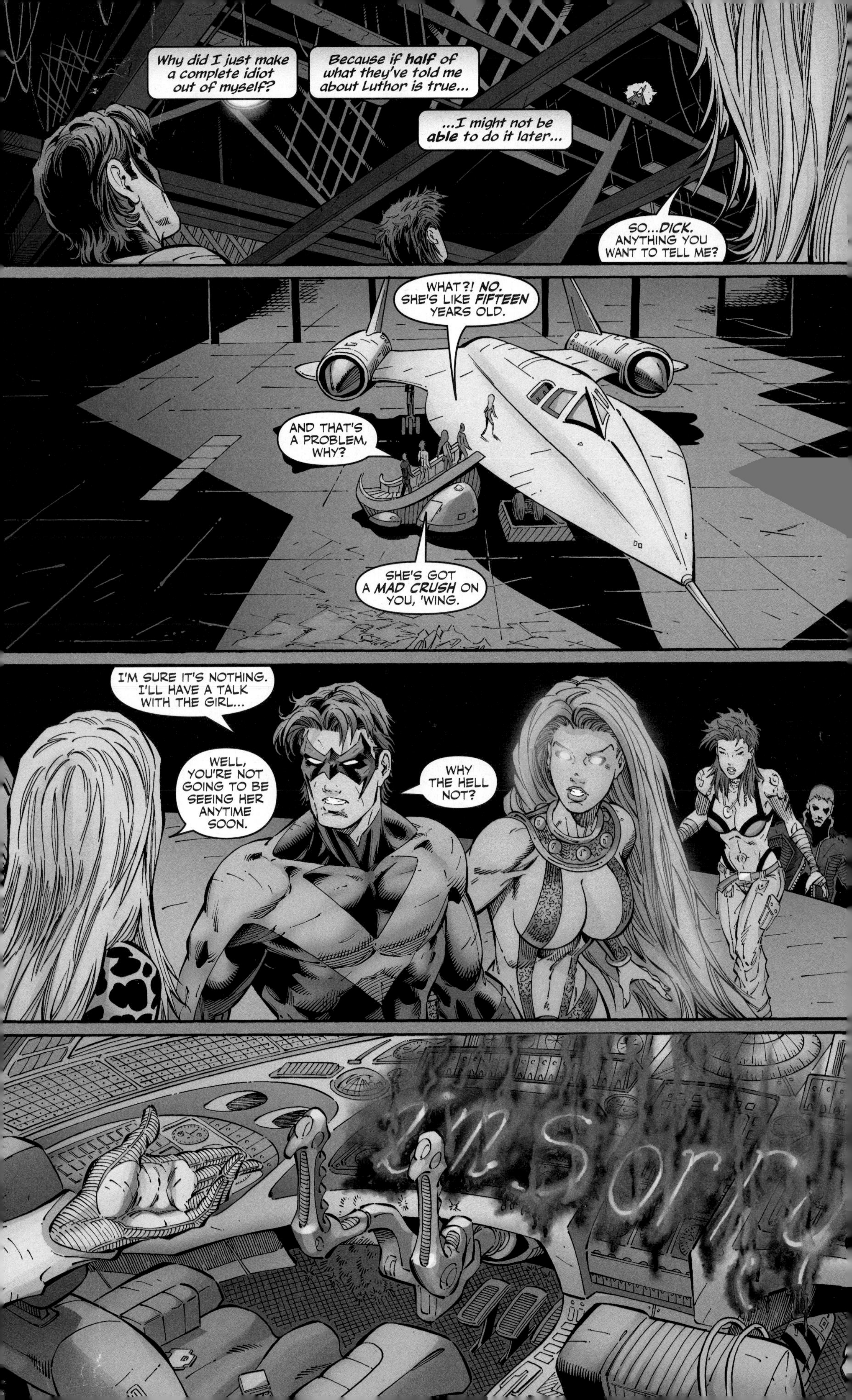
Why did I just make a complete idiot out of myself?
Because if half of what they've told me about Luthor is true...
...I might not be able to do it later...
SO...DICK. ANYTHING YOU WANT TO TELL ME?
WHAT?! NO. SHE'S LIKE FIFTEEN YEARS OLD.
AND THAT'S A PROBLEM, WHY?
SHE'S GOT A MAD CRUSH ON YOU, 'WING.
I'M SURE IT'S NOTHING. I'LL HAVE A TALK WITH THE GIRL...
WELL, YOU'RE NOT GOING TO BE SEEING HER ANYTIME SOON.
WHY THE HELL NOT?
I'm Sorry

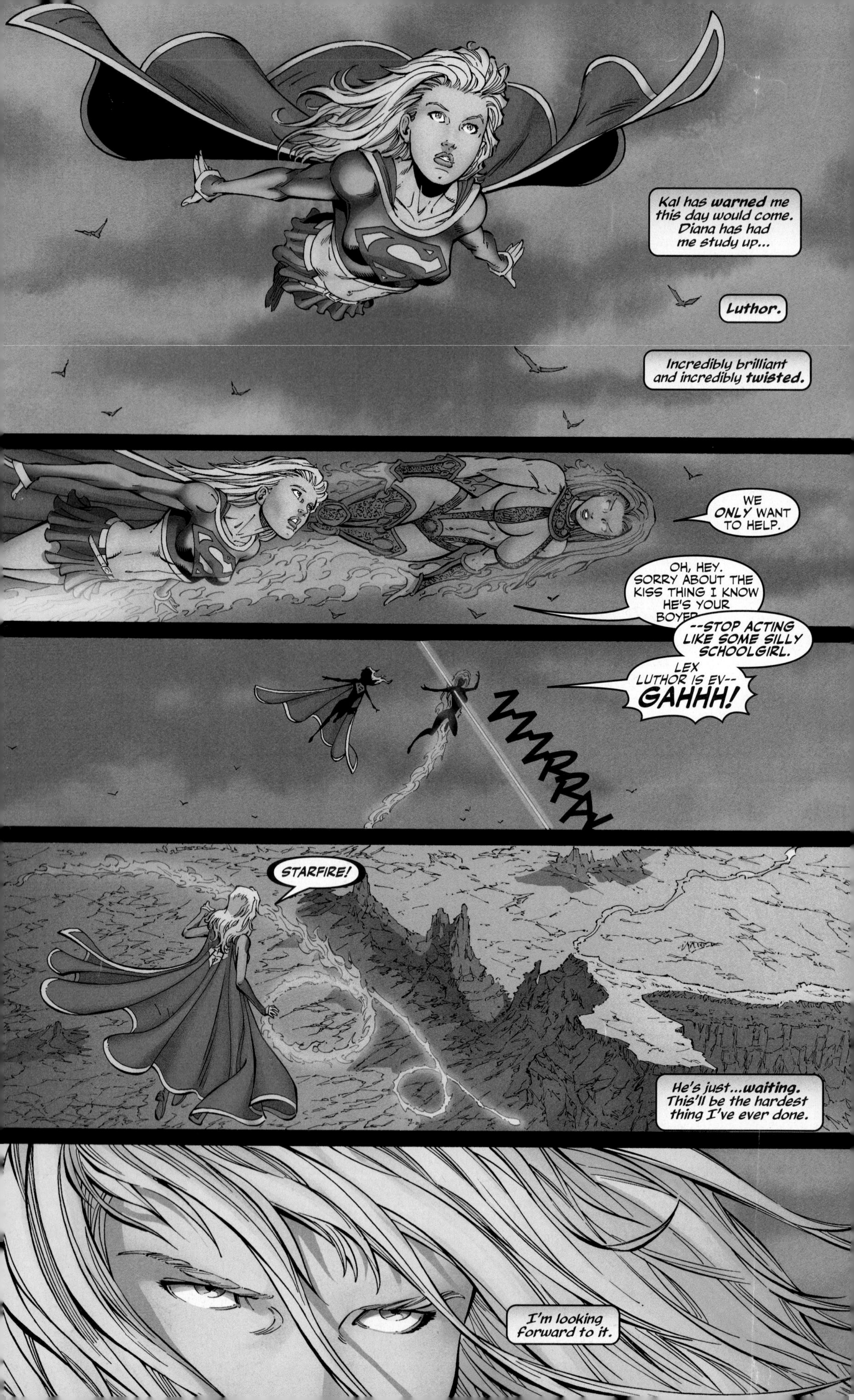
Kal has warned me this day would come. Diana has had me study up...
Luthor.
Incredibly brilliant and incredibly twisted.
WE ONLY WANT TO HELP.
OH, HEY. SORRY ABOUT THE KISS THING I KNOW HE'S YOUR BOYFR--
--STOP ACTING LIKE SOME SILLY SCHOOLGIRL.
LEX LUTHOR IS EV-- GAHHH!
VVVRRRAM
STARFIRE!
He's just...waiting. This'll be the hardest thing I've ever done.
I'm looking forward to it.

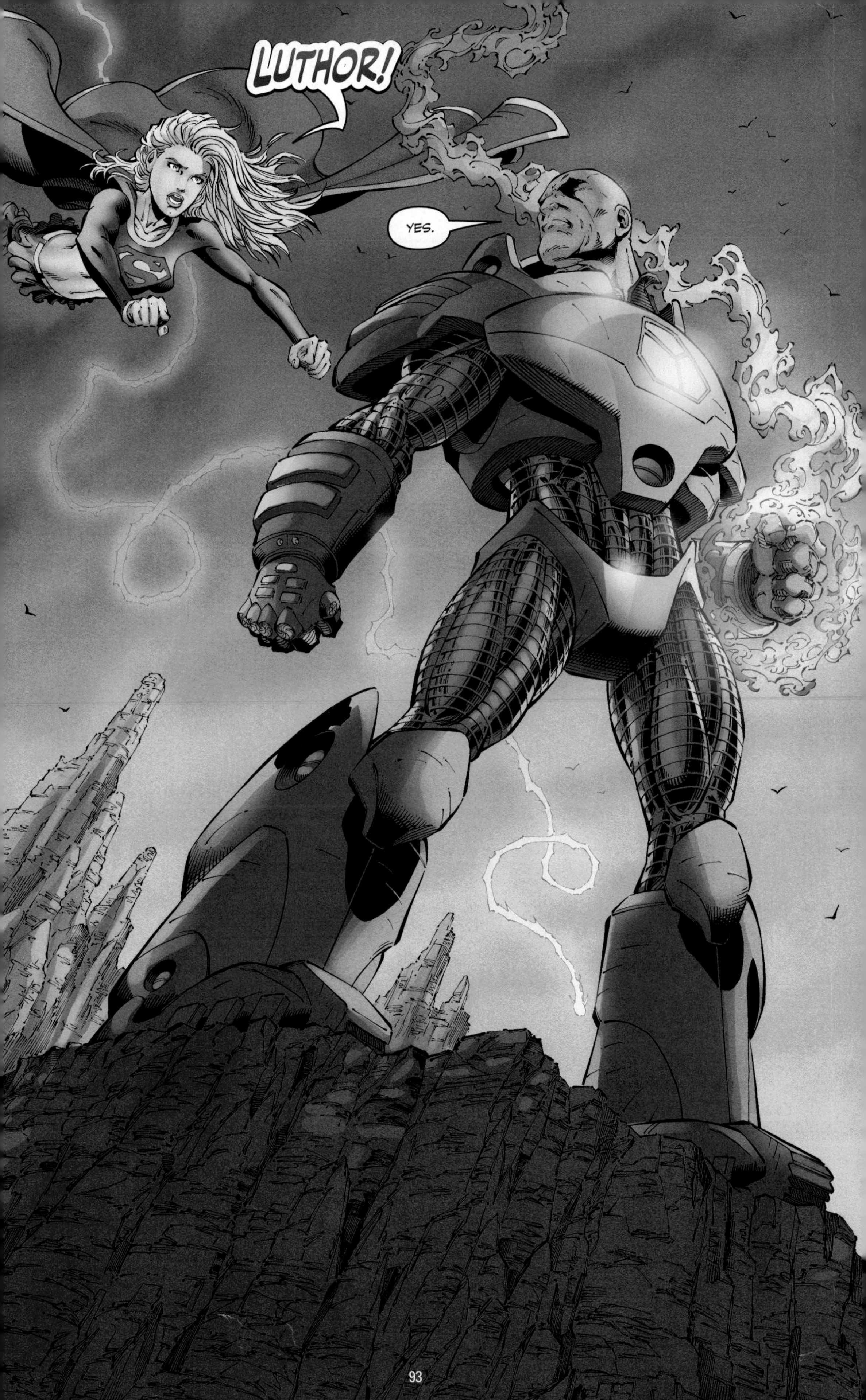
LUTHOR!
YES.

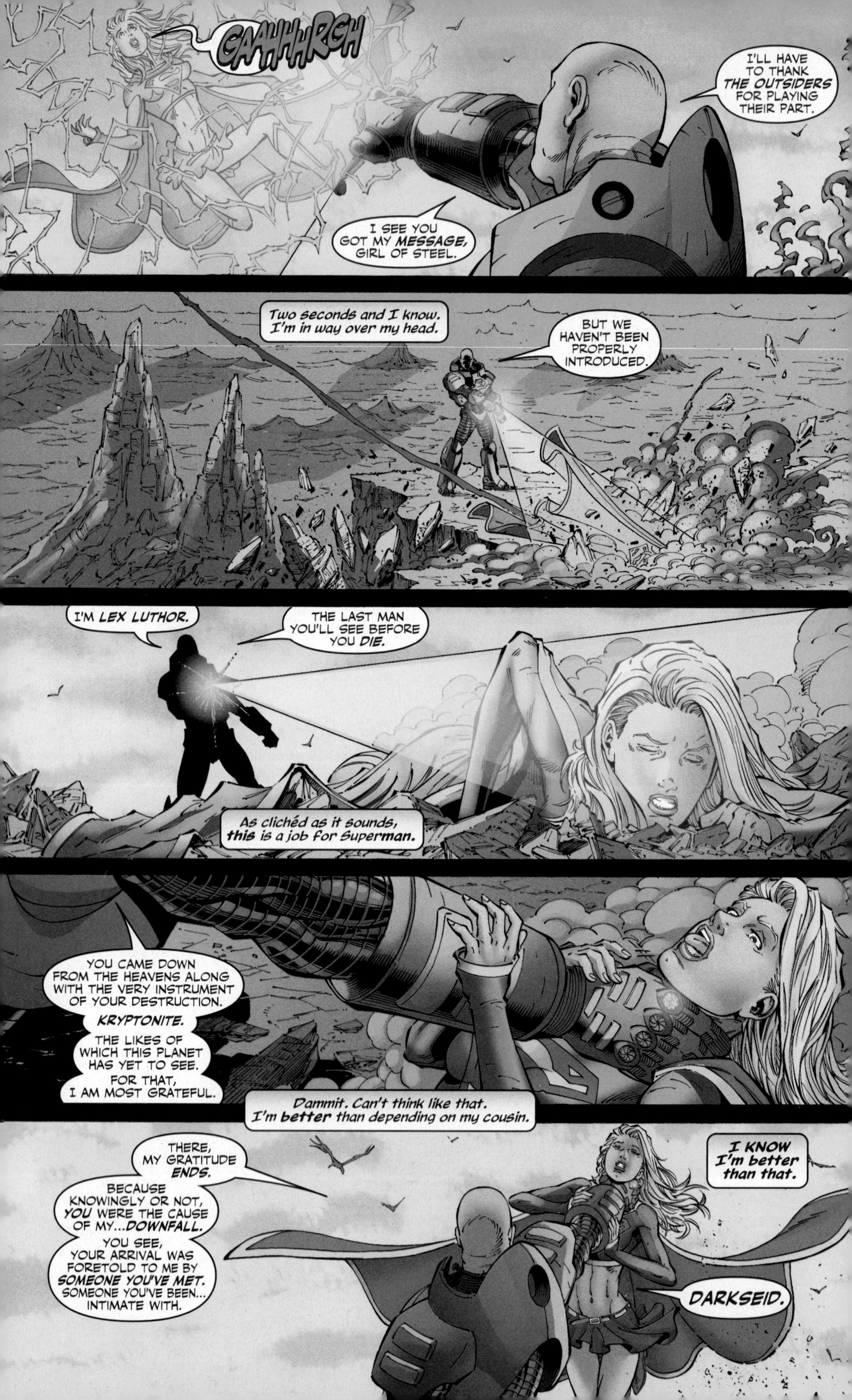
GAAHHHRGH
I'LL HAVE TO THANK THE OUTSIDERS FOR PLAYING THEIR PART.
I SEE YOU GOT MY MESSAGE, GIRL OF STEEL.
Two seconds and I know. I'm in way over my head.
BUT WE HAVEN'T BEEN PROPERLY INTRODUCED.
I'M LEX LUTHOR.
THE LAST MAN YOU'LL SEE BEFORE YOU DIE.
As clichéd as it sounds, this is a job for Superman.
YOU CAME DOWN FROM THE HEAVENS ALONG WITH THE VERY INSTRUMENT OF YOUR DESTRUCTION.
KRYPTONITE.
THE LIKES OF WHICH THIS PLANET HAS YET TO SEE.
FOR THAT, I AM MOST GRATEFUL.
Dammit. Can't think like that. I'm better than depending on my cousin.
THERE, MY GRATITUDE ENDS.
BECAUSE KNOWINGLY OR NOT, YOU WERE THE CAUSE OF MY...DOWNFALL.
YOU SEE, YOUR ARRIVAL WAS FORETOLD TO ME BY SOMEONE YOU'VE MET. SOMEONE YOU'VE BEEN... INTIMATE WITH.
I KNOW I'm better than that.
DARKSEID.

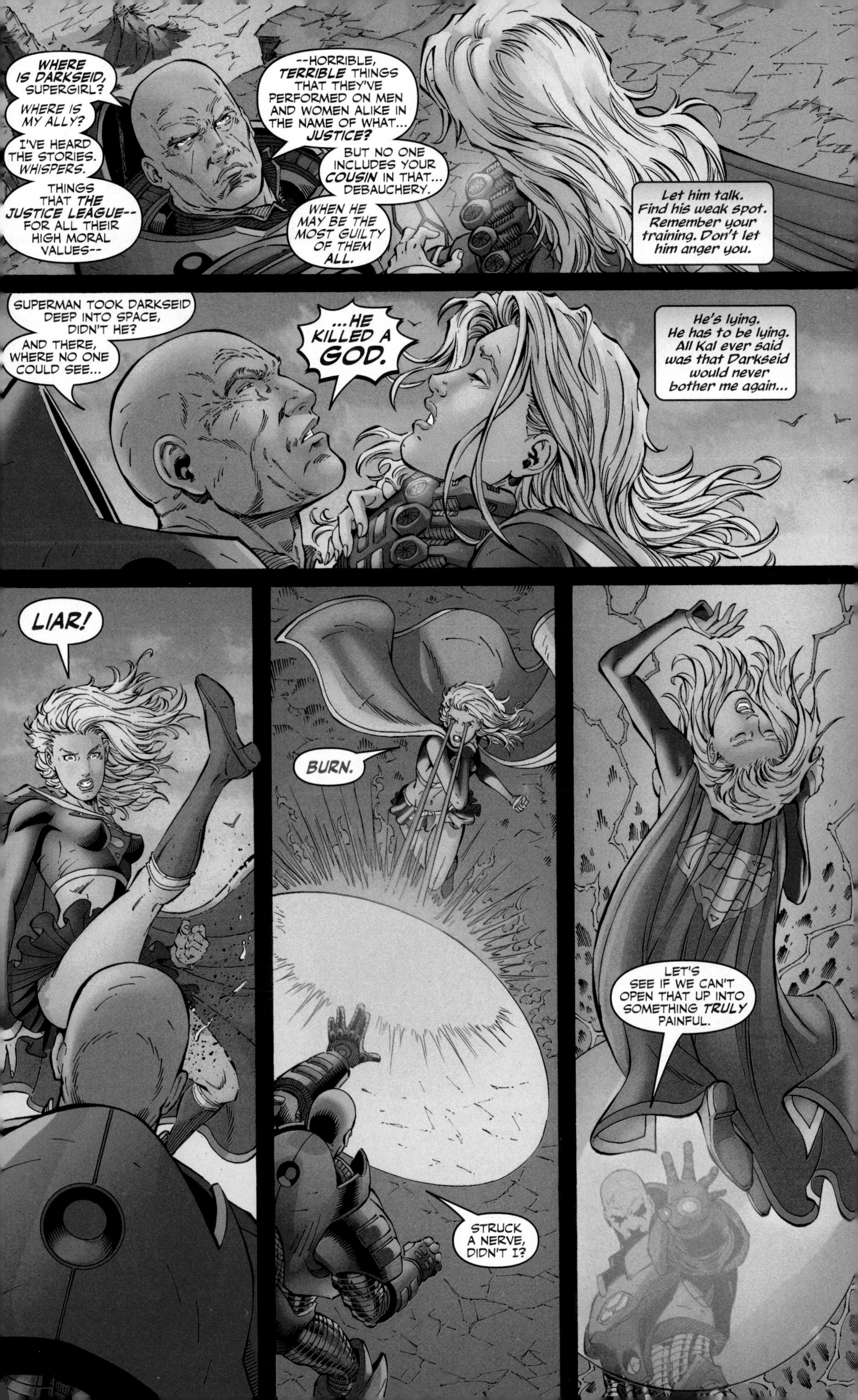
WHERE IS DARKSEID, SUPERGIRL?
WHERE IS MY ALLY?
I'VE HEARD THE STORIES. WHISPERS.
THINGS THAT THE JUSTICE LEAGUE-- FOR ALL THEIR HIGH MORAL VALUES--
--HORRIBLE, TERRIBLE THINGS THAT THEY'VE PERFORMED ON MEN AND WOMEN ALIKE IN THE NAME OF WHAT... JUSTICE?
BUT NO ONE INCLUDES YOUR COUSIN IN THAT... DEBAUCHERY.
WHEN HE MAY BE THE MOST GUILTY OF THEM ALL.
Let him talk. Find his weak spot. Remember your training. Don't let him anger you.
SUPERMAN TOOK DARKSEID DEEP INTO SPACE, DIDN'T HE?
AND THERE, WHERE NO ONE COULD SEE...
...HE KILLED A GOD.
He's lying. He has to be lying. All Kal ever said was that Darkseid would never bother me again...
LIAR!
BURN.
STRUCK A NERVE, DIDN'T I?
LET'S SEE IF WE CAN'T OPEN THAT UP INTO SOMETHING TRULY PAINFUL.

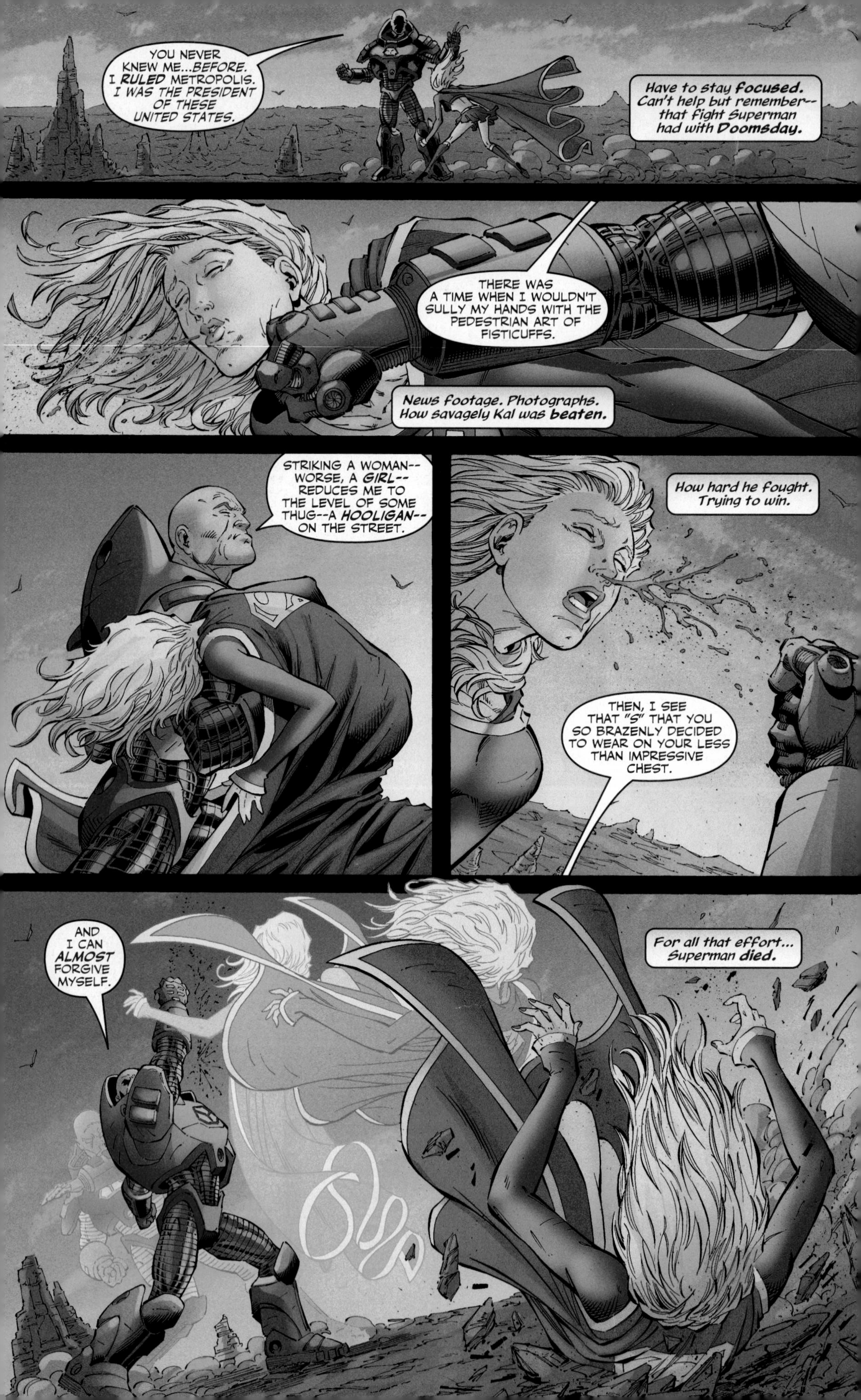
YOU NEVER KNEW ME...BEFORE. I RULED METROPOLIS. I WAS THE PRESIDENT OF THESE UNITED STATES.
Have to stay focused. Can't help but remember--that fight Superman had with Doomsday.
THERE WAS A TIME WHEN I WOULDN'T SULLY MY HANDS WITH THE PEDESTRIAN ART OF FISTICUFFS.
News footage. Photographs. How savagely Kal was beaten.
STRIKING A WOMAN--WORSE, A GIRL--REDUCES ME TO THE LEVEL OF SOME THUG--A HOOLIGAN--ON THE STREET.
How hard he fought. Trying to win.
THEN, I SEE THAT "S" THAT YOU SO BRAZENLY DECIDED TO WEAR ON YOUR LESS THAN IMPRESSIVE CHEST.
AND I CAN ALMOST FORGIVE MYSELF.
For all that effort... Superman died.

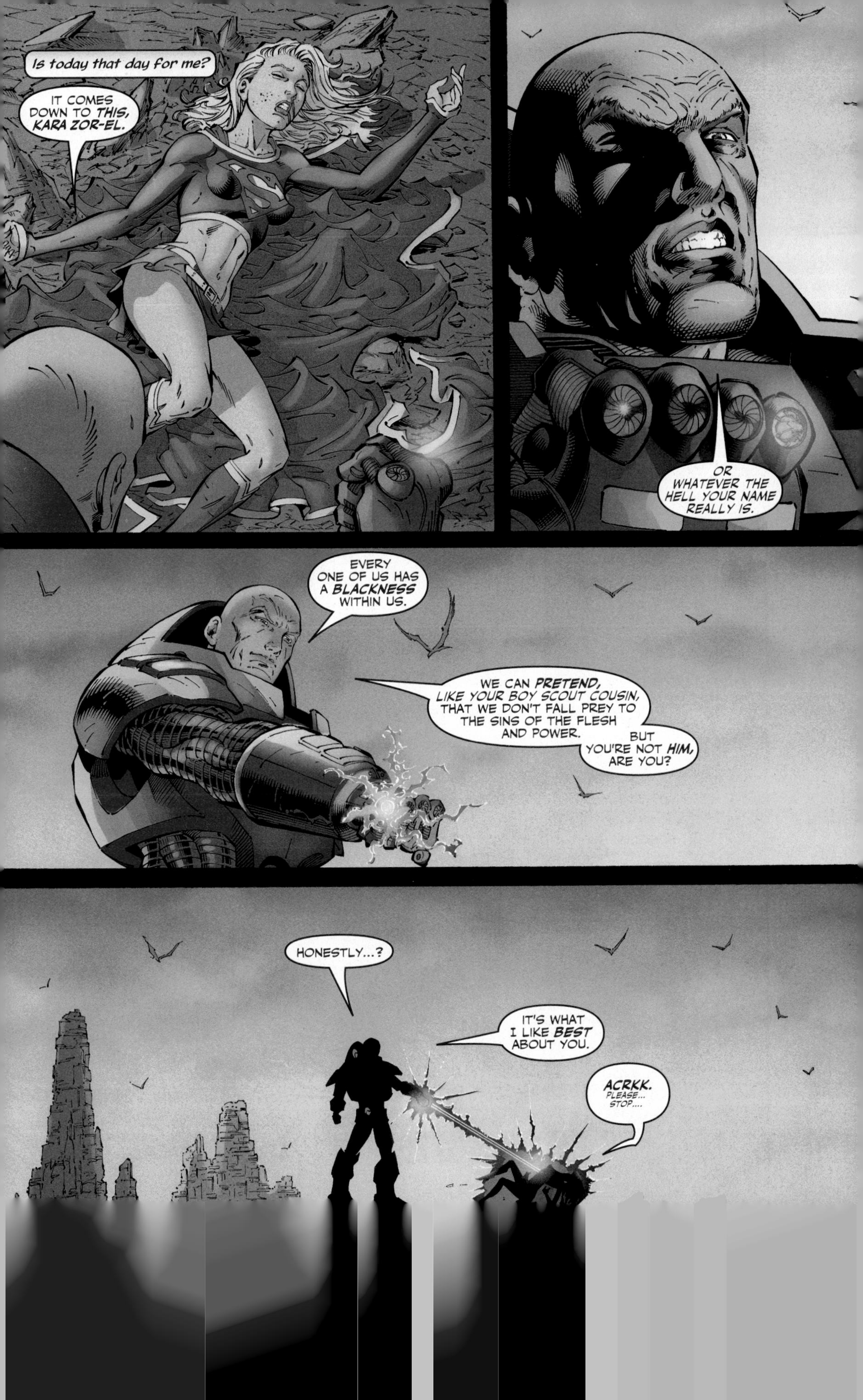
Is today that day for me?
IT COMES DOWN TO THIS, KARA ZOR-EL.
OR WHATEVER THE HELL YOUR NAME REALLY IS.
EVERY ONE OF US HAS A BLACKNESS WITHIN US.
WE CAN PRETEND, LIKE YOUR BOY SCOUT COUSIN, THAT WE DON'T FALL PREY TO THE SINS OF THE FLESH AND POWER.
BUT YOU'RE NOT HIM, ARE YOU?
HONESTLY...?
IT'S WHAT I LIKE BEST ABOUT YOU.
ACRKK. PLEASE... STOP....

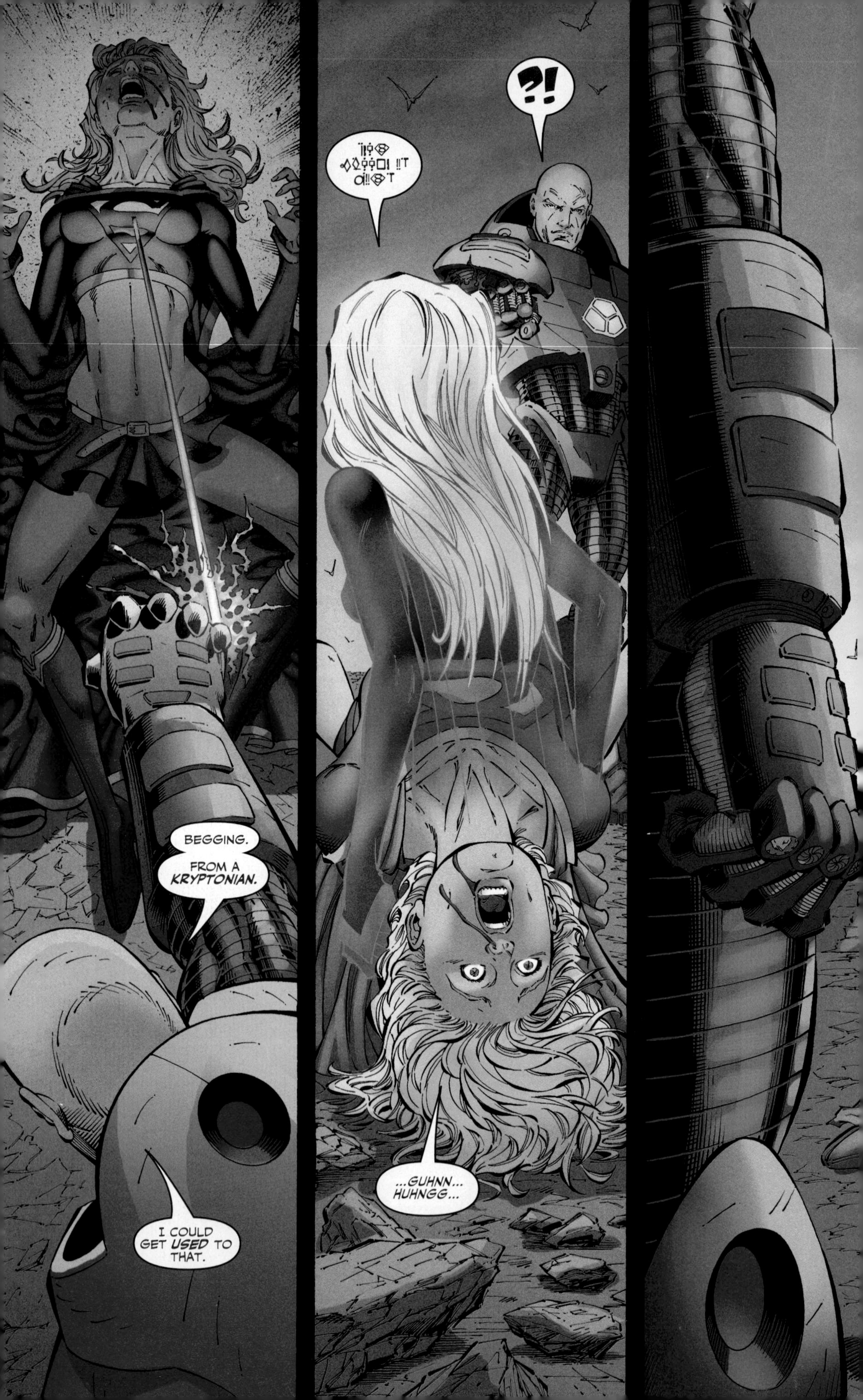
BEGGING.
FROM A KRYPTONIAN.
I COULD GET USED TO THAT.
?!
...GUHNN... HUHNGG...

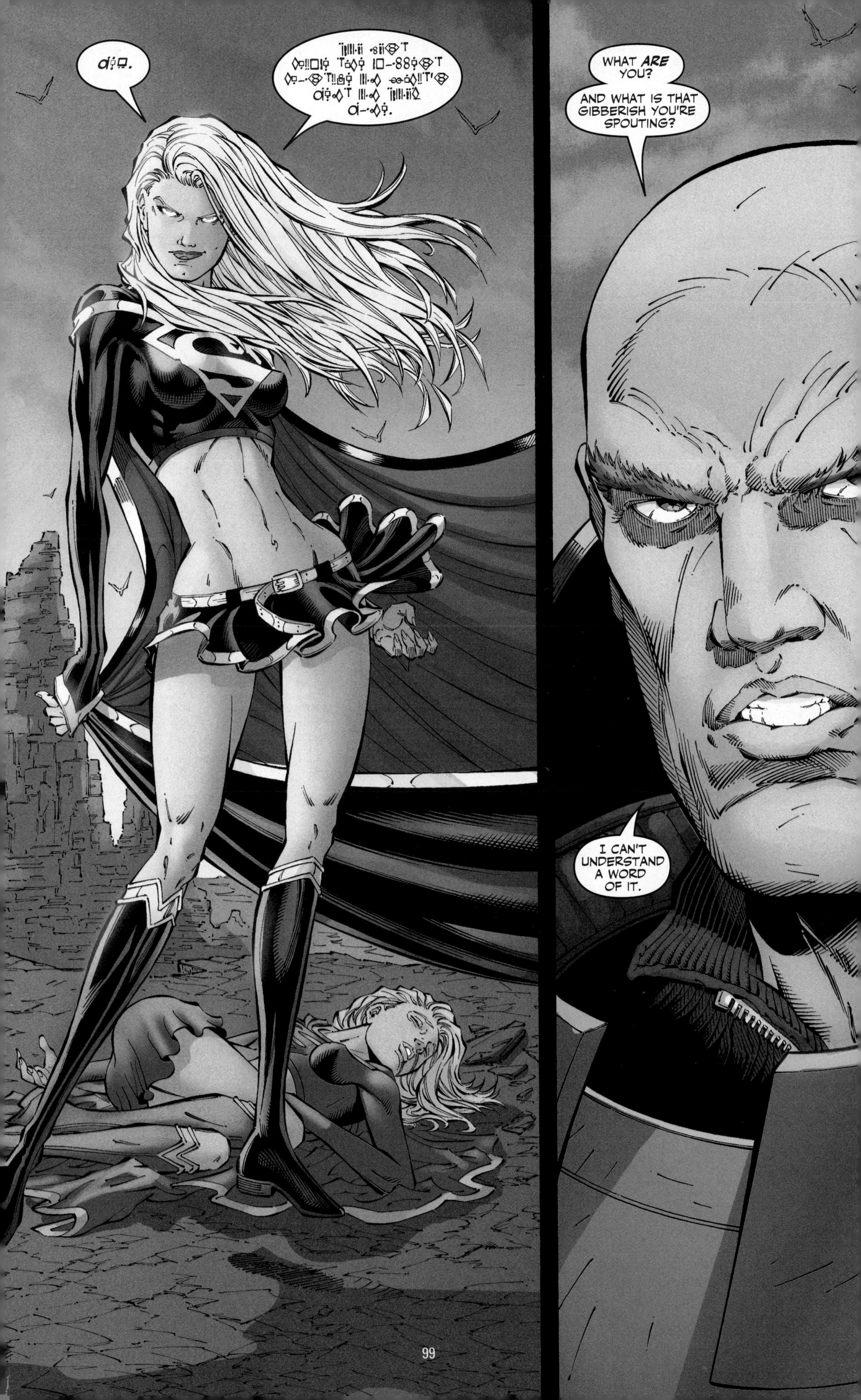
WHAT ARE YOU?
AND WHAT IS THAT GIBBERISH YOU'RE SPOUTING?
I CAN'T UNDERSTAND A WORD OF IT.

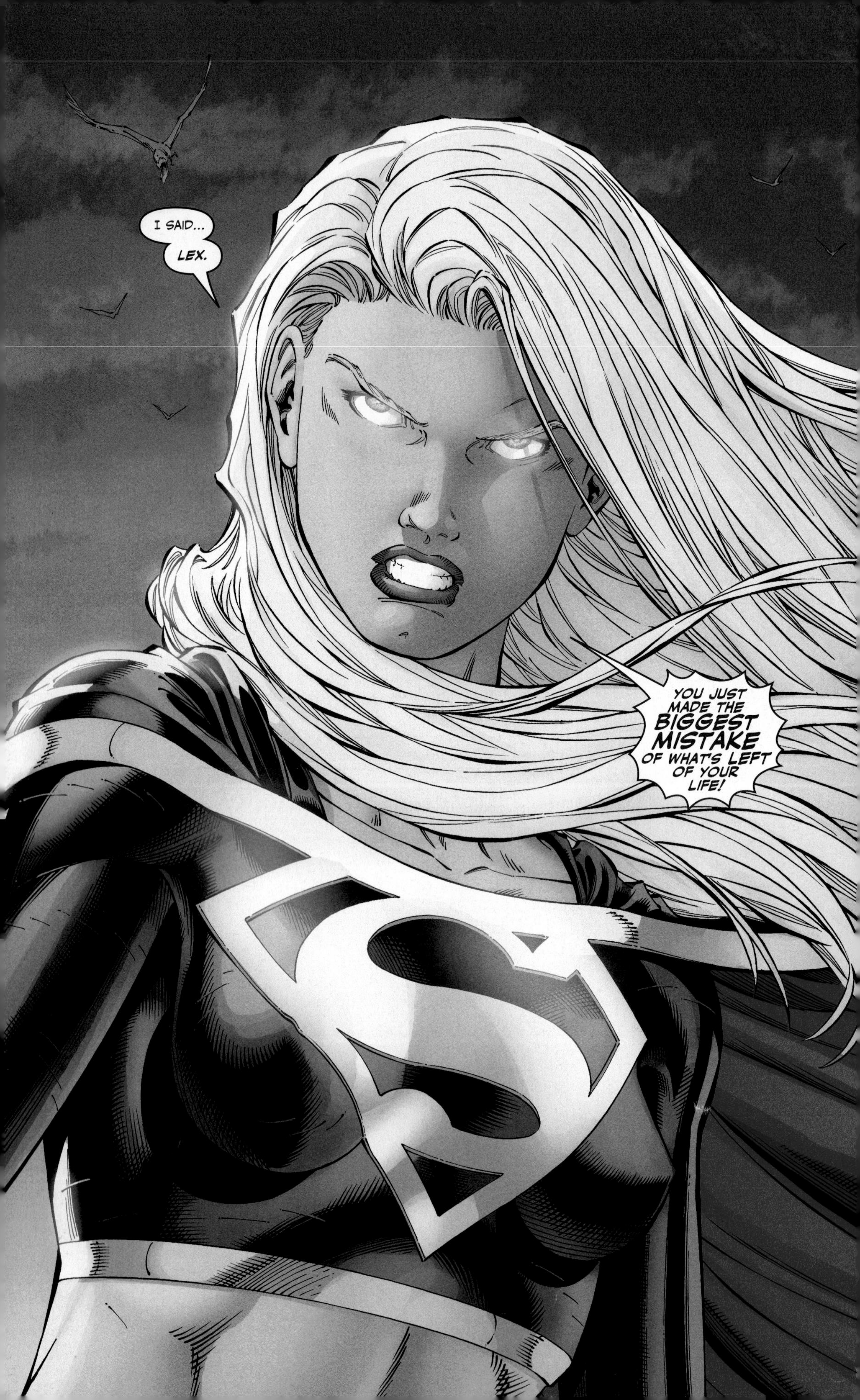
I SAID...
LEX.
YOU JUST MADE THE BIGGEST MISTAKE OF WHAT'S LEFT OF YOUR LIFE!

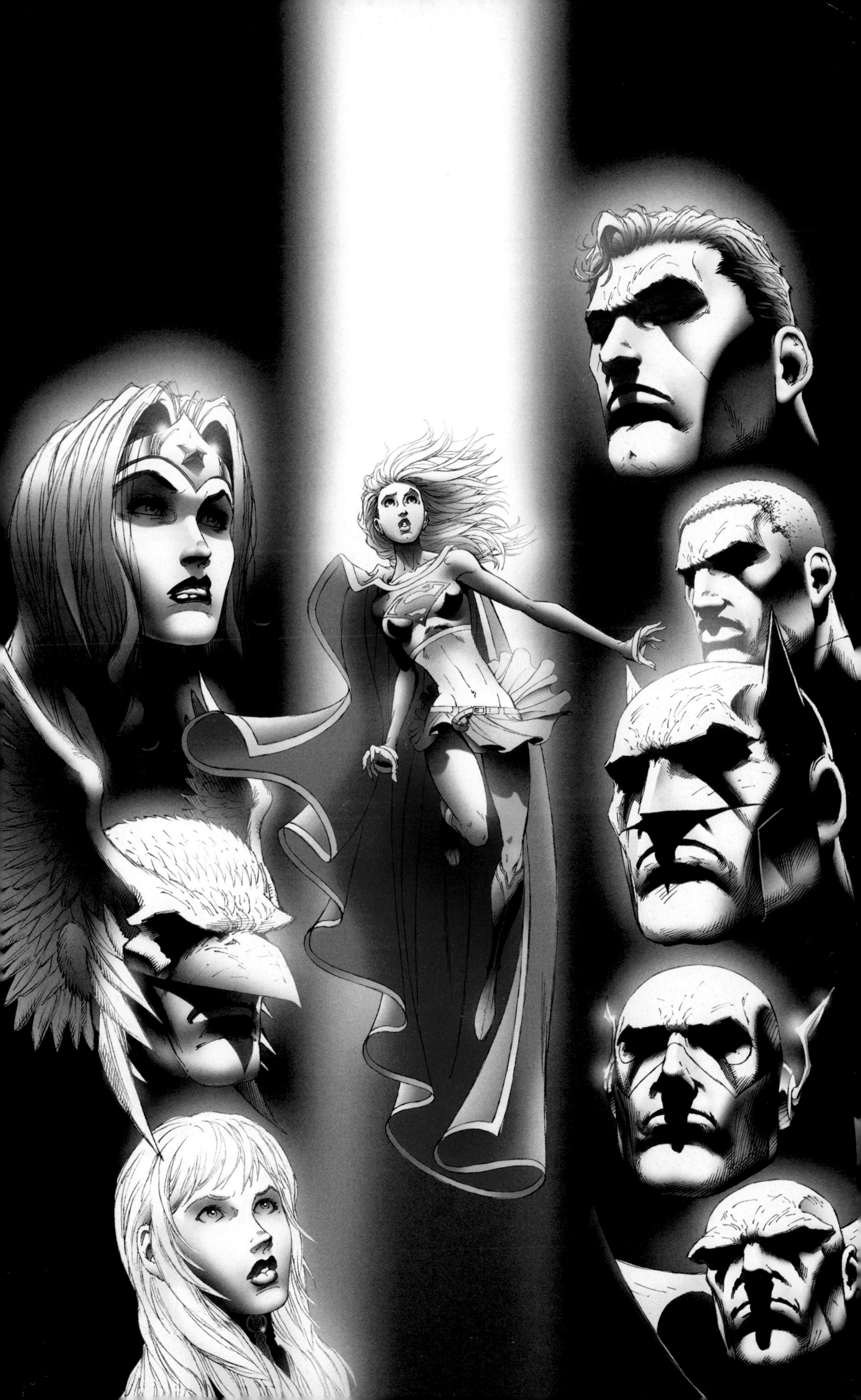

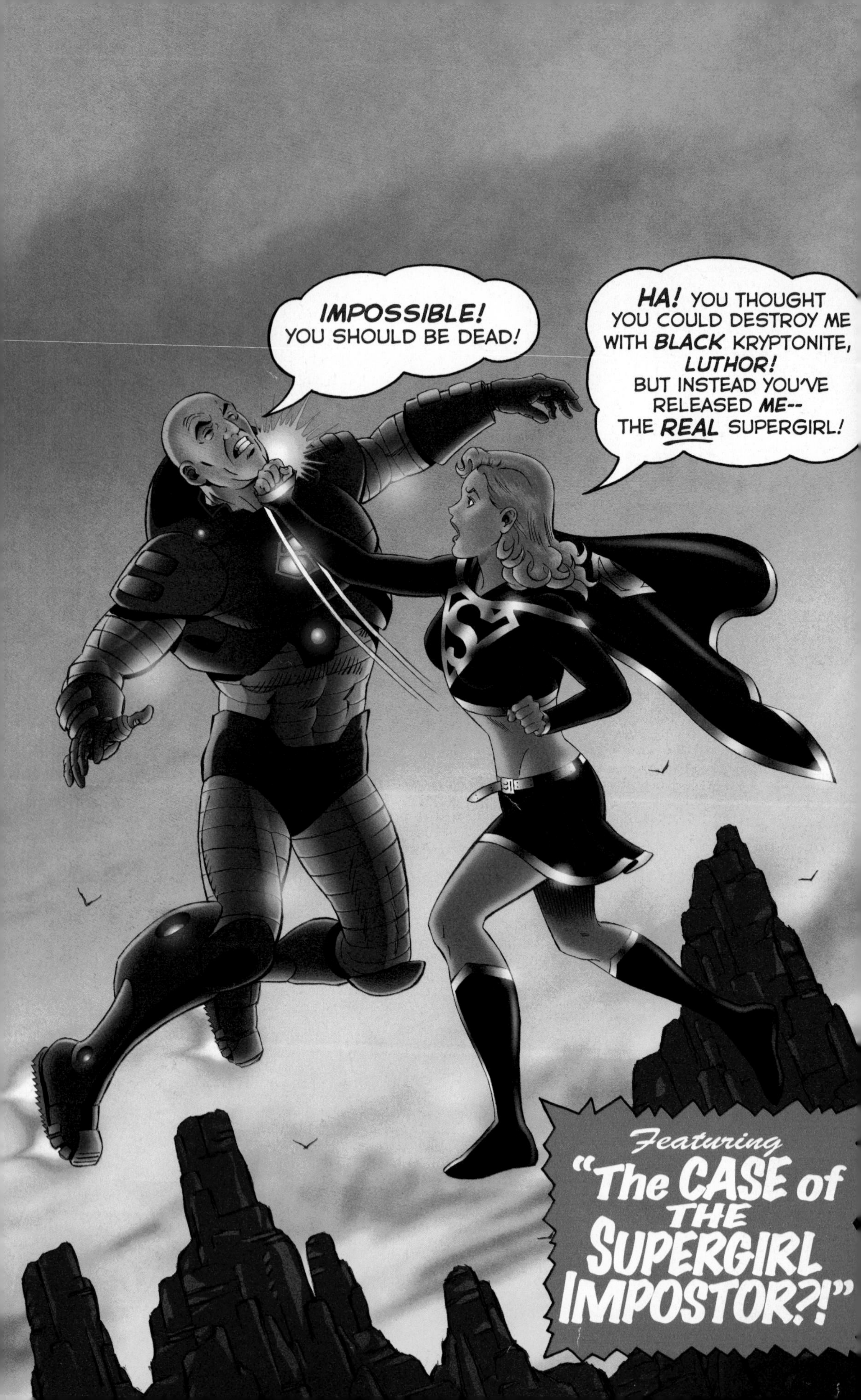
IMPOSSIBLE! YOU SHOULD BE DEAD!
HA! YOU THOUGHT YOU COULD DESTROY ME WITH BLACK KRYPTONITE, LUTHOR! BUT INSTEAD YOU'VE RELEASED ME-- THE REAL SUPERGIRL!
Featuring "The CASE of THE SUPERGIRL IMPOSTOR?!"

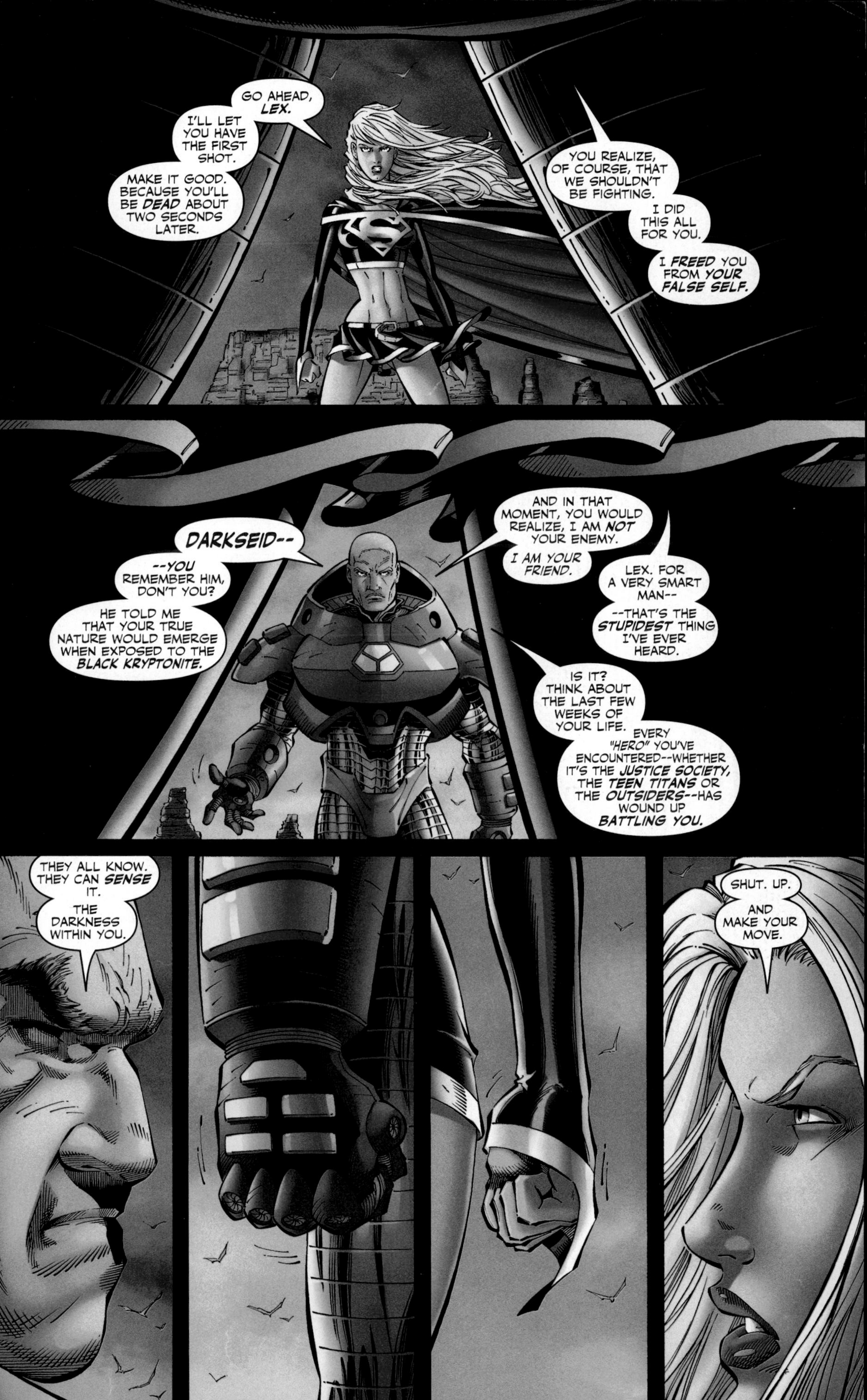
GO AHEAD, LEX.
I'LL LET YOU HAVE THE FIRST SHOT.
MAKE IT GOOD. BECAUSE YOU'LL BE DEAD ABOUT TWO SECONDS LATER.
YOU REALIZE, OF COURSE, THAT WE SHOULDN'T BE FIGHTING.
I DID THIS ALL FOR YOU.
I FREED YOU FROM YOUR FALSE SELF.
DARKSEID--
--YOU REMEMBER HIM, DON'T YOU?
HE TOLD ME THAT YOUR TRUE NATURE WOULD EMERGE WHEN EXPOSED TO THE BLACK KRYPTONITE.
AND IN THAT MOMENT, YOU WOULD REALIZE, I AM NOT YOUR ENEMY.
I AM YOUR FRIEND.
LEX. FOR A VERY SMART MAN--
--THAT'S THE STUPIDEST THING I'VE EVER HEARD.
IS IT? THINK ABOUT THE LAST FEW WEEKS OF YOUR LIFE.
EVERY "HERO" YOU'VE ENCOUNTERED--WHETHER IT'S THE JUSTICE SOCIETY, THE TEEN TITANS OR THE OUTSIDERS--HAS WOUND UP BATTLING YOU.
THEY ALL KNOW. THEY CAN SENSE IT.
THE DARKNESS WITHIN YOU.
SHUT. UP.
AND MAKE YOUR MOVE.

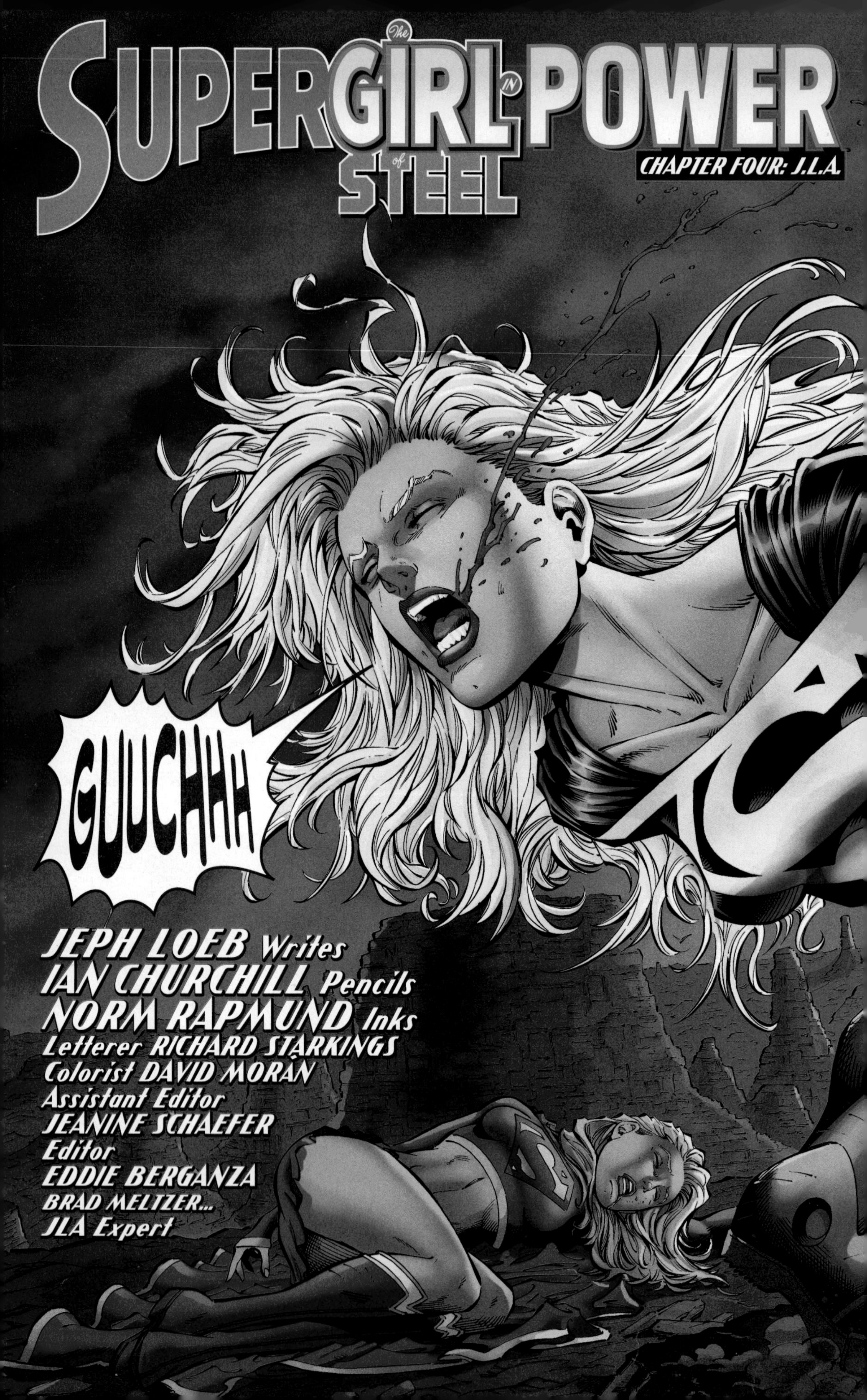
The SUPERGIRL in POWER of STEEL
CHAPTER FOUR: J.L.A.
GUUCHHH
JEPH LOEB Writes
IAN CHURCHILL Pencils
NORM RAPMUND Inks
Letterer RICHARD STARKINGS
Colorist DAVID MORAN
Assistant Editor
JEANINE SCHAEFER
Editor
EDDIE BERGANZA
BRAD MELTZER...
JLA Expert

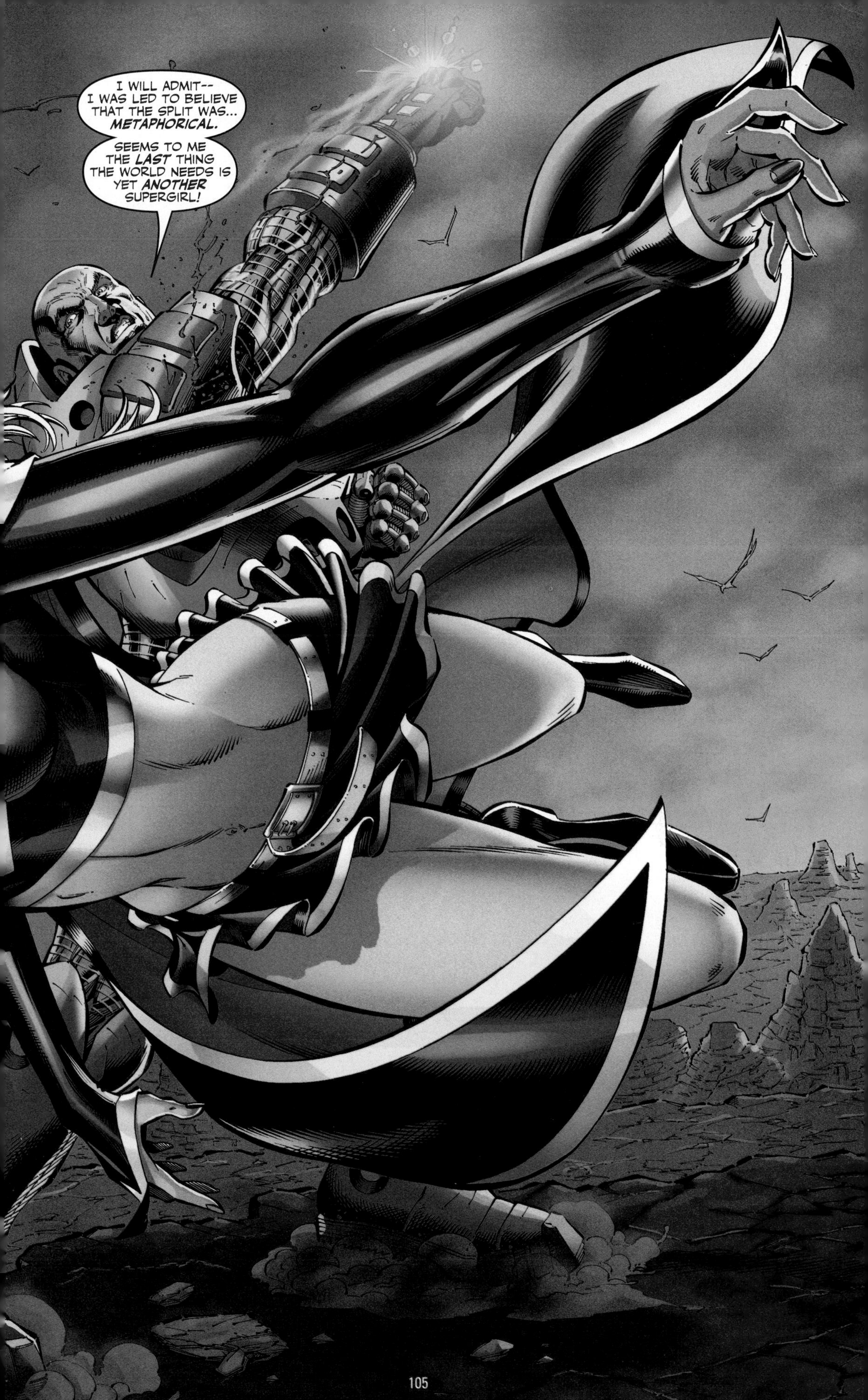
I WILL ADMIT-- I WAS LED TO BELIEVE THAT THE SPLIT WAS... METAPHORICAL.
SEEMS TO ME THE LAST THING THE WORLD NEEDS IS YET ANOTHER SUPERGIRL!

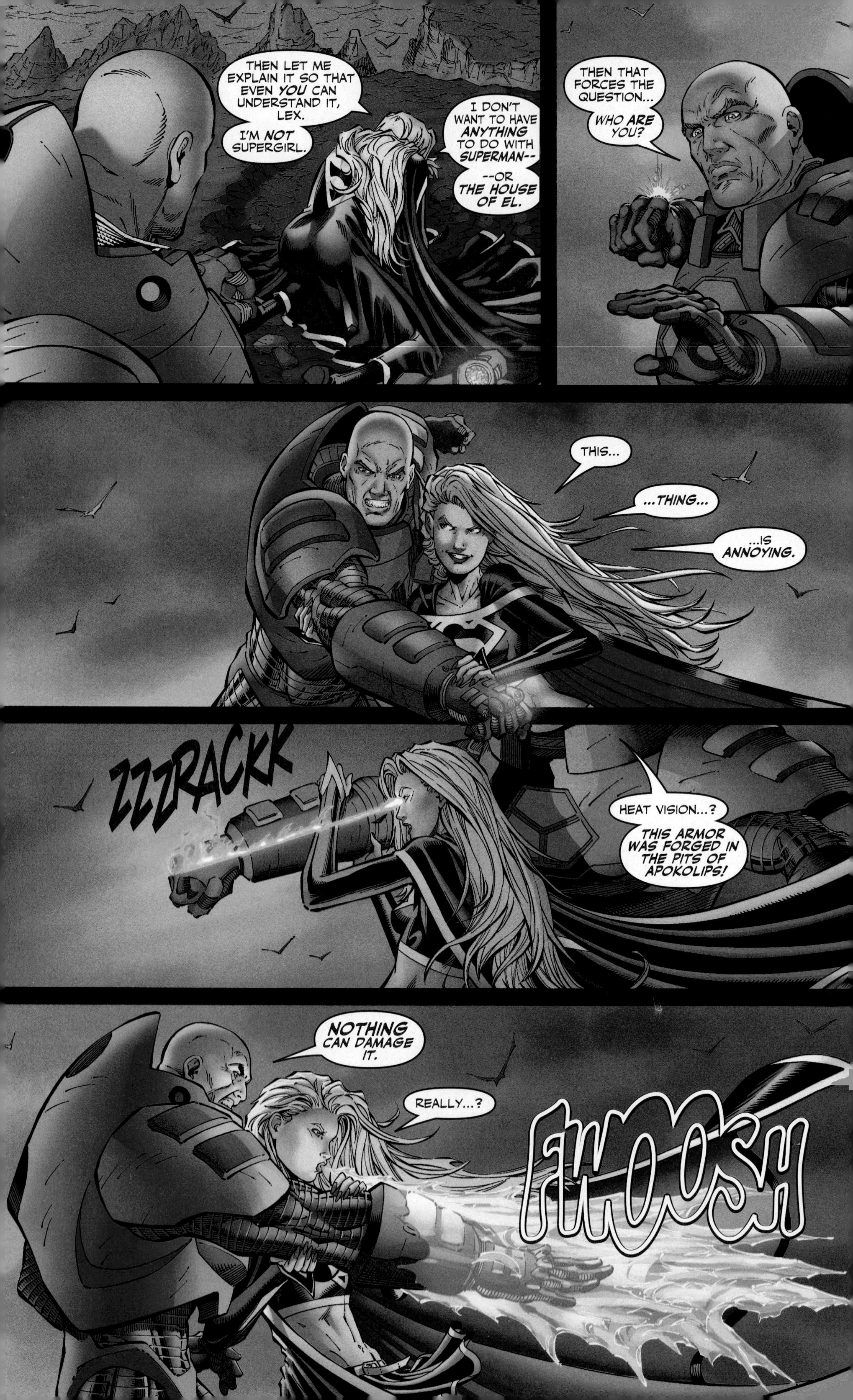
THEN LET ME EXPLAIN IT SO THAT EVEN YOU CAN UNDERSTAND IT, LEX.
I'M NOT SUPERGIRL.
I DON'T WANT TO HAVE ANYTHING TO DO WITH SUPERMAN--
--OR THE HOUSE OF EL.
THEN THAT FORCES THE QUESTION...
WHO ARE YOU?
THIS...
...THING...
...IS ANNOYING.
ZZZRACKK
HEAT VISION...?
THIS ARMOR WAS FORGED IN THE PITS OF APOKOLIPS!
NOTHING CAN DAMAGE IT.
REALLY...?
FWOOSH

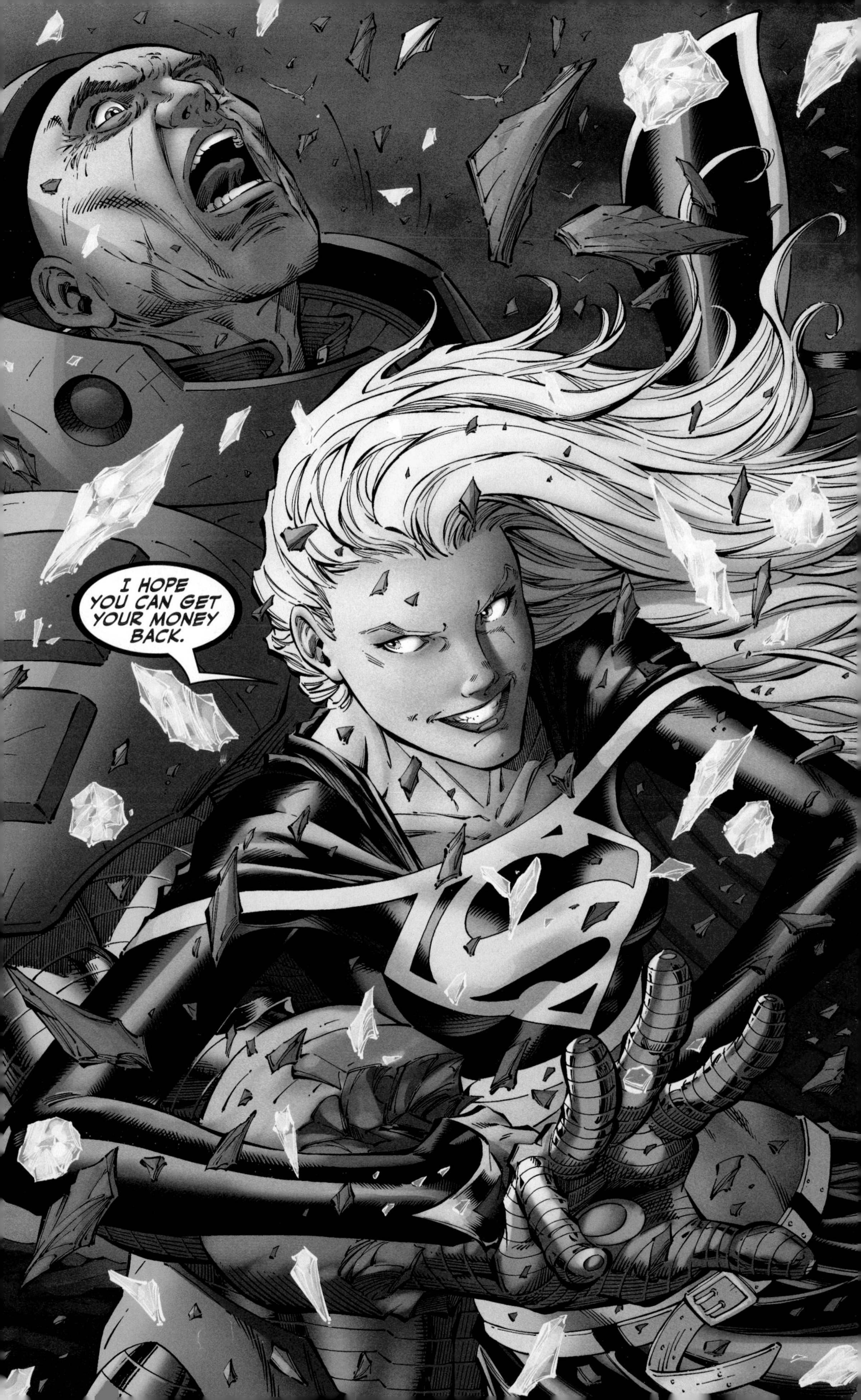
I HOPE YOU CAN GET YOUR MONEY BACK.

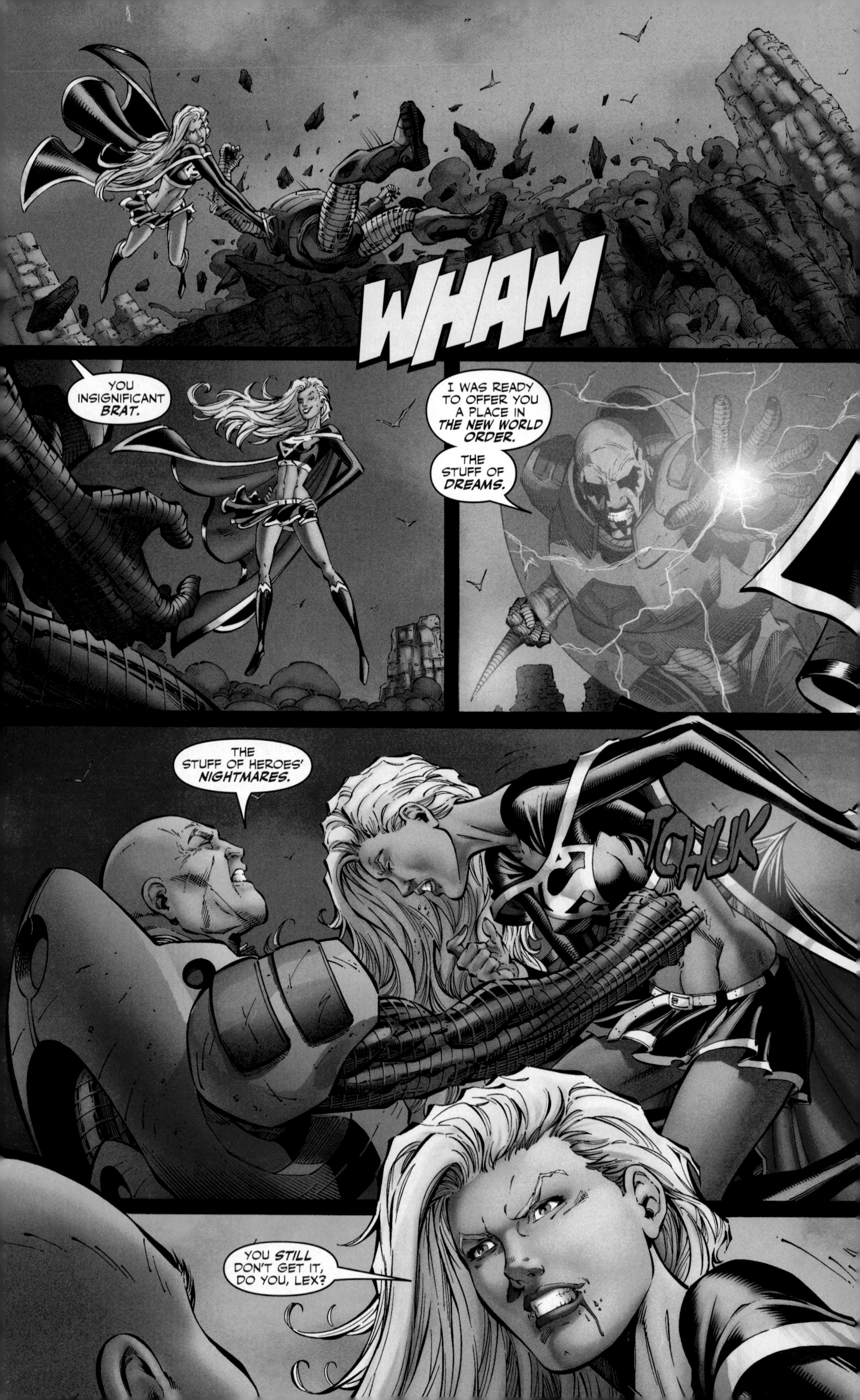
WHAM
YOU INSIGNIFICANT BRAT.
I WAS READY TO OFFER YOU A PLACE IN THE NEW WORLD ORDER.
THE STUFF OF DREAMS.
THE STUFF OF HEROES' NIGHTMARES.
TCHUK
YOU STILL DON'T GET IT, DO YOU, LEX?

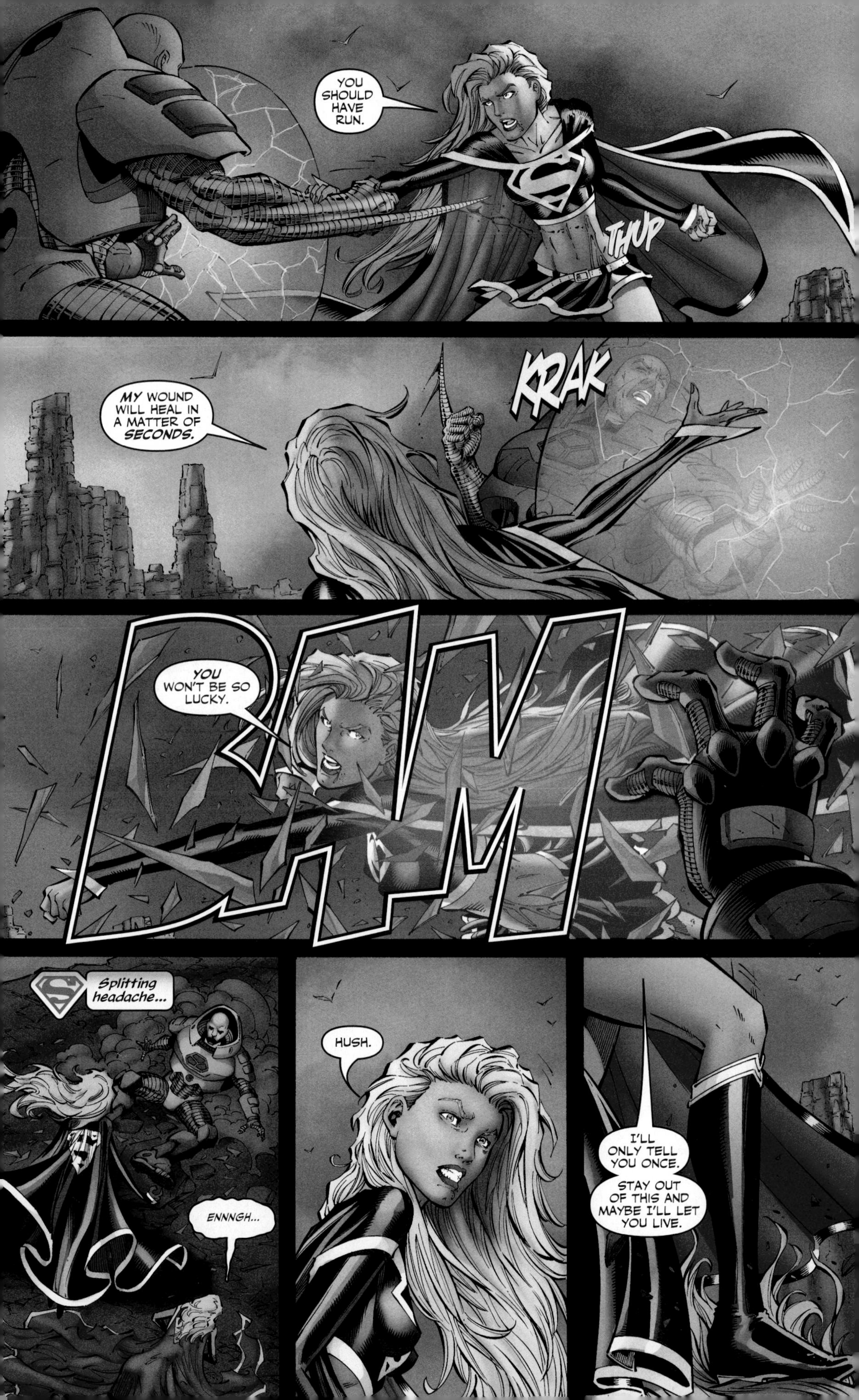

YOU SHOULD HAVE RUN.
THUP
KRAK
MY WOUND WILL HEAL IN A MATTER OF SECONDS.
BAM
YOU WON'T BE SO LUCKY.
Splitting headache...
ENNNGH...
HUSH.
I'LL ONLY TELL YOU ONCE.
STAY OUT OF THIS AND MAYBE I'LL LET YOU LIVE.

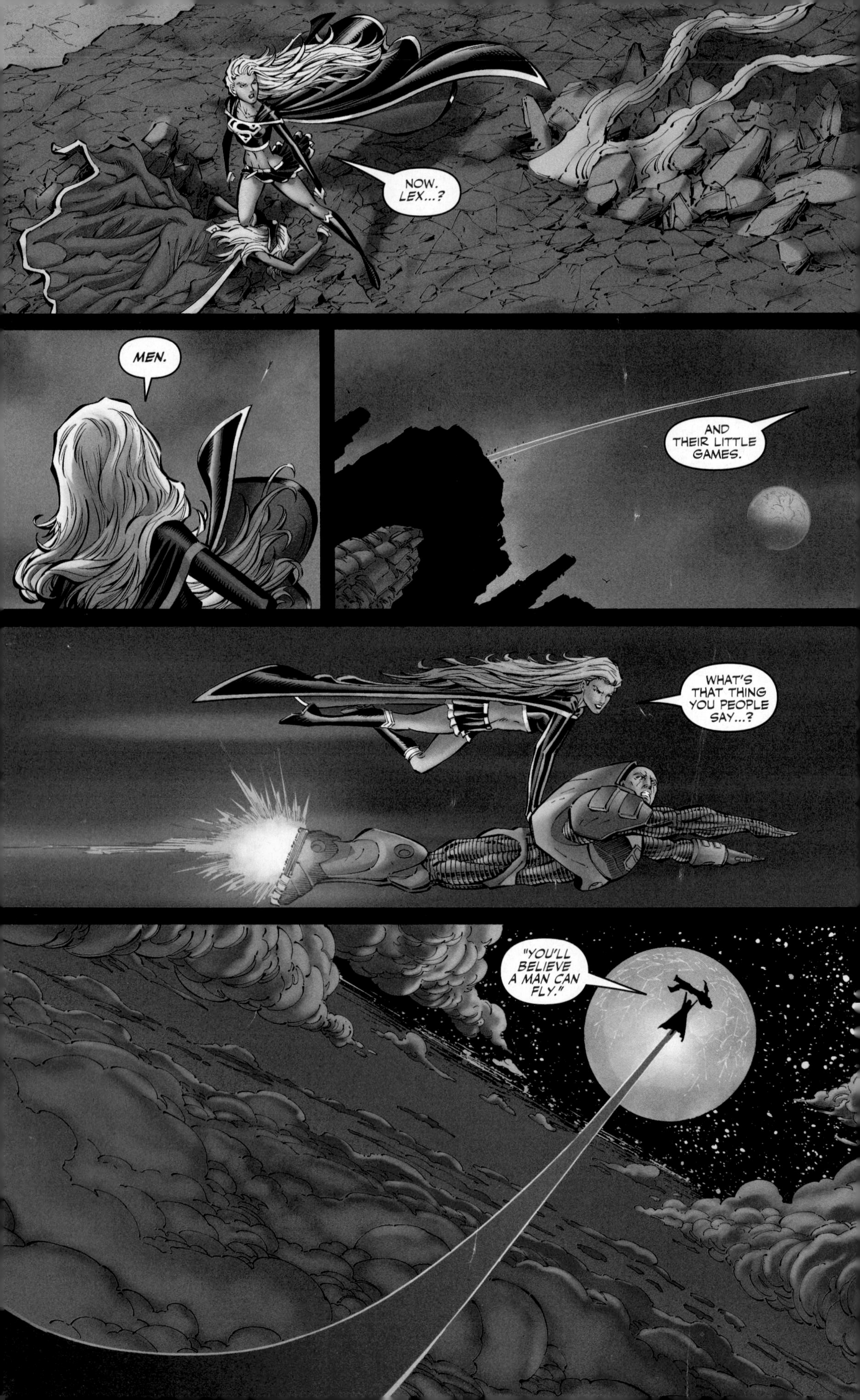
NOW. LEX...?
MEN.
AND THEIR LITTLE GAMES.
WHAT'S THAT THING YOU PEOPLE SAY...?
"YOU'LL BELIEVE A MAN CAN FLY."

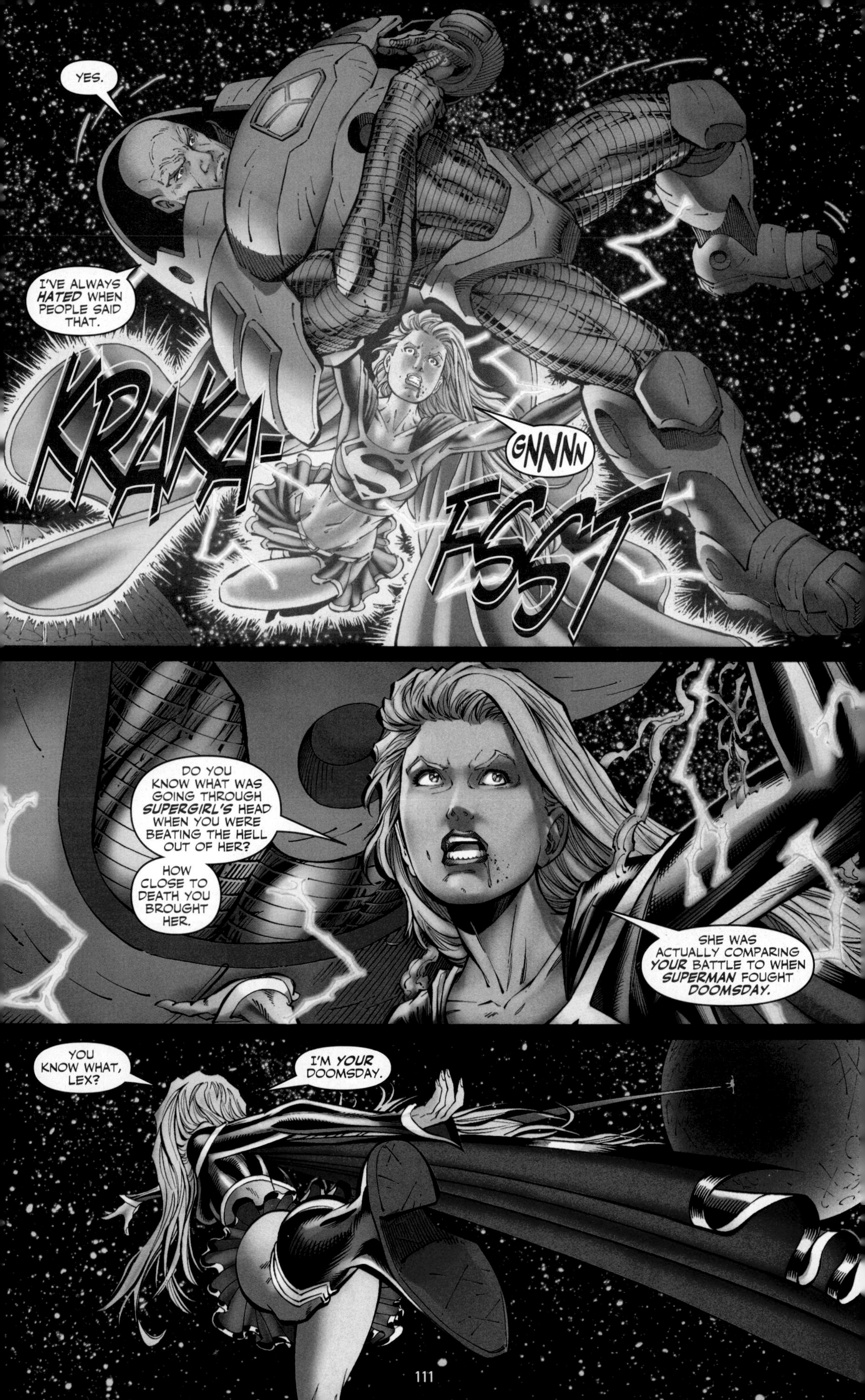
YES.
I'VE ALWAYS *HATED* WHEN PEOPLE SAID THAT.
KRAKA-
GNNNN
FSSST
DO YOU KNOW WHAT WAS GOING THROUGH *SUPERGIRL'S* HEAD WHEN YOU WERE BEATING THE HELL OUT OF HER?
HOW CLOSE TO DEATH YOU BROUGHT HER.
SHE WAS ACTUALLY COMPARING *YOUR* BATTLE TO WHEN *SUPERMAN* FOUGHT *DOOMSDAY.*
YOU KNOW WHAT, LEX?
I'M *YOUR* DOOMSDAY.

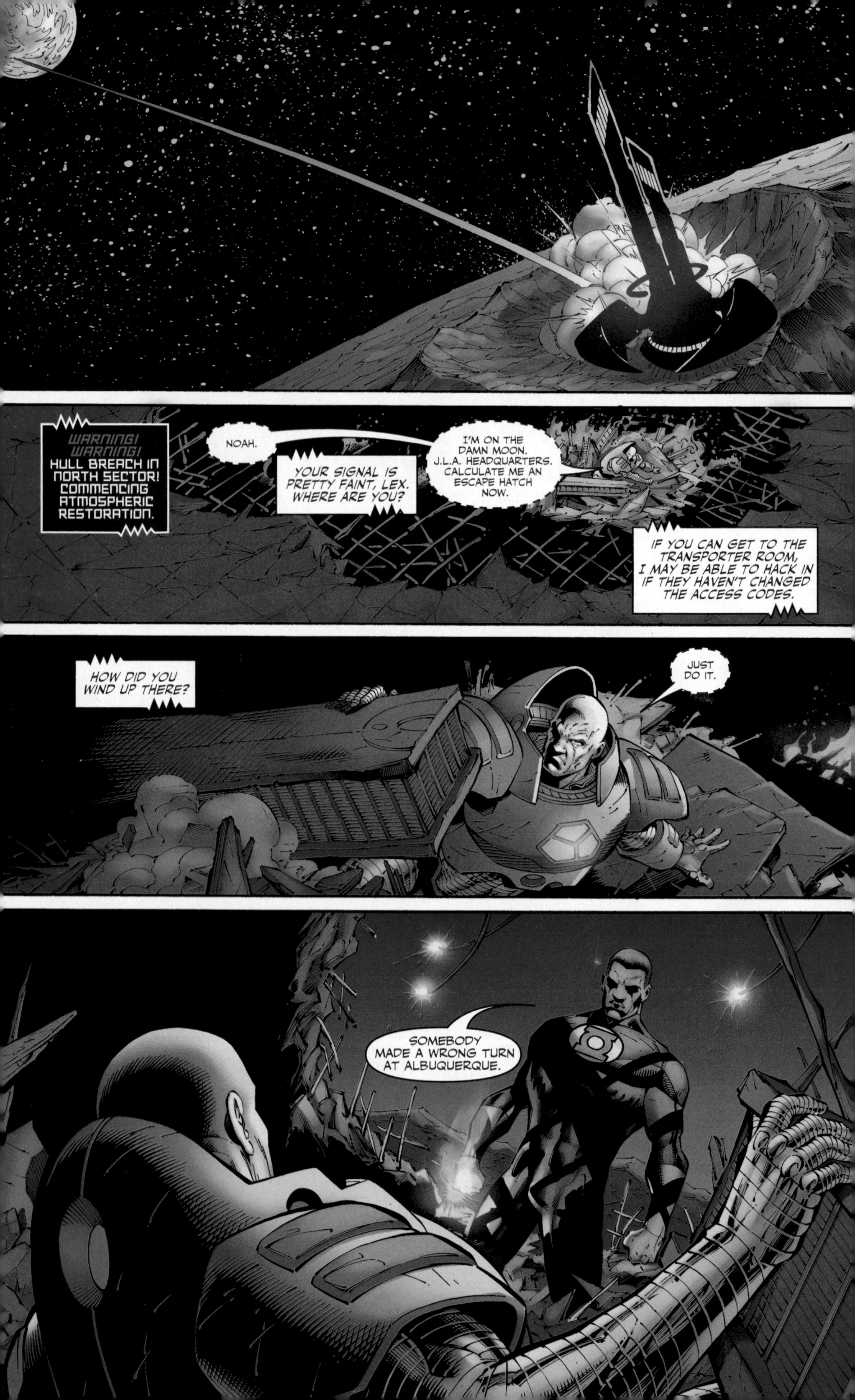
WARNING! WARNING! HULL BREACH IN NORTH SECTOR! COMMENCING ATMOSPHERIC RESTORATION.
NOAH.
YOUR SIGNAL IS PRETTY FAINT, LEX. WHERE ARE YOU?
I'M ON THE DAMN MOON. J.L.A. HEADQUARTERS. CALCULATE ME AN ESCAPE HATCH NOW.
IF YOU CAN GET TO THE TRANSPORTER ROOM, I MAY BE ABLE TO HACK IN IF THEY HAVEN'T CHANGED THE ACCESS CODES.
HOW DID YOU WIND UP THERE?
JUST DO IT.
SOMEBODY MADE A WRONG TURN AT ALBUQUERQUE.

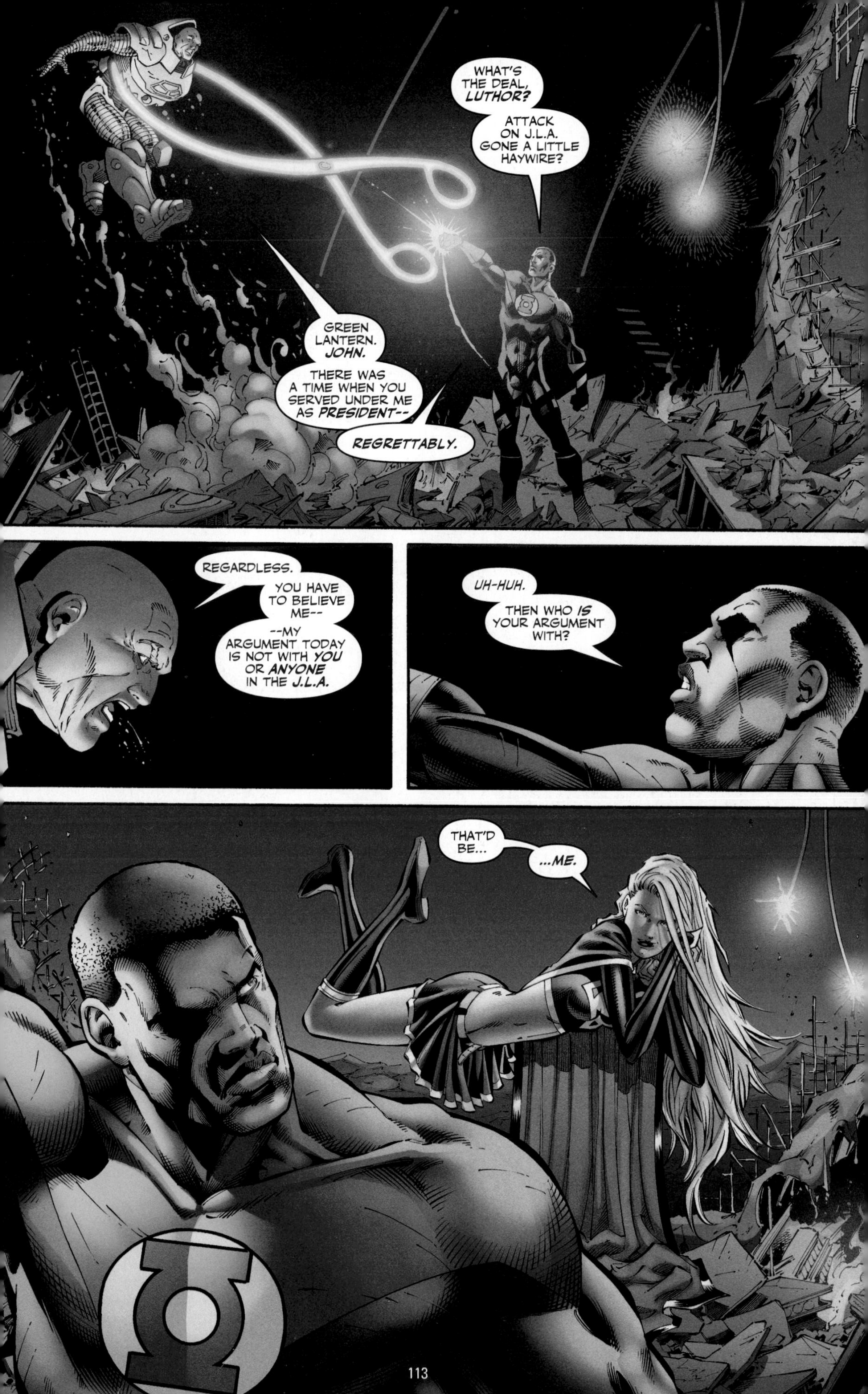
WHAT'S THE DEAL, *LUTHOR?*
ATTACK ON J.L.A. GONE A LITTLE HAYWIRE?
GREEN LANTERN. *JOHN.*
THERE WAS A TIME WHEN YOU SERVED UNDER ME AS *PRESIDENT*--
REGRETTABLY.
REGARDLESS.
YOU HAVE TO BELIEVE ME--
--MY ARGUMENT TODAY IS NOT WITH *YOU* OR *ANYONE* IN THE *J.L.A.*
UH-HUH.
THEN WHO *IS* YOUR ARGUMENT WITH?
THAT'D BE...
...ME.

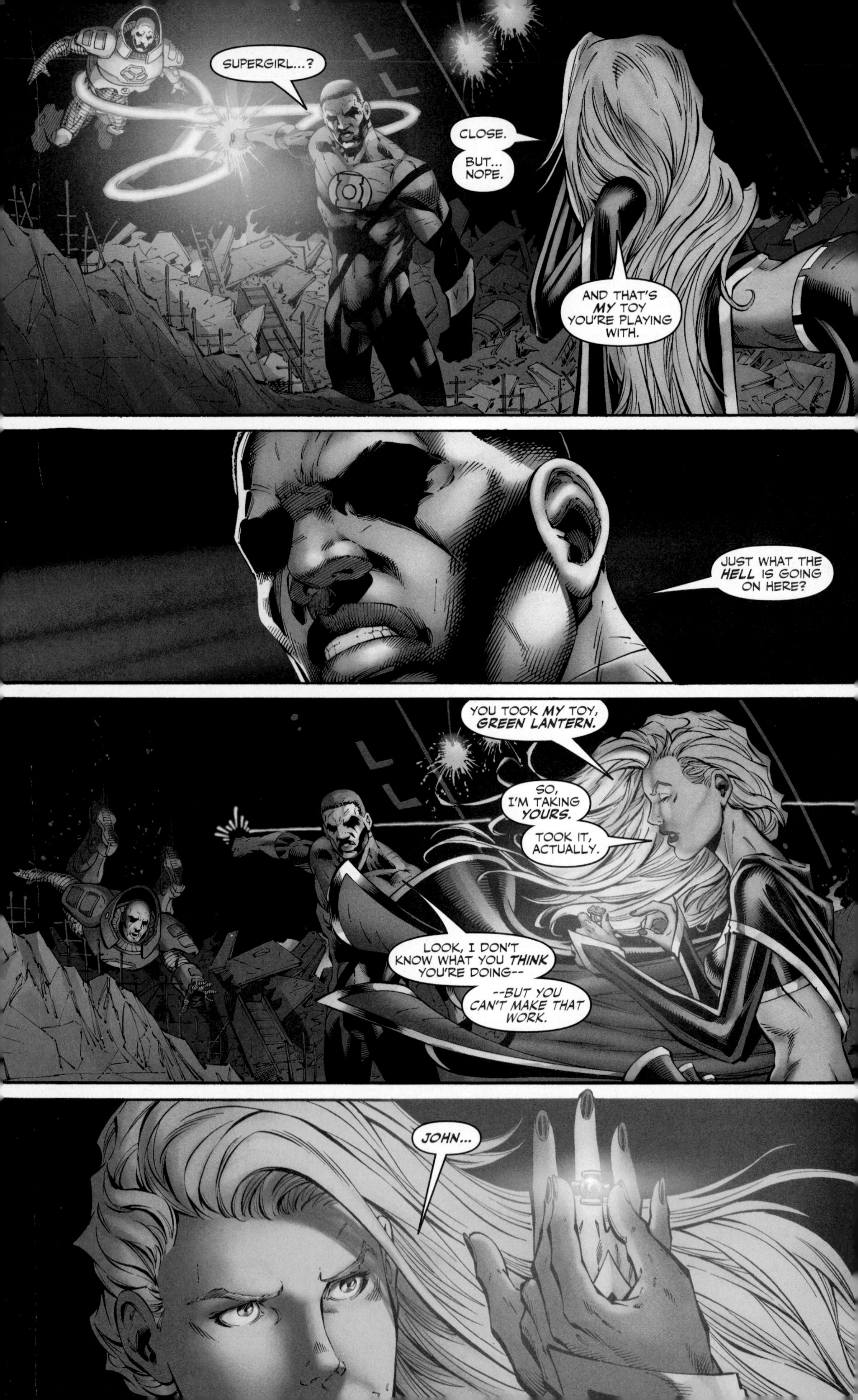
SUPERGIRL...?
CLOSE.
BUT... NOPE.
AND THAT'S MY TOY YOU'RE PLAYING WITH.
JUST WHAT THE HELL IS GOING ON HERE?
YOU TOOK MY TOY, GREEN LANTERN.
SO, I'M TAKING YOURS.
TOOK IT, ACTUALLY.
LOOK, I DON'T KNOW WHAT YOU THINK YOU'RE DOING--
--BUT YOU CAN'T MAKE THAT WORK.
JOHN...

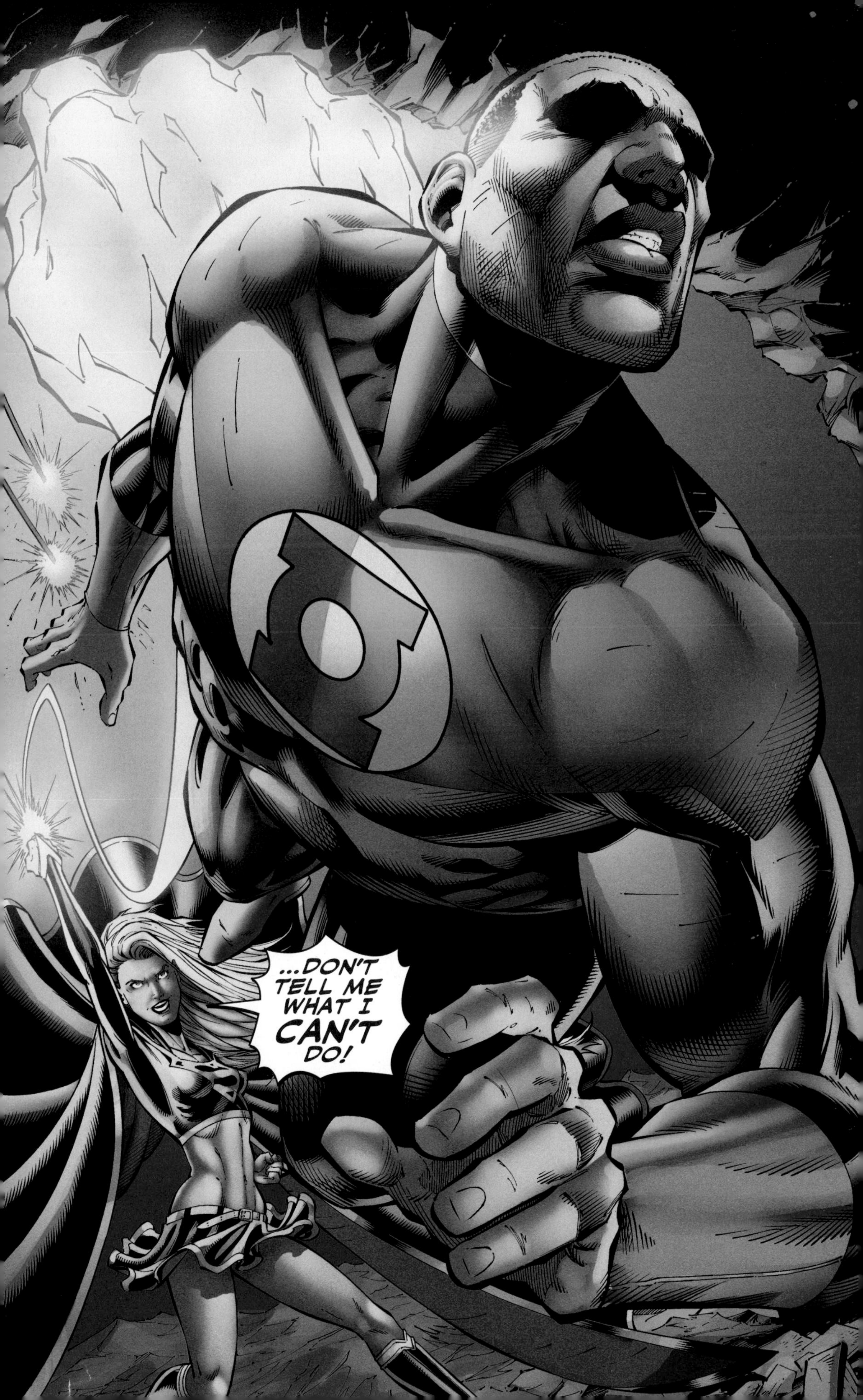
...DON'T TELL ME WHAT I CAN'T DO!

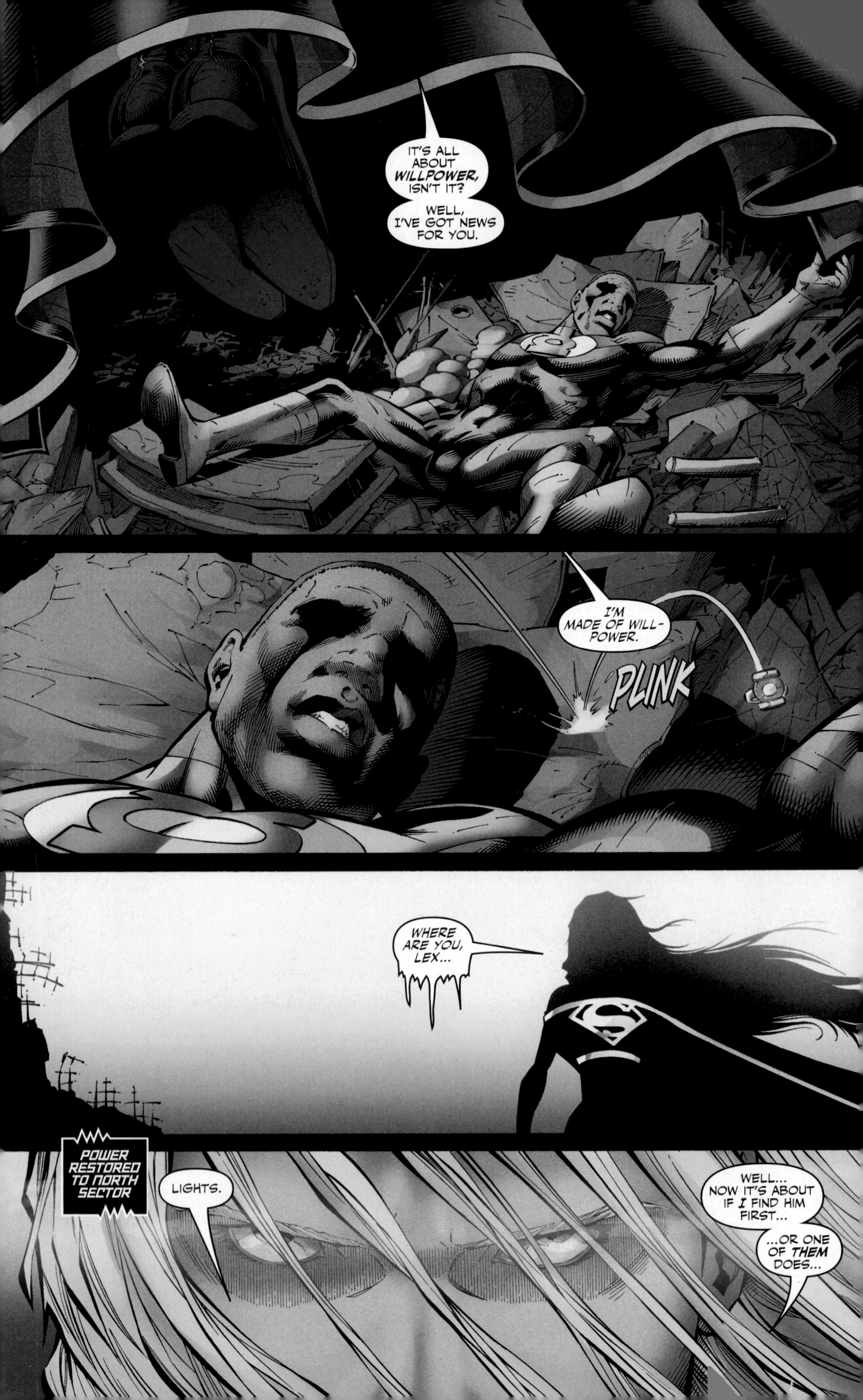
IT'S ALL ABOUT WILLPOWER, ISN'T IT?
WELL, I'VE GOT NEWS FOR YOU.
I'M MADE OF WILL-POWER.
PLINK
WHERE ARE YOU, LEX...
POWER RESTORED TO NORTH SECTOR
LIGHTS.
WELL... NOW IT'S ABOUT IF I FIND HIM FIRST...
...OR ONE OF THEM DOES...

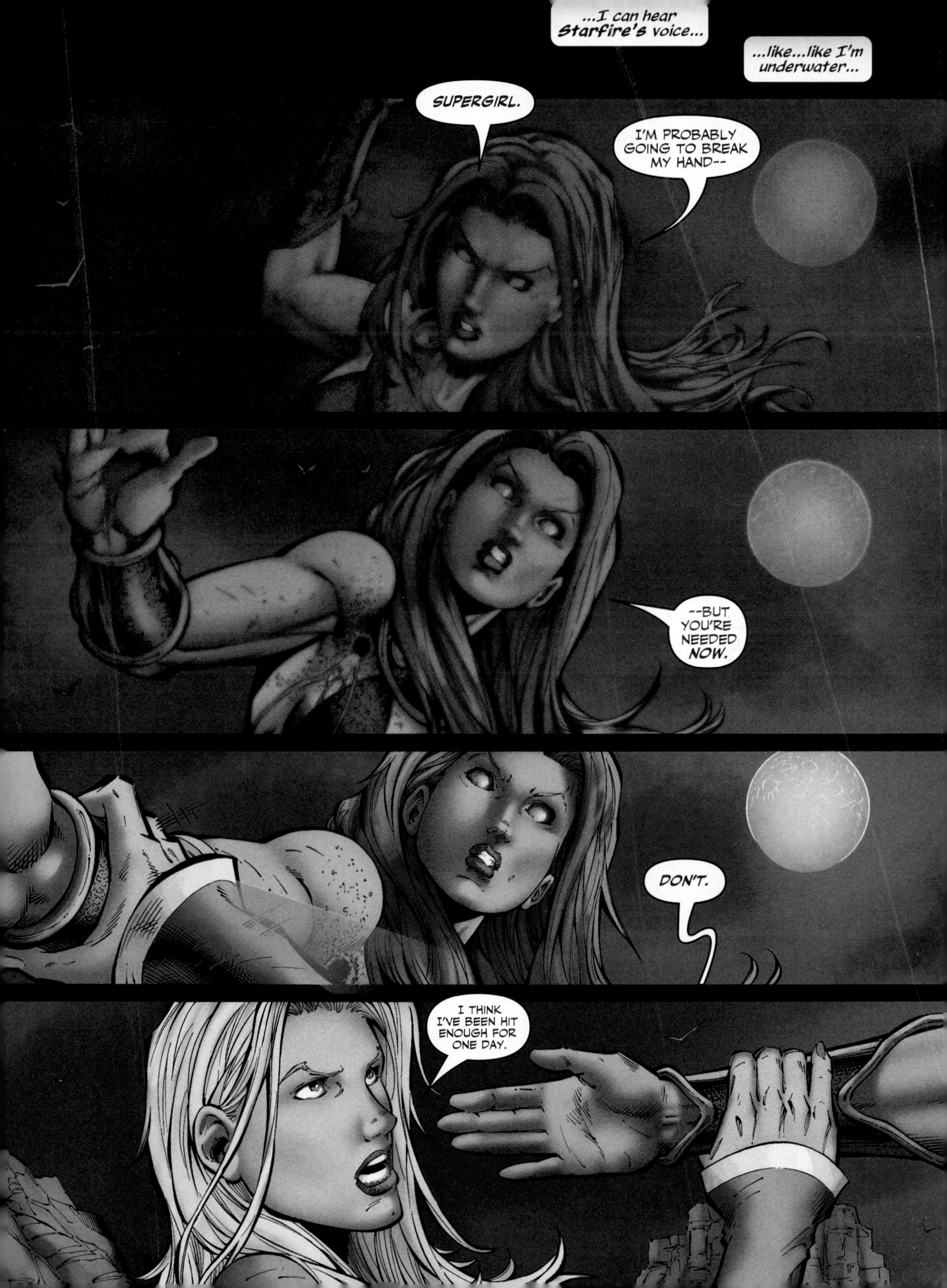
...I can hear Starfire's voice...
...like...like I'm underwater...
SUPERGIRL.
I'M PROBABLY GOING TO BREAK MY HAND--
--BUT YOU'RE NEEDED NOW.
DON'T.
I THINK I'VE BEEN HIT ENOUGH FOR ONE DAY.

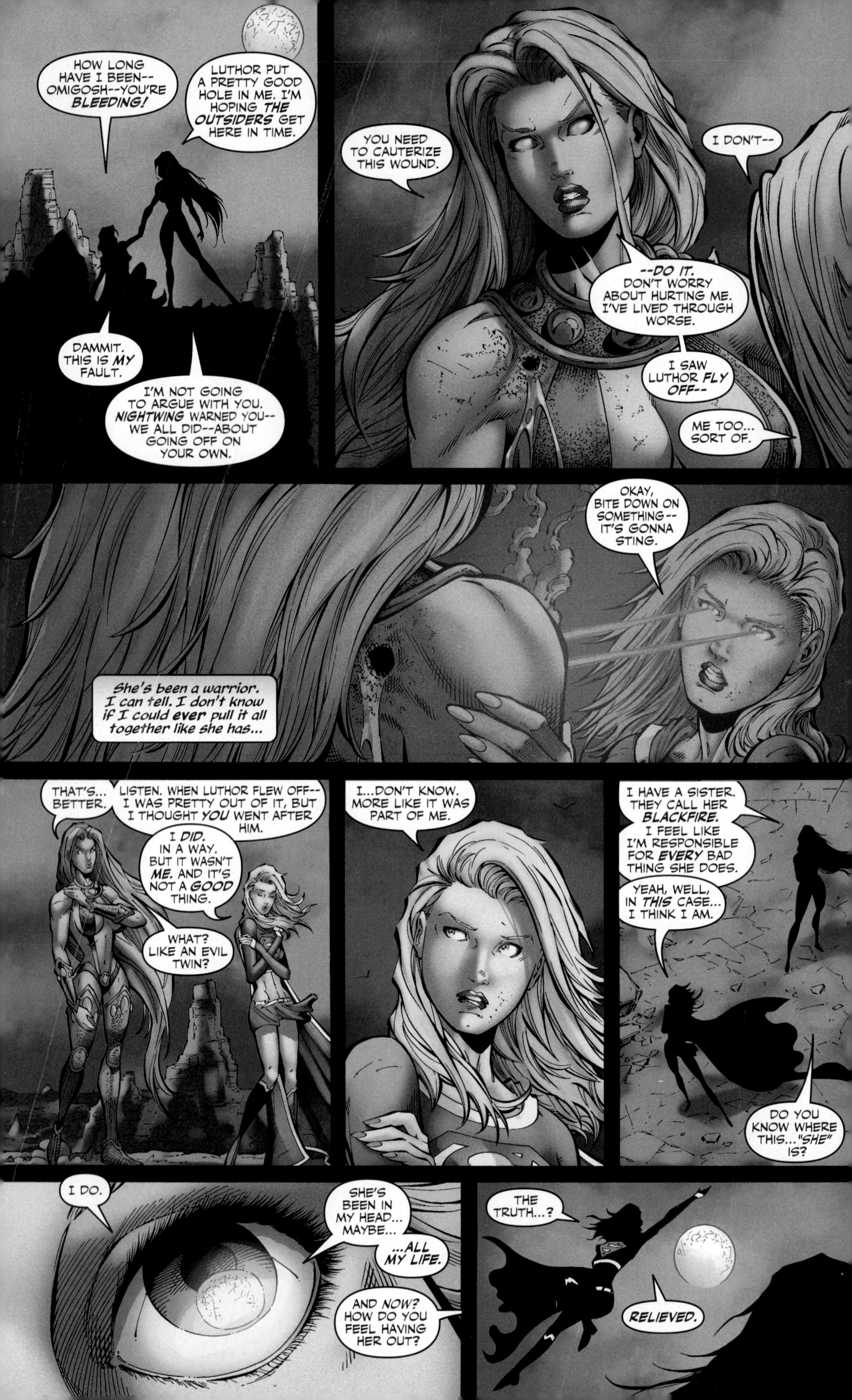
HOW LONG HAVE I BEEN-- OMIGOSH--YOU'RE BLEEDING!
LUTHOR PUT A PRETTY GOOD HOLE IN ME. I'M HOPING THE OUTSIDERS GET HERE IN TIME.
DAMMIT. THIS IS MY FAULT.
I'M NOT GOING TO ARGUE WITH YOU. NIGHTWING WARNED YOU-- WE ALL DID--ABOUT GOING OFF ON YOUR OWN.
YOU NEED TO CAUTERIZE THIS WOUND.
I DON'T--
--DO IT. DON'T WORRY ABOUT HURTING ME. I'VE LIVED THROUGH WORSE.
I SAW LUTHOR FLY OFF--
ME TOO... SORT OF.
OKAY, BITE DOWN ON SOMETHING-- IT'S GONNA STING.
She's been a warrior. I can tell. I don't know if I could ever pull it all together like she has...
THAT'S... BETTER.
LISTEN. WHEN LUTHOR FLEW OFF-- I WAS PRETTY OUT OF IT, BUT I THOUGHT YOU WENT AFTER HIM.
I DID. IN A WAY. BUT IT WASN'T ME. AND IT'S NOT A GOOD THING.
WHAT? LIKE AN EVIL TWIN?
I...DON'T KNOW. MORE LIKE IT WAS PART OF ME.
I HAVE A SISTER. THEY CALL HER BLACKFIRE. I FEEL LIKE I'M RESPONSIBLE FOR EVERY BAD THING SHE DOES.
YEAH, WELL, IN THIS CASE... I THINK I AM.
DO YOU KNOW WHERE THIS..."SHE" IS?
I DO.
SHE'S BEEN IN MY HEAD... MAYBE...
...ALL MY LIFE.
AND NOW? HOW DO YOU FEEL HAVING HER OUT?
THE TRUTH...?
RELIEVED.

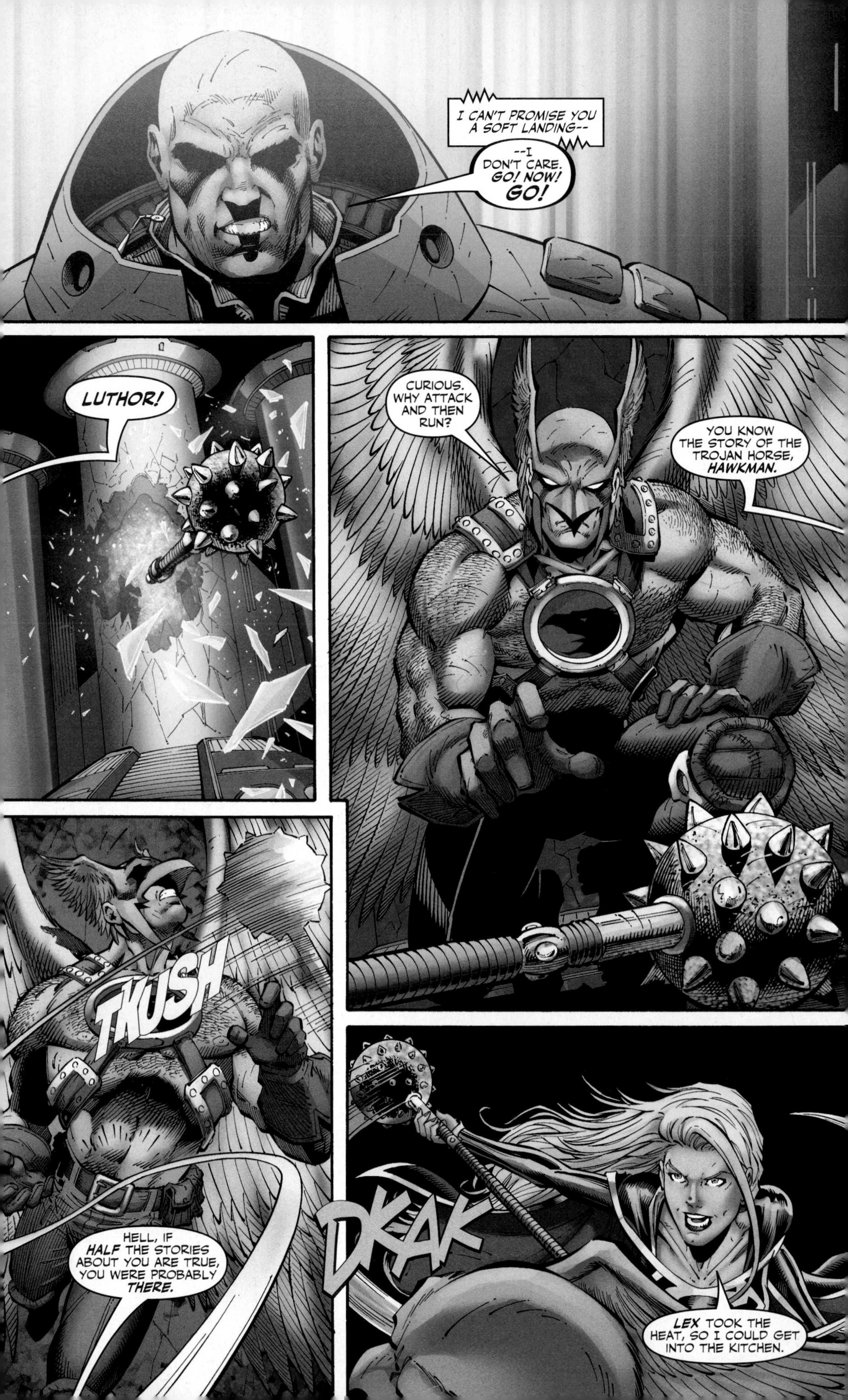

I CAN'T PROMISE YOU A SOFT LANDING--
--I DON'T CARE. GO! NOW! GO!
LUTHOR!
CURIOUS. WHY ATTACK AND THEN RUN?
YOU KNOW THE STORY OF THE TROJAN HORSE, HAWKMAN.
TKUSH
HELL, IF HALF THE STORIES ABOUT YOU ARE TRUE, YOU WERE PROBABLY THERE.
DKAK
LEX TOOK THE HEAT, SO I COULD GET INTO THE KITCHEN.

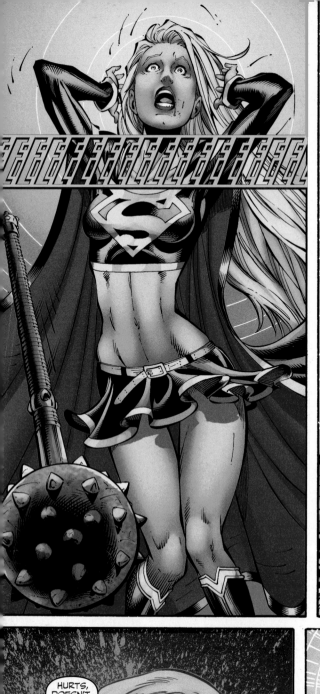

HUNNNNHH

HURTS, DOESN'T IT?

HYPERSONICS. ONLY *TWO* PEOPLE AND A *DOG* CAN HEAR IT AT THAT DECIBEL.

STAY *DOWN,* SUPERGIRL. TELL ME WHAT'S GOING ON HERE OR I CAN MAKE IT MUCH WORSE.

THEN, YOU'VE MADE *TWO* MISTAKES...

HOW'S THAT?

YOU SHOULD HAVE *KILLED* ME WHEN YOU HAD THE CHANCE...

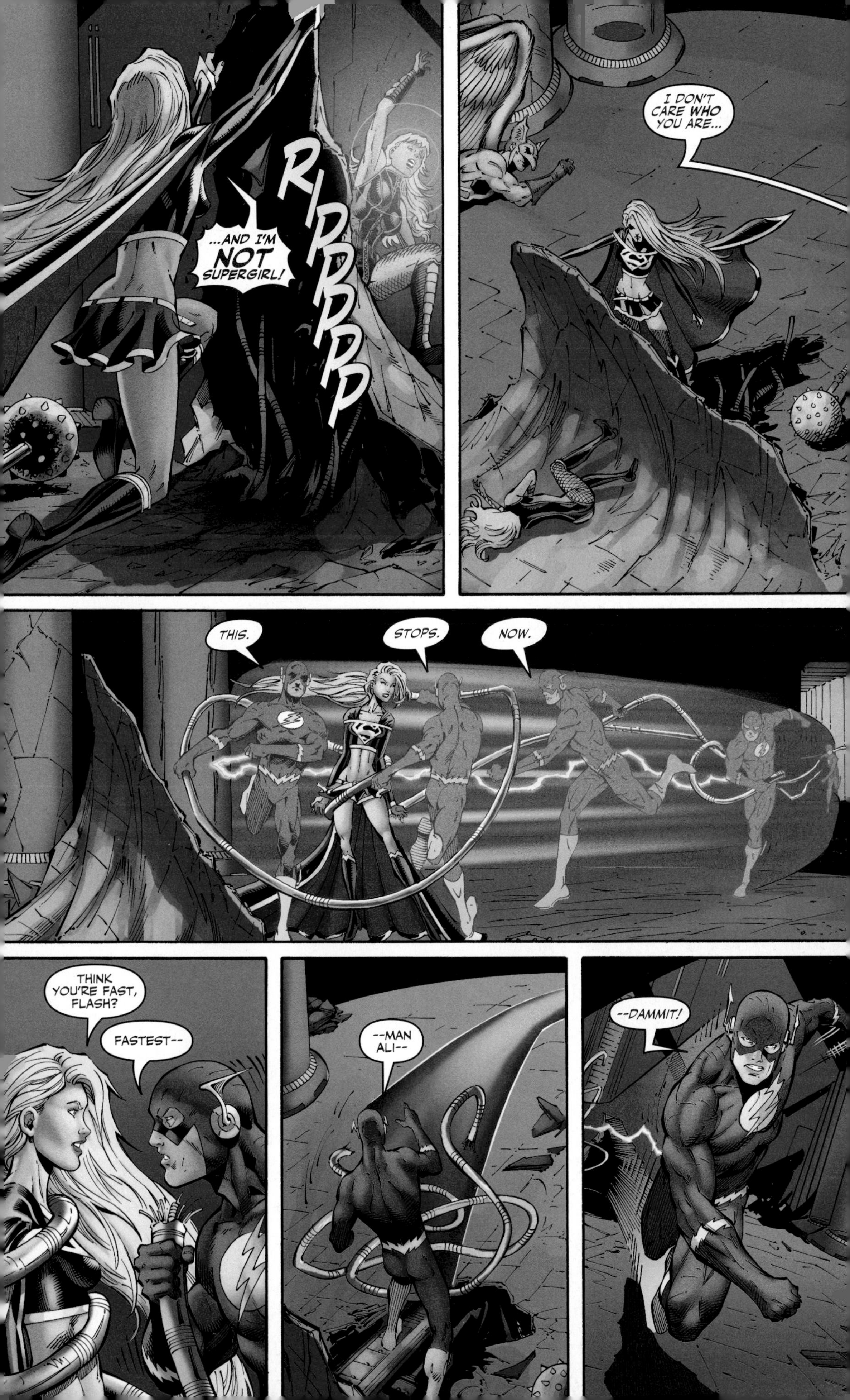
...AND I'M NOT SUPERGIRL!
RIPPPPP
I DON'T CARE WHO YOU ARE...
THIS.
STOPS.
NOW.
THINK YOU'RE FAST, FLASH?
FASTEST--
--MAN ALI--
--DAMMIT!

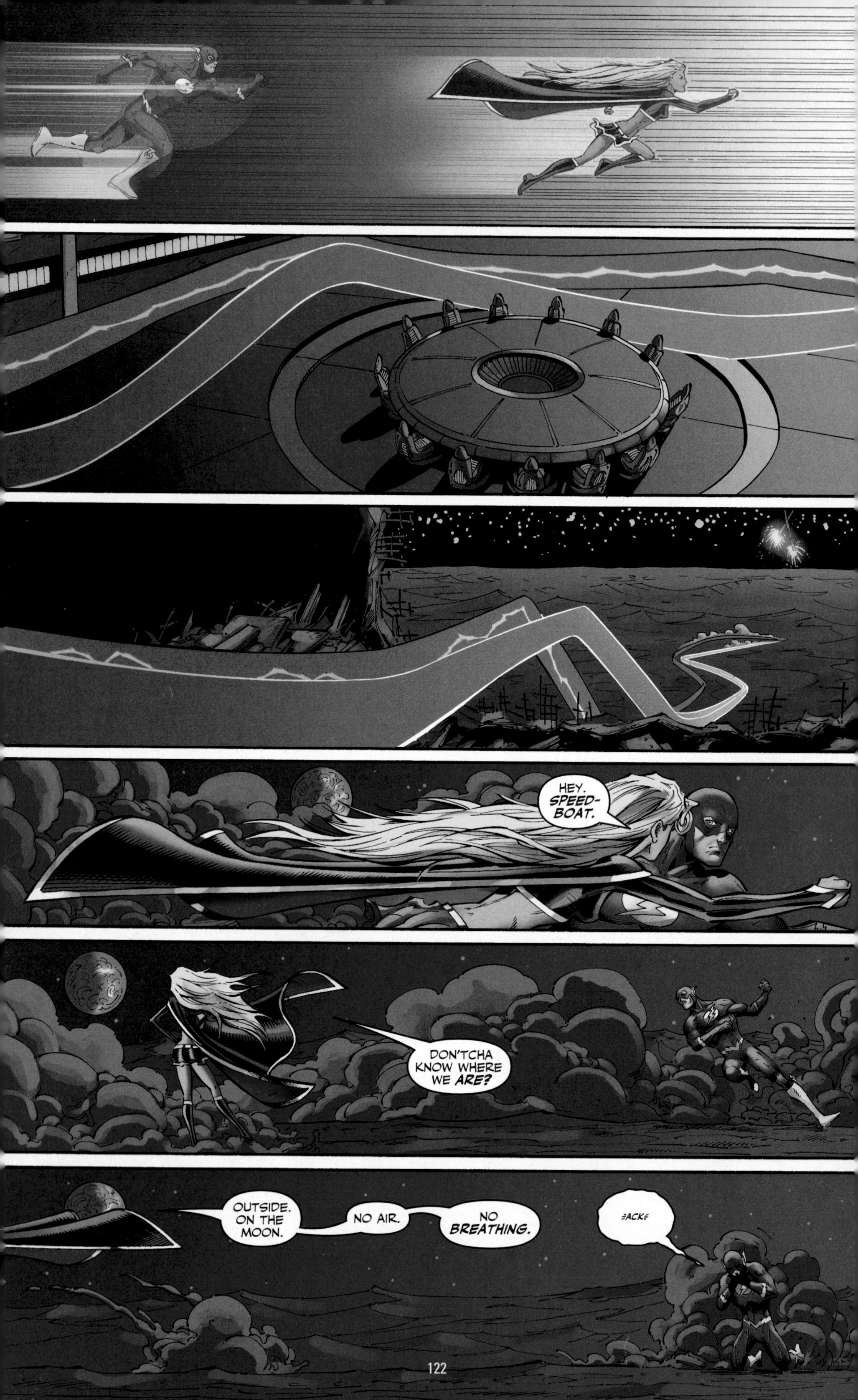
HEY. SPEED-BOAT.
DON'TCHA KNOW WHERE WE ARE?
OUTSIDE. ON THE MOON.
NO AIR.
NO BREATHING.
ACK

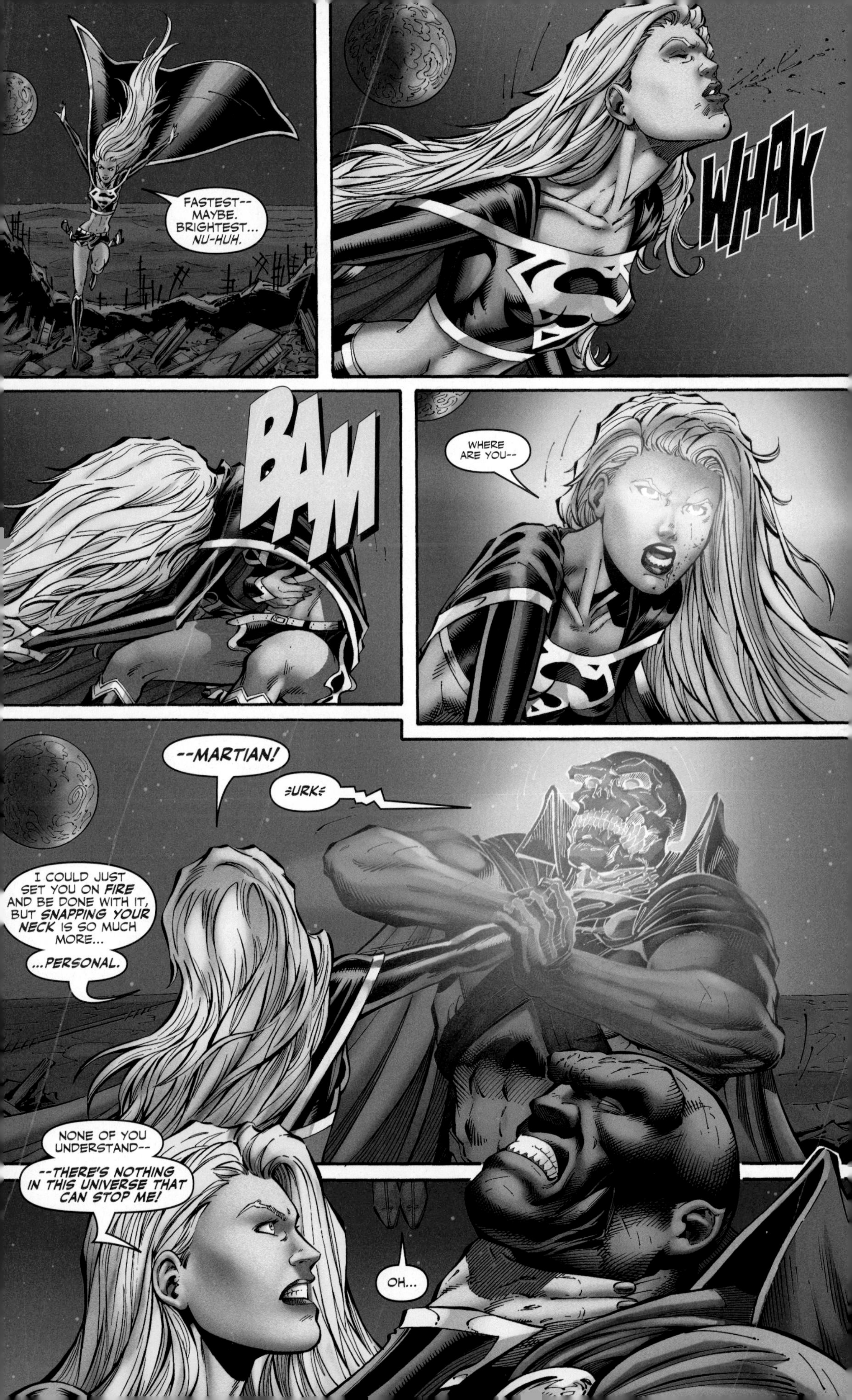
FASTEST--
MAYBE.
BRIGHTEST...
NU-HUH.
WHAK
BAM
WHERE ARE YOU--
--MARTIAN!
URK
I COULD JUST SET YOU ON FIRE AND BE DONE WITH IT, BUT SNAPPING YOUR NECK IS SO MUCH MORE...
...PERSONAL.
NONE OF YOU UNDERSTAND--
--THERE'S NOTHING IN THIS UNIVERSE THAT CAN STOP ME!
OH...

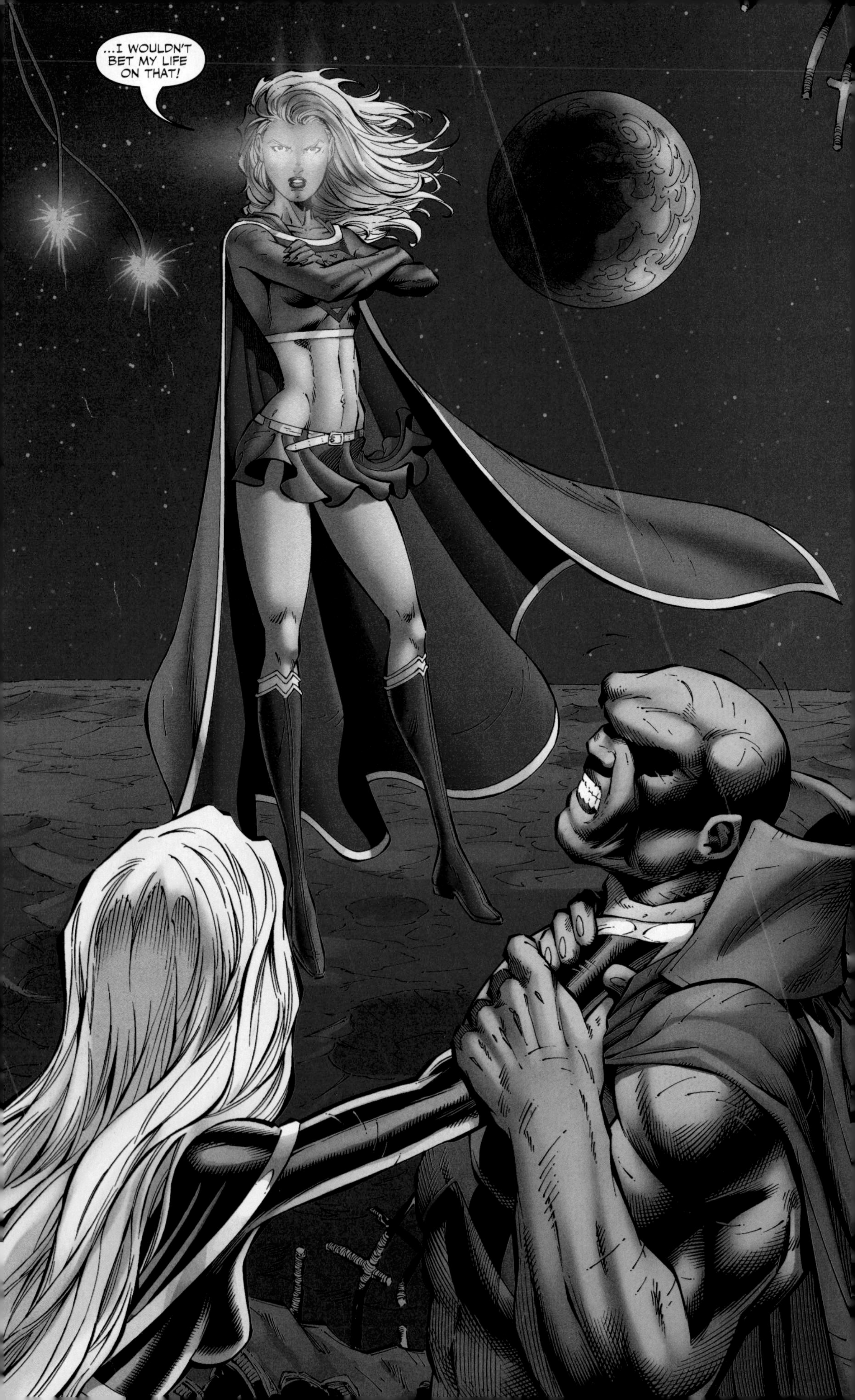
...I WOULDN'T BET MY LIFE ON THAT!

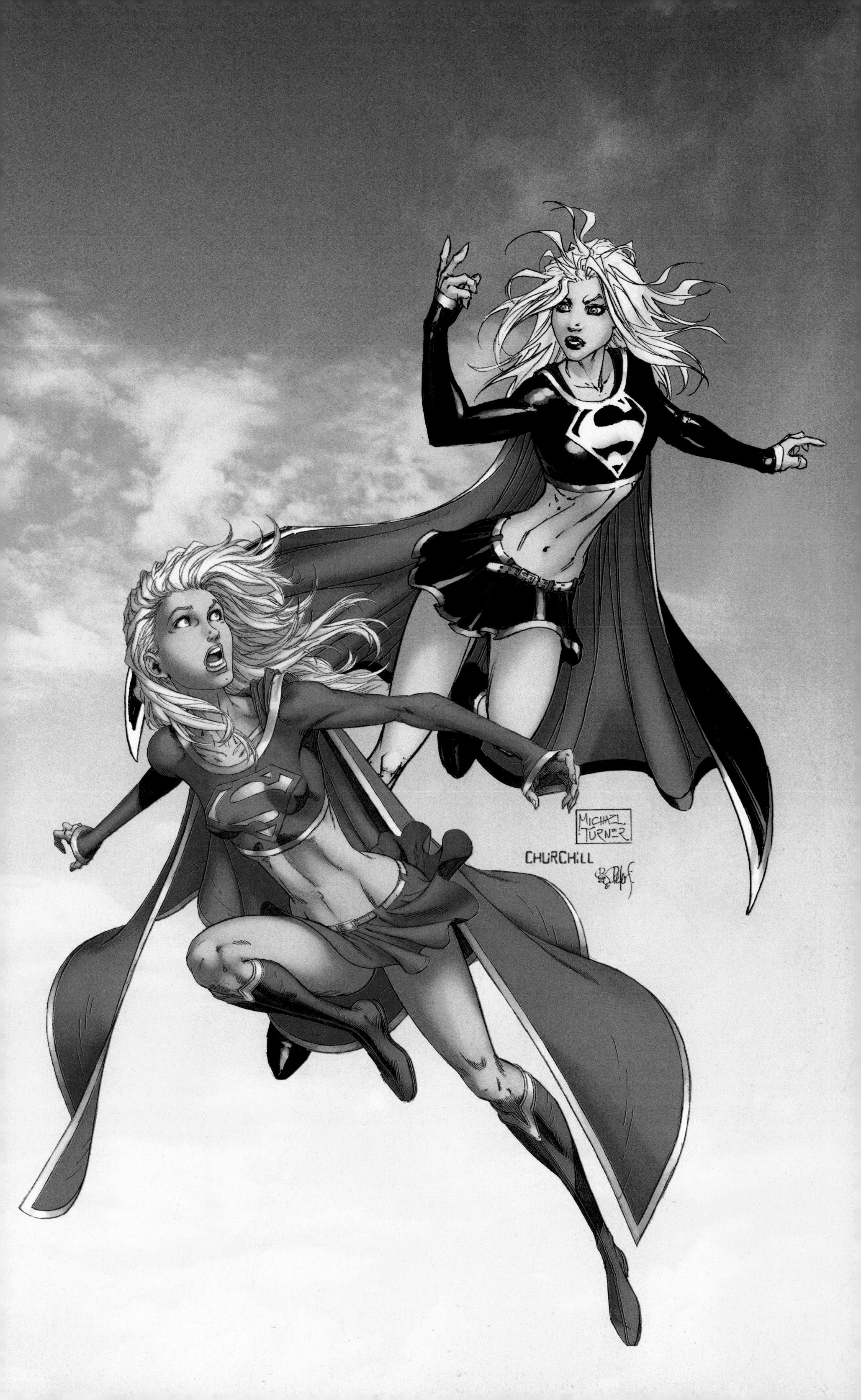
MICHAEL TURNER
CHURCHILL

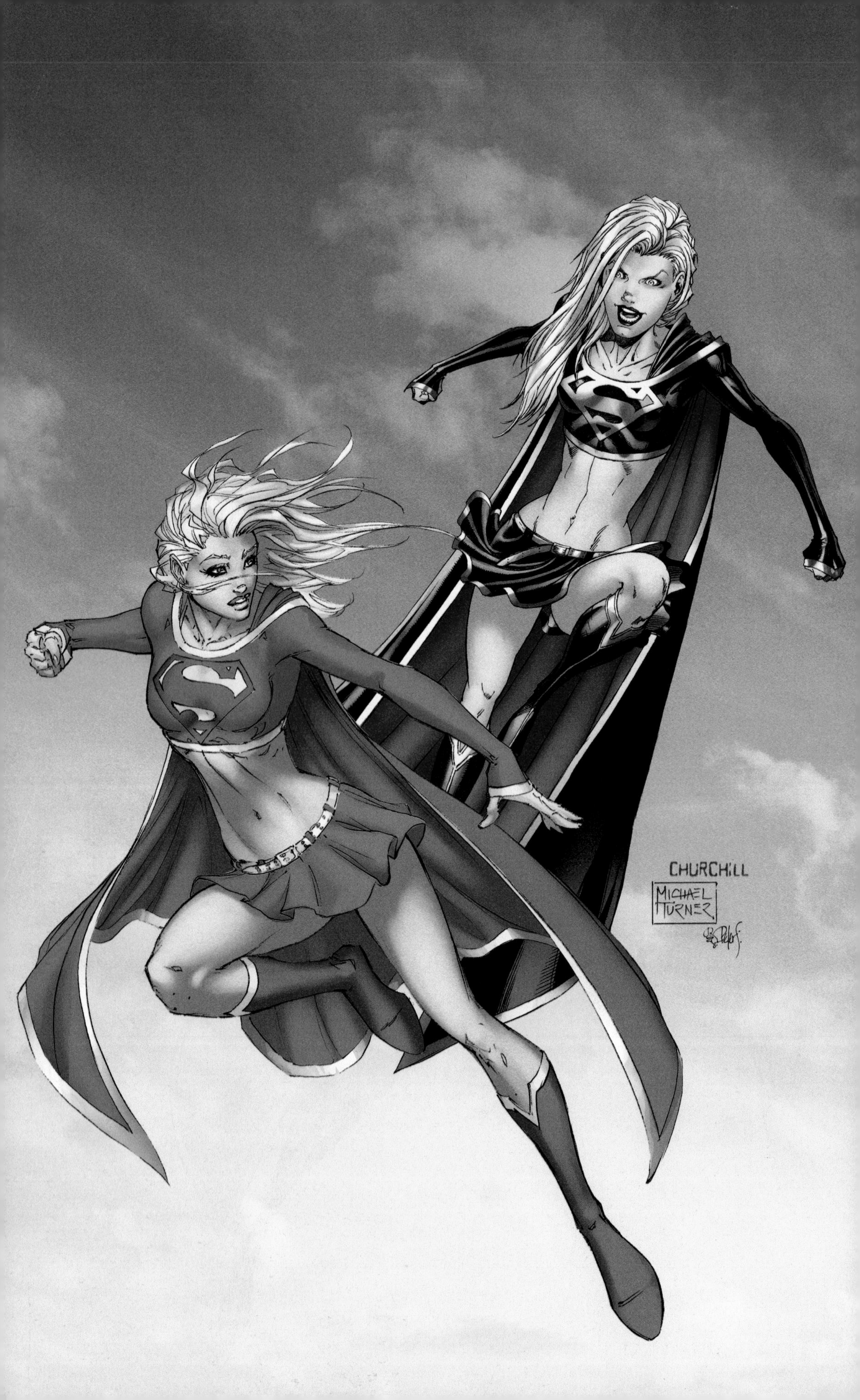
CHURCHILL
MICHAEL TURNER

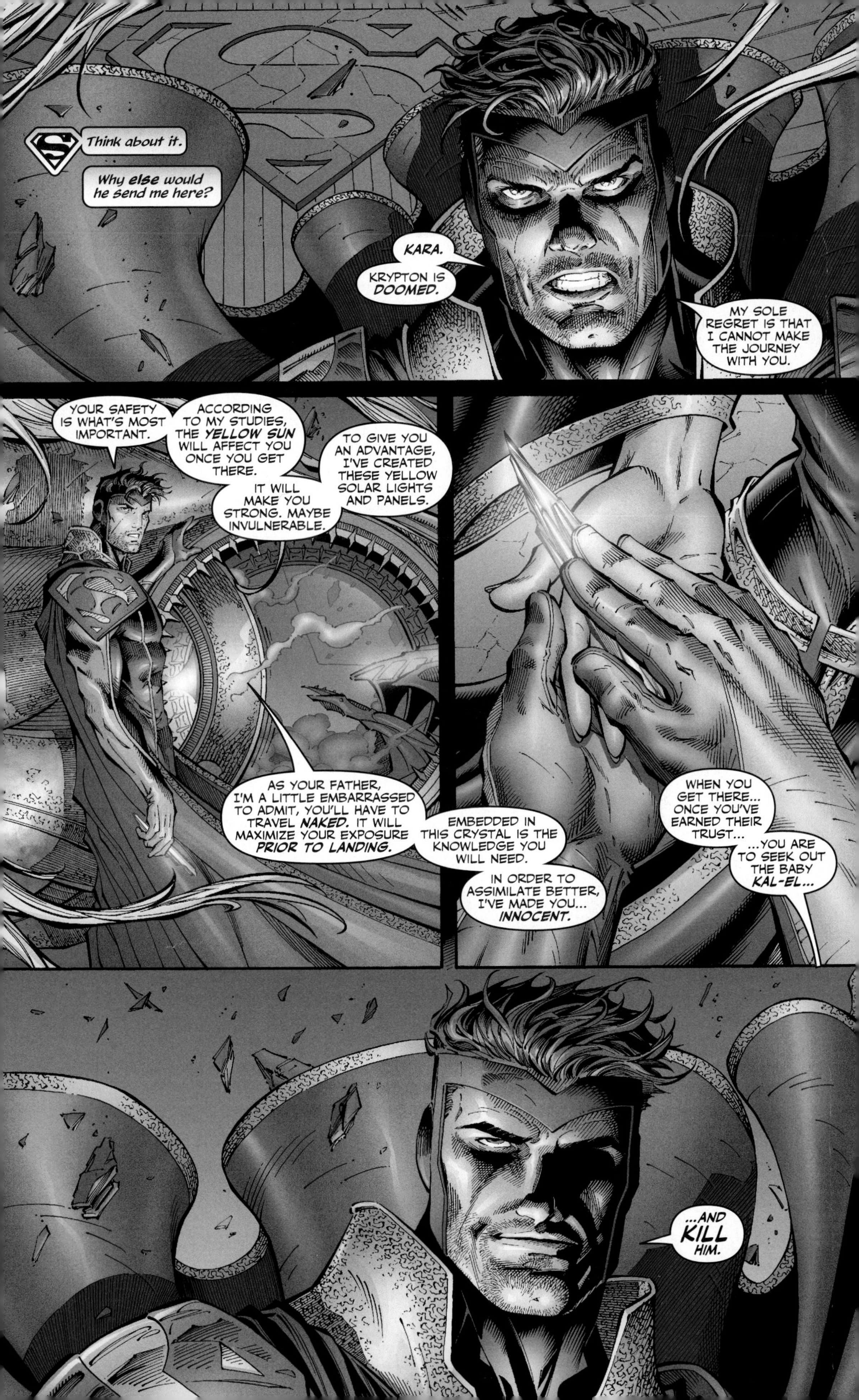
Think about it.
Why else would he send me here?
KARA.
KRYPTON IS DOOMED.
MY SOLE REGRET IS THAT I CANNOT MAKE THE JOURNEY WITH YOU.
YOUR SAFETY IS WHAT'S MOST IMPORTANT.
ACCORDING TO MY STUDIES, THE YELLOW SUN WILL AFFECT YOU ONCE YOU GET THERE.
IT WILL MAKE YOU STRONG. MAYBE INVULNERABLE.
TO GIVE YOU AN ADVANTAGE, I'VE CREATED THESE YELLOW SOLAR LIGHTS AND PANELS.
AS YOUR FATHER, I'M A LITTLE EMBARRASSED TO ADMIT, YOU'LL HAVE TO TRAVEL NAKED. IT WILL MAXIMIZE YOUR EXPOSURE PRIOR TO LANDING.
EMBEDDED IN THIS CRYSTAL IS THE KNOWLEDGE YOU WILL NEED.
IN ORDER TO ASSIMILATE BETTER, I'VE MADE YOU... INNOCENT.
WHEN YOU GET THERE... ONCE YOU'VE EARNED THEIR TRUST...
...YOU ARE TO SEEK OUT THE BABY KAL-EL...
...AND KILL HIM.

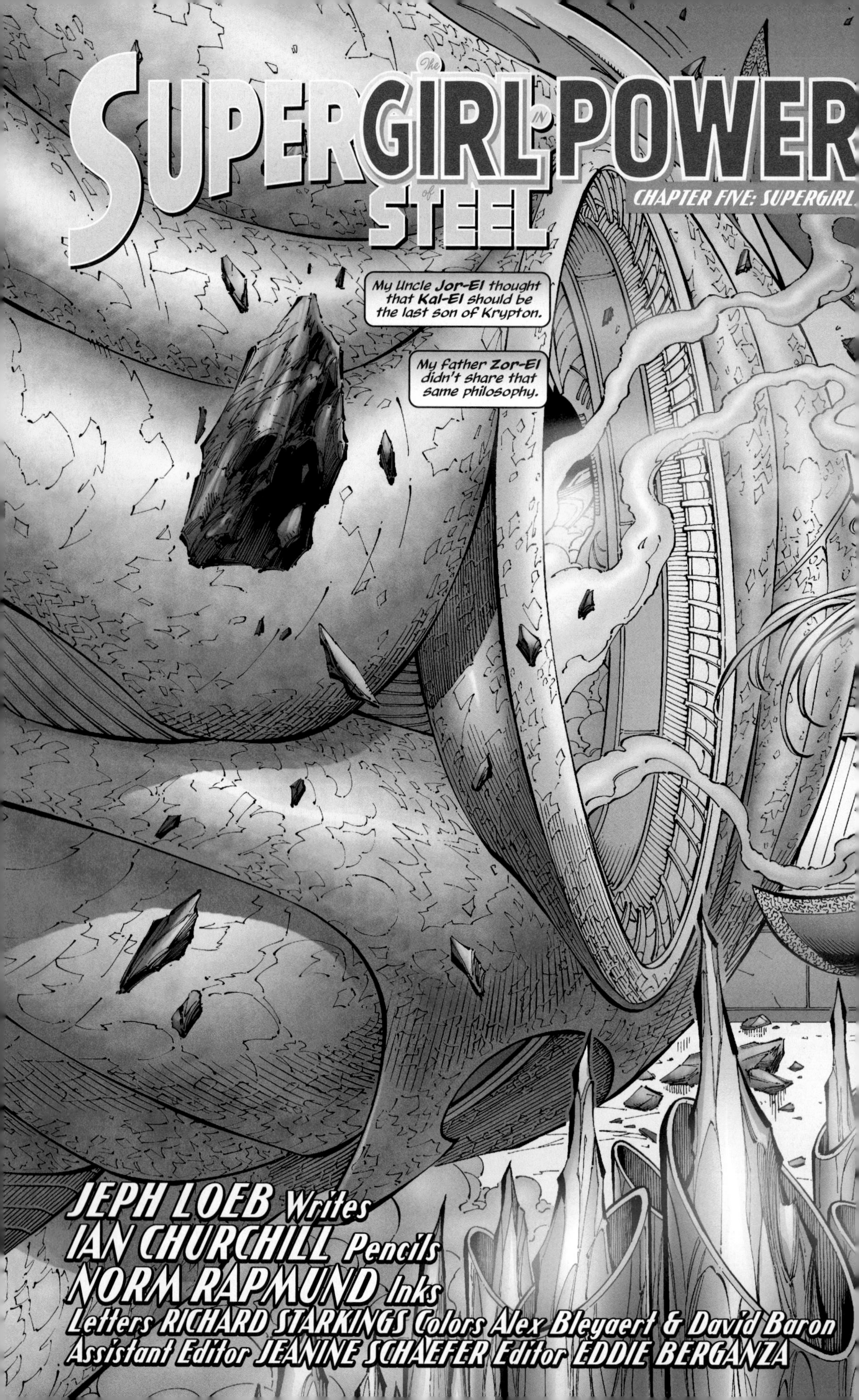

The SUPERGIRL in POWER of STEEL
CHAPTER FIVE: SUPERGIRL
My Uncle Jor-El thought that Kal-El should be the last son of Krypton.
My father Zor-El didn't share that same philosophy.
JEPH LOEB Writes
IAN CHURCHILL Pencils
NORM RAPMUND Inks
Letters RICHARD STARKINGS Colors Alex Bleyaert & David Baron
Assistant Editor JEANINE SCHAEFER Editor EDDIE BERGANZA

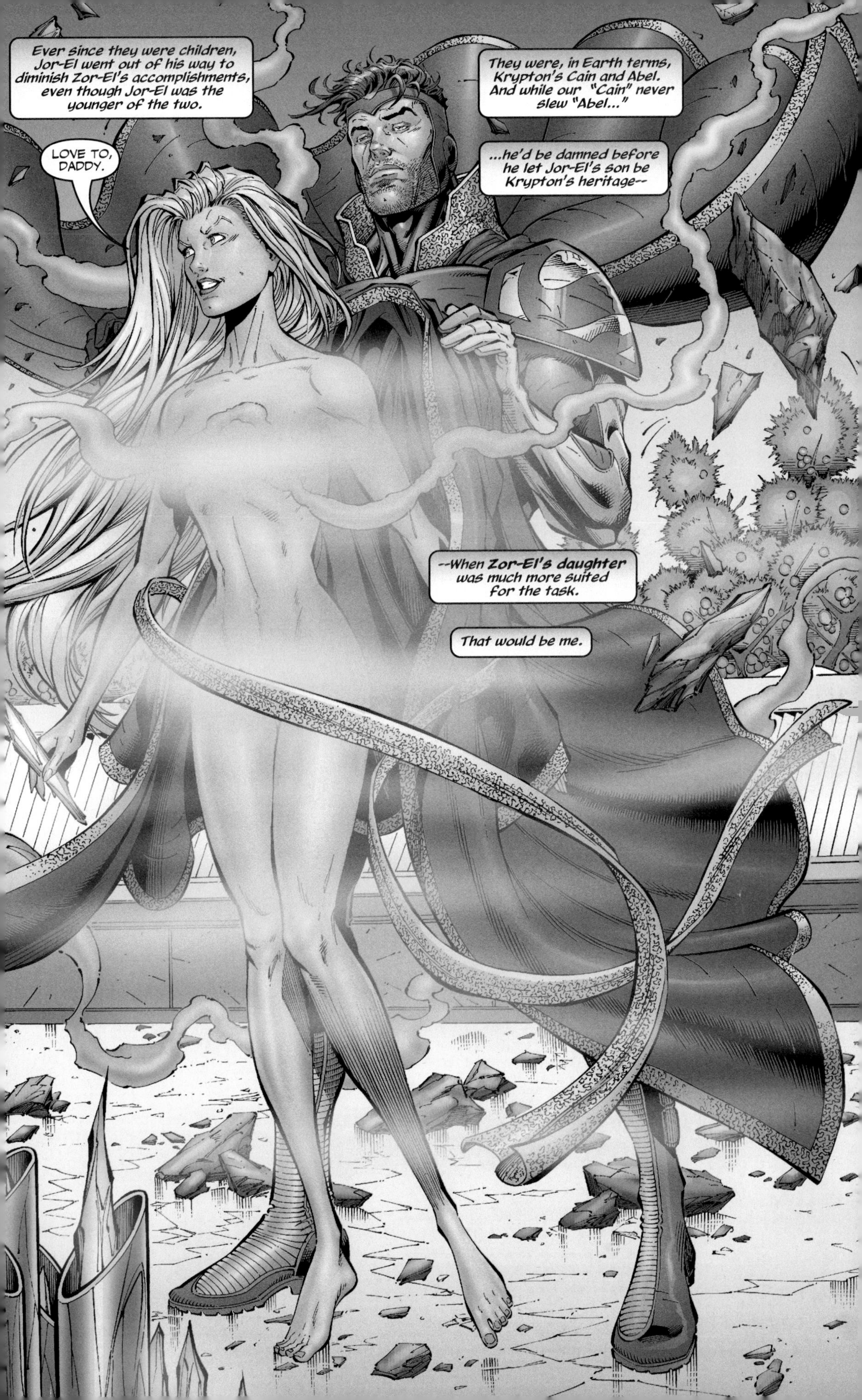
Ever since they were children, Jor-El went out of his way to diminish Zor-El's accomplishments, even though Jor-El was the younger of the two.
LOVE TO, DADDY.
They were, in Earth terms, Krypton's Cain and Abel. And while our "Cain" never slew "Abel..."
...he'd be damned before he let Jor-El's son be Krypton's heritage--
--When Zor-El's daughter was much more suited for the task.
That would be me.

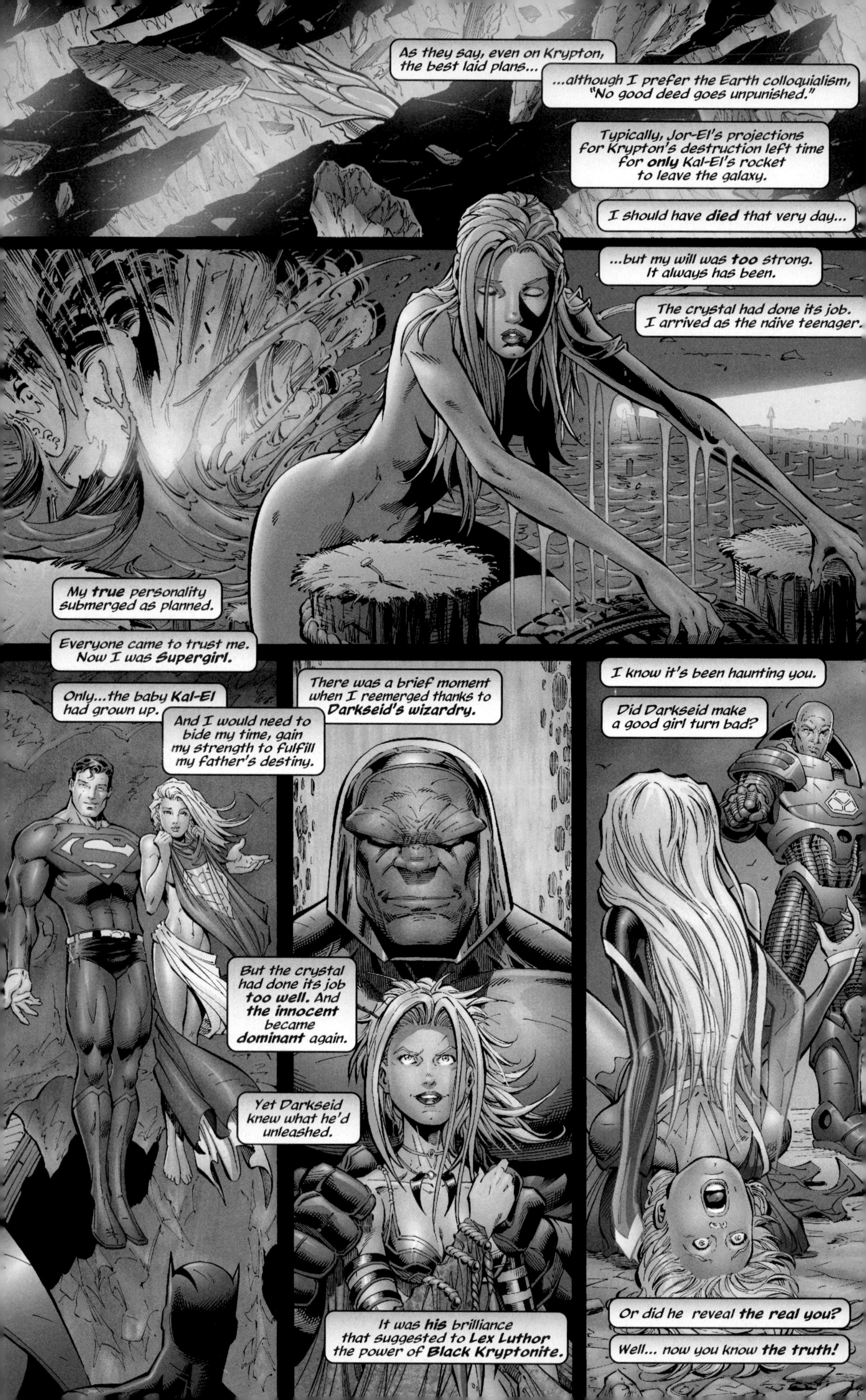
As they say, even on Krypton, the best laid plans...
...although I prefer the Earth colloquialism, "No good deed goes unpunished."
Typically, Jor-El's projections for Krypton's destruction left time for only Kal-El's rocket to leave the galaxy.
I should have died that very day...
...but my will was too strong. It always has been.
The crystal had done its job. I arrived as the naïve teenager.
My true personality submerged as planned.
Everyone came to trust me. Now I was Supergirl.
Only...the baby Kal-El had grown up.
And I would need to bide my time, gain my strength to fulfill my father's destiny.
There was a brief moment when I reemerged thanks to Darkseid's wizardry.
But the crystal had done its job too well. And the innocent became dominant again.
Yet Darkseid knew what he'd unleashed.
It was his brilliance that suggested to Lex Luthor the power of Black Kryptonite.
I know it's been haunting you.
Did Darkseid make a good girl turn bad?
Or did he reveal the real you?
Well... now you know the truth!

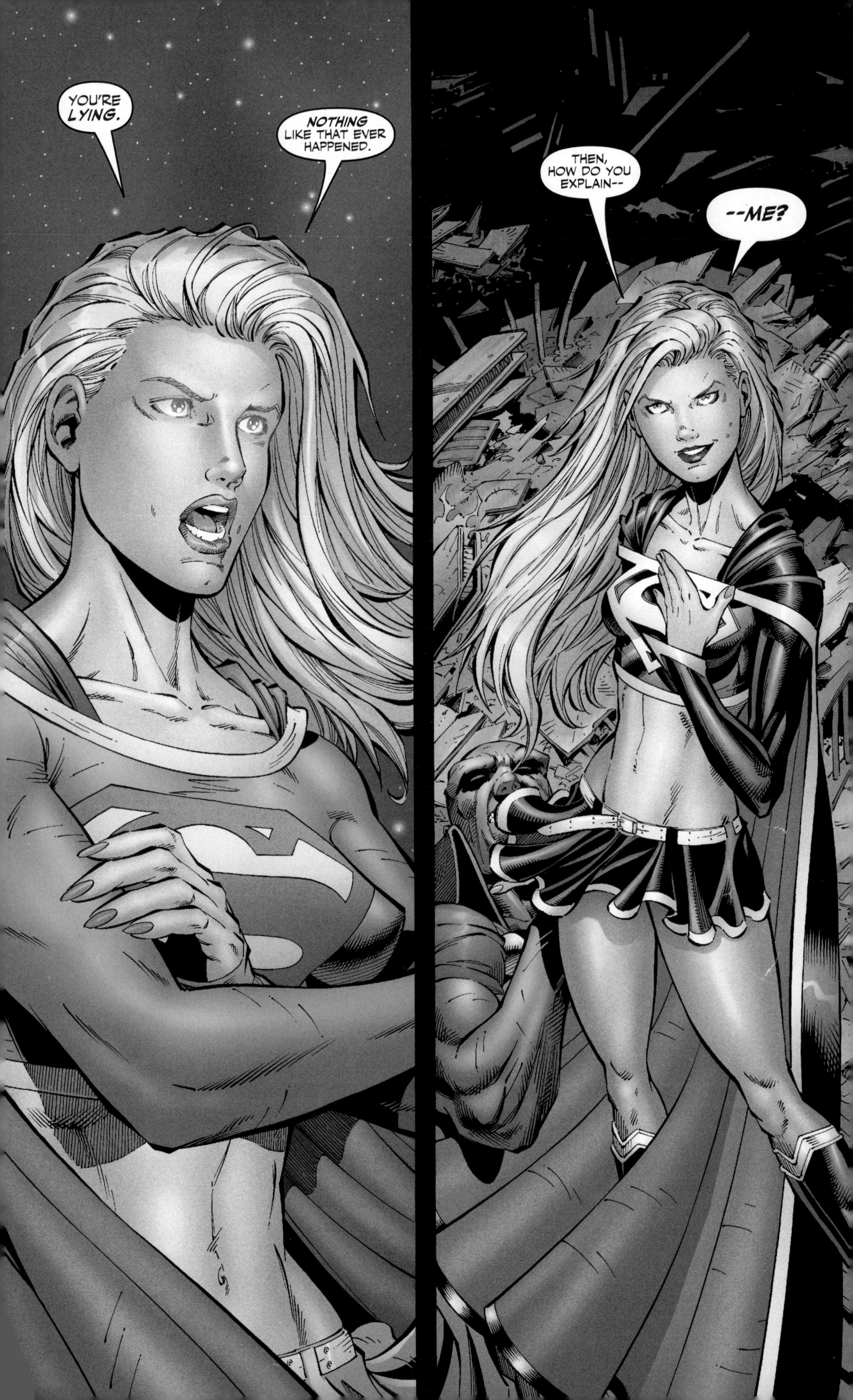
YOU'RE *LYING.*
NOTHING LIKE THAT EVER HAPPENED.
THEN, HOW DO YOU EXPLAIN--
--ME?

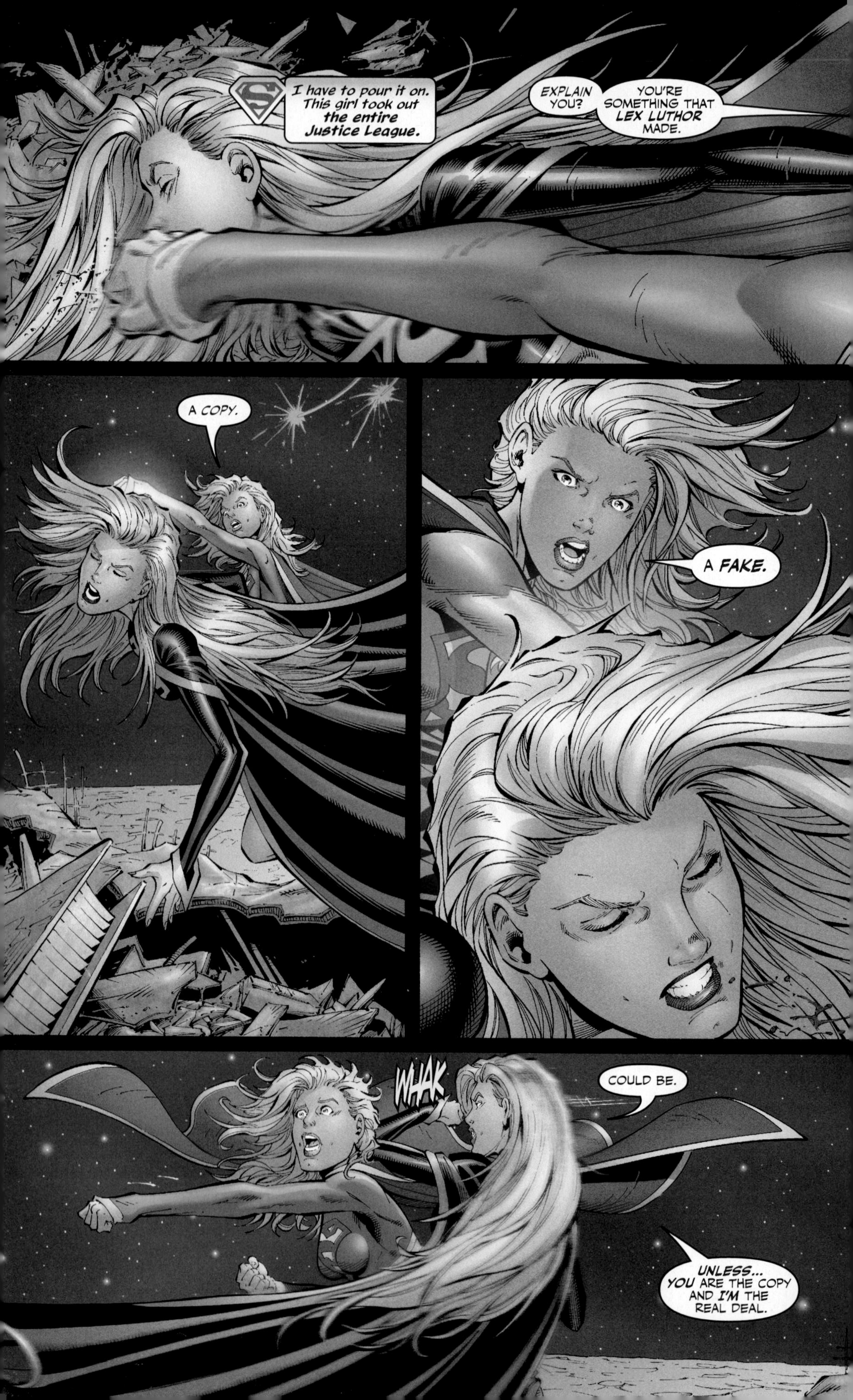

I have to pour it on. This girl took out the entire Justice League.
EXPLAIN YOU?
YOU'RE SOMETHING THAT LEX LUTHOR MADE.
A COPY.
A FAKE.
WHAK
COULD BE.
UNLESS... YOU ARE THE COPY AND I'M THE REAL DEAL.

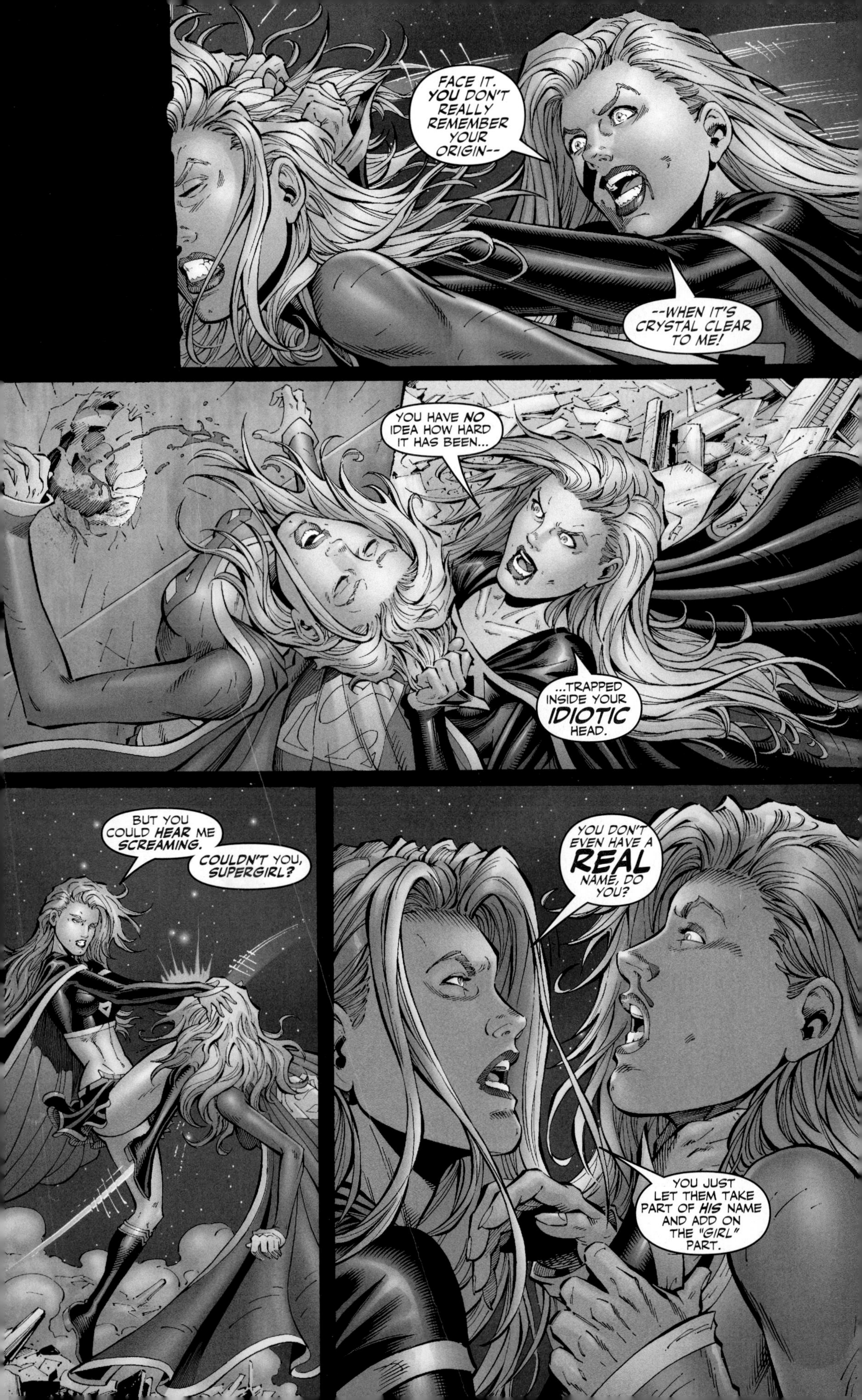
FACE IT. YOU DON'T REALLY REMEMBER YOUR ORIGIN--
--WHEN IT'S CRYSTAL CLEAR TO ME!
YOU HAVE NO IDEA HOW HARD IT HAS BEEN...
...TRAPPED INSIDE YOUR IDIOTIC HEAD.
BUT YOU COULD HEAR ME SCREAMING.
COULDN'T YOU, SUPERGIRL?
YOU DON'T EVEN HAVE A REAL NAME, DO YOU?
YOU JUST LET THEM TAKE PART OF HIS NAME AND ADD ON THE "GIRL" PART.

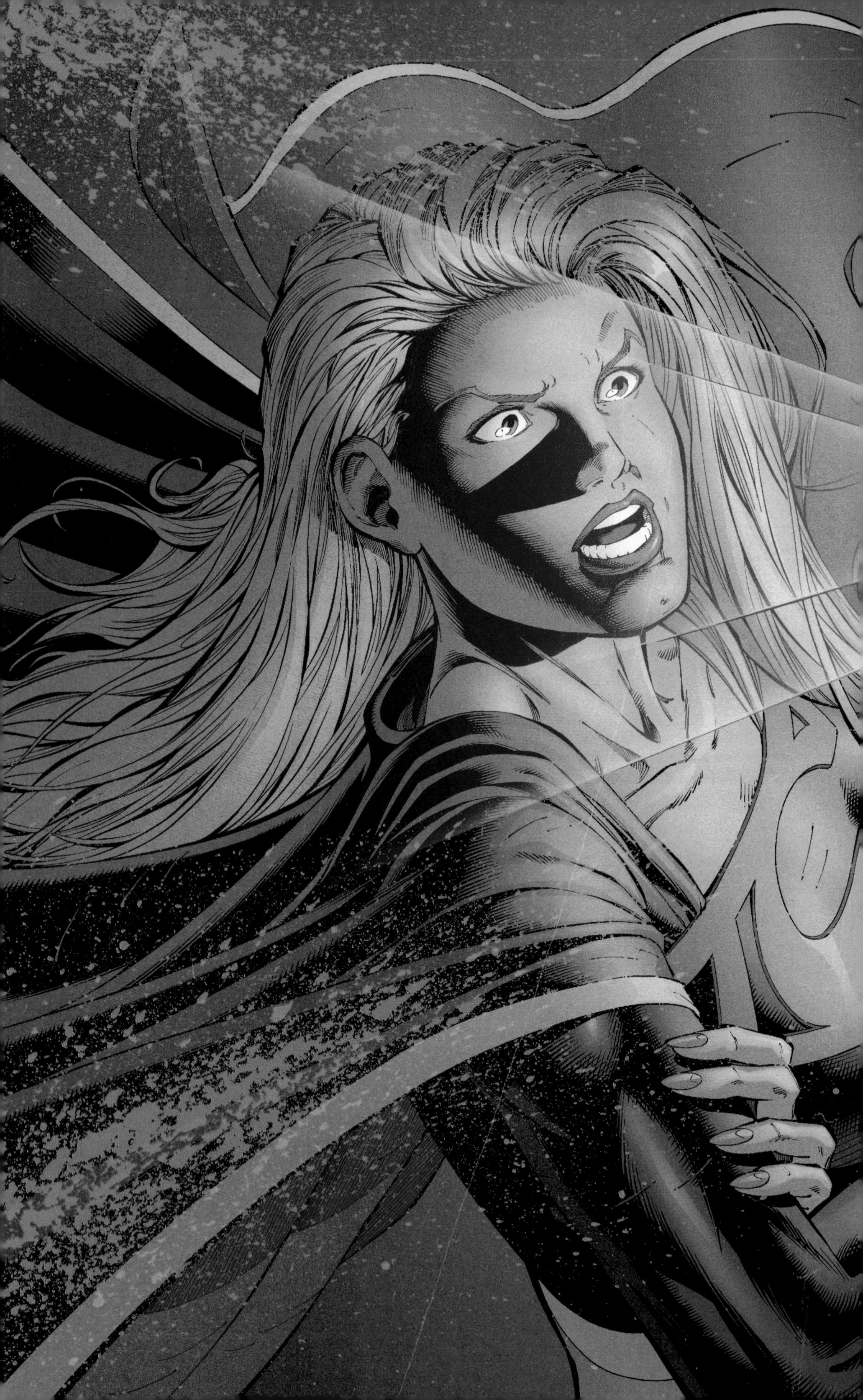

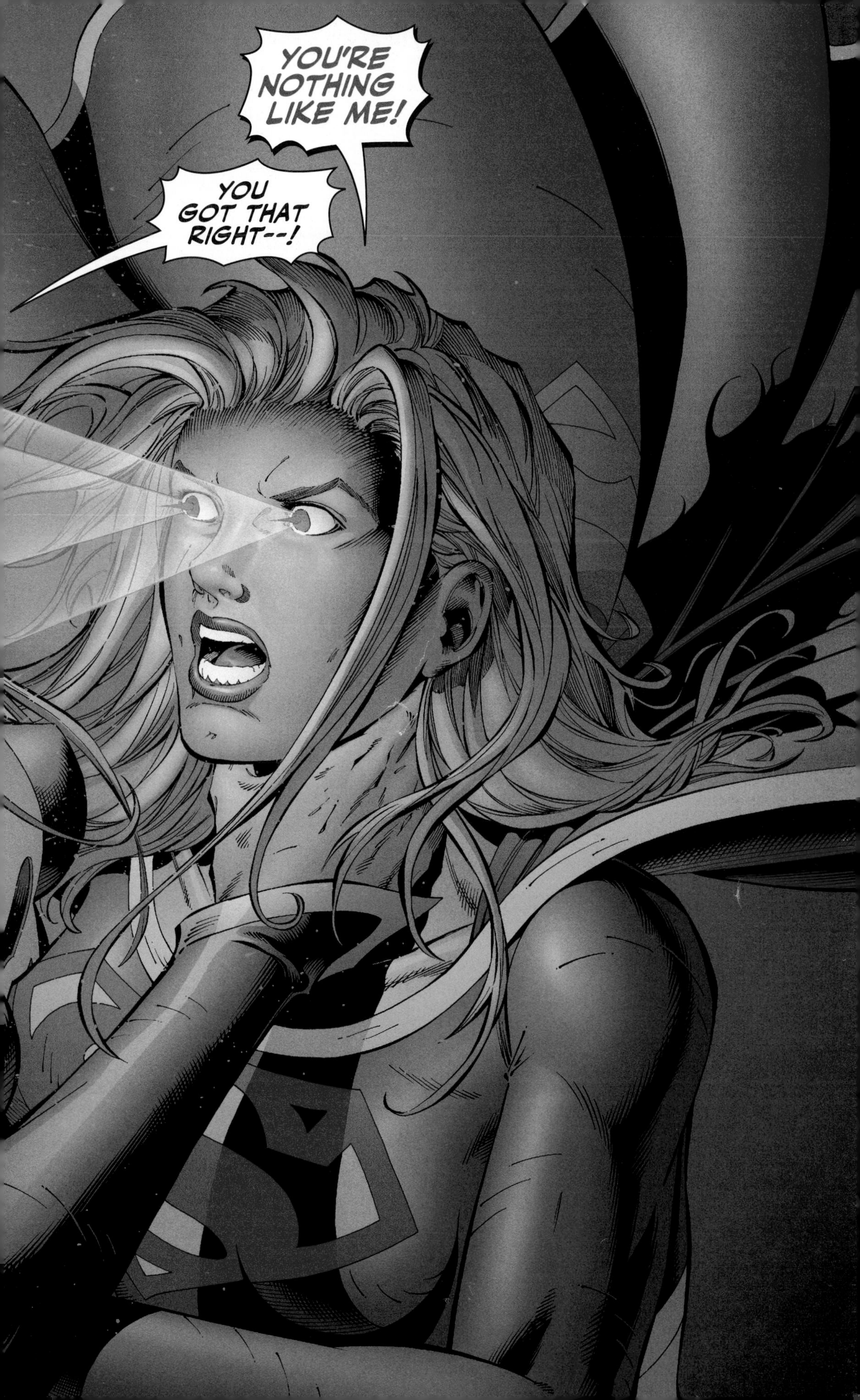
YOU'RE NOTHING LIKE ME!
YOU GOT THAT RIGHT--!

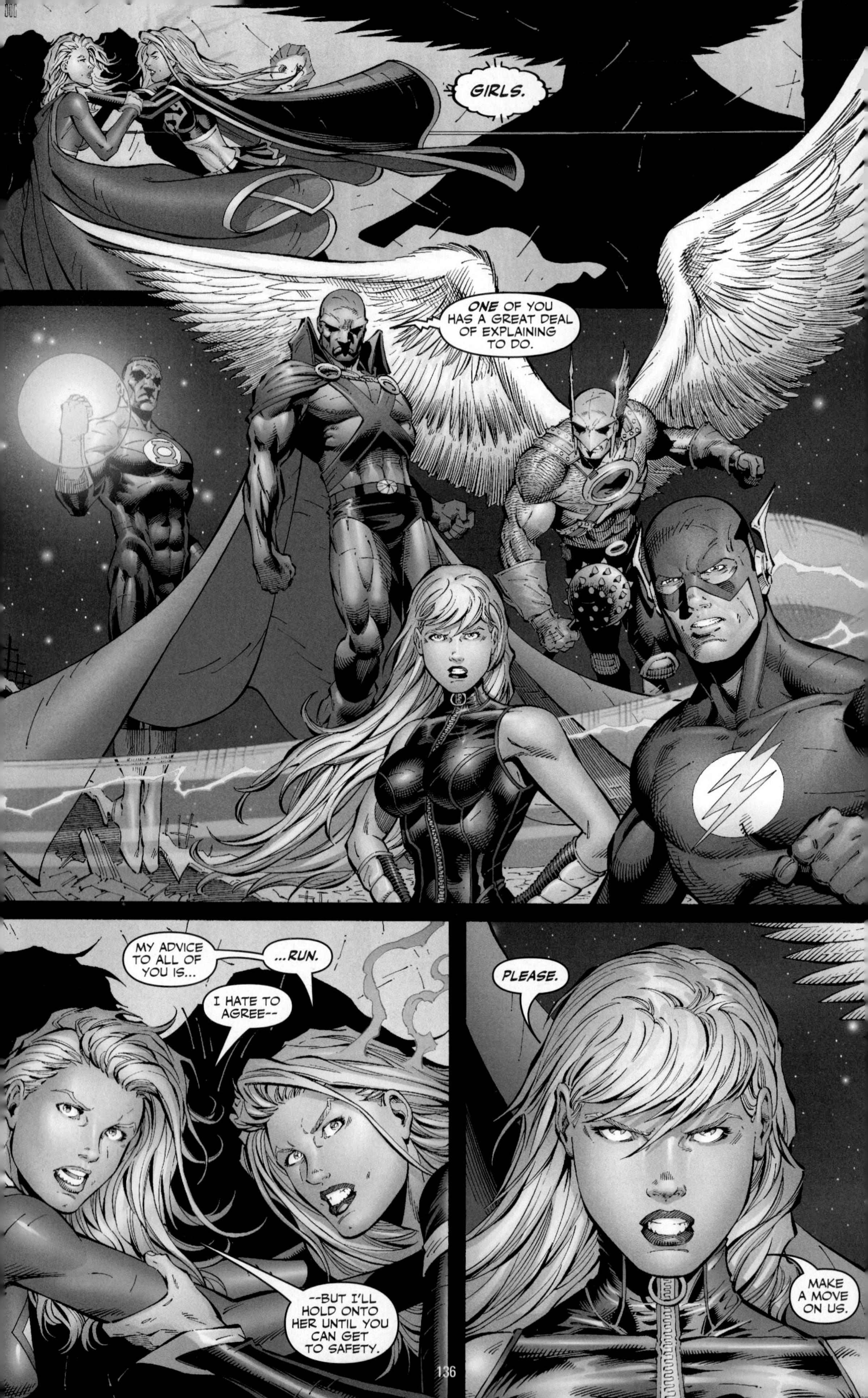
GIRLS.
ONE OF YOU HAS A GREAT DEAL OF EXPLAINING TO DO.
MY ADVICE TO ALL OF YOU IS...
...RUN.
I HATE TO AGREE--
--BUT I'LL HOLD ONTO HER UNTIL YOU CAN GET TO SAFETY.
PLEASE.
MAKE A MOVE ON US.

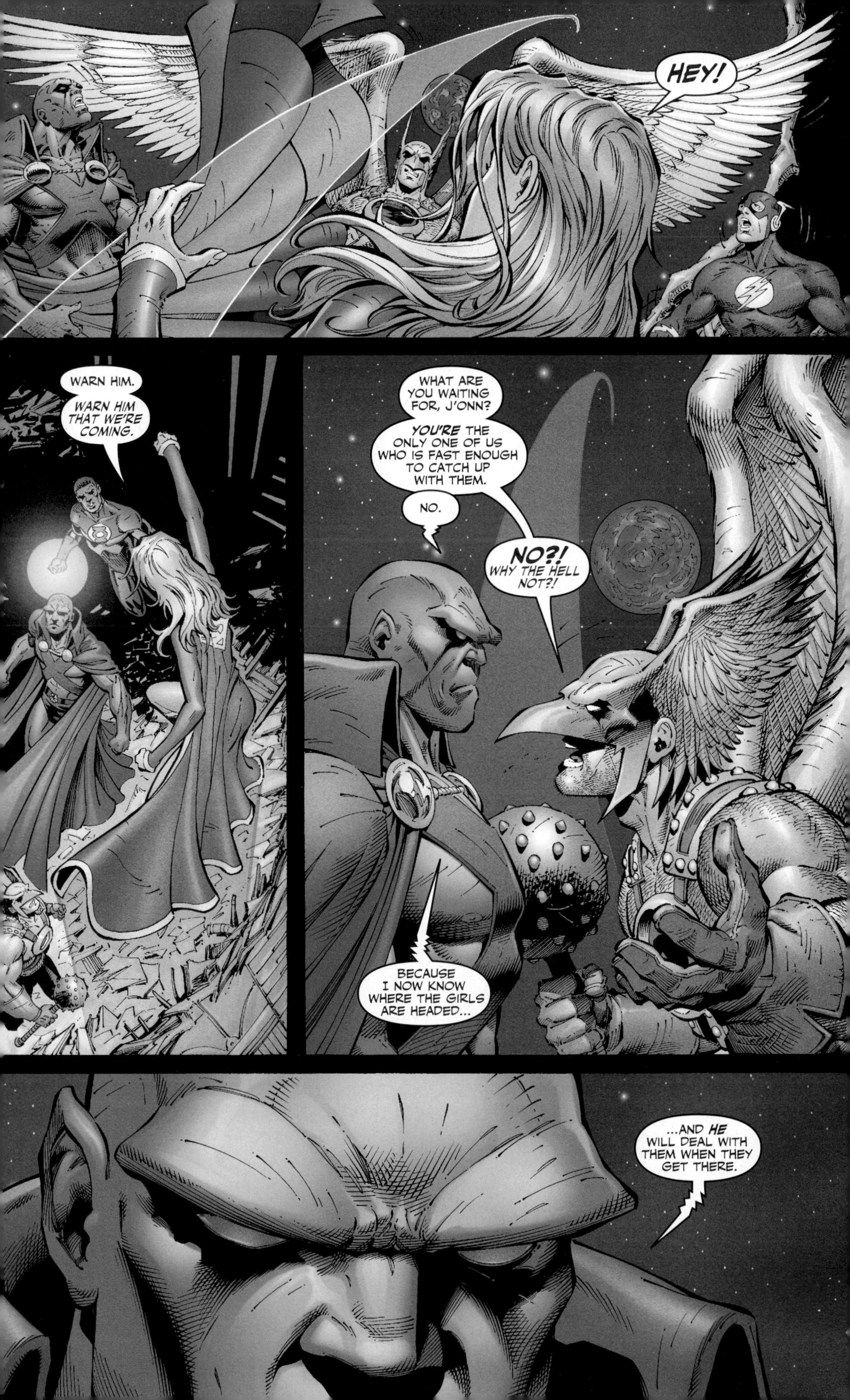
HEY!
WARN HIM.
WARN HIM THAT WE'RE COMING.
WHAT ARE YOU WAITING FOR, J'ONN?
YOU'RE THE ONLY ONE OF US WHO IS FAST ENOUGH TO CATCH UP WITH THEM.
NO.
NO?! WHY THE HELL NOT?!
BECAUSE I NOW KNOW WHERE THE GIRLS ARE HEADED...
...AND HE WILL DEAL WITH THEM WHEN THEY GET THERE.

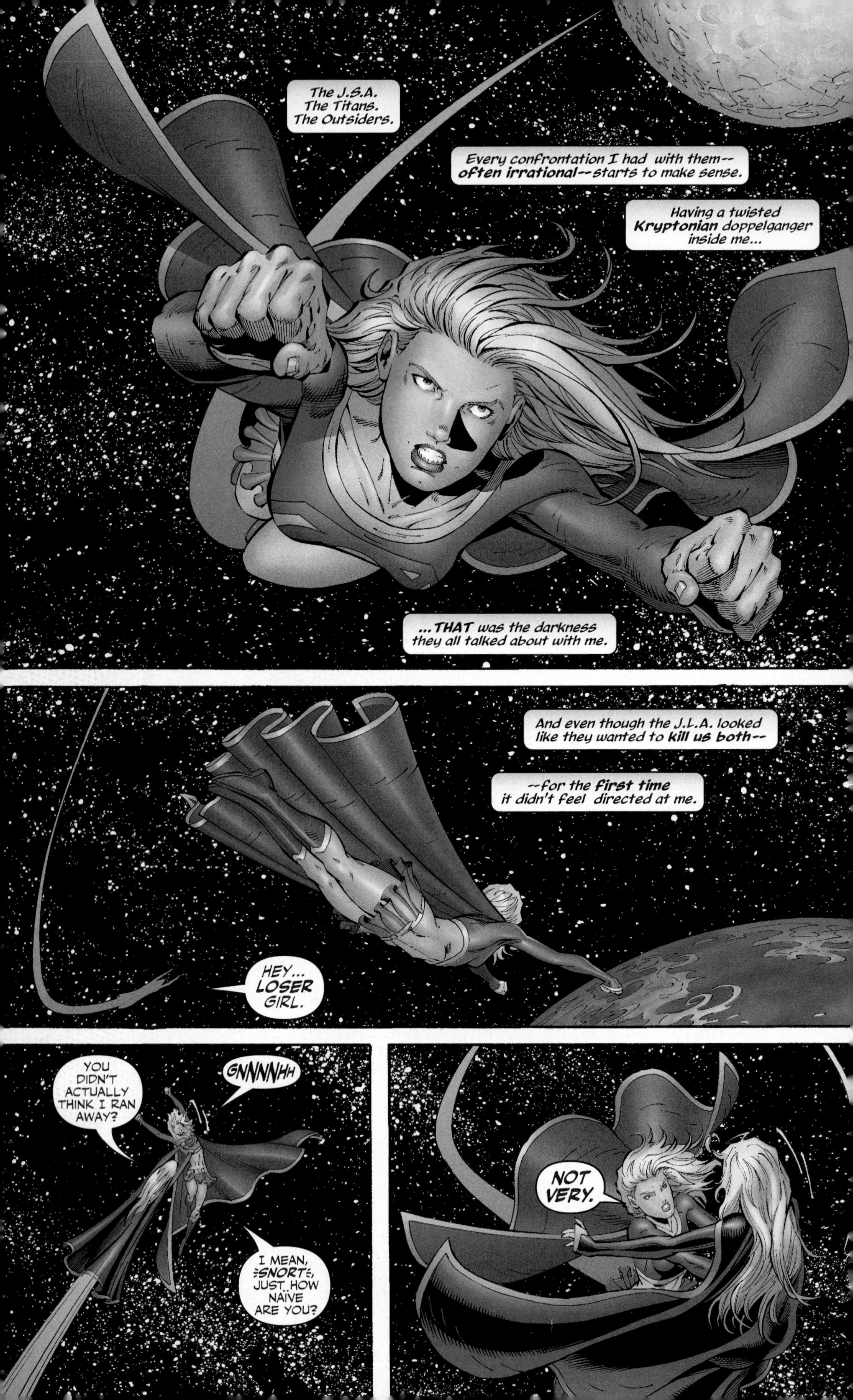

The J.S.A.
The Titans.
The Outsiders.
Every confrontation I had with them-- often irrational--starts to make sense.
Having a twisted Kryptonian doppelganger inside me...
...THAT was the darkness they all talked about with me.
And even though the J.L.A. looked like they wanted to kill us both--
--for the first time it didn't feel directed at me.
HEY... LOSER GIRL.
YOU DIDN'T ACTUALLY THINK I RAN AWAY?
GNNNNHH
I MEAN, SNORT, JUST HOW NAÏVE ARE YOU?
NOT VERY.

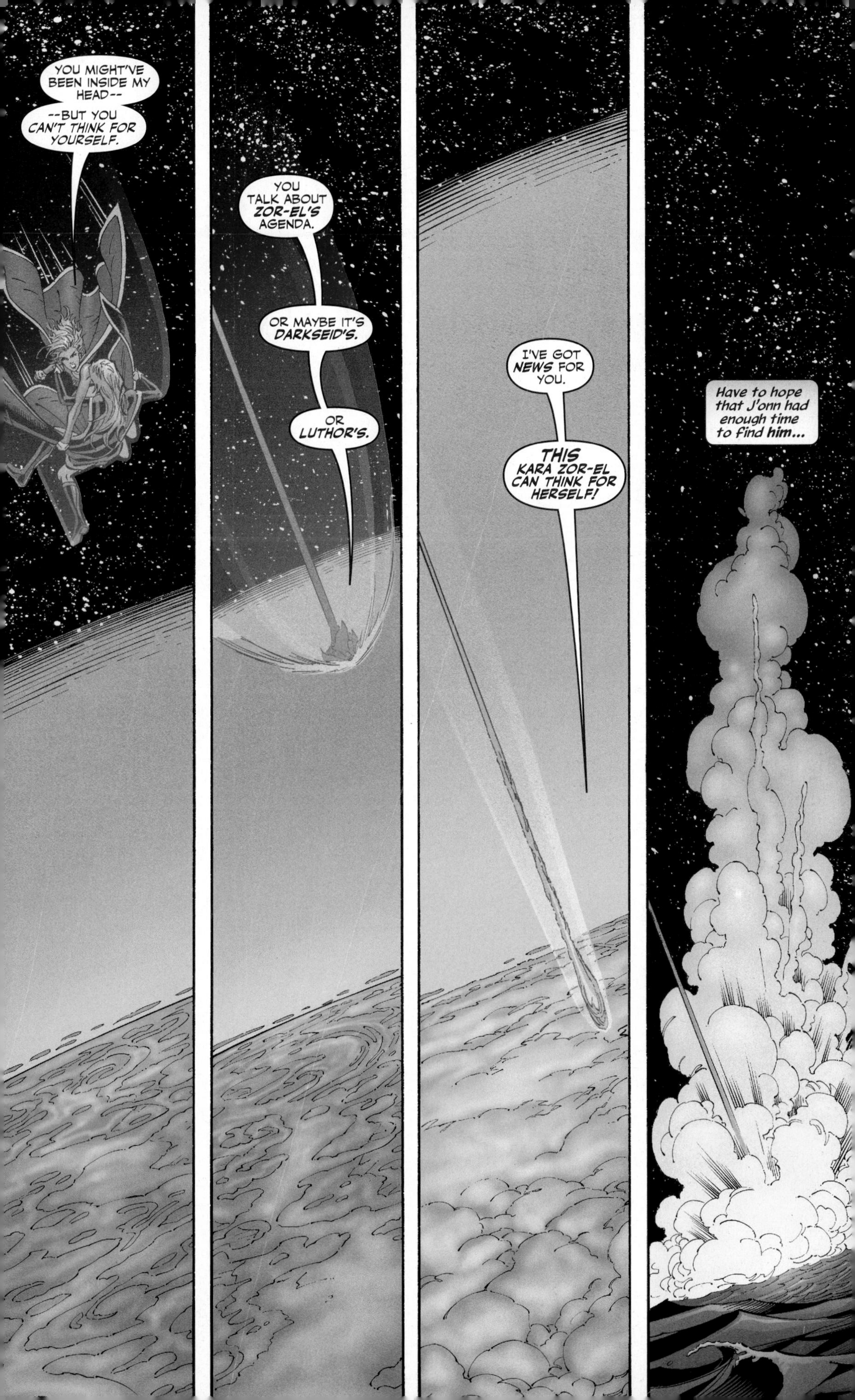
YOU MIGHT'VE BEEN INSIDE MY HEAD--
--BUT YOU CAN'T THINK FOR YOURSELF.
YOU TALK ABOUT ZOR-EL'S AGENDA.
OR MAYBE IT'S DARKSEID'S.
OR LUTHOR'S.
I'VE GOT NEWS FOR YOU.
THIS KARA ZOR-EL CAN THINK FOR HERSELF!
Have to hope that J'onn had enough time to find him...

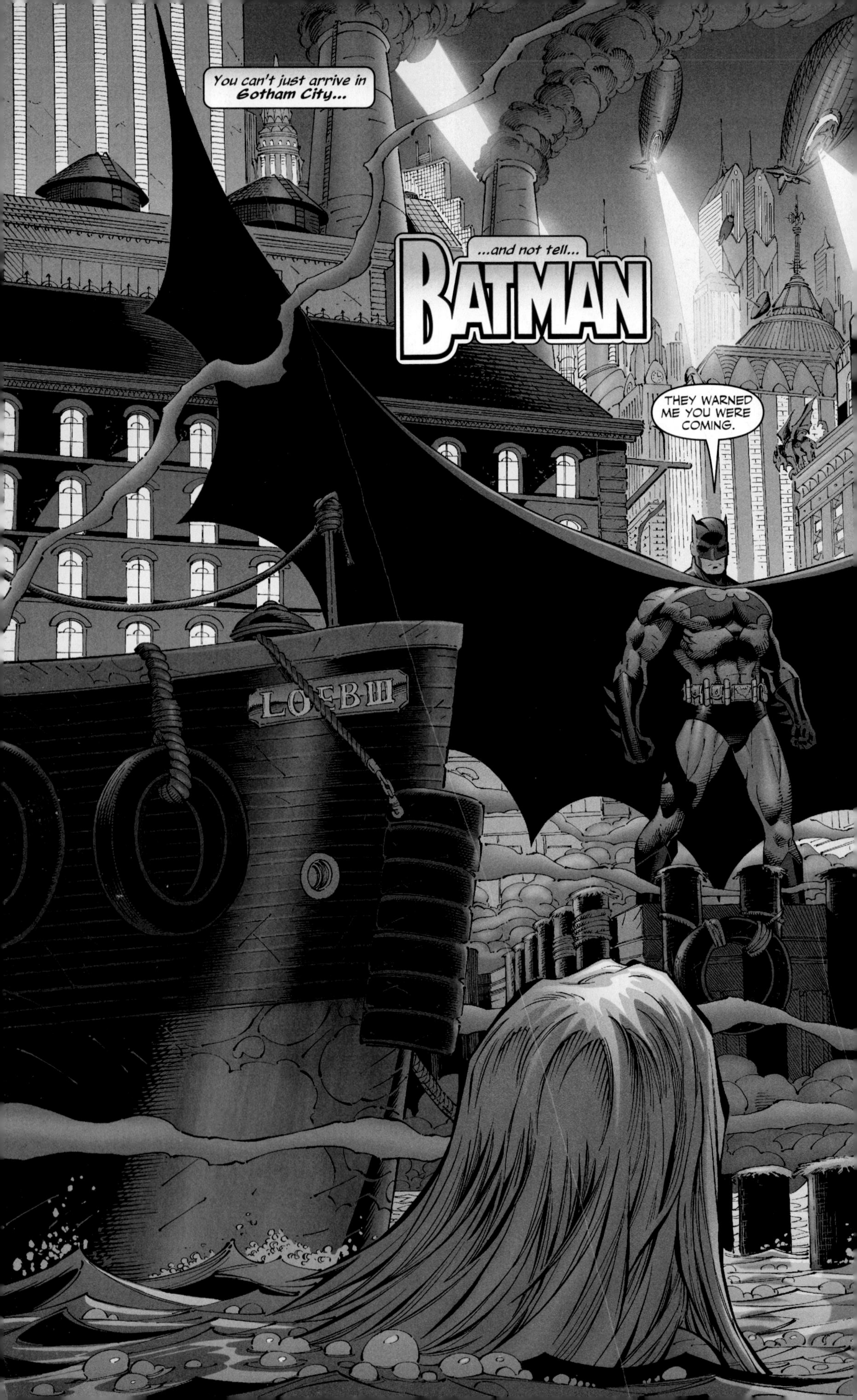
You can't just arrive in Gotham City...
...and not tell...
BATMAN
THEY WARNED ME YOU WERE COMING.
LOEB III

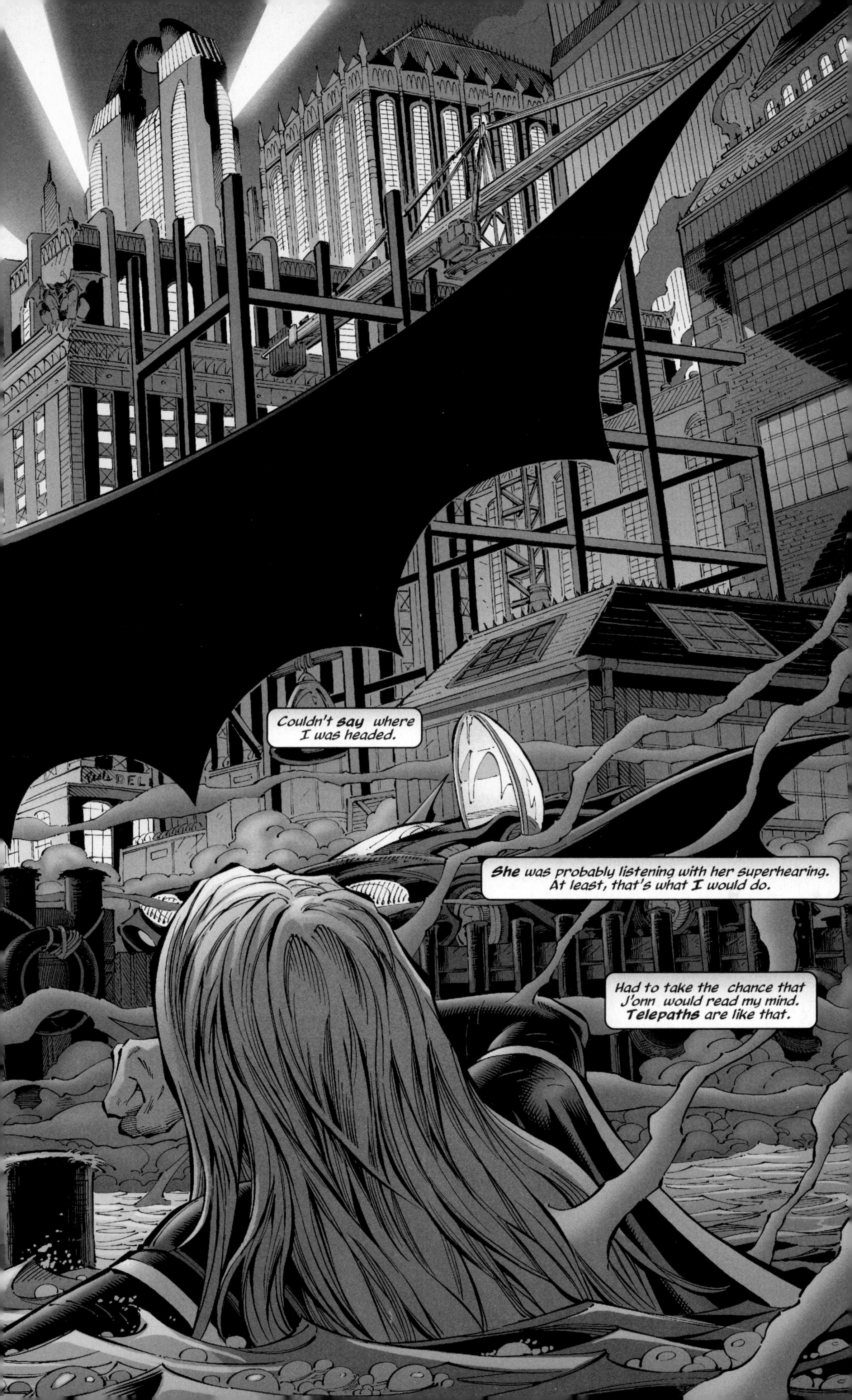
Couldn't say where I was headed.
She was probably listening with her superhearing. At least, that's what I would do.
Had to take the chance that J'onn would read my mind. Telepaths are like that.

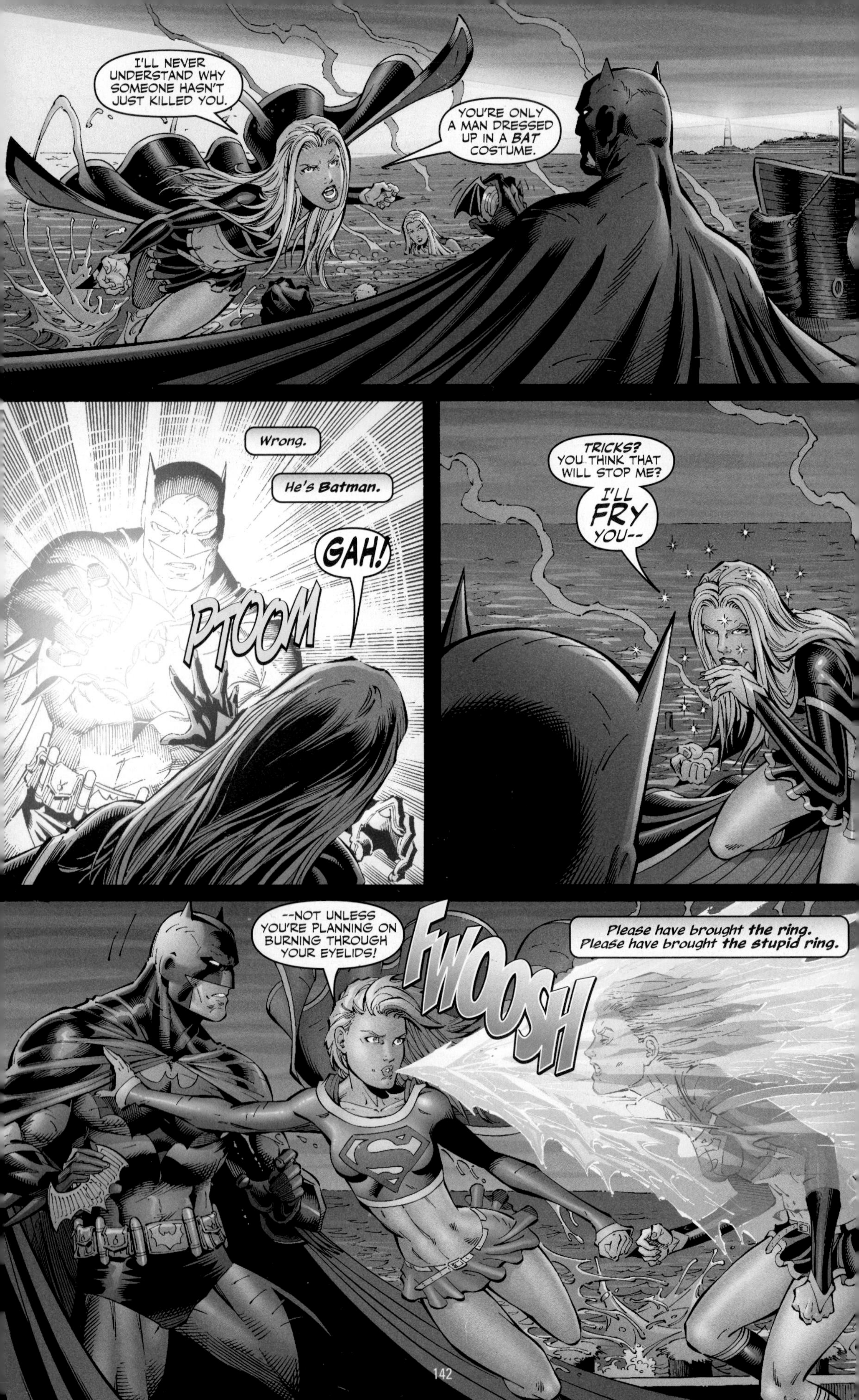
I'LL NEVER UNDERSTAND WHY SOMEONE HASN'T JUST KILLED YOU.
YOU'RE ONLY A MAN DRESSED UP IN A *BAT* COSTUME.
Wrong.
He's Batman.
GAH!
PTOOM
TRICKS? YOU THINK THAT WILL STOP ME?
I'LL FRY YOU--
--NOT UNLESS YOU'RE PLANNING ON BURNING THROUGH YOUR EYELIDS!
FWOOSH
Please have brought the ring.
Please have brought the stupid ring.

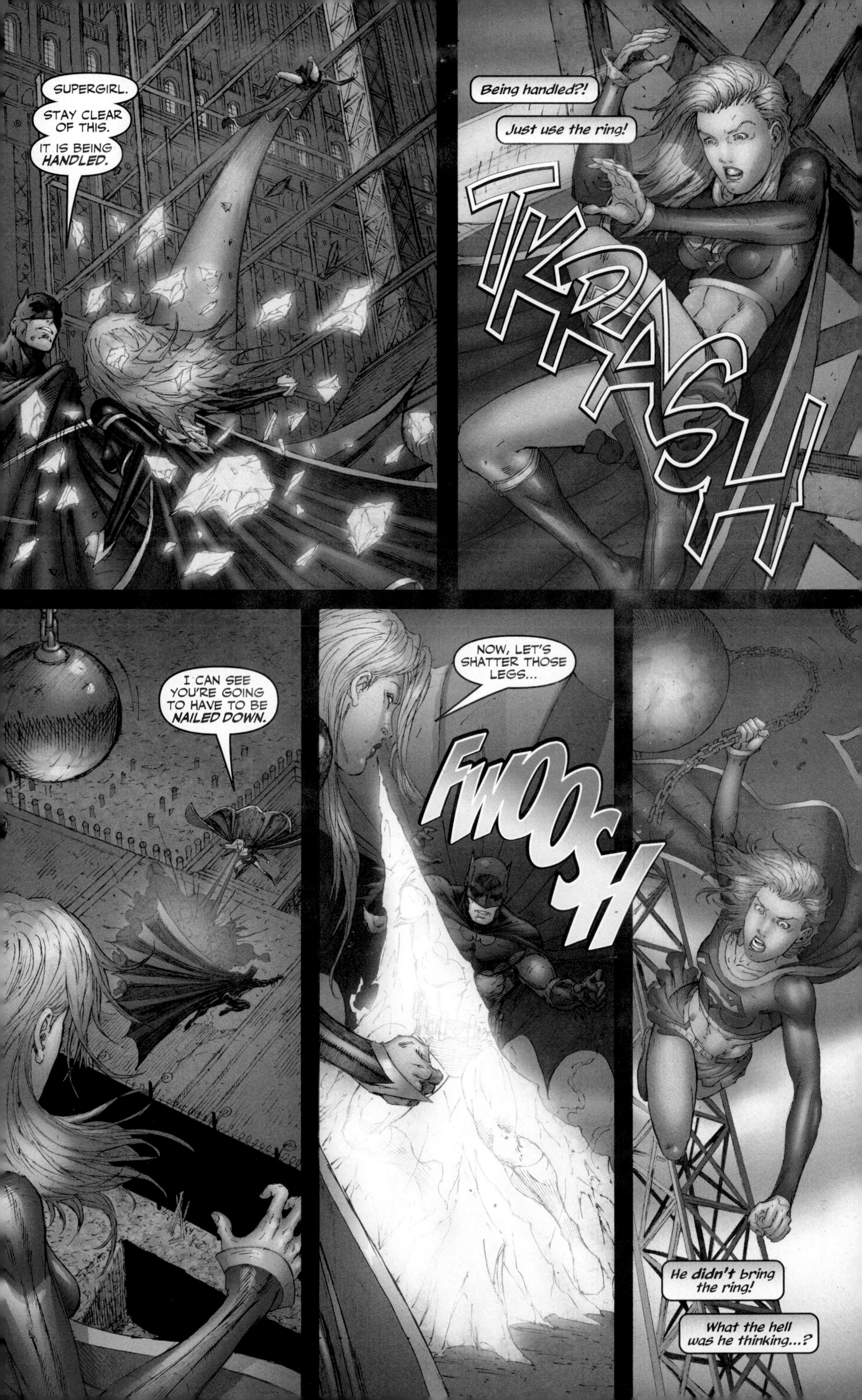
SUPERGIRL.
STAY CLEAR OF THIS.
IT IS BEING *HANDLED.*
Being handled?!
Just use the ring!
TKRASH
I CAN SEE YOU'RE GOING TO HAVE TO BE *NAILED DOWN.*
NOW, LET'S SHATTER THOSE LEGS...
FWOOSH
He *didn't* bring the ring!
What the hell was he thinking...?

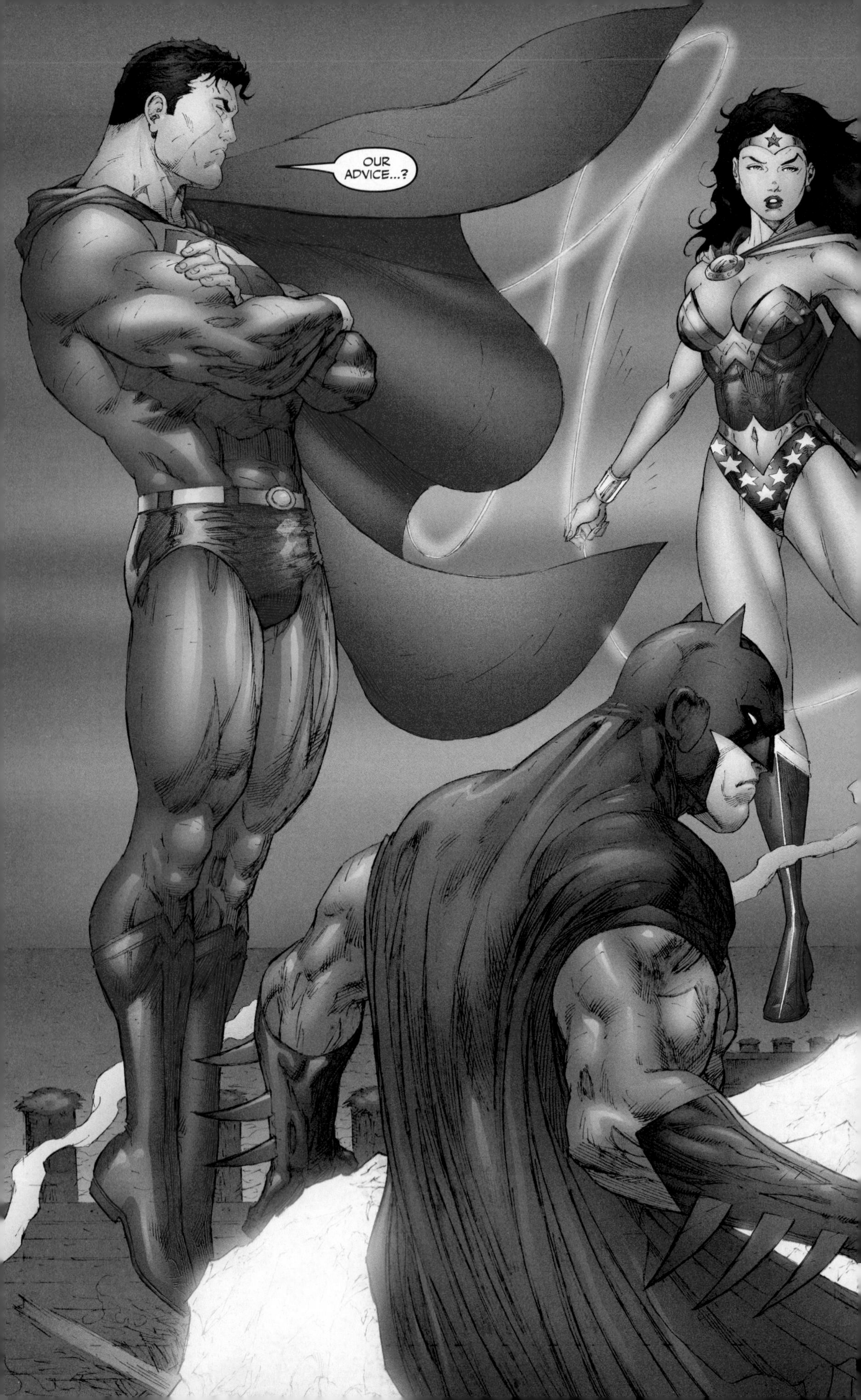
OUR ADVICE...?

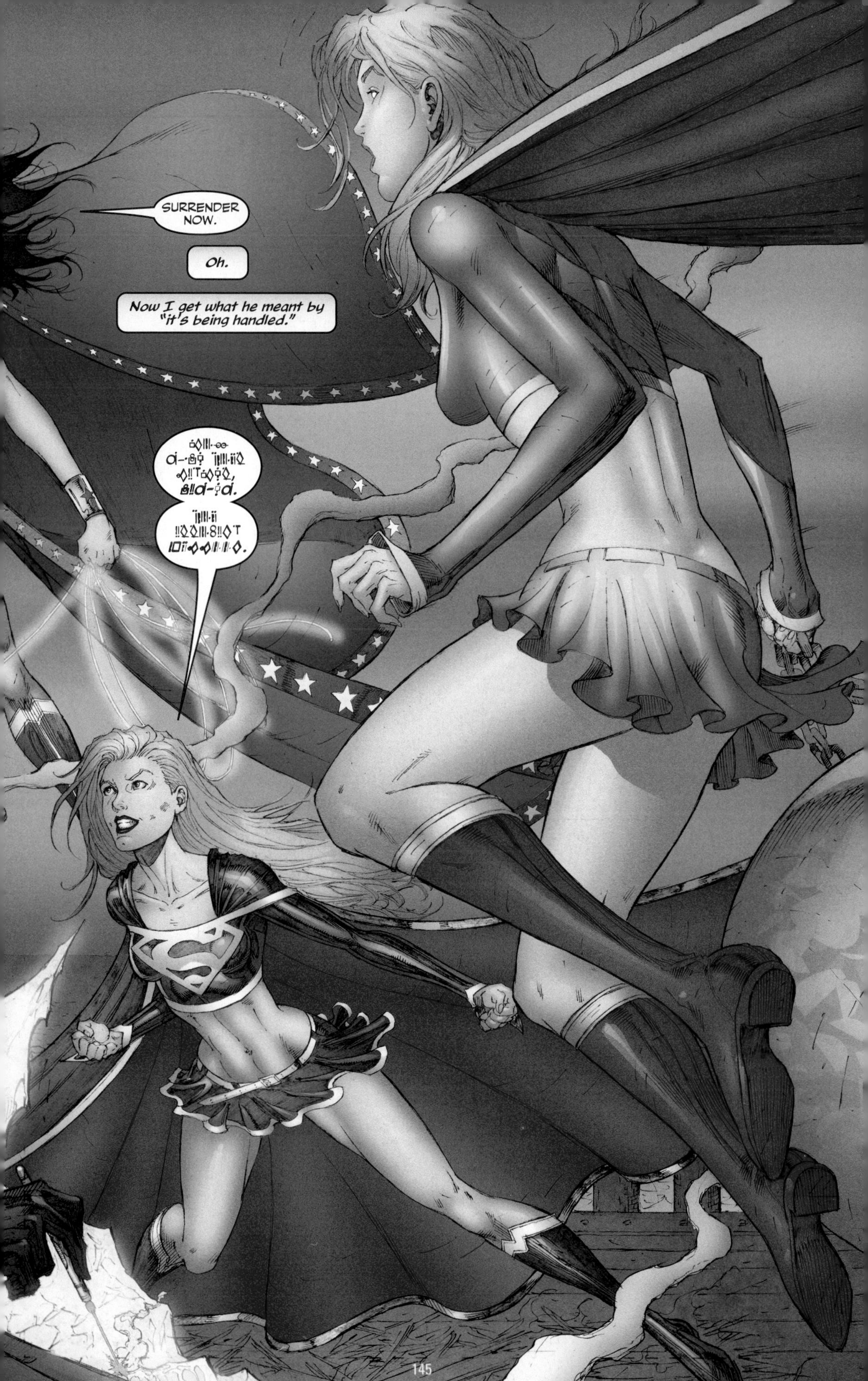
SURRENDER NOW.
Oh.
Now I get what he meant by "it's being handled."

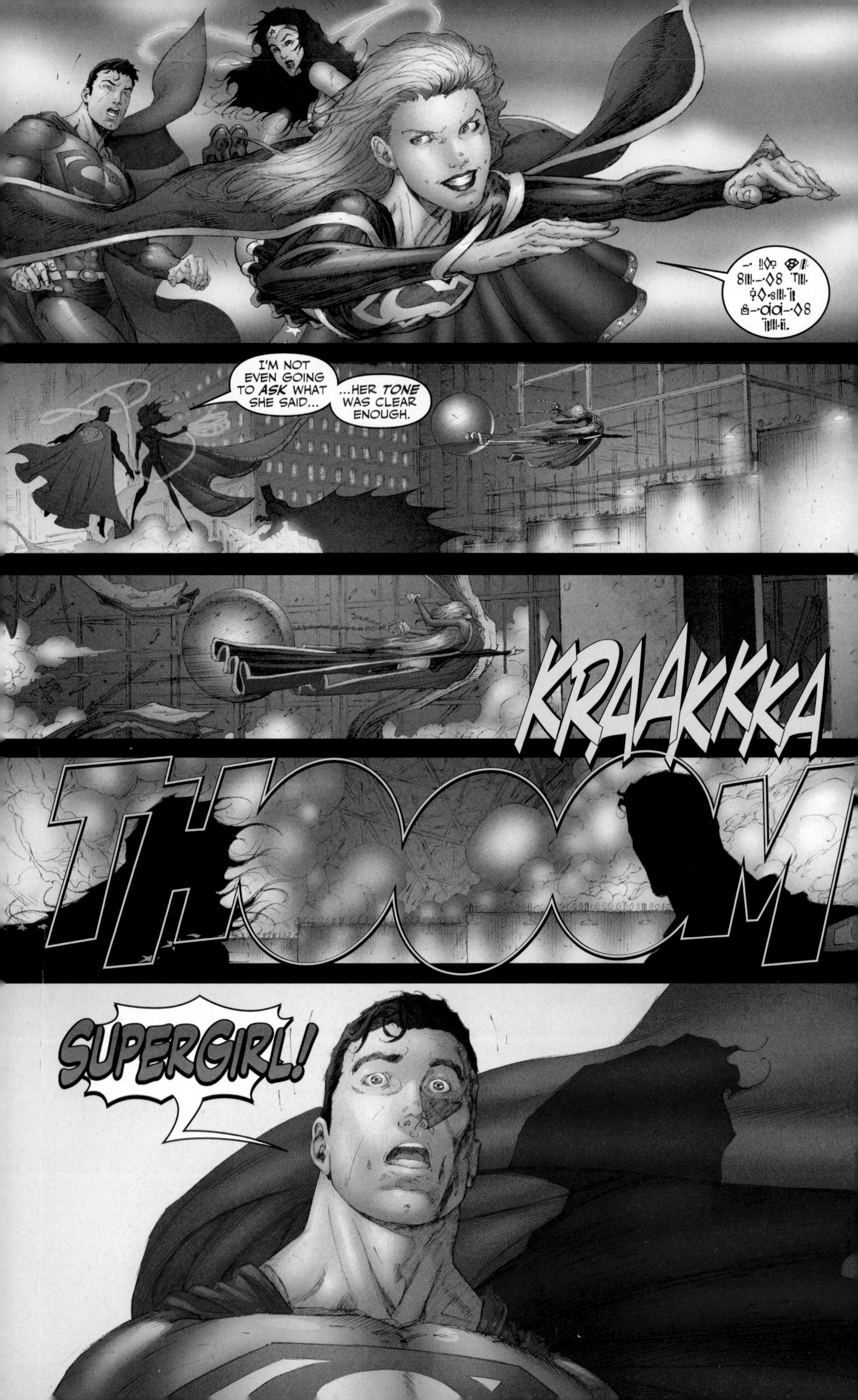
I'M NOT EVEN GOING TO ASK WHAT SHE SAID...
...HER TONE WAS CLEAR ENOUGH.
KRAAKKA
THOOOM
SUPERGIRL!

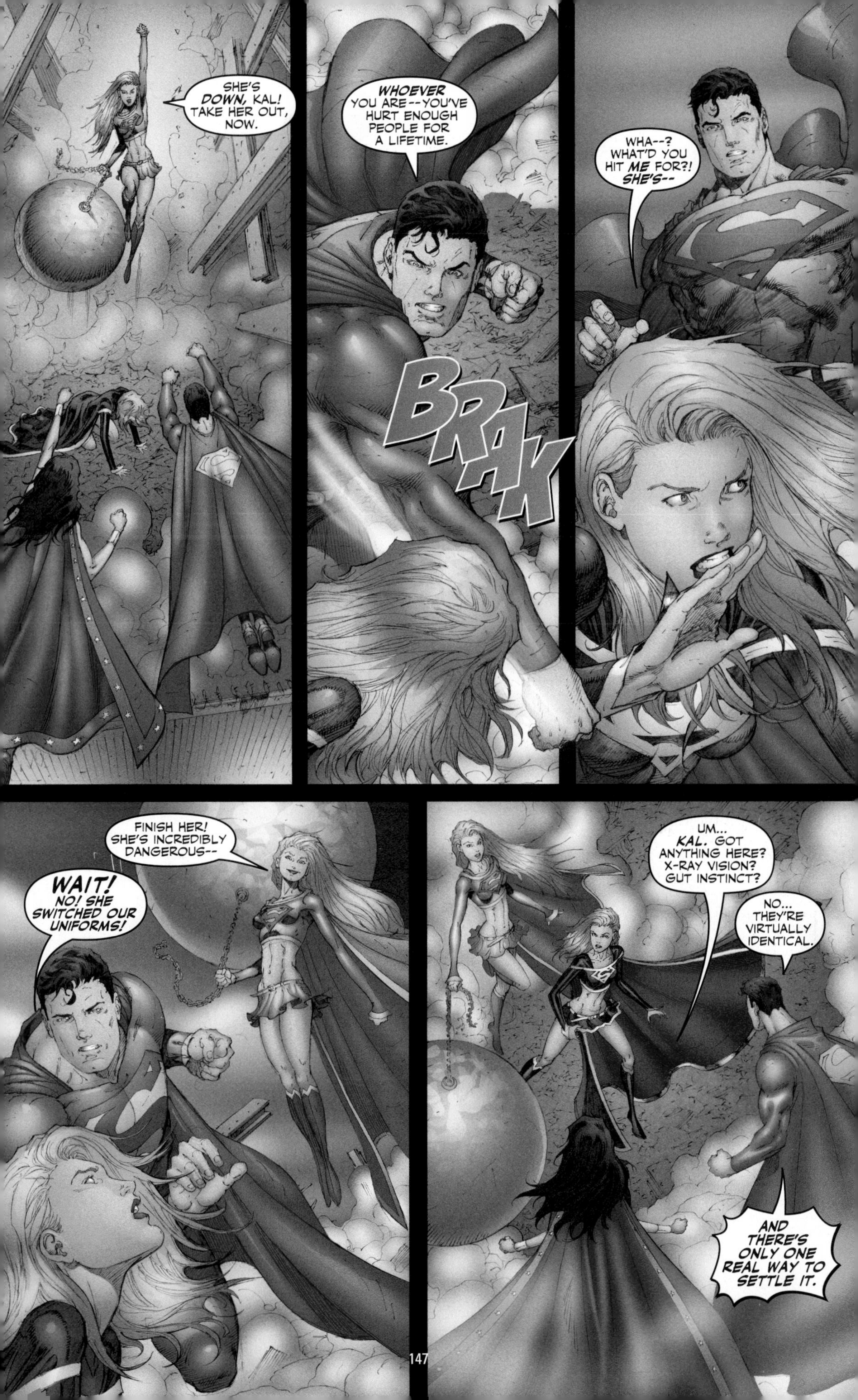

SHE'S DOWN, KAL! TAKE HER OUT, NOW.
WHOEVER YOU ARE--YOU'VE HURT ENOUGH PEOPLE FOR A LIFETIME.
BRAK
WHA--? WHAT'D YOU HIT ME FOR?! SHE'S--
FINISH HER! SHE'S INCREDIBLY DANGEROUS--
WAIT! NO! SHE SWITCHED OUR UNIFORMS!
UM... KAL. GOT ANYTHING HERE? X-RAY VISION? GUT INSTINCT?
NO... THEY'RE VIRTUALLY IDENTICAL.
AND THERE'S ONLY ONE REAL WAY TO SETTLE IT.

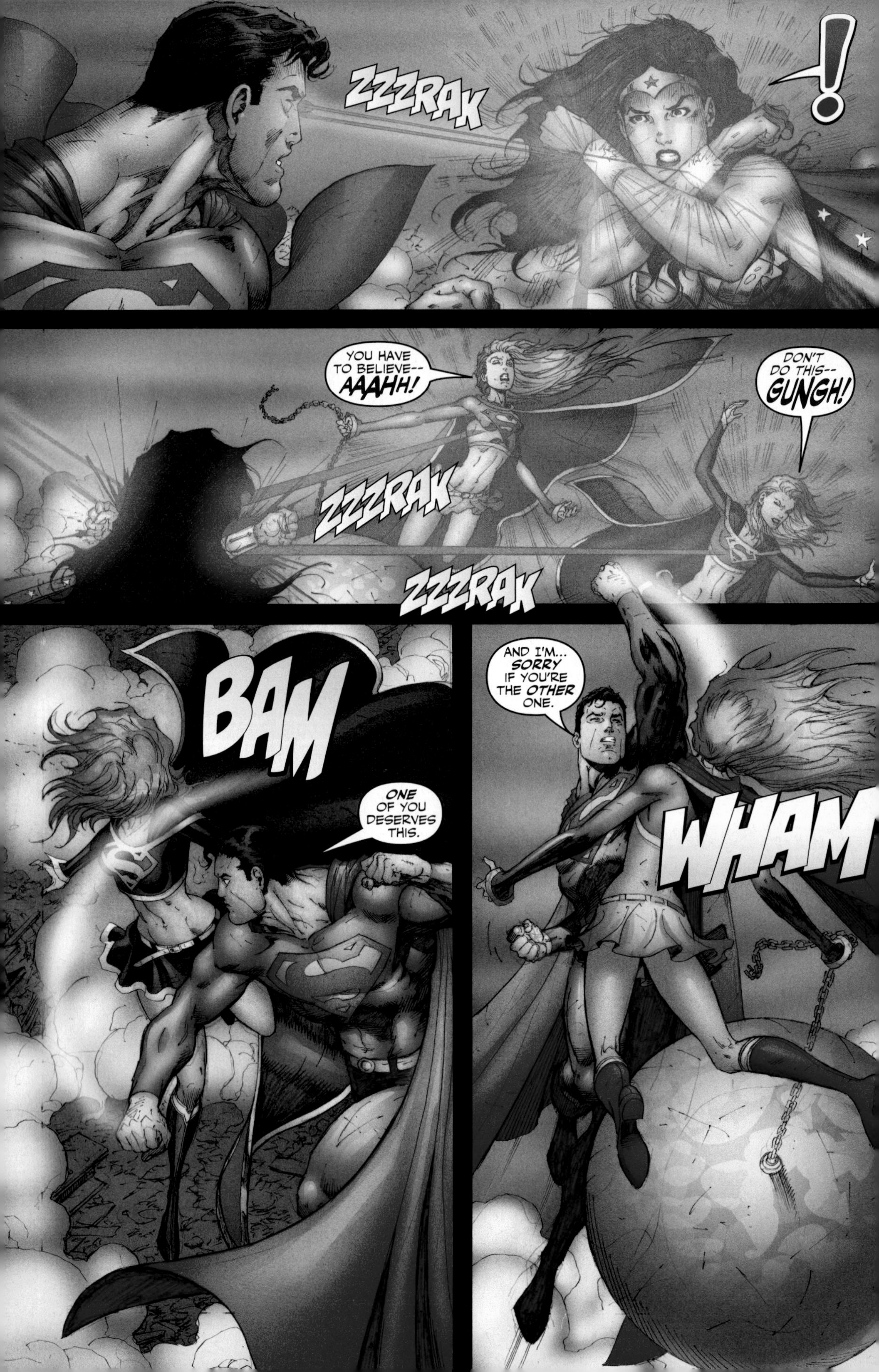
ZZZRAK
!
YOU HAVE TO BELIEVE-- AAAHH!
DON'T DO THIS-- GUNGH!
ZZZRAK
ZZZRAK
BAM
ONE OF YOU DESERVES THIS.
AND I'M... SORRY IF YOU'RE THE OTHER ONE.
WHAM

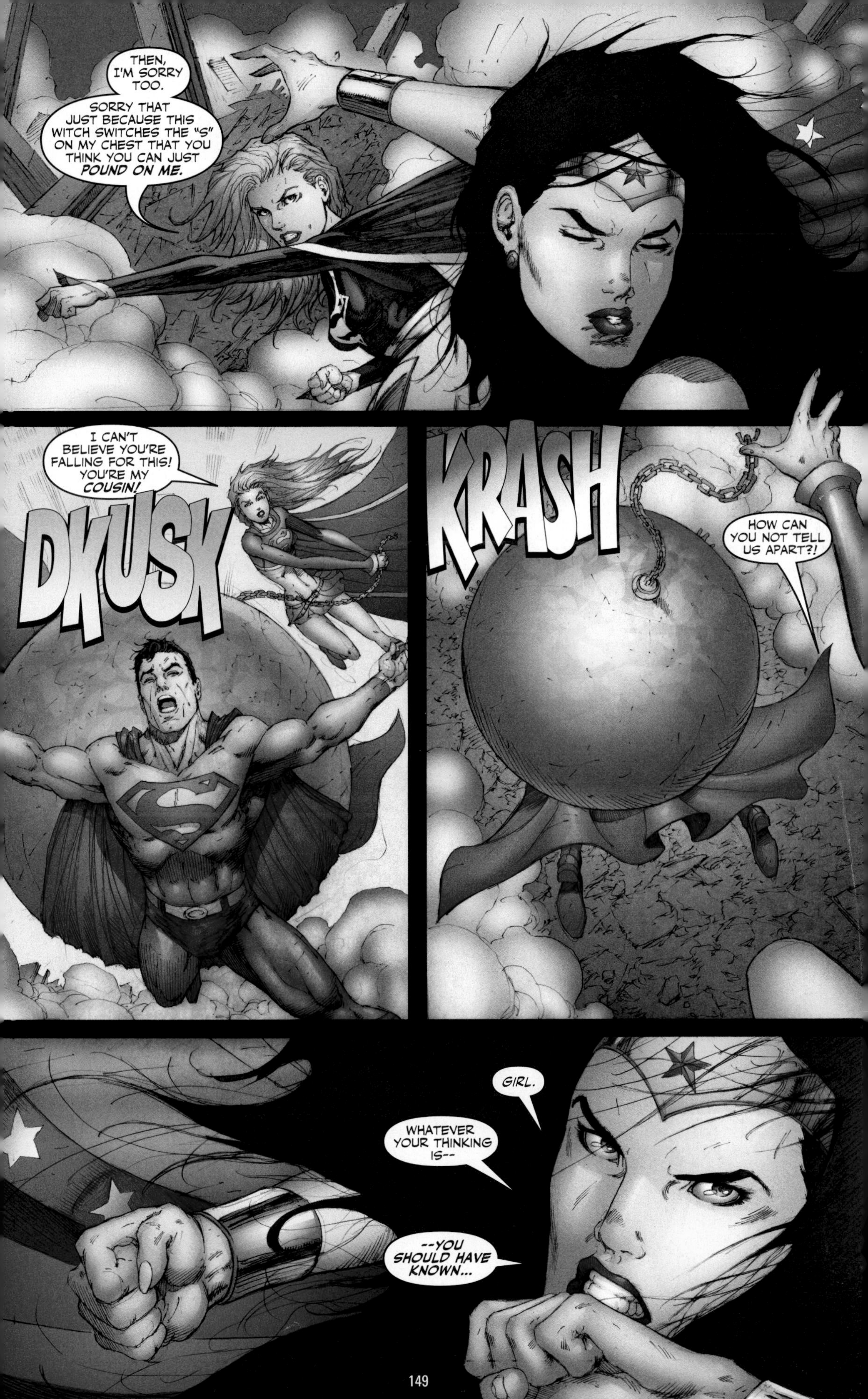
THEN, I'M SORRY TOO.
SORRY THAT JUST BECAUSE THIS WITCH SWITCHES THE "S" ON MY CHEST THAT YOU THINK YOU CAN JUST POUND ON ME.
I CAN'T BELIEVE YOU'RE FALLING FOR THIS! YOU'RE MY COUSIN!
DKUSK
KRASH
HOW CAN YOU NOT TELL US APART?!
GIRL.
WHATEVER YOUR THINKING IS--
--YOU SHOULD HAVE KNOWN...

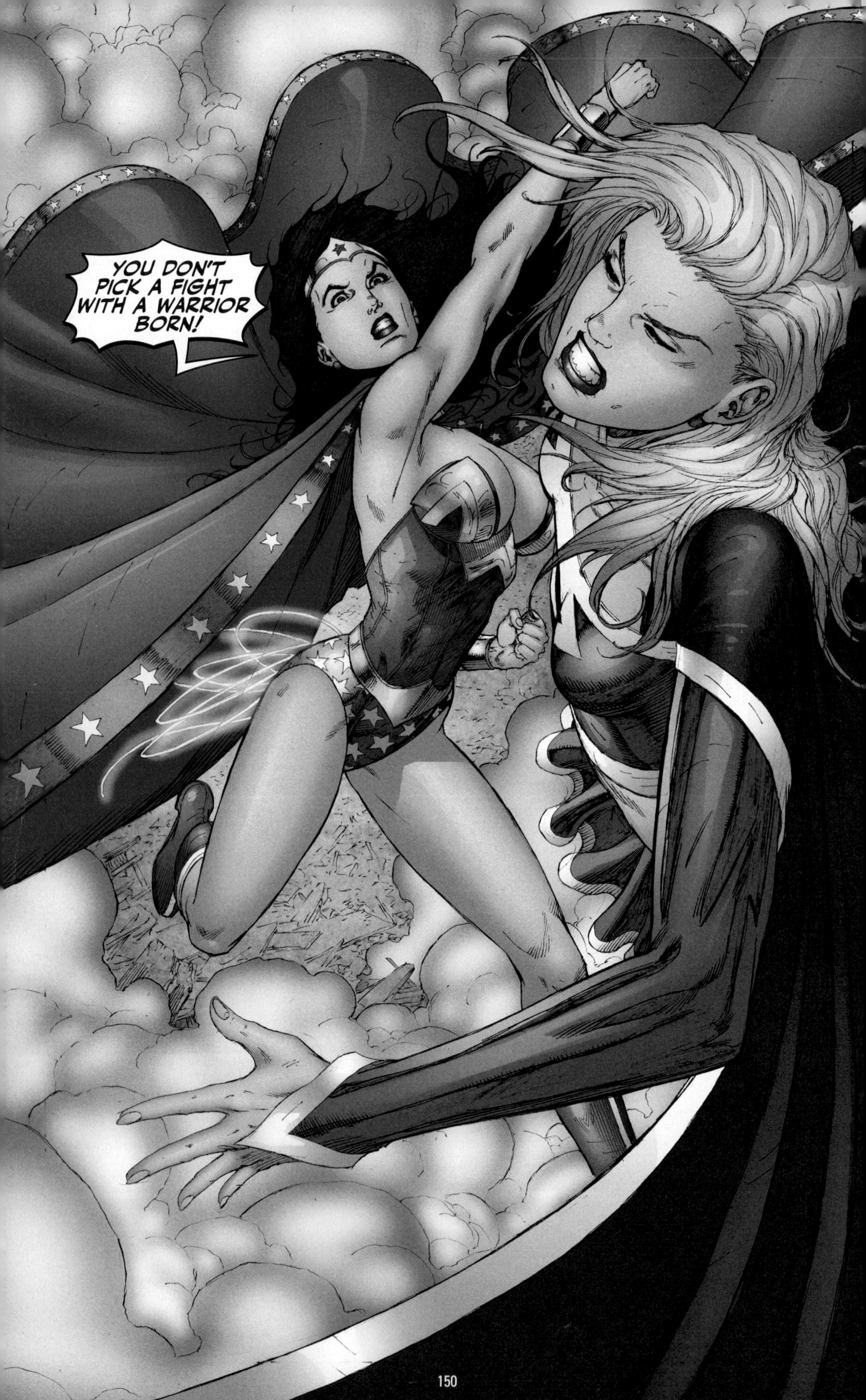
YOU DON'T PICK A FIGHT WITH A WARRIOR BORN!

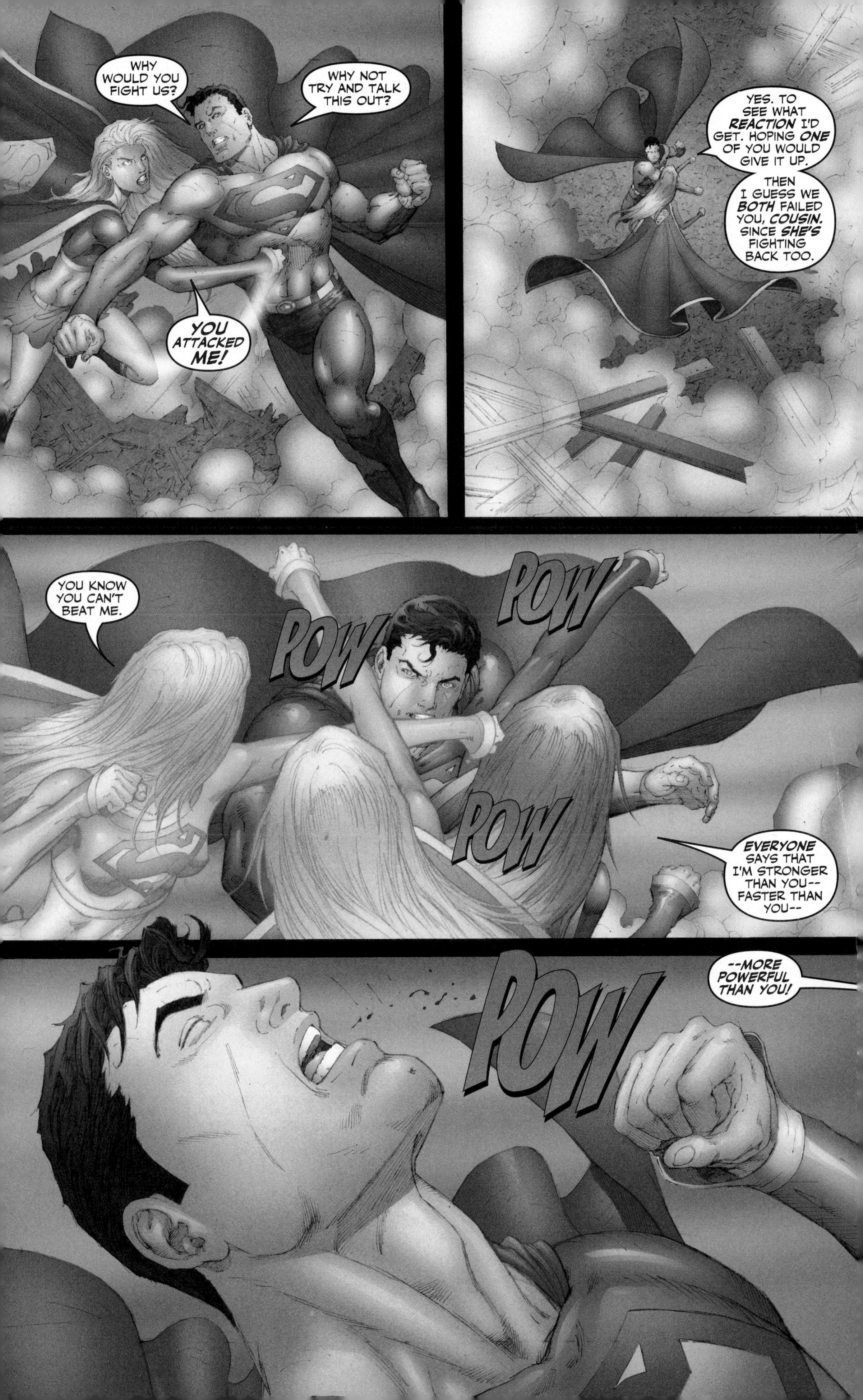
WHY WOULD YOU FIGHT US?
WHY NOT TRY AND TALK THIS OUT?
YOU ATTACKED ME!
YES. TO SEE WHAT REACTION I'D GET. HOPING ONE OF YOU WOULD GIVE IT UP.
THEN I GUESS WE BOTH FAILED YOU, COUSIN. SINCE SHE'S FIGHTING BACK TOO.
YOU KNOW YOU CAN'T BEAT ME.
POW
POW
POW
EVERYONE SAYS THAT I'M STRONGER THAN YOU-- FASTER THAN YOU--
--MORE POWERFUL THAN YOU!
POW

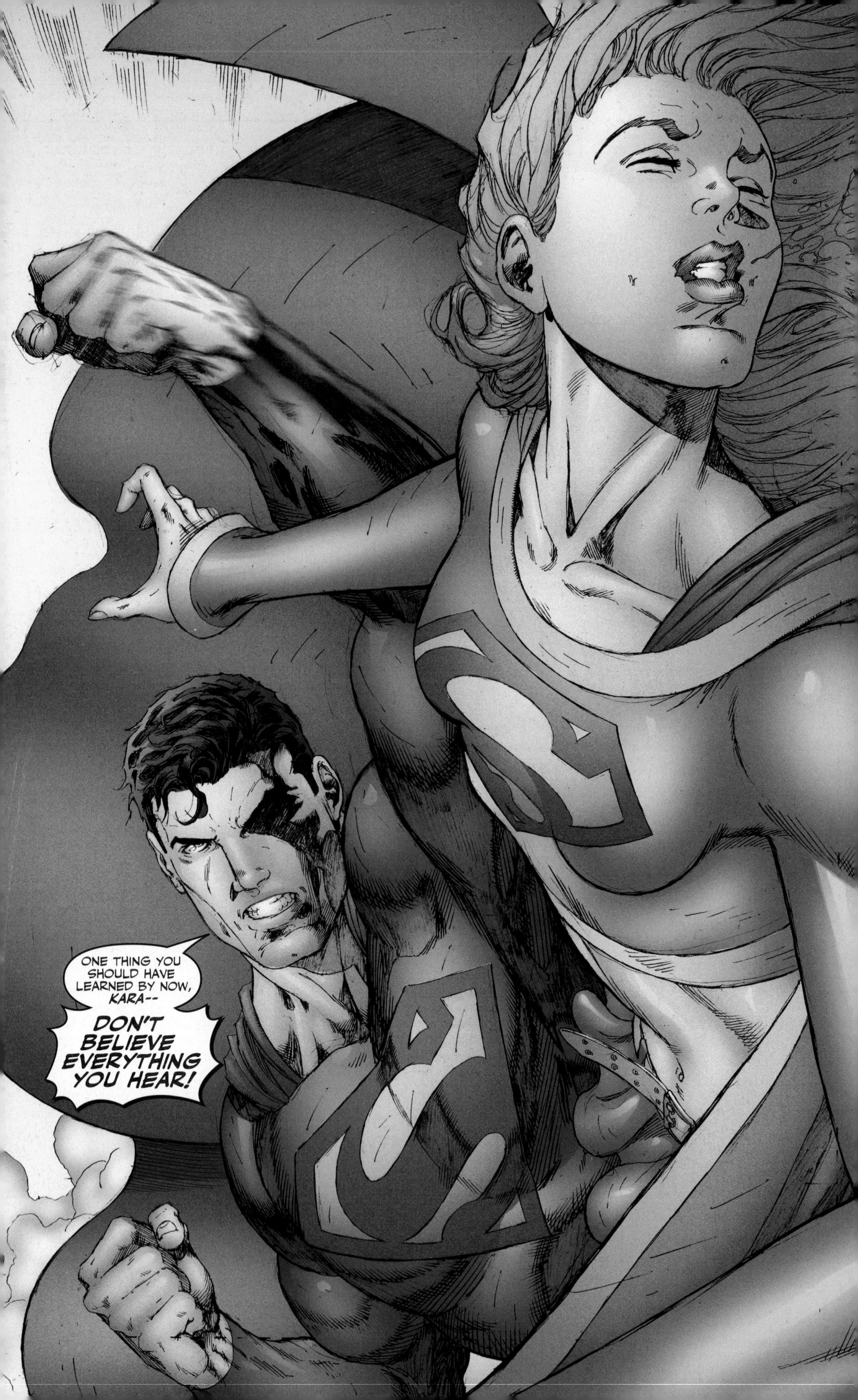
ONE THING YOU SHOULD HAVE LEARNED BY NOW, KARA--
DON'T BELIEVE EVERYTHING YOU HEAR!

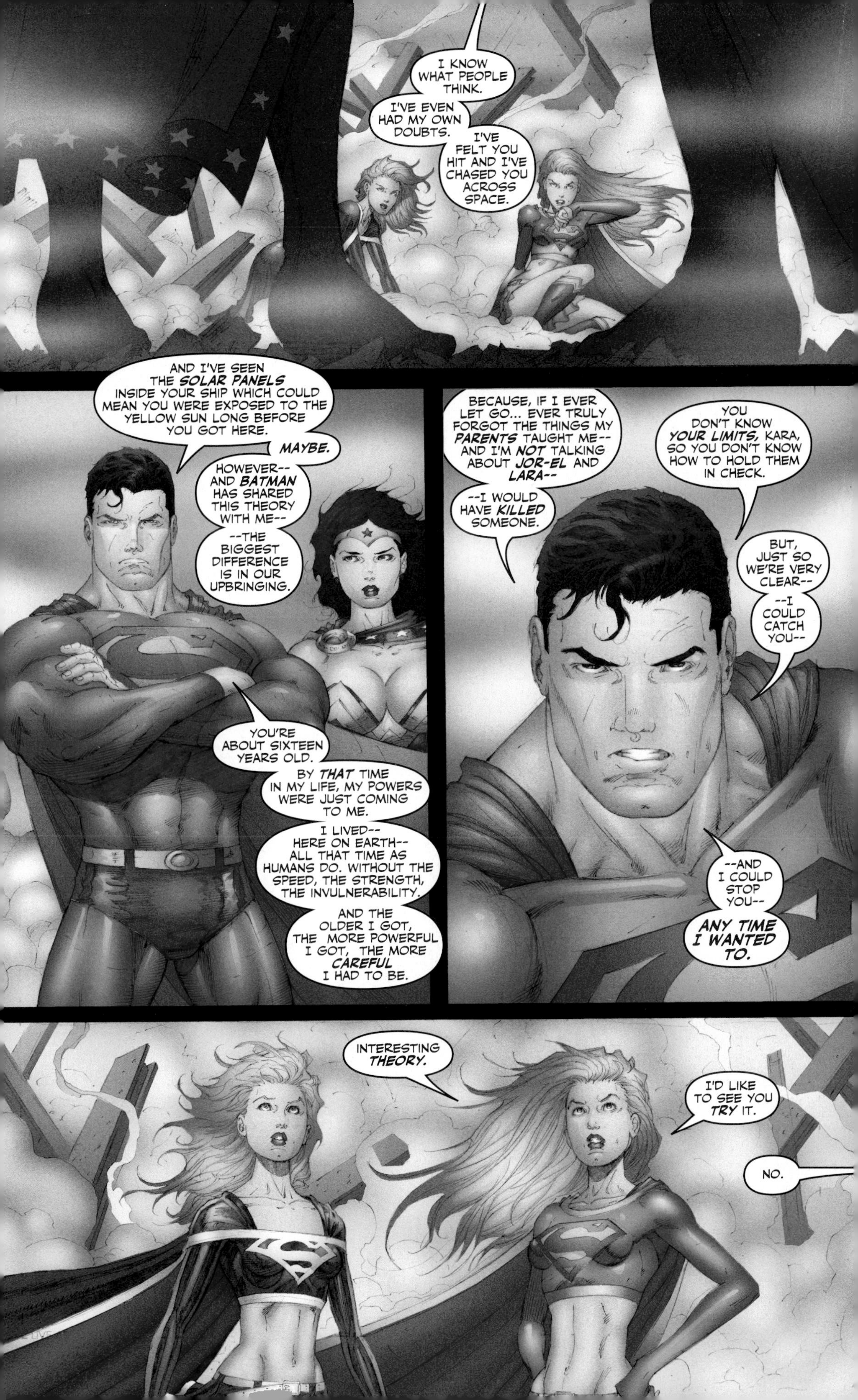
I KNOW WHAT PEOPLE THINK.
I'VE EVEN HAD MY OWN DOUBTS.
I'VE FELT YOU HIT AND I'VE CHASED YOU ACROSS SPACE.
AND I'VE SEEN THE SOLAR PANELS INSIDE YOUR SHIP WHICH COULD MEAN YOU WERE EXPOSED TO THE YELLOW SUN LONG BEFORE YOU GOT HERE.
MAYBE.
HOWEVER-- AND BATMAN HAS SHARED THIS THEORY WITH ME--
--THE BIGGEST DIFFERENCE IS IN OUR UPBRINGING.
YOU'RE ABOUT SIXTEEN YEARS OLD.
BY THAT TIME IN MY LIFE, MY POWERS WERE JUST COMING TO ME.
I LIVED-- HERE ON EARTH-- ALL THAT TIME AS HUMANS DO. WITHOUT THE SPEED, THE STRENGTH, THE INVULNERABILITY.
AND THE OLDER I GOT, THE MORE POWERFUL I GOT, THE MORE CAREFUL I HAD TO BE.
BECAUSE, IF I EVER LET GO... EVER TRULY FORGOT THE THINGS MY PARENTS TAUGHT ME-- AND I'M NOT TALKING ABOUT JOR-EL AND LARA--
--I WOULD HAVE KILLED SOMEONE.
YOU DON'T KNOW YOUR LIMITS, KARA, SO YOU DON'T KNOW HOW TO HOLD THEM IN CHECK.
BUT, JUST SO WE'RE VERY CLEAR--
--I COULD CATCH YOU--
--AND I COULD STOP YOU--
ANY TIME I WANTED TO.
INTERESTING THEORY.
I'D LIKE TO SEE YOU TRY IT.
NO.

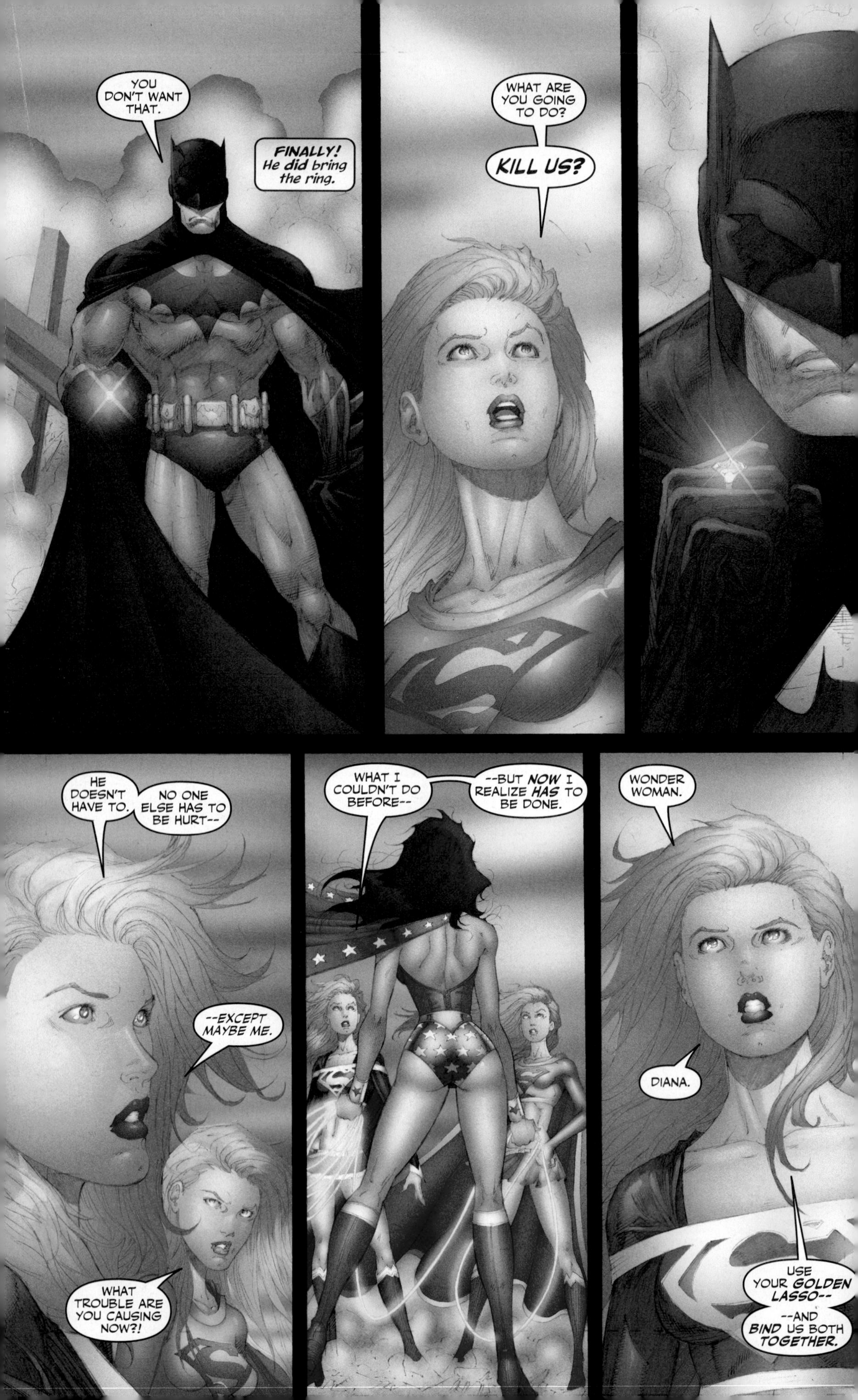
YOU DON'T WANT THAT.
FINALLY! He did bring the ring.
WHAT ARE YOU GOING TO DO? KILL US?
HE DOESN'T HAVE TO.
NO ONE ELSE HAS TO BE HURT--
--EXCEPT MAYBE ME.
WHAT TROUBLE ARE YOU CAUSING NOW?!
WHAT I COULDN'T DO BEFORE--
--BUT NOW I REALIZE HAS TO BE DONE.
WONDER WOMAN.
DIANA.
USE YOUR GOLDEN LASSO--
--AND BIND US BOTH TOGETHER.

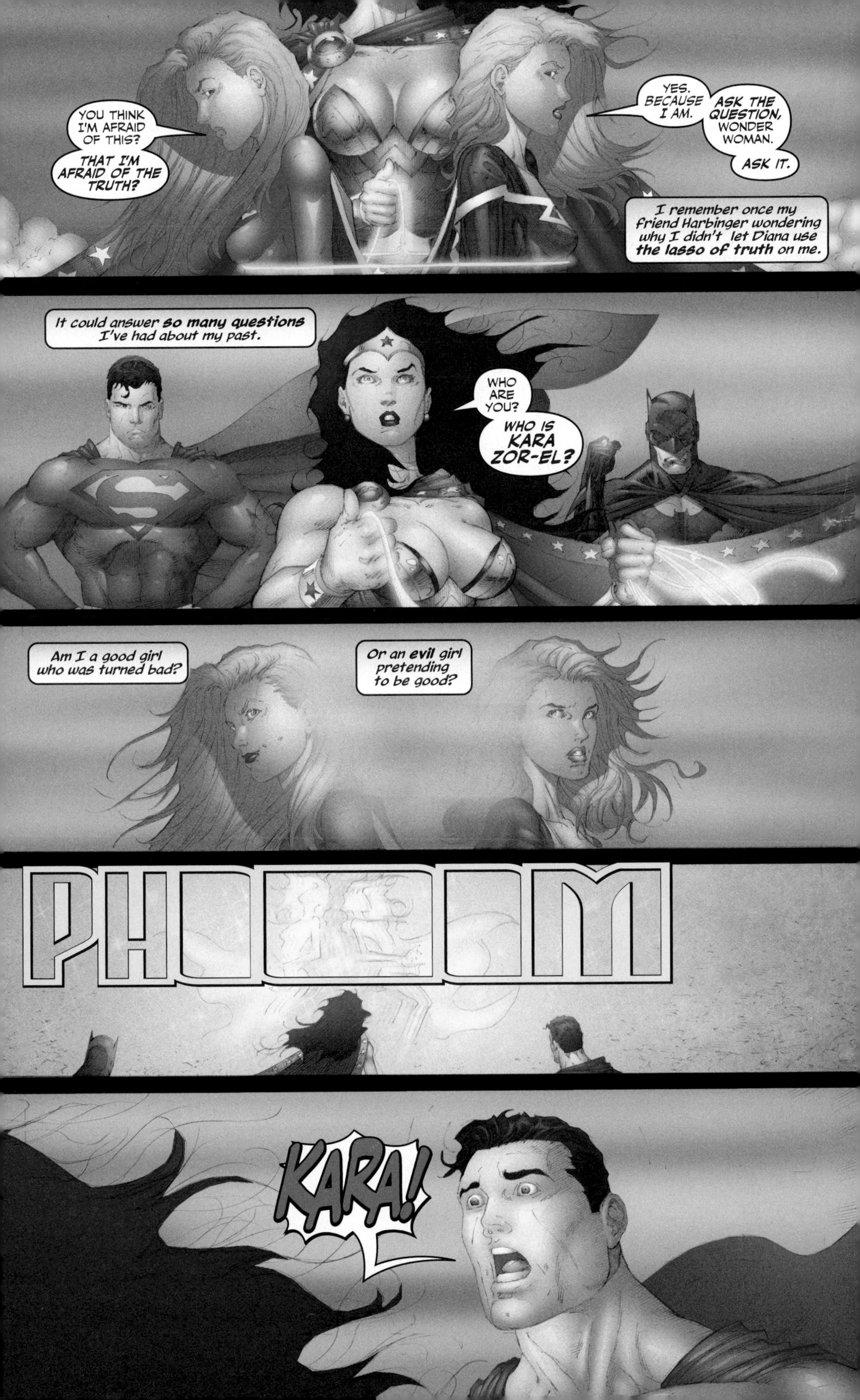
YOU THINK I'M AFRAID OF THIS?
THAT I'M AFRAID OF THE TRUTH?
YES. BECAUSE I AM.
ASK THE QUESTION, WONDER WOMAN.
ASK IT.
I remember once my friend Harbinger wondering why I didn't let Diana use the lasso of truth on me.
It could answer so many questions I've had about my past.
WHO ARE YOU?
WHO IS KARA ZOR-EL?
Am I a good girl who was turned bad?
Or an evil girl pretending to be good?
PHOOOOM
KARA!

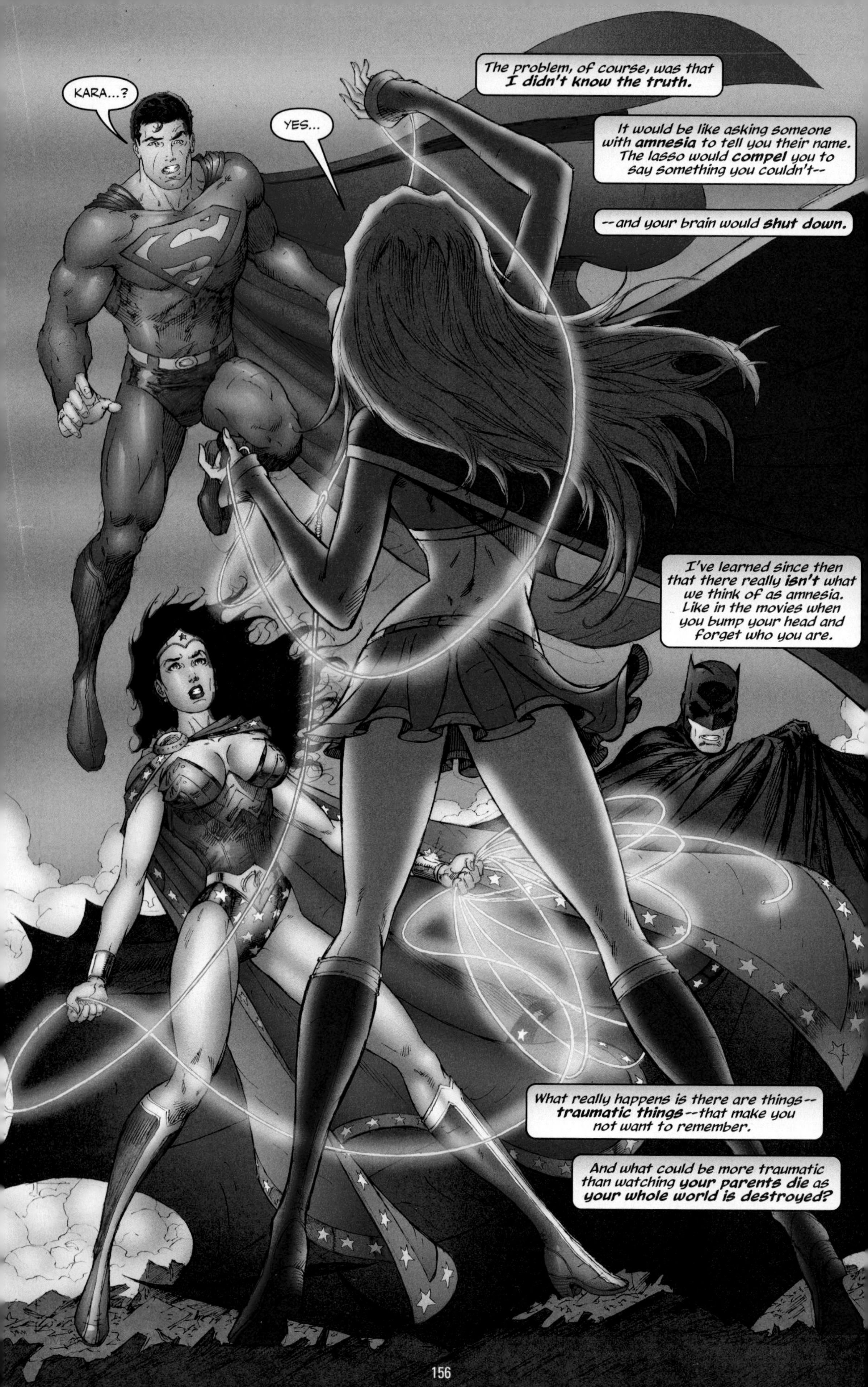
KARA...?
YES...
The problem, of course, was that I didn't know the truth.
It would be like asking someone with amnesia to tell you their name. The lasso would compel you to say something you couldn't--
--and your brain would shut down.
I've learned since then that there really isn't what we think of as amnesia. Like in the movies when you bump your head and forget who you are.
What really happens is there are things--traumatic things--that make you not want to remember.
And what could be more traumatic than watching your parents die as your whole world is destroyed?

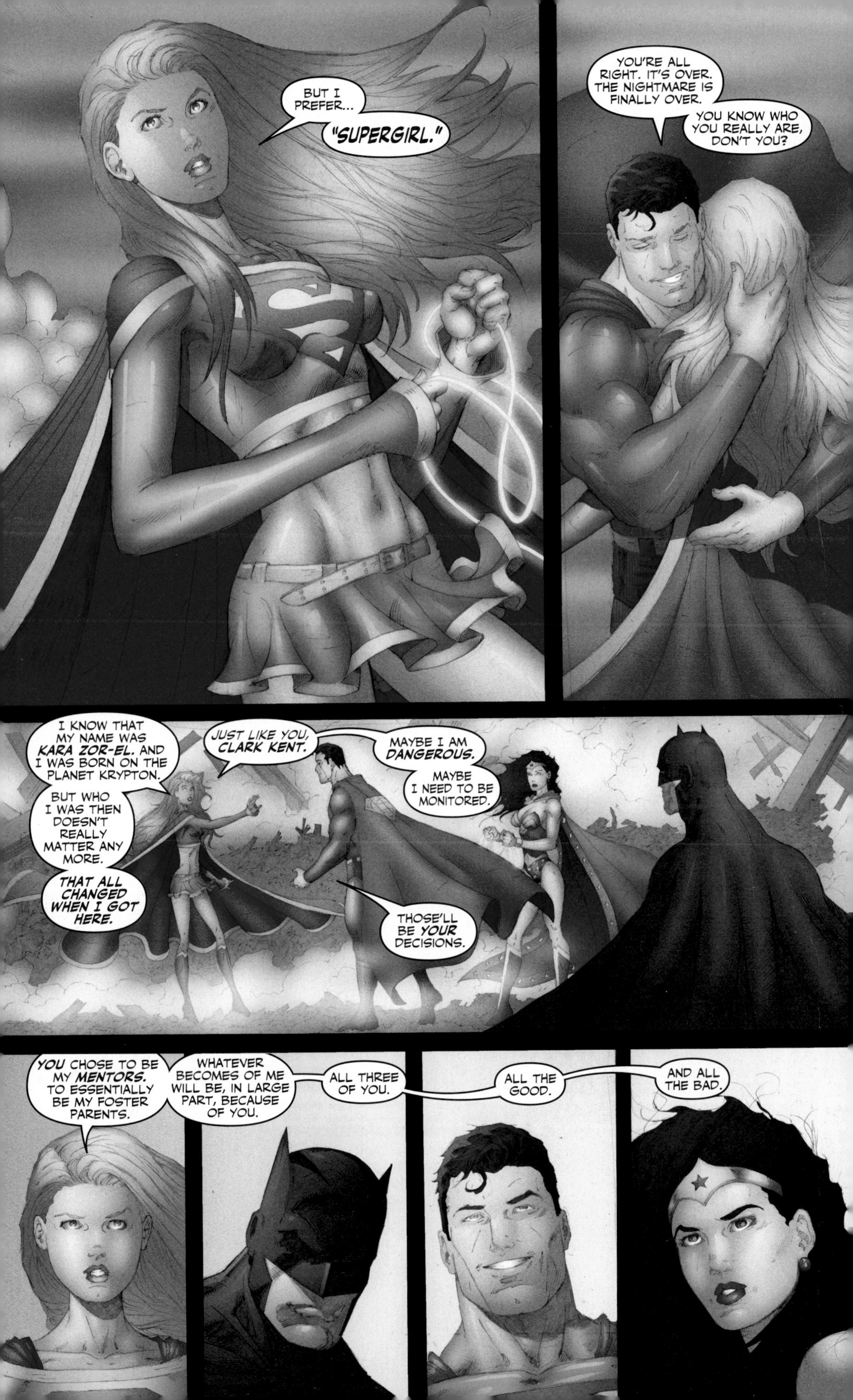
BUT I PREFER...
"SUPERGIRL."
YOU'RE ALL RIGHT. IT'S OVER. THE NIGHTMARE IS FINALLY OVER.
YOU KNOW WHO YOU REALLY ARE, DON'T YOU?
I KNOW THAT MY NAME WAS KARA ZOR-EL. AND I WAS BORN ON THE PLANET KRYPTON.
BUT WHO I WAS THEN DOESN'T REALLY MATTER ANY MORE.
THAT ALL CHANGED WHEN I GOT HERE.
JUST LIKE YOU, CLARK KENT.
MAYBE I AM DANGEROUS.
MAYBE I NEED TO BE MONITORED.
THOSE'LL BE YOUR DECISIONS.
YOU CHOSE TO BE MY MENTORS. TO ESSENTIALLY BE MY FOSTER PARENTS.
WHATEVER BECOMES OF ME WILL BE, IN LARGE PART, BECAUSE OF YOU.
ALL THREE OF YOU.
ALL THE GOOD.
AND ALL THE BAD.

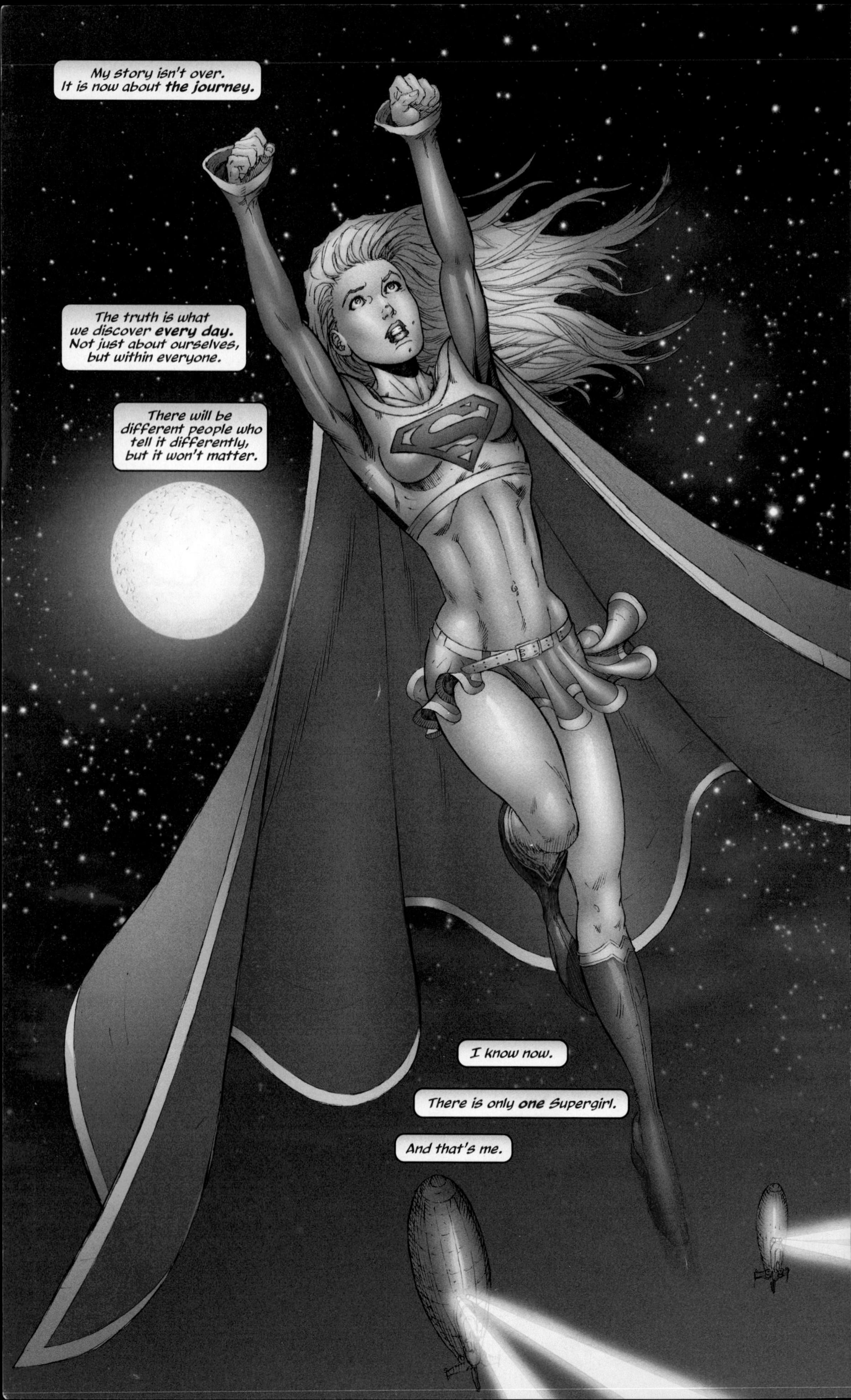
My story isn't over.
It is now about **the journey.**
The truth is what we discover **every day.** Not just about ourselves, but within everyone.
There will be different people who tell it differently, but it won't matter.
I know now.
There is only **one** Supergirl.
And that's me.

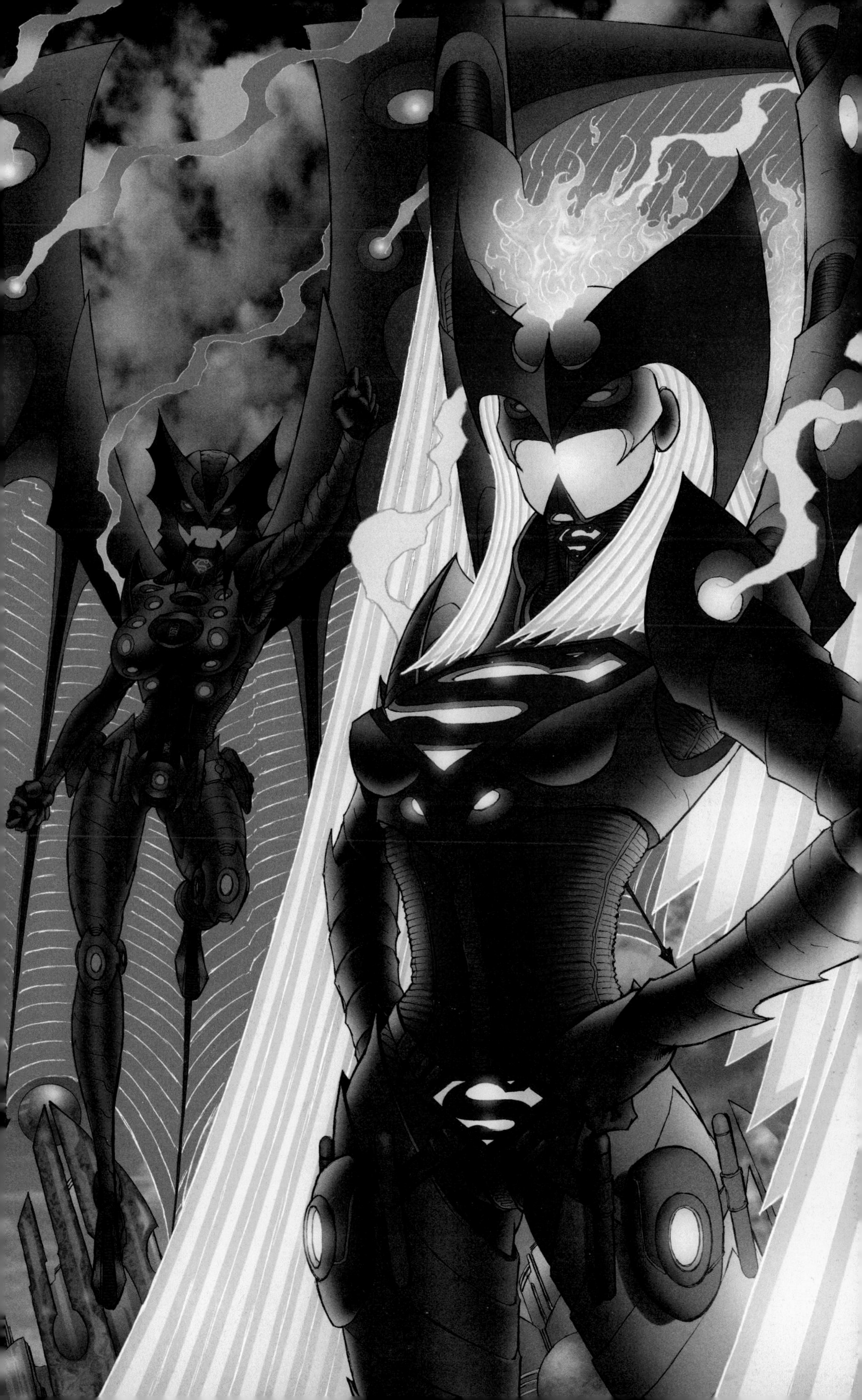

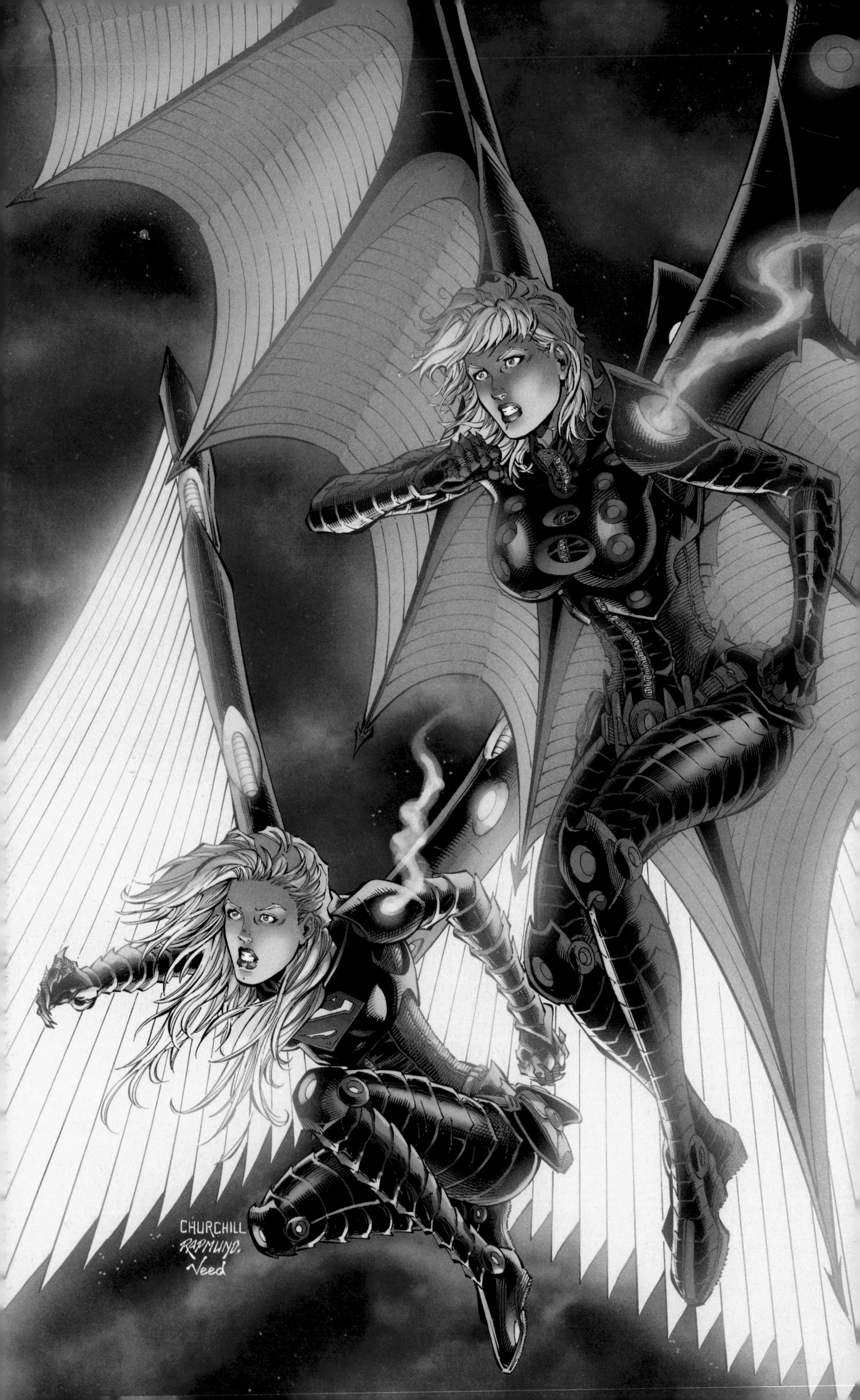
CHURCHILL
RAPMUND
Veed

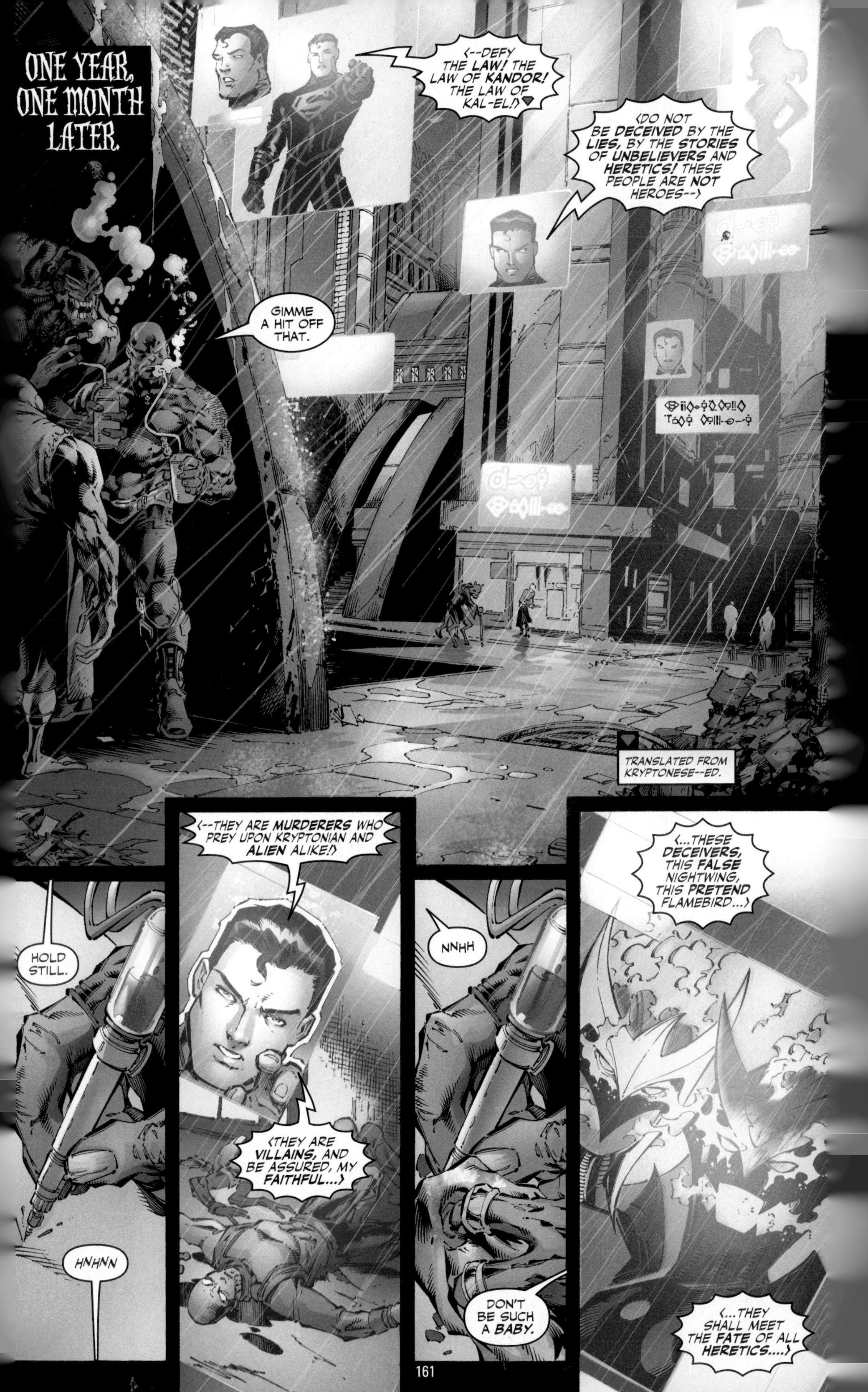
ONE YEAR, ONE MONTH LATER.
‹--DEFY THE LAW! THE LAW OF KANDOR! THE LAW OF KAL-EL!›
‹DO NOT BE DECEIVED BY THE LIES, BY THE STORIES OF UNBELIEVERS AND HERETICS! THESE PEOPLE ARE NOT HEROES--›
GIMME A HIT OFF THAT.
TRANSLATED FROM KRYPTONESE--ED.
HOLD STILL.
HNHNN
‹--THEY ARE MURDERERS WHO PREY UPON KRYPTONIAN AND ALIEN ALIKE!›
‹THEY ARE VILLAINS, AND BE ASSURED, MY FAITHFUL...›
NNHH
DON'T BE SUCH A BABY.
‹...THESE DECEIVERS, THIS FALSE NIGHTWING, THIS PRETEND FLAMEBIRD...›
‹...THEY SHALL MEET THE FATE OF ALL HERETICS....›

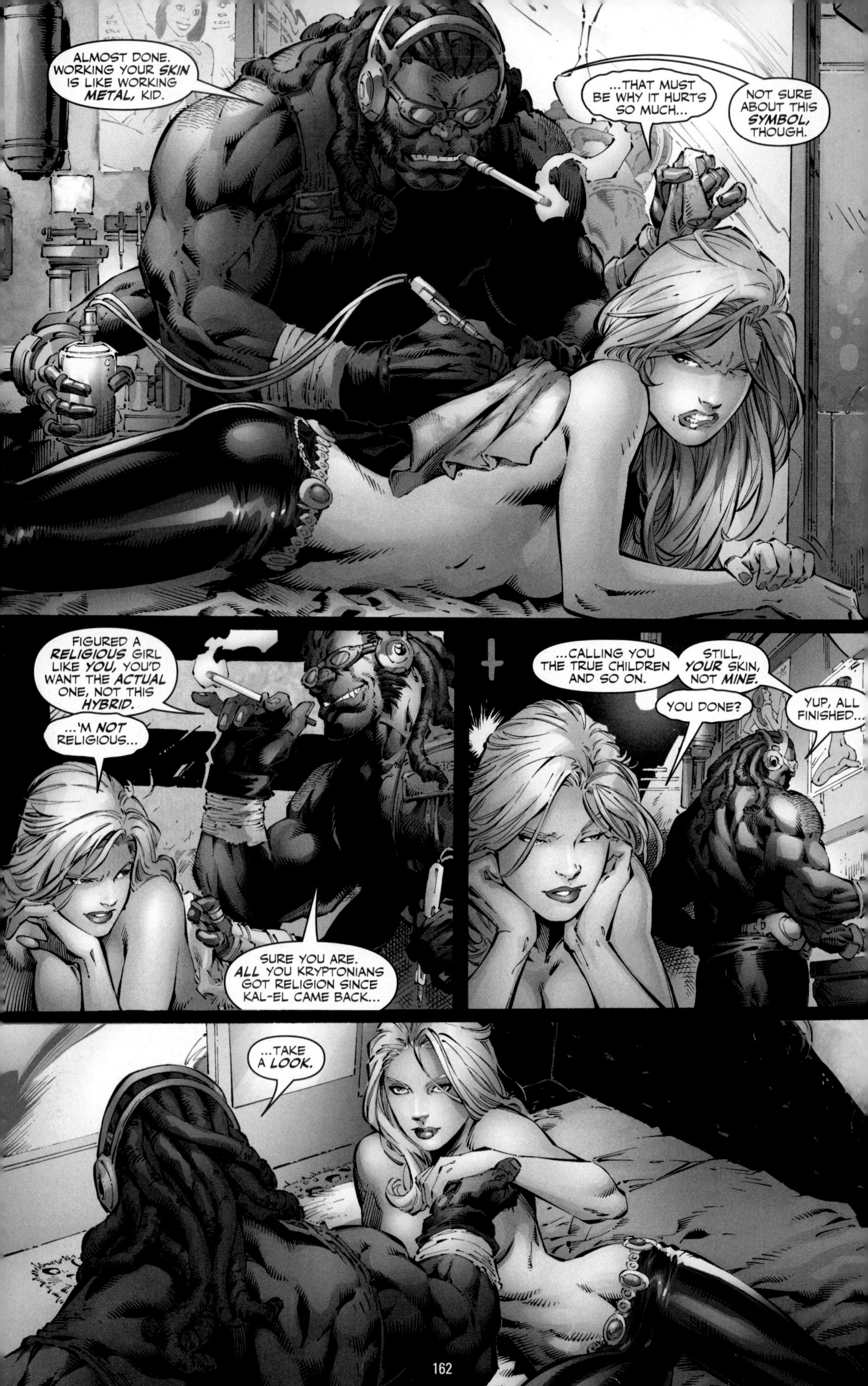

ALMOST DONE. WORKING YOUR SKIN IS LIKE WORKING METAL, KID.
...THAT MUST BE WHY IT HURTS SO MUCH...
NOT SURE ABOUT THIS SYMBOL, THOUGH.
FIGURED A RELIGIOUS GIRL LIKE YOU, YOU'D WANT THE ACTUAL ONE, NOT THIS HYBRID.
...'M NOT RELIGIOUS...
SURE YOU ARE. ALL YOU KRYPTONIANS GOT RELIGION SINCE KAL-EL CAME BACK...
...CALLING YOU THE TRUE CHILDREN AND SO ON.
STILL, YOUR SKIN, NOT MINE.
YOU DONE?
YUP, ALL FINISHED...
...TAKE A LOOK.

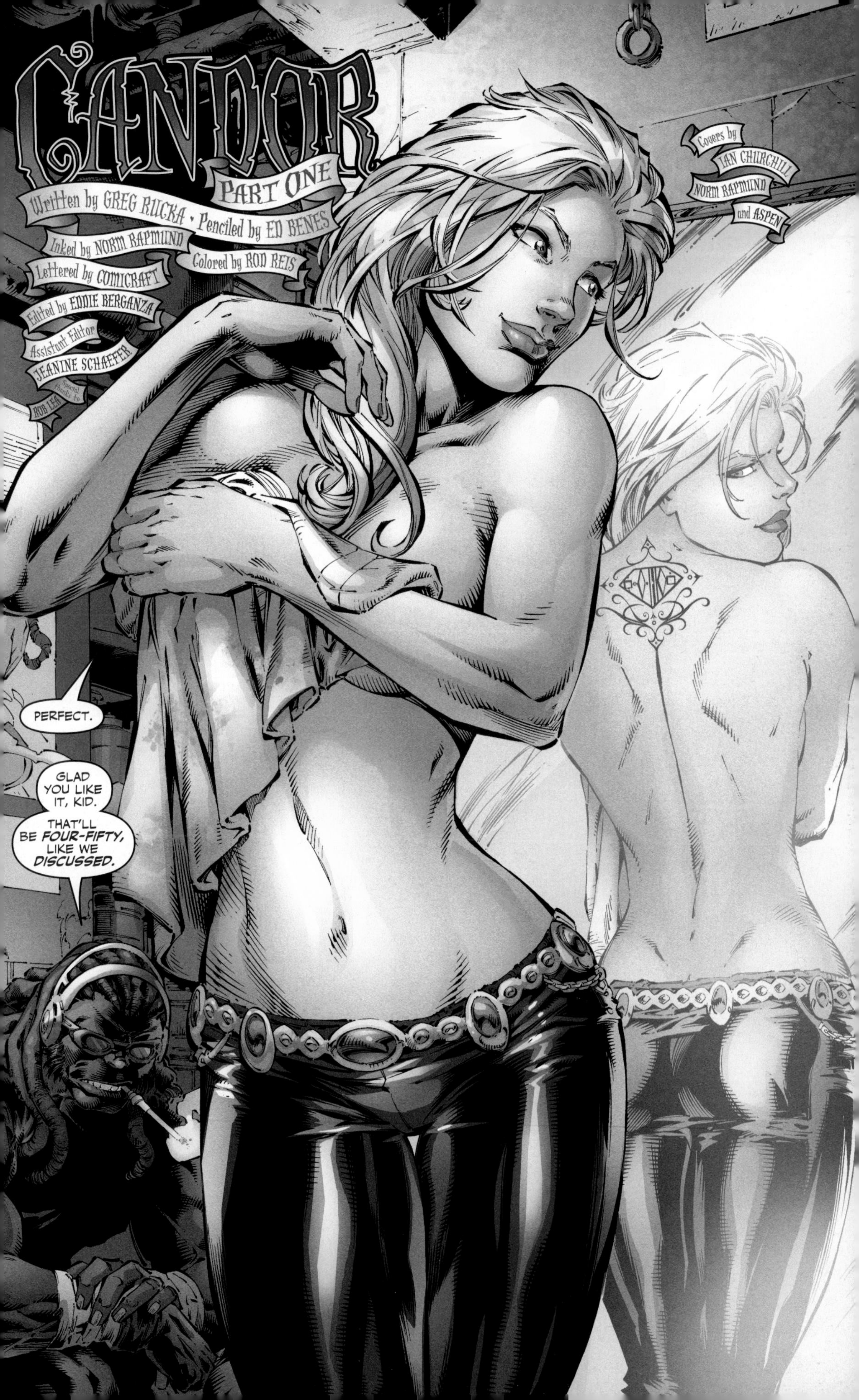
CANDOR
PART ONE
Written by GREG RUCKA • Penciled by ED BENES
Inked by NORM RAPMUND
Colored by ROD REIS
Lettered by COMICRAFT
Edited by EDDIE BERGANZA
Assistant Editor JEANINE SCHAEFER
Special thanks to ROB LEA
Covers by IAN CHURCHILL NORM RAPMUND and ASPEN
PERFECT.
GLAD YOU LIKE IT, KID.
THAT'LL BE FOUR-FIFTY, LIKE WE DISCUSSED.

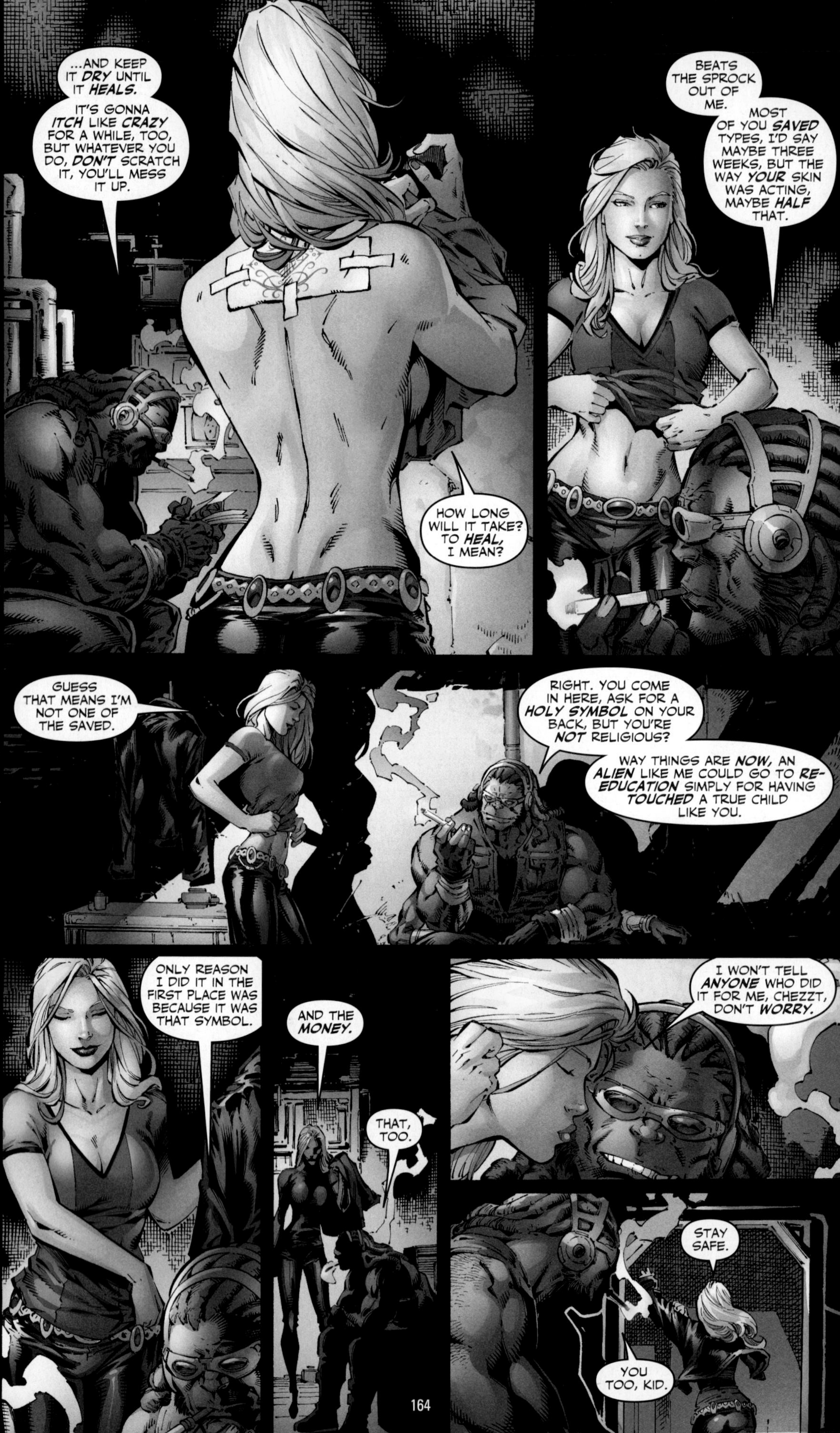
...AND KEEP IT DRY UNTIL IT HEALS.
IT'S GONNA ITCH LIKE CRAZY FOR A WHILE, TOO, BUT WHATEVER YOU DO, DON'T SCRATCH IT, YOU'LL MESS IT UP.
HOW LONG WILL IT TAKE? TO HEAL, I MEAN?
BEATS THE SPROCK OUT OF ME.
MOST OF YOU SAVED TYPES, I'D SAY MAYBE THREE WEEKS, BUT THE WAY YOUR SKIN WAS ACTING, MAYBE HALF THAT.
GUESS THAT MEANS I'M NOT ONE OF THE SAVED.
RIGHT. YOU COME IN HERE, ASK FOR A HOLY SYMBOL ON YOUR BACK, BUT YOU'RE NOT RELIGIOUS?
WAY THINGS ARE NOW, AN ALIEN LIKE ME COULD GO TO RE-EDUCATION SIMPLY FOR HAVING TOUCHED A TRUE CHILD LIKE YOU.
ONLY REASON I DID IT IN THE FIRST PLACE WAS BECAUSE IT WAS THAT SYMBOL.
AND THE MONEY.
THAT, TOO.
I WON'T TELL ANYONE WHO DID IT FOR ME, CHEZZT, DON'T WORRY.
STAY SAFE.
YOU TOO, KID.

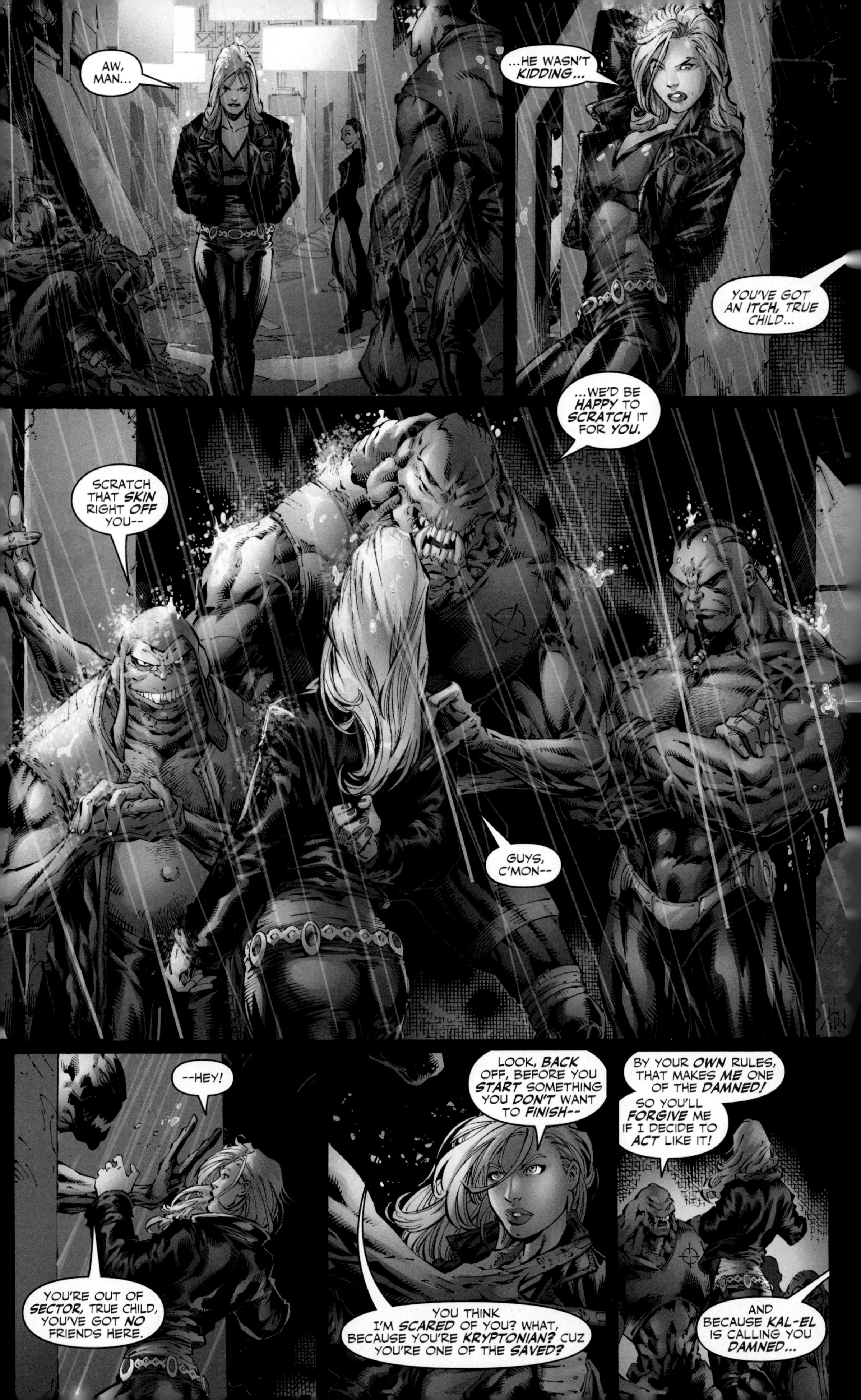
AW, MAN...
...HE WASN'T KIDDING...
YOU'VE GOT AN ITCH, TRUE CHILD...
...WE'D BE HAPPY TO SCRATCH IT FOR YOU.
SCRATCH THAT SKIN RIGHT OFF YOU--
GUYS, C'MON--
--HEY!
YOU'RE OUT OF SECTOR, TRUE CHILD, YOU'VE GOT NO FRIENDS HERE.
LOOK, BACK OFF, BEFORE YOU START SOMETHING YOU DON'T WANT TO FINISH--
YOU THINK I'M SCARED OF YOU? WHAT, BECAUSE YOU'RE KRYPTONIAN? CUZ YOU'RE ONE OF THE SAVED?
AND BECAUSE KAL-EL IS CALLING YOU DAMNED...
BY YOUR OWN RULES, THAT MAKES ME ONE OF THE DAMNED!
SO YOU'LL FORGIVE ME IF I DECIDE TO ACT LIKE IT!

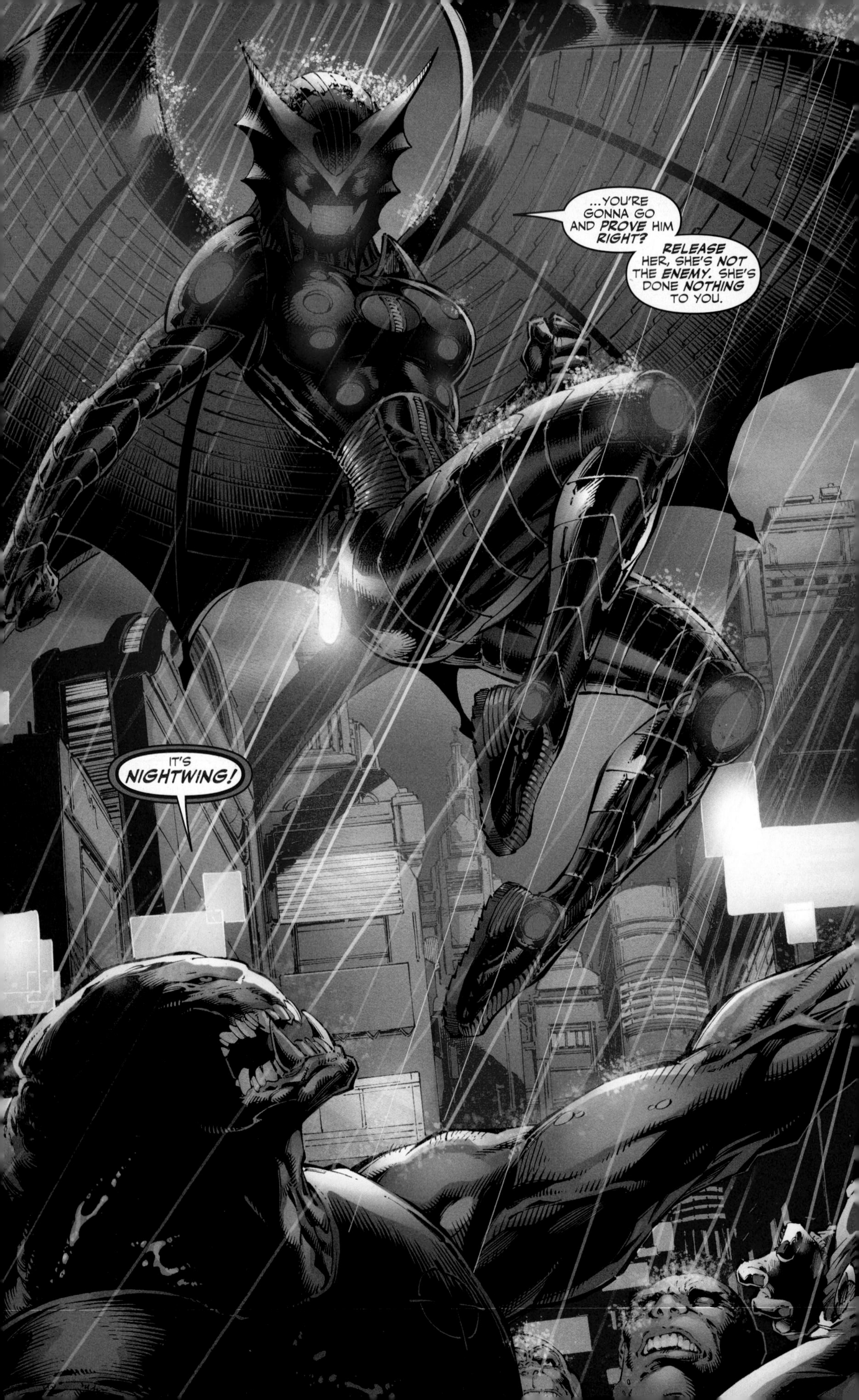
...YOU'RE GONNA GO AND PROVE HIM RIGHT?
RELEASE HER, SHE'S NOT THE ENEMY. SHE'S DONE NOTHING TO YOU.
IT'S NIGHTWING!

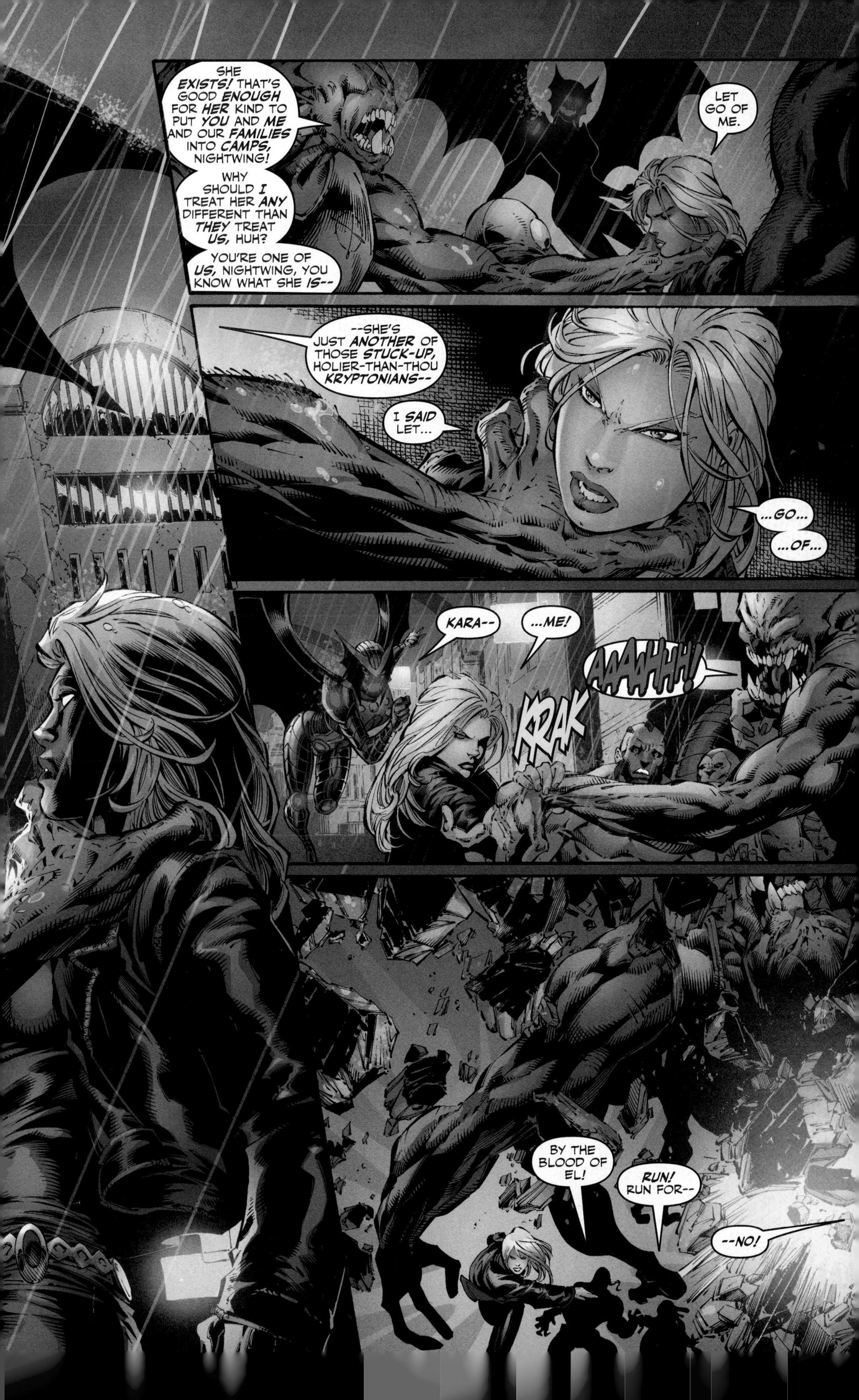
SHE EXISTS! THAT'S GOOD ENOUGH FOR HER KIND TO PUT YOU AND ME AND OUR FAMILIES INTO CAMPS, NIGHTWING!
WHY SHOULD I TREAT HER ANY DIFFERENT THAN THEY TREAT US, HUH?
YOU'RE ONE OF US, NIGHTWING, YOU KNOW WHAT SHE IS--
LET GO OF ME.
--SHE'S JUST ANOTHER OF THOSE STUCK-UP, HOLIER-THAN-THOU KRYPTONIANS--
I SAID LET...
...GO...
...OF...
KARA--
...ME!
AAAAHHH!
KRAK
BY THE BLOOD OF EL!
RUN! RUN FOR--
--NO!

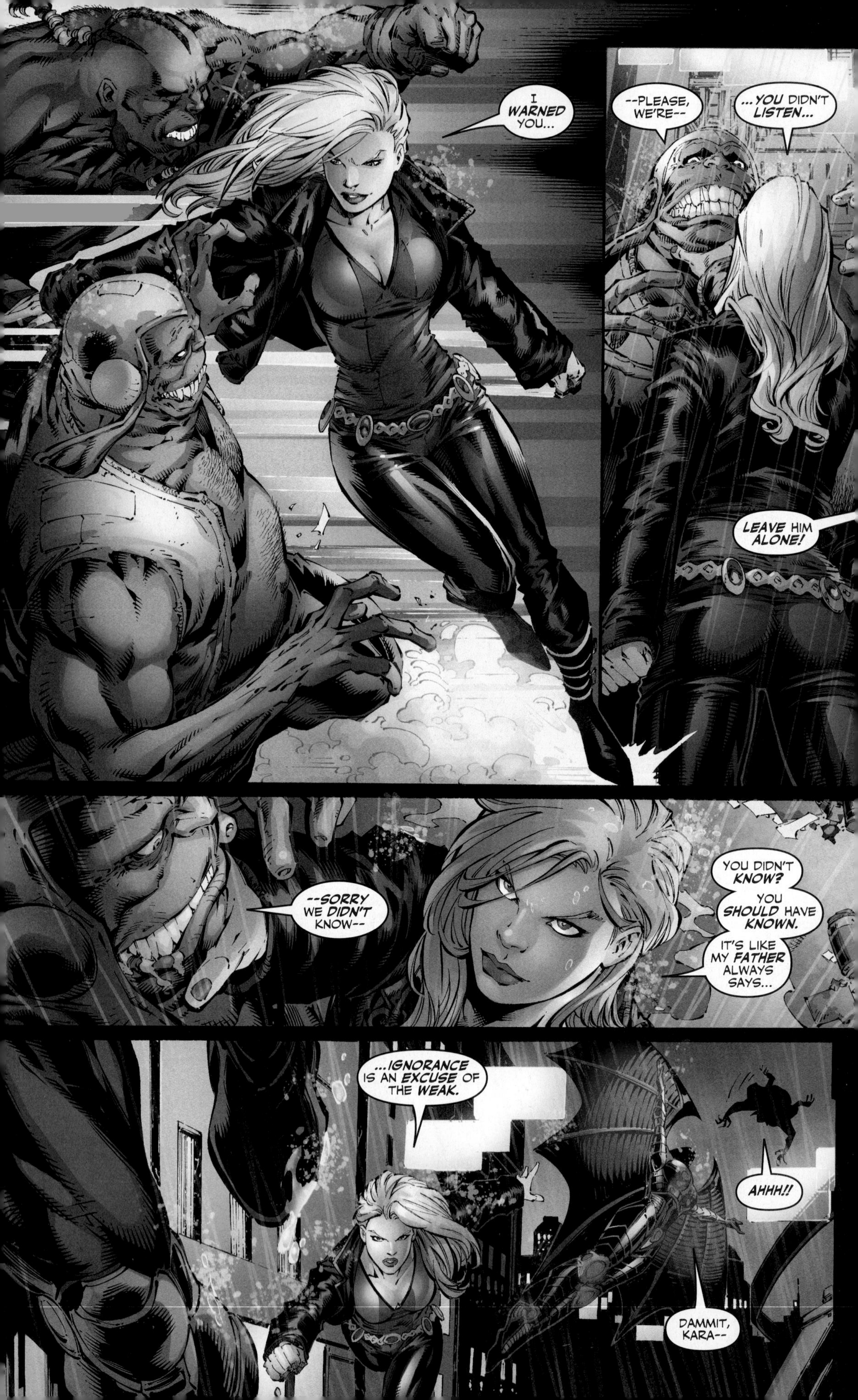

I WARNED YOU...
--PLEASE, WE'RE--
...YOU DIDN'T LISTEN...
LEAVE HIM ALONE!
--SORRY WE DIDN'T KNOW--
YOU DIDN'T KNOW?
YOU SHOULD HAVE KNOWN.
IT'S LIKE MY FATHER ALWAYS SAYS...
...IGNORANCE IS AN EXCUSE OF THE WEAK.
AHHH!!
DAMMIT, KARA--

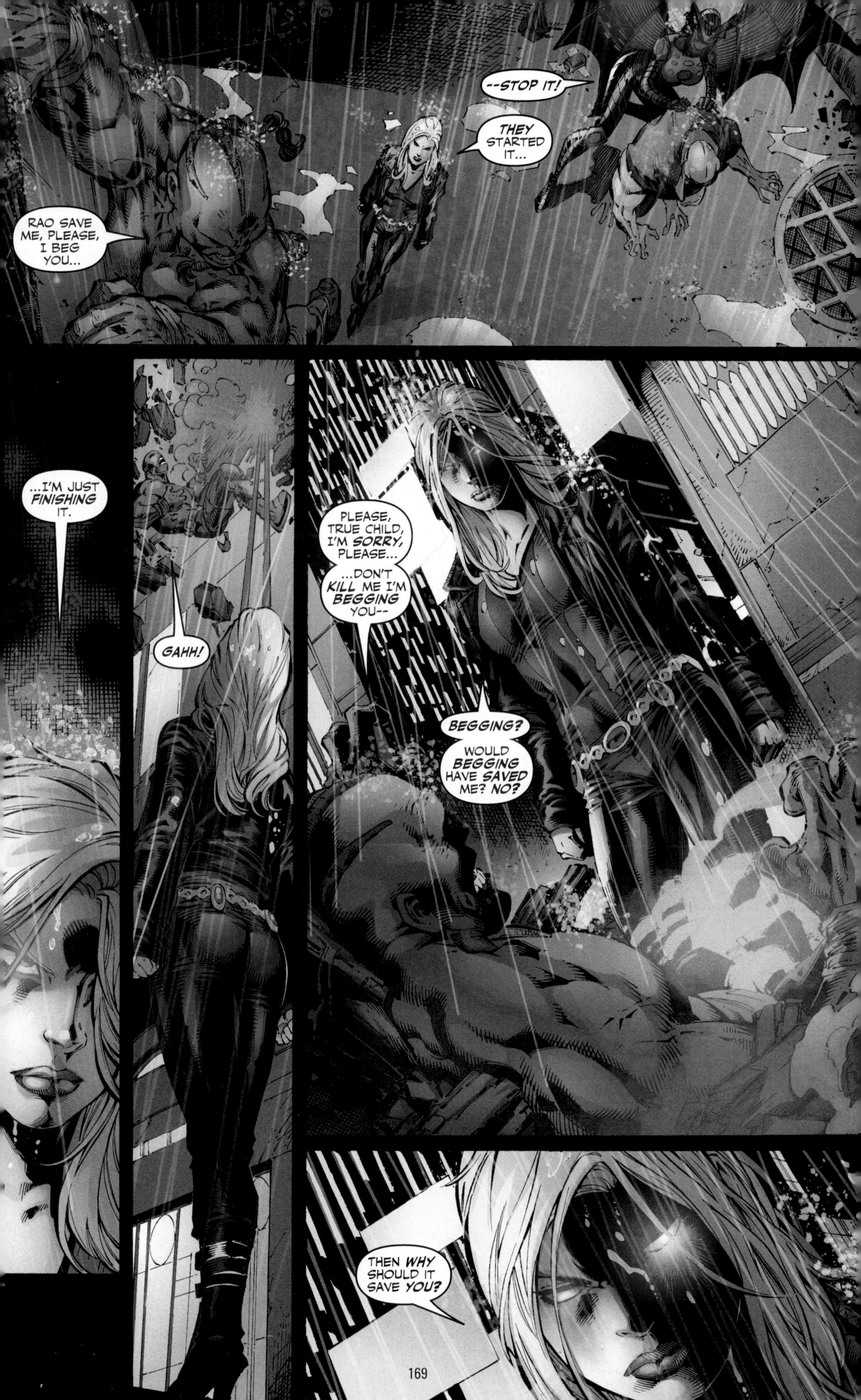
--STOP IT!
THEY STARTED IT...
RAO SAVE ME, PLEASE, I BEG YOU...
...I'M JUST FINISHING IT.
GAHH!
PLEASE, TRUE CHILD, I'M SORRY, PLEASE...
...DON'T KILL ME I'M BEGGING YOU--
BEGGING?
WOULD BEGGING HAVE SAVED ME? NO?
THEN WHY SHOULD IT SAVE YOU?

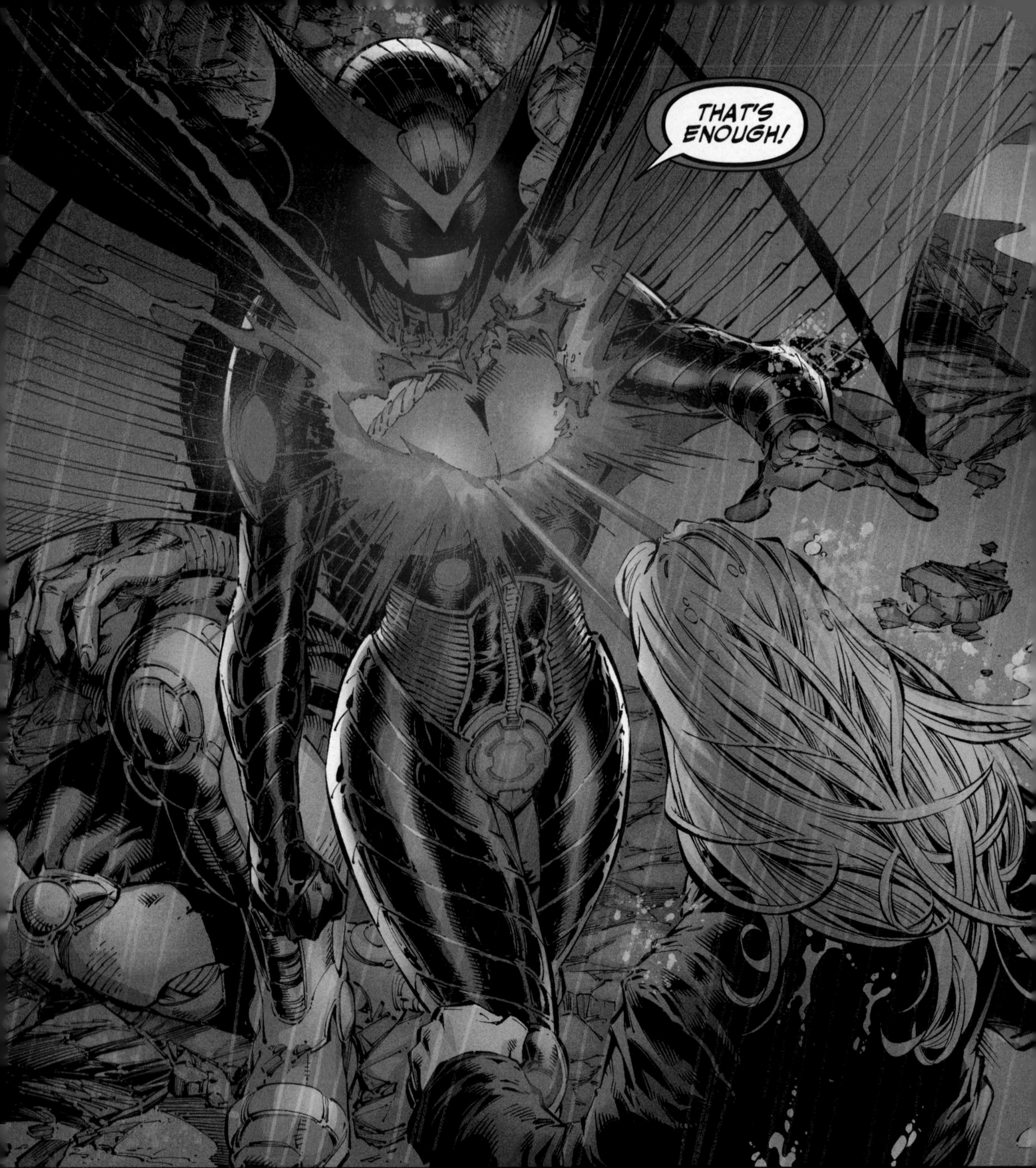
THAT'S ENOUGH!

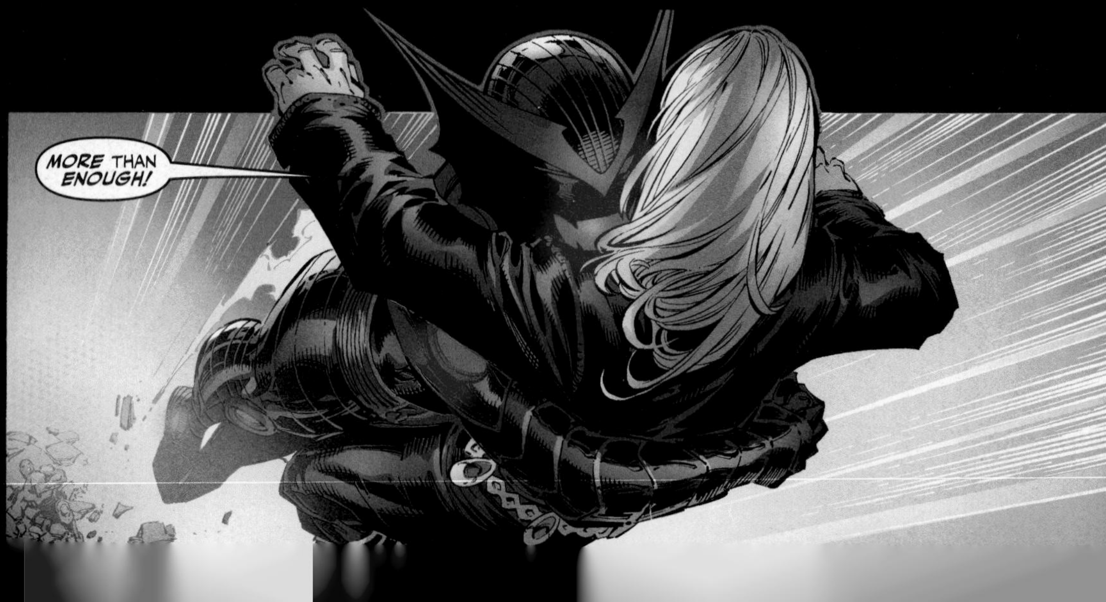
MORE THAN ENOUGH!

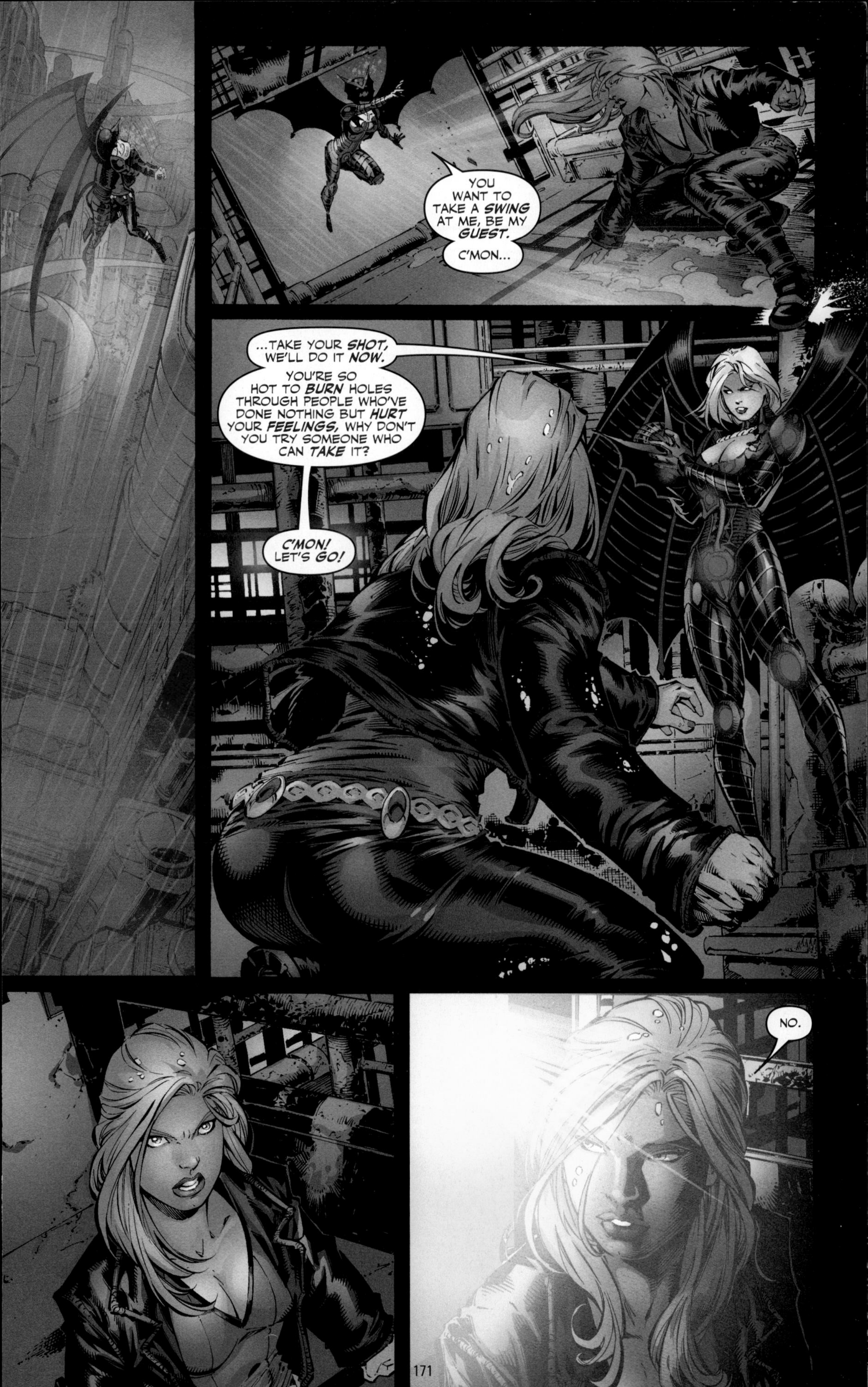
YOU WANT TO TAKE A *SWING* AT ME, BE MY *GUEST.*
C'MON...
...TAKE YOUR *SHOT,* WE'LL DO IT *NOW.*
YOU'RE SO HOT TO *BURN* HOLES THROUGH PEOPLE WHO'VE DONE NOTHING BUT *HURT* YOUR *FEELINGS,* WHY DON'T YOU TRY SOMEONE WHO CAN *TAKE* IT?
C'MON! LET'S *GO!*
NO.

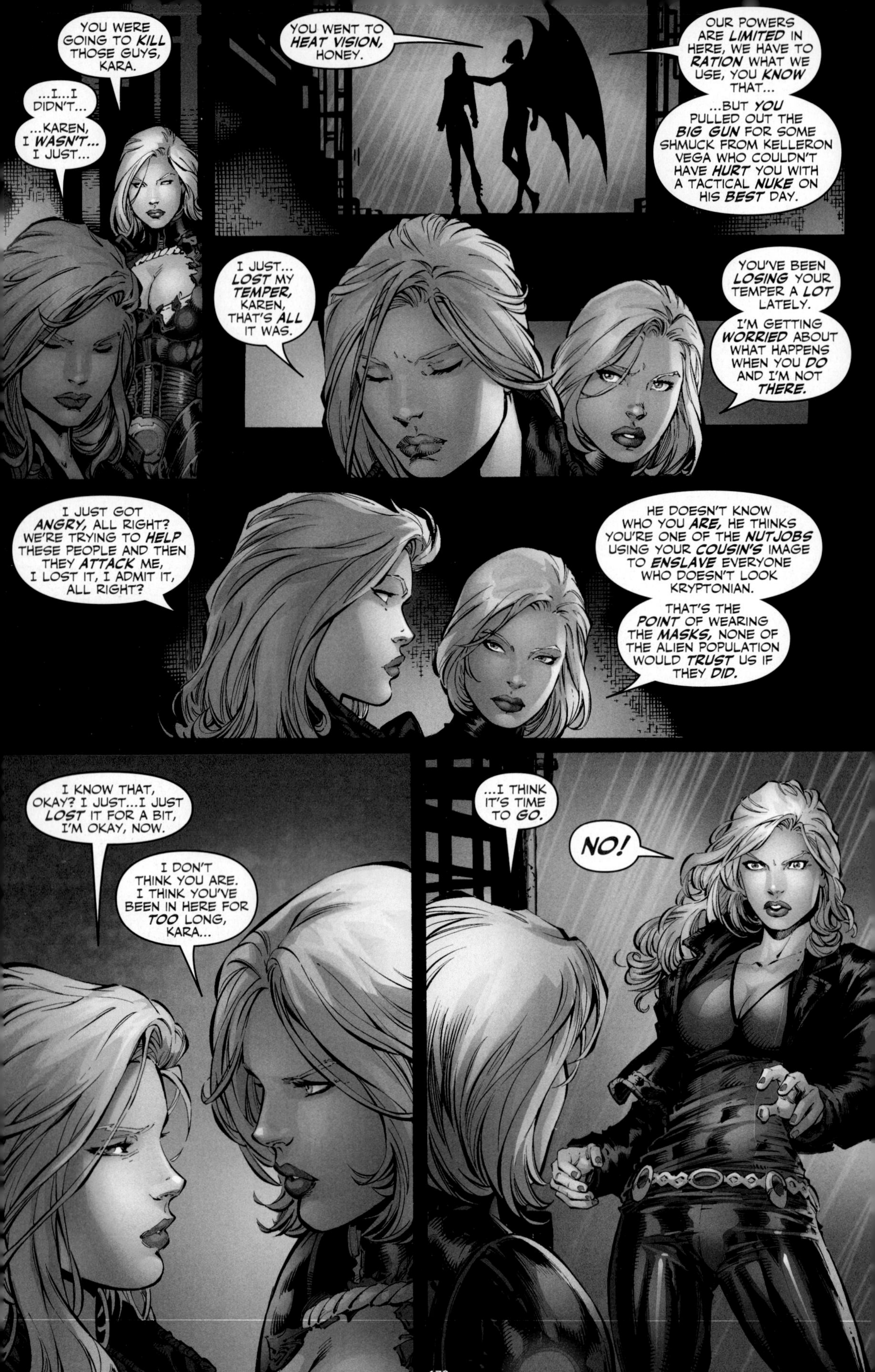
YOU WERE GOING TO KILL THOSE GUYS, KARA.
...I...I DIDN'T...
...KAREN, I WASN'T... I JUST...
YOU WENT TO HEAT VISION, HONEY.
OUR POWERS ARE LIMITED IN HERE, WE HAVE TO RATION WHAT WE USE, YOU KNOW THAT...
...BUT YOU PULLED OUT THE BIG GUN FOR SOME SHMUCK FROM KELLERON VEGA WHO COULDN'T HAVE HURT YOU WITH A TACTICAL NUKE ON HIS BEST DAY.
I JUST... LOST MY TEMPER, KAREN, THAT'S ALL IT WAS.
YOU'VE BEEN LOSING YOUR TEMPER A LOT LATELY.
I'M GETTING WORRIED ABOUT WHAT HAPPENS WHEN YOU DO AND I'M NOT THERE.
I JUST GOT ANGRY, ALL RIGHT? WE'RE TRYING TO HELP THESE PEOPLE AND THEN THEY ATTACK ME, I LOST IT, I ADMIT IT, ALL RIGHT?
HE DOESN'T KNOW WHO YOU ARE, HE THINKS YOU'RE ONE OF THE NUTJOBS USING YOUR COUSIN'S IMAGE TO ENSLAVE EVERYONE WHO DOESN'T LOOK KRYPTONIAN.
THAT'S THE POINT OF WEARING THE MASKS, NONE OF THE ALIEN POPULATION WOULD TRUST US IF THEY DID.
I KNOW THAT, OKAY? I JUST...I JUST LOST IT FOR A BIT, I'M OKAY, NOW.
I DON'T THINK YOU ARE. I THINK YOU'VE BEEN IN HERE FOR TOO LONG, KARA...
...I THINK IT'S TIME TO GO.
NO!

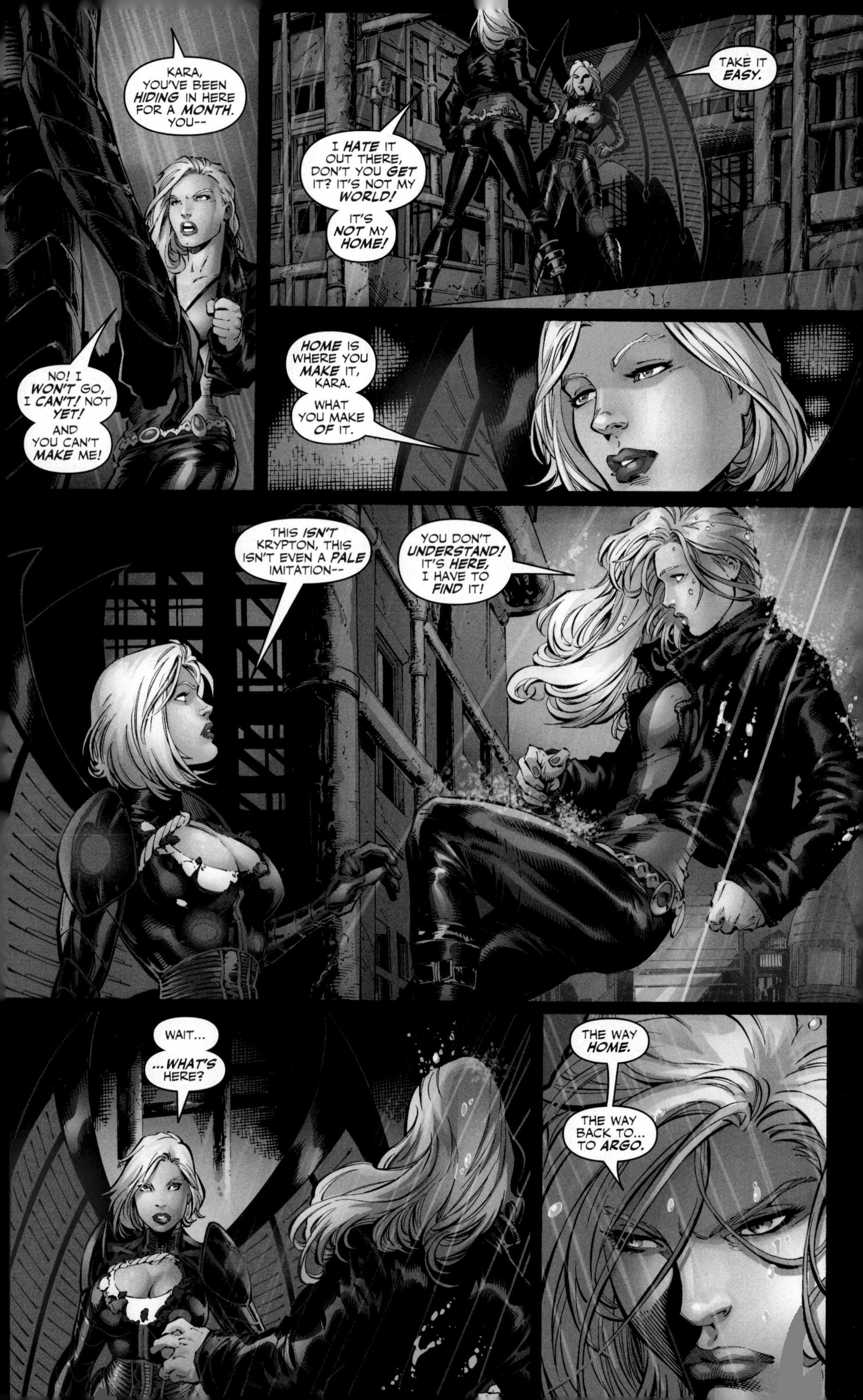
KARA, YOU'VE BEEN HIDING IN HERE FOR A MONTH. YOU--
I HATE IT OUT THERE, DON'T YOU GET IT? IT'S NOT MY WORLD!
IT'S NOT MY HOME!
TAKE IT EASY.
NO! I WON'T GO, I CAN'T! NOT YET!
AND YOU CAN'T MAKE ME!
HOME IS WHERE YOU MAKE IT, KARA.
WHAT YOU MAKE OF IT.
THIS ISN'T KRYPTON, THIS ISN'T EVEN A PALE IMITATION--
YOU DON'T UNDERSTAND! IT'S HERE, I HAVE TO FIND IT!
WAIT...
...WHAT'S HERE?
THE WAY HOME.
THE WAY BACK TO... TO ARGO.

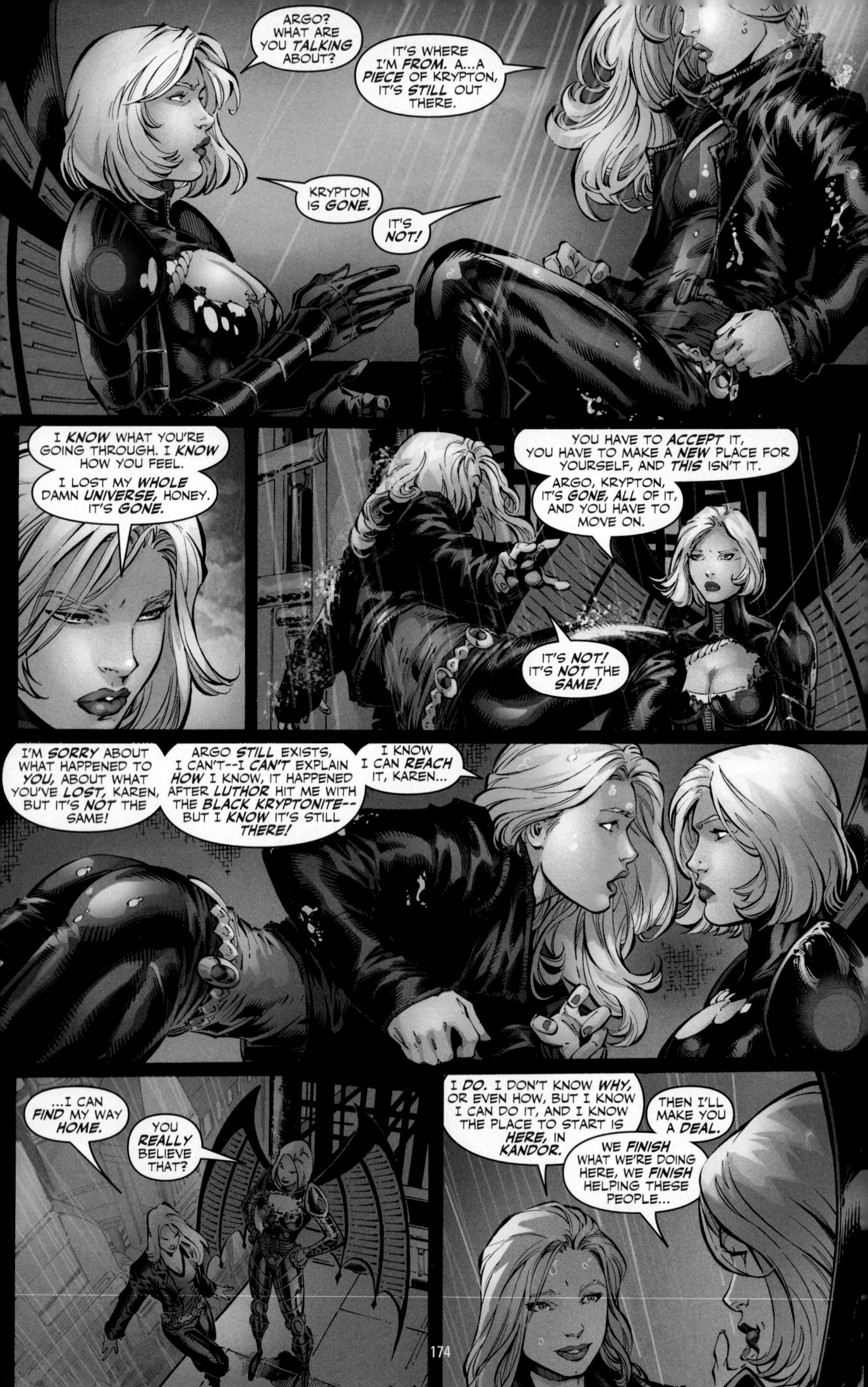
ARGO? WHAT ARE YOU TALKING ABOUT?
IT'S WHERE I'M FROM. A...A PIECE OF KRYPTON, IT'S STILL OUT THERE.
KRYPTON IS GONE.
IT'S NOT!
I KNOW WHAT YOU'RE GOING THROUGH. I KNOW HOW YOU FEEL.
I LOST MY WHOLE DAMN UNIVERSE, HONEY. IT'S GONE.
YOU HAVE TO ACCEPT IT, YOU HAVE TO MAKE A NEW PLACE FOR YOURSELF, AND THIS ISN'T IT.
ARGO, KRYPTON, IT'S GONE, ALL OF IT, AND YOU HAVE TO MOVE ON.
IT'S NOT! IT'S NOT THE SAME!
I'M SORRY ABOUT WHAT HAPPENED TO YOU, ABOUT WHAT YOU'VE LOST, KAREN, BUT IT'S NOT THE SAME!
ARGO STILL EXISTS, I CAN'T--I CAN'T EXPLAIN HOW I KNOW, IT HAPPENED AFTER LUTHOR HIT ME WITH THE BLACK KRYPTONITE-- BUT I KNOW IT'S STILL THERE!
I KNOW I CAN REACH IT, KAREN...
...I CAN FIND MY WAY HOME.
YOU REALLY BELIEVE THAT?
I DO. I DON'T KNOW WHY, OR EVEN HOW, BUT I KNOW I CAN DO IT, AND I KNOW THE PLACE TO START IS HERE, IN KANDOR.
THEN I'LL MAKE YOU A DEAL.
WE FINISH WHAT WE'RE DOING HERE, WE FINISH HELPING THESE PEOPLE...

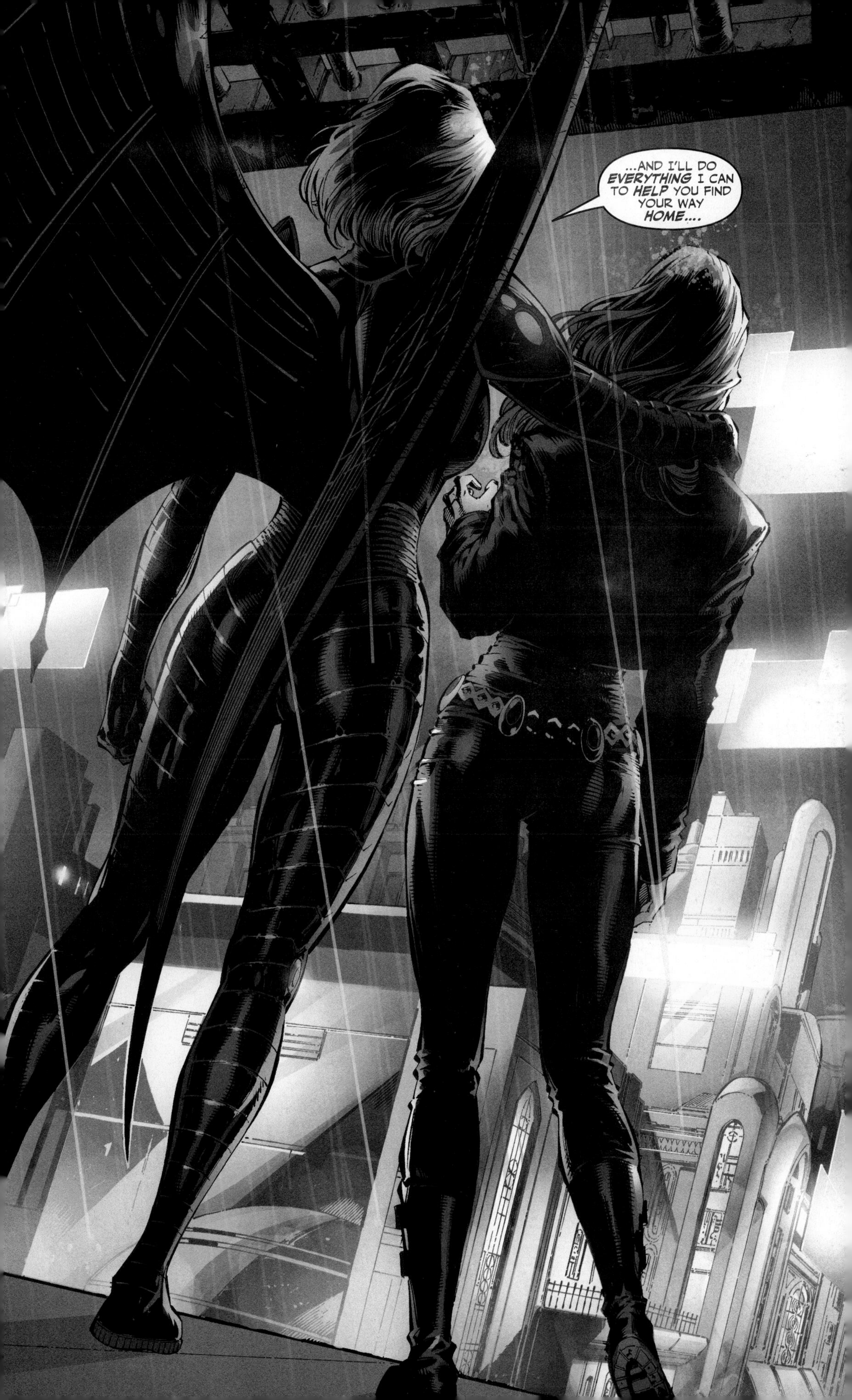
...AND I'LL DO EVERYTHING I CAN TO HELP YOU FIND YOUR WAY HOME....

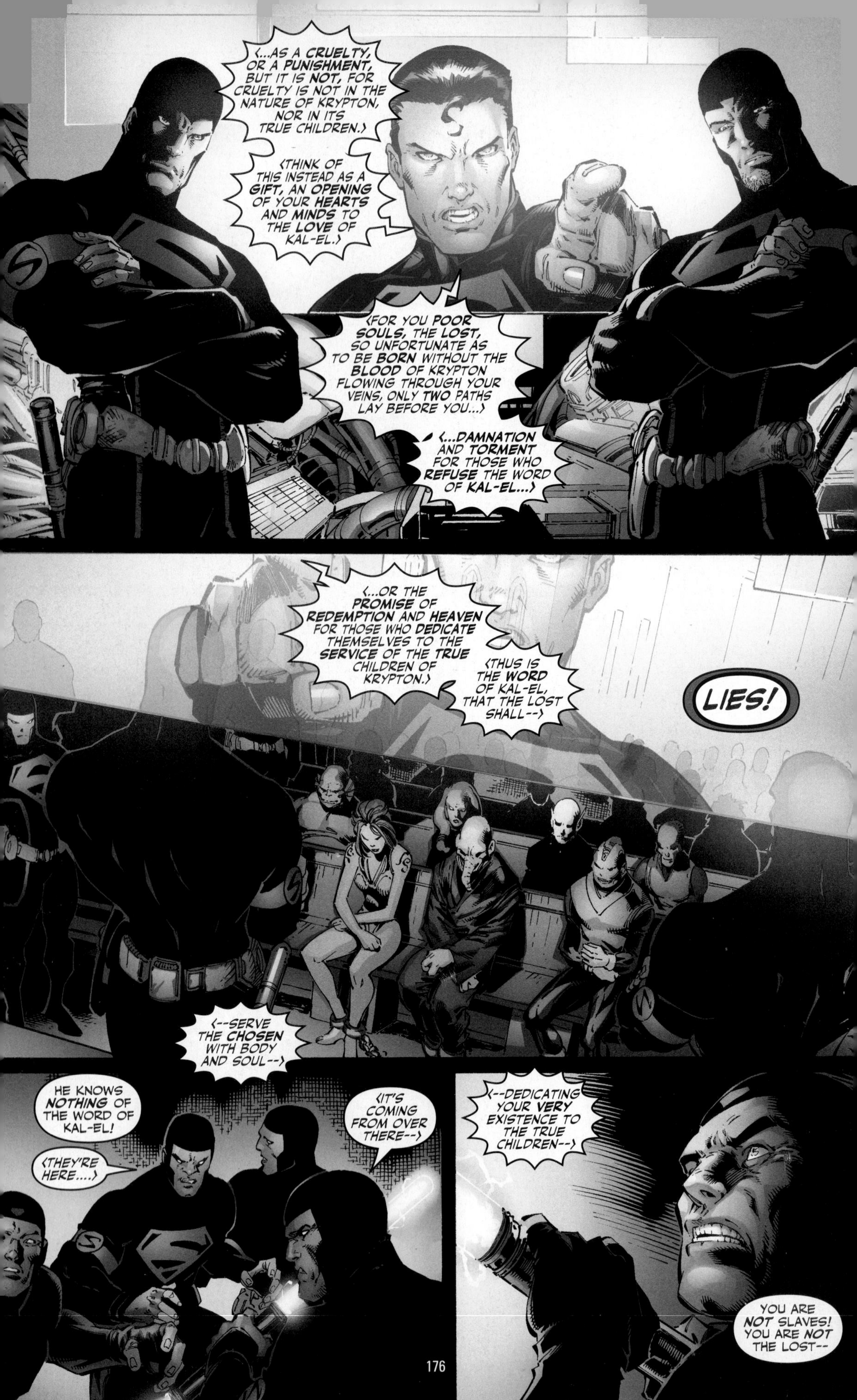

‹...AS A CRUELTY, OR A PUNISHMENT, BUT IT IS NOT, FOR CRUELTY IS NOT IN THE NATURE OF KRYPTON, NOR IN ITS TRUE CHILDREN.›
‹THINK OF THIS INSTEAD AS A GIFT, AN OPENING OF YOUR HEARTS AND MINDS TO THE LOVE OF KAL-EL.›
‹FOR YOU POOR SOULS, THE LOST, SO UNFORTUNATE AS TO BE BORN WITHOUT THE BLOOD OF KRYPTON FLOWING THROUGH YOUR VEINS, ONLY TWO PATHS LAY BEFORE YOU...›
‹...DAMNATION AND TORMENT FOR THOSE WHO REFUSE THE WORD OF KAL-EL...›
‹...OR THE PROMISE OF REDEMPTION AND HEAVEN FOR THOSE WHO DEDICATE THEMSELVES TO THE SERVICE OF THE TRUE CHILDREN OF KRYPTON.›
‹THUS IS THE WORD OF KAL-EL, THAT THE LOST SHALL--›
LIES!
‹--SERVE THE CHOSEN WITH BODY AND SOUL--›
HE KNOWS NOTHING OF THE WORD OF KAL-EL!
‹THEY'RE HERE....›
‹IT'S COMING FROM OVER THERE--›
‹--DEDICATING YOUR VERY EXISTENCE TO THE TRUE CHILDREN--›
YOU ARE NOT SLAVES! YOU ARE NOT THE LOST--

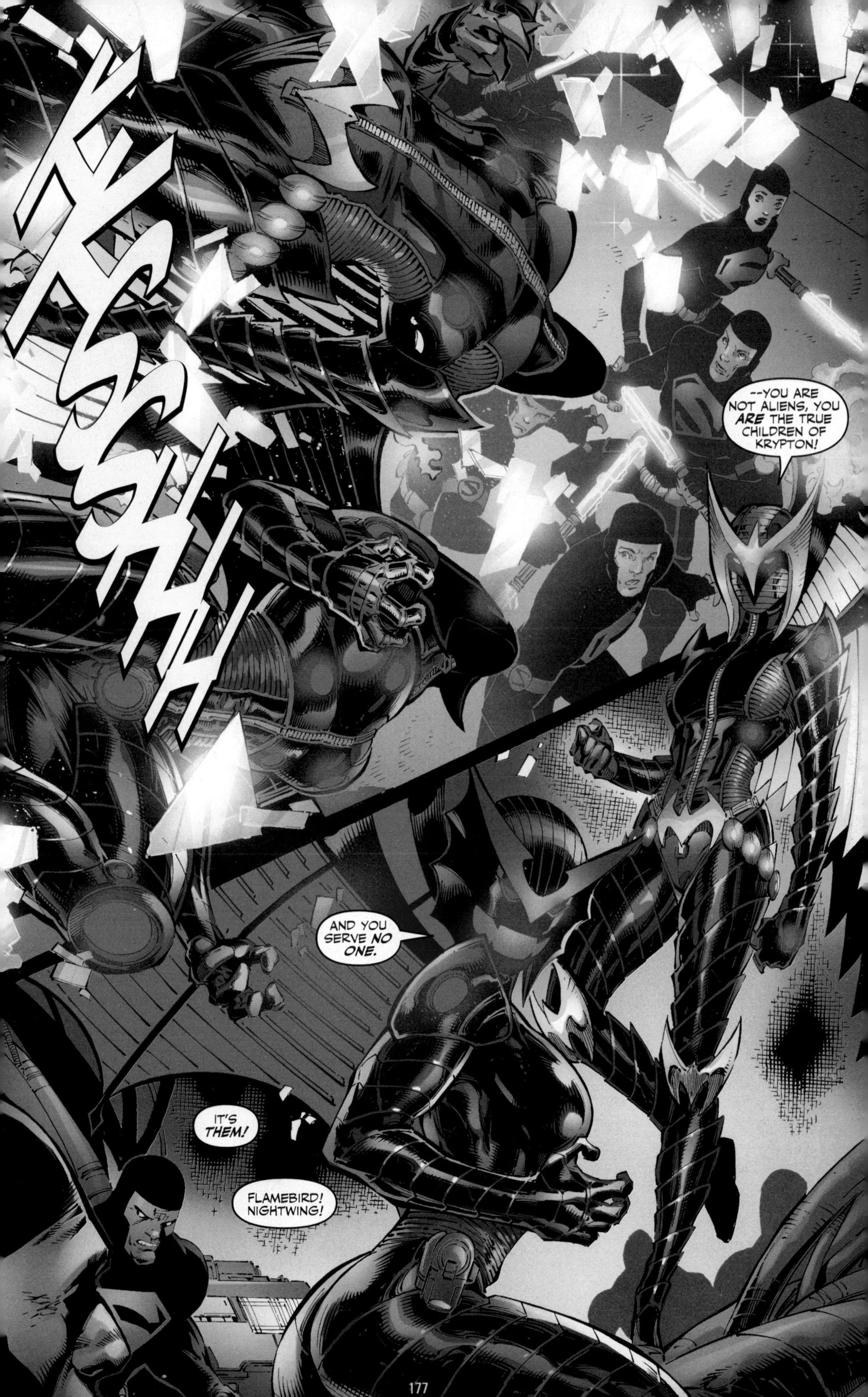
KKSSSHH
--YOU ARE NOT ALIENS, YOU ARE THE TRUE CHILDREN OF KRYPTON!
AND YOU SERVE NO ONE.
IT'S THEM!
FLAMEBIRD! NIGHTWING!

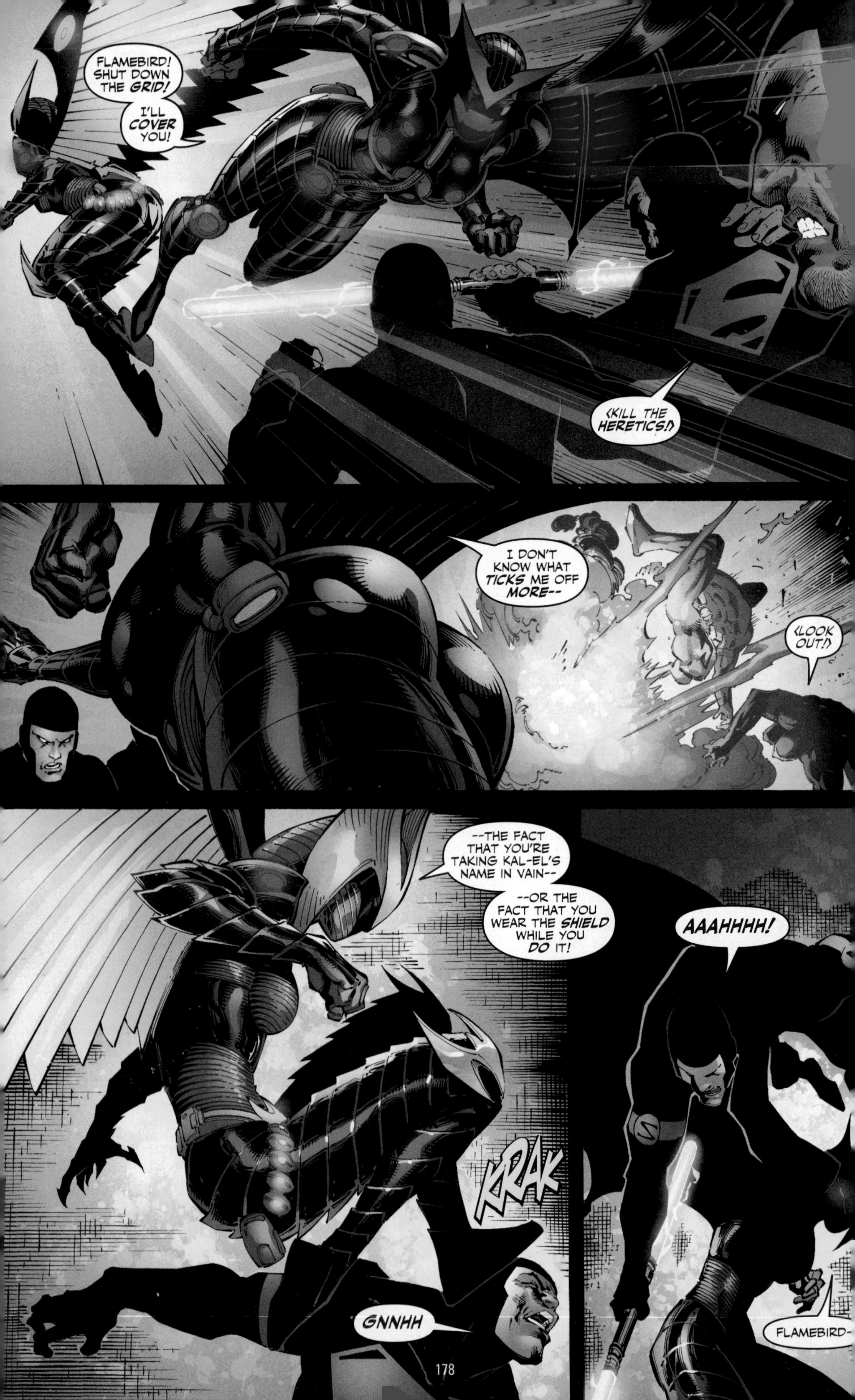
FLAMEBIRD! SHUT DOWN THE GRID!
I'LL COVER YOU!
‹KILL THE HERETICS!›
I DON'T KNOW WHAT TICKS ME OFF MORE--
‹LOOK OUT!›
--THE FACT THAT YOU'RE TAKING KAL-EL'S NAME IN VAIN--
--OR THE FACT THAT YOU WEAR THE SHIELD WHILE YOU DO IT!
KRAK
GNNHH
AAAHHHH!
FLAMEBIRD-

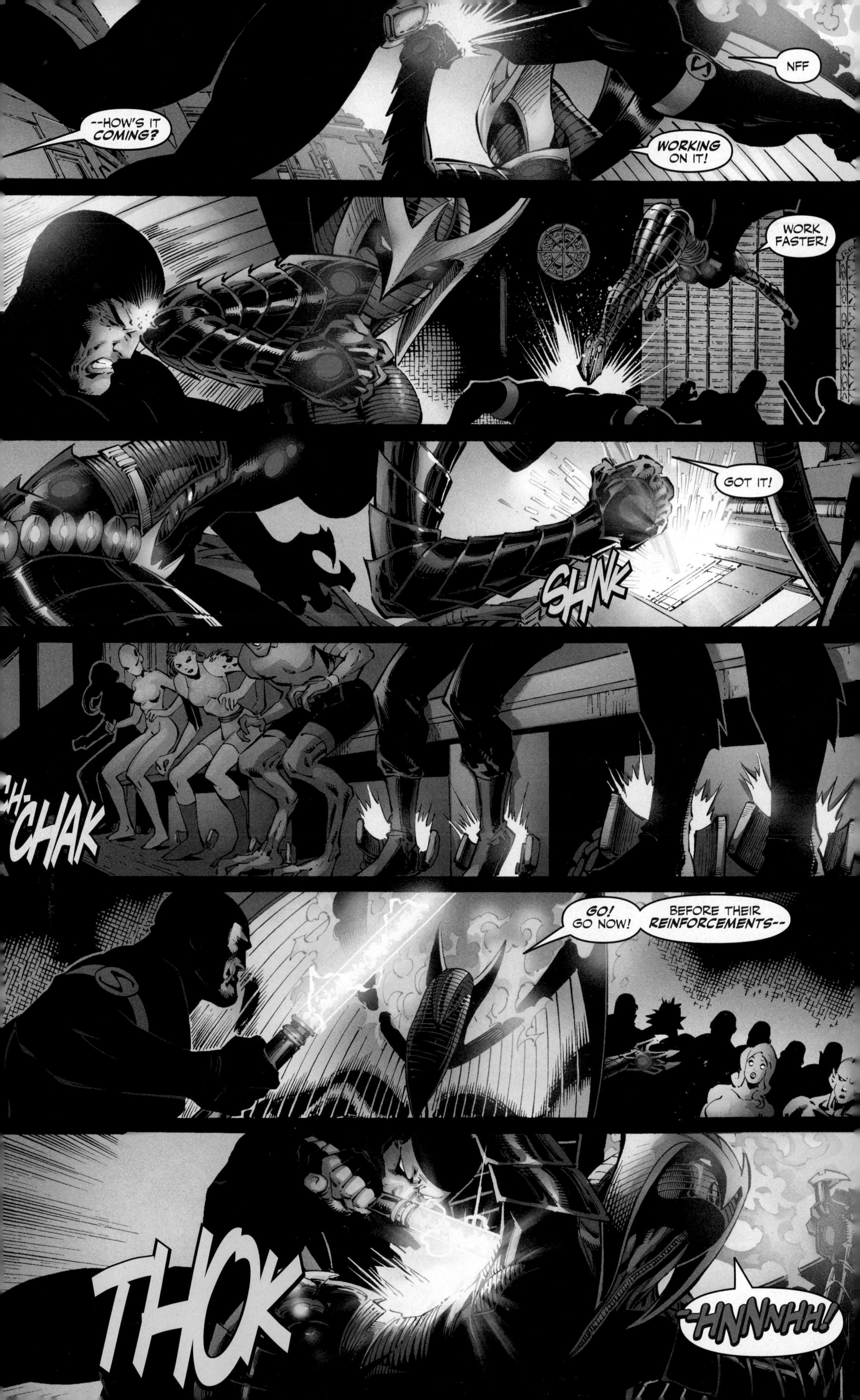
NFF
--HOW'S IT COMING?
WORKING ON IT!
WORK FASTER!
GOT IT!
SHNK
CH-CHAK
GO! GO NOW!
BEFORE THEIR REINFORCEMENTS--
THOK
-HNNNHH!

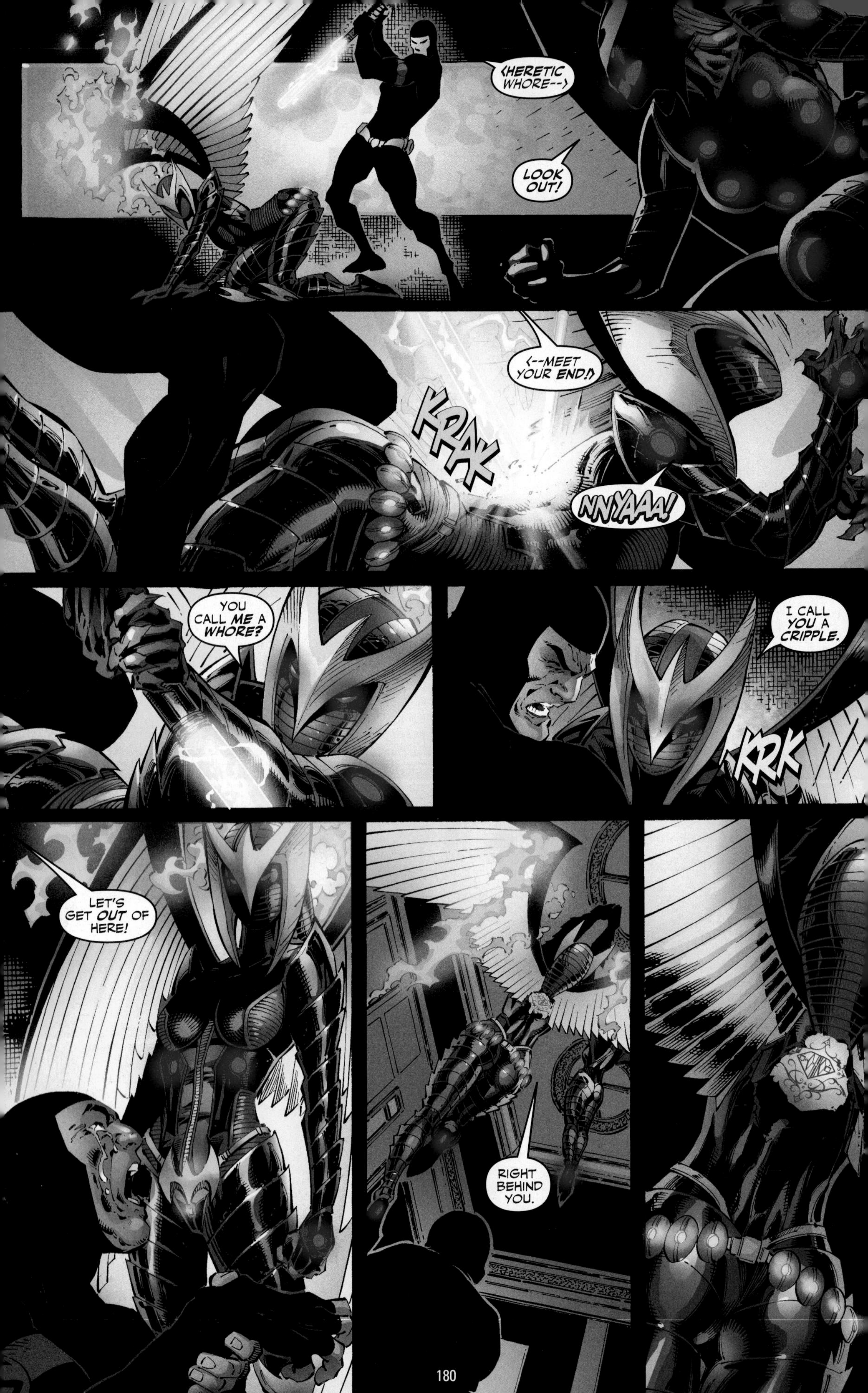
‹HERETIC WHORE--›
LOOK OUT!
‹--MEET YOUR END!›
KRAK
NNYAAA!
YOU CALL ME A WHORE?
I CALL YOU A CRIPPLE.
KRK
LET'S GET OUT OF HERE!
RIGHT BEHIND YOU.

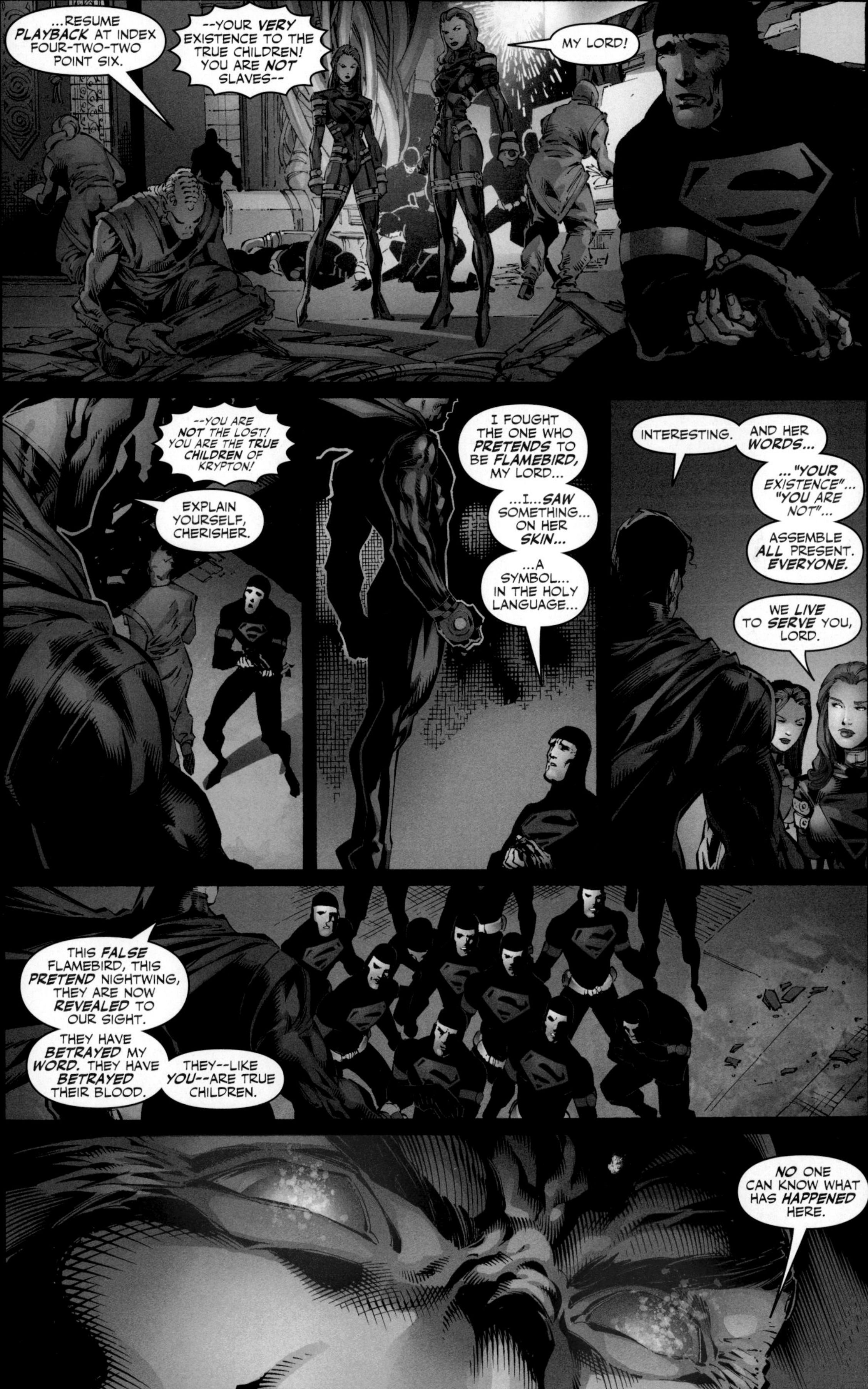
...RESUME PLAYBACK AT INDEX FOUR-TWO-TWO POINT SIX.
--YOUR VERY EXISTENCE TO THE TRUE CHILDREN! YOU ARE NOT SLAVES--
MY LORD!
--YOU ARE NOT THE LOST! YOU ARE THE TRUE CHILDREN OF KRYPTON!
EXPLAIN YOURSELF, CHERISHER.
I FOUGHT THE ONE WHO PRETENDS TO BE FLAMEBIRD, MY LORD...
...I...SAW SOMETHING... ON HER SKIN...
...A SYMBOL... IN THE HOLY LANGUAGE...
INTERESTING.
AND HER WORDS...
..."YOUR EXISTENCE"... "YOU ARE NOT"...
ASSEMBLE ALL PRESENT. EVERYONE.
WE LIVE TO SERVE YOU, LORD.
THIS FALSE FLAMEBIRD, THIS PRETEND NIGHTWING, THEY ARE NOW REVEALED TO OUR SIGHT.
THEY HAVE BETRAYED MY WORD. THEY HAVE BETRAYED THEIR BLOOD.
THEY--LIKE YOU--ARE TRUE CHILDREN.
NO ONE CAN KNOW WHAT HAS HAPPENED HERE.

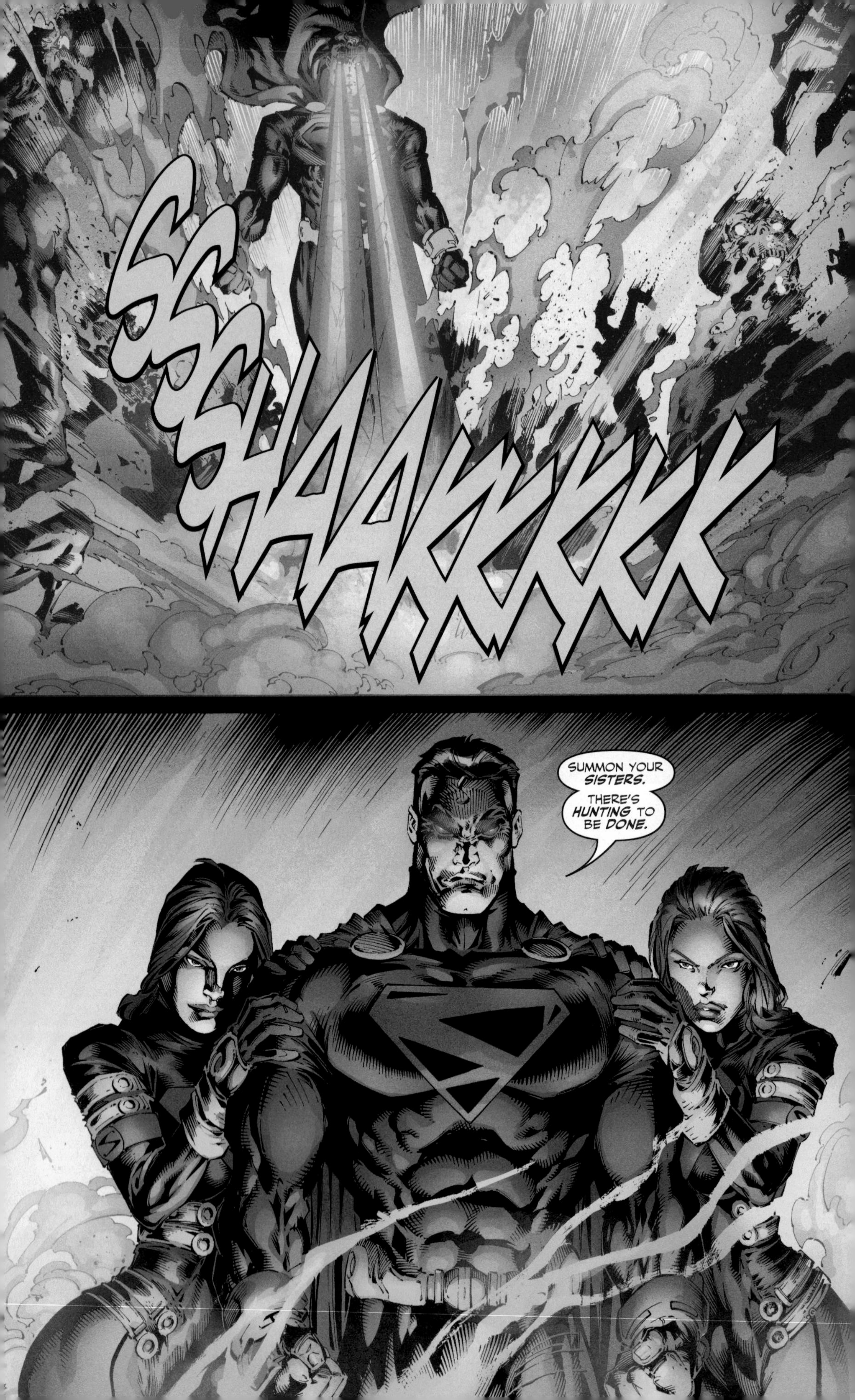
SUMMON YOUR *SISTERS.*
THERE'S *HUNTING* TO BE *DONE.*

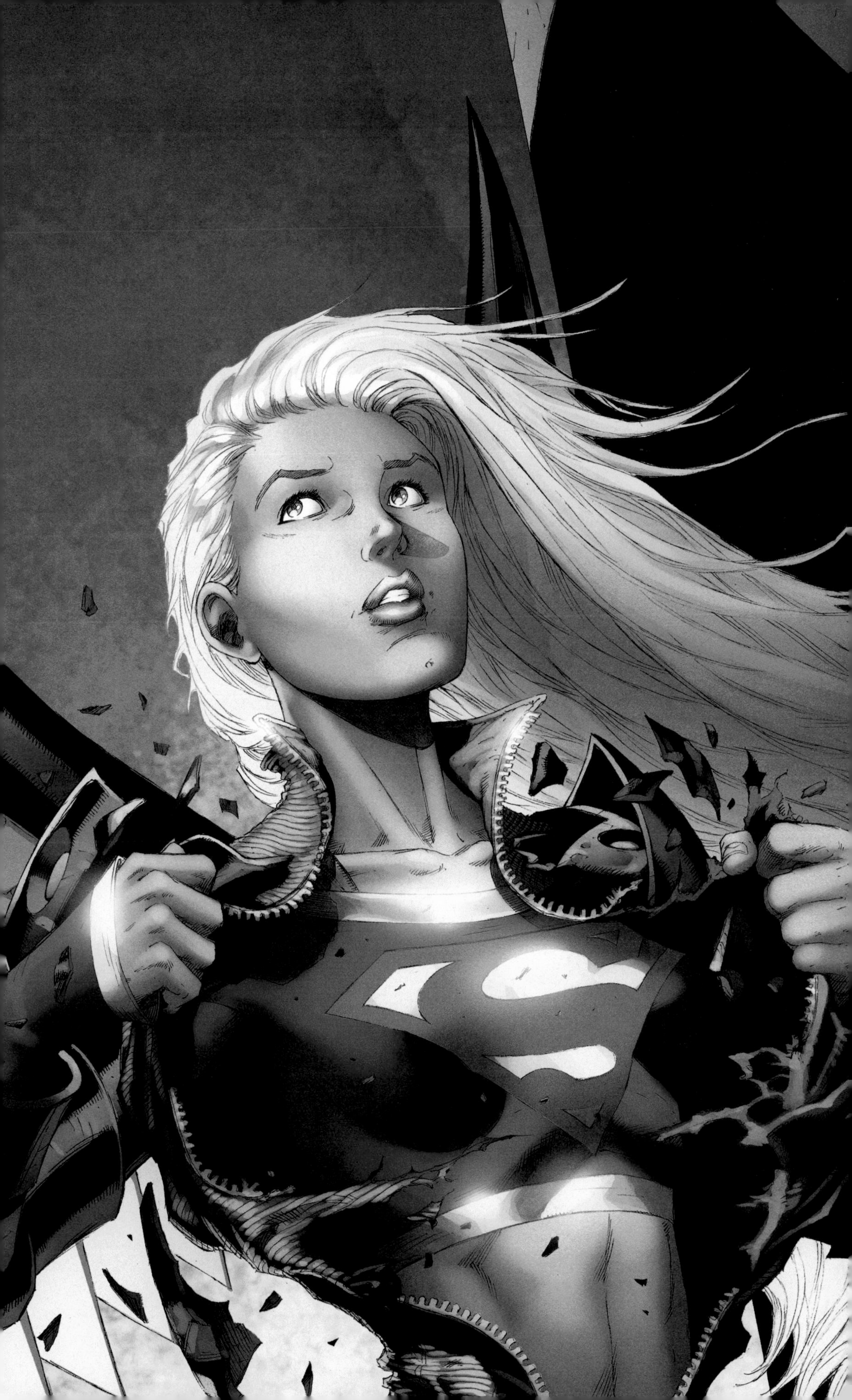

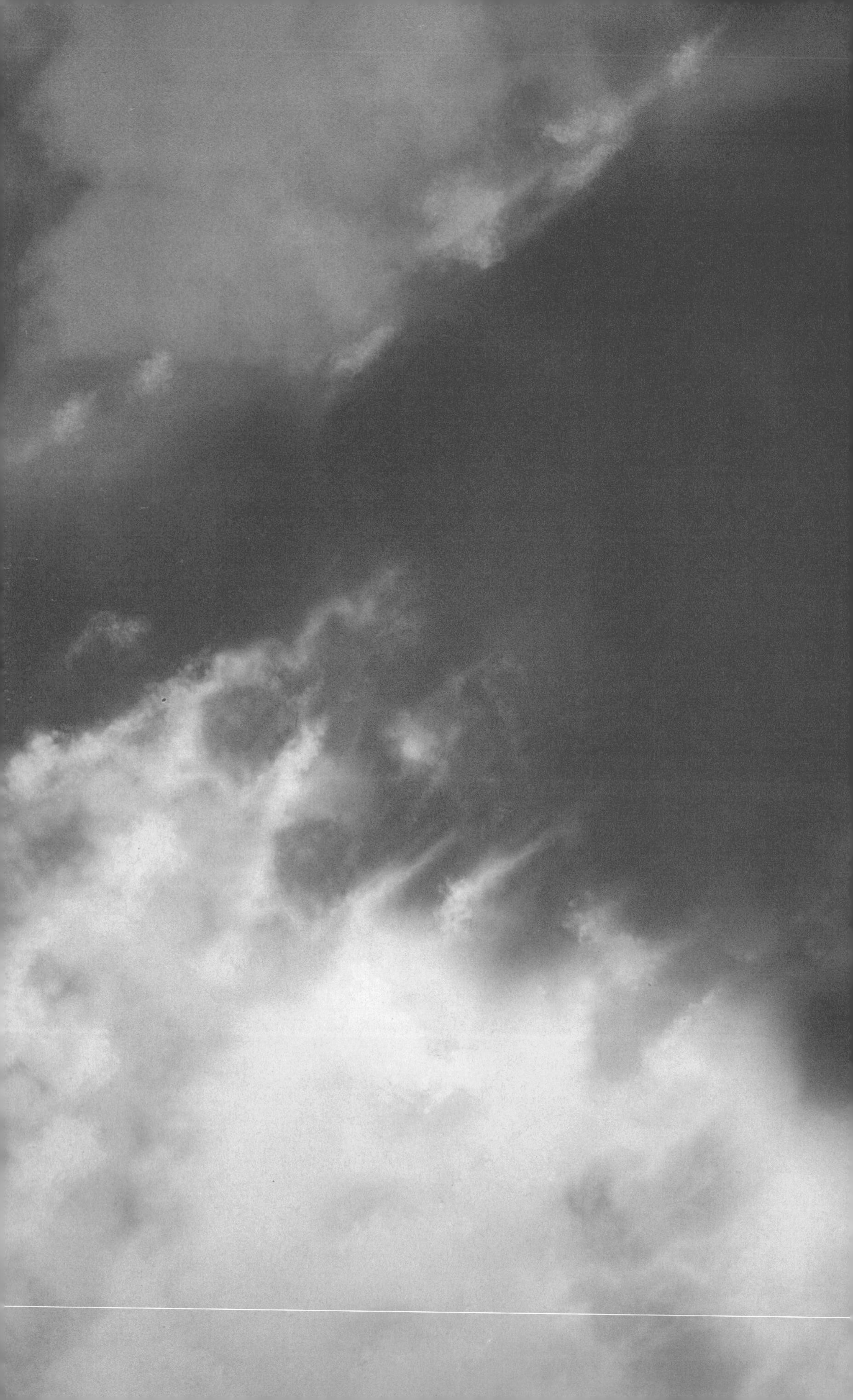

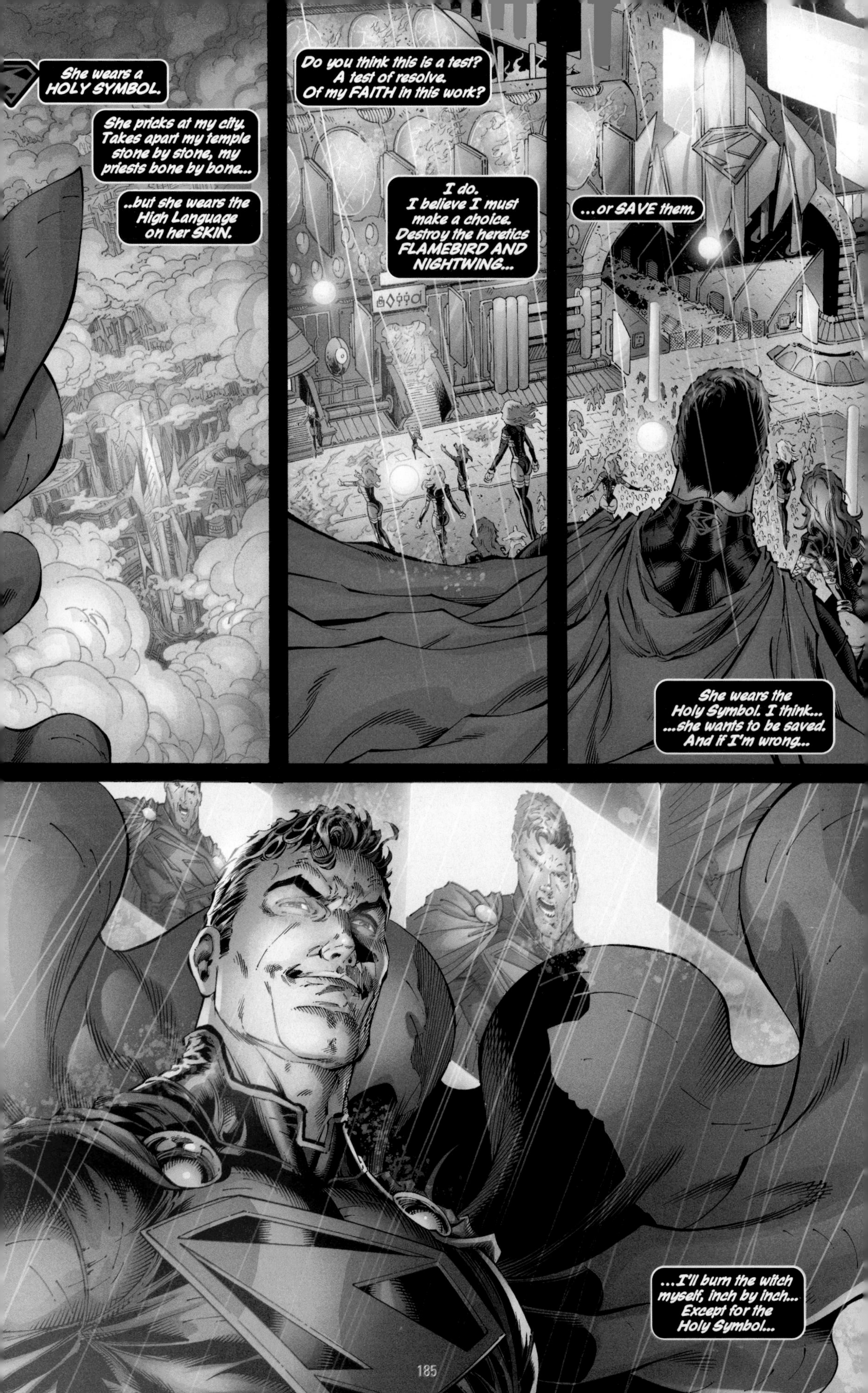
She wears a HOLY SYMBOL.
She pricks at my city. Takes apart my temple stone by stone, my priests bone by bone...
..but she wears the High Language on her SKIN.
Do you think this is a test? A test of resolve. Of my FAITH in this work?
I do. I believe I must make a choice. Destroy the heretics FLAMEBIRD AND NIGHTWING...
...or SAVE them.
She wears the Holy Symbol. I think... ...she wants to be saved. And if I'm wrong...
...I'll burn the witch myself, inch by inch... Except for the Holy Symbol...

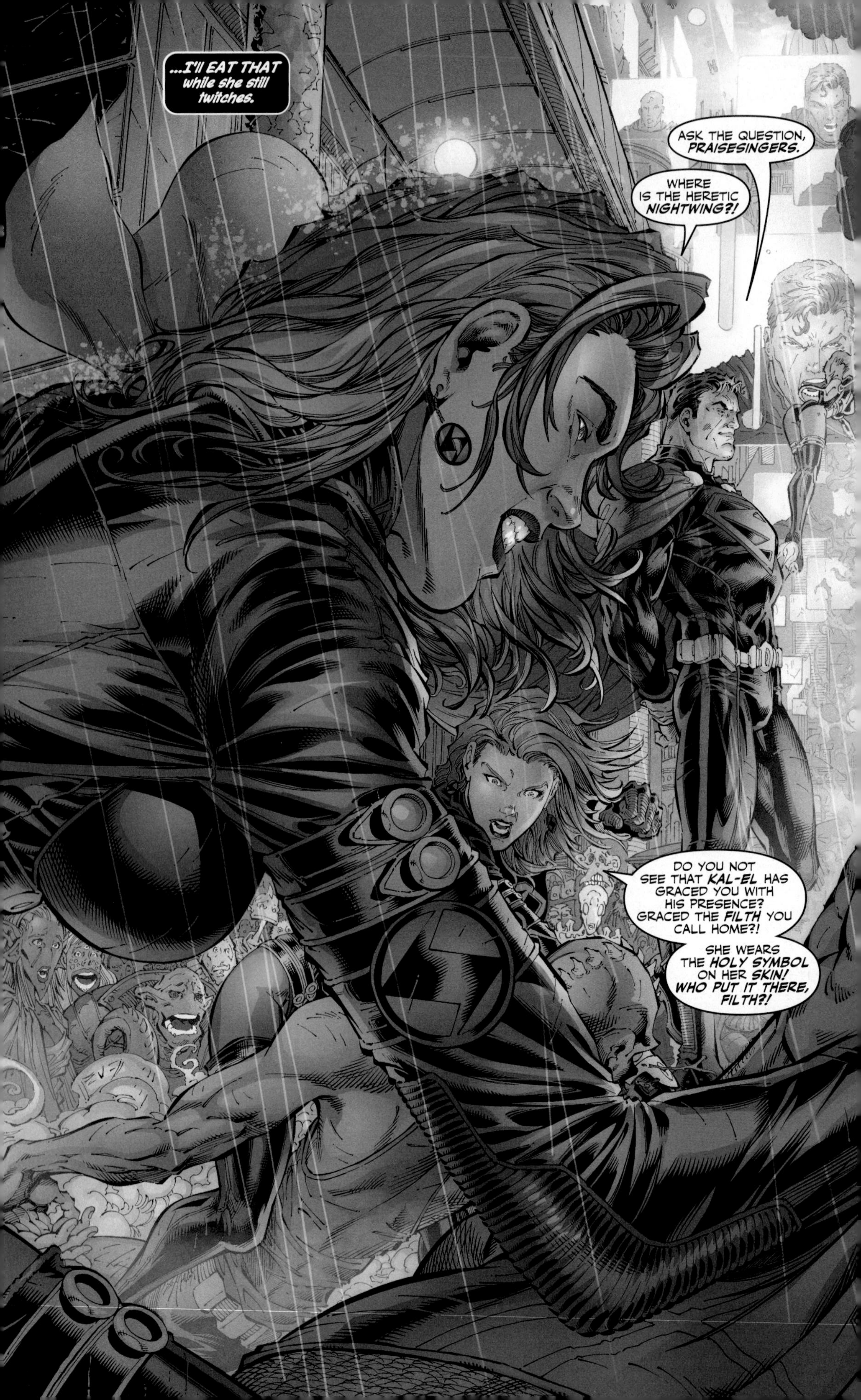
...I'll EAT THAT while she still twitches.
ASK THE QUESTION, PRAISESINGERS.
WHERE IS THE HERETIC NIGHTWING?!
DO YOU NOT SEE THAT KAL-EL HAS GRACED YOU WITH HIS PRESENCE? GRACED THE FILTH YOU CALL HOME?!
SHE WEARS THE HOLY SYMBOL ON HER SKIN! WHO PUT IT THERE, FILTH?!

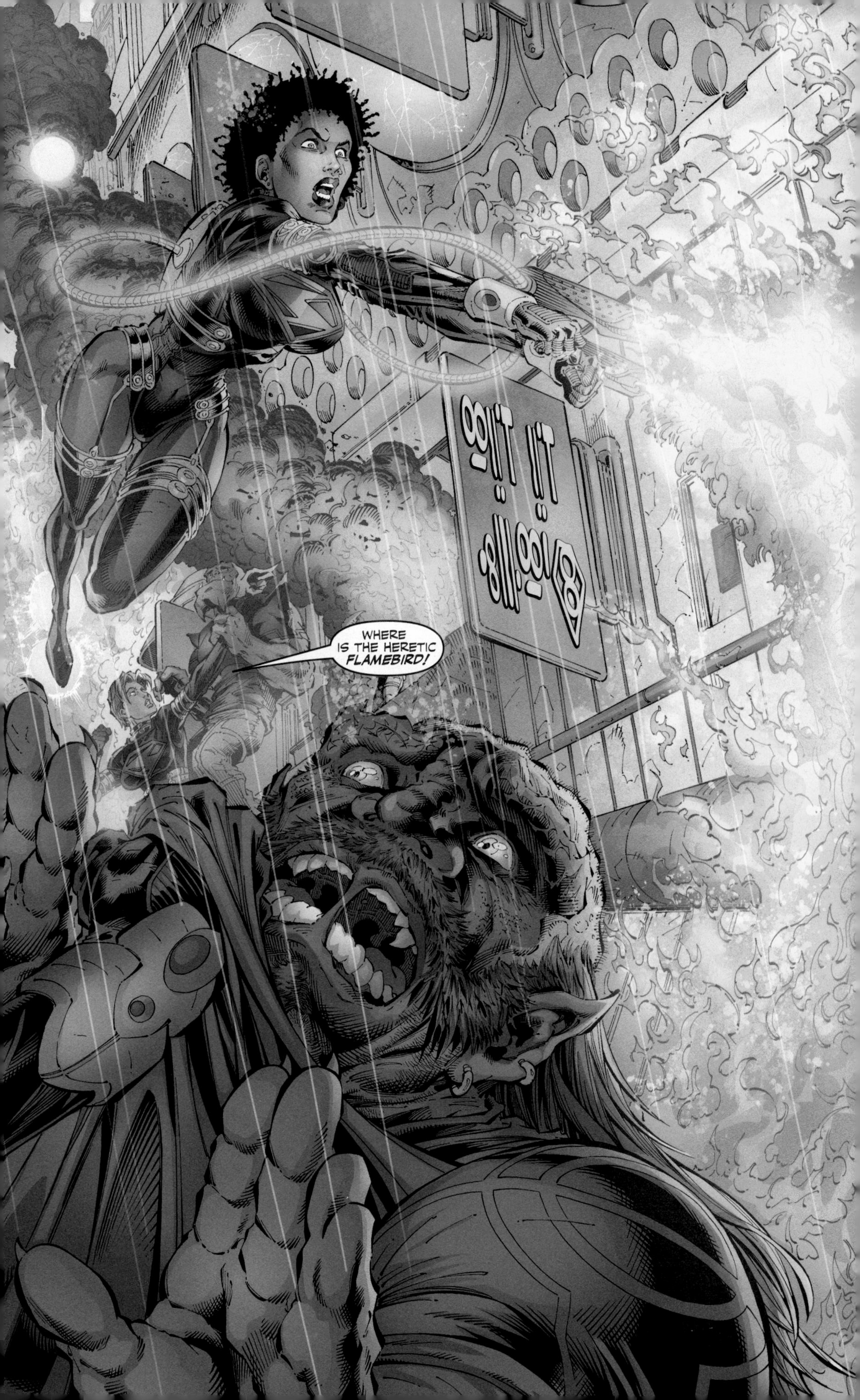
WHERE IS THE HERETIC FLAMEBIRD!

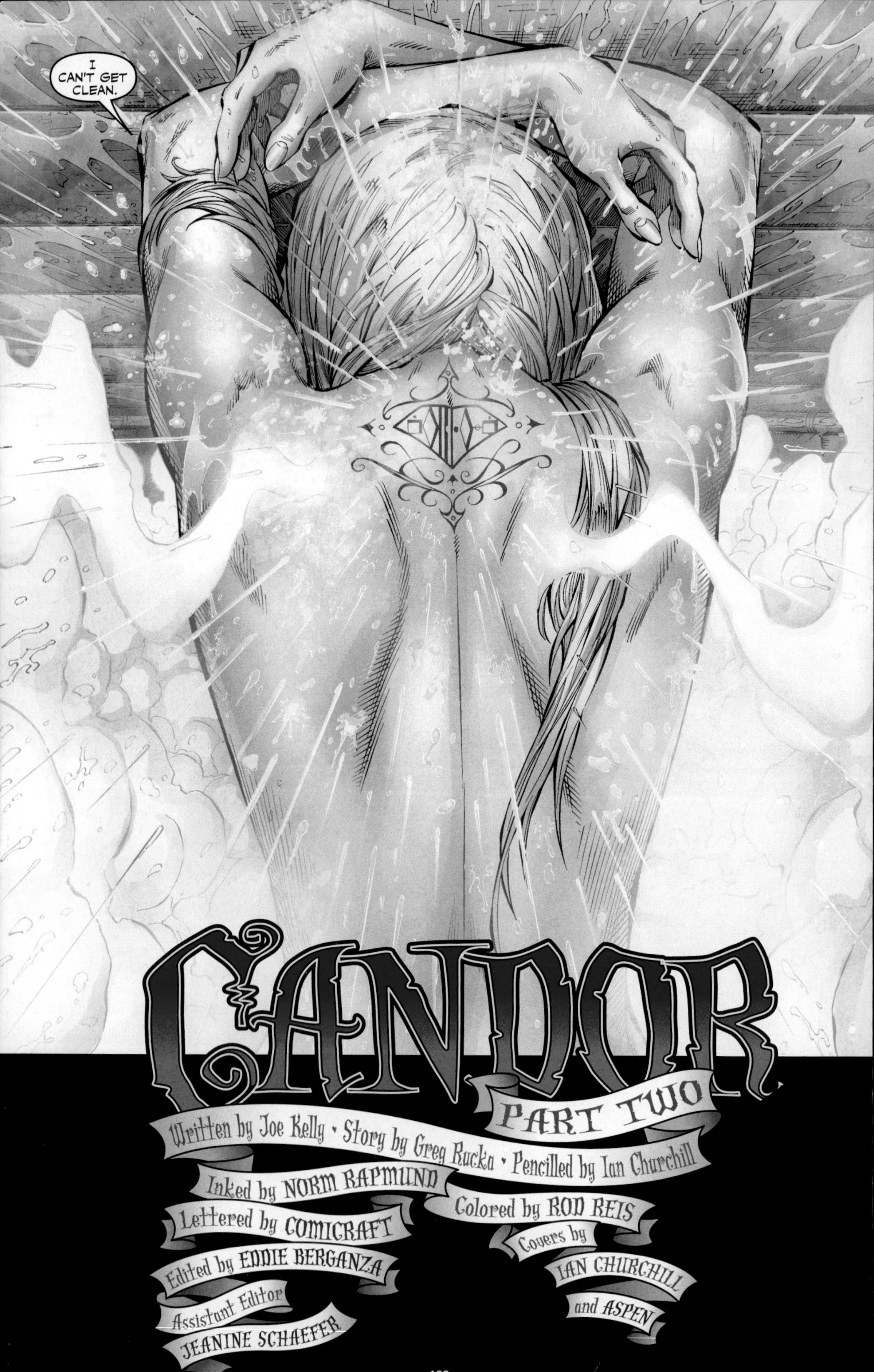
I CAN'T GET CLEAN.
CANDOR
PART TWO
Written by Joe Kelly • Story by Greg Rucka • Pencilled by Ian Churchill
Inked by NORM RAPMUND
Colored by ROD REIS
Lettered by COMICRAFT
Covers by IAN CHURCHILL and ASPEN
Edited by EDDIE BERGANZA
Assistant Editor JEANINE SCHAEFER

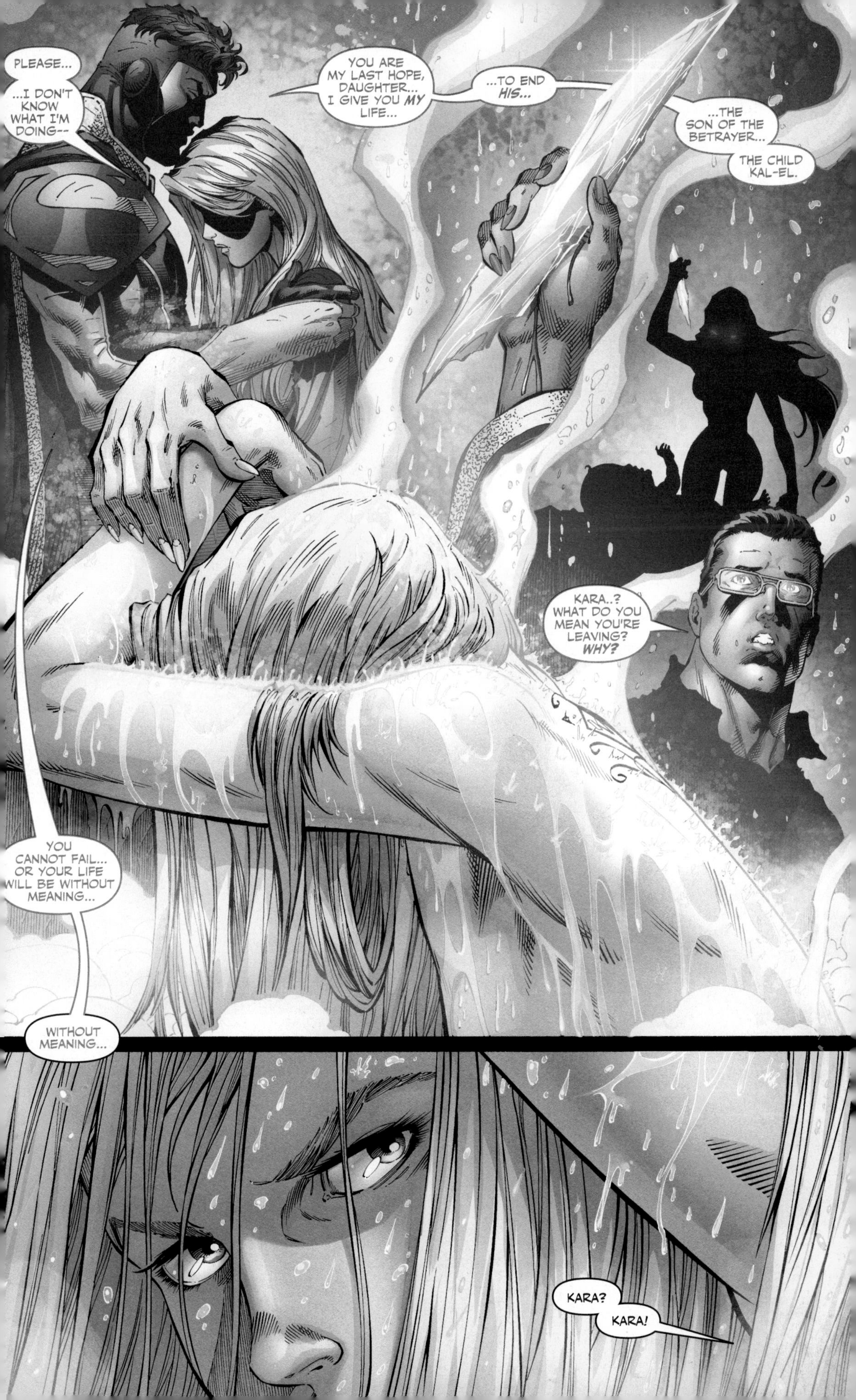
PLEASE...
...I DON'T KNOW WHAT I'M DOING--
YOU ARE MY LAST HOPE, DAUGHTER... I GIVE YOU *MY* LIFE...
...TO END *HIS*...
...THE SON OF THE BETRAYER...
THE CHILD KAL-EL.
KARA..? WHAT DO YOU MEAN YOU'RE LEAVING? *WHY?*
YOU CANNOT FAIL... OR YOUR LIFE WILL BE WITHOUT MEANING...
WITHOUT MEANING...
KARA?
KARA!

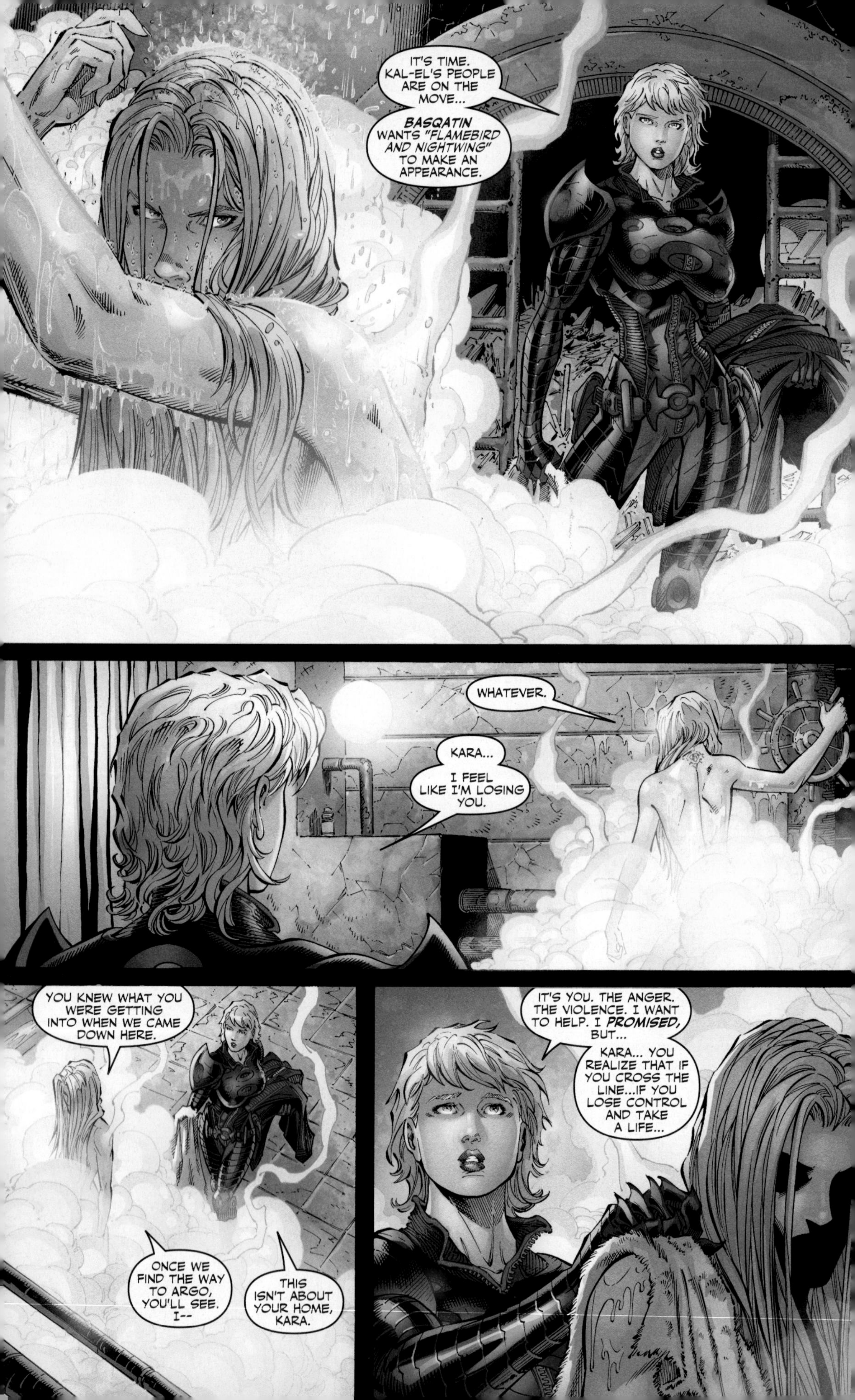
IT'S TIME. KAL-EL'S PEOPLE ARE ON THE MOVE...
BASQATIN WANTS "FLAMEBIRD AND NIGHTWING" TO MAKE AN APPEARANCE.
WHATEVER.
KARA...
I FEEL LIKE I'M LOSING YOU.
YOU KNEW WHAT YOU WERE GETTING INTO WHEN WE CAME DOWN HERE.
ONCE WE FIND THE WAY TO ARGO, YOU'LL SEE. I--
THIS ISN'T ABOUT YOUR HOME, KARA.
IT'S YOU. THE ANGER. THE VIOLENCE. I WANT TO HELP. I PROMISED, BUT...
KARA... YOU REALIZE THAT IF YOU CROSS THE LINE...IF YOU LOSE CONTROL AND TAKE A LIFE...

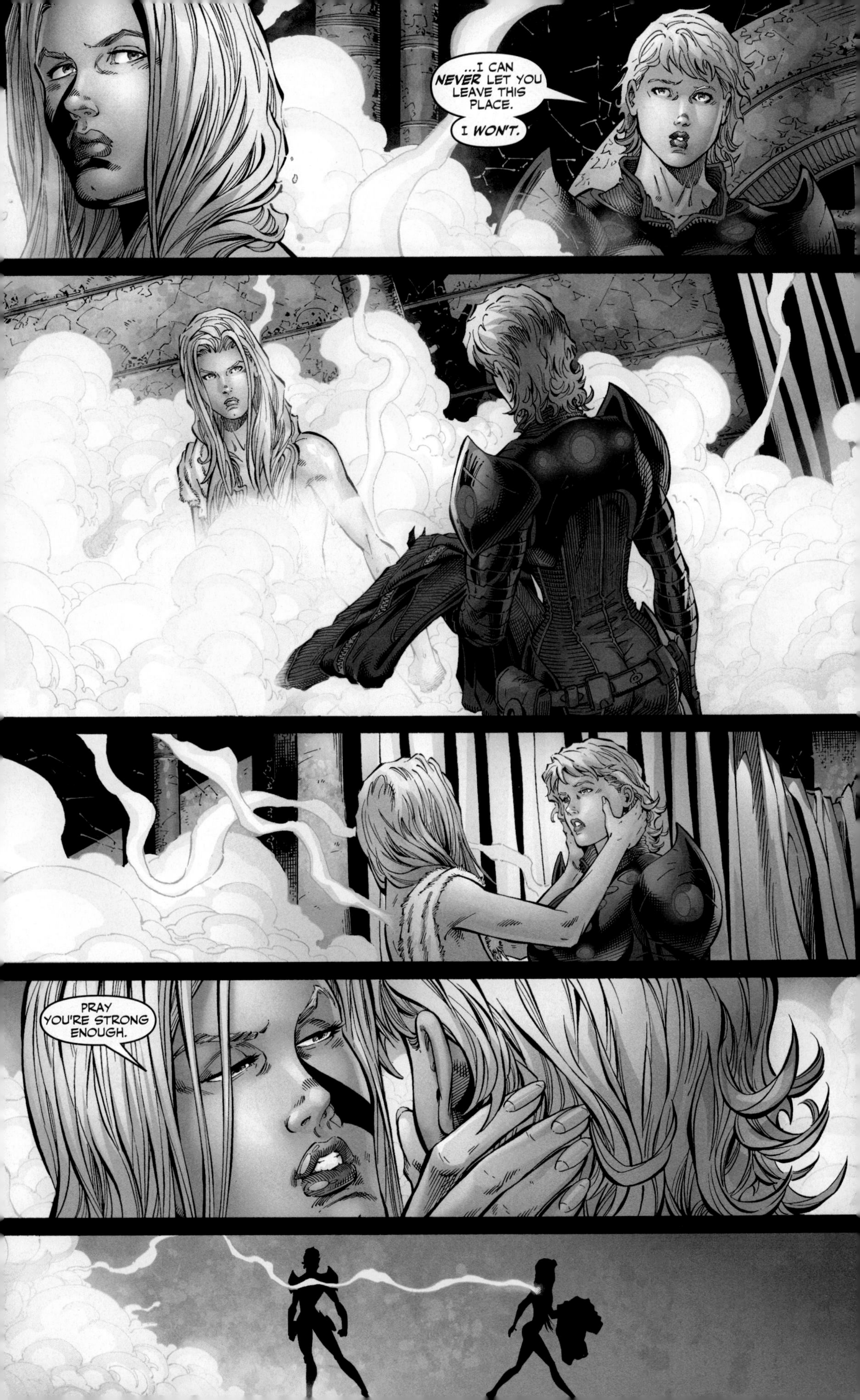
...I CAN NEVER LET YOU LEAVE THIS PLACE.
I WON'T.
PRAY YOU'RE STRONG ENOUGH.

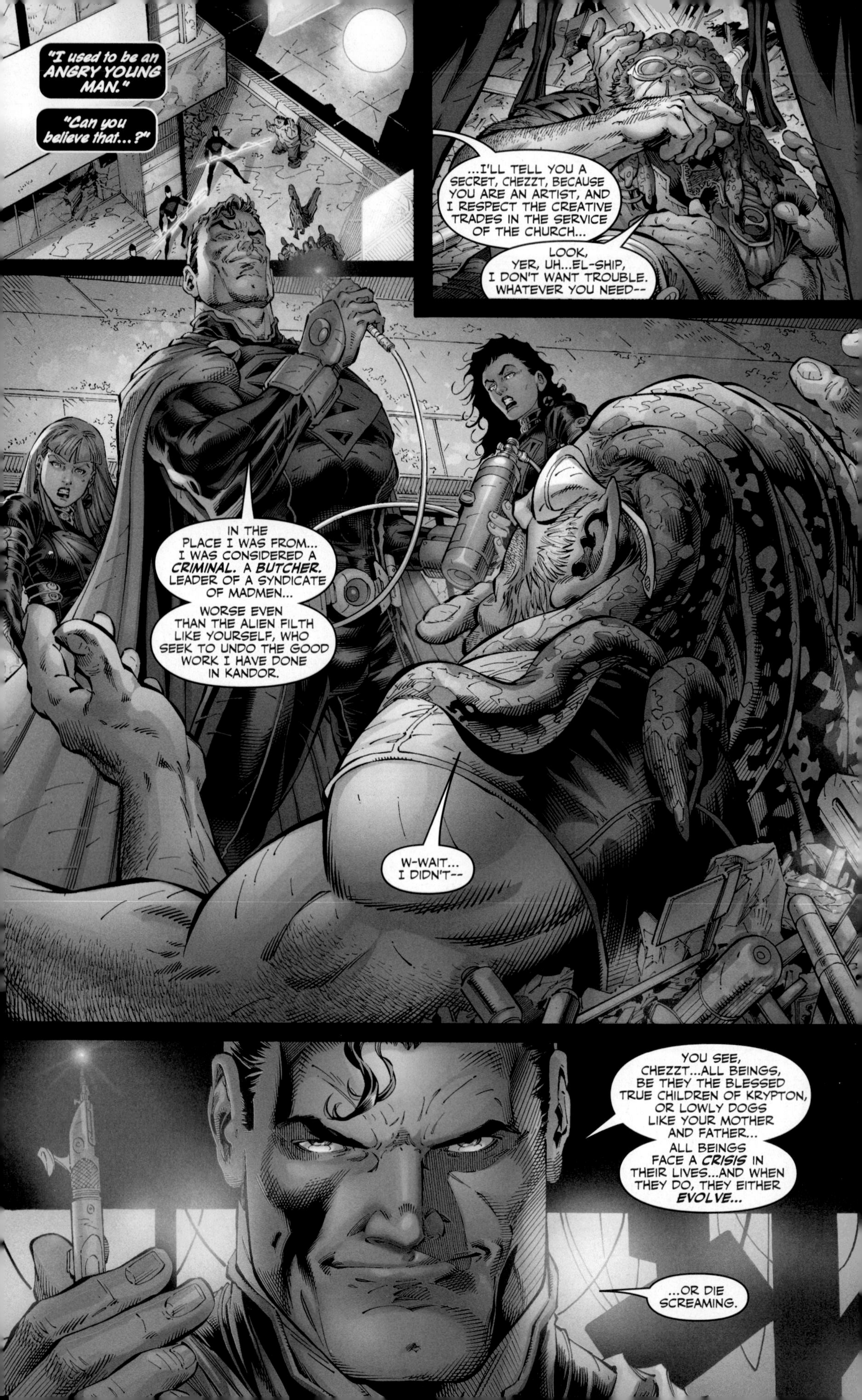
"I used to be an ANGRY YOUNG MAN."
"Can you believe that...?"
...I'LL TELL YOU A SECRET, CHEZZT, BECAUSE YOU ARE AN ARTIST, AND I RESPECT THE CREATIVE TRADES IN THE SERVICE OF THE CHURCH...
LOOK, YER, UH...EL-SHIP, I DON'T WANT TROUBLE. WHATEVER YOU NEED--
IN THE PLACE I WAS FROM... I WAS CONSIDERED A CRIMINAL. A BUTCHER. LEADER OF A SYNDICATE OF MADMEN...
WORSE EVEN THAN THE ALIEN FILTH LIKE YOURSELF, WHO SEEK TO UNDO THE GOOD WORK I HAVE DONE IN KANDOR.
W-WAIT... I DIDN'T--
YOU SEE, CHEZZT...ALL BEINGS, BE THEY THE BLESSED TRUE CHILDREN OF KRYPTON, OR LOWLY DOGS LIKE YOUR MOTHER AND FATHER...
ALL BEINGS FACE A CRISIS IN THEIR LIVES...AND WHEN THEY DO, THEY EITHER EVOLVE...
...OR DIE SCREAMING.

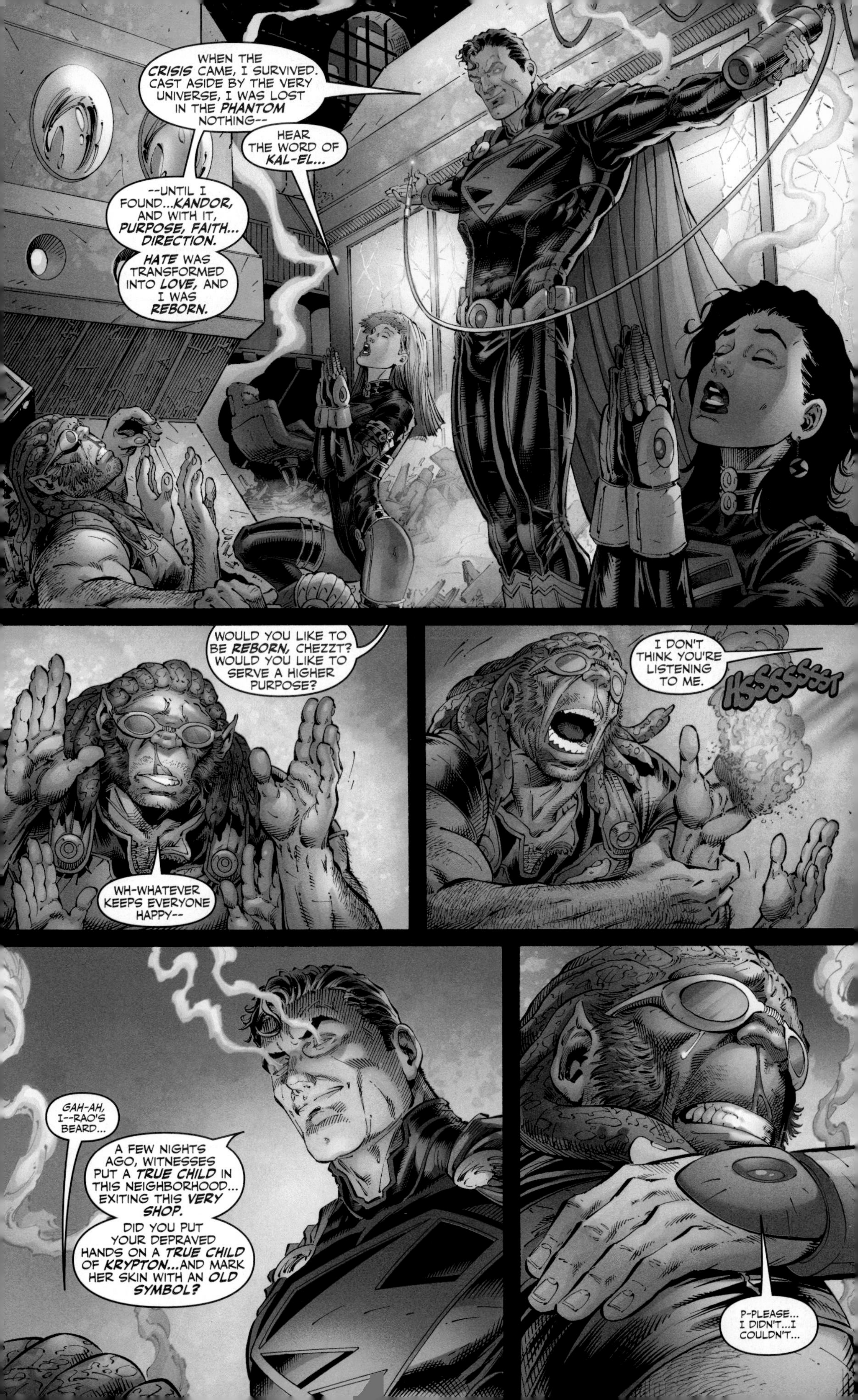
WHEN THE CRISIS CAME, I SURVIVED. CAST ASIDE BY THE VERY UNIVERSE, I WAS LOST IN THE PHANTOM NOTHING--
HEAR THE WORD OF KAL-EL...
--UNTIL I FOUND...KANDOR, AND WITH IT, PURPOSE, FAITH... DIRECTION.
HATE WAS TRANSFORMED INTO LOVE, AND I WAS REBORN.
WOULD YOU LIKE TO BE REBORN, CHEZZT? WOULD YOU LIKE TO SERVE A HIGHER PURPOSE?
WH-WHATEVER KEEPS EVERYONE HAPPY--
I DON'T THINK YOU'RE LISTENING TO ME.
HSSSSSSST
GAH-AH, I--RAO'S BEARD...
A FEW NIGHTS AGO, WITNESSES PUT A TRUE CHILD IN THIS NEIGHBORHOOD... EXITING THIS VERY SHOP.
DID YOU PUT YOUR DEPRAVED HANDS ON A TRUE CHILD OF KRYPTON...AND MARK HER SKIN WITH AN OLD SYMBOL?
P-PLEASE... I DIDN'T...I COULDN'T...

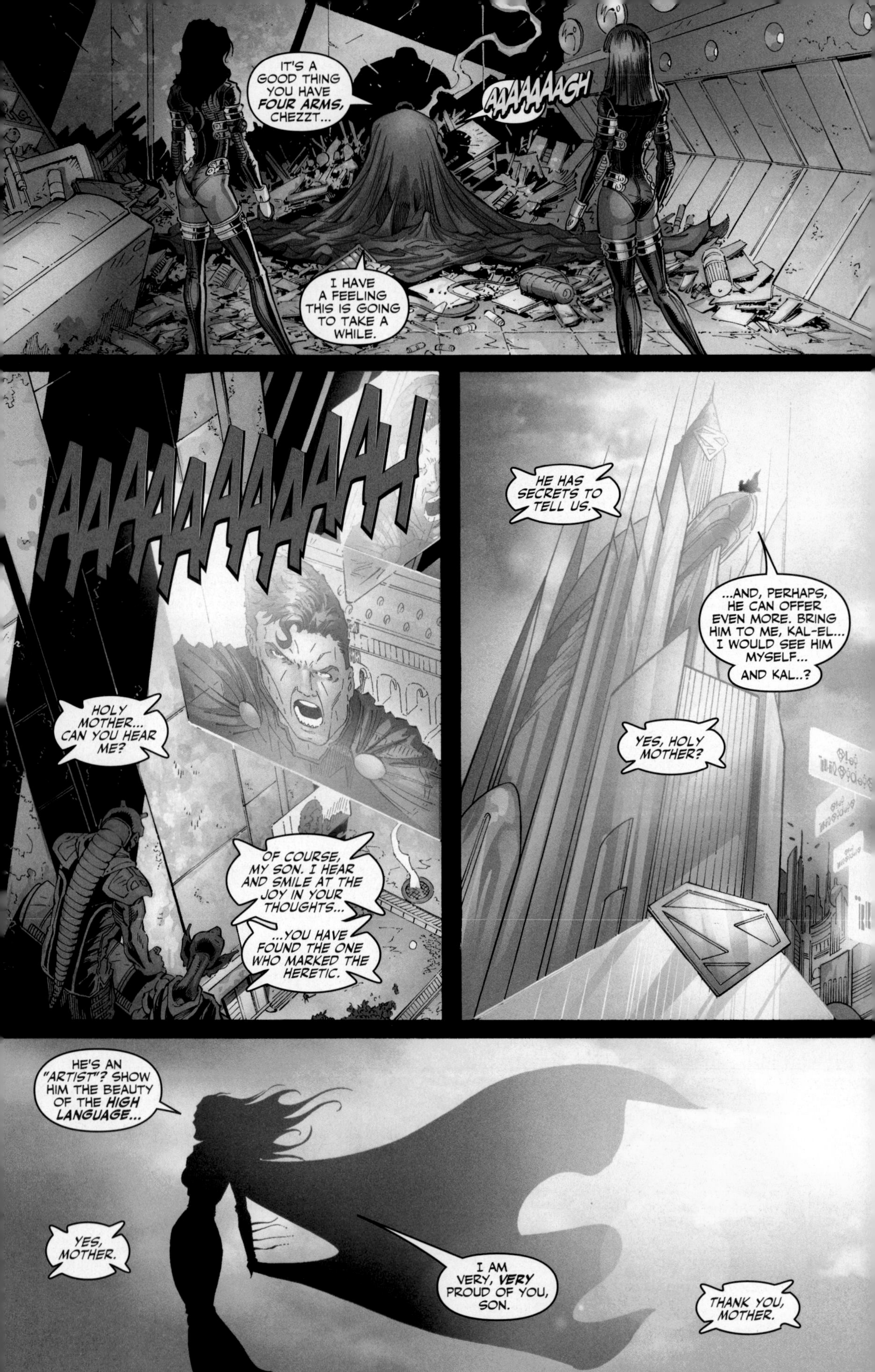
IT'S A GOOD THING YOU HAVE **FOUR ARMS,** CHEZZT...
AAAAAAAGH
I HAVE A FEELING THIS IS GOING TO TAKE A WHILE.
AAAAAAAAAAAH
HOLY MOTHER... CAN YOU HEAR ME?
OF COURSE, MY SON. I HEAR AND SMILE AT THE JOY IN YOUR THOUGHTS...
...YOU HAVE FOUND THE ONE WHO MARKED THE HERETIC.
HE HAS SECRETS TO TELL US.
...AND, PERHAPS, HE CAN OFFER EVEN MORE. BRING HIM TO ME, KAL-EL... I WOULD SEE HIM MYSELF...
AND KAL..?
YES, HOLY MOTHER?
HE'S AN "ARTIST"? SHOW HIM THE BEAUTY OF THE **HIGH LANGUAGE...**
YES, MOTHER.
I AM VERY, **VERY** PROUD OF YOU, SON.
THANK YOU, MOTHER.

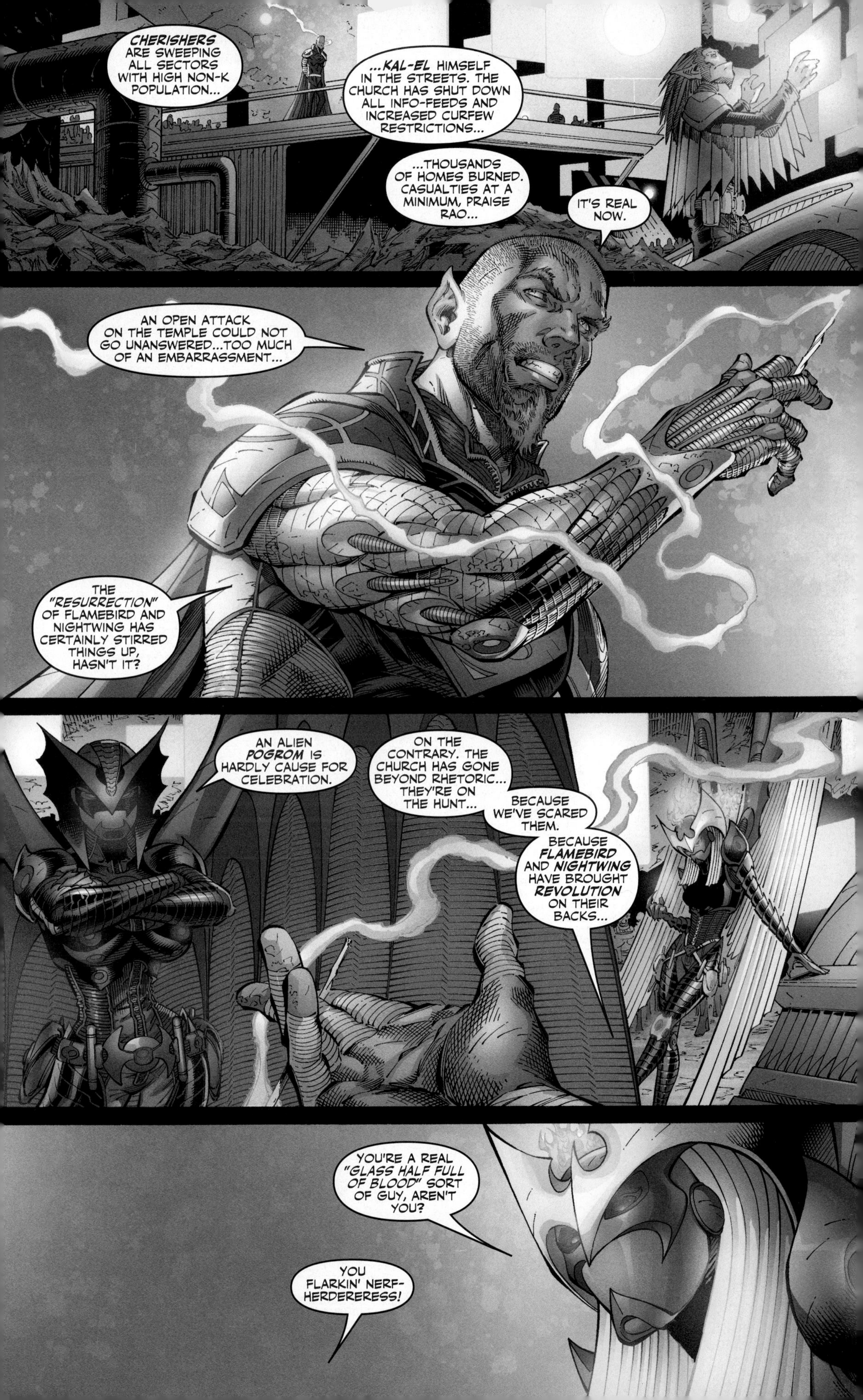
CHERISHERS ARE SWEEPING ALL SECTORS WITH HIGH NON-K POPULATION...
...KAL-EL HIMSELF IN THE STREETS. THE CHURCH HAS SHUT DOWN ALL INFO-FEEDS AND INCREASED CURFEW RESTRICTIONS...
...THOUSANDS OF HOMES BURNED. CASUALTIES AT A MINIMUM, PRAISE RAO...
IT'S REAL NOW.
AN OPEN ATTACK ON THE TEMPLE COULD NOT GO UNANSWERED...TOO MUCH OF AN EMBARRASSMENT...
THE "RESURRECTION" OF FLAMEBIRD AND NIGHTWING HAS CERTAINLY STIRRED THINGS UP, HASN'T IT?
AN ALIEN POGROM IS HARDLY CAUSE FOR CELEBRATION.
ON THE CONTRARY. THE CHURCH HAS GONE BEYOND RHETORIC... THEY'RE ON THE HUNT...
BECAUSE WE'VE SCARED THEM.
BECAUSE FLAMEBIRD AND NIGHTWING HAVE BROUGHT REVOLUTION ON THEIR BACKS...
YOU'RE A REAL "GLASS HALF FULL OF BLOOD" SORT OF GUY, AREN'T YOU?
YOU FLARKIN' NERF-HERDERERESS!

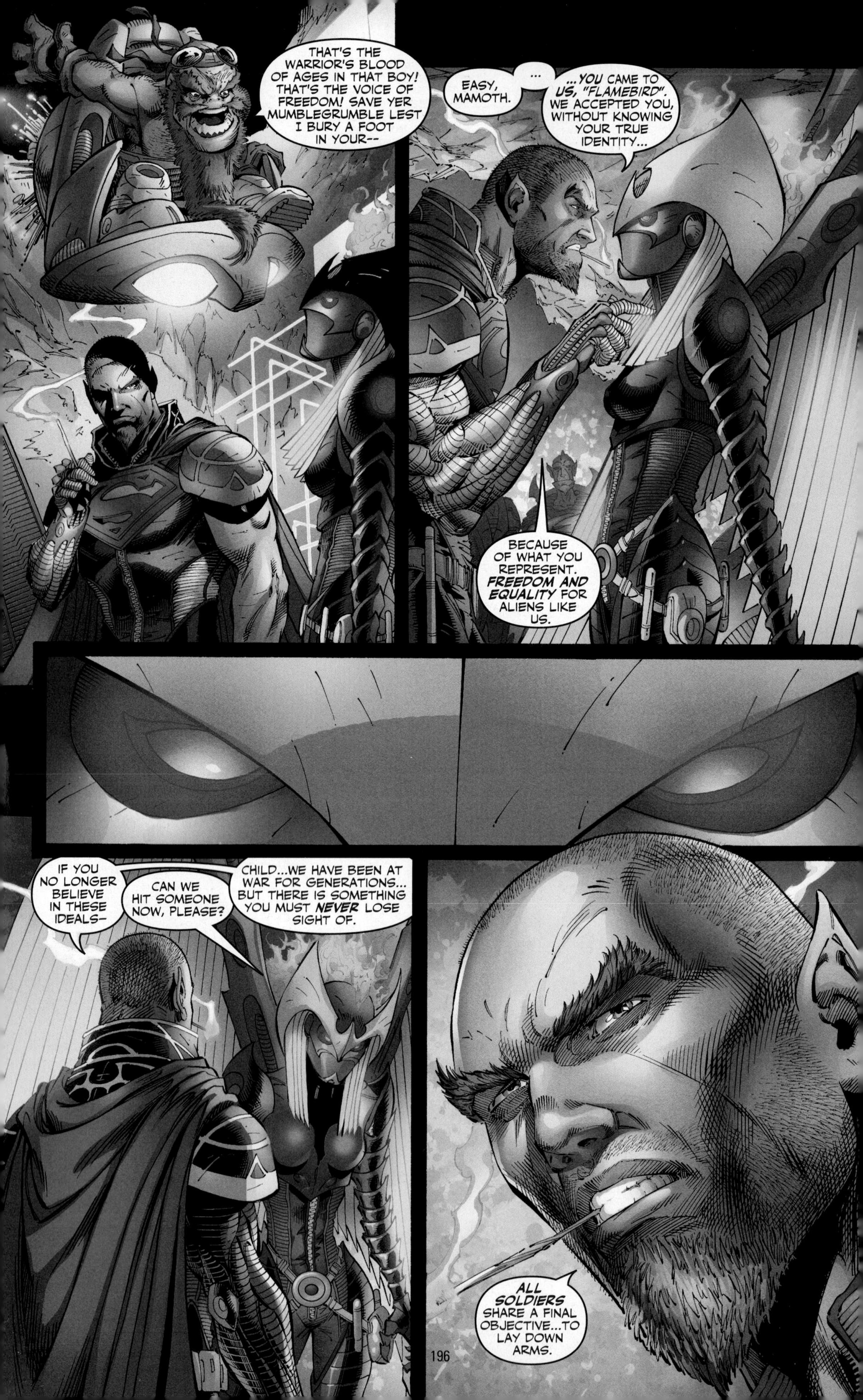
THAT'S THE WARRIOR'S BLOOD OF AGES IN THAT BOY! THAT'S THE VOICE OF FREEDOM! SAVE YER MUMBLEGRUMBLE LEST I BURY A FOOT IN YOUR--
EASY, MAMOTH.
...
...YOU CAME TO US, "FLAMEBIRD". WE ACCEPTED YOU, WITHOUT KNOWING YOUR TRUE IDENTITY...
BECAUSE OF WHAT YOU REPRESENT. FREEDOM AND EQUALITY FOR ALIENS LIKE US.
IF YOU NO LONGER BELIEVE IN THESE IDEALS-
CAN WE HIT SOMEONE NOW, PLEASE?
CHILD...WE HAVE BEEN AT WAR FOR GENERATIONS... BUT THERE IS SOMETHING YOU MUST NEVER LOSE SIGHT OF.
ALL SOLDIERS SHARE A FINAL OBJECTIVE...TO LAY DOWN ARMS.

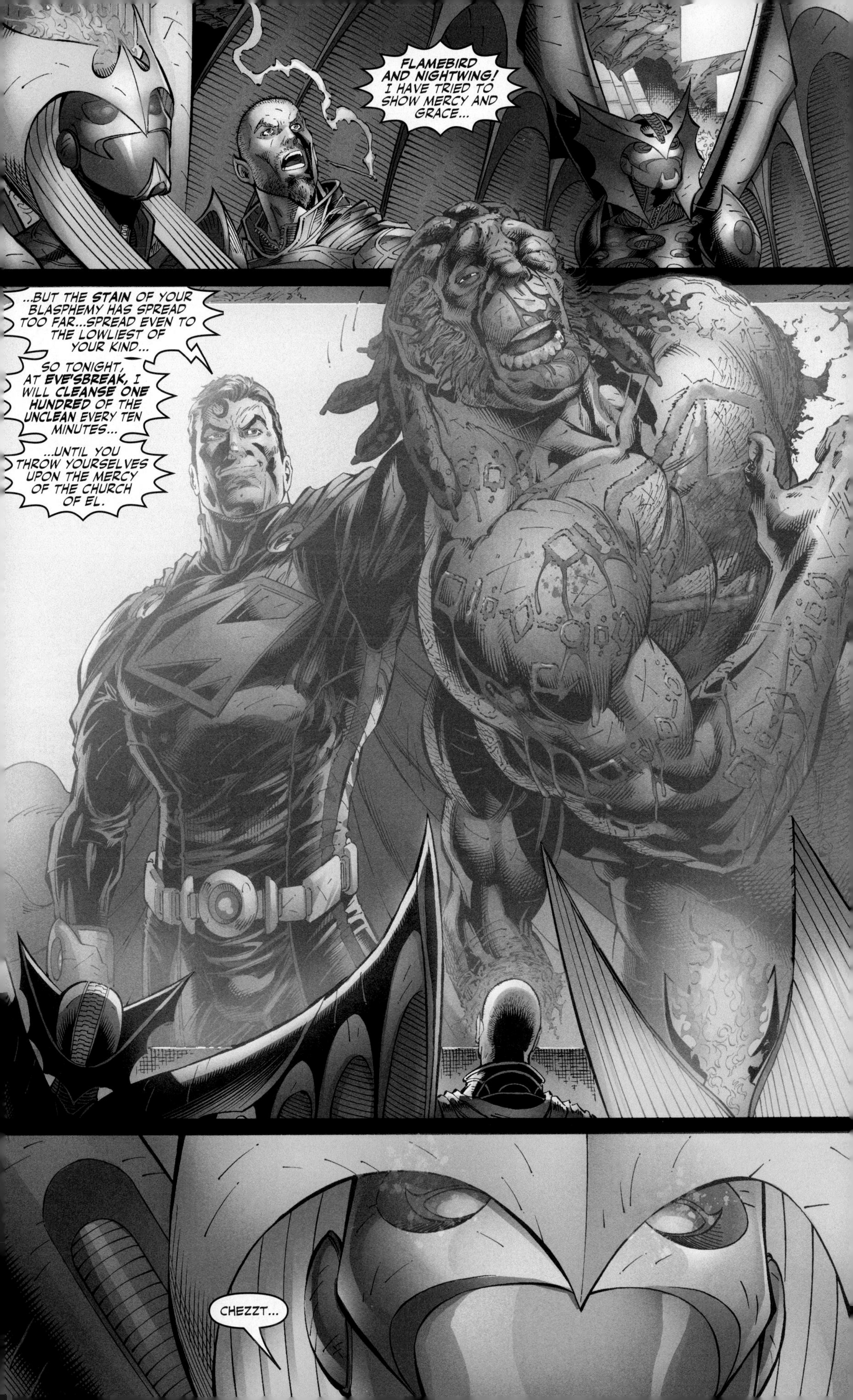
FLAMEBIRD AND NIGHTWING! I HAVE TRIED TO SHOW MERCY AND GRACE...
...BUT THE STAIN OF YOUR BLASPHEMY HAS SPREAD TOO FAR...SPREAD EVEN TO THE LOWLIEST OF YOUR KIND...
SO TONIGHT, AT EVE'SBREAK, I WILL CLEANSE ONE HUNDRED OF THE UNCLEAN EVERY TEN MINUTES...
...UNTIL YOU THROW YOURSELVES UPON THE MERCY OF THE CHURCH OF EL.
CHEZZT...

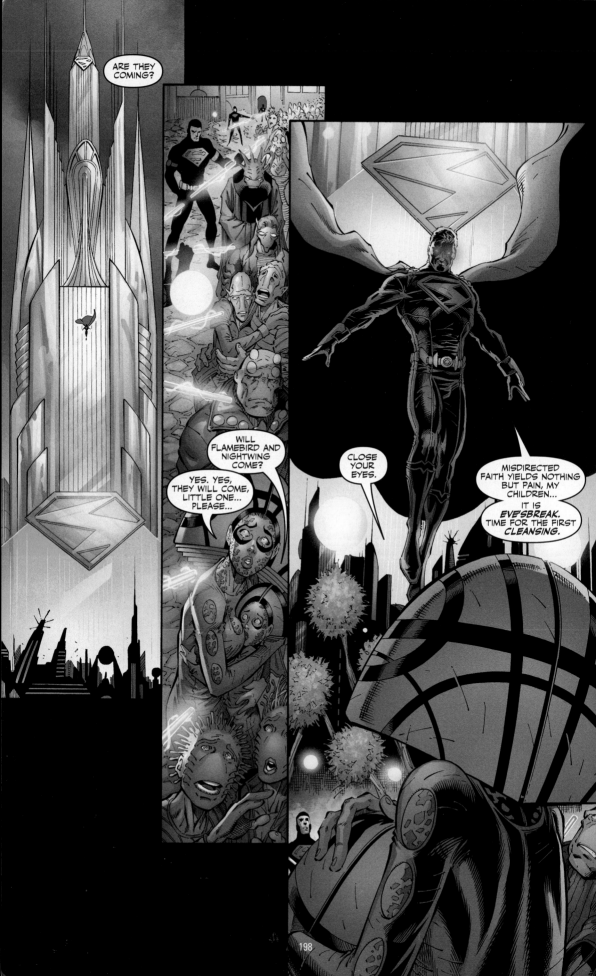

ARE THEY COMING?

WILL FLAMEBIRD AND NIGHTWING COME?

YES. YES, THEY WILL COME, LITTLE ONE... PLEASE...

CLOSE YOUR EYES.

MISDIRECTED FAITH YIELDS NOTHING BUT PAIN, MY CHILDREN...

IT IS *EVE'SBREAK*. TIME FOR THE FIRST *CLEANSING*.

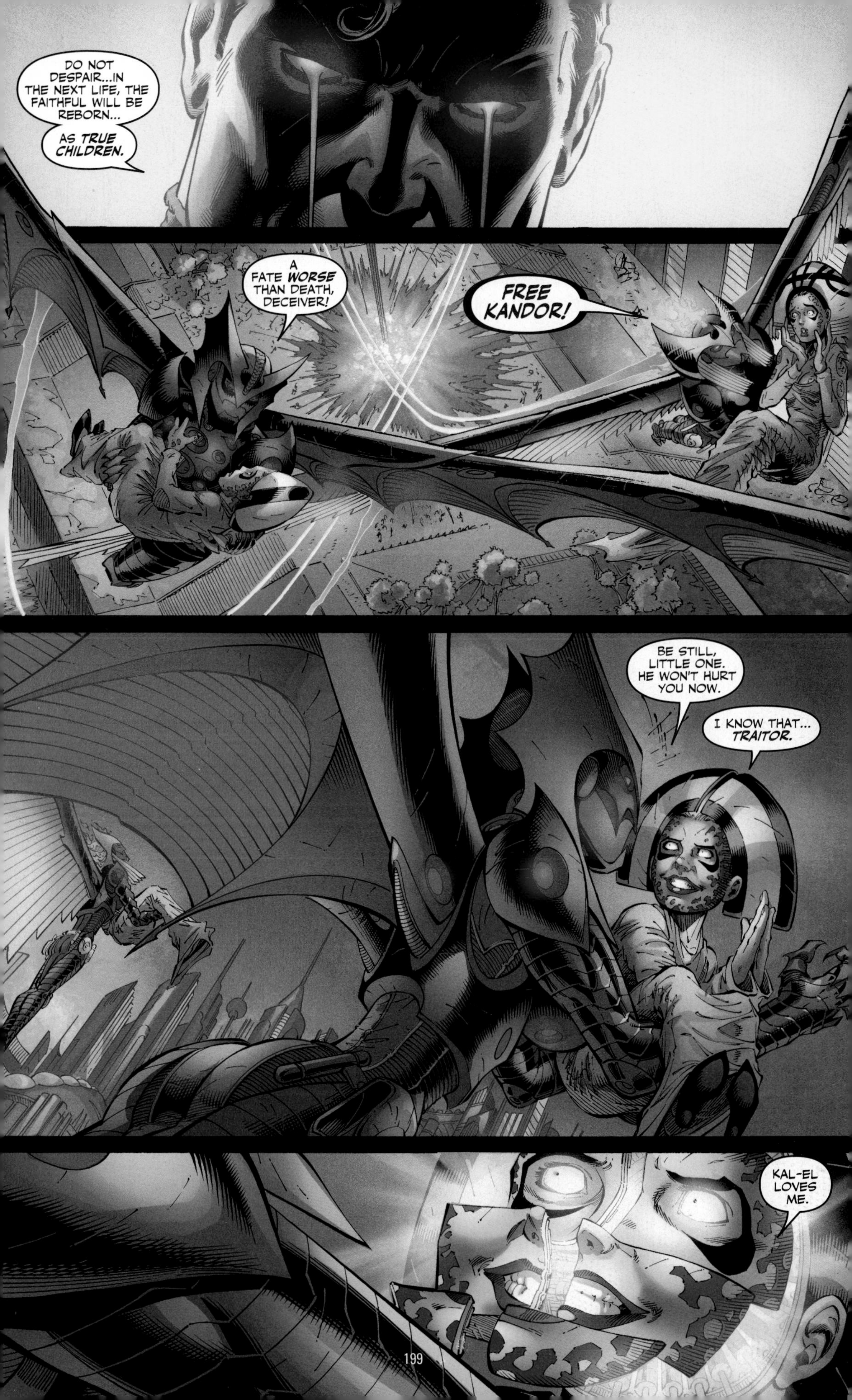
DO NOT DESPAIR...IN THE NEXT LIFE, THE FAITHFUL WILL BE REBORN...
AS TRUE CHILDREN.
A FATE WORSE THAN DEATH, DECEIVER!
FREE KANDOR!
BE STILL, LITTLE ONE. HE WON'T HURT YOU NOW.
I KNOW THAT... TRAITOR.
KAL-EL LOVES ME.

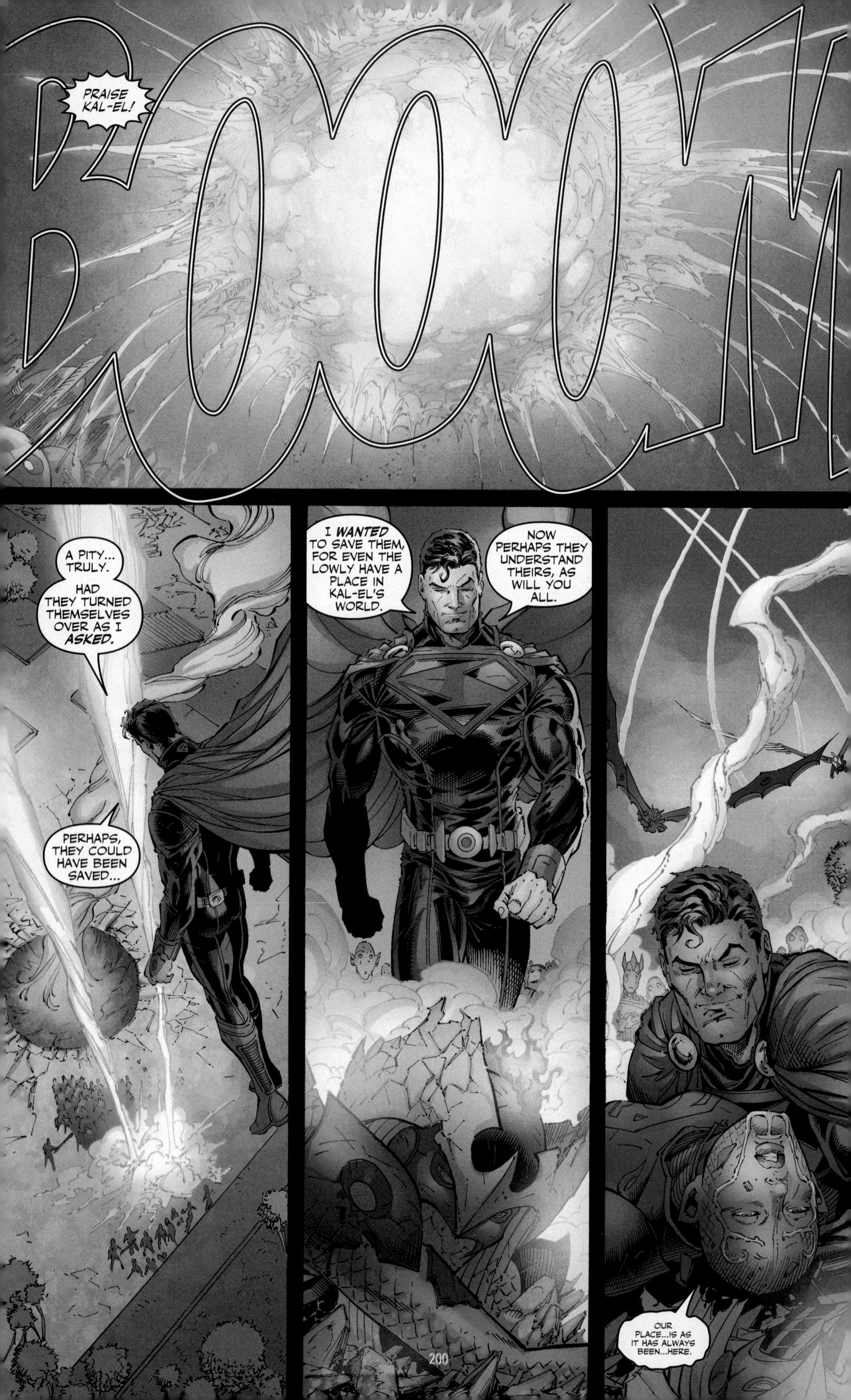
PRAISE KAL-EL!
BOOOOOM
A PITY... TRULY.
HAD THEY TURNED THEMSELVES OVER AS I *ASKED.*
PERHAPS, THEY COULD HAVE BEEN SAVED...
I *WANTED* TO SAVE THEM, FOR EVEN THE LOWLY HAVE A PLACE IN KAL-EL'S WORLD.
NOW PERHAPS THEY UNDERSTAND THEIRS, AS WILL YOU ALL.
OUR PLACE...IS AS IT HAS ALWAYS BEEN...HERE.

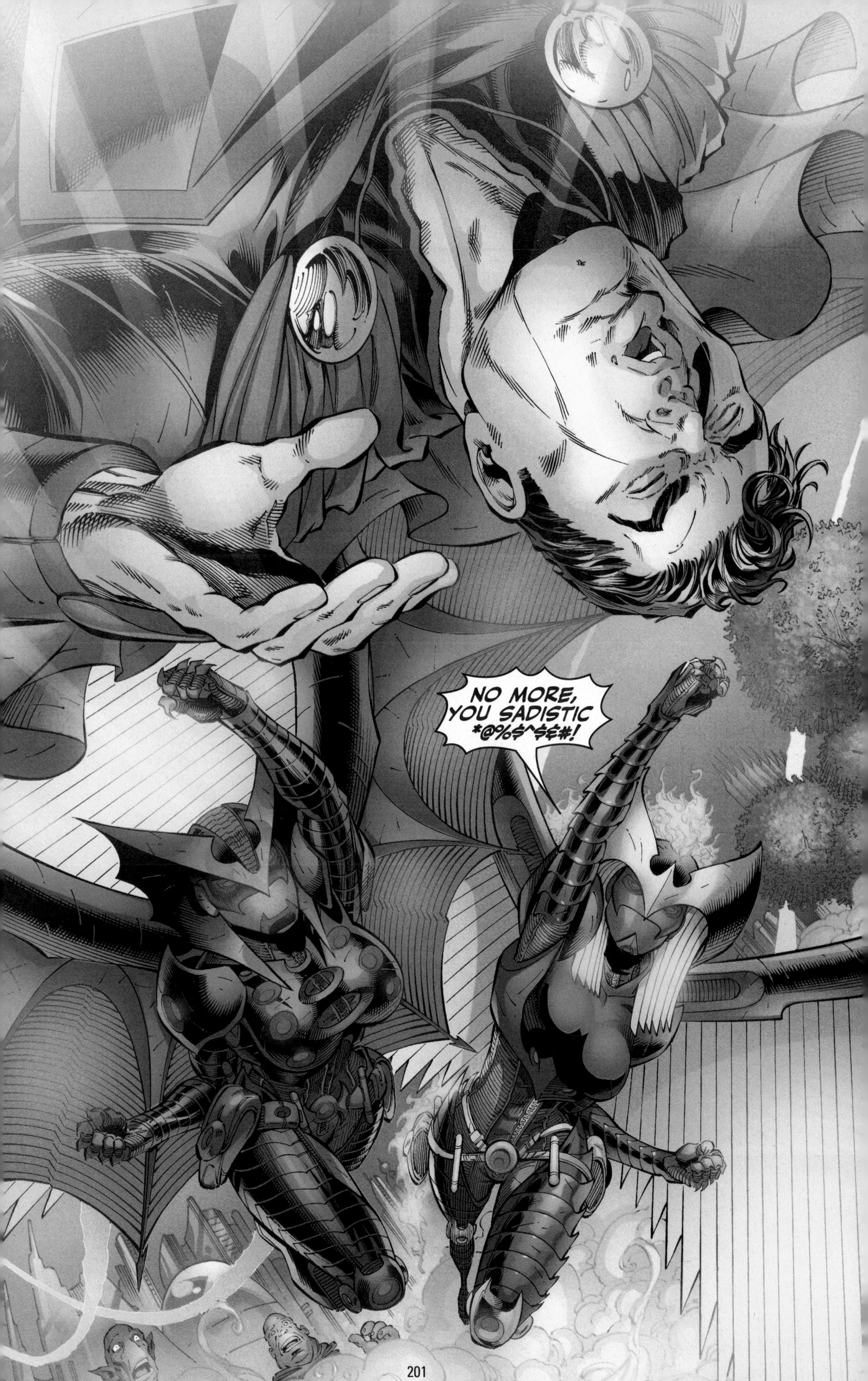
NO MORE, YOU SADISTIC *@%$^$€#!

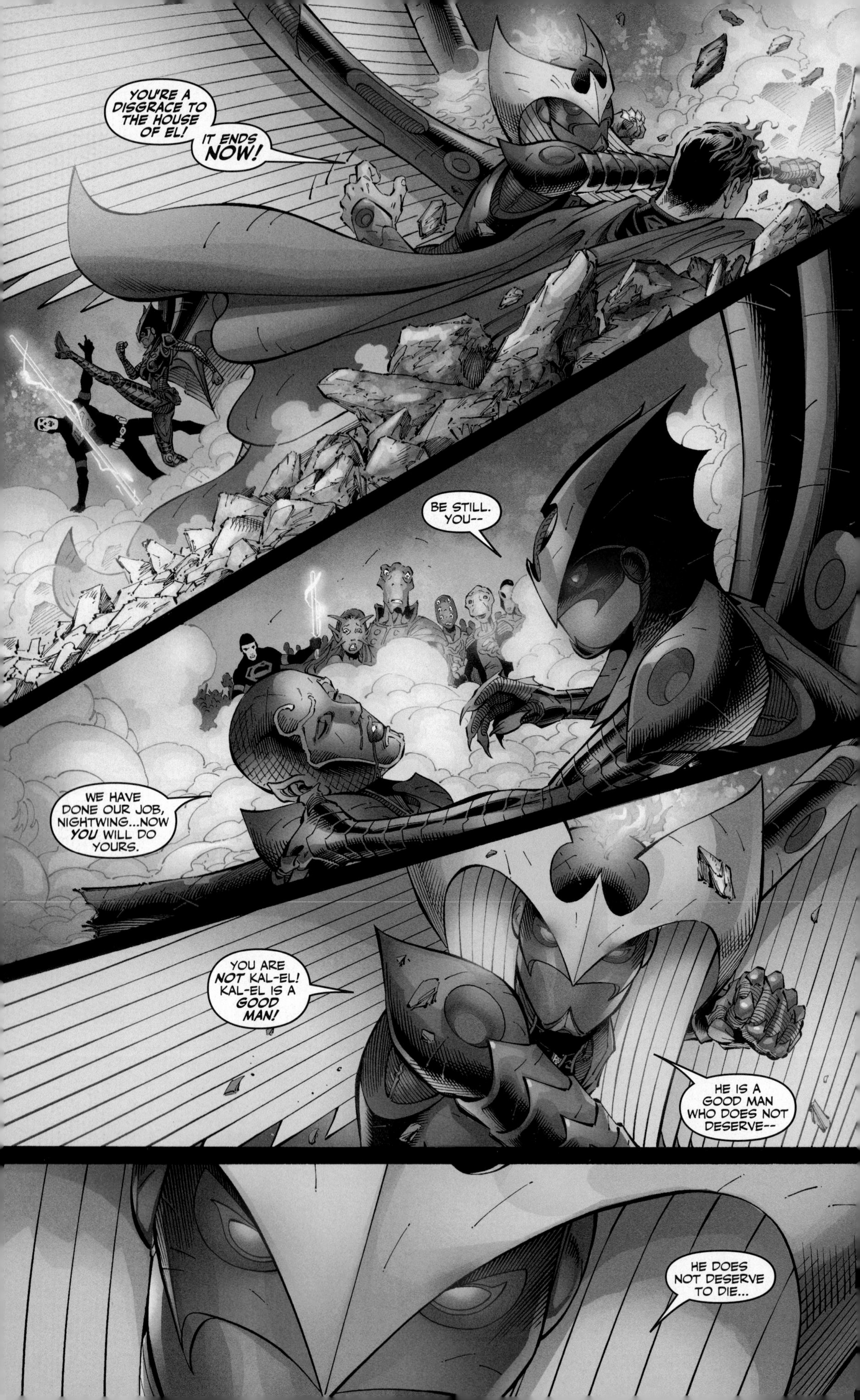
YOU'RE A DISGRACE TO THE HOUSE OF EL!
IT ENDS NOW!
BE STILL. YOU--
WE HAVE DONE OUR JOB, NIGHTWING...NOW YOU WILL DO YOURS.
YOU ARE NOT KAL-EL! KAL-EL IS A GOOD MAN!
HE IS A GOOD MAN WHO DOES NOT DESERVE--
HE DOES NOT DESERVE TO DIE...

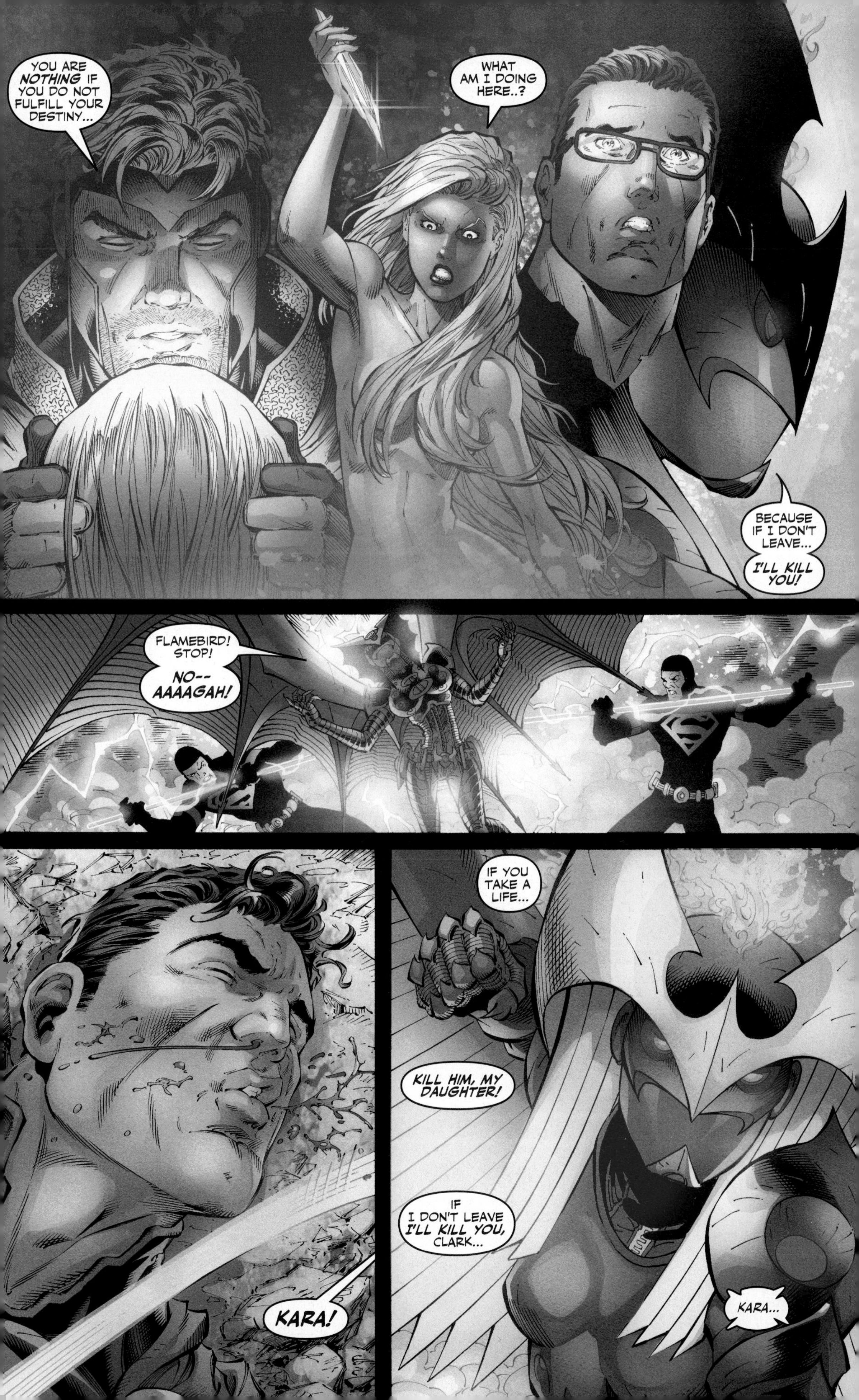
YOU ARE NOTHING IF YOU DO NOT FULFILL YOUR DESTINY...
WHAT AM I DOING HERE..?
BECAUSE IF I DON'T LEAVE...
I'LL KILL YOU!
FLAMEBIRD! STOP!
NO-- AAAAGAH!
KARA!
IF YOU TAKE A LIFE...
KILL HIM, MY DAUGHTER!
IF I DON'T LEAVE I'LL KILL YOU, CLARK...
KARA...

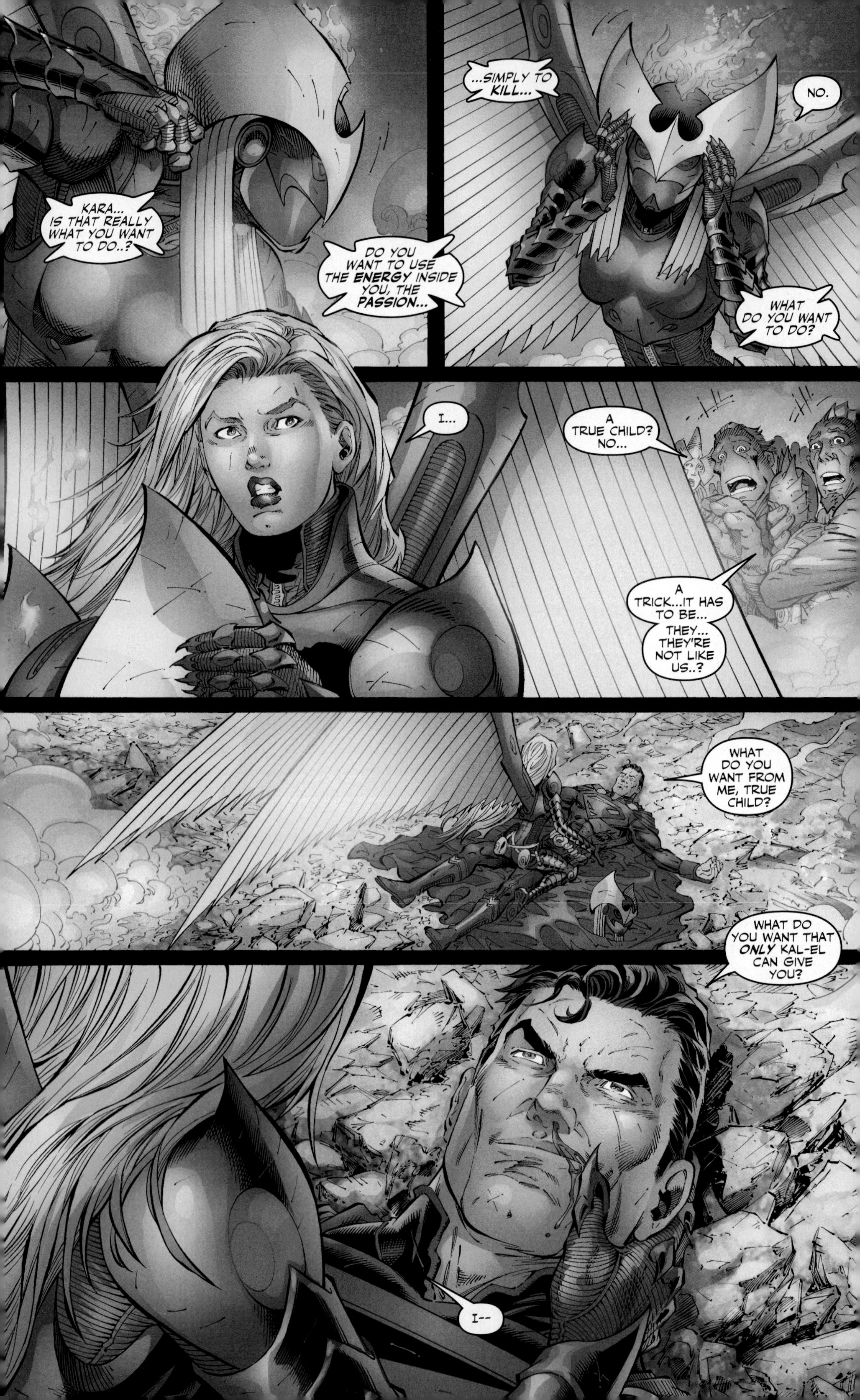
KARA... IS THAT REALLY WHAT YOU WANT TO DO..?
DO YOU WANT TO USE THE ENERGY INSIDE YOU, THE PASSION...
...SIMPLY TO KILL...
NO.
WHAT DO YOU WANT TO DO?
I...
A TRUE CHILD? NO...
A TRICK...IT HAS TO BE... THEY... THEY'RE NOT LIKE US..?
WHAT DO YOU WANT FROM ME, TRUE CHILD?
WHAT DO YOU WANT THAT ONLY KAL-EL CAN GIVE YOU?
I--

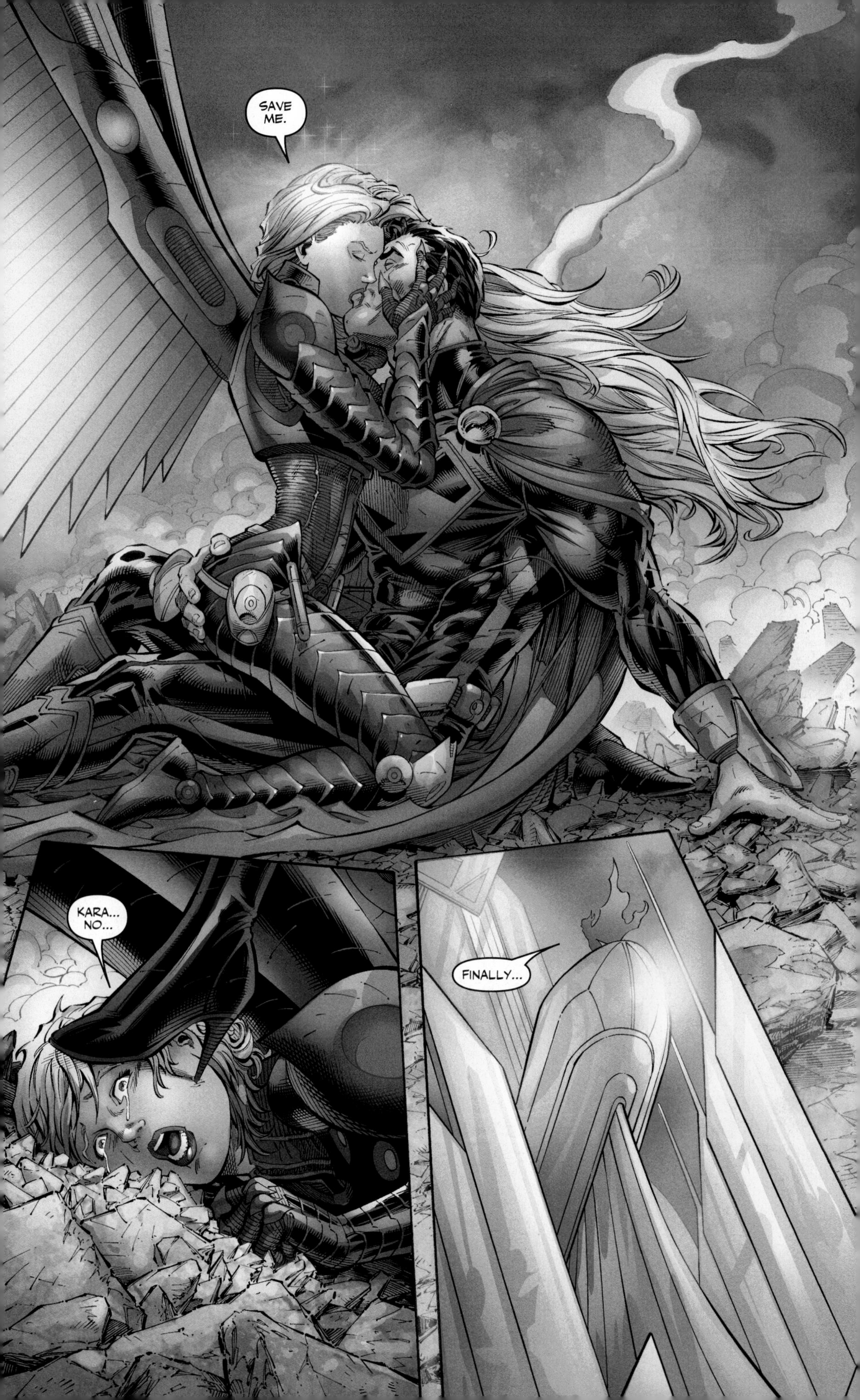
SAVE ME.
KARA... NO...
FINALLY...

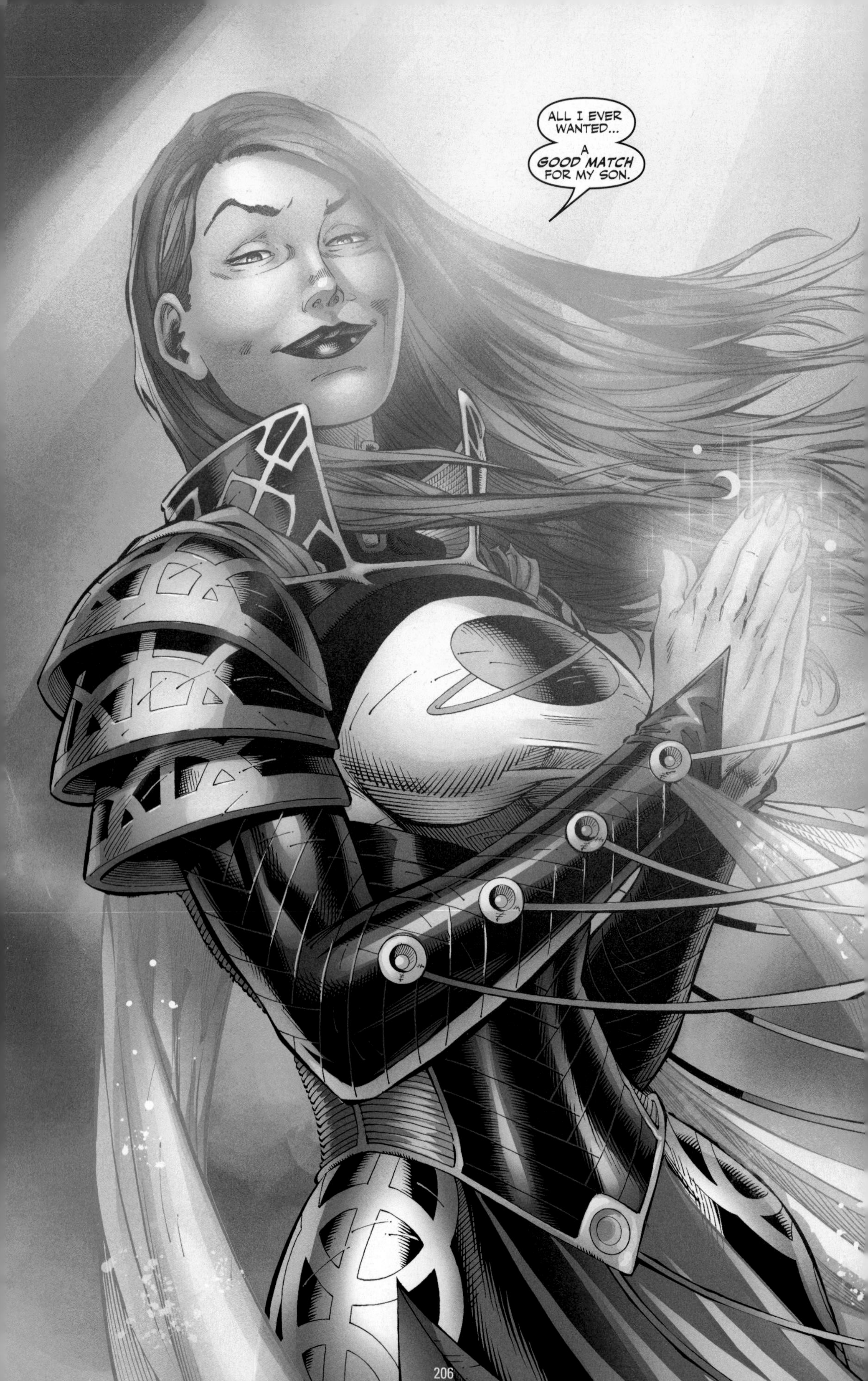
ALL I EVER WANTED... A GOOD MATCH FOR MY SON.

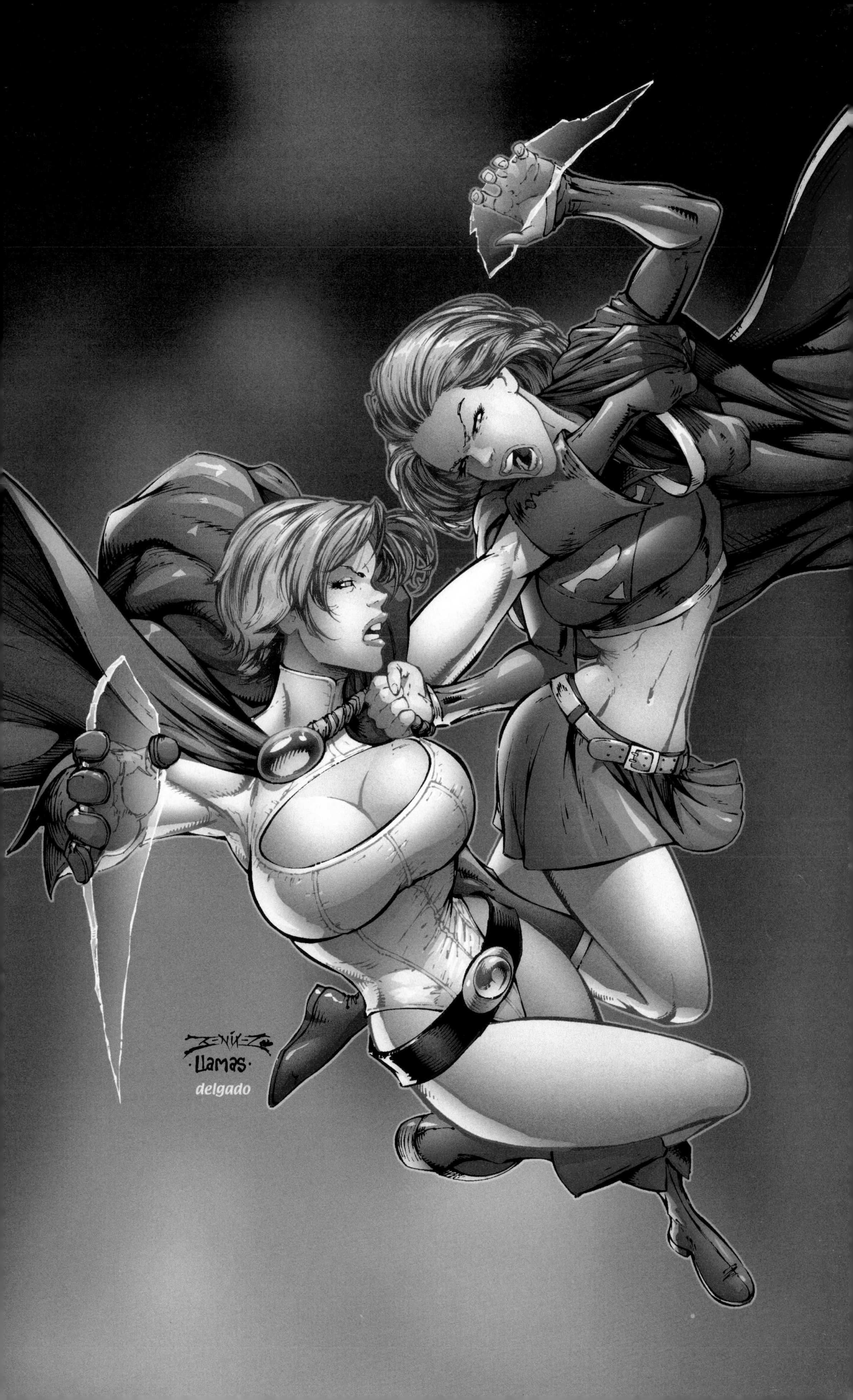
Llamas
delgado

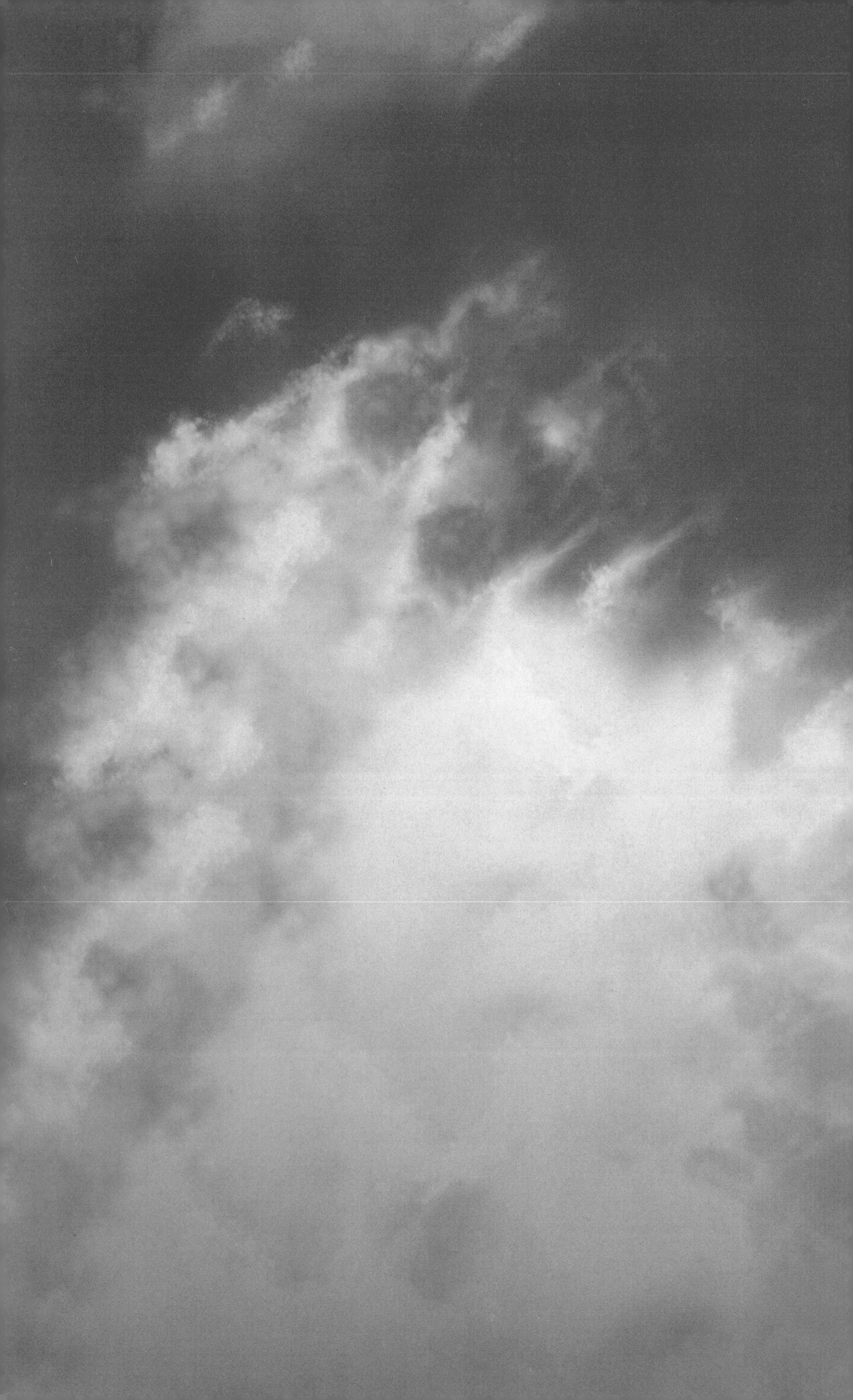

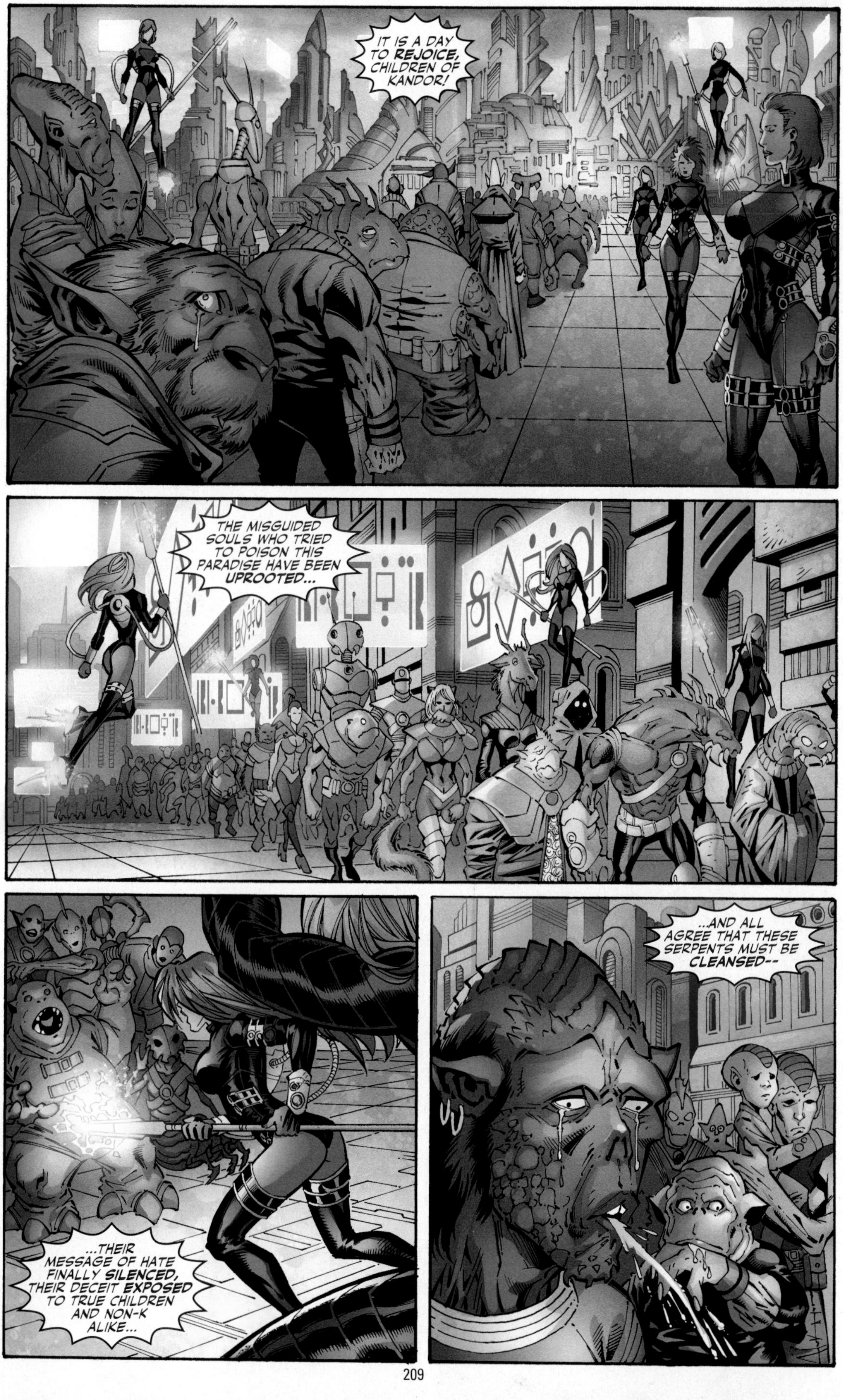
IT IS A DAY TO REJOICE, CHILDREN OF KANDOR!
THE MISGUIDED SOULS WHO TRIED TO POISON THIS PARADISE HAVE BEEN UPROOTED...
...THEIR MESSAGE OF HATE FINALLY SILENCED, THEIR DECEIT EXPOSED TO TRUE CHILDREN AND NON-K ALIKE...
...AND ALL AGREE THAT THESE SERPENTS MUST BE CLEANSED--

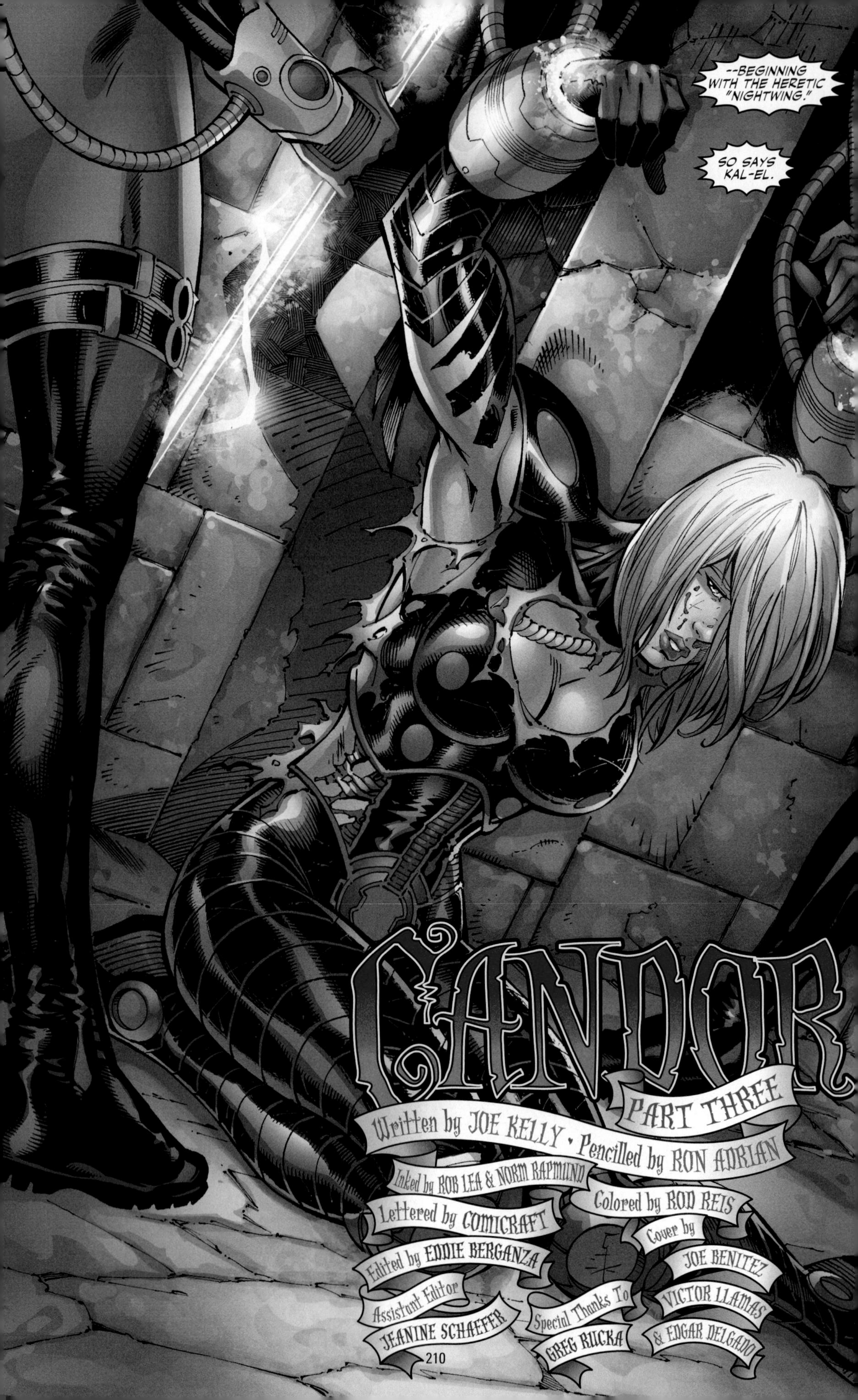
--BEGINNING WITH THE HERETIC "NIGHTWING."
SO SAYS KAL-EL.
CANDOR
PART THREE
Written by JOE KELLY • Pencilled by RON ADRIAN
Inked by ROB LEA & NORM RAPMUND
Lettered by COMICRAFT
Colored by ROD REIS
Edited by EDDIE BERGANZA
Cover by JOE BENITEZ
Assistant Editor JEANINE SCHAEFER
Special Thanks To GREG RUCKA
VICTOR LLAMAS & EDGAR DELGADO

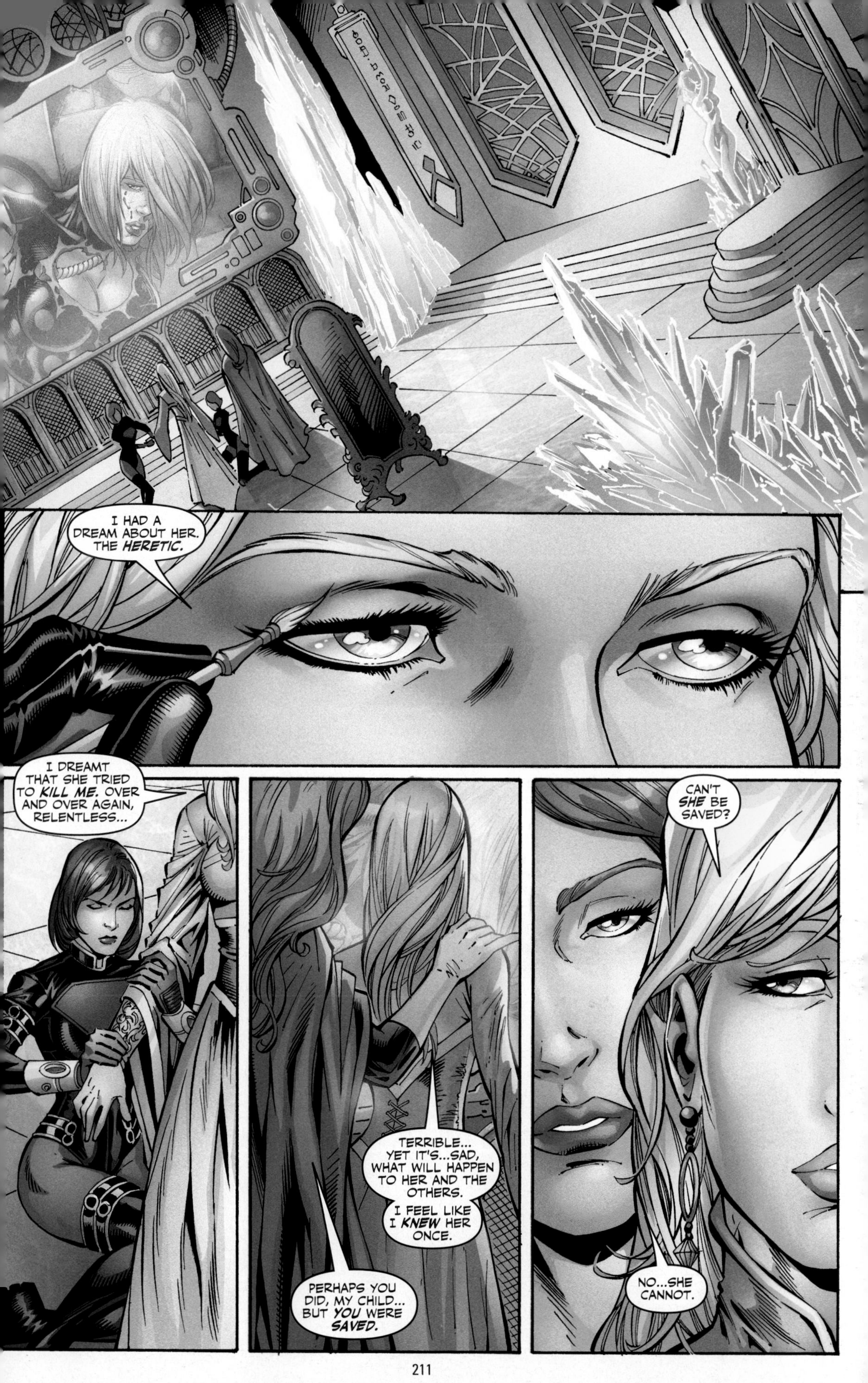

I HAD A DREAM ABOUT HER. THE HERETIC.
I DREAMT THAT SHE TRIED TO KILL ME. OVER AND OVER AGAIN, RELENTLESS...
TERRIBLE... YET IT'S...SAD, WHAT WILL HAPPEN TO HER AND THE OTHERS.
I FEEL LIKE I KNEW HER ONCE.
PERHAPS YOU DID, MY CHILD... BUT YOU WERE SAVED.
CAN'T SHE BE SAVED?
NO...SHE CANNOT.

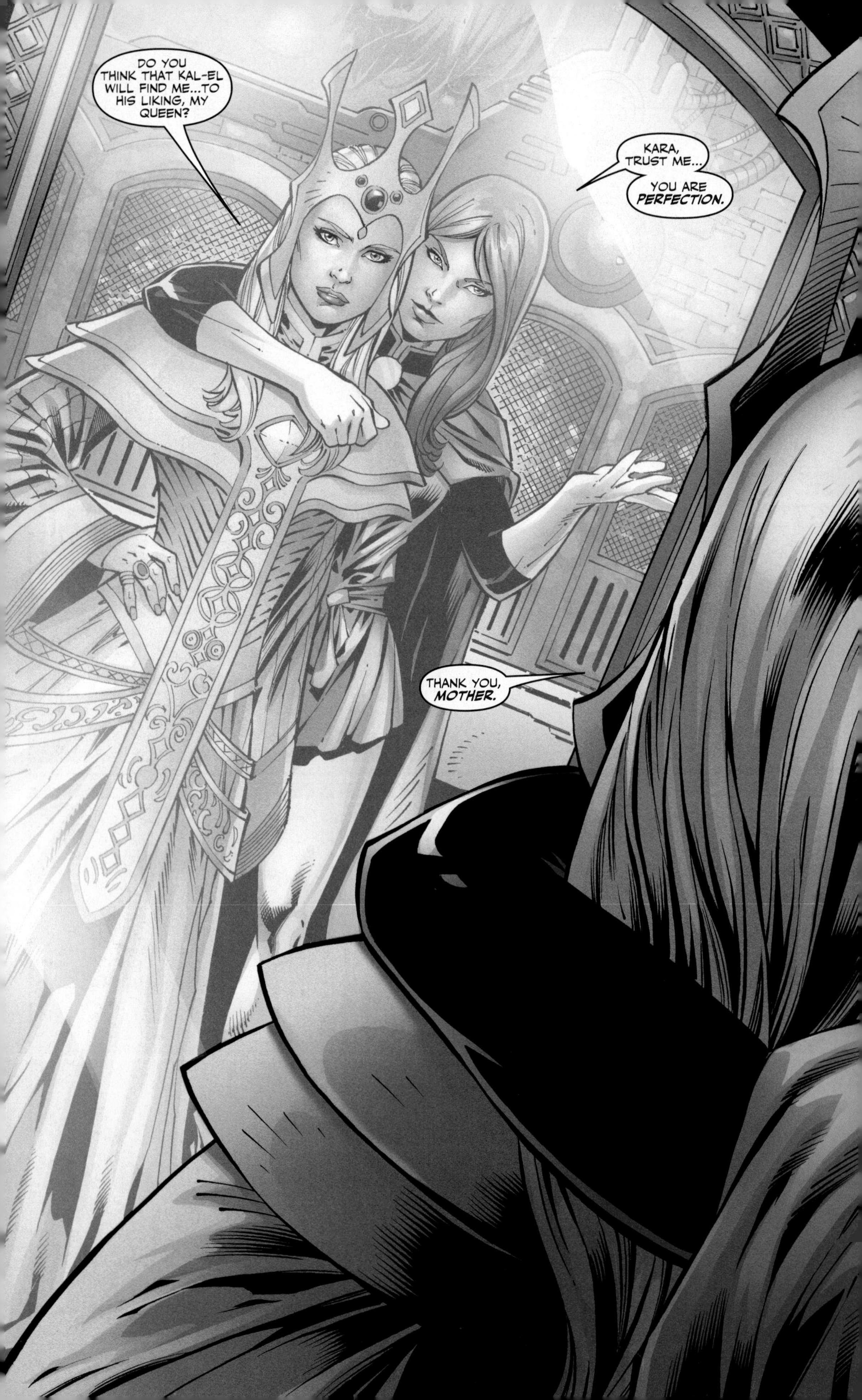
DO YOU THINK THAT KAL-EL WILL FIND ME...TO HIS LIKING, MY QUEEN?
KARA, TRUST ME...
YOU ARE *PERFECTION.*
THANK YOU, *MOTHER.*

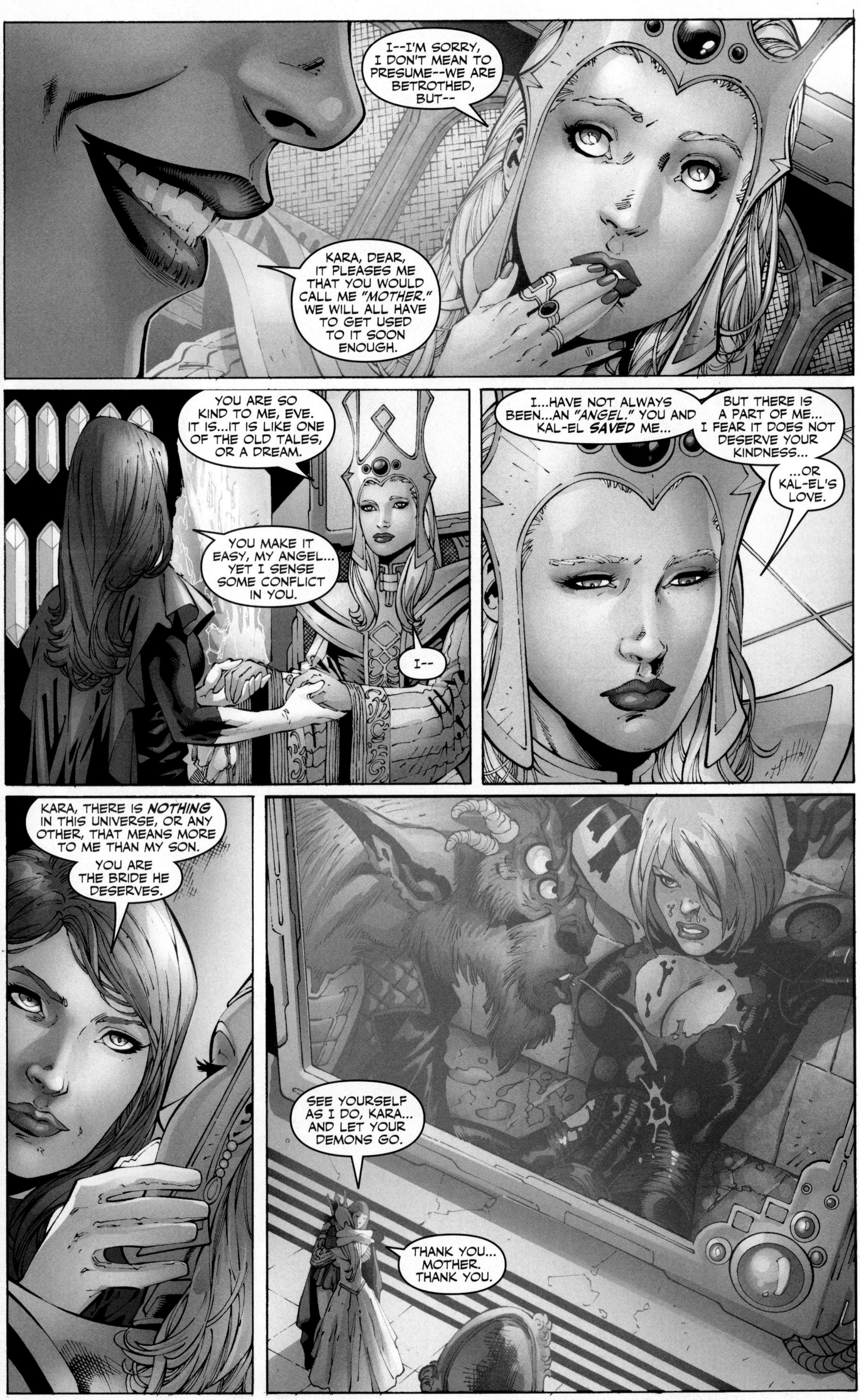
I--I'M SORRY, I DON'T MEAN TO PRESUME--WE ARE BETROTHED, BUT--
KARA, DEAR, IT PLEASES ME THAT YOU WOULD CALL ME "MOTHER." WE WILL ALL HAVE TO GET USED TO IT SOON ENOUGH.
YOU ARE SO KIND TO ME, EVE. IT IS...IT IS LIKE ONE OF THE OLD TALES, OR A DREAM.
YOU MAKE IT EASY, MY ANGEL... YET I SENSE SOME CONFLICT IN YOU.
I--
I...HAVE NOT ALWAYS BEEN...AN "ANGEL." YOU AND KAL-EL SAVED ME...
BUT THERE IS A PART OF ME... I FEAR IT DOES NOT DESERVE YOUR KINDNESS...
...OR KAL-EL'S LOVE.
KARA, THERE IS NOTHING IN THIS UNIVERSE, OR ANY OTHER, THAT MEANS MORE TO ME THAN MY SON.
YOU ARE THE BRIDE HE DESERVES.
SEE YOURSELF AS I DO, KARA... AND LET YOUR DEMONS GO.
THANK YOU... MOTHER. THANK YOU.

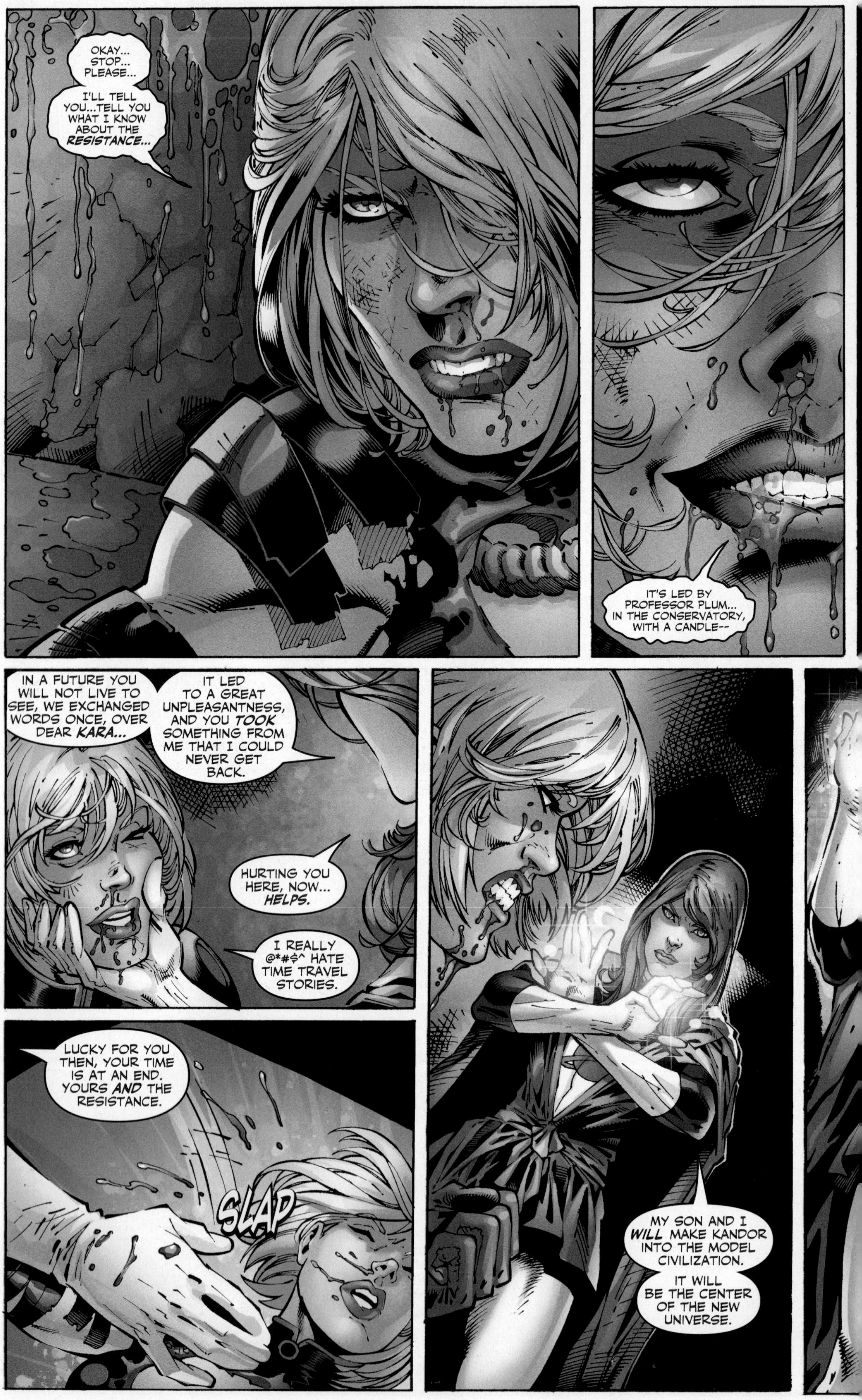

OKAY... STOP... PLEASE...
I'LL TELL YOU...TELL YOU WHAT I KNOW ABOUT THE RESISTANCE...
IT'S LED BY PROFESSOR PLUM... IN THE CONSERVATORY, WITH A CANDLE--
IN A FUTURE YOU WILL NOT LIVE TO SEE, WE EXCHANGED WORDS ONCE, OVER DEAR KARA...
IT LED TO A GREAT UNPLEASANTNESS, AND YOU TOOK SOMETHING FROM ME THAT I COULD NEVER GET BACK.
HURTING YOU HERE, NOW... HELPS.
I REALLY @*#$^ HATE TIME TRAVEL STORIES.
LUCKY FOR YOU THEN, YOUR TIME IS AT AN END. YOURS AND THE RESISTANCE.
SLAP
MY SON AND I WILL MAKE KANDOR INTO THE MODEL CIVILIZATION.
IT WILL BE THE CENTER OF THE NEW UNIVERSE.

YOU ARE A STUBBORN ONE, KAREN.

EVERYWHEN AND EVERYWHERE WE HAVE CROSSED DESTINIES...

KRAK

...ALWAYS THE MISBEGOTTEN STEPCHILD WHO CANNOT BEHAVE.

YOU'LL FORGIVE ME IF I DON'T KNOW WHAT THE HELL YOU'RE TALKING ABOUT.

Y-YOU'RE TELEPATHIC...

KARA...YOU'RE CONTROLLING... KARA--

HARDLY. SHE REQUIRED LITTLE MORE THAN A NUDGE TO EMBRACE MY VISION FOR HER IN KANDOR.

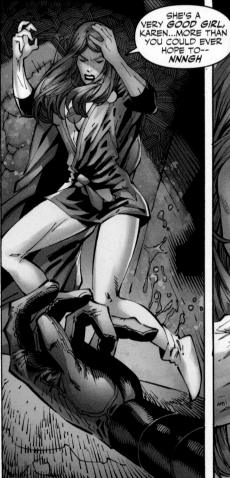

SHE'S A VERY GOOD GIRL, KAREN...MORE THAN YOU COULD EVER HOPE TO-- NNNGH

KARA?

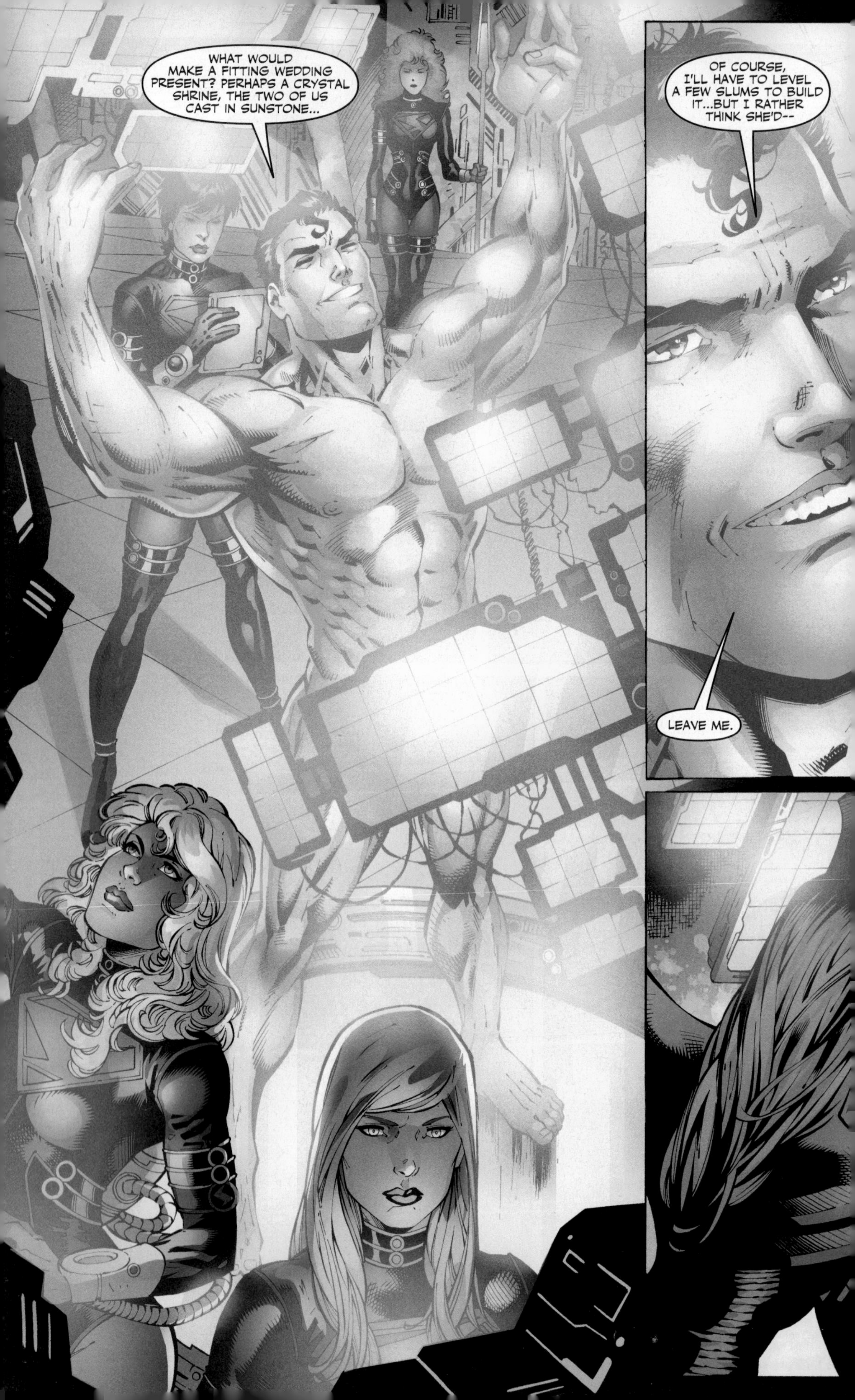
WHAT WOULD MAKE A FITTING WEDDING PRESENT? PERHAPS A CRYSTAL SHRINE, THE TWO OF US CAST IN SUNSTONE...
OF COURSE, I'LL HAVE TO LEVEL A FEW SLUMS TO BUILD IT...BUT I RATHER THINK SHE'D--
LEAVE ME.

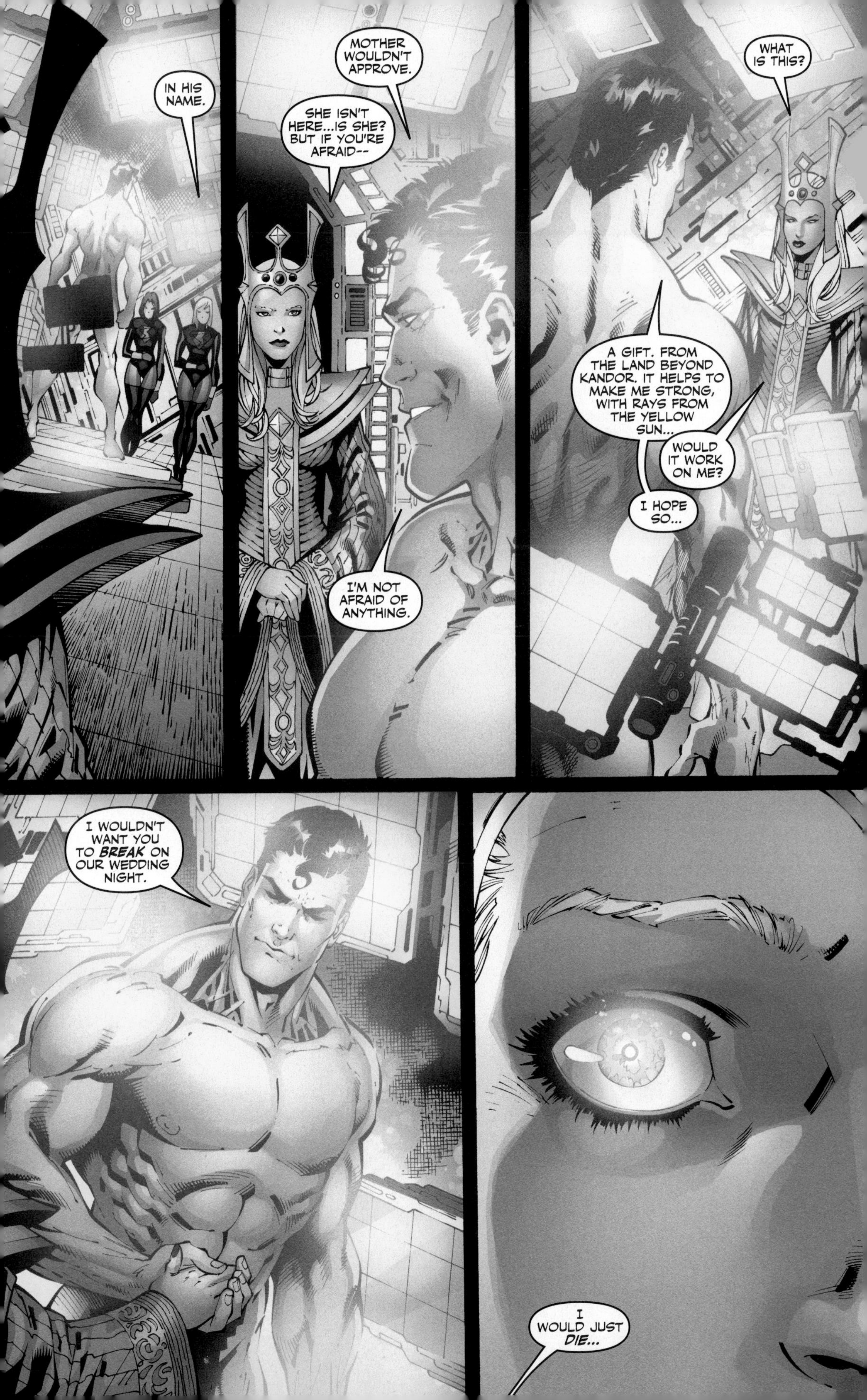
IN HIS NAME.
MOTHER WOULDN'T APPROVE.
SHE ISN'T HERE...IS SHE? BUT IF YOU'RE AFRAID--
I'M NOT AFRAID OF ANYTHING.
WHAT IS THIS?
A GIFT. FROM THE LAND BEYOND KANDOR. IT HELPS TO MAKE ME STRONG, WITH RAYS FROM THE YELLOW SUN...
WOULD IT WORK ON ME?
I HOPE SO...
I WOULDN'T WANT YOU TO BREAK ON OUR WEDDING NIGHT.
I WOULD JUST DIE...

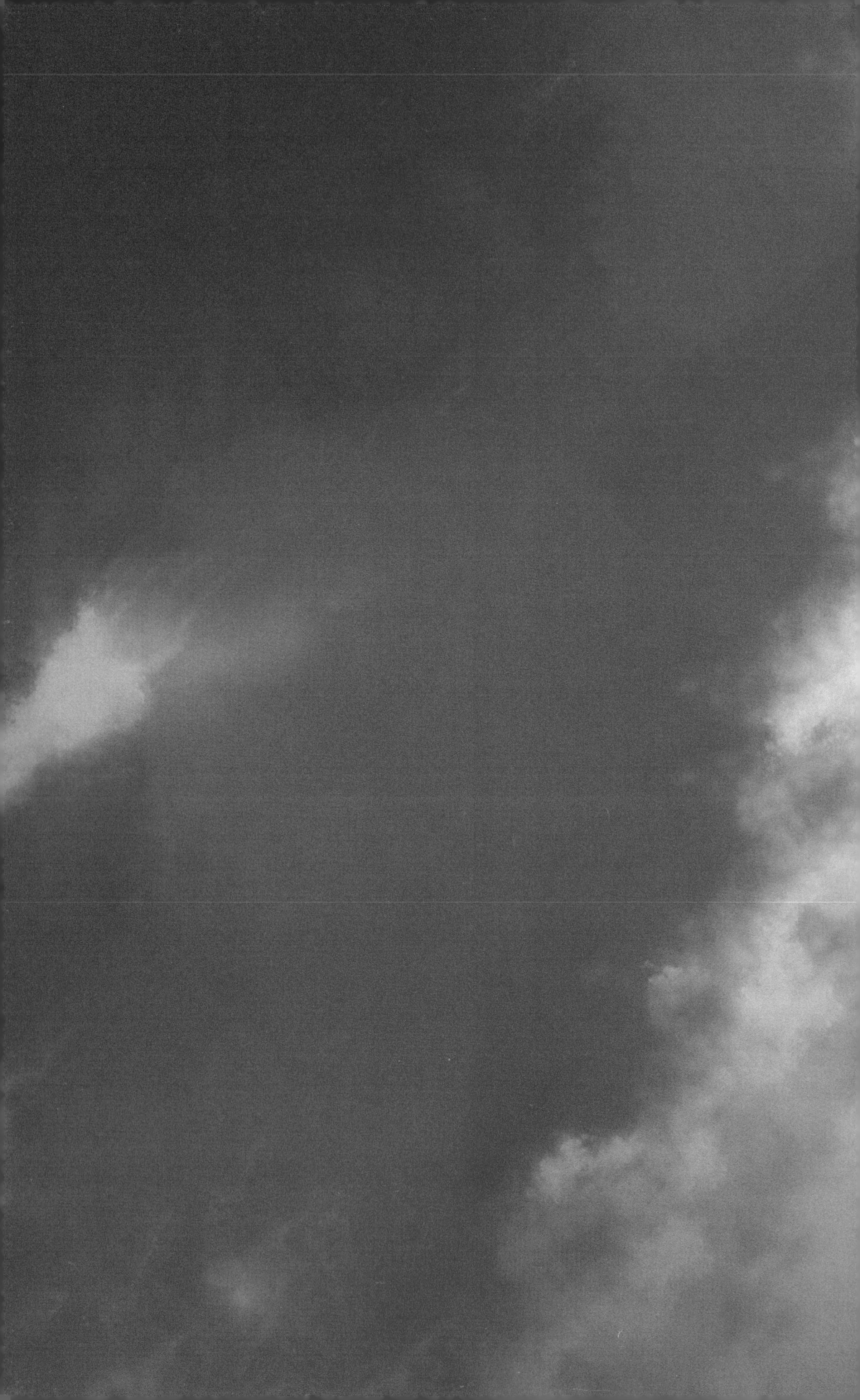

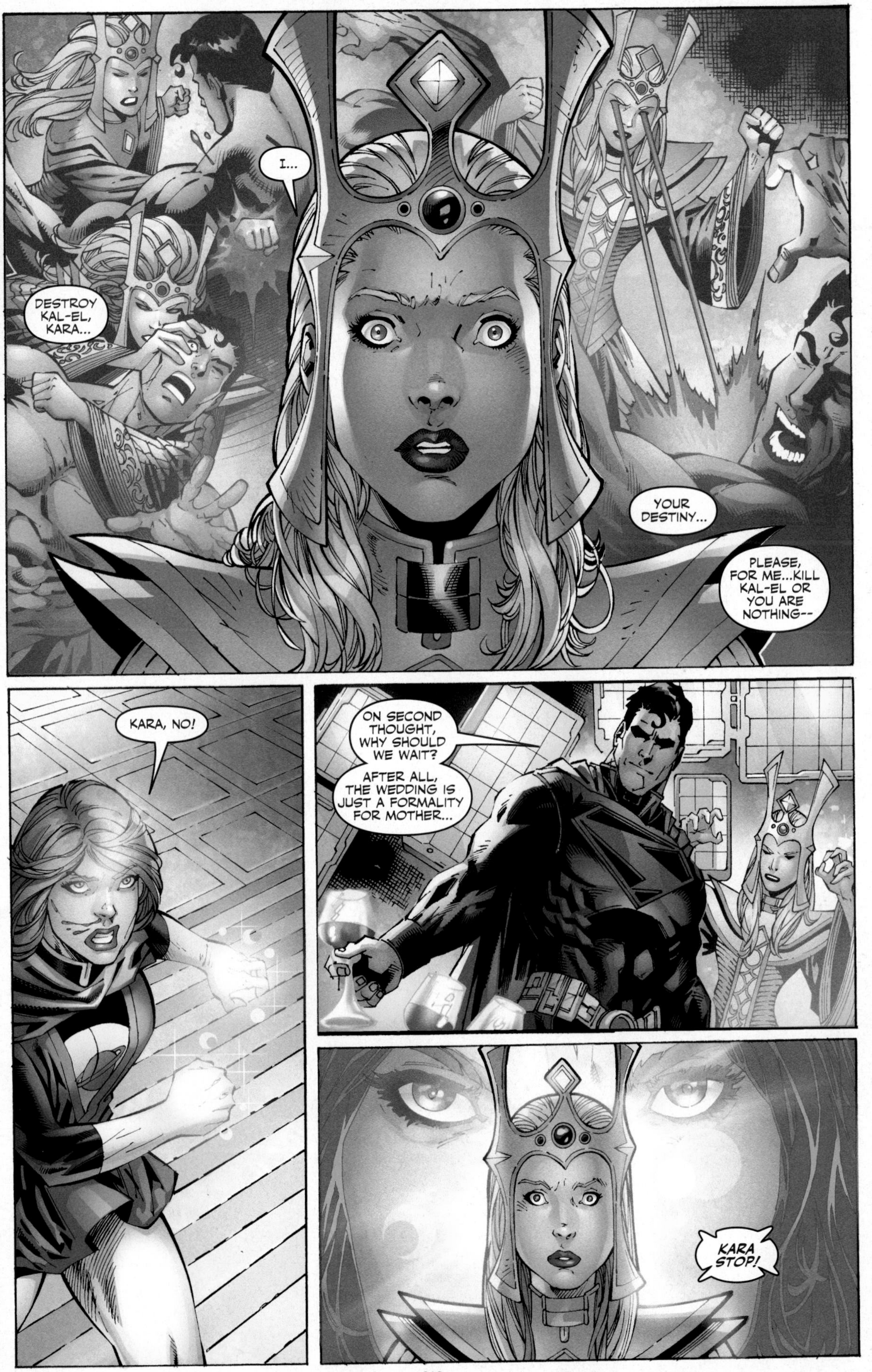
I...
DESTROY KAL-EL, KARA...
YOUR DESTINY...
PLEASE, FOR ME...KILL KAL-EL OR YOU ARE NOTHING--
KARA, NO!
ON SECOND THOUGHT, WHY SHOULD WE WAIT?
AFTER ALL, THE WEDDING IS JUST A FORMALITY FOR MOTHER...
KARA STOP!

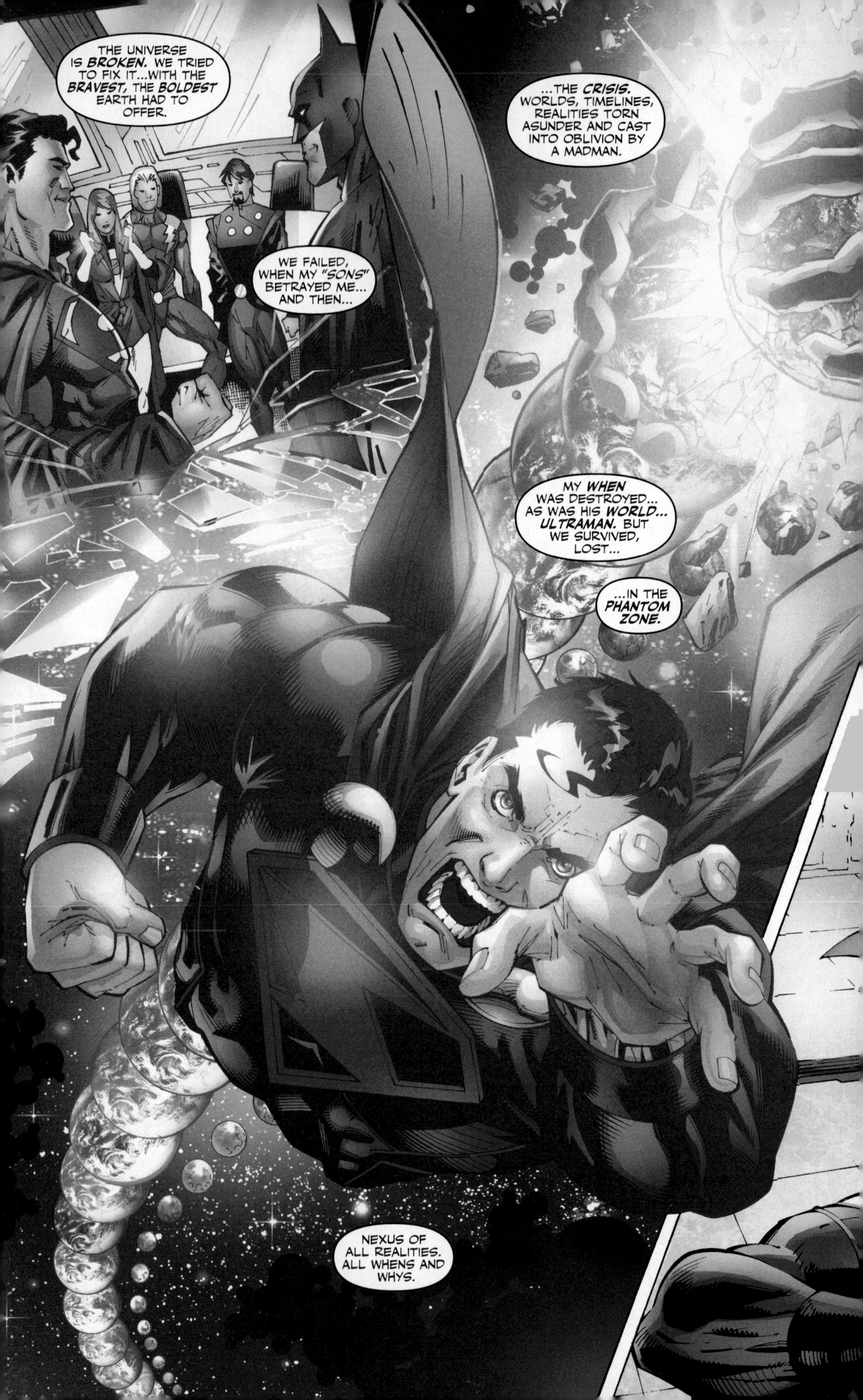
THE UNIVERSE IS BROKEN. WE TRIED TO FIX IT...WITH THE BRAVEST, THE BOLDEST EARTH HAD TO OFFER.
WE FAILED, WHEN MY "SONS" BETRAYED ME... AND THEN...
...THE CRISIS. WORLDS, TIMELINES, REALITIES TORN ASUNDER AND CAST INTO OBLIVION BY A MADMAN.
MY WHEN WAS DESTROYED... AS WAS HIS WORLD... ULTRAMAN. BUT WE SURVIVED, LOST...
...IN THE PHANTOM ZONE.
NEXUS OF ALL REALITIES. ALL WHENS AND WHYS.

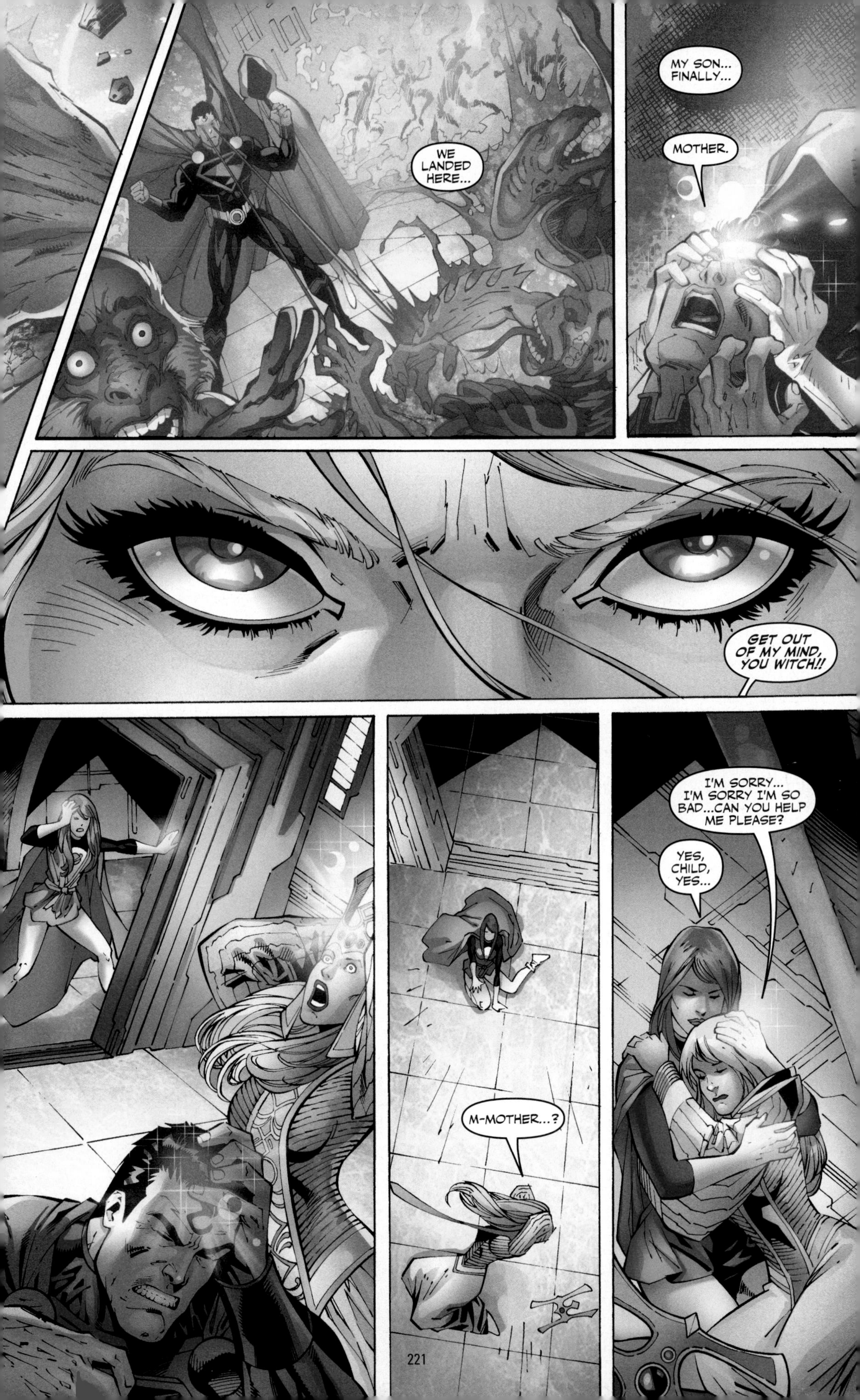
WE LANDED HERE...
MY SON... FINALLY...
MOTHER.
GET OUT OF MY MIND, YOU WITCH!!
M-MOTHER...?
I'M SORRY... I'M SORRY I'M SO BAD...CAN YOU HELP ME PLEASE?
YES, CHILD, YES...

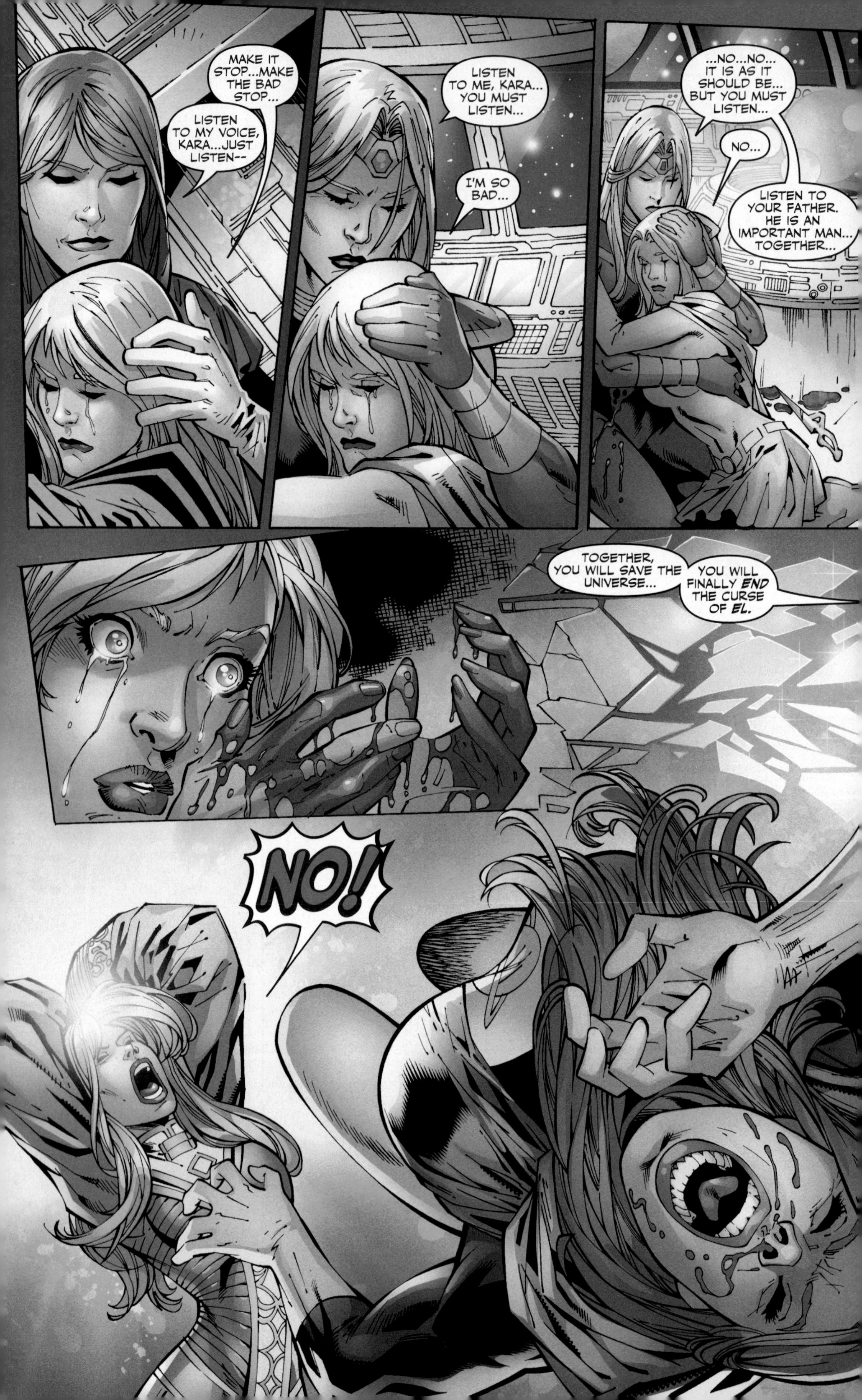
MAKE IT STOP...MAKE THE BAD STOP...
LISTEN TO MY VOICE, KARA...JUST LISTEN--
LISTEN TO ME, KARA... YOU MUST LISTEN...
I'M SO BAD...
...NO...NO... IT IS AS IT SHOULD BE... BUT YOU MUST LISTEN...
NO...
LISTEN TO YOUR FATHER. HE IS AN IMPORTANT MAN... TOGETHER...
TOGETHER, YOU WILL SAVE THE UNIVERSE...
YOU WILL FINALLY END THE CURSE OF EL.
NO!

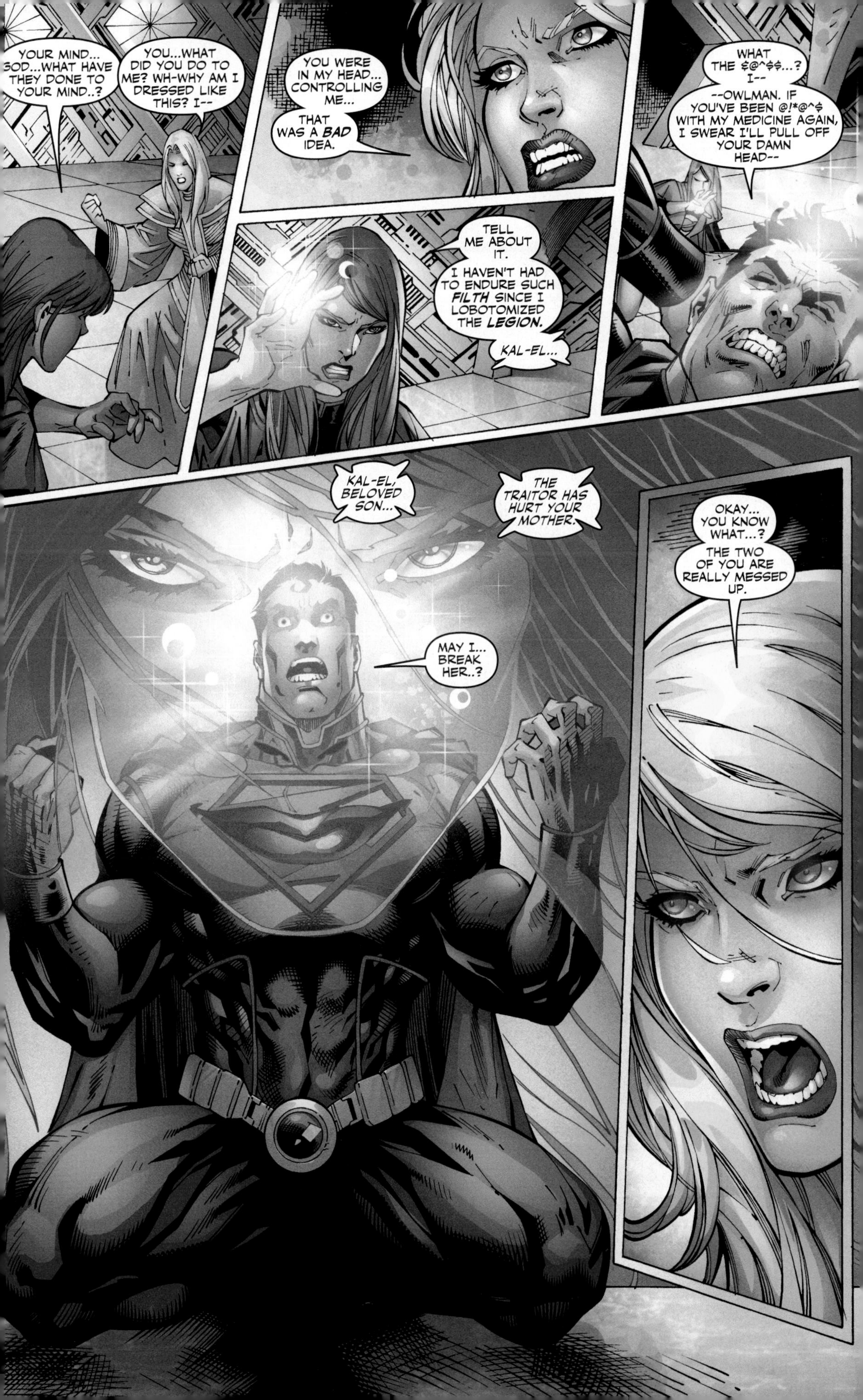
YOUR MIND... GOD...WHAT HAVE THEY DONE TO YOUR MIND..?
YOU...WHAT DID YOU DO TO ME? WH-WHY AM I DRESSED LIKE THIS? I--
YOU WERE IN MY HEAD... CONTROLLING ME...
THAT WAS A BAD IDEA.
WHAT THE $@^$$...? I--
--OWLMAN. IF YOU'VE BEEN @!*@^$ WITH MY MEDICINE AGAIN, I SWEAR I'LL PULL OFF YOUR DAMN HEAD--
TELL ME ABOUT IT.
I HAVEN'T HAD TO ENDURE SUCH FILTH SINCE I LOBOTOMIZED THE LEGION.
KAL-EL...
KAL-EL, BELOVED SON...
THE TRAITOR HAS HURT YOUR MOTHER.
MAY I... BREAK HER..?
OKAY... YOU KNOW WHAT...?
THE TWO OF YOU ARE REALLY MESSED UP.

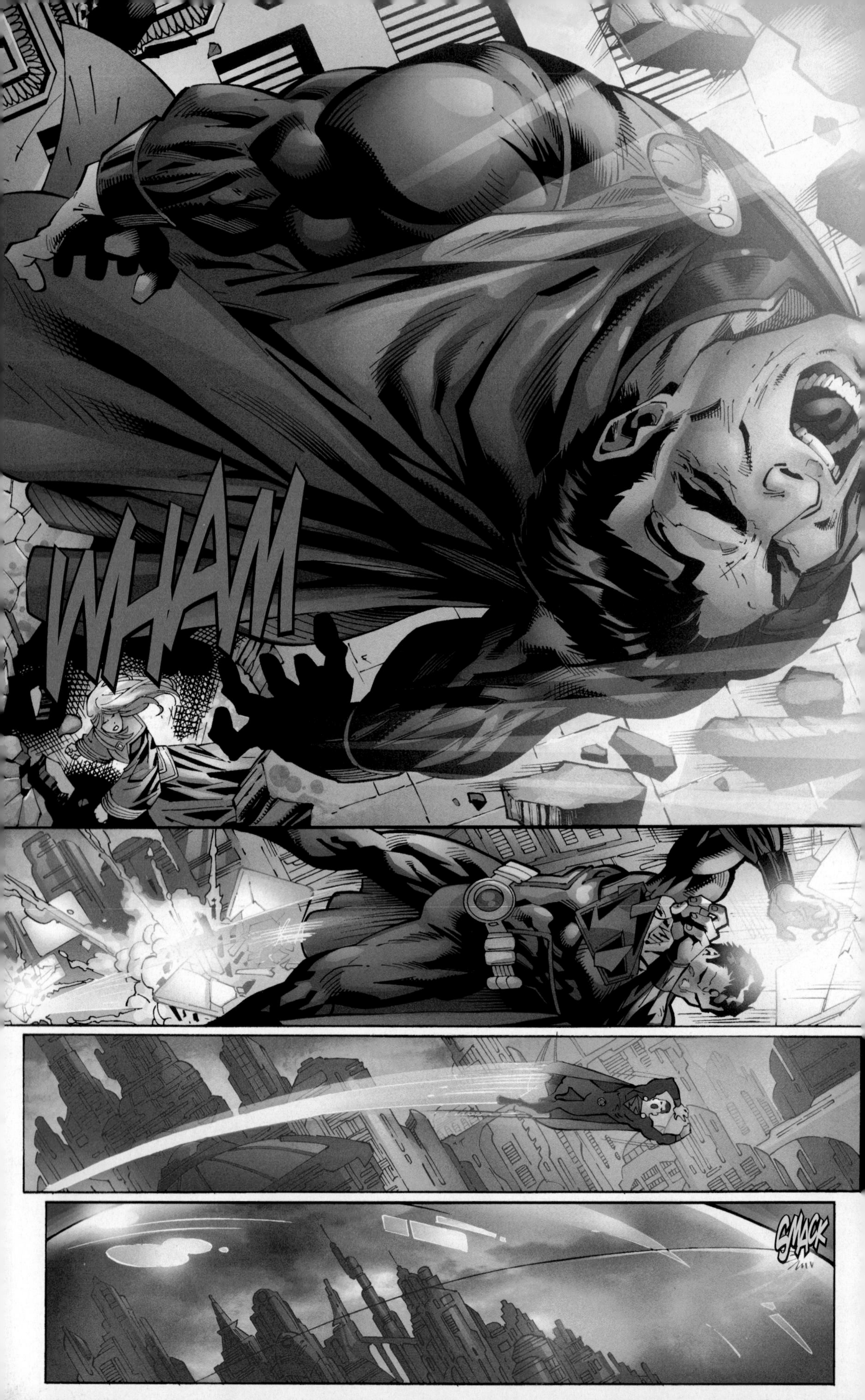
WHAM
SMACK

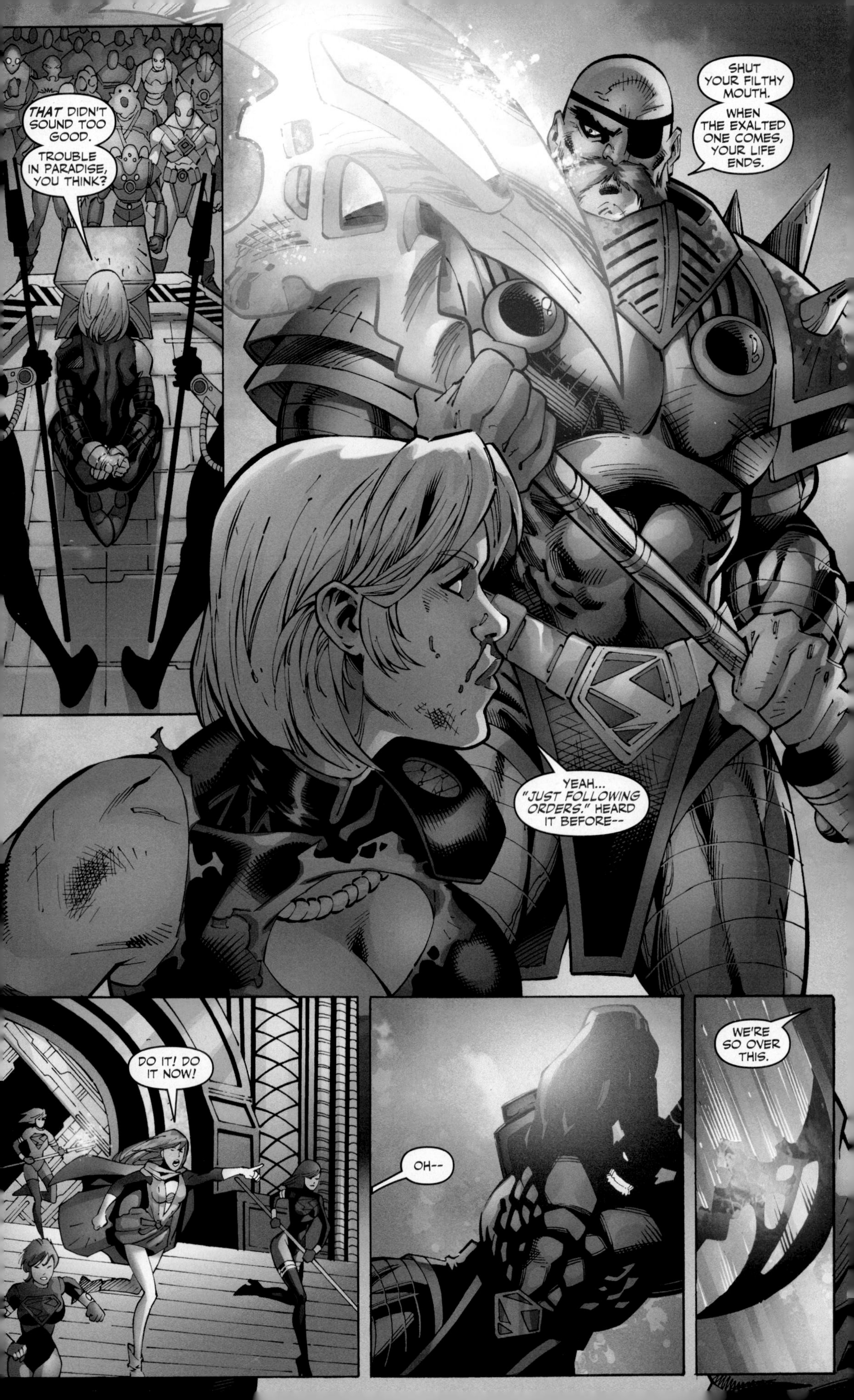
THAT DIDN'T SOUND TOO GOOD.
TROUBLE IN PARADISE, YOU THINK?
SHUT YOUR FILTHY MOUTH.
WHEN THE EXALTED ONE COMES, YOUR LIFE ENDS.
YEAH... "JUST FOLLOWING ORDERS." HEARD IT BEFORE--
DO IT! DO IT NOW!
OH--
WE'RE SO OVER THIS.

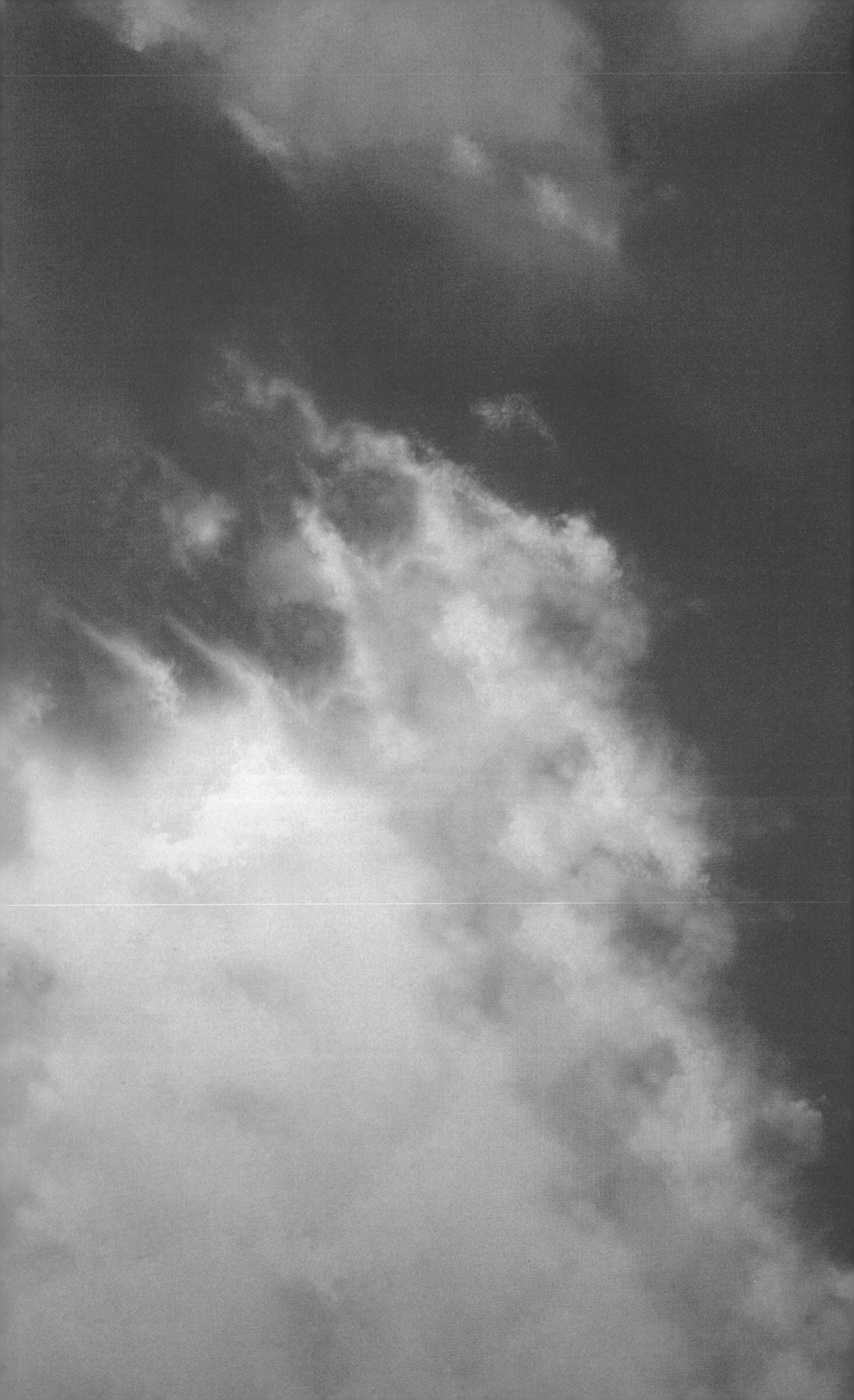

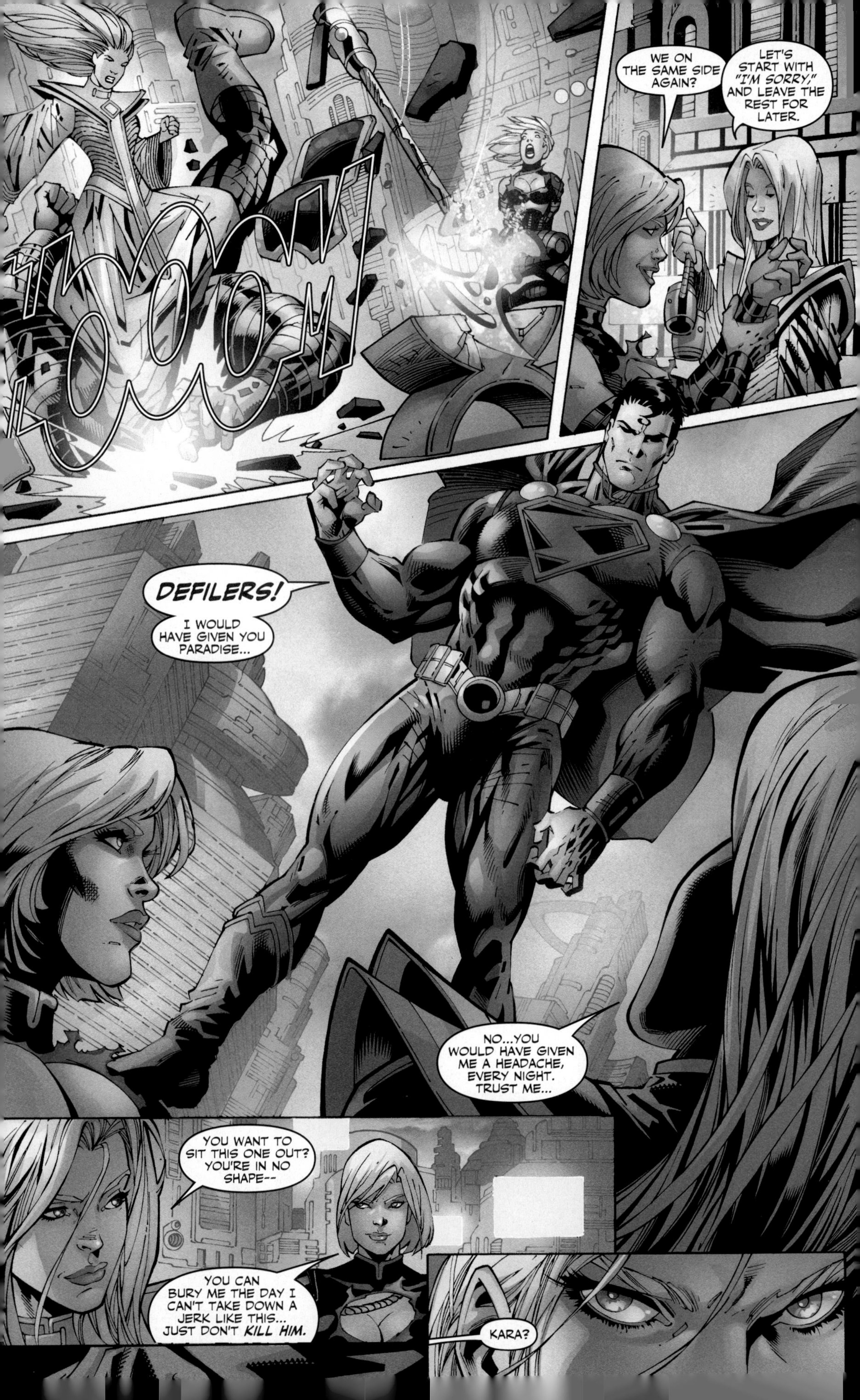
WOOOOM
WE ON THE SAME SIDE AGAIN?
LET'S START WITH "I'M SORRY," AND LEAVE THE REST FOR LATER.
DEFILERS!
I WOULD HAVE GIVEN YOU PARADISE...
NO...YOU WOULD HAVE GIVEN ME A HEADACHE, EVERY NIGHT. TRUST ME...
YOU WANT TO SIT THIS ONE OUT? YOU'RE IN NO SHAPE--
YOU CAN BURY ME THE DAY I CAN'T TAKE DOWN A JERK LIKE THIS... JUST DON'T KILL HIM.
KARA?

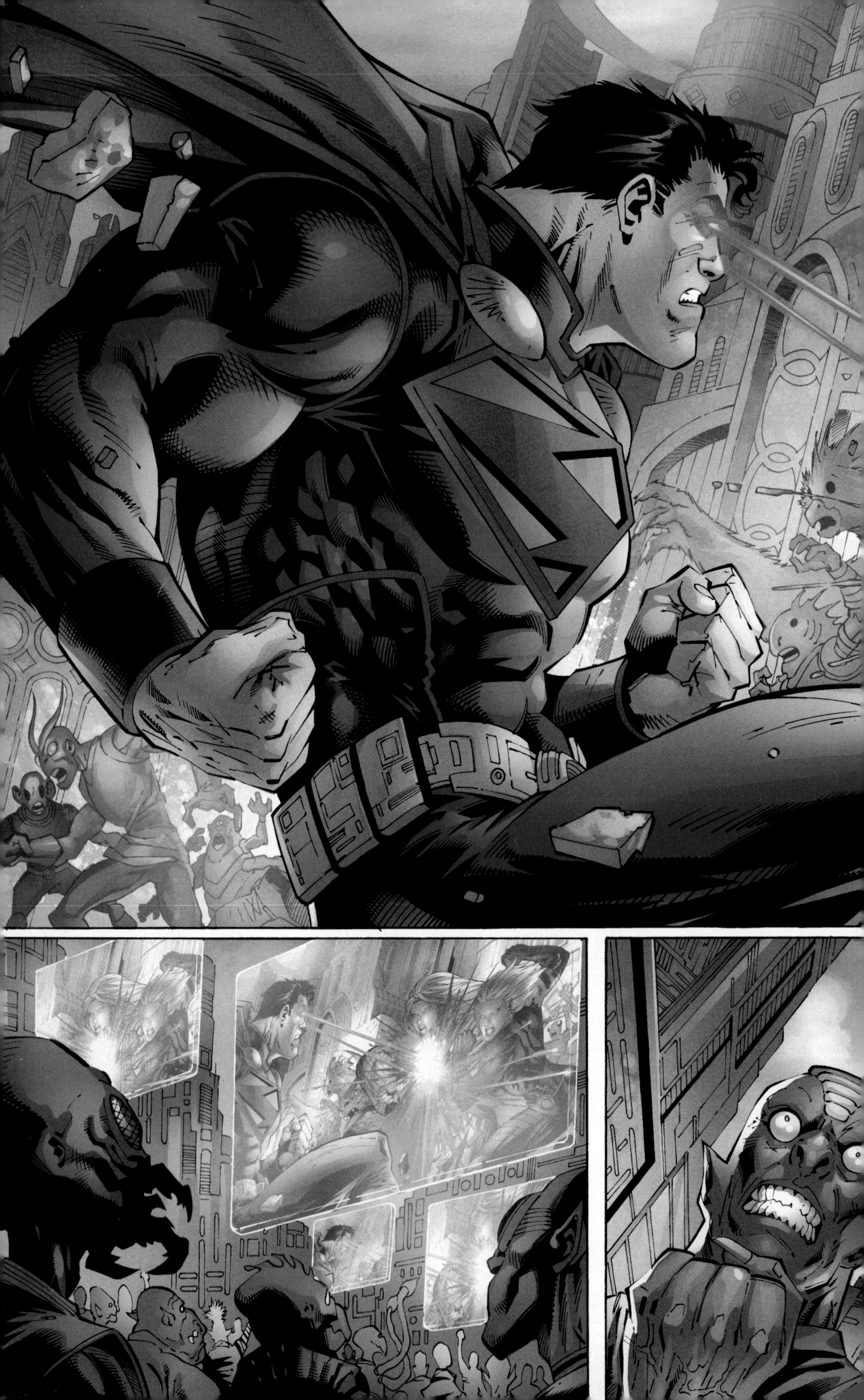

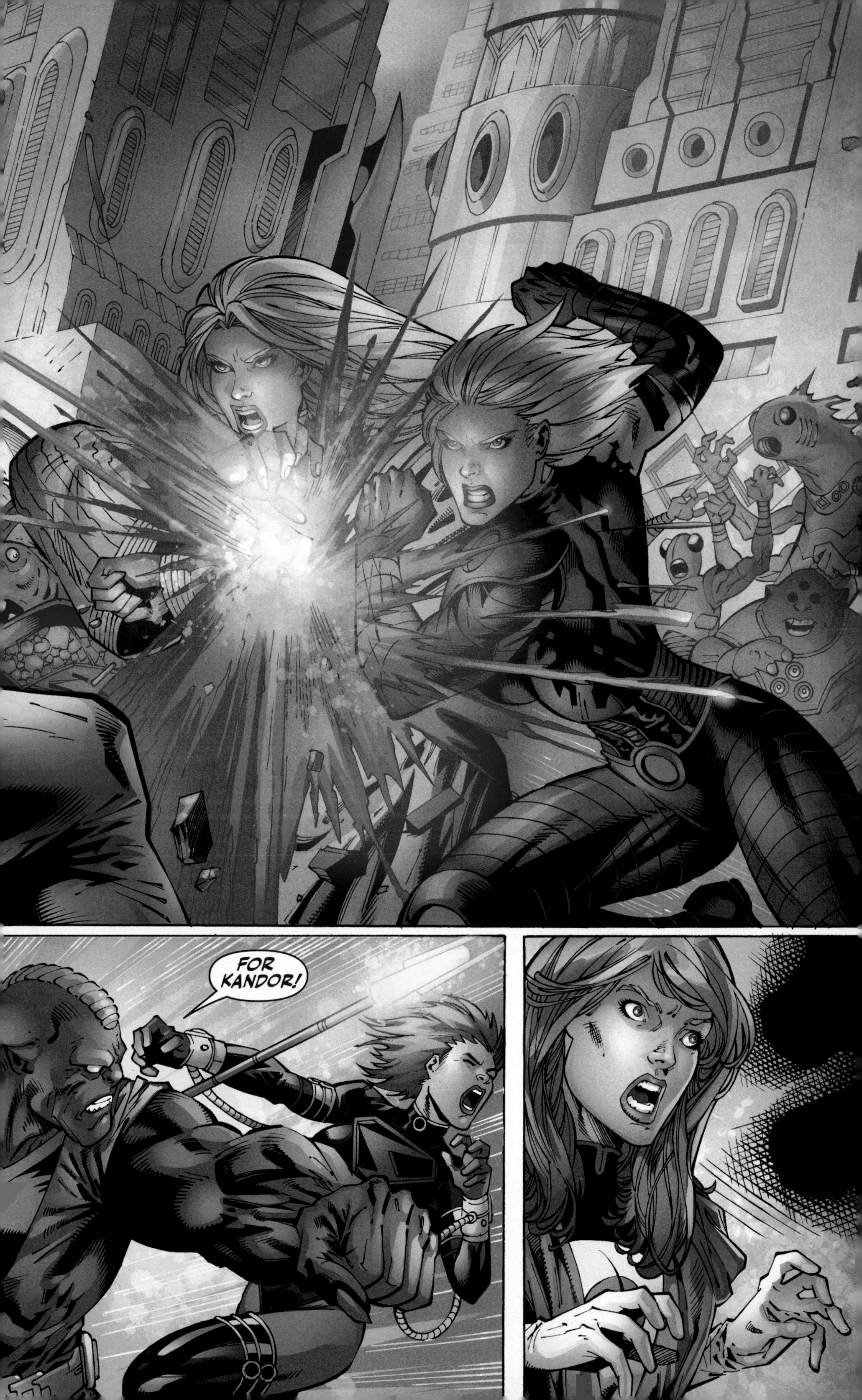
FOR KANDOR!

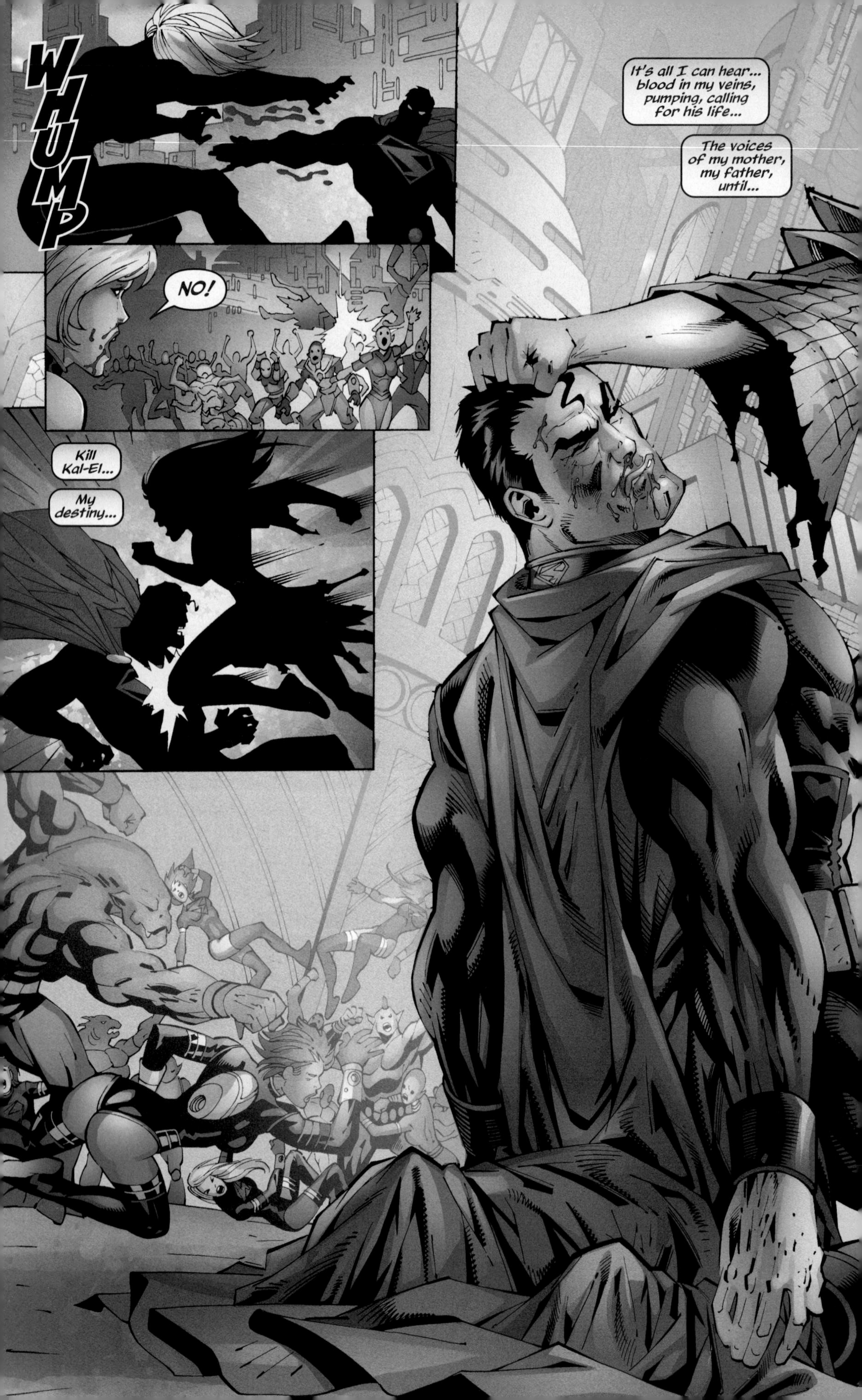
WHUMP
It's all I can hear... blood in my veins, pumping, calling for his life...
The voices of my mother, my father, until...
NO!
Kill Kal-El...
My destiny...

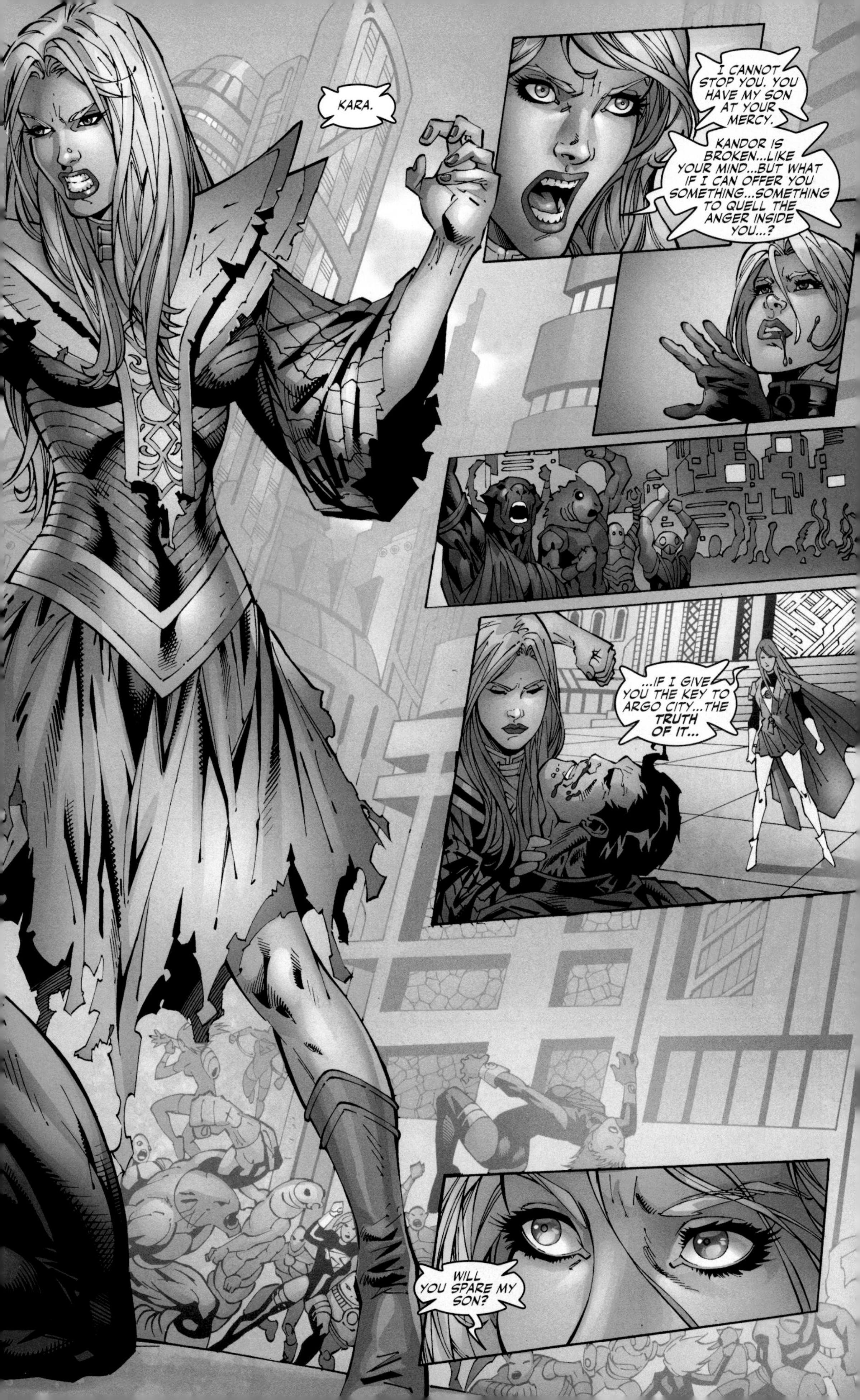
KARA.
I CANNOT STOP YOU. YOU HAVE MY SON AT YOUR MERCY.
KANDOR IS BROKEN...LIKE YOUR MIND...BUT WHAT IF I CAN OFFER YOU SOMETHING...SOMETHING TO QUELL THE ANGER INSIDE YOU...?
...IF I GIVE YOU THE KEY TO ARGO CITY...THE TRUTH OF IT...
WILL YOU SPARE MY SON?

PROVE IT.

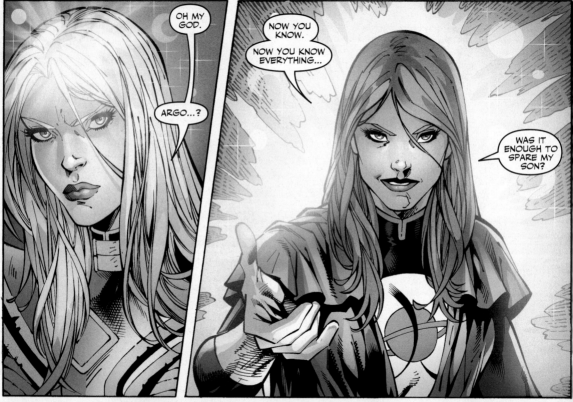

OH MY GOD.

ARGO...?

NOW YOU KNOW.

NOW YOU KNOW EVERYTHING...

WAS IT ENOUGH TO SPARE MY SON?

KARA...?

WHAT HAPPENED? KARA...?

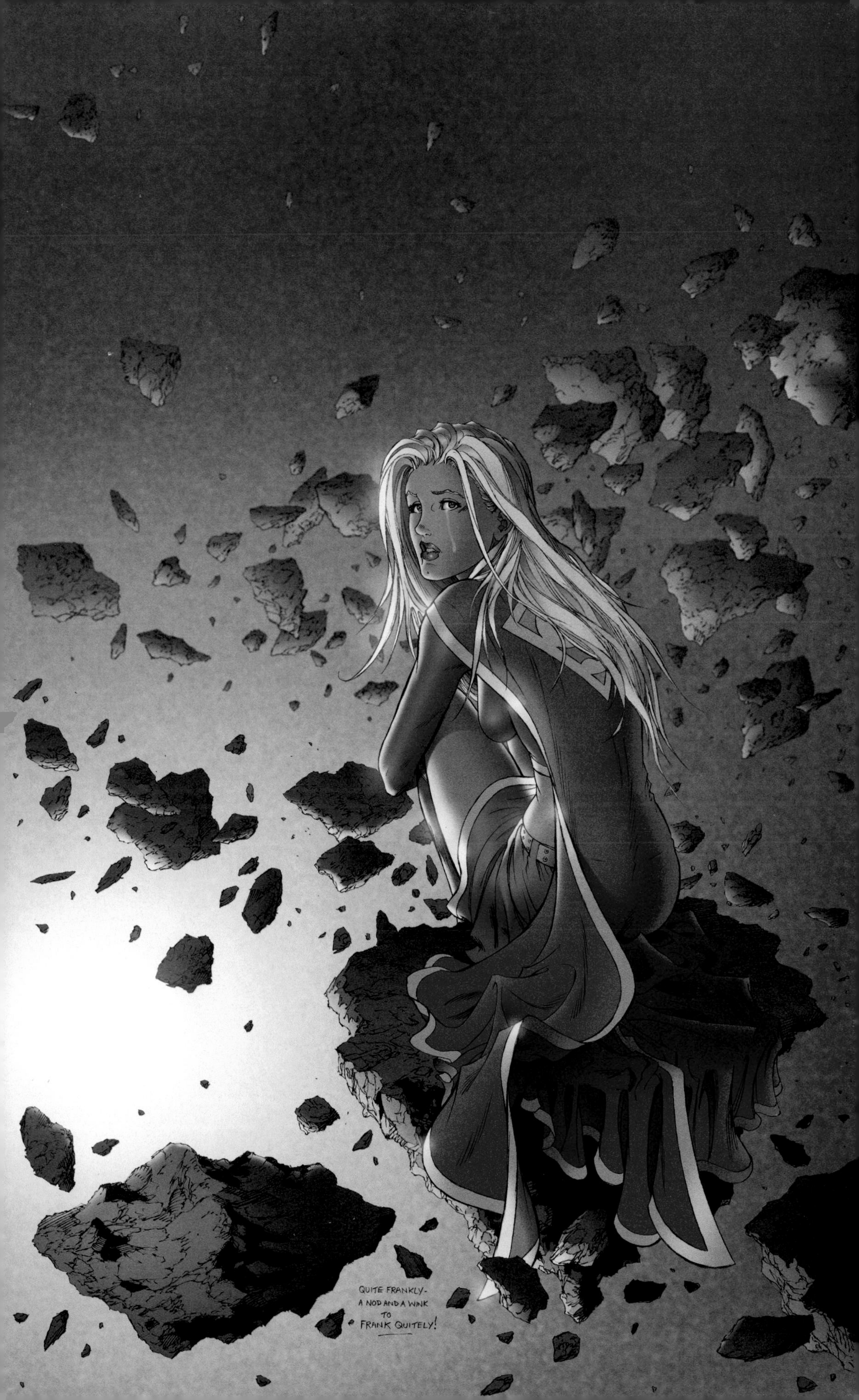
QUITE FRANKLY-
A NOD AND A WINK
TO
FRANK QUITELY!

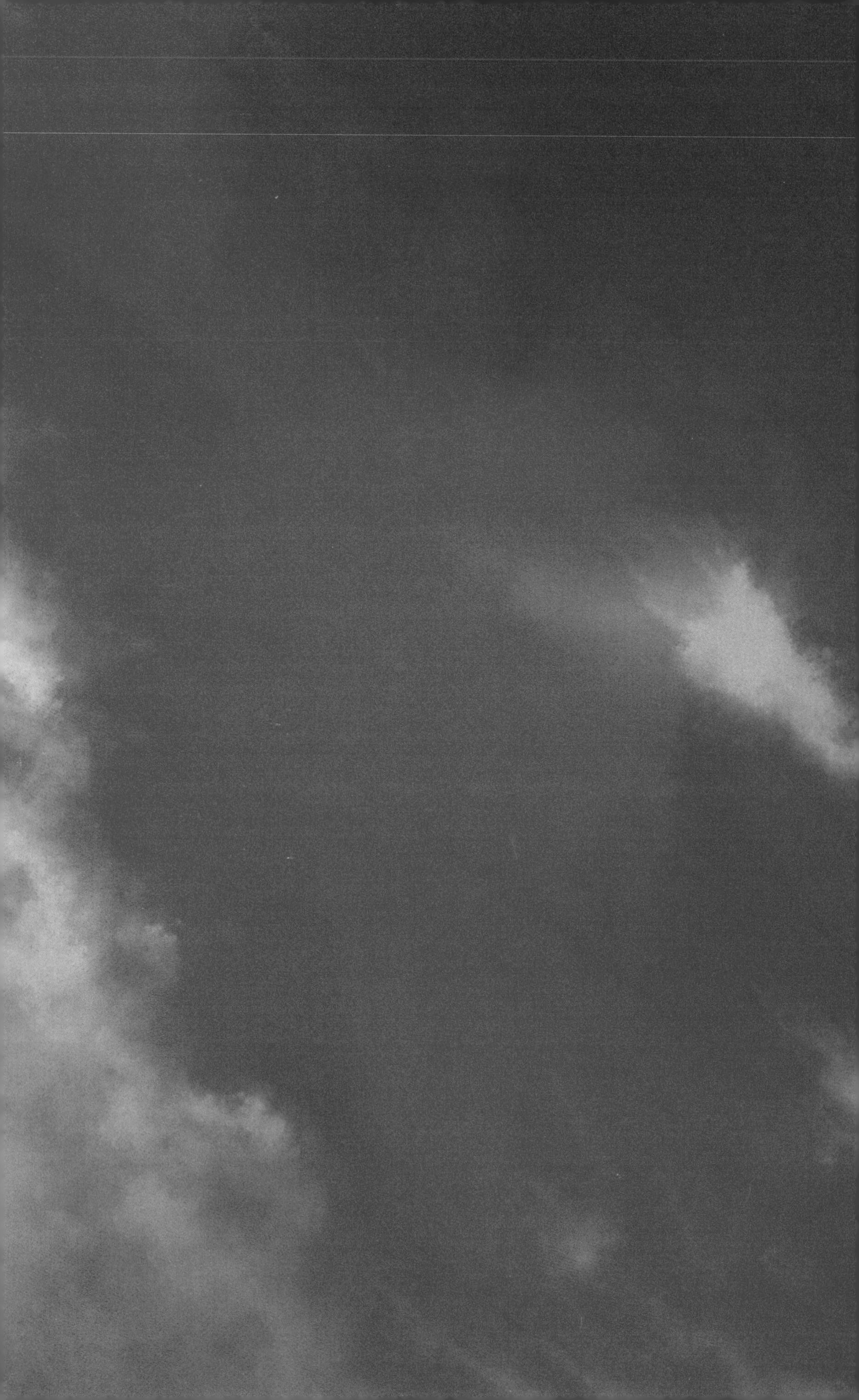

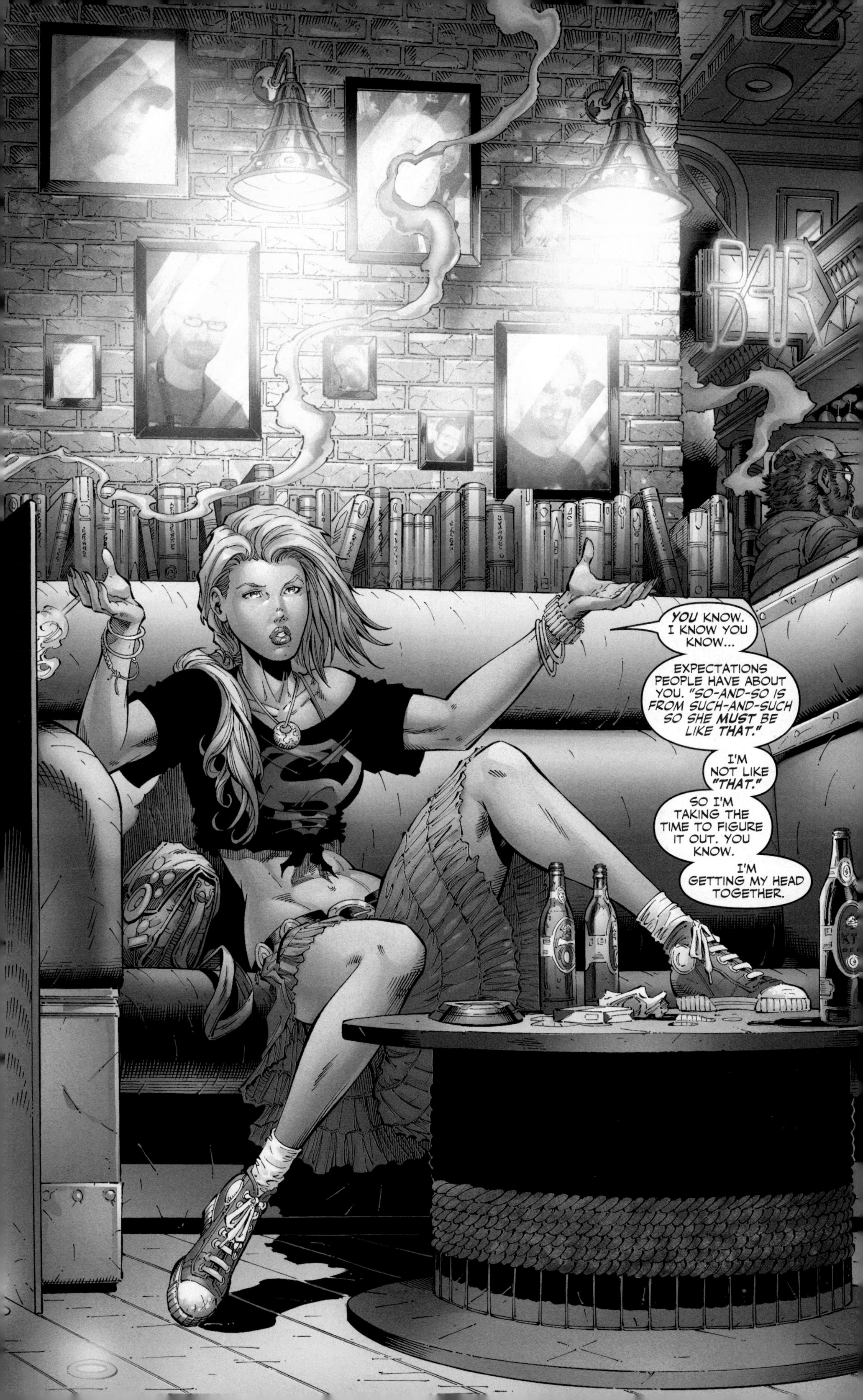
YOU KNOW. I KNOW YOU KNOW...
EXPECTATIONS PEOPLE HAVE ABOUT YOU. "SO-AND-SO IS FROM SUCH-AND-SUCH SO SHE MUST BE LIKE THAT."
I'M NOT LIKE "THAT."
SO I'M TAKING THE TIME TO FIGURE IT OUT. YOU KNOW.
I'M GETTING MY HEAD TOGETHER.
BAR

HOW'S THAT WORKING OUT FOR YOU?

I STARTED SMOKING.

YOU LIKE IT?

IT'S *DISGUSTING.*

I JUST QUIT SMOKING.

CONGRATULATIONS. I QUIT LAST YEAR. HARD, THOUGH.

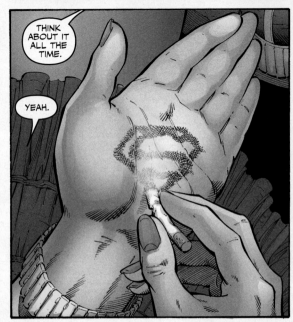

THINK ABOUT IT ALL THE TIME.

YEAH.

WHY DID YOU AGREE TO GO OUT WITH ME?

WHY NOT?

THAT'S NOT AN ANSWER.

IT'S ALL I GOT RIGHT NOW, SWEETHEART. SORRY.

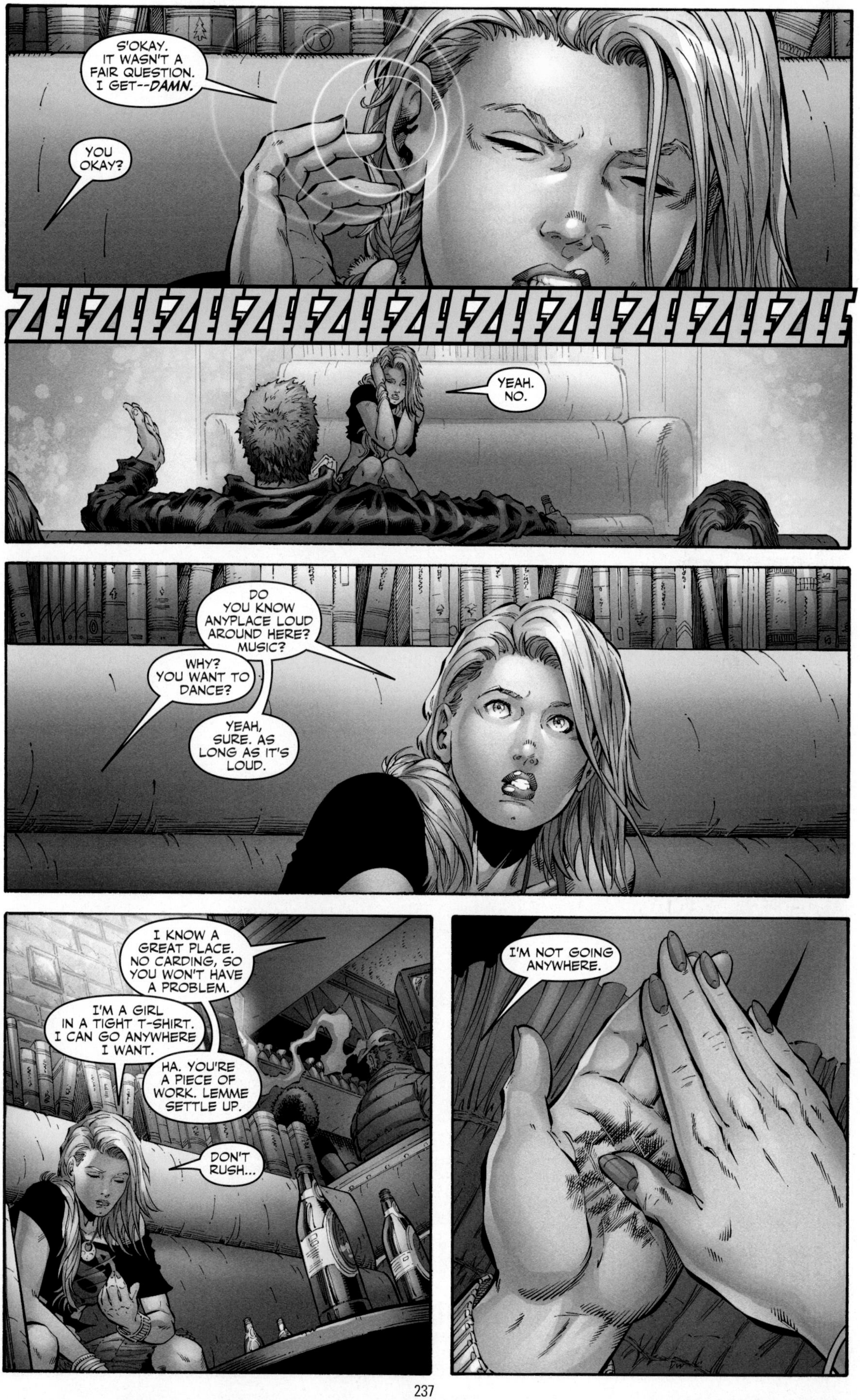
S'OKAY. IT WASN'T A FAIR QUESTION. I GET--DAMN.
YOU OKAY?
ZEEZEEZEEZEEZEEZEEZEEZEEZEEZEE
YEAH. NO.
DO YOU KNOW ANYPLACE LOUD AROUND HERE? MUSIC?
WHY? YOU WANT TO DANCE?
YEAH, SURE. AS LONG AS IT'S LOUD.
I KNOW A GREAT PLACE. NO CARDING, SO YOU WON'T HAVE A PROBLEM.
I'M A GIRL IN A TIGHT T-SHIRT. I CAN GO ANYWHERE I WANT.
HA. YOU'RE A PIECE OF WORK. LEMME SETTLE UP.
DON'T RUSH...
I'M NOT GOING ANYWHERE.

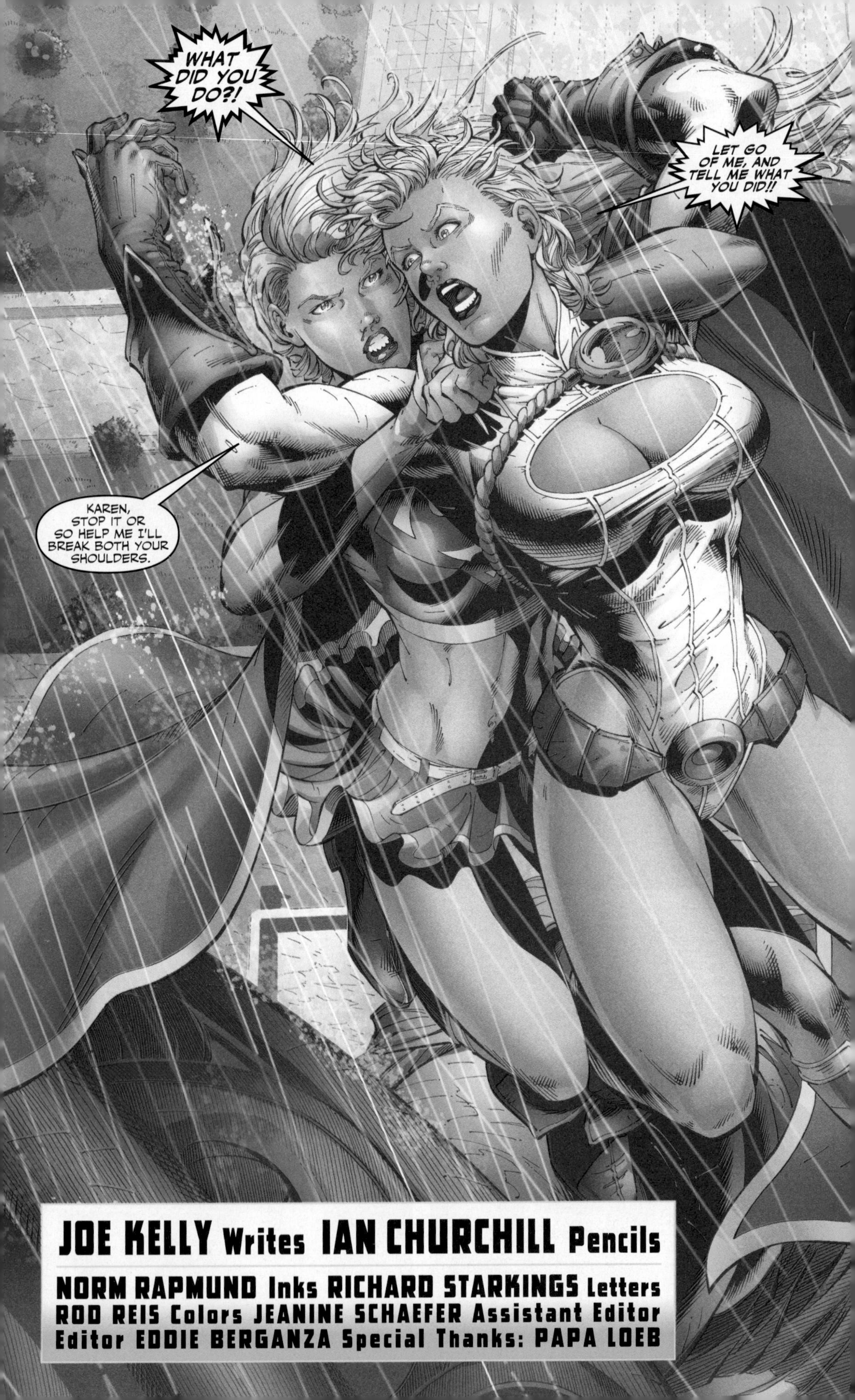
WHAT DID YOU DO?!
LET GO OF ME, AND TELL ME WHAT YOU DID!!
KAREN, STOP IT OR SO HELP ME I'LL BREAK BOTH YOUR SHOULDERS.
JOE KELLY Writes IAN CHURCHILL Pencils
NORM RAPMUND Inks RICHARD STARKINGS Letters
ROD REIS Colors JEANINE SCHAEFER Assistant Editor
Editor EDDIE BERGANZA Special Thanks: PAPA LOEB

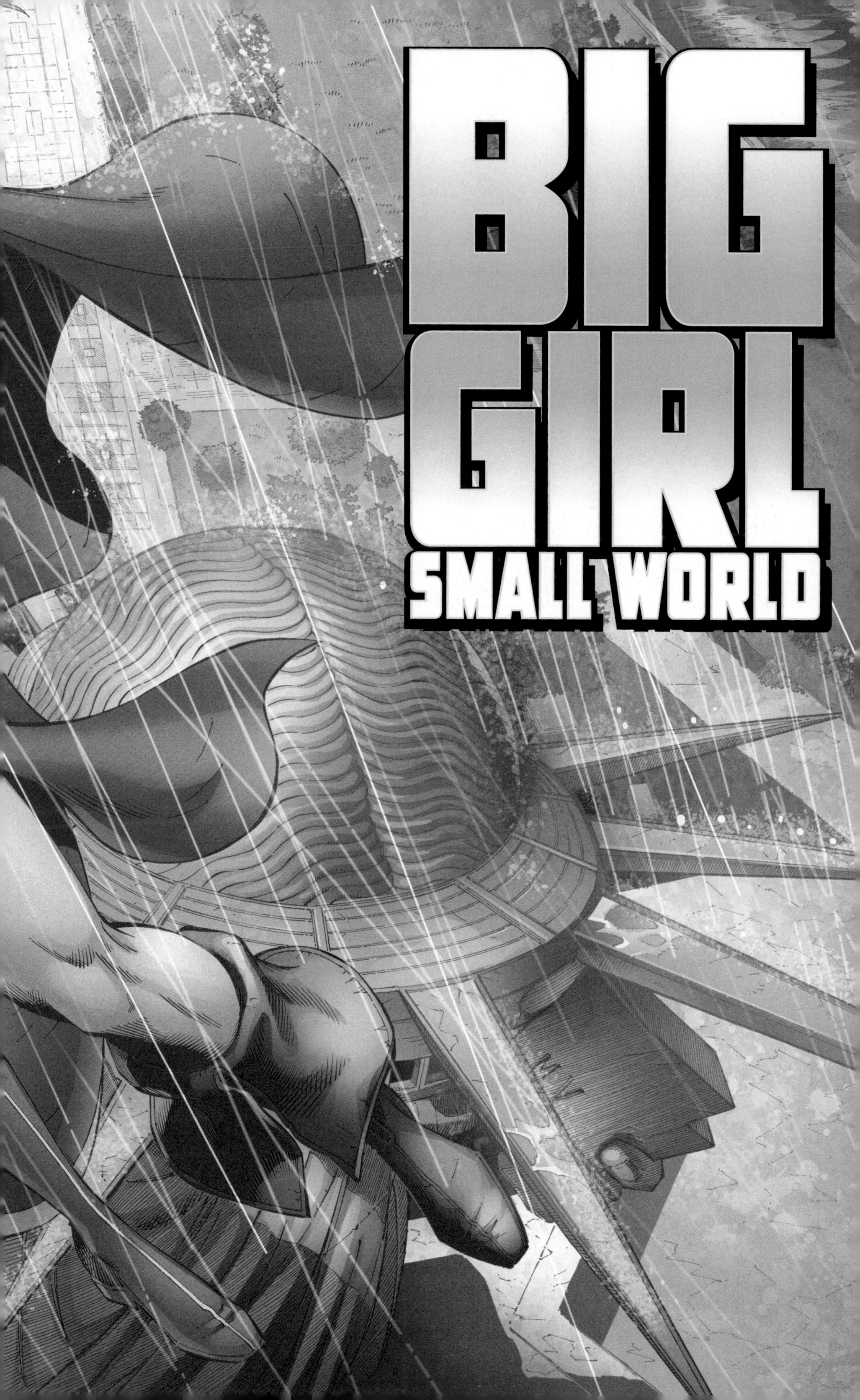
BIG
GIRL
SMALL WORLD

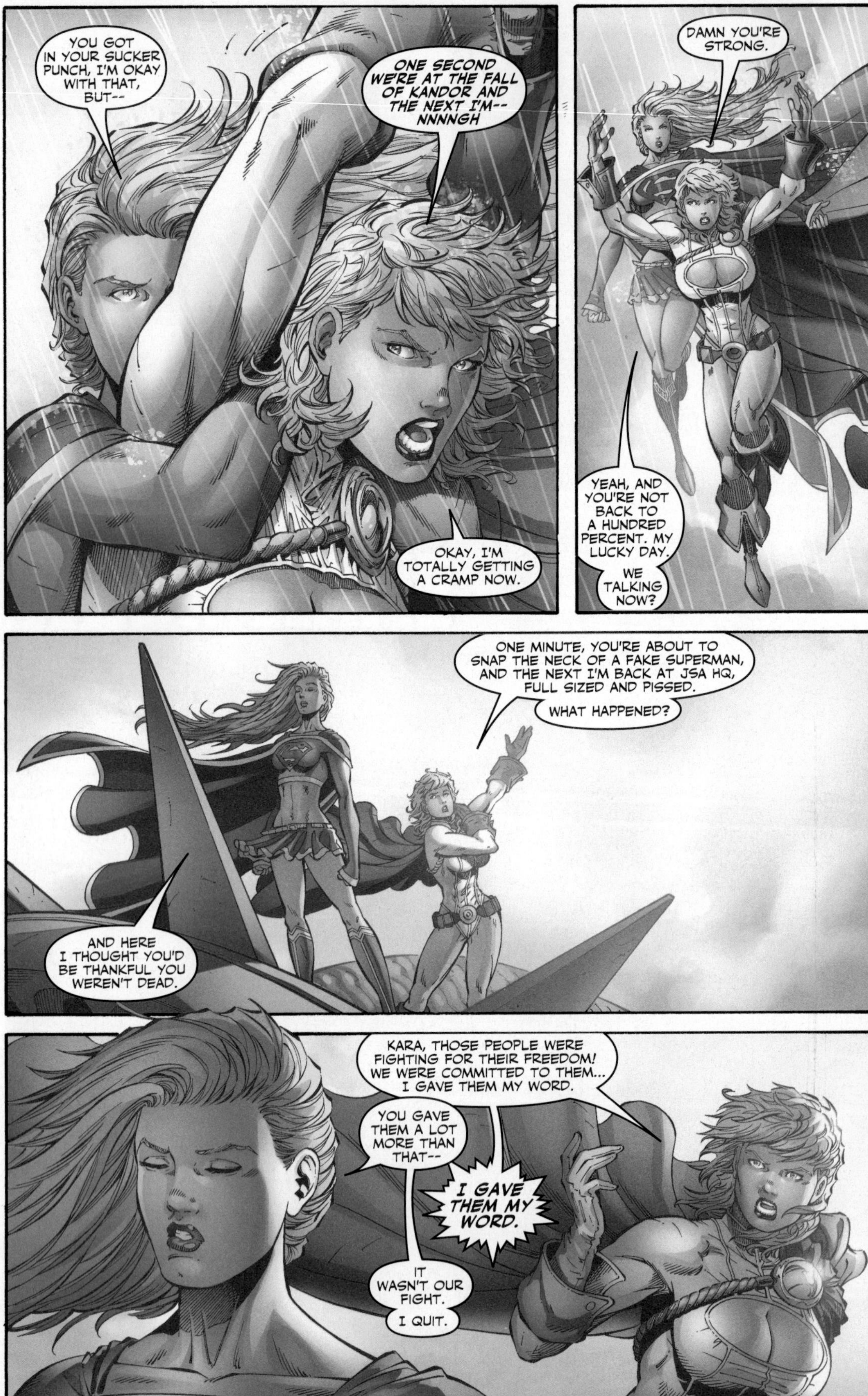
YOU GOT IN YOUR SUCKER PUNCH, I'M OKAY WITH THAT, BUT--
ONE SECOND WE'RE AT THE FALL OF KANDOR AND THE NEXT I'M-- NNNNGH
OKAY, I'M TOTALLY GETTING A CRAMP NOW.
DAMN YOU'RE STRONG.
YEAH, AND YOU'RE NOT BACK TO A HUNDRED PERCENT. MY LUCKY DAY.
WE TALKING NOW?
ONE MINUTE, YOU'RE ABOUT TO SNAP THE NECK OF A FAKE SUPERMAN, AND THE NEXT I'M BACK AT JSA HQ, FULL SIZED AND PISSED.
WHAT HAPPENED?
AND HERE I THOUGHT YOU'D BE THANKFUL YOU WEREN'T DEAD.
KARA, THOSE PEOPLE WERE FIGHTING FOR THEIR FREEDOM! WE WERE COMMITTED TO THEM... I GAVE THEM MY WORD.
YOU GAVE THEM A LOT MORE THAN THAT--
I GAVE THEM MY WORD.
IT WASN'T OUR FIGHT.
I QUIT.

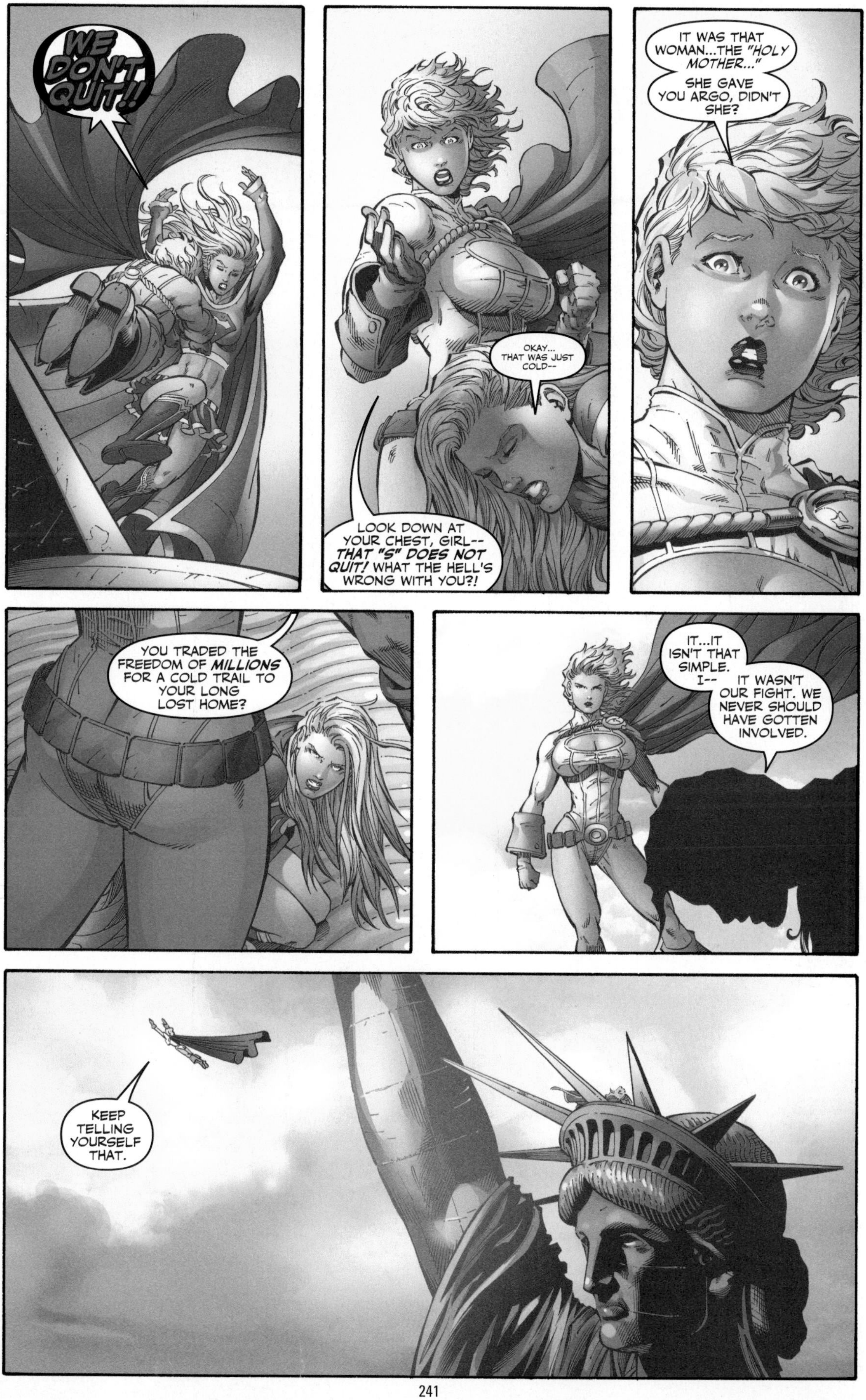
WE DON'T QUIT!!
OKAY... THAT WAS JUST COLD--
LOOK DOWN AT YOUR CHEST, GIRL-- THAT "S" DOES NOT QUIT! WHAT THE HELL'S WRONG WITH YOU?!
IT WAS THAT WOMAN...THE "HOLY MOTHER..."
SHE GAVE YOU ARGO, DIDN'T SHE?
YOU TRADED THE FREEDOM OF MILLIONS FOR A COLD TRAIL TO YOUR LONG LOST HOME?
IT...IT ISN'T THAT SIMPLE. I--
IT WASN'T OUR FIGHT. WE NEVER SHOULD HAVE GOTTEN INVOLVED.
KEEP TELLING YOURSELF THAT.

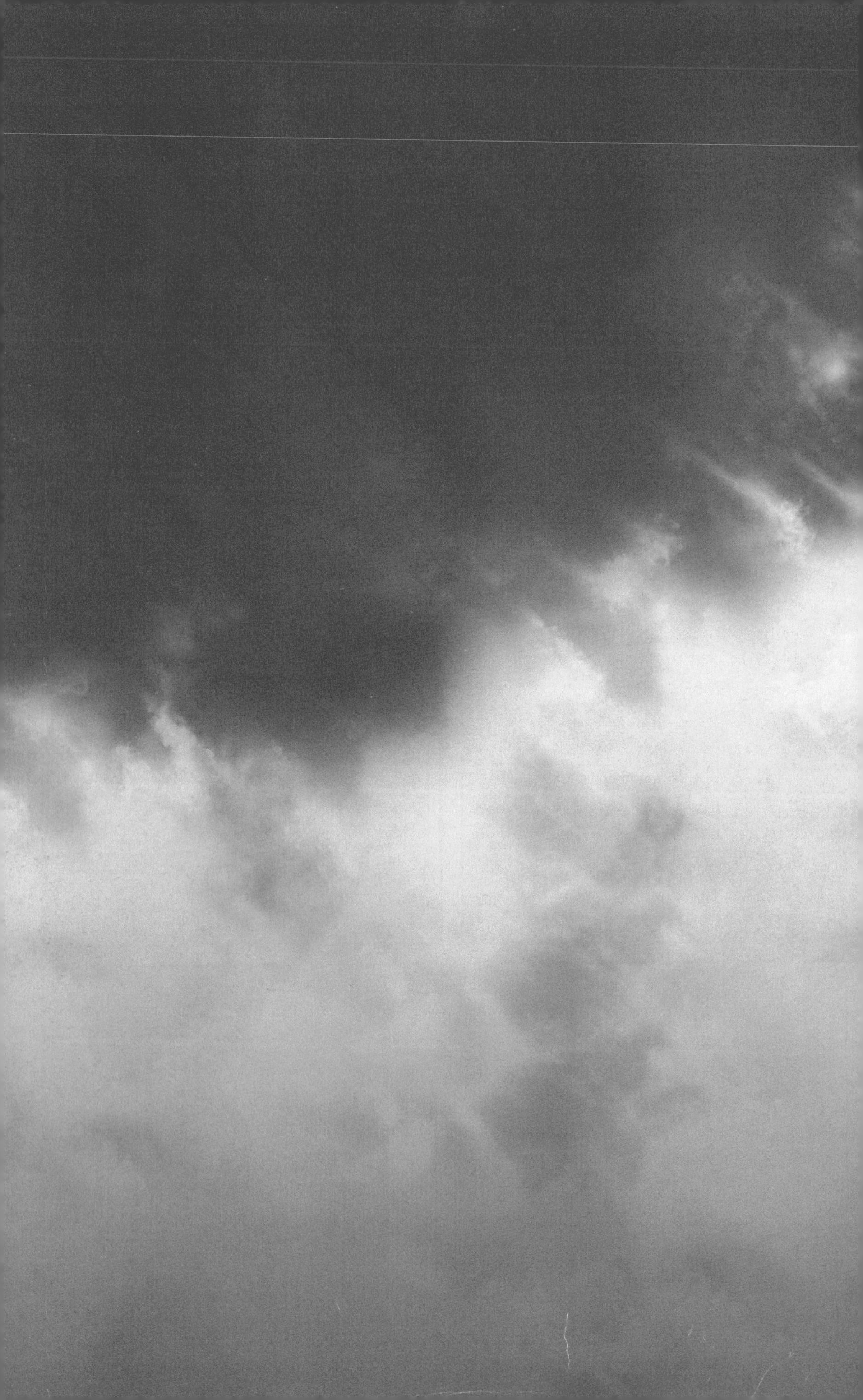

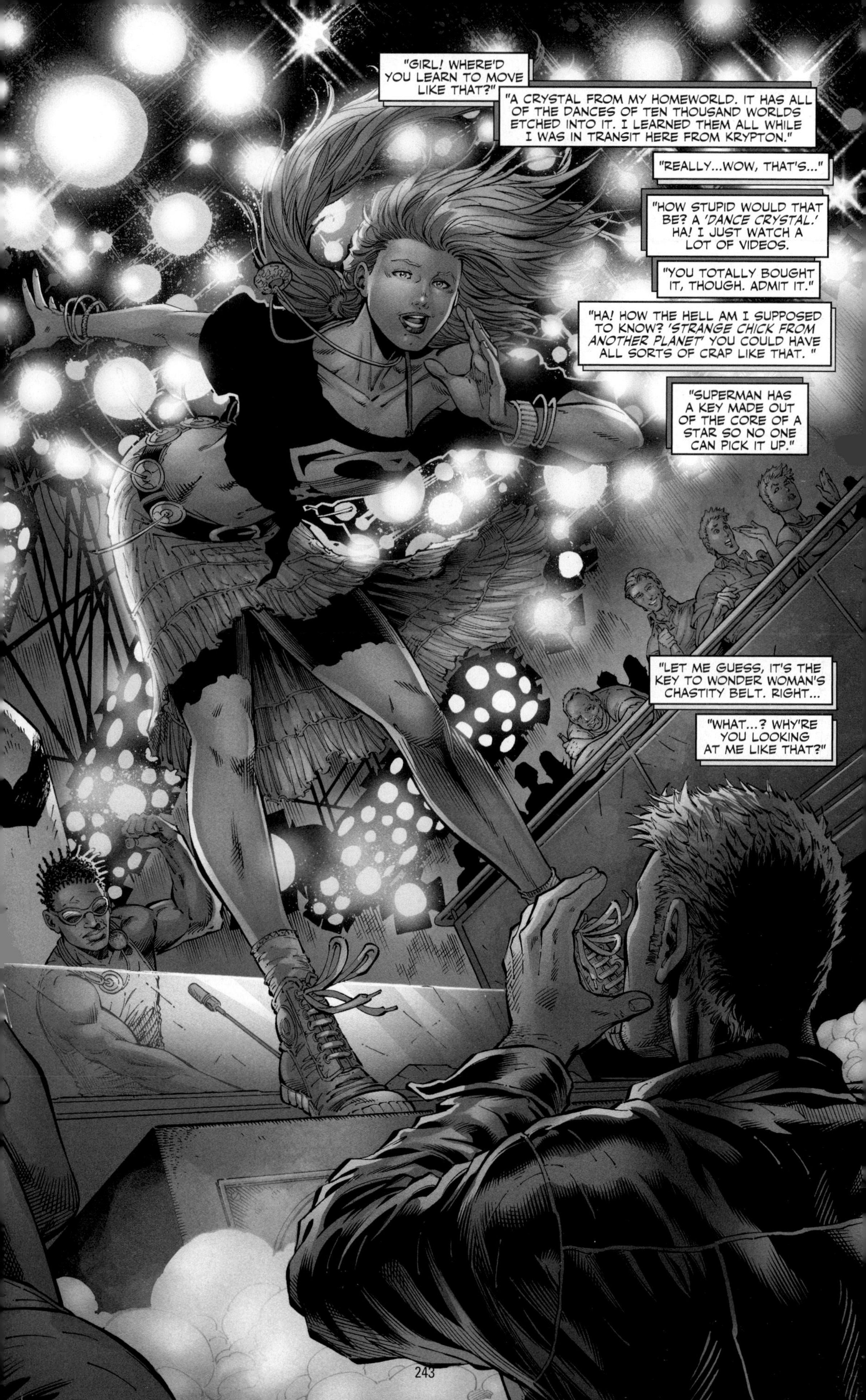
"GIRL! WHERE'D YOU LEARN TO MOVE LIKE THAT?"
"A CRYSTAL FROM MY HOMEWORLD. IT HAS ALL OF THE DANCES OF TEN THOUSAND WORLDS ETCHED INTO IT. I LEARNED THEM ALL WHILE I WAS IN TRANSIT HERE FROM KRYPTON."
"REALLY...WOW, THAT'S..."
"HOW STUPID WOULD THAT BE? A 'DANCE CRYSTAL.' HA! I JUST WATCH A LOT OF VIDEOS.
"YOU TOTALLY BOUGHT IT, THOUGH. ADMIT IT."
"HA! HOW THE HELL AM I SUPPOSED TO KNOW? 'STRANGE CHICK FROM ANOTHER PLANET' YOU COULD HAVE ALL SORTS OF CRAP LIKE THAT. "
"SUPERMAN HAS A KEY MADE OUT OF THE CORE OF A STAR SO NO ONE CAN PICK IT UP."
"LET ME GUESS, IT'S THE KEY TO WONDER WOMAN'S CHASTITY BELT. RIGHT...
"WHAT...? WHY'RE YOU LOOKING AT ME LIKE THAT?"

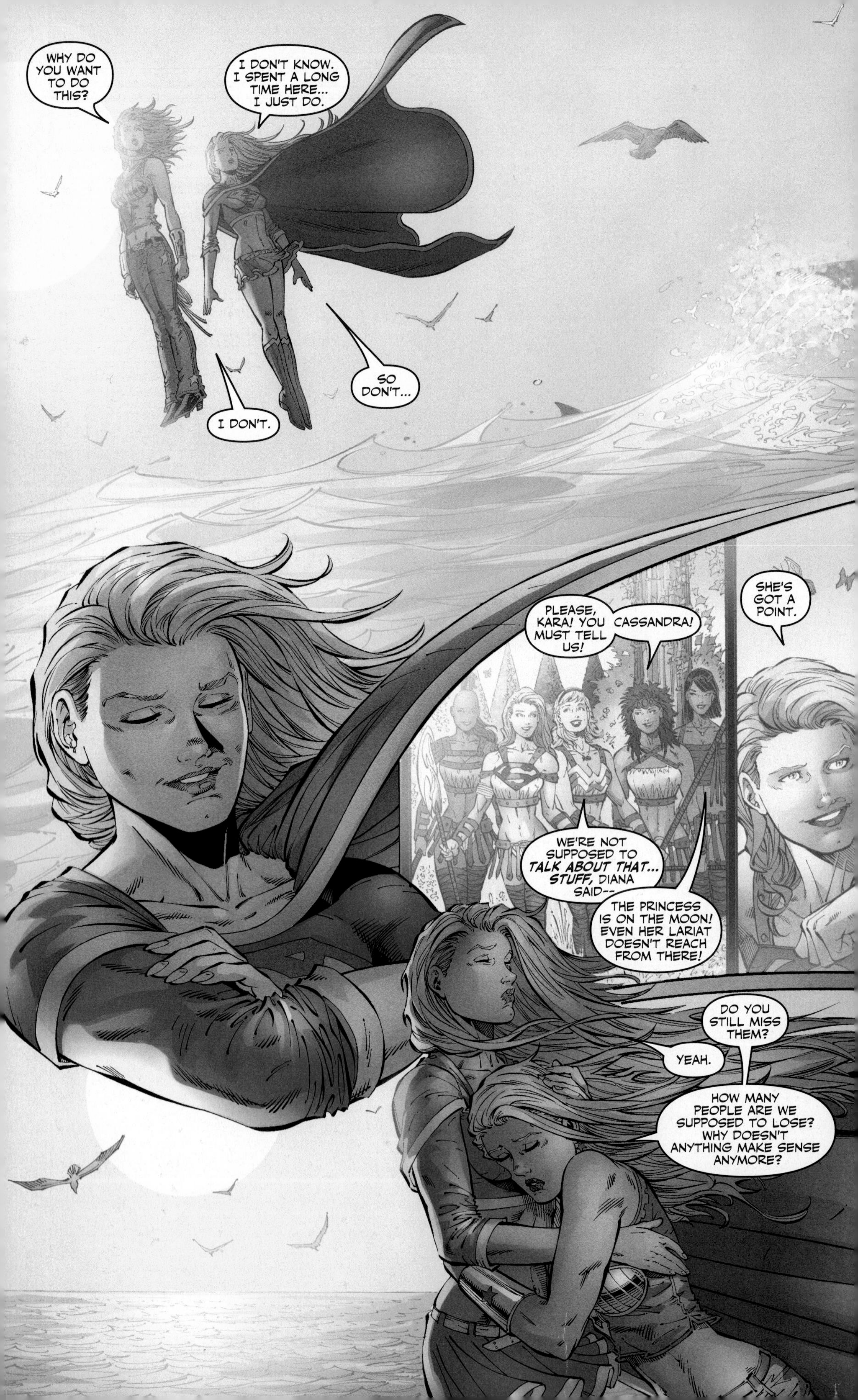
WHY DO YOU WANT TO DO THIS?
I DON'T KNOW. I SPENT A LONG TIME HERE... I JUST DO.
SO DON'T...
I DON'T.
PLEASE, KARA! YOU MUST TELL US!
CASSANDRA!
SHE'S GOT A POINT.
WE'RE NOT SUPPOSED TO TALK ABOUT THAT... STUFF, DIANA SAID--
THE PRINCESS IS ON THE MOON! EVEN HER LARIAT DOESN'T REACH FROM THERE!
DO YOU STILL MISS THEM?
YEAH.
HOW MANY PEOPLE ARE WE SUPPOSED TO LOSE? WHY DOESN'T ANYTHING MAKE SENSE ANYMORE?

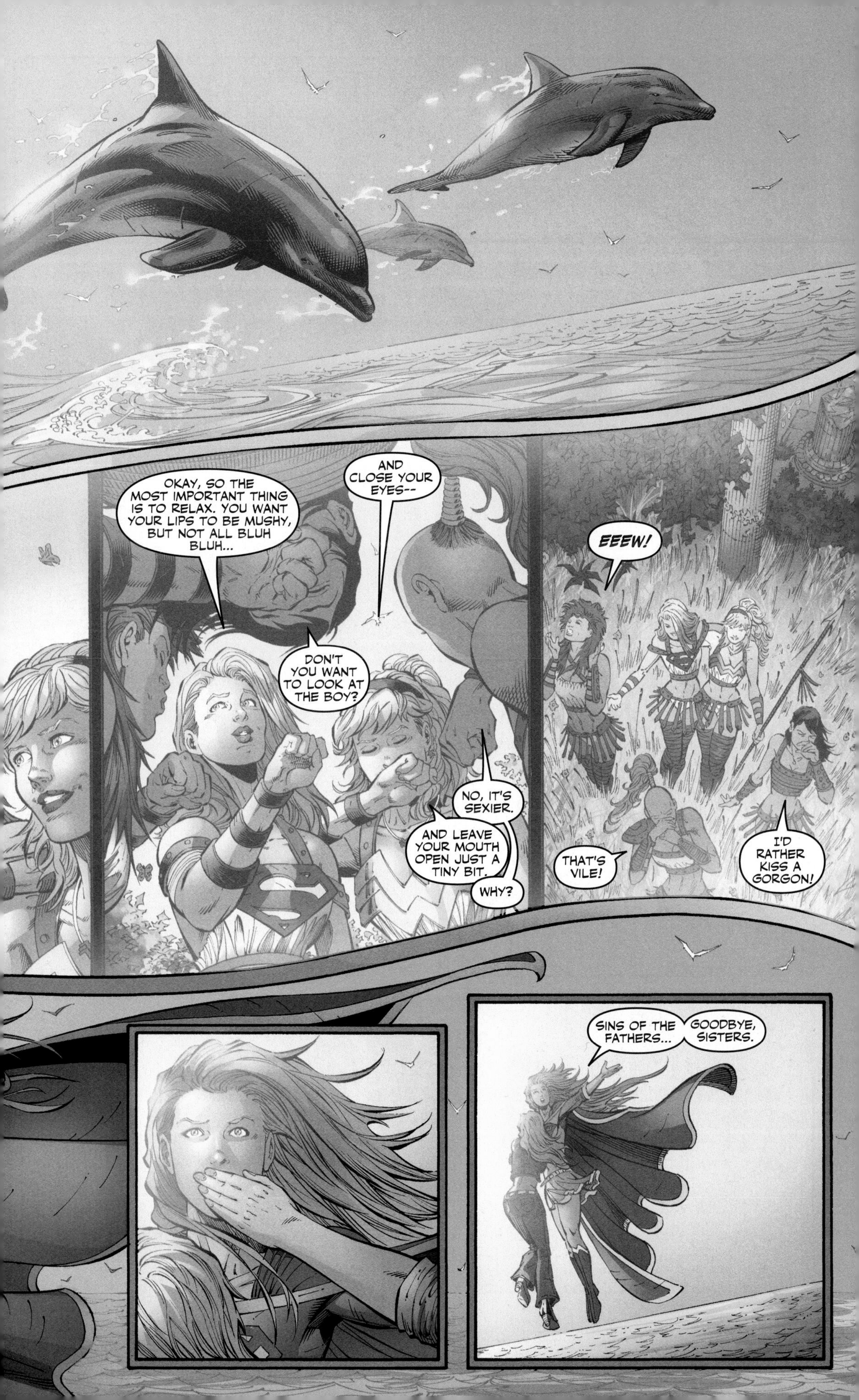
OKAY, SO THE MOST IMPORTANT THING IS TO RELAX. YOU WANT YOUR LIPS TO BE MUSHY, BUT NOT ALL BLUH BLUH...
AND CLOSE YOUR EYES--
DON'T YOU WANT TO LOOK AT THE BOY?
NO, IT'S SEXIER.
AND LEAVE YOUR MOUTH OPEN JUST A TINY BIT.
WHY?
EEEW!
THAT'S VILE!
I'D RATHER KISS A GORGON!
SINS OF THE FATHERS...
GOODBYE, SISTERS.

I RESERVE THE RIGHT TO KILL YOU, IF YOU SAY "NICE S."

YOU KNOW, YOU DON'T TALK LIKE A SIXTEEN-YEAR-OLD.

'CAUSE I'M NOT. I WAS IN SEMI-LUCID SUSPENDED ANIMATION FOR A LONG TIME.

"DANCE CRYSTALS"?

NO, SERIOUSLY... INTERSTELLAR SPACE SHIP, WARP DRIVES... IT'S ALL IN MY ORIGIN STORY. YOU SHOULD LOOK IT UP.

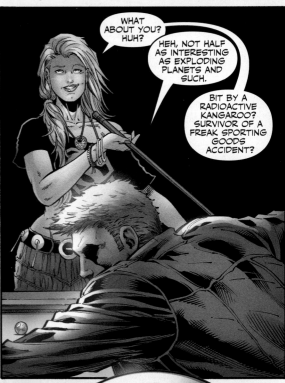

WHAT ABOUT YOU? HUH?

HEH, NOT HALF AS INTERESTING AS EXPLODING PLANETS AND SUCH.

BIT BY A RADIOACTIVE KANGAROO? SURVIVOR OF A FREAK SPORTING GOODS ACCIDENT?

MY FATHER WAS MURDERED.

OH.

THAT SUCKS.

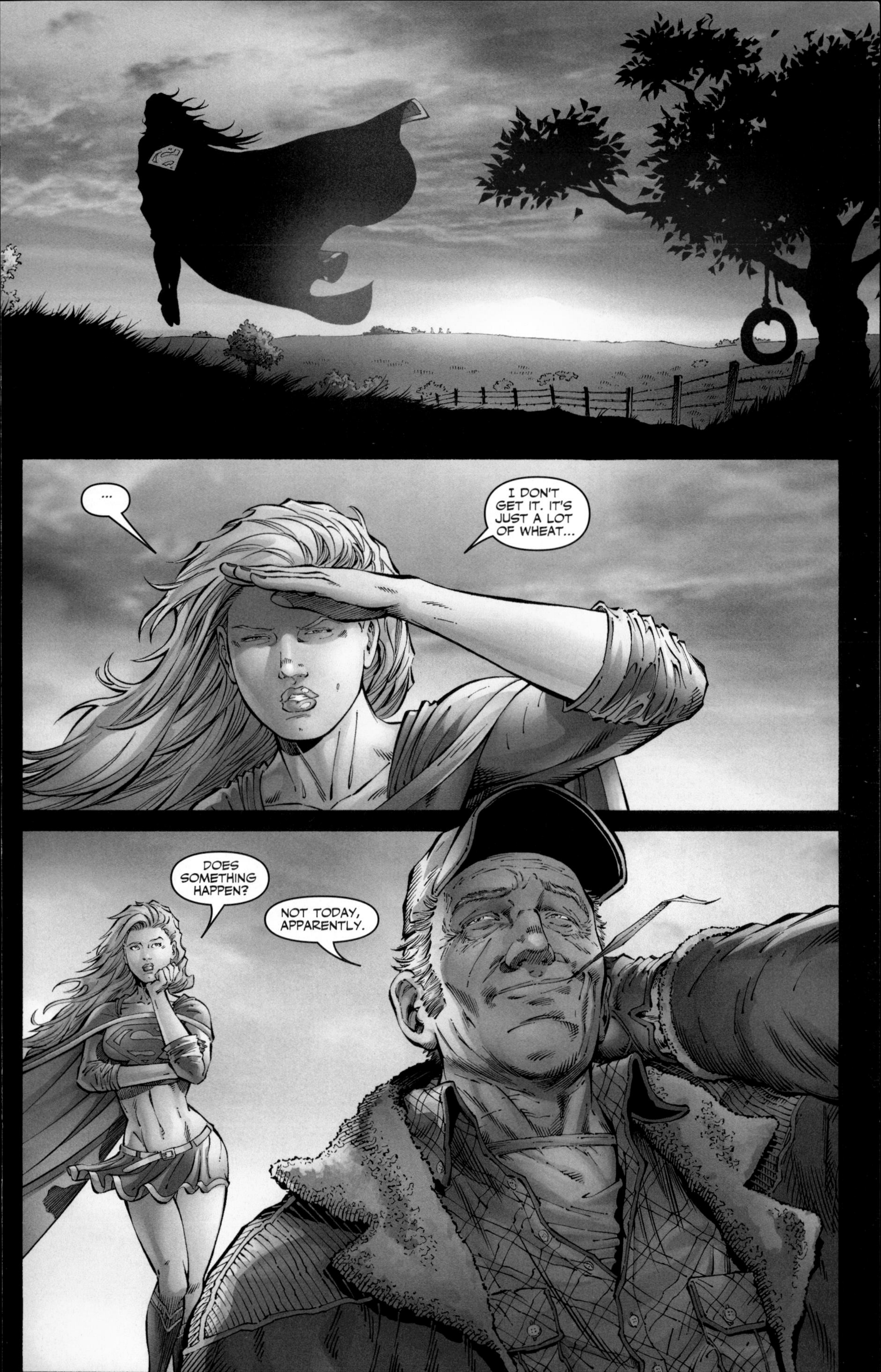
...
I DON'T GET IT. IT'S JUST A LOT OF WHEAT...
DOES SOMETHING HAPPEN?
NOT TODAY, APPARENTLY.

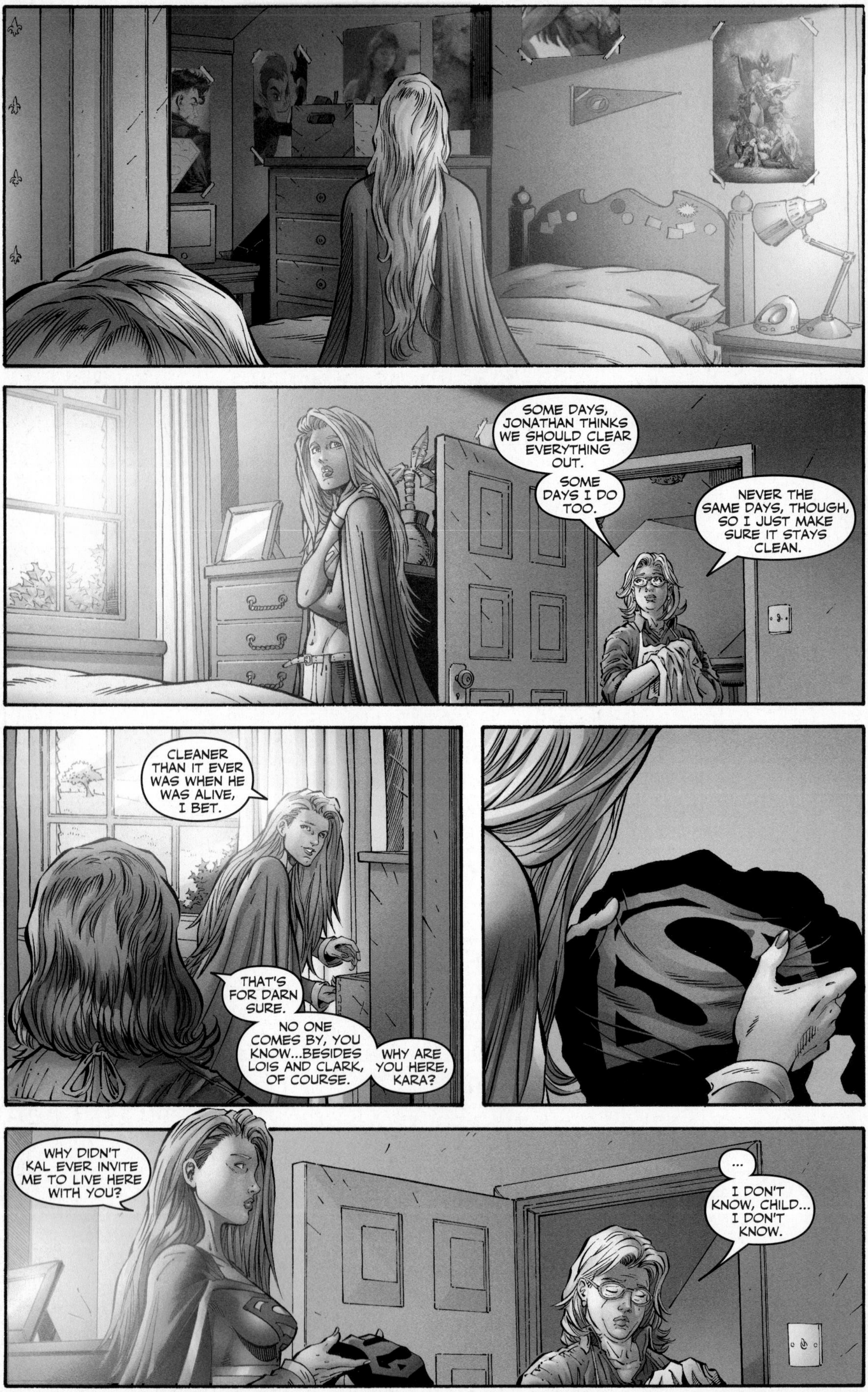
SOME DAYS, JONATHAN THINKS WE SHOULD CLEAR EVERYTHING OUT.
SOME DAYS I DO TOO.
NEVER THE SAME DAYS, THOUGH, SO I JUST MAKE SURE IT STAYS CLEAN.
CLEANER THAN IT EVER WAS WHEN HE WAS ALIVE, I BET.
THAT'S FOR DARN SURE.
NO ONE COMES BY, YOU KNOW...BESIDES LOIS AND CLARK, OF COURSE.
WHY ARE YOU HERE, KARA?
WHY DIDN'T KAL EVER INVITE ME TO LIVE HERE WITH YOU?
...
I DON'T KNOW, CHILD... I DON'T KNOW.

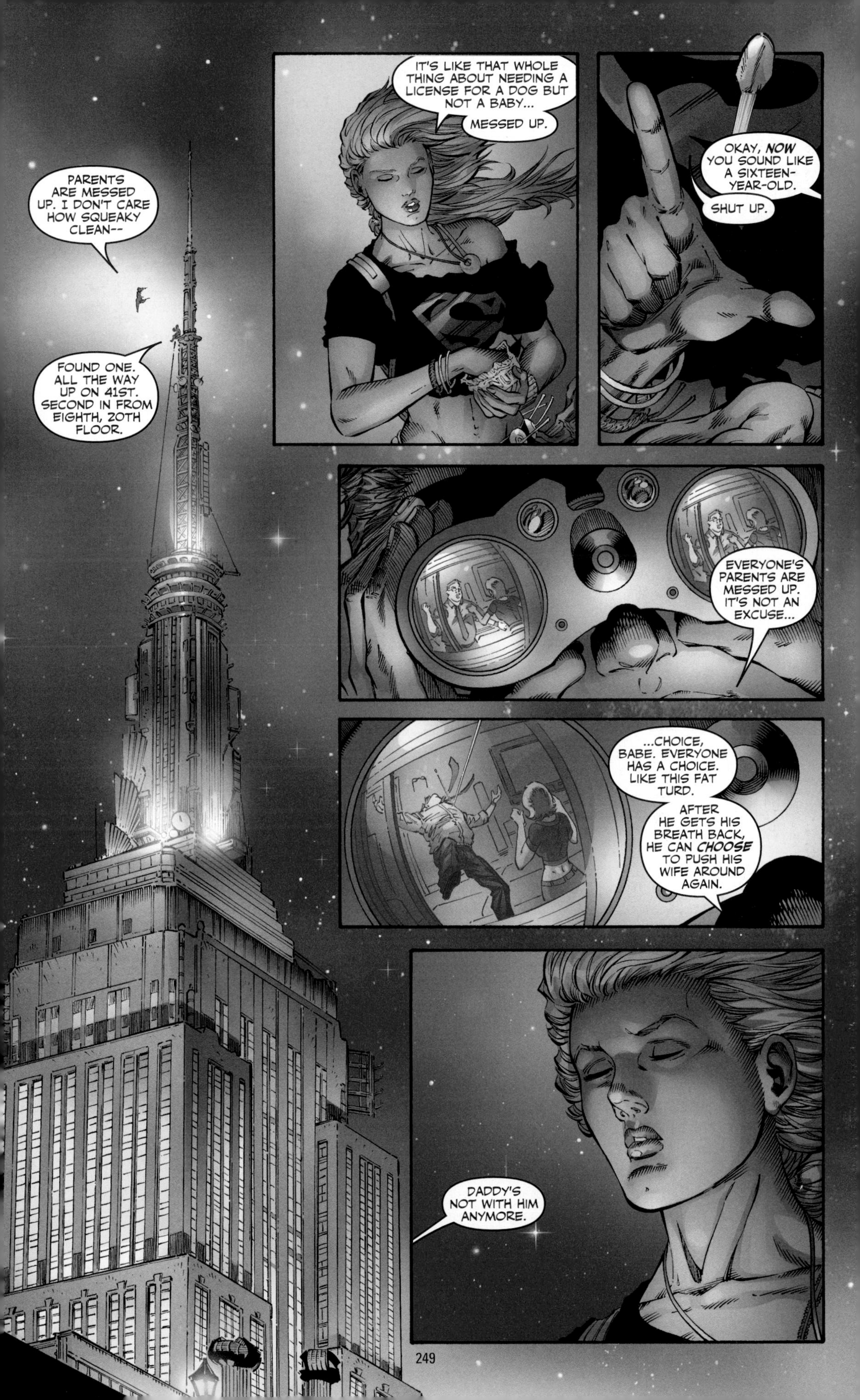
PARENTS ARE MESSED UP. I DON'T CARE HOW SQUEAKY CLEAN--
FOUND ONE. ALL THE WAY UP ON 41ST. SECOND IN FROM EIGHTH, 20TH FLOOR.
IT'S LIKE THAT WHOLE THING ABOUT NEEDING A LICENSE FOR A DOG BUT NOT A BABY...
MESSED UP.
OKAY, NOW YOU SOUND LIKE A SIXTEEN-YEAR-OLD.
SHUT UP.
EVERYONE'S PARENTS ARE MESSED UP. IT'S NOT AN EXCUSE...
...CHOICE, BABE. EVERYONE HAS A CHOICE. LIKE THIS FAT TURD.
AFTER HE GETS HIS BREATH BACK, HE CAN CHOOSE TO PUSH HIS WIFE AROUND AGAIN.
DADDY'S NOT WITH HIM ANYMORE.

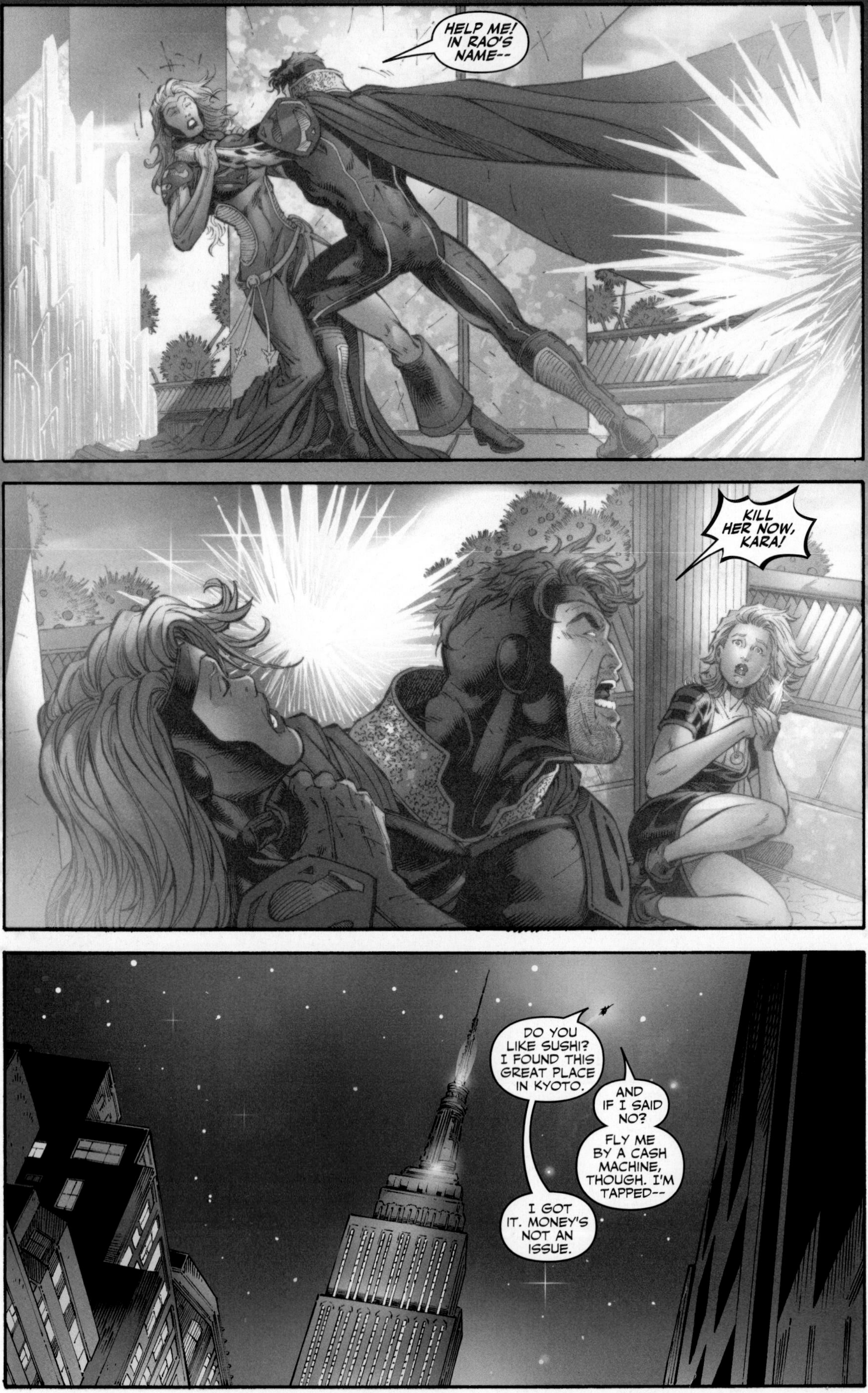
HELP ME! IN RAO'S NAME--
KILL HER NOW, KARA!
DO YOU LIKE SUSHI? I FOUND THIS GREAT PLACE IN KYOTO.
AND IF I SAID NO?
FLY ME BY A CASH MACHINE, THOUGH. I'M TAPPED--
I GOT IT. MONEY'S NOT AN ISSUE.

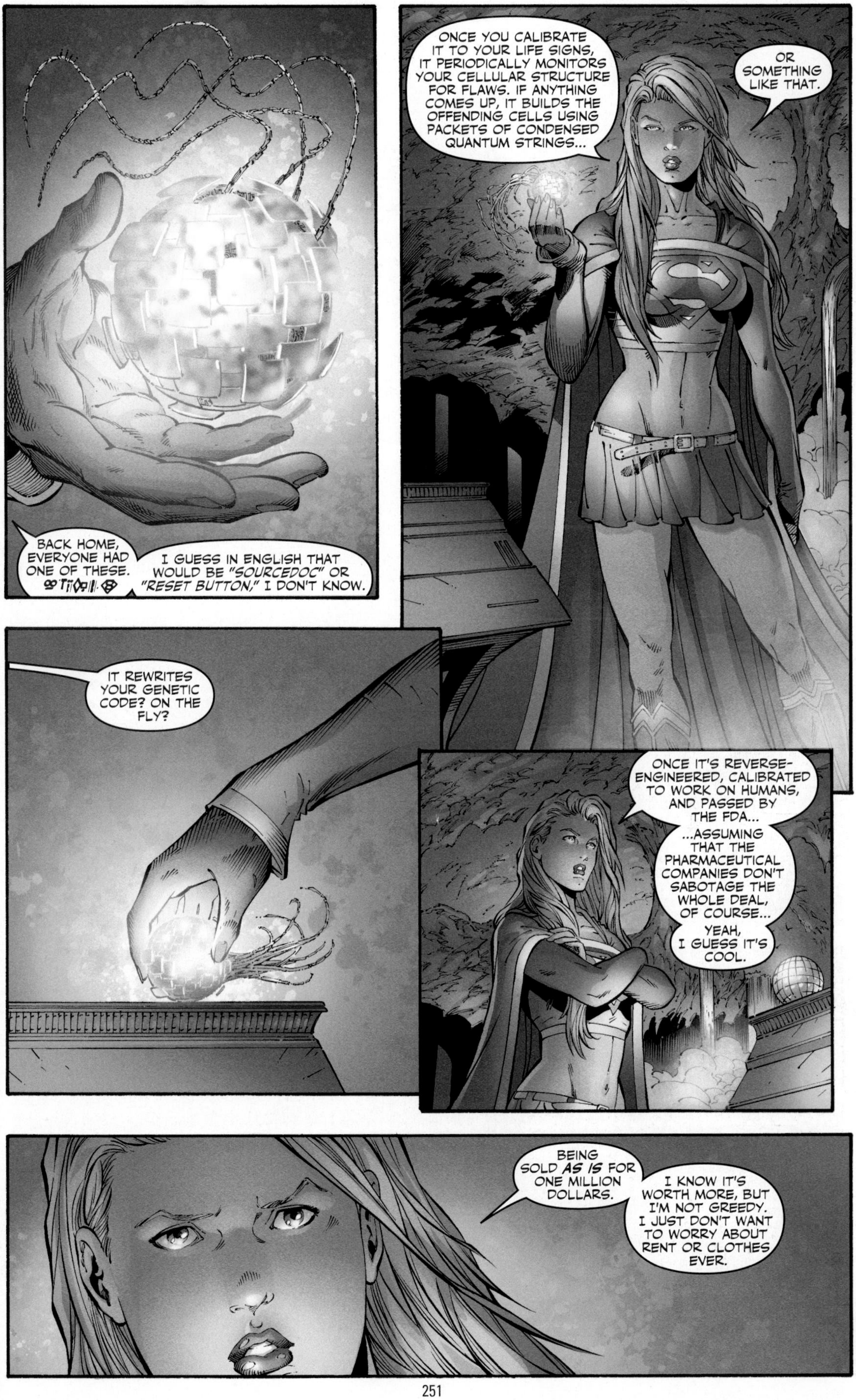
BACK HOME, EVERYONE HAD ONE OF THESE.
I GUESS IN ENGLISH THAT WOULD BE "SOURCEDOC" OR "RESET BUTTON," I DON'T KNOW.
ONCE YOU CALIBRATE IT TO YOUR LIFE SIGNS, IT PERIODICALLY MONITORS YOUR CELLULAR STRUCTURE FOR FLAWS. IF ANYTHING COMES UP, IT BUILDS THE OFFENDING CELLS USING PACKETS OF CONDENSED QUANTUM STRINGS...
OR SOMETHING LIKE THAT.
IT REWRITES YOUR GENETIC CODE? ON THE FLY?
ONCE IT'S REVERSE-ENGINEERED, CALIBRATED TO WORK ON HUMANS, AND PASSED BY THE FDA...
...ASSUMING THAT THE PHARMACEUTICAL COMPANIES DON'T SABOTAGE THE WHOLE DEAL, OF COURSE...
YEAH, I GUESS IT'S COOL.
BEING SOLD AS IS FOR ONE MILLION DOLLARS.
I KNOW IT'S WORTH MORE, BUT I'M NOT GREEDY. I JUST DON'T WANT TO WORRY ABOUT RENT OR CLOTHES EVER.

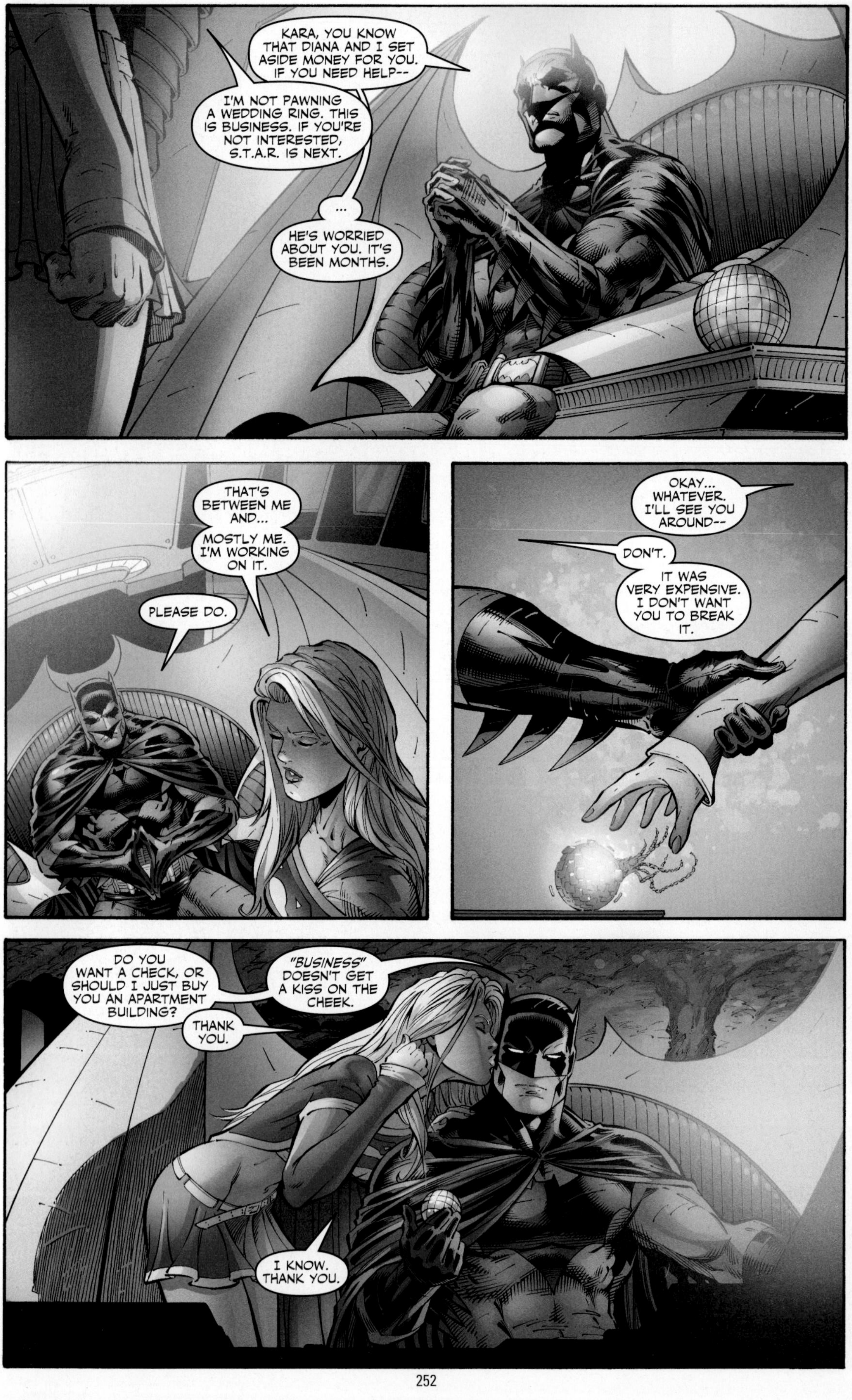
KARA, YOU KNOW THAT DIANA AND I SET ASIDE MONEY FOR YOU. IF YOU NEED HELP--
I'M NOT PAWNING A WEDDING RING. THIS IS BUSINESS. IF YOU'RE NOT INTERESTED, S.T.A.R. IS NEXT.
...
HE'S WORRIED ABOUT YOU. IT'S BEEN MONTHS.
THAT'S BETWEEN ME AND...
MOSTLY ME. I'M WORKING ON IT.
PLEASE DO.
OKAY... WHATEVER. I'LL SEE YOU AROUND--
DON'T.
IT WAS VERY EXPENSIVE. I DON'T WANT YOU TO BREAK IT.
DO YOU WANT A CHECK, OR SHOULD I JUST BUY YOU AN APARTMENT BUILDING?
"BUSINESS" DOESN'T GET A KISS ON THE CHEEK.
THANK YOU.
I KNOW. THANK YOU.

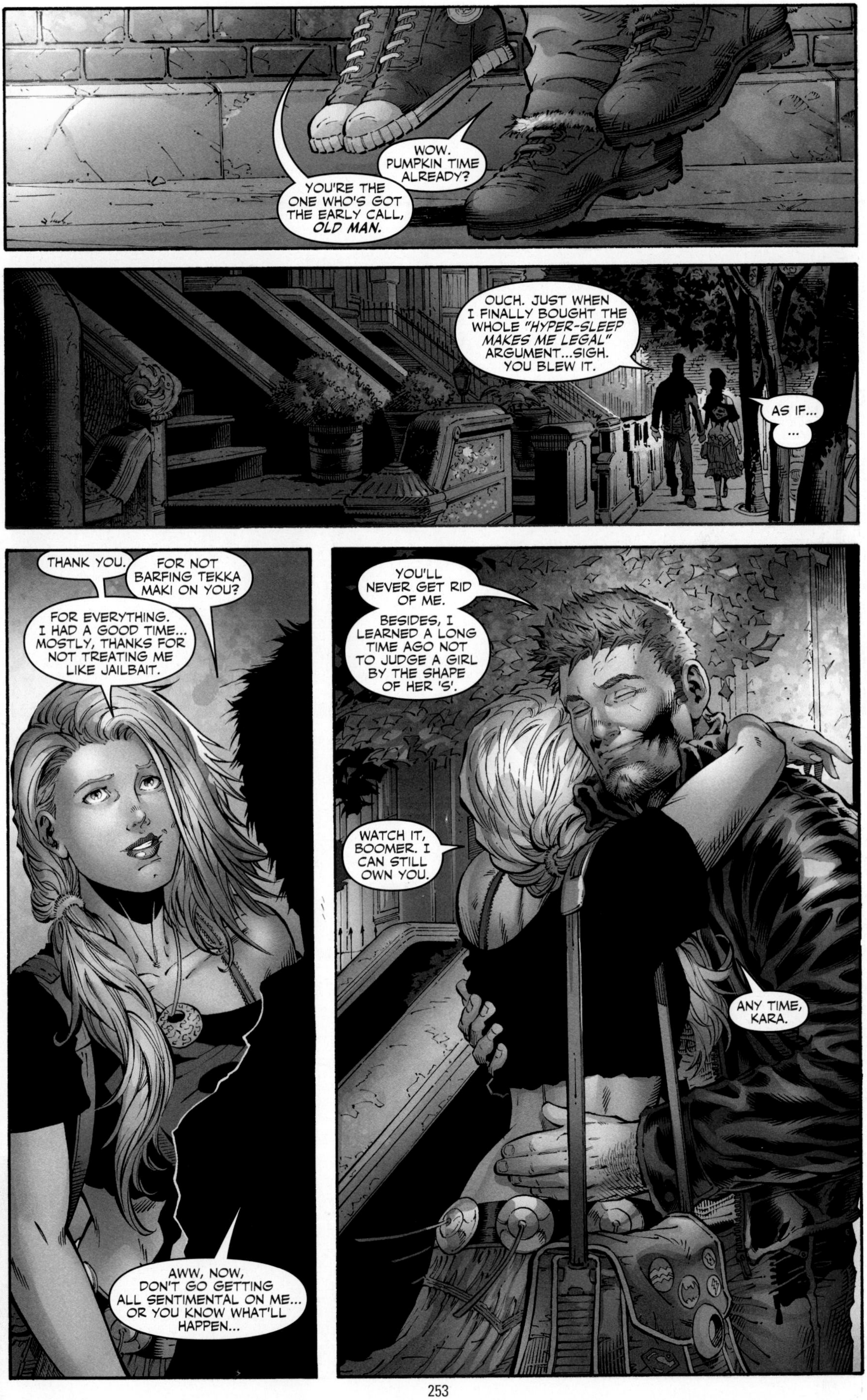
WOW. PUMPKIN TIME ALREADY?
YOU'RE THE ONE WHO'S GOT THE EARLY CALL, OLD MAN.
OUCH. JUST WHEN I FINALLY BOUGHT THE WHOLE "HYPER-SLEEP MAKES ME LEGAL" ARGUMENT...SIGH. YOU BLEW IT.
AS IF... ...
THANK YOU.
FOR NOT BARFING TEKKA MAKI ON YOU?
FOR EVERYTHING. I HAD A GOOD TIME... MOSTLY, THANKS FOR NOT TREATING ME LIKE JAILBAIT.
AWW, NOW, DON'T GO GETTING ALL SENTIMENTAL ON ME... OR YOU KNOW WHAT'LL HAPPEN...
YOU'LL NEVER GET RID OF ME.
BESIDES, I LEARNED A LONG TIME AGO NOT TO JUDGE A GIRL BY THE SHAPE OF HER 'S'.
WATCH IT, BOOMER. I CAN STILL OWN YOU.
ANY TIME, KARA.

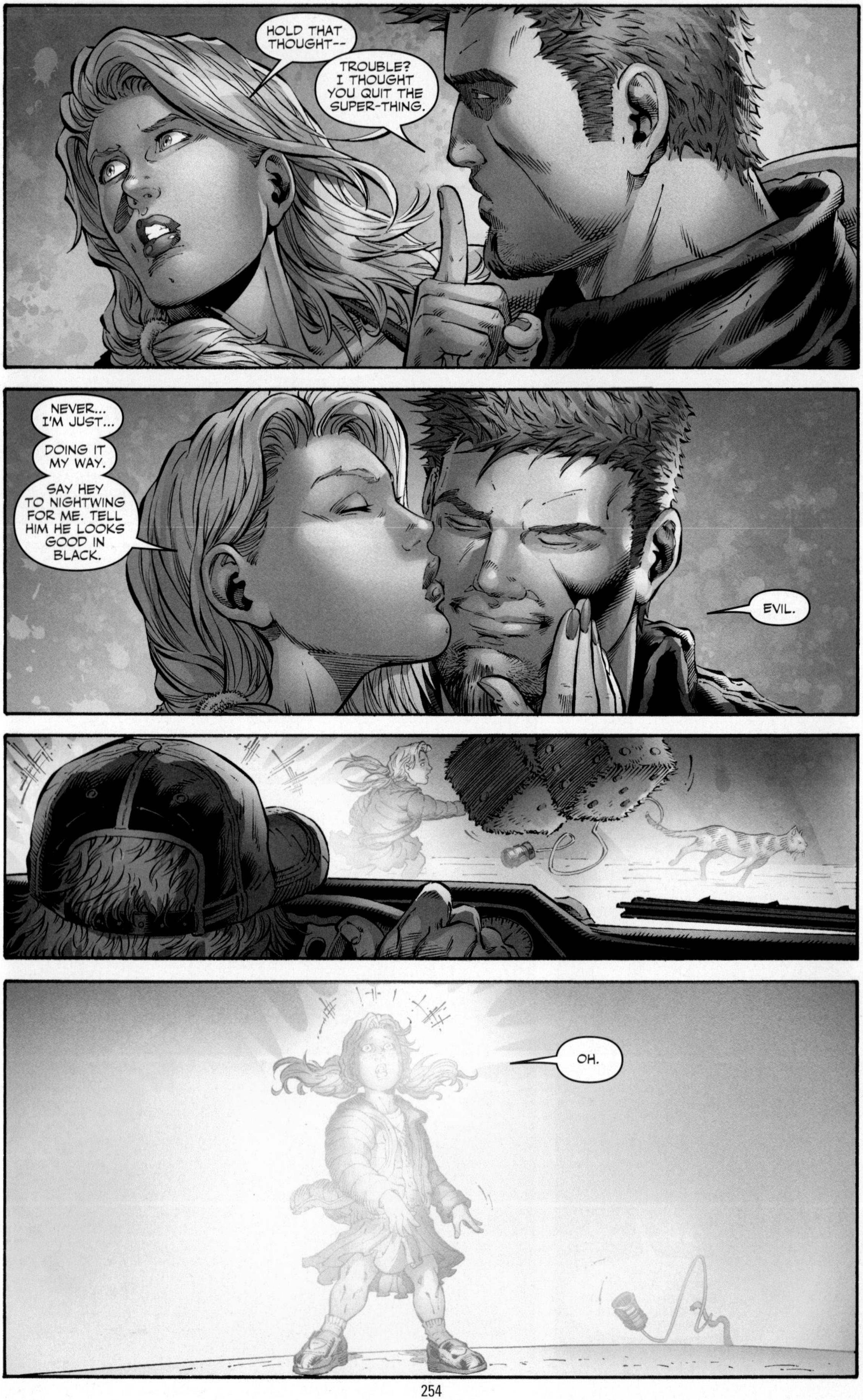
HOLD THAT THOUGHT--
TROUBLE? I THOUGHT YOU QUIT THE SUPER-THING.
NEVER... I'M JUST...
DOING IT MY WAY.
SAY HEY TO NIGHTWING FOR ME. TELL HIM HE LOOKS GOOD IN BLACK.
EVIL.
OH.

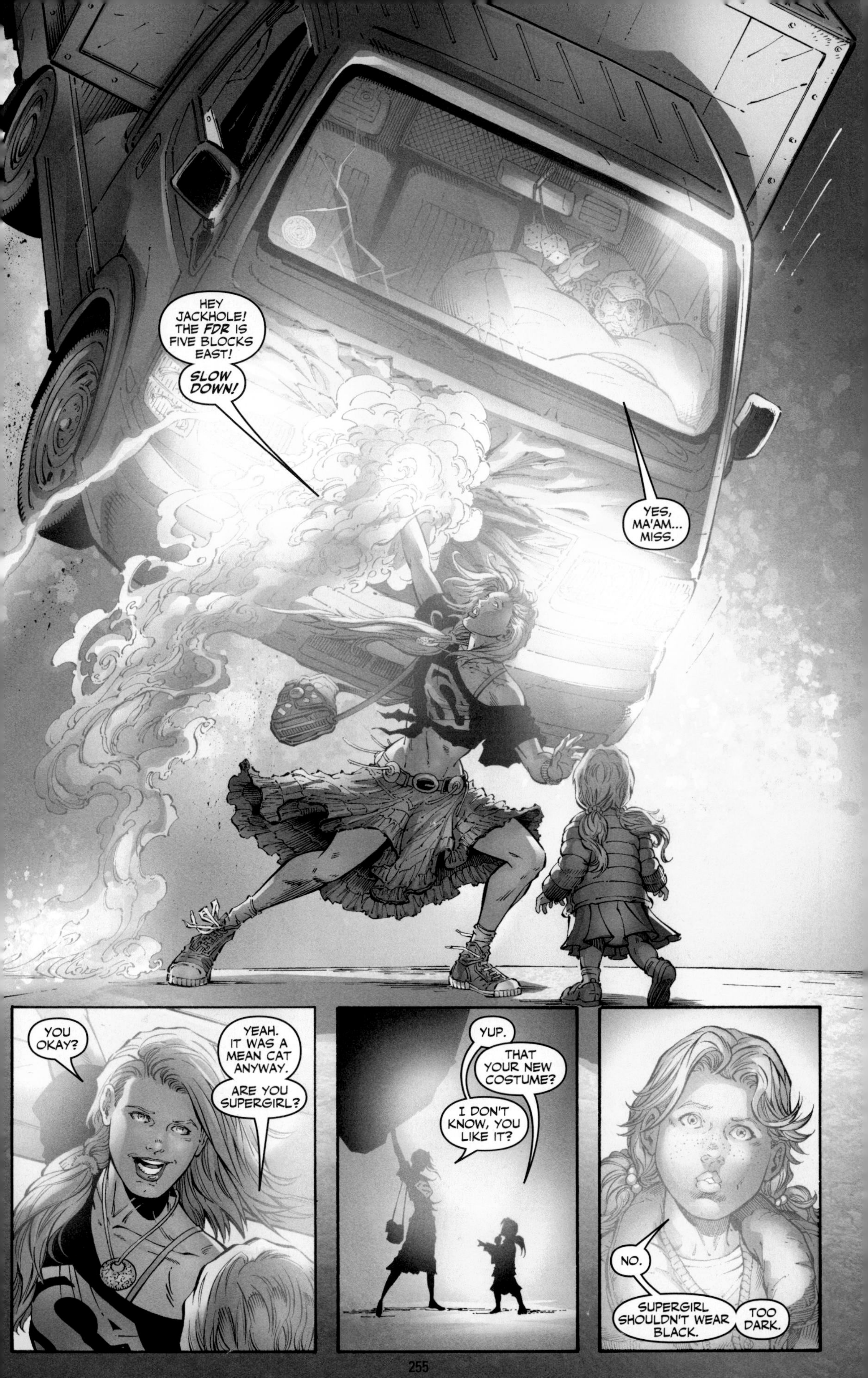
HEY JACKHOLE! THE FDR IS FIVE BLOCKS EAST!
SLOW DOWN!
YES, MA'AM... MISS.
YOU OKAY?
YEAH. IT WAS A MEAN CAT ANYWAY.
ARE YOU SUPERGIRL?
YUP.
THAT YOUR NEW COSTUME?
I DON'T KNOW, YOU LIKE IT?
NO.
SUPERGIRL SHOULDN'T WEAR BLACK.
TOO DARK.

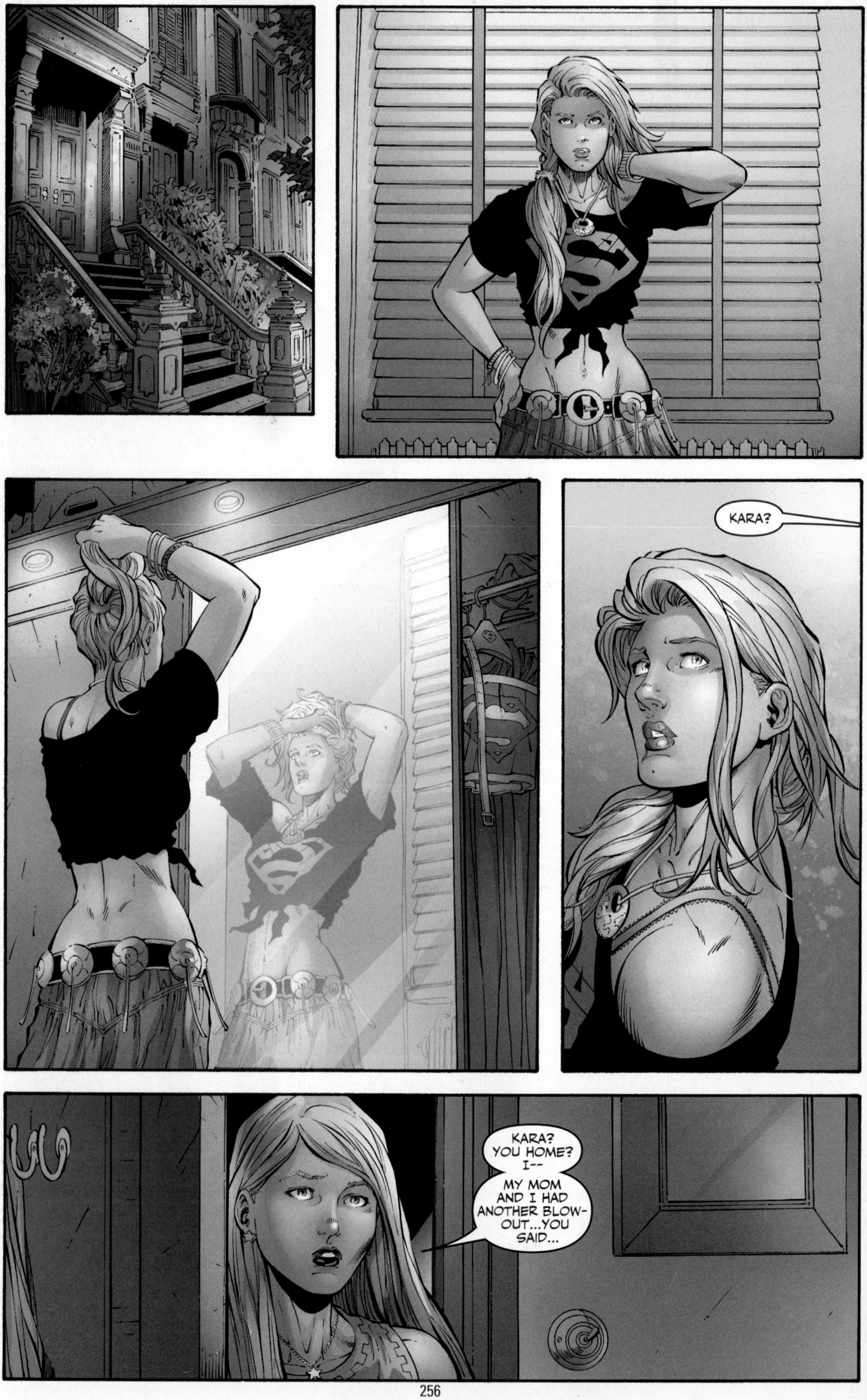
KARA?
KARA? YOU HOME? I--
MY MOM AND I HAD ANOTHER BLOW-OUT...YOU SAID...

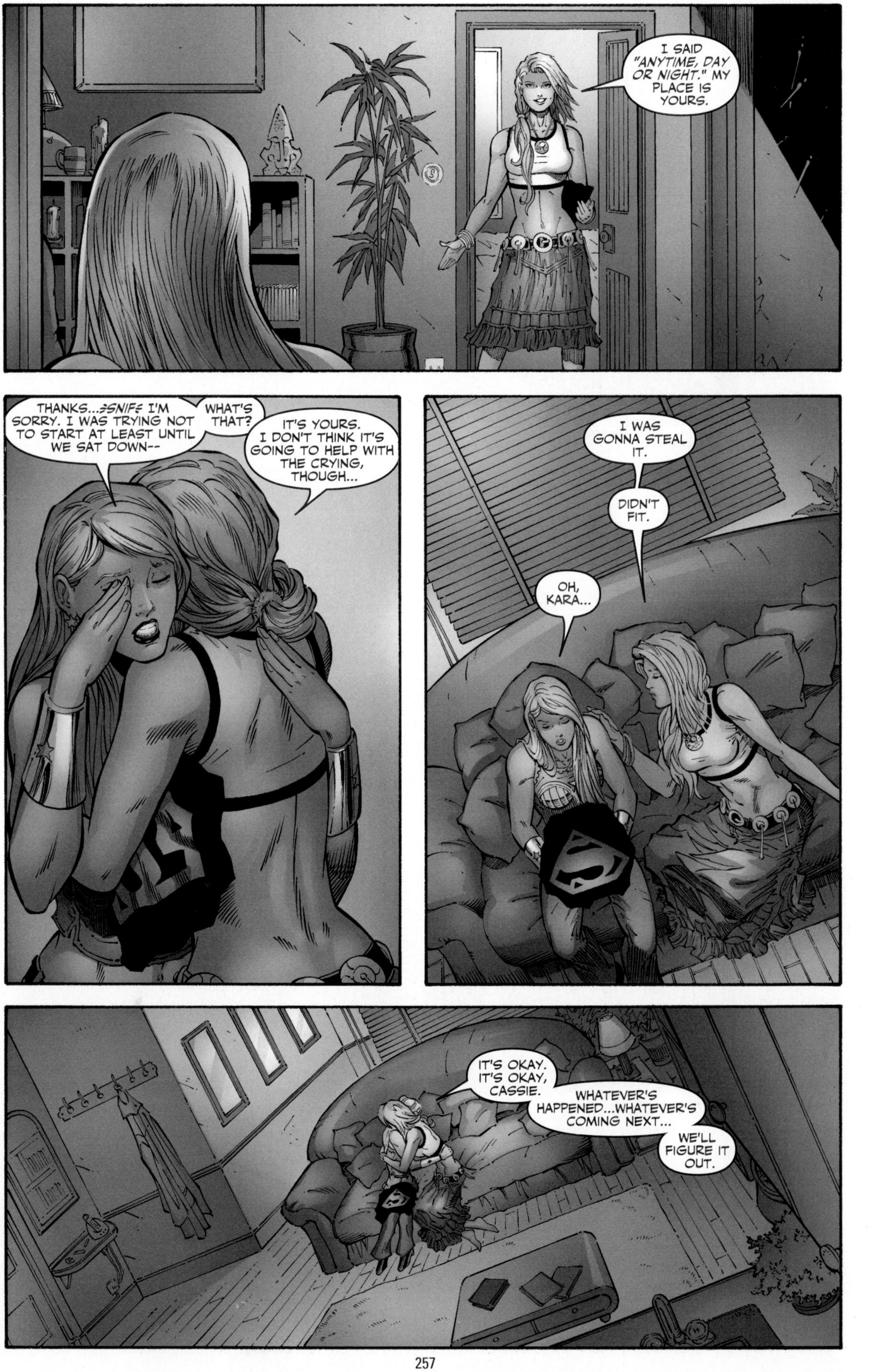
I SAID "ANYTIME, DAY OR NIGHT." MY PLACE IS YOURS.
THANKS... SNIF I'M SORRY. I WAS TRYING NOT TO START AT LEAST UNTIL WE SAT DOWN--
WHAT'S THAT?
IT'S YOURS. I DON'T THINK IT'S GOING TO HELP WITH THE CRYING, THOUGH...
I WAS GONNA STEAL IT.
DIDN'T FIT.
OH, KARA...
IT'S OKAY. IT'S OKAY, CASSIE.
WHATEVER'S HAPPENED...WHATEVER'S COMING NEXT...
WE'LL FIGURE IT OUT.

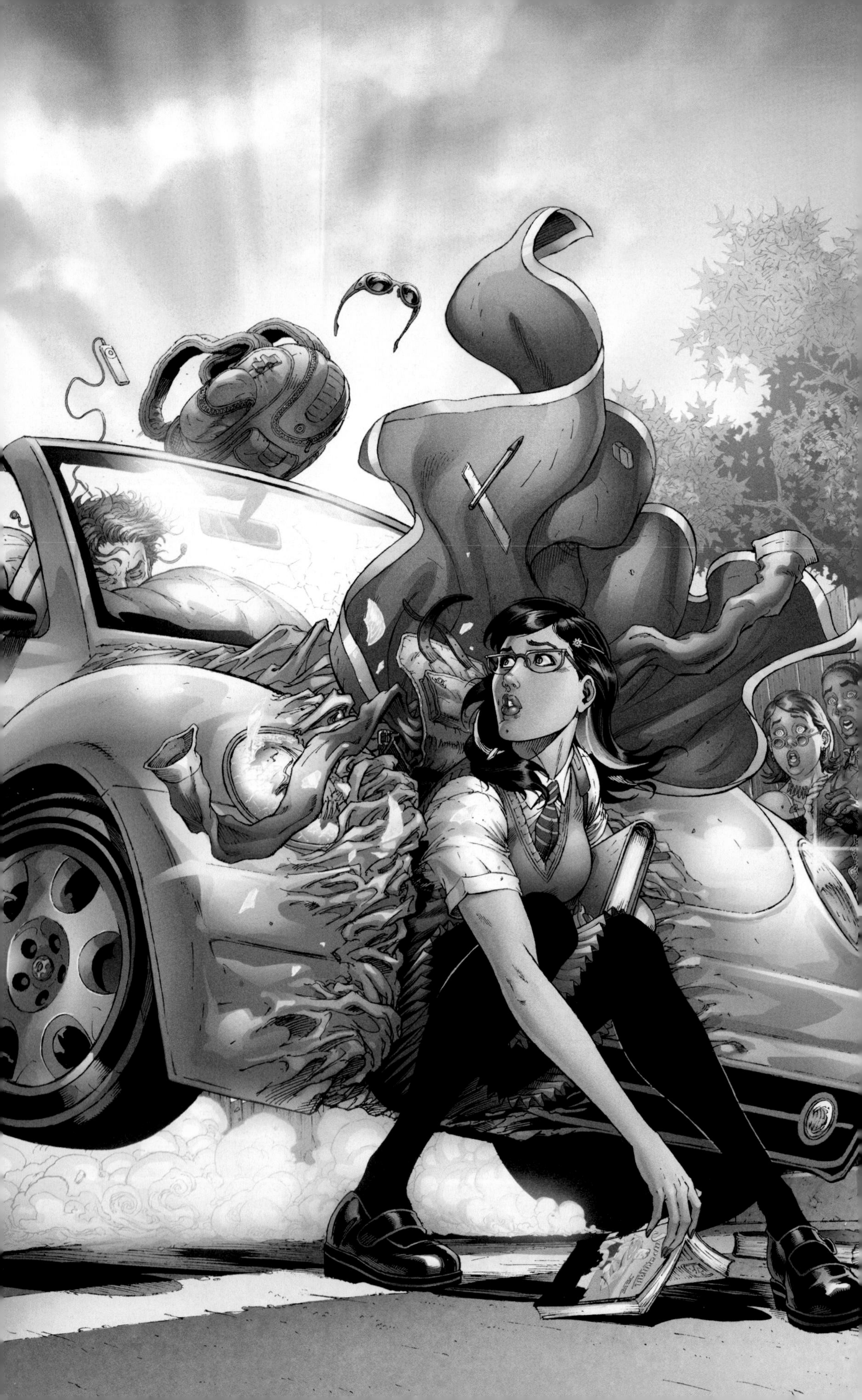

LOOK, I'M NOT SAYING I'M AN EXPERT. DROPPED OUTTA SCHOOL AT FIFTEEN--

AND YET, YOU'RE STILL TALKING. WEIRD.

BECAUSE BOOMER DOESN'T KNOW WHEN TO QWIT, DOES HE, PWETTY KITTY?

ROWRR?!

NO, BECAUSE FIFTEEN WAS OLD ENOUGH FOR ME TO LEARN THAT HIGH SCHOOL IS NO PLACE FOR KIDS.

AND IF THAT THING'S "PWETTY," I'M BRAD PITT.

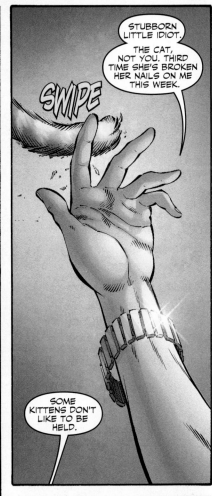

STUBBORN LITTLE IDIOT. THE CAT, NOT YOU. THIRD TIME SHE'S BROKEN HER NAILS ON ME THIS WEEK.

SWIPE

SOME KITTENS DON'T LIKE TO BE HELD.

IGNORING YOU, THANKS. SO THESE ARE SUPPOSED TO HELP ME "BLEND IN"?

HEH. NO, I DOUBT YOU'LL DO THAT. IF YOU'RE GOING THROUGH WITH THIS INSANITY...

...THEY'RE TO HELP YOU SURVIVE.

"ESCAPE FROM ALCATRAZ"? "SHAWSHANK REDEMPTION"? "LOCK UP"?

THESE ARE PRISON FILMS.

YOU EVER SPEAK TO A GROUP OF 16-YEAR-OLD GIRLS?

CELL BLOCK

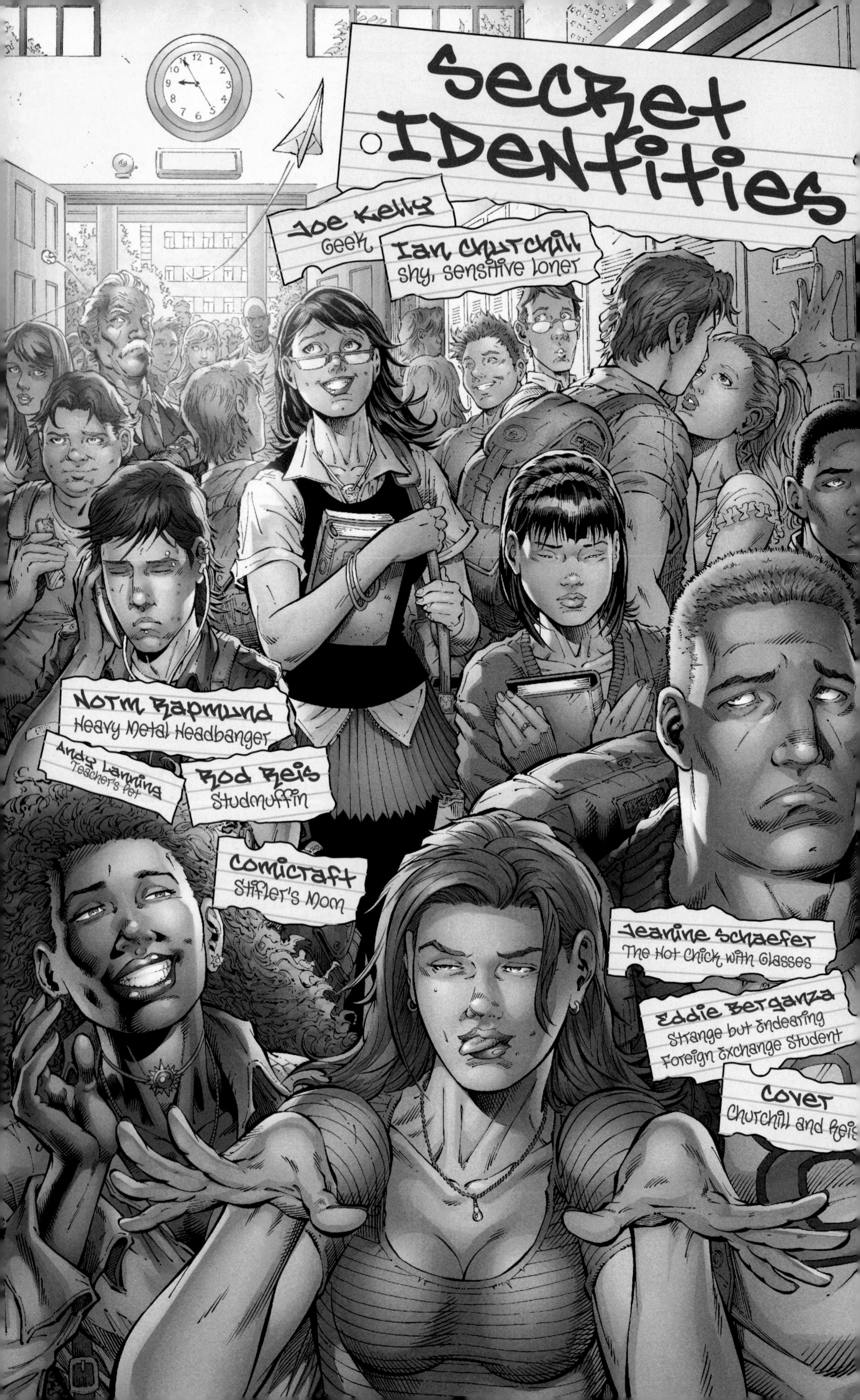

Secret Identities
Joe Kelly
Geek
Ian Churchill
Shy, Sensitive Loner
Norm Rapmund
Heavy Metal Headbanger
Andy Lanning
Teacher's Pet
Rod Reis
Studmuffin
Comicraft
Stifler's Mom
Jeanine Schaefer
The Hot Chick with Glasses
Eddie Berganza
Strange but Endearing
Foreign Exchange Student
Cover
Churchill and Reis

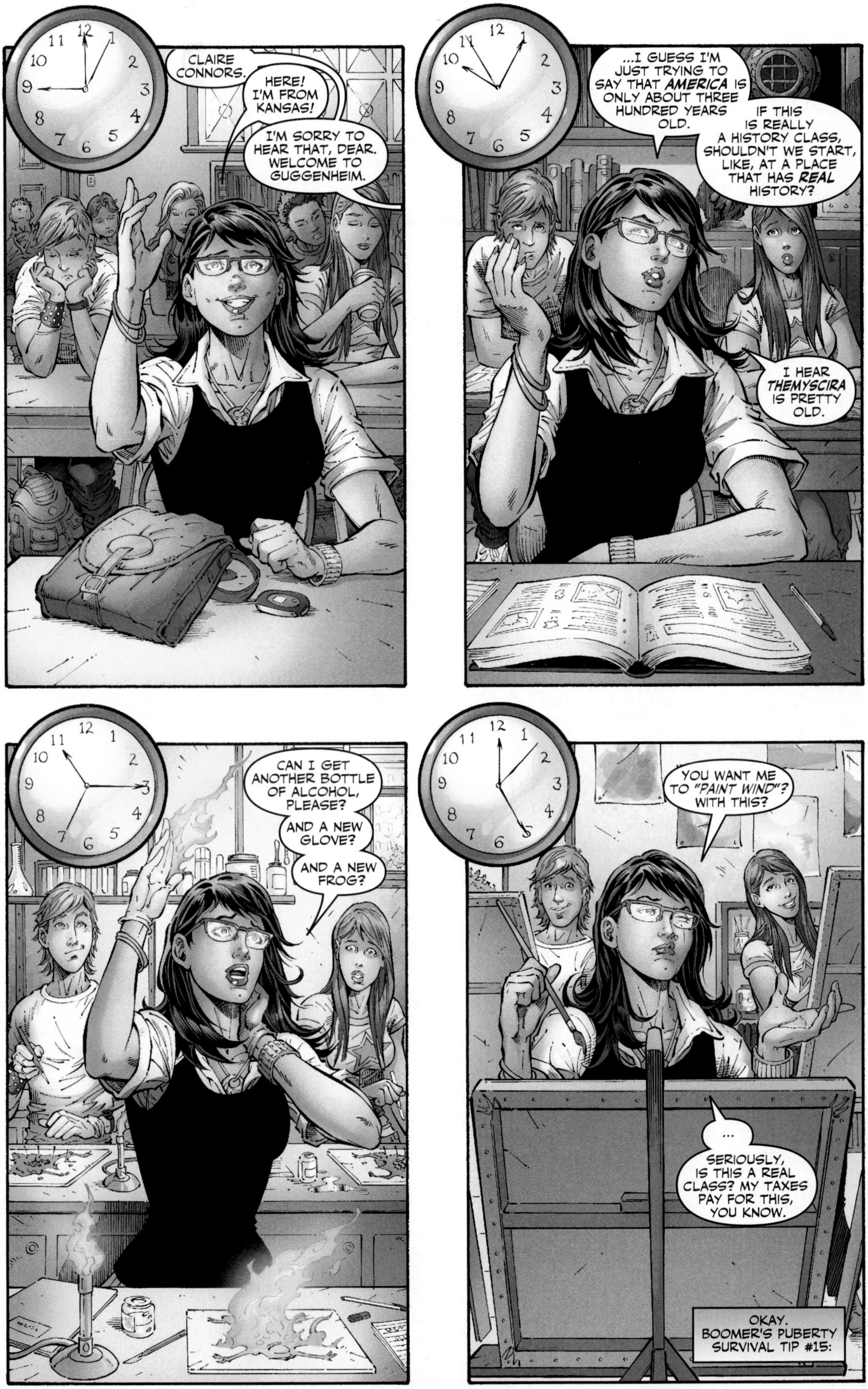
CLAIRE CONNORS.
HERE! I'M FROM KANSAS!
I'M SORRY TO HEAR THAT, DEAR. WELCOME TO GUGGENHEIM.
...I GUESS I'M JUST TRYING TO SAY THAT AMERICA IS ONLY ABOUT THREE HUNDRED YEARS OLD.
IF THIS IS REALLY A HISTORY CLASS, SHOULDN'T WE START, LIKE, AT A PLACE THAT HAS REAL HISTORY?
I HEAR THEMYSCIRA IS PRETTY OLD.
CAN I GET ANOTHER BOTTLE OF ALCOHOL, PLEASE?
AND A NEW GLOVE?
AND A NEW FROG?
YOU WANT ME TO "PAINT WIND"? WITH THIS?
...
SERIOUSLY, IS THIS A REAL CLASS? MY TAXES PAY FOR THIS, YOU KNOW.
OKAY. BOOMER'S PUBERTY SURVIVAL TIP #15:

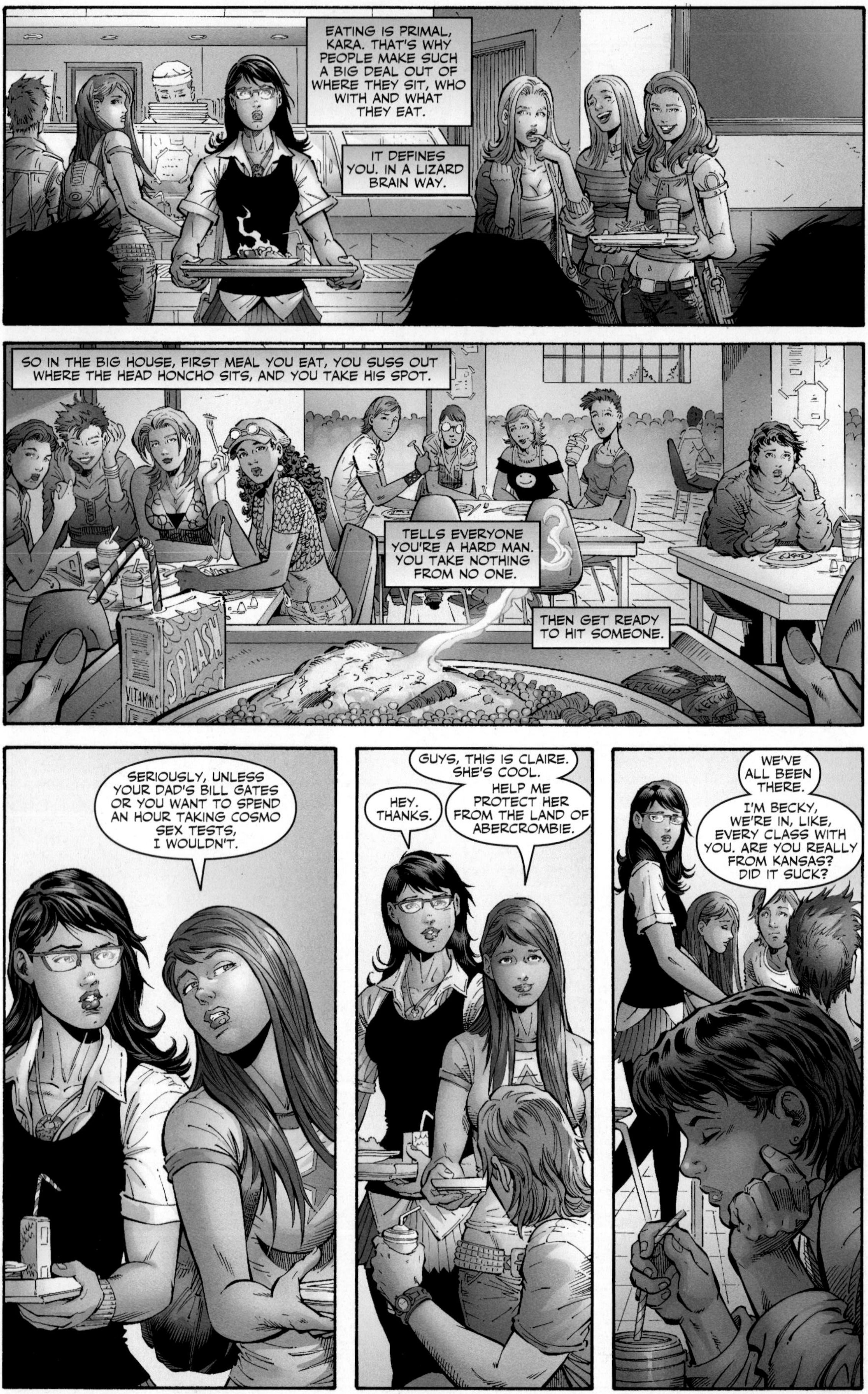
EATING IS PRIMAL, KARA. THAT'S WHY PEOPLE MAKE SUCH A BIG DEAL OUT OF WHERE THEY SIT, WHO WITH AND WHAT THEY EAT.
IT DEFINES YOU. IN A LIZARD BRAIN WAY.
SO IN THE BIG HOUSE, FIRST MEAL YOU EAT, YOU SUSS OUT WHERE THE HEAD HONCHO SITS, AND YOU TAKE HIS SPOT.
TELLS EVERYONE YOU'RE A HARD MAN. YOU TAKE NOTHING FROM NO ONE.
THEN GET READY TO HIT SOMEONE.
SPLASH
VITAMIN C
KETCHUP
SERIOUSLY, UNLESS YOUR DAD'S BILL GATES OR YOU WANT TO SPEND AN HOUR TAKING COSMO SEX TESTS, I WOULDN'T.
HEY. THANKS.
GUYS, THIS IS CLAIRE. SHE'S COOL.
HELP ME PROTECT HER FROM THE LAND OF ABERCROMBIE.
WE'VE ALL BEEN THERE.
I'M BECKY, WE'RE IN, LIKE, EVERY CLASS WITH YOU. ARE YOU REALLY FROM KANSAS? DID IT SUCK?

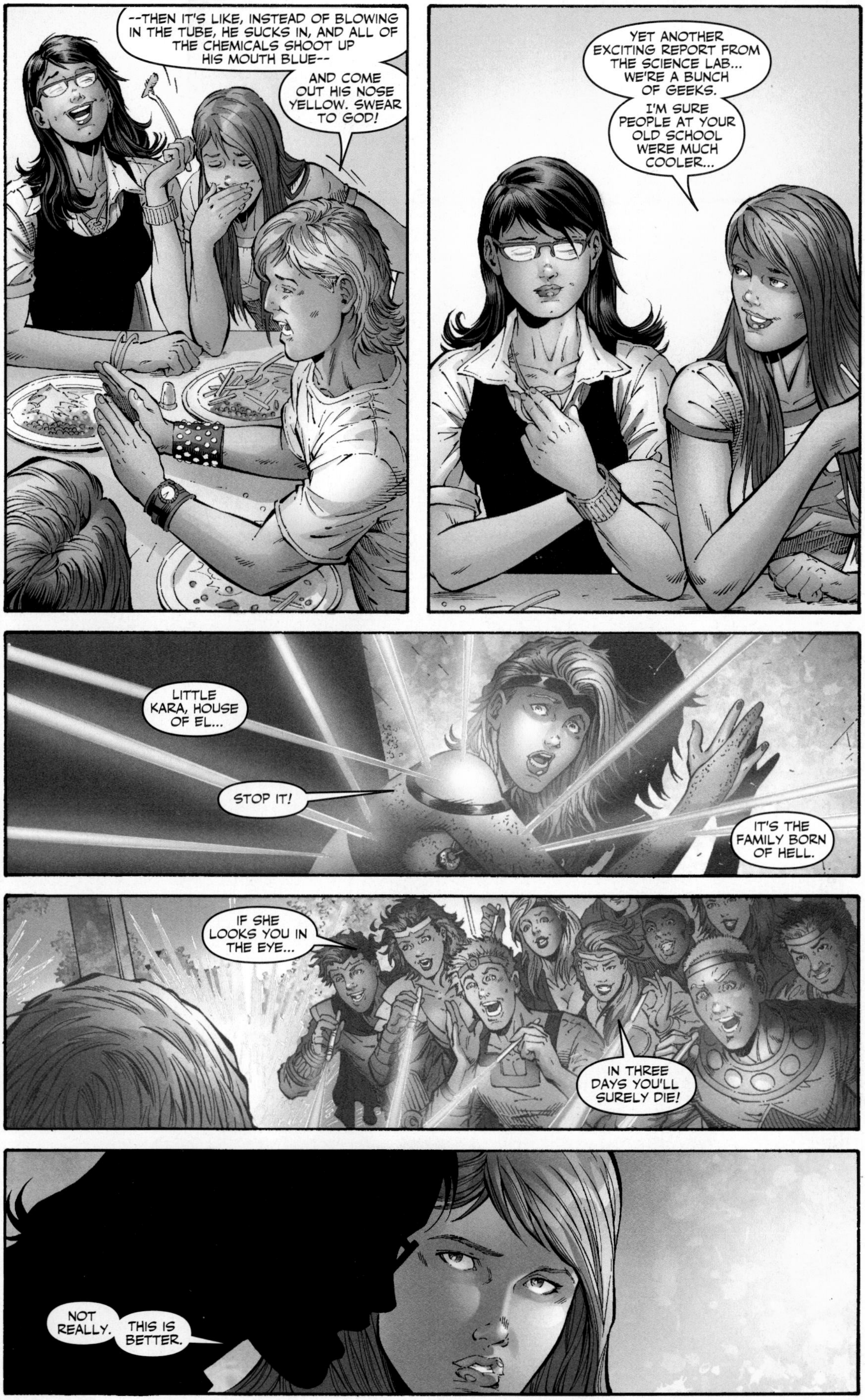
--THEN IT'S LIKE, INSTEAD OF BLOWING IN THE TUBE, HE SUCKS IN, AND ALL OF THE CHEMICALS SHOOT UP HIS MOUTH BLUE--
AND COME OUT HIS NOSE YELLOW. SWEAR TO GOD!
YET ANOTHER EXCITING REPORT FROM THE SCIENCE LAB... WE'RE A BUNCH OF GEEKS.
I'M SURE PEOPLE AT YOUR OLD SCHOOL WERE MUCH COOLER...
LITTLE KARA, HOUSE OF EL...
STOP IT!
IT'S THE FAMILY BORN OF HELL.
IF SHE LOOKS YOU IN THE EYE...
IN THREE DAYS YOU'LL SURELY DIE!
NOT REALLY.
THIS IS BETTER.

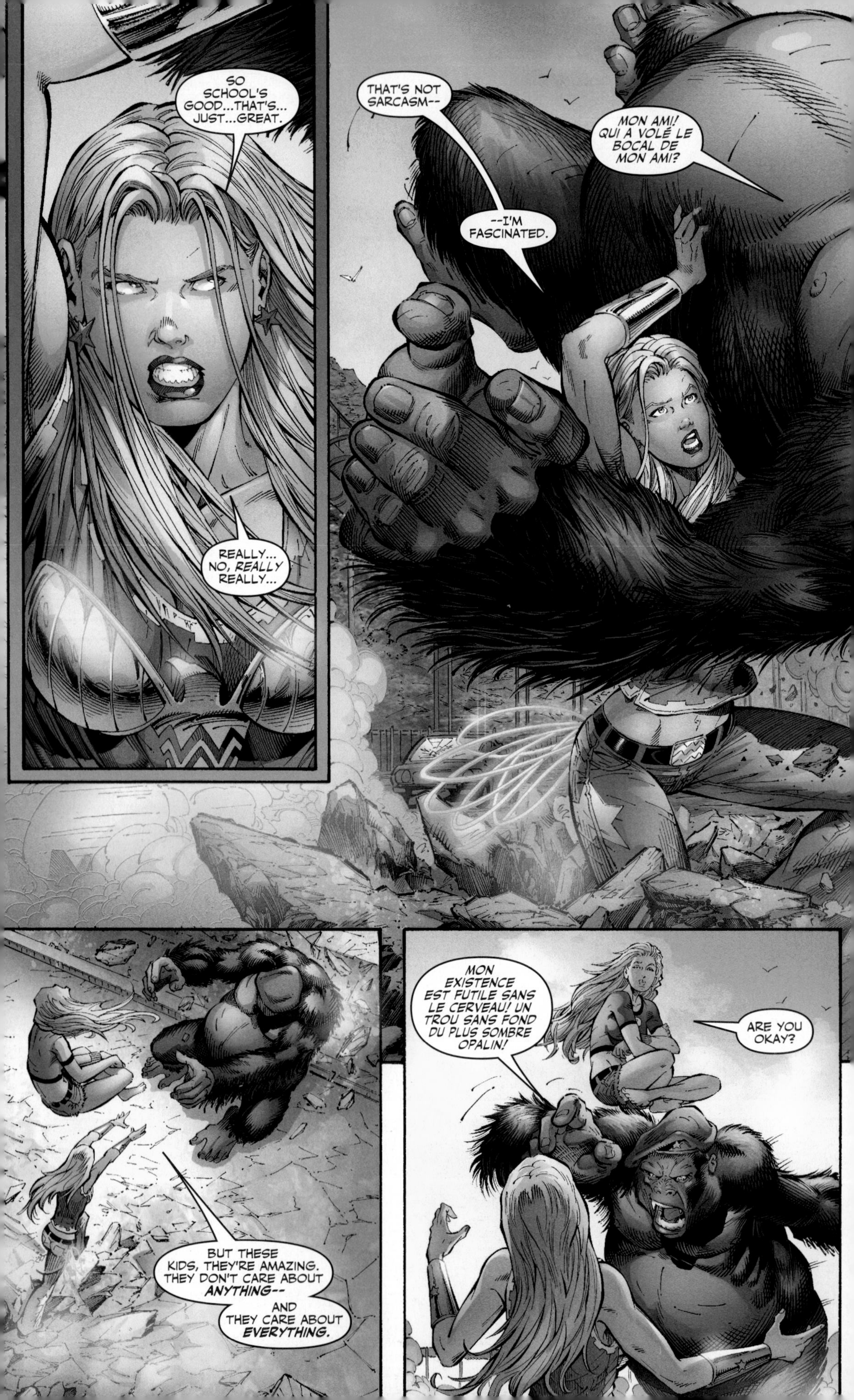
SO SCHOOL'S GOOD...THAT'S... JUST...GREAT.
REALLY... NO, REALLY REALLY...
THAT'S NOT SARCASM--
--I'M FASCINATED.
MON AMI! QUI A VOLÉ LE BOCAL DE MON AMI?
BUT THESE KIDS, THEY'RE AMAZING. THEY DON'T CARE ABOUT ANYTHING--
AND THEY CARE ABOUT EVERYTHING.
MON EXISTENCE EST FUTILE SANS LE CERVEAU! UN TROU SANS FOND DU PLUS SOMBRE OPALIN!
ARE YOU OKAY?

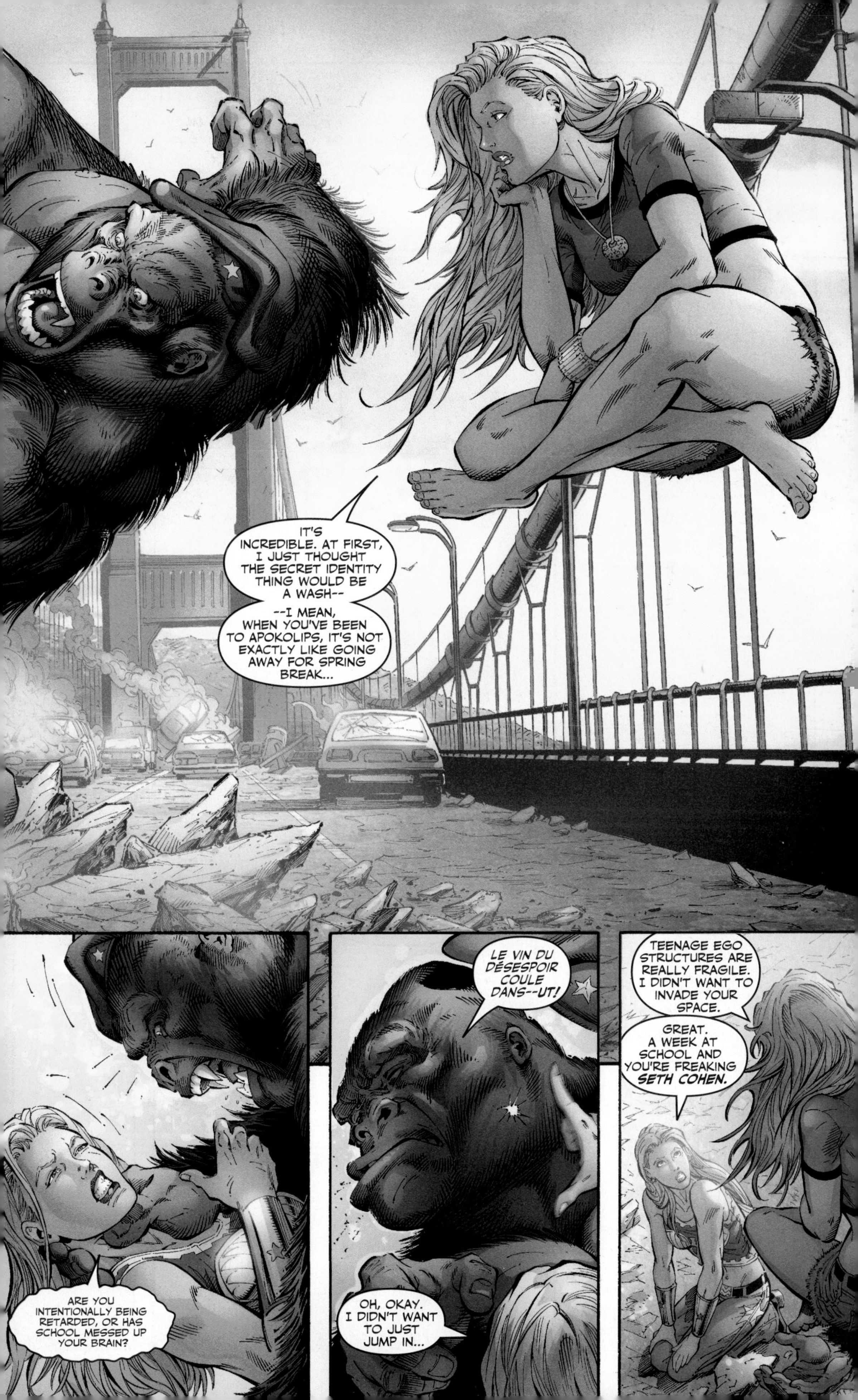

IT'S INCREDIBLE. AT FIRST, I JUST THOUGHT THE SECRET IDENTITY THING WOULD BE A WASH--
--I MEAN, WHEN YOU'VE BEEN TO APOKOLIPS, IT'S NOT EXACTLY LIKE GOING AWAY FOR SPRING BREAK...
ARE YOU INTENTIONALLY BEING RETARDED, OR HAS SCHOOL MESSED UP YOUR BRAIN?
LE VIN DU DÉSESPOIR COULE DANS--UT!
OH, OKAY. I DIDN'T WANT TO JUST JUMP IN...
TEENAGE EGO STRUCTURES ARE REALLY FRAGILE. I DIDN'T WANT TO INVADE YOUR SPACE.
GREAT. A WEEK AT SCHOOL AND YOU'RE FREAKING SETH COHEN.

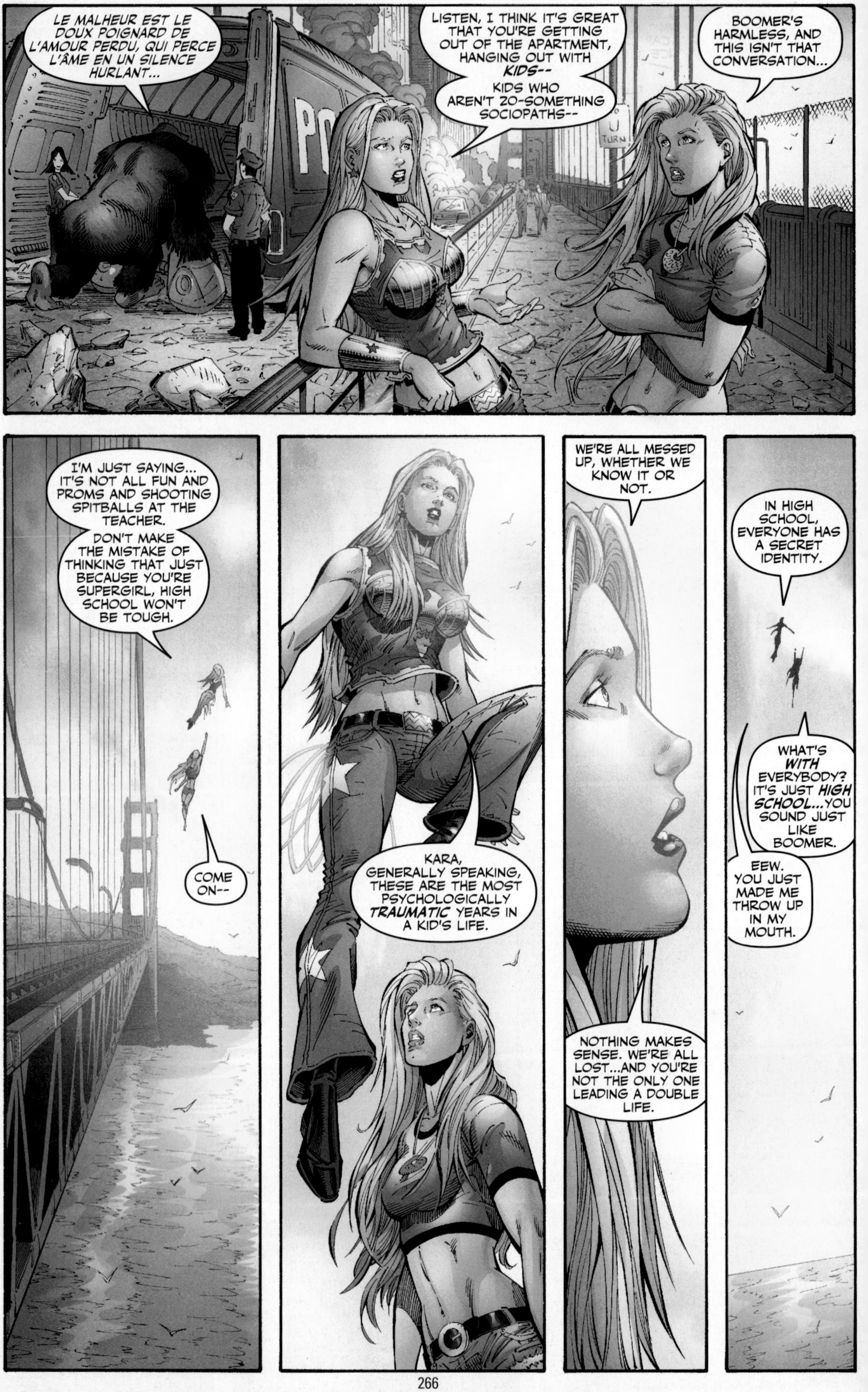
LE MALHEUR EST LE DOUX POIGNARD DE L'AMOUR PERDU, QUI PERCE L'ÂME EN UN SILENCE HURLANT...
LISTEN, I THINK IT'S GREAT THAT YOU'RE GETTING OUT OF THE APARTMENT, HANGING OUT WITH KIDS--
KIDS WHO AREN'T 20-SOMETHING SOCIOPATHS--
BOOMER'S HARMLESS, AND THIS ISN'T THAT CONVERSATION...
U TURN
I'M JUST SAYING... IT'S NOT ALL FUN AND PROMS AND SHOOTING SPITBALLS AT THE TEACHER.
DON'T MAKE THE MISTAKE OF THINKING THAT JUST BECAUSE YOU'RE SUPERGIRL, HIGH SCHOOL WON'T BE TOUGH.
COME ON--
KARA, GENERALLY SPEAKING, THESE ARE THE MOST PSYCHOLOGICALLY TRAUMATIC YEARS IN A KID'S LIFE.
WE'RE ALL MESSED UP, WHETHER WE KNOW IT OR NOT.
NOTHING MAKES SENSE. WE'RE ALL LOST...AND YOU'RE NOT THE ONLY ONE LEADING A DOUBLE LIFE.
IN HIGH SCHOOL, EVERYONE HAS A SECRET IDENTITY.
WHAT'S WITH EVERYBODY? IT'S JUST HIGH SCHOOL...YOU SOUND JUST LIKE BOOMER.
EEW. YOU JUST MADE ME THROW UP IN MY MOUTH.

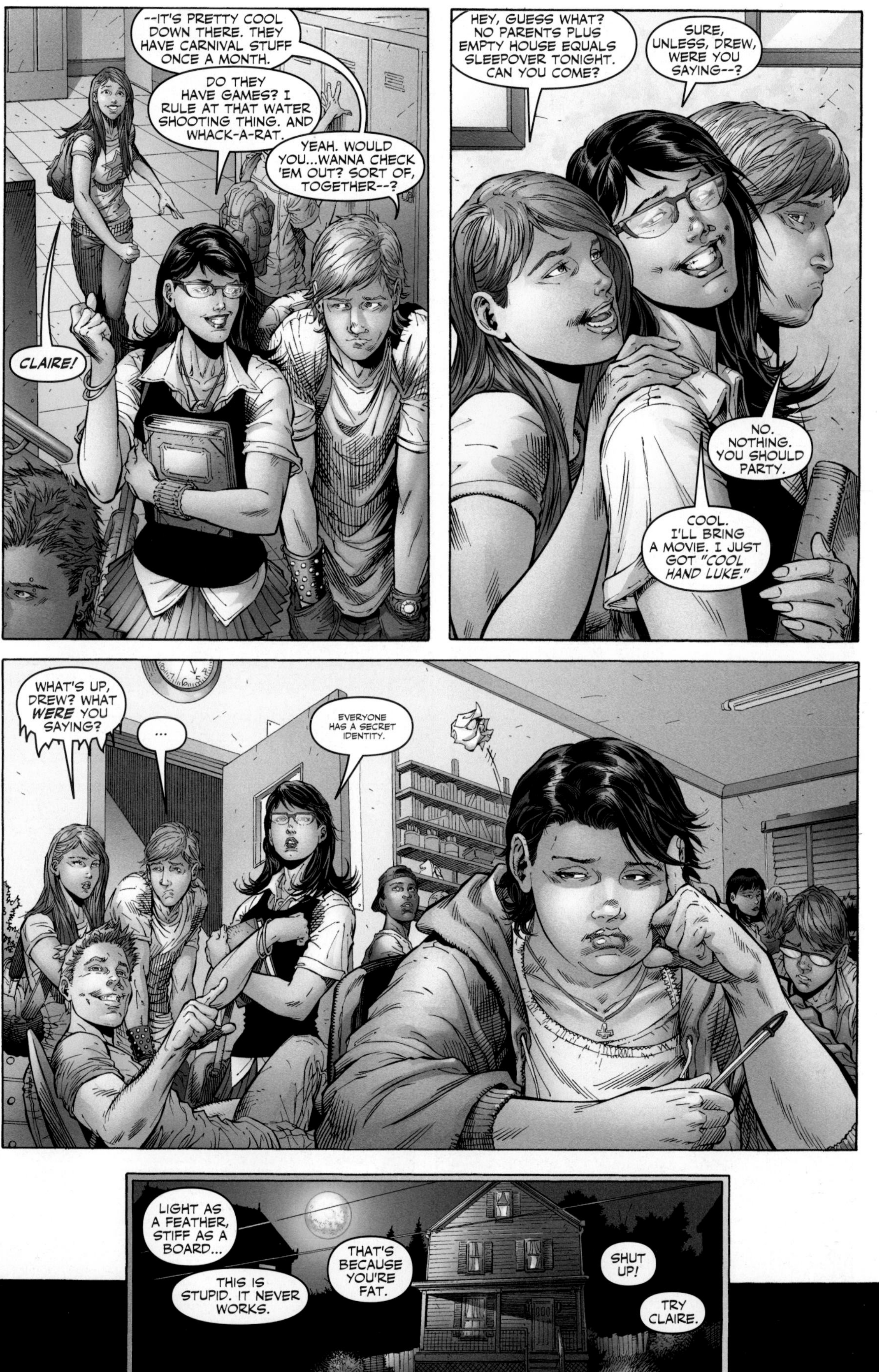
--IT'S PRETTY COOL DOWN THERE. THEY HAVE CARNIVAL STUFF ONCE A MONTH.
DO THEY HAVE GAMES? I RULE AT THAT WATER SHOOTING THING. AND WHACK-A-RAT.
YEAH. WOULD YOU...WANNA CHECK 'EM OUT? SORT OF, TOGETHER--?
CLAIRE!
HEY, GUESS WHAT? NO PARENTS PLUS EMPTY HOUSE EQUALS SLEEPOVER TONIGHT. CAN YOU COME?
SURE, UNLESS, DREW, WERE YOU SAYING--?
NO. NOTHING. YOU SHOULD PARTY.
COOL. I'LL BRING A MOVIE. I JUST GOT "COOL HAND LUKE."
WHAT'S UP, DREW? WHAT WERE YOU SAYING?
...
EVERYONE HAS A SECRET IDENTITY.
LIGHT AS A FEATHER, STIFF AS A BOARD...
THIS IS STUPID. IT NEVER WORKS.
THAT'S BECAUSE YOU'RE FAT.
SHUT UP!
TRY CLAIRE.

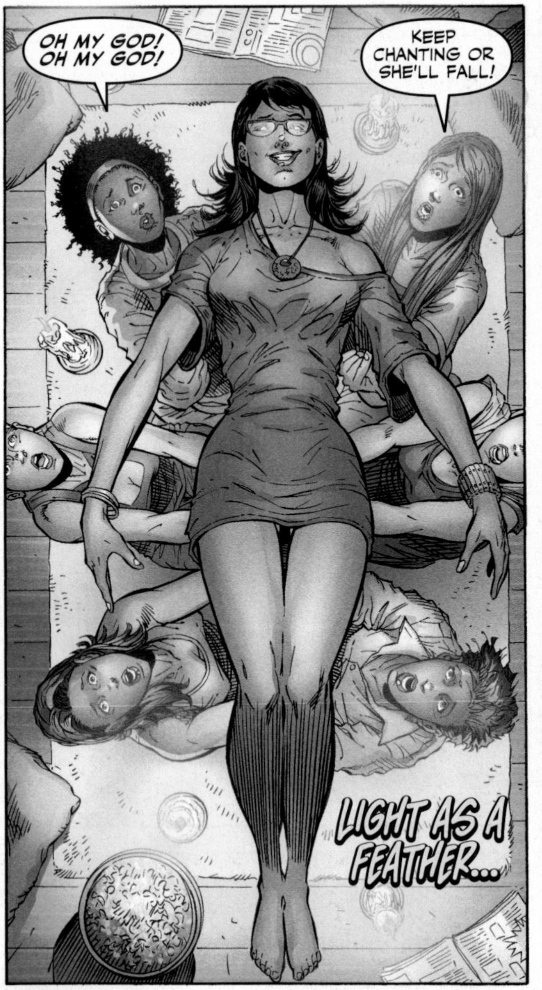
OH MY GOD! OH MY GOD!
KEEP CHANTING OR SHE'LL FALL!
LIGHT AS A FEATHER...

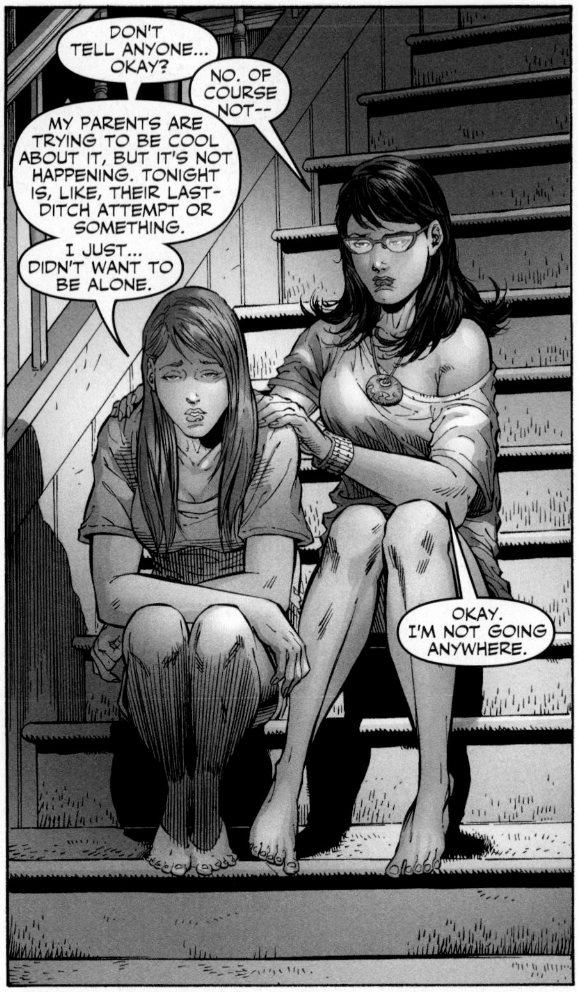
DON'T TELL ANYONE... OKAY?
NO. OF COURSE NOT--
MY PARENTS ARE TRYING TO BE COOL ABOUT IT, BUT IT'S NOT HAPPENING. TONIGHT IS, LIKE, THEIR LAST-DITCH ATTEMPT OR SOMETHING.
I JUST... DIDN'T WANT TO BE ALONE.
OKAY. I'M NOT GOING ANYWHERE.

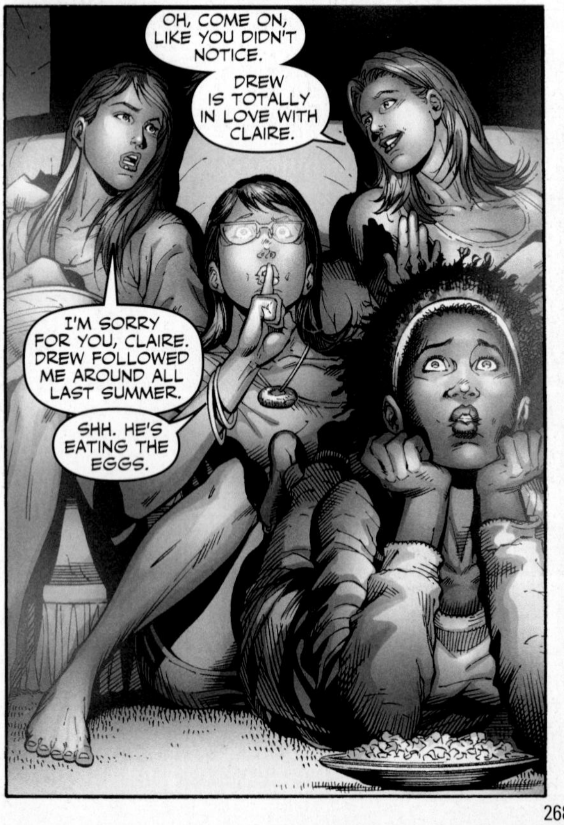
OH, COME ON, LIKE YOU DIDN'T NOTICE.
DREW IS TOTALLY IN LOVE WITH CLAIRE.
I'M SORRY FOR YOU, CLAIRE. DREW FOLLOWED ME AROUND ALL LAST SUMMER.
SHH. HE'S EATING THE EGGS.

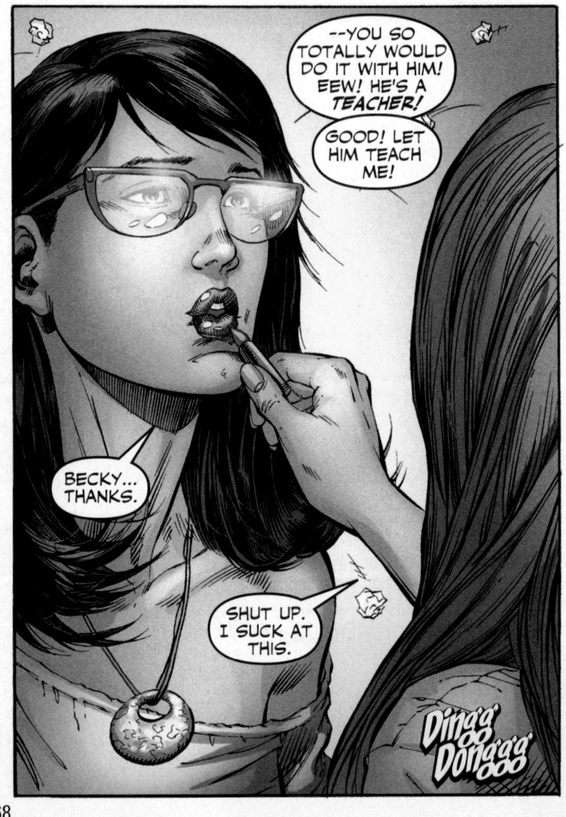
--YOU SO TOTALLY WOULD DO IT WITH HIM! EEW! HE'S A TEACHER!
GOOD! LET HIM TEACH ME!
BECKY... THANKS.
SHUT UP. I SUCK AT THIS.
Ding'a'a' Dong'a'a'

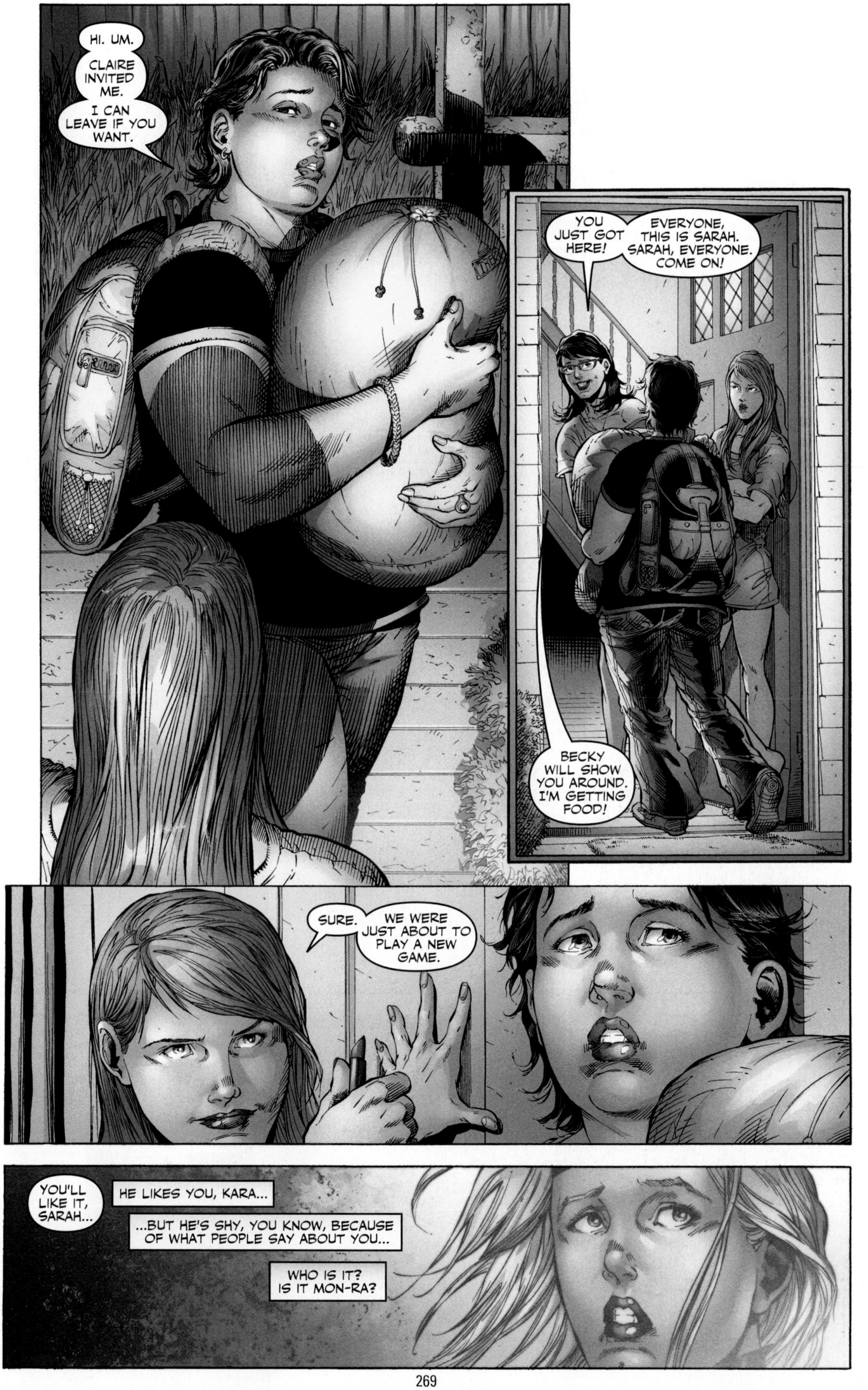
HI. UM.
CLAIRE INVITED ME.
I CAN LEAVE IF YOU WANT.
YOU JUST GOT HERE!
EVERYONE, THIS IS SARAH. SARAH, EVERYONE. COME ON!
BECKY WILL SHOW YOU AROUND. I'M GETTING FOOD!
SURE.
WE WERE JUST ABOUT TO PLAY A NEW GAME.
YOU'LL LIKE IT, SARAH...
HE LIKES YOU, KARA...
...BUT HE'S SHY, YOU KNOW, BECAUSE OF WHAT PEOPLE SAY ABOUT YOU...
WHO IS IT? IS IT MON-RA?

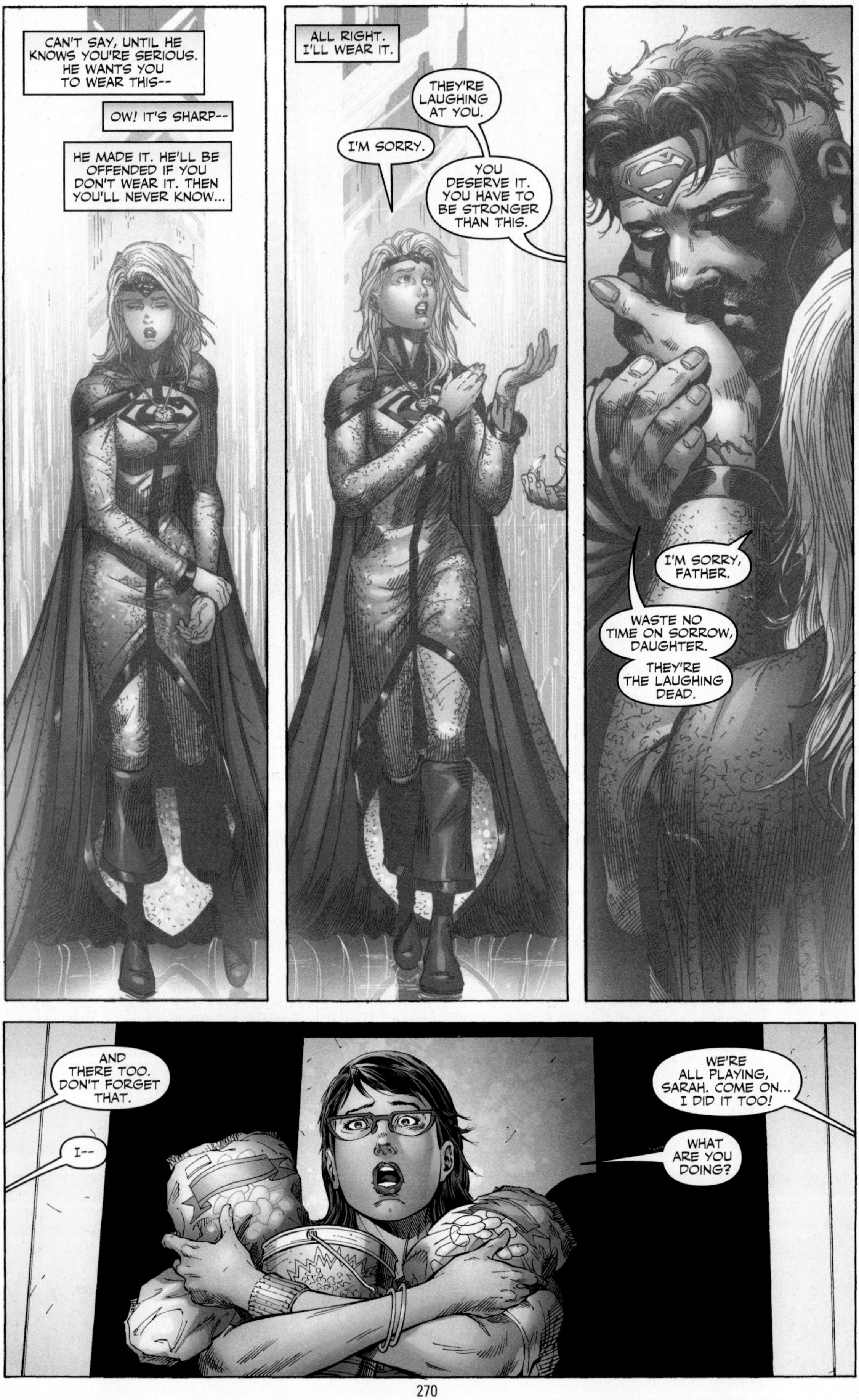
CAN'T SAY, UNTIL HE KNOWS YOU'RE SERIOUS. HE WANTS YOU TO WEAR THIS--
OW! IT'S SHARP--
HE MADE IT. HE'LL BE OFFENDED IF YOU DON'T WEAR IT. THEN YOU'LL NEVER KNOW...
ALL RIGHT. I'LL WEAR IT.
THEY'RE LAUGHING AT YOU.
I'M SORRY.
YOU DESERVE IT. YOU HAVE TO BE STRONGER THAN THIS.
I'M SORRY, FATHER.
WASTE NO TIME ON SORROW, DAUGHTER.
THEY'RE THE LAUGHING DEAD.
AND THERE TOO. DON'T FORGET THAT.
I--
WE'RE ALL PLAYING, SARAH. COME ON... I DID IT TOO!
WHAT ARE YOU DOING?

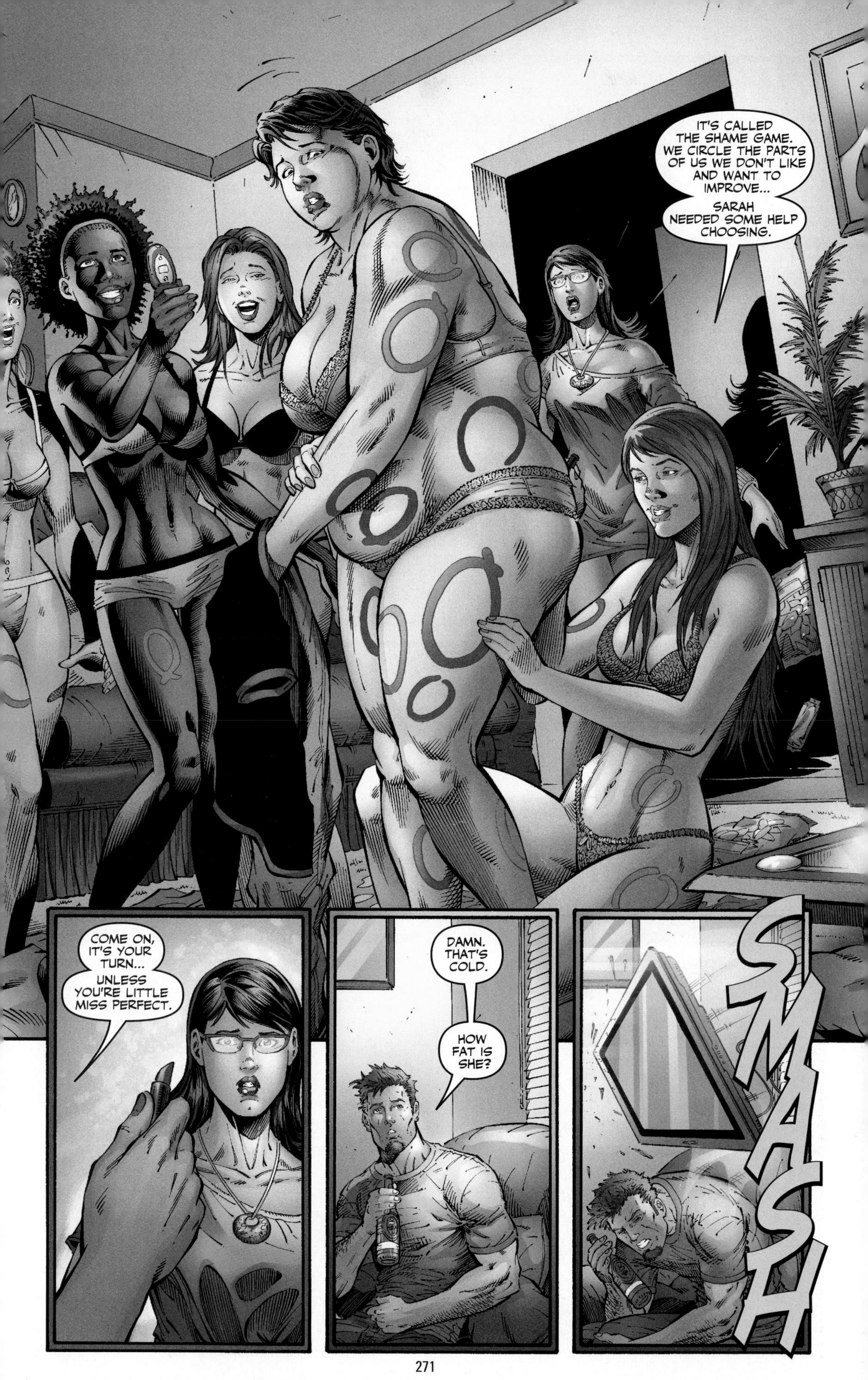
IT'S CALLED THE SHAME GAME. WE CIRCLE THE PARTS OF US WE DON'T LIKE AND WANT TO IMPROVE...
SARAH NEEDED SOME HELP CHOOSING.
COME ON, IT'S YOUR TURN...
UNLESS YOU'RE LITTLE MISS PERFECT.
DAMN. THAT'S COLD.
HOW FAT IS SHE?
SMASH

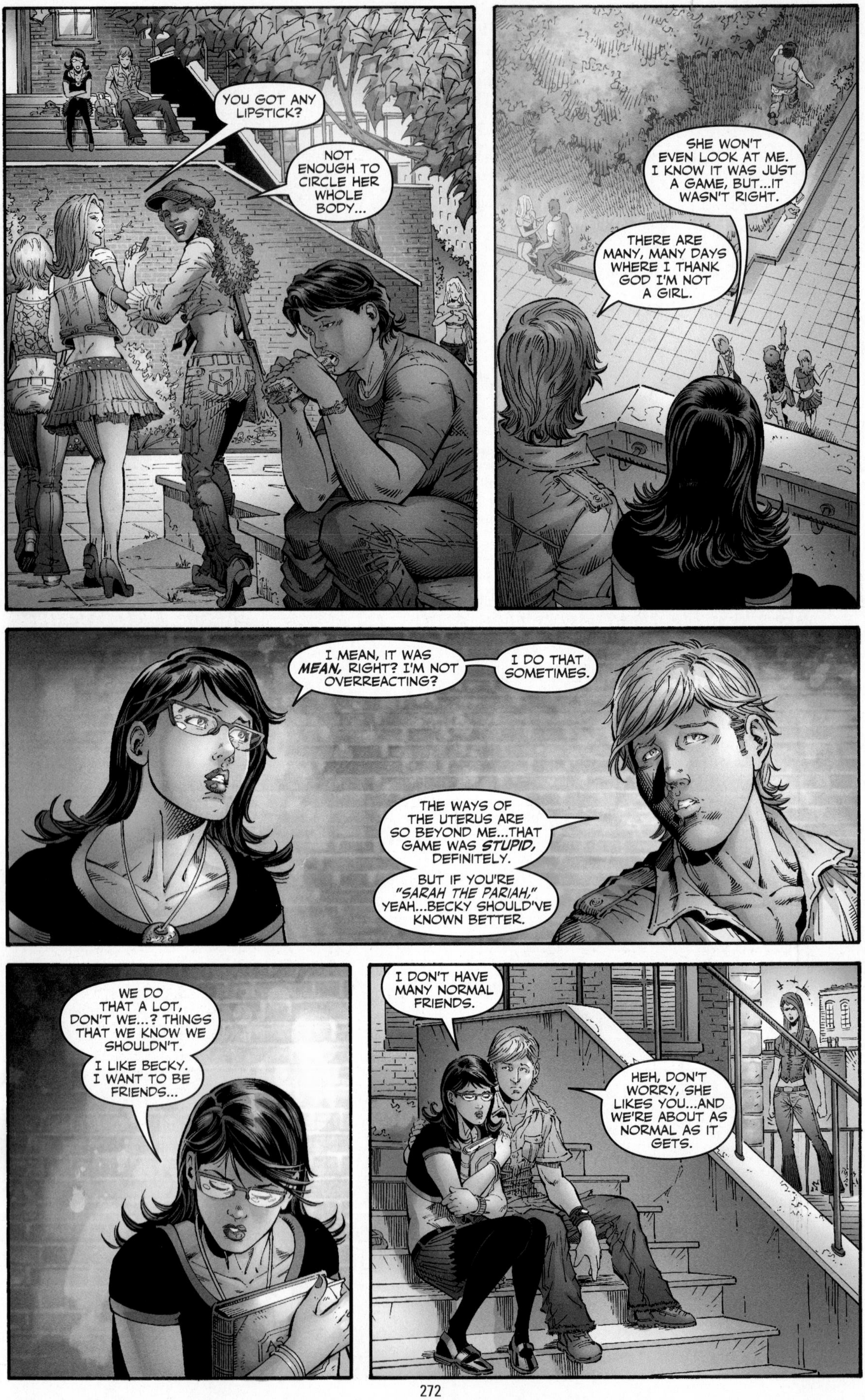
YOU GOT ANY LIPSTICK?
NOT ENOUGH TO CIRCLE HER WHOLE BODY...
SHE WON'T EVEN LOOK AT ME. I KNOW IT WAS JUST A GAME, BUT...IT WASN'T RIGHT.
THERE ARE MANY, MANY DAYS WHERE I THANK GOD I'M NOT A GIRL.
I MEAN, IT WAS MEAN, RIGHT? I'M NOT OVERREACTING?
I DO THAT SOMETIMES.
THE WAYS OF THE UTERUS ARE SO BEYOND ME...THAT GAME WAS STUPID, DEFINITELY.
BUT IF YOU'RE "SARAH THE PARIAH," YEAH...BECKY SHOULD'VE KNOWN BETTER.
WE DO THAT A LOT, DON'T WE...? THINGS THAT WE KNOW WE SHOULDN'T.
I LIKE BECKY. I WANT TO BE FRIENDS...
I DON'T HAVE MANY NORMAL FRIENDS.
HEH, DON'T WORRY, SHE LIKES YOU...AND WE'RE ABOUT AS NORMAL AS IT GETS.

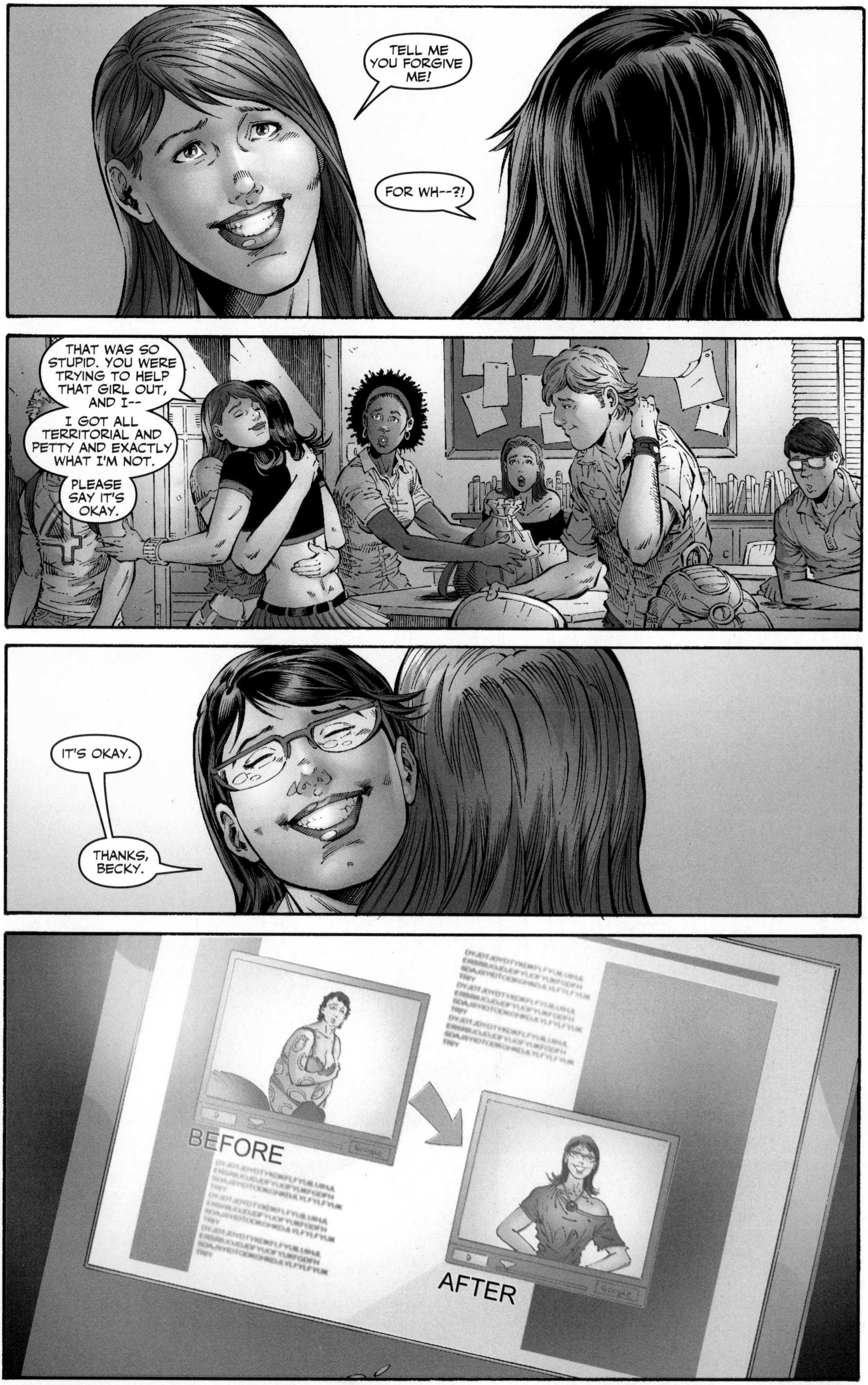
TELL ME YOU FORGIVE ME!
FOR WH--?!
THAT WAS SO STUPID. YOU WERE TRYING TO HELP THAT GIRL OUT, AND I--
I GOT ALL TERRITORIAL AND PETTY AND EXACTLY WHAT I'M NOT.
PLEASE SAY IT'S OKAY.
IT'S OKAY.
THANKS, BECKY.
BEFORE
AFTER

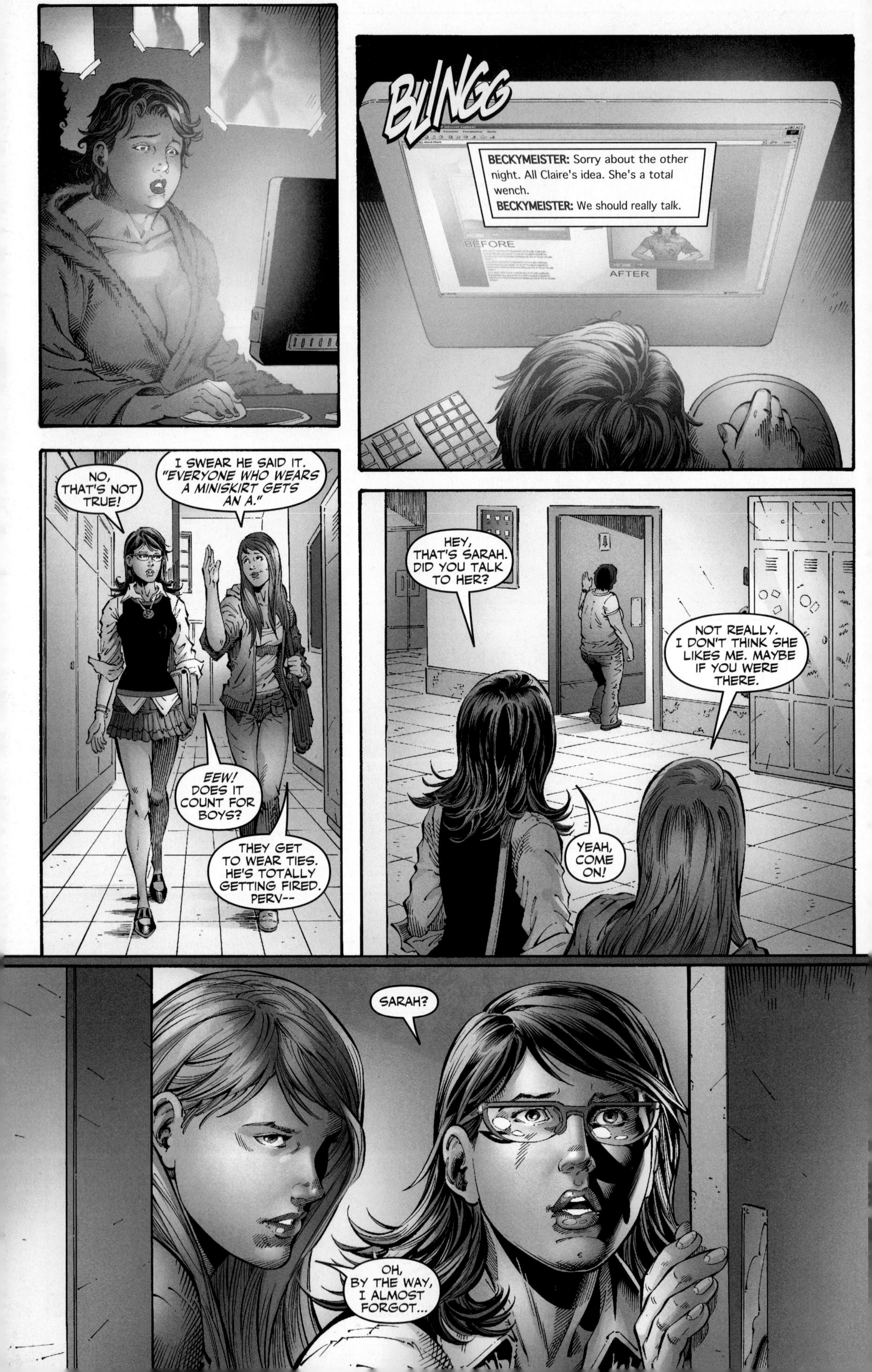
BLINGG
BECKYMEISTER: Sorry about the other night. All Claire's idea. She's a total wench.
BECKYMEISTER: We should really talk.
BEFORE
AFTER
NO, THAT'S NOT TRUE!
I SWEAR HE SAID IT. "EVERYONE WHO WEARS A MINISKIRT GETS AN A."
EEW! DOES IT COUNT FOR BOYS?
THEY GET TO WEAR TIES. HE'S TOTALLY GETTING FIRED. PERV--
HEY, THAT'S SARAH. DID YOU TALK TO HER?
NOT REALLY. I DON'T THINK SHE LIKES ME. MAYBE IF YOU WERE THERE.
YEAH, COME ON!
SARAH?
OH, BY THE WAY, I ALMOST FORGOT...

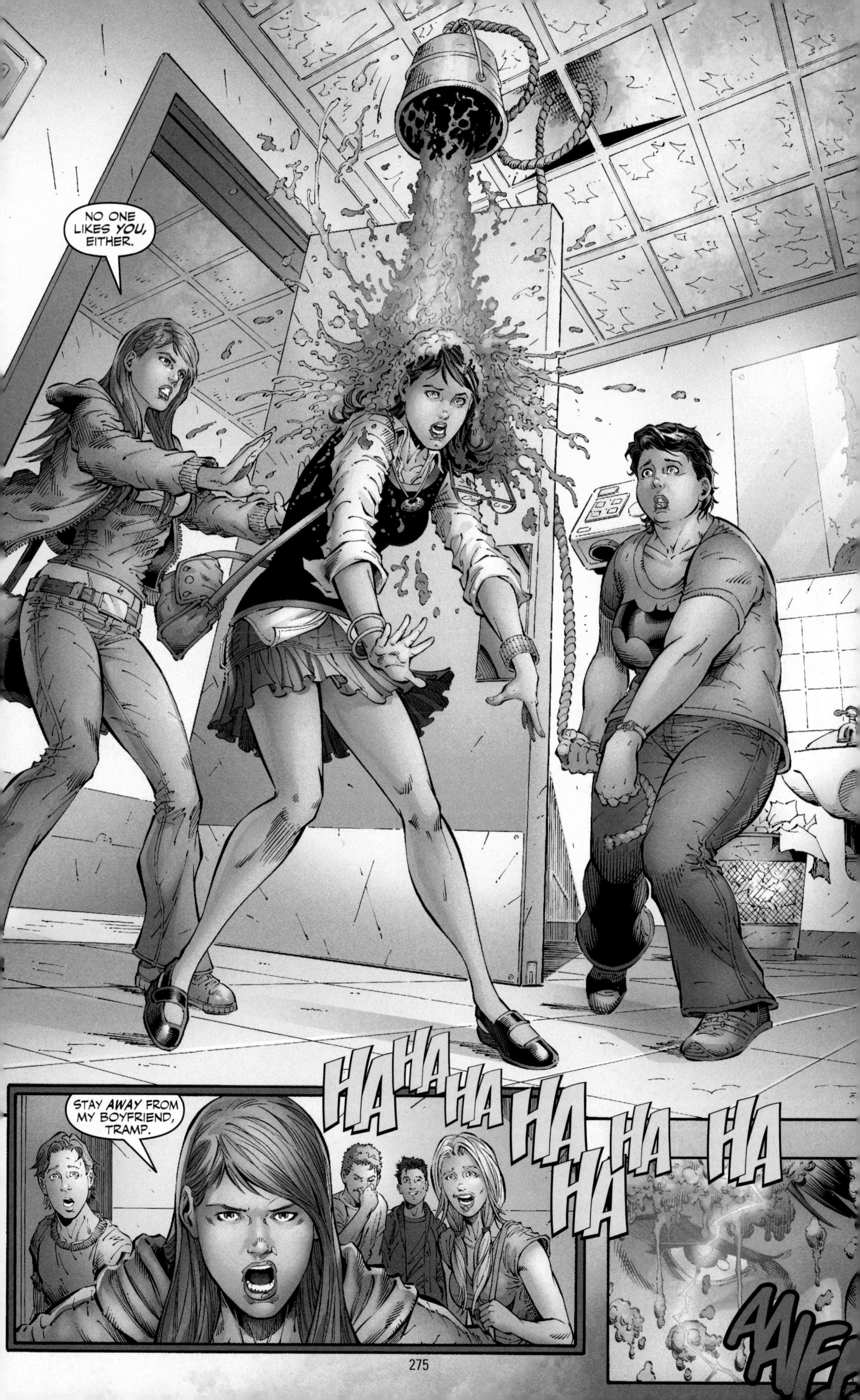
NO ONE LIKES *YOU*, EITHER.
STAY *AWAY* FROM MY BOYFRIEND, TRAMP.
HA HA HA HA HA HA HA

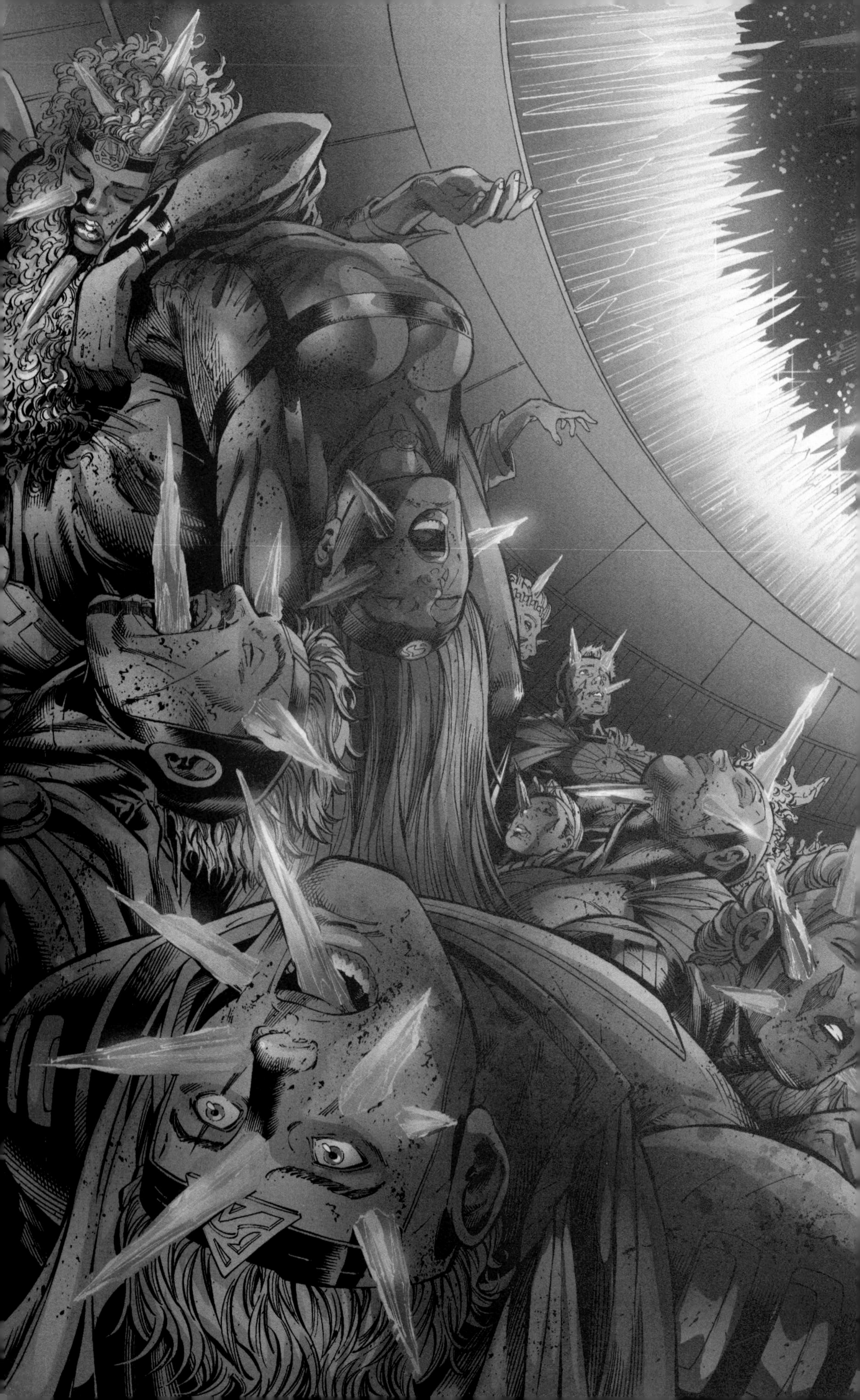

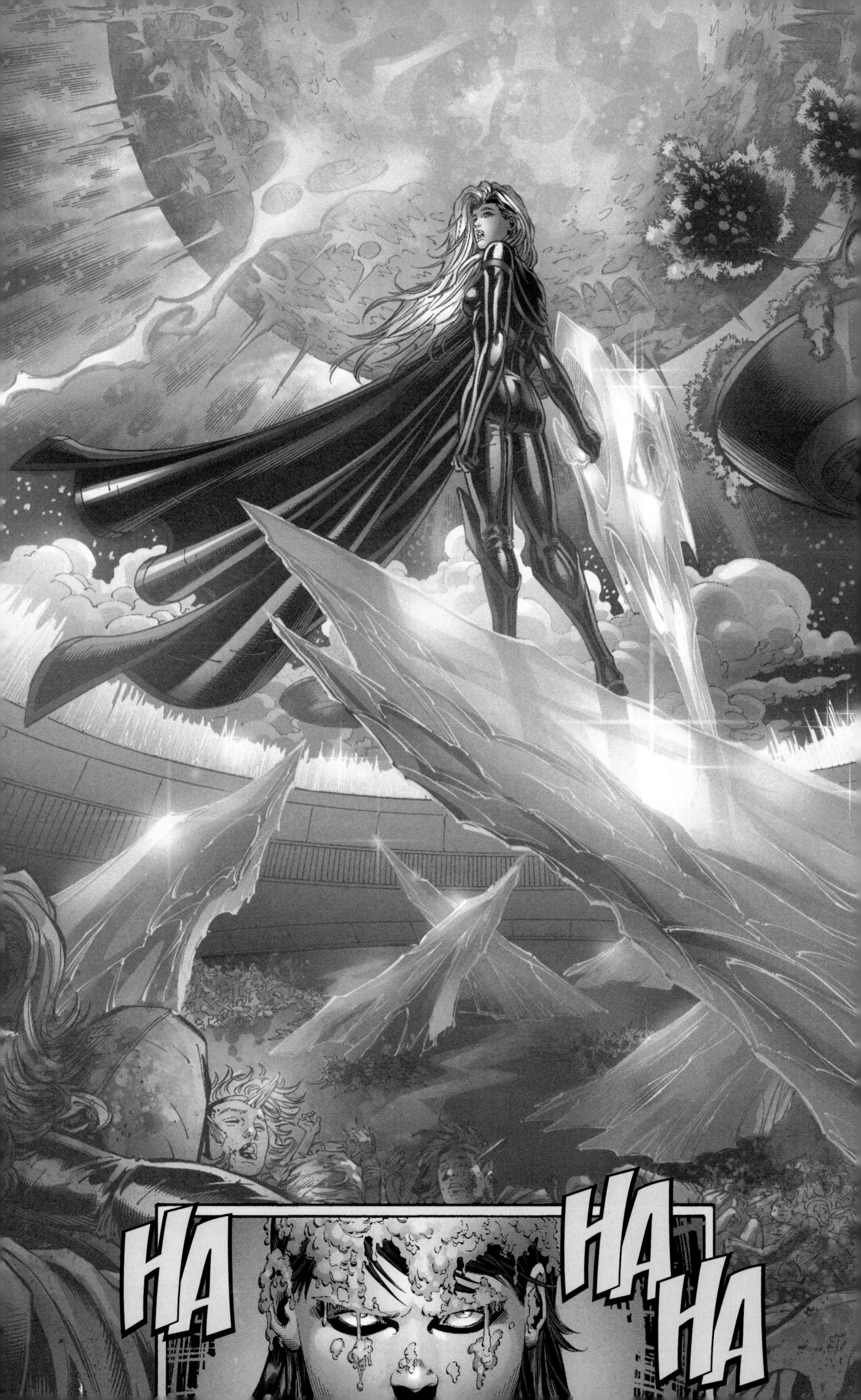
HA
HA
HA
HA

I--

BECKY.

WHAT'RE YOU GONNA DO?

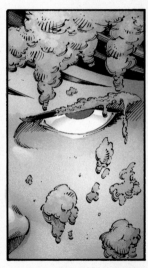

YOU JERKS!

THIS IS FUNNY? SHUT UP! STOP LAUGHING!

DON'T LOOK AT THEM. THEY DON'T EVEN EXIST. OKAY?

YOU WANT TO GO TO THE NURSE? YOU WANT ME TO TAKE YOU HOME?

YOU-- YOU'RE--

ABERCROMBIE AND WITCH, YEAH, I KNOW.

SECRET IDENTITIES SUCK, DON'T THEY?

THANK YOU FOR TRYING TO HELP.

I'M SORRY I NEVER TRIED TO TALK TO YOU.

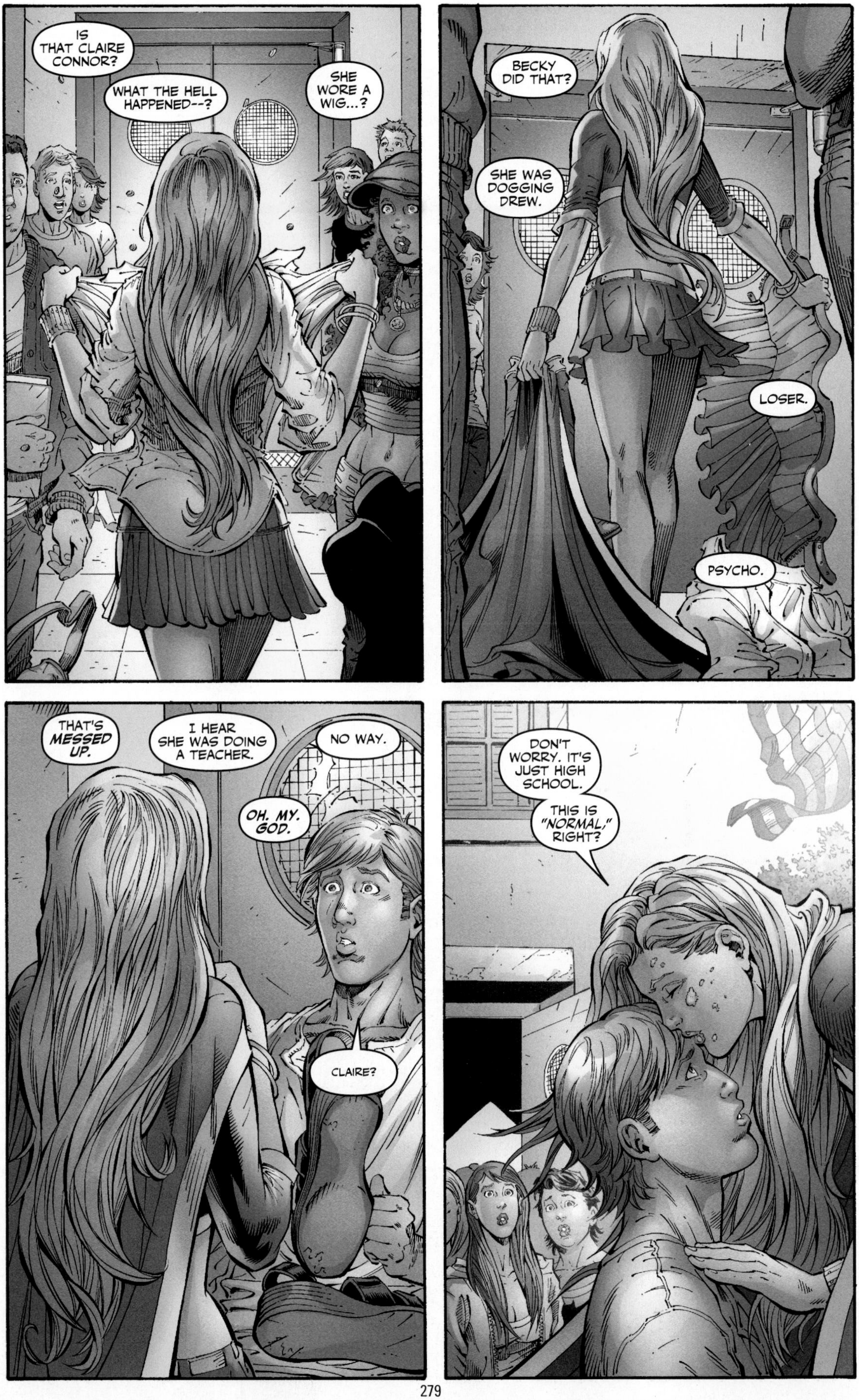
IS THAT CLAIRE CONNOR?
WHAT THE HELL HAPPENED--?
SHE WORE A WIG...?
BECKY DID THAT?
SHE WAS DOGGING DREW.
LOSER.
PSYCHO.
THAT'S *MESSED UP.*
I HEAR SHE WAS DOING A TEACHER.
NO WAY.
OH. MY. GOD.
CLAIRE?
DON'T WORRY. IT'S JUST HIGH SCHOOL.
THIS IS *"NORMAL,"* RIGHT?

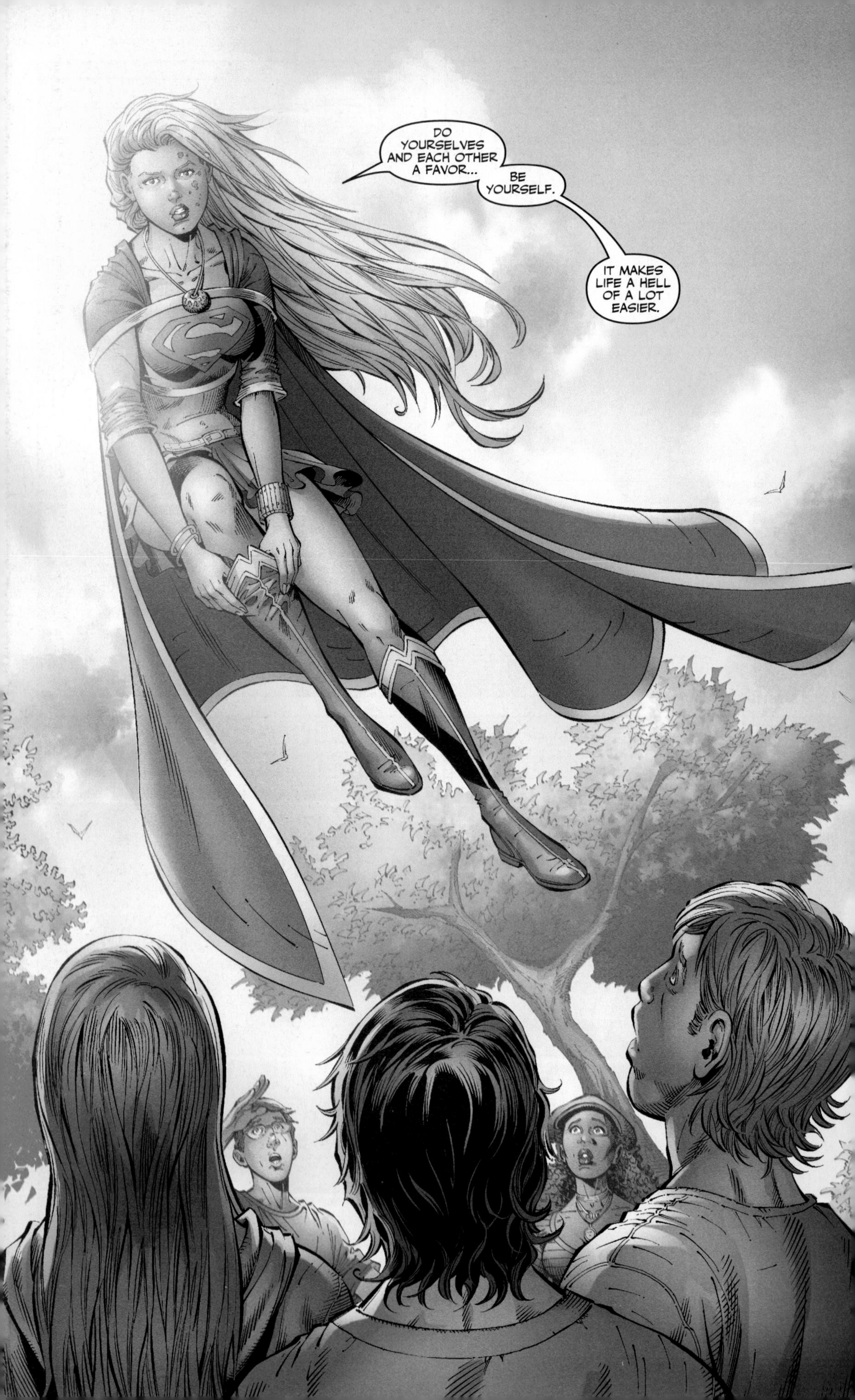
DO YOURSELVES AND EACH OTHER A FAVOR...
BE YOURSELF.
IT MAKES LIFE A HELL OF A LOT EASIER.

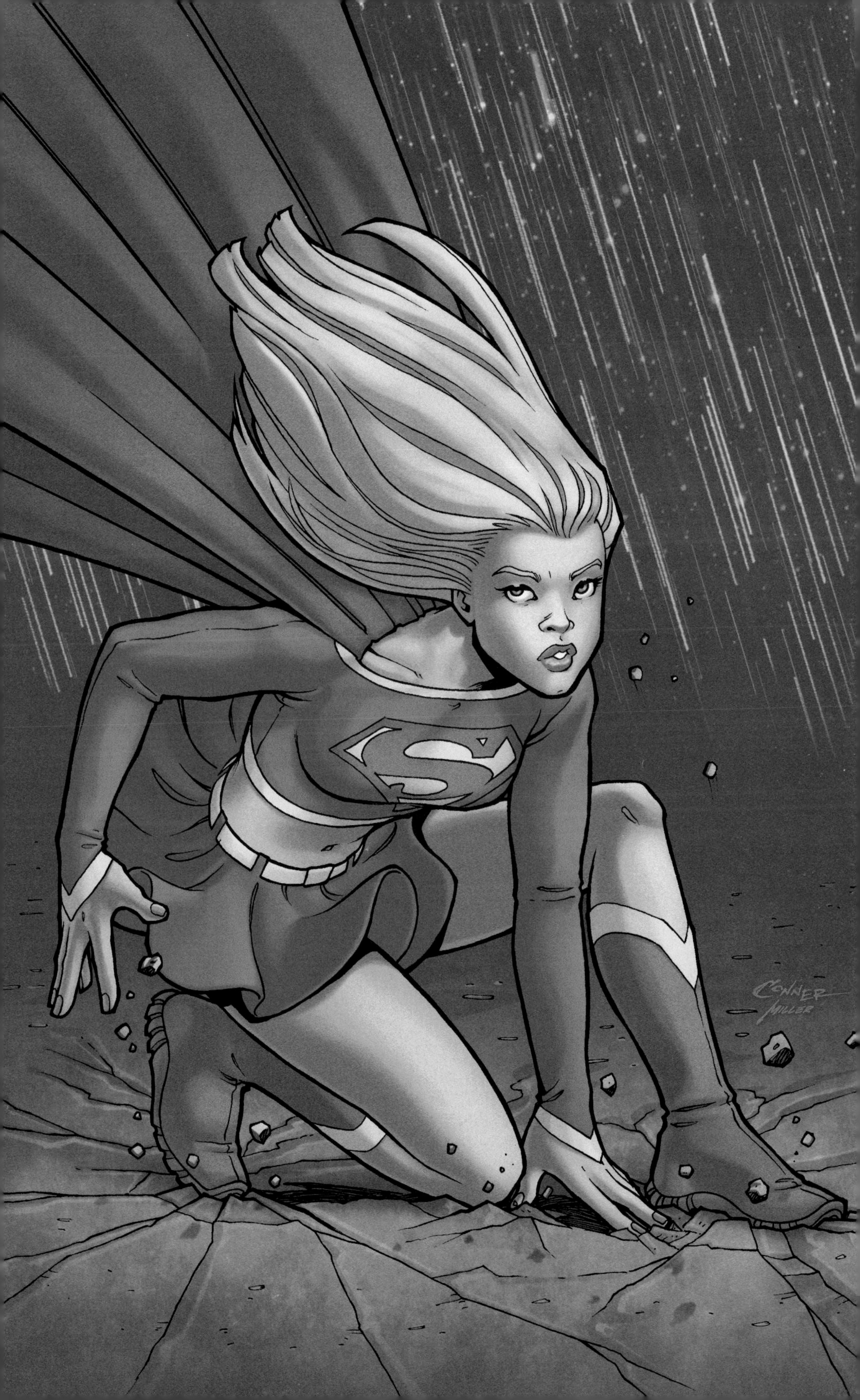
CONNER
MILLER

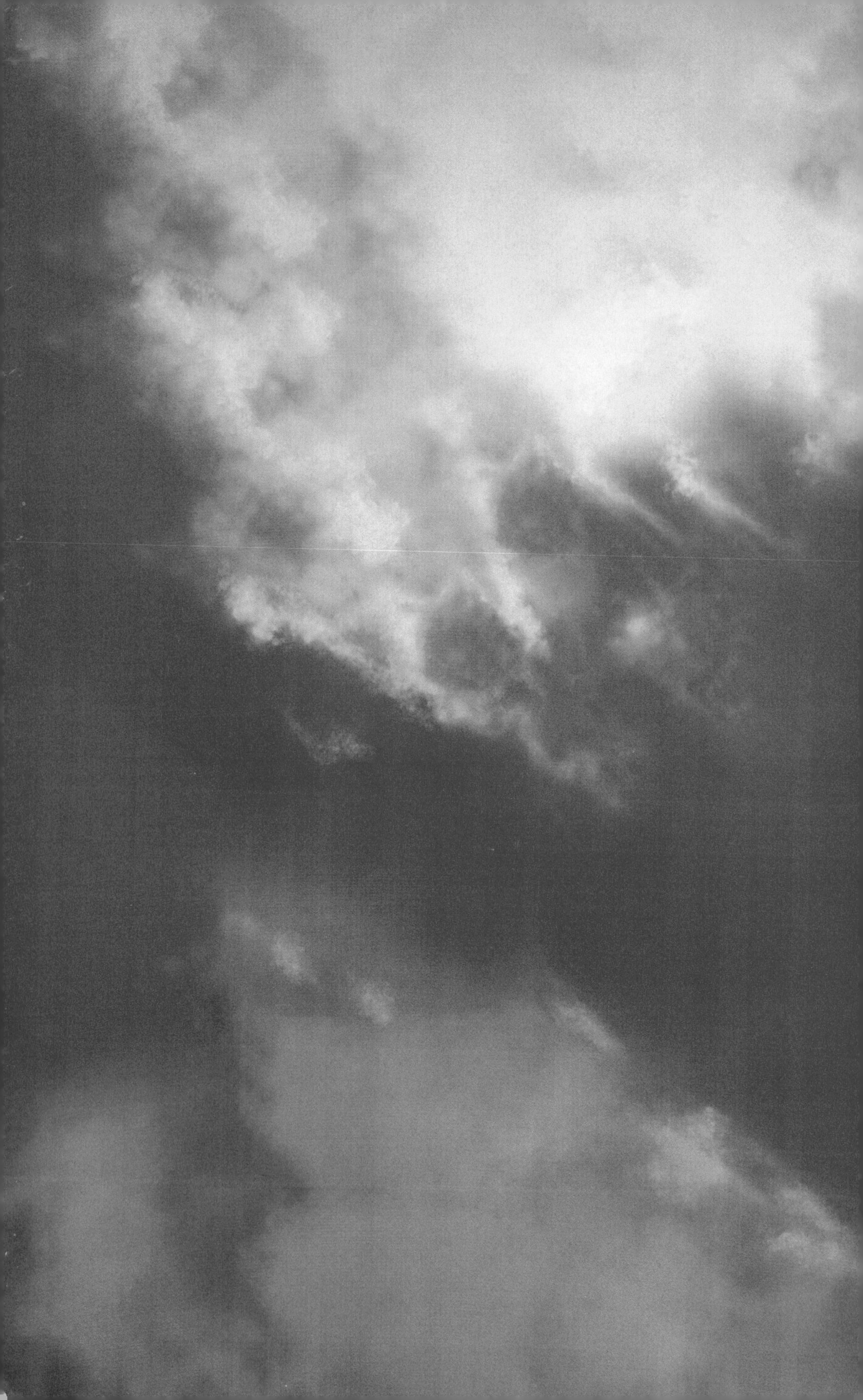

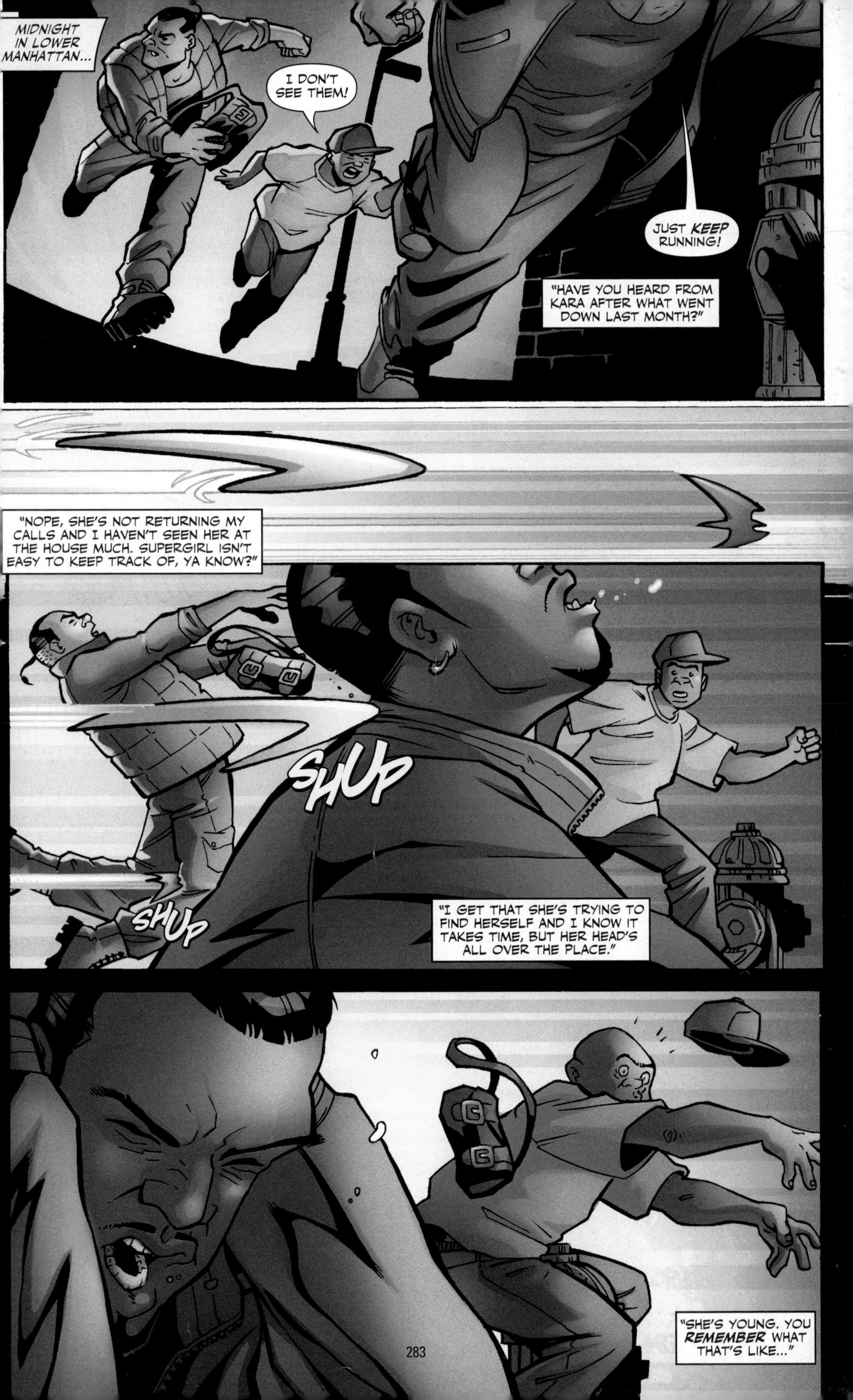
MIDNIGHT IN LOWER MANHATTAN...
I DON'T SEE THEM!
JUST KEEP RUNNING!
"HAVE YOU HEARD FROM KARA AFTER WHAT WENT DOWN LAST MONTH?"
"NOPE, SHE'S NOT RETURNING MY CALLS AND I HAVEN'T SEEN HER AT THE HOUSE MUCH. SUPERGIRL ISN'T EASY TO KEEP TRACK OF, YA KNOW?"
SHUP
SHUP
"I GET THAT SHE'S TRYING TO FIND HERSELF AND I KNOW IT TAKES TIME, BUT HER HEAD'S ALL OVER THE PLACE."
"SHE'S YOUNG. YOU REMEMBER WHAT THAT'S LIKE..."

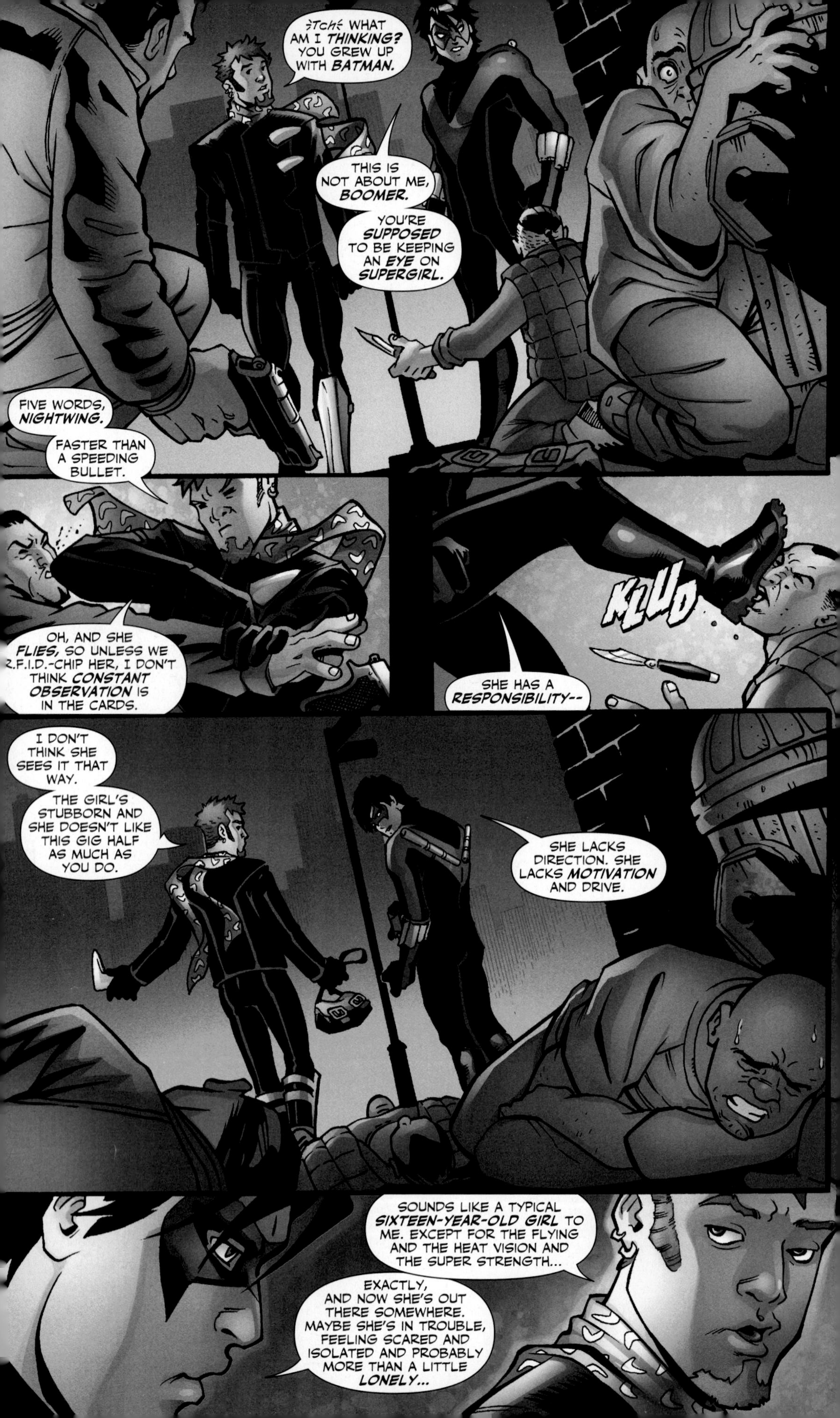

TCH WHAT AM I THINKING? YOU GREW UP WITH BATMAN.
THIS IS NOT ABOUT ME, BOOMER.
YOU'RE SUPPOSED TO BE KEEPING AN EYE ON SUPERGIRL.
FIVE WORDS, NIGHTWING.
FASTER THAN A SPEEDING BULLET.
OH, AND SHE FLIES, SO UNLESS WE R.F.I.D.-CHIP HER, I DON'T THINK CONSTANT OBSERVATION IS IN THE CARDS.
KLUD
SHE HAS A RESPONSIBILITY--
I DON'T THINK SHE SEES IT THAT WAY.
THE GIRL'S STUBBORN AND SHE DOESN'T LIKE THIS GIG HALF AS MUCH AS YOU DO.
SHE LACKS DIRECTION. SHE LACKS MOTIVATION AND DRIVE.
SOUNDS LIKE A TYPICAL SIXTEEN-YEAR-OLD GIRL TO ME. EXCEPT FOR THE FLYING AND THE HEAT VISION AND THE SUPER STRENGTH...
EXACTLY, AND NOW SHE'S OUT THERE SOMEWHERE. MAYBE SHE'S IN TROUBLE, FEELING SCARED AND ISOLATED AND PROBABLY MORE THAN A LITTLE LONELY...

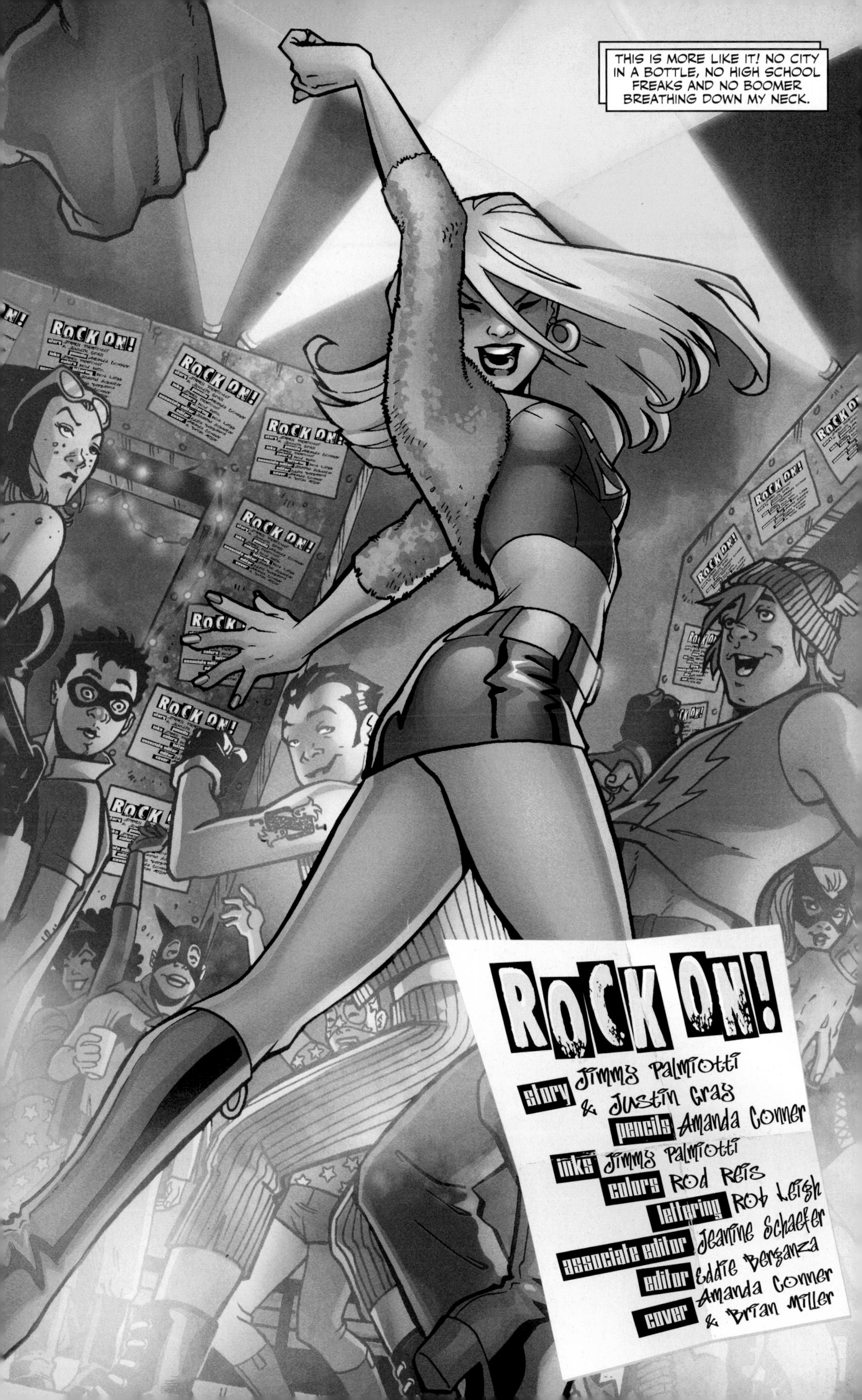
THIS IS MORE LIKE IT! NO CITY IN A BOTTLE, NO HIGH SCHOOL FREAKS AND NO BOOMER BREATHING DOWN MY NECK.
ROCK ON!
story Jimmy Palmiotti & Justin Gray
pencils Amanda Conner
inks Jimmy Palmiotti
colors Rod Reis
lettering Rob Leigh
associate editor Jeanine Schaefer
editor Eddie Berganza
cover Amanda Conner & Brian Miller

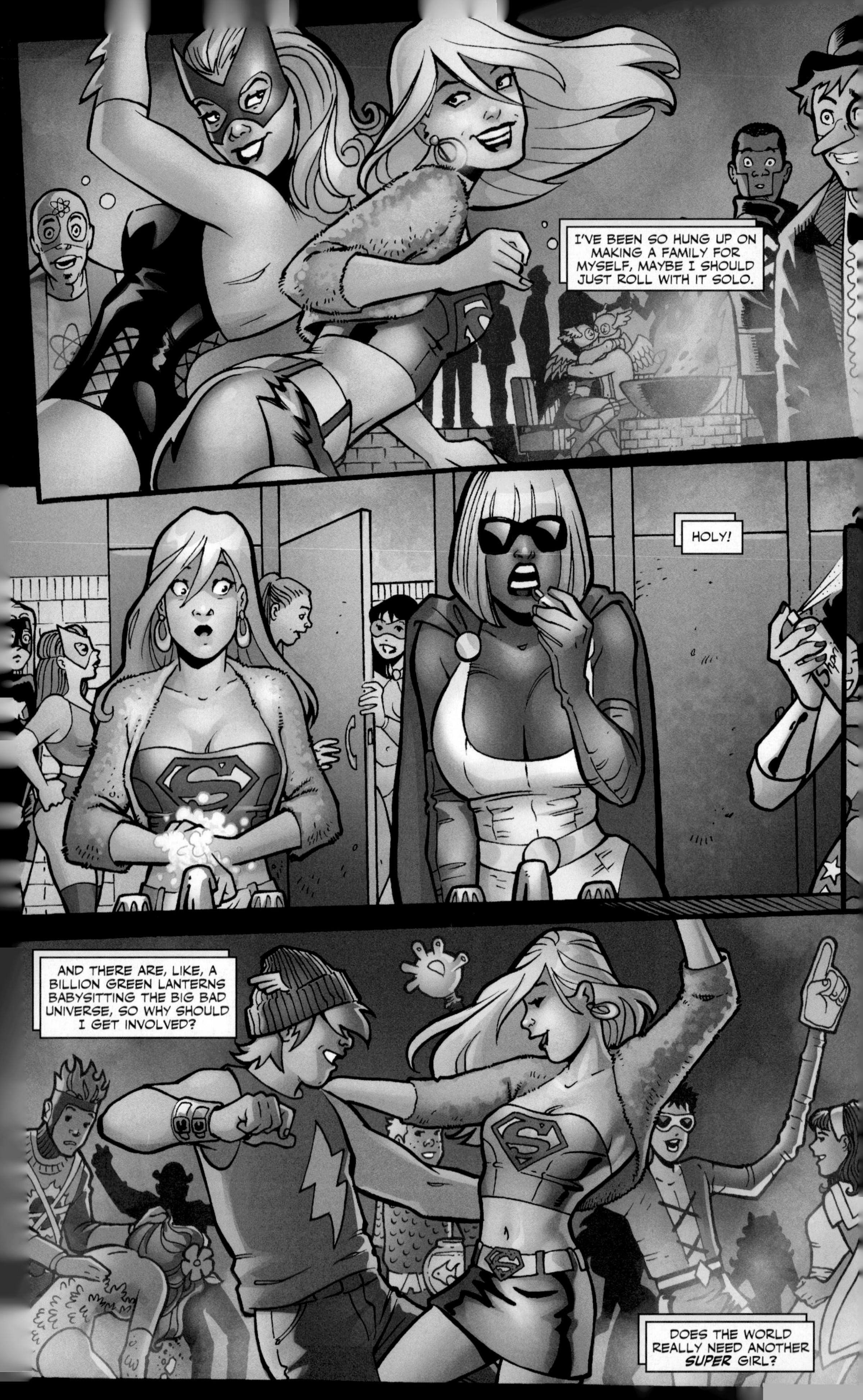
I'VE BEEN SO HUNG UP ON MAKING A FAMILY FOR MYSELF, MAYBE I SHOULD JUST ROLL WITH IT SOLO.
HOLY!
AND THERE ARE, LIKE, A BILLION GREEN LANTERNS BABYSITTING THE BIG BAD UNIVERSE, SO WHY SHOULD I GET INVOLVED?
DOES THE WORLD REALLY NEED ANOTHER *SUPER* GIRL?

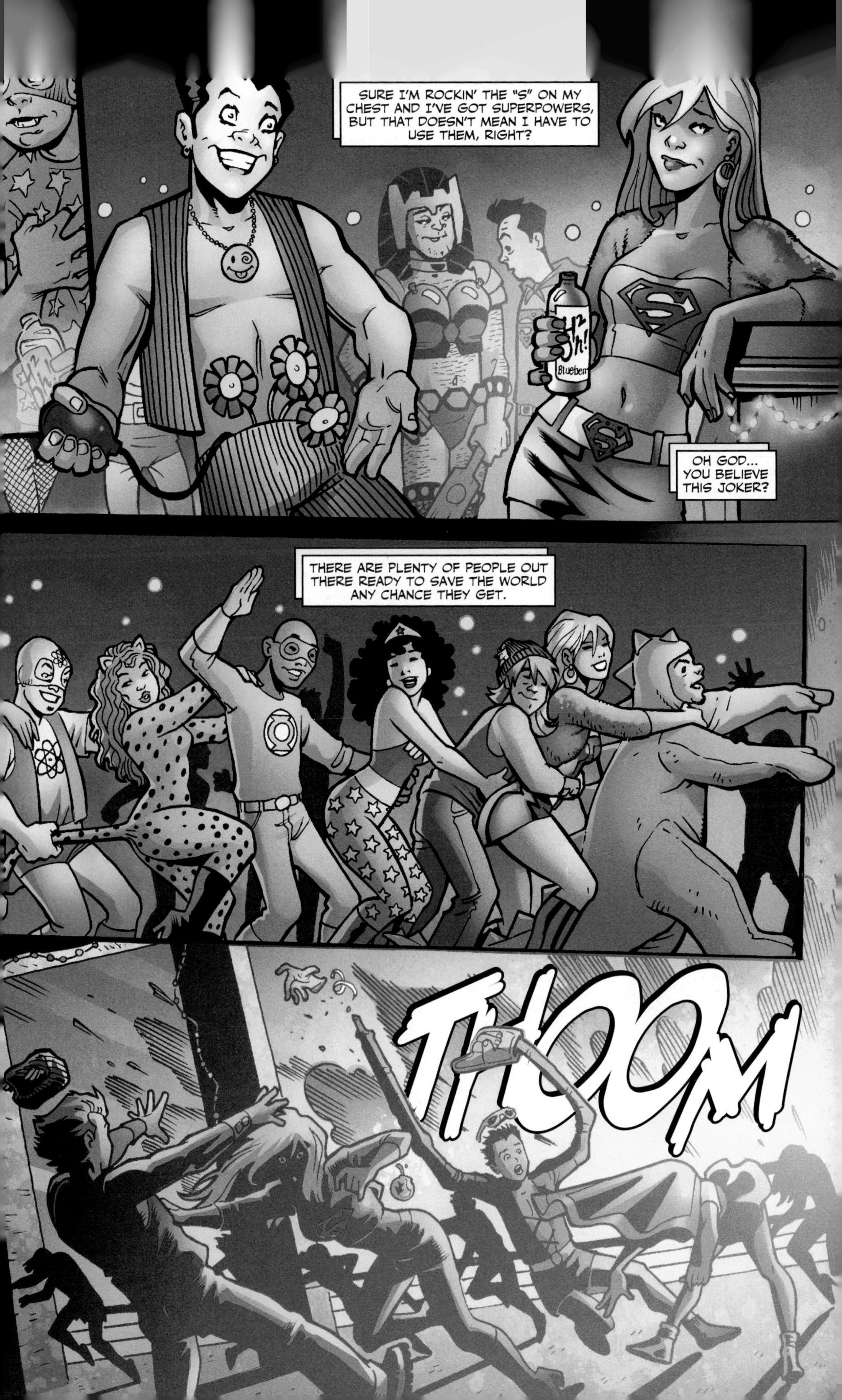
SURE I'M ROCKIN' THE "S" ON MY CHEST AND I'VE GOT SUPERPOWERS, BUT THAT DOESN'T MEAN I HAVE TO USE THEM, RIGHT?
OH GOD... YOU BELIEVE THIS JOKER?
THERE ARE PLENTY OF PEOPLE OUT THERE READY TO SAVE THE WORLD ANY CHANCE THEY GET.
THOOM

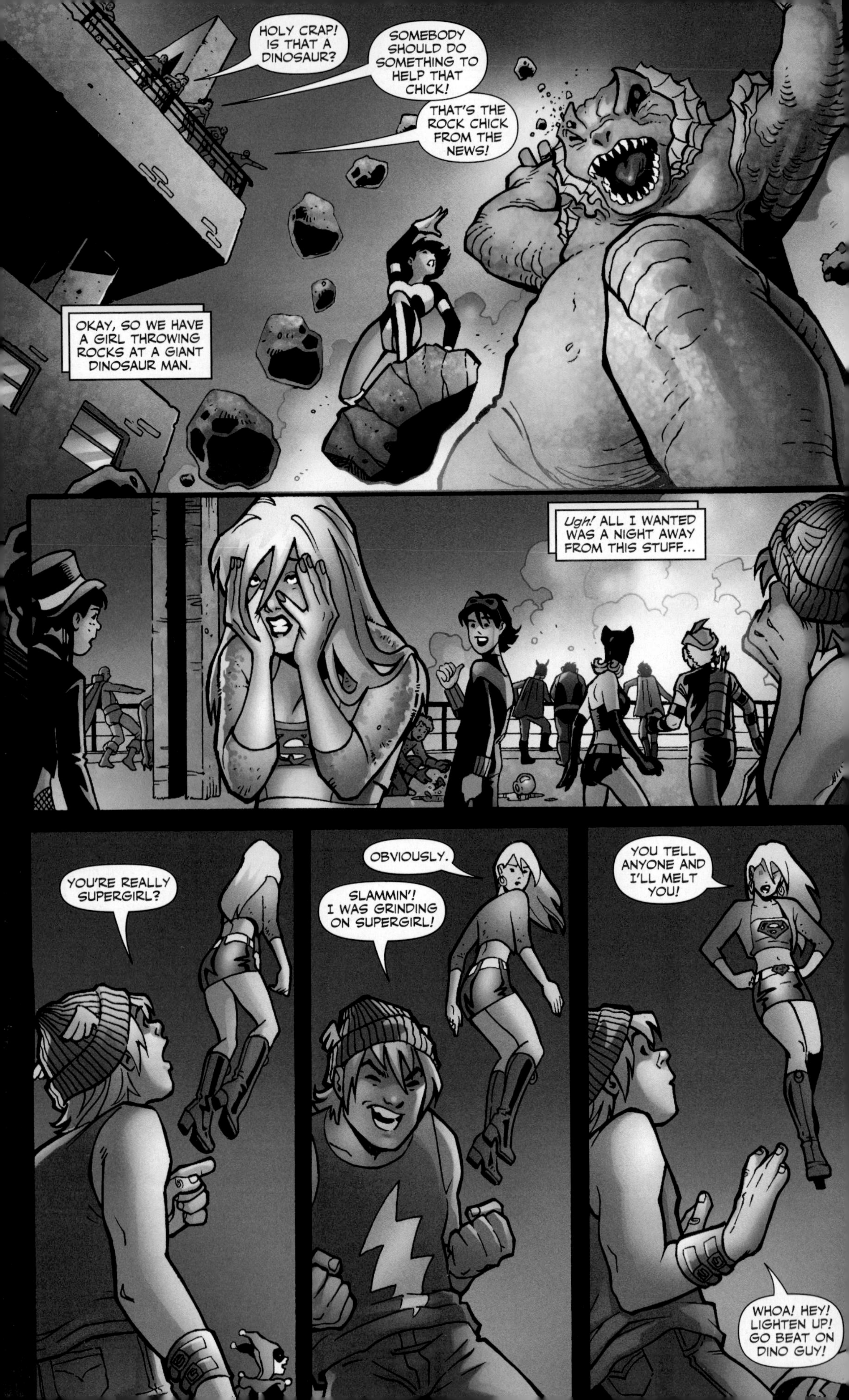
HOLY CRAP! IS THAT A DINOSAUR?
SOMEBODY SHOULD DO SOMETHING TO HELP THAT CHICK!
THAT'S THE ROCK CHICK FROM THE NEWS!
OKAY, SO WE HAVE A GIRL THROWING ROCKS AT A GIANT DINOSAUR MAN.
Ugh! ALL I WANTED WAS A NIGHT AWAY FROM THIS STUFF...
YOU'RE REALLY SUPERGIRL?
OBVIOUSLY.
SLAMMIN'! I WAS GRINDING ON SUPERGIRL!
YOU TELL ANYONE AND I'LL MELT YOU!
WHOA! HEY! LIGHTEN UP! GO BEAT ON DINO GUY!

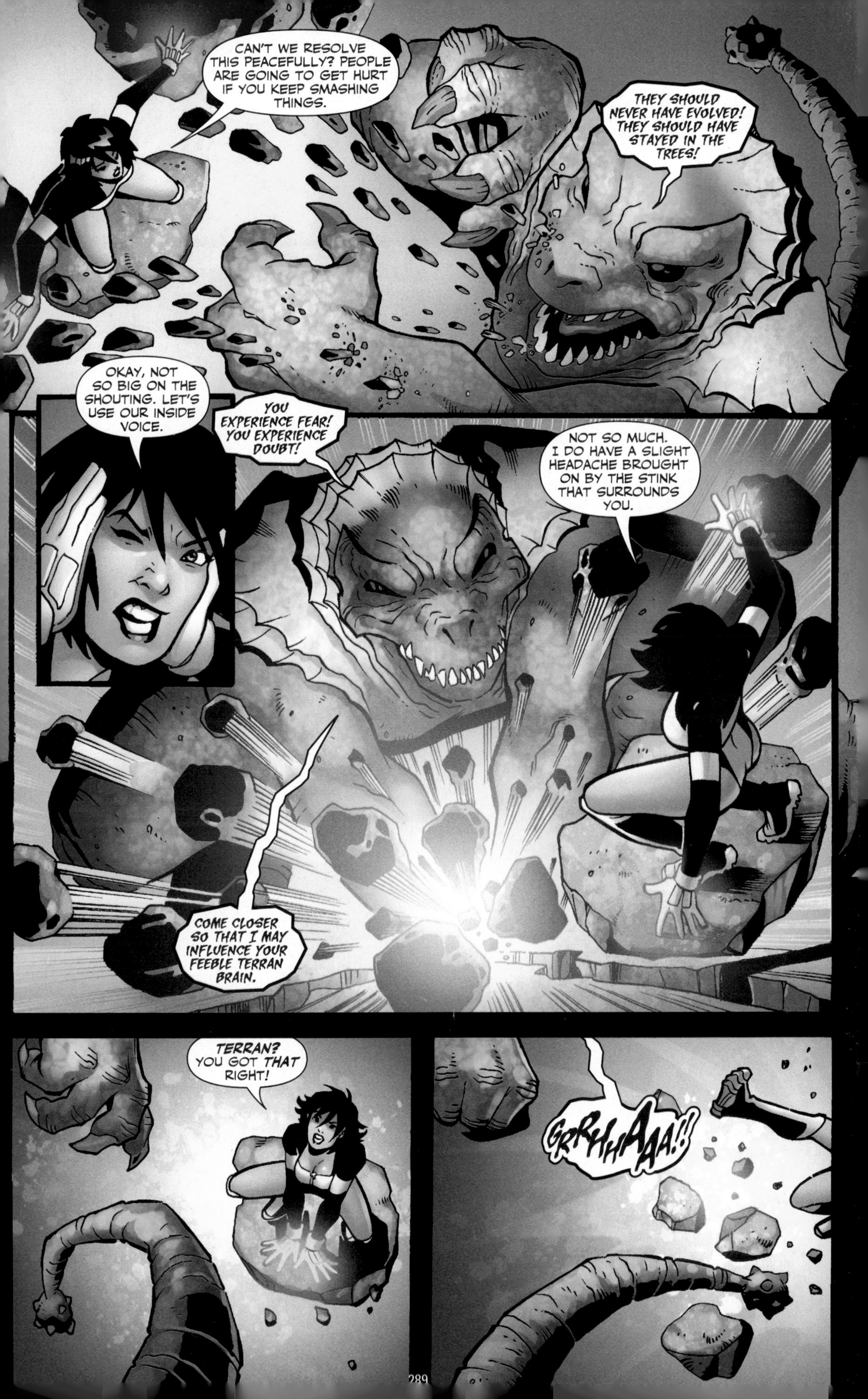
CAN'T WE RESOLVE THIS PEACEFULLY? PEOPLE ARE GOING TO GET HURT IF YOU KEEP SMASHING THINGS.
THEY SHOULD NEVER HAVE EVOLVED! THEY SHOULD HAVE STAYED IN THE TREES!
OKAY, NOT SO BIG ON THE SHOUTING. LET'S USE OUR INSIDE VOICE.
YOU EXPERIENCE FEAR! YOU EXPERIENCE DOUBT!
NOT SO MUCH. I DO HAVE A SLIGHT HEADACHE BROUGHT ON BY THE STINK THAT SURROUNDS YOU.
COME CLOSER SO THAT I MAY INFLUENCE YOUR FEEBLE TERRAN BRAIN.
TERRAN? YOU GOT THAT RIGHT!
GRRHHAAA!!

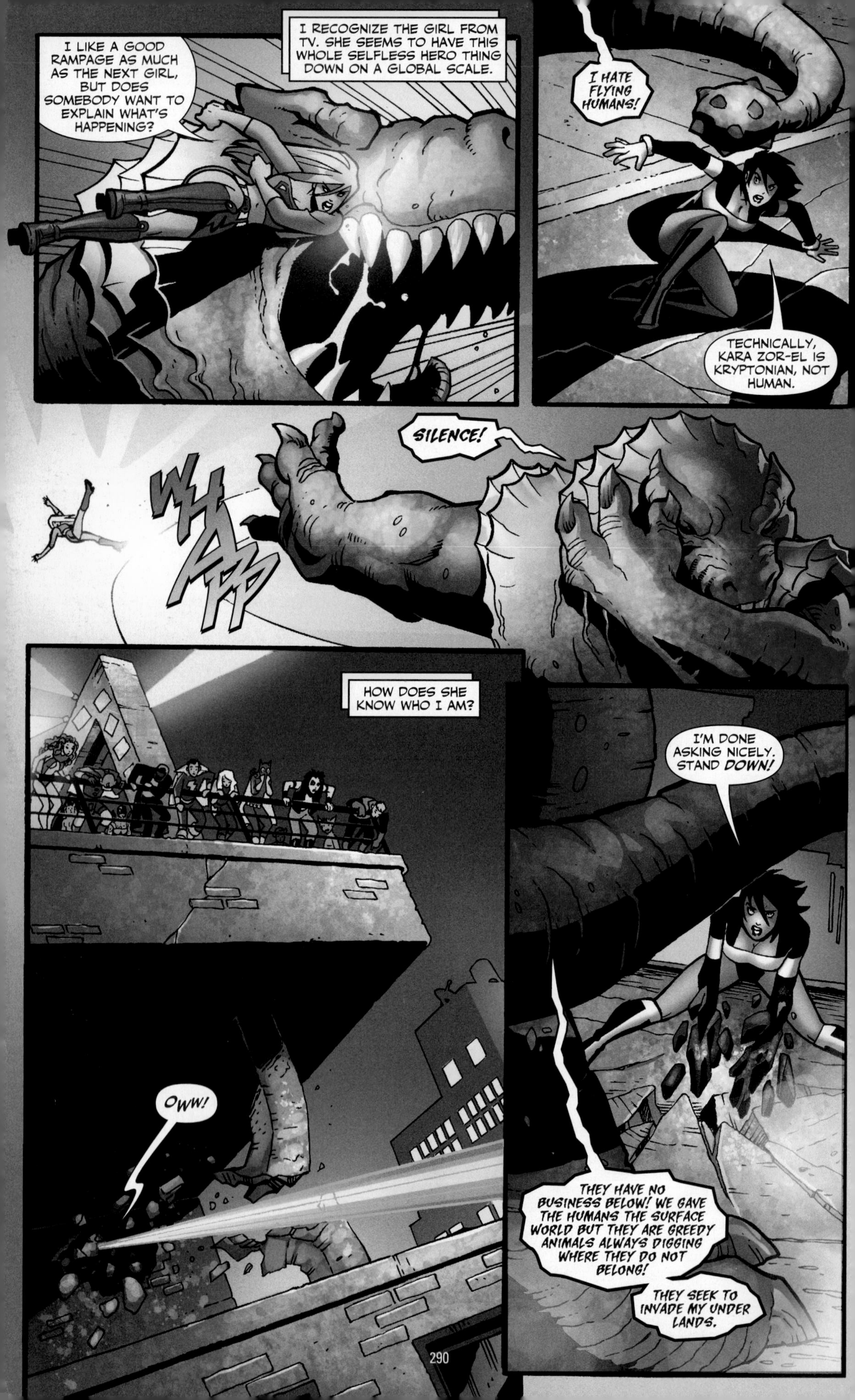
I LIKE A GOOD RAMPAGE AS MUCH AS THE NEXT GIRL, BUT DOES SOMEBODY WANT TO EXPLAIN WHAT'S HAPPENING?
I RECOGNIZE THE GIRL FROM TV. SHE SEEMS TO HAVE THIS WHOLE SELFLESS HERO THING DOWN ON A GLOBAL SCALE.
I HATE FLYING HUMANS!
TECHNICALLY, KARA ZOR-EL IS KRYPTONIAN, NOT HUMAN.
SILENCE!
WHAPP
HOW DOES SHE KNOW WHO I AM?
OWW!
I'M DONE ASKING NICELY. STAND DOWN!
THEY HAVE NO BUSINESS BELOW! WE GAVE THE HUMANS THE SURFACE WORLD BUT THEY ARE GREEDY ANIMALS ALWAYS DIGGING WHERE THEY DO NOT BELONG!
THEY SEEK TO INVADE MY UNDER LANDS.

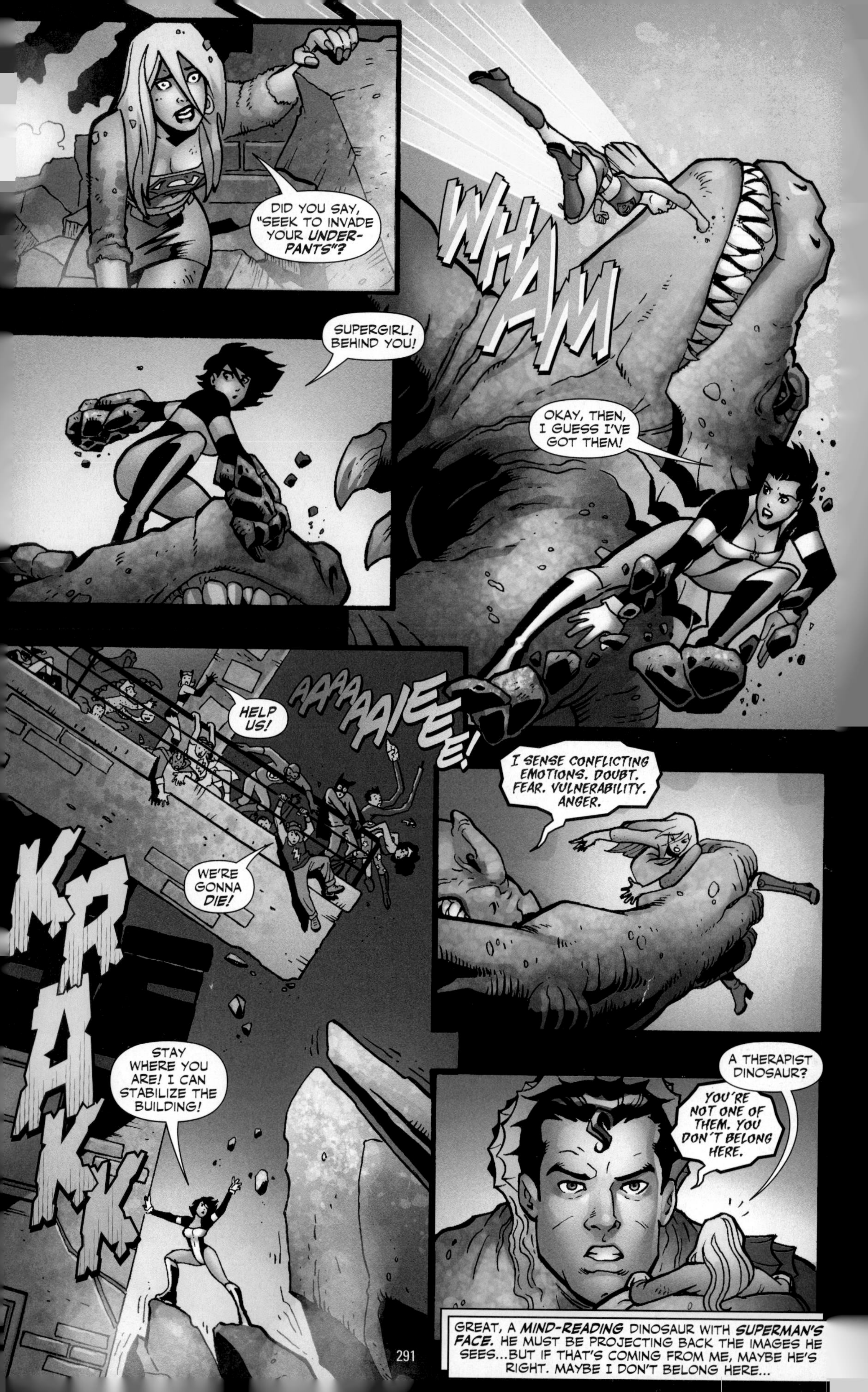
DID YOU SAY, "SEEK TO INVADE YOUR UNDER-PANTS"?
WHAM
SUPERGIRL! BEHIND YOU!
OKAY, THEN, I GUESS I'VE GOT THEM!
HELP US!
AAAAAAIEEEE!
WE'RE GONNA DIE!
I SENSE CONFLICTING EMOTIONS. DOUBT. FEAR. VULNERABILITY. ANGER.
KRAKK
STAY WHERE YOU ARE! I CAN STABILIZE THE BUILDING!
A THERAPIST DINOSAUR?
YOU'RE NOT ONE OF THEM. YOU DON'T BELONG HERE.
GREAT, A MIND-READING DINOSAUR WITH SUPERMAN'S FACE. HE MUST BE PROJECTING BACK THE IMAGES HE SEES...BUT IF THAT'S COMING FROM ME, MAYBE HE'S RIGHT. MAYBE I DON'T BELONG HERE...

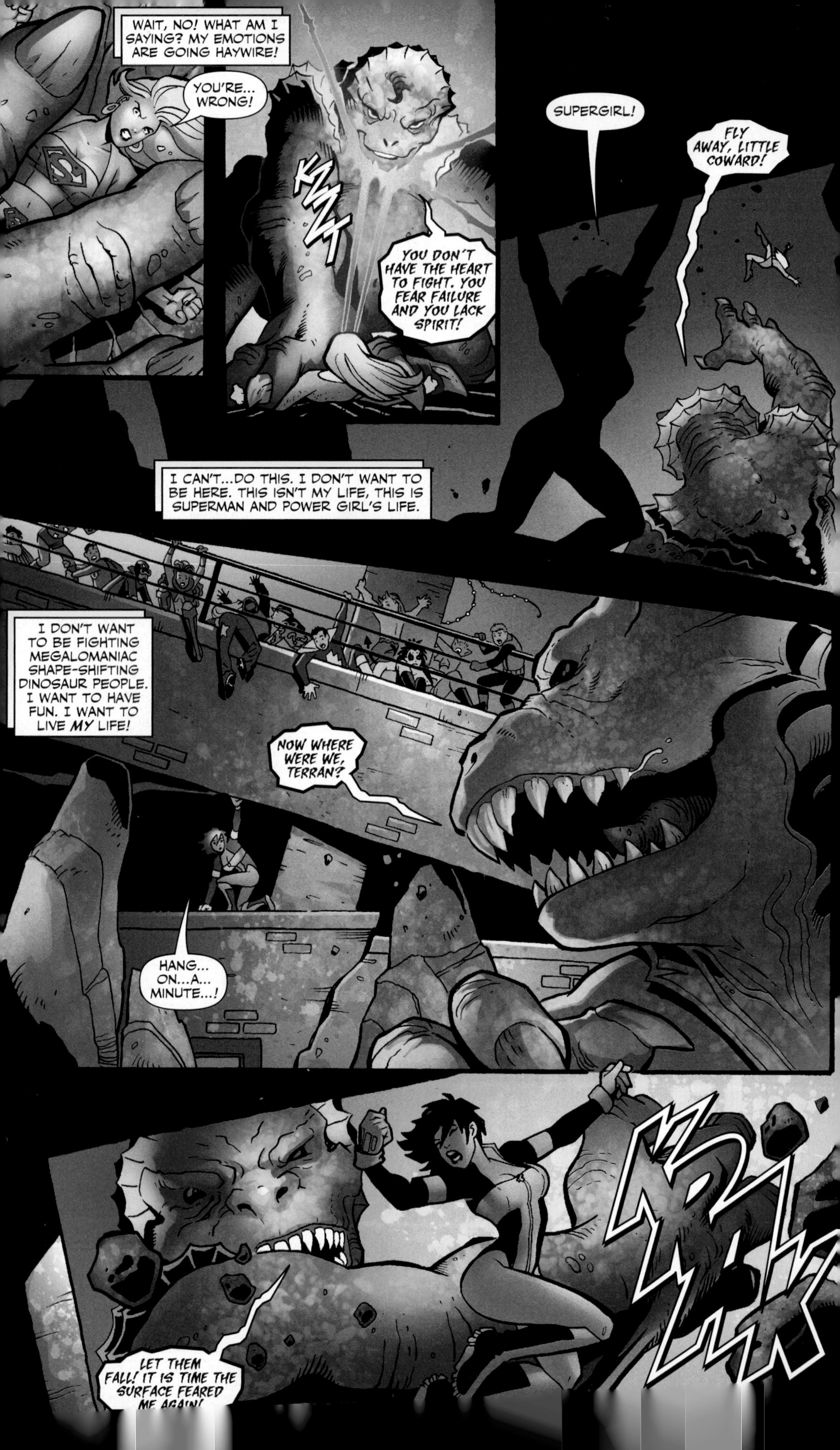

WAIT, NO! WHAT AM I SAYING? MY EMOTIONS ARE GOING HAYWIRE!
YOU'RE... WRONG!
KNNK
YOU DON'T HAVE THE HEART TO FIGHT. YOU FEAR FAILURE AND YOU LACK SPIRIT!
SUPERGIRL!
FLY AWAY, LITTLE COWARD!
I CAN'T...DO THIS. I DON'T WANT TO BE HERE. THIS ISN'T MY LIFE, THIS IS SUPERMAN AND POWER GIRL'S LIFE.
I DON'T WANT TO BE FIGHTING MEGALOMANIAC SHAPE-SHIFTING DINOSAUR PEOPLE. I WANT TO HAVE FUN. I WANT TO LIVE MY LIFE!
NOW WHERE WERE WE, TERRAN?
HANG... ON...A... MINUTE...!
LET THEM FALL! IT IS TIME THE SURFACE FEARED ME AGAIN!

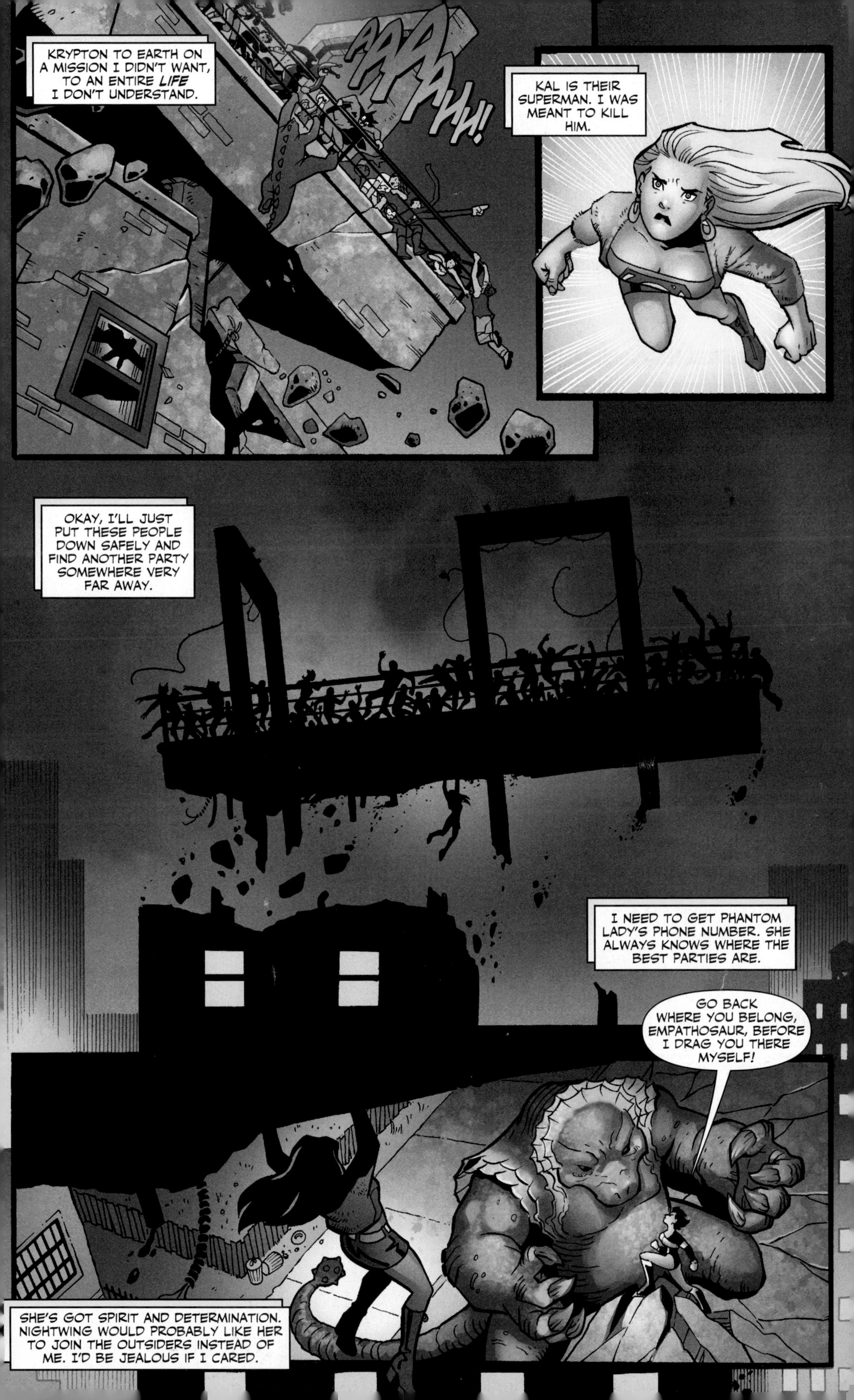
KRYPTON TO EARTH ON A MISSION I DIDN'T WANT, TO AN ENTIRE *LIFE* I DON'T UNDERSTAND.
AAAAAHH!
KAL IS THEIR SUPERMAN. I WAS MEANT TO KILL HIM.
OKAY, I'LL JUST PUT THESE PEOPLE DOWN SAFELY AND FIND ANOTHER PARTY SOMEWHERE VERY FAR AWAY.
I NEED TO GET PHANTOM LADY'S PHONE NUMBER. SHE ALWAYS KNOWS WHERE THE BEST PARTIES ARE.
GO BACK WHERE YOU BELONG, EMPATHOSAUR, BEFORE I DRAG YOU THERE MYSELF!
SHE'S GOT SPIRIT AND DETERMINATION. NIGHTWING WOULD PROBABLY LIKE HER TO JOIN THE OUTSIDERS INSTEAD OF ME. I'D BE JEALOUS IF I CARED.

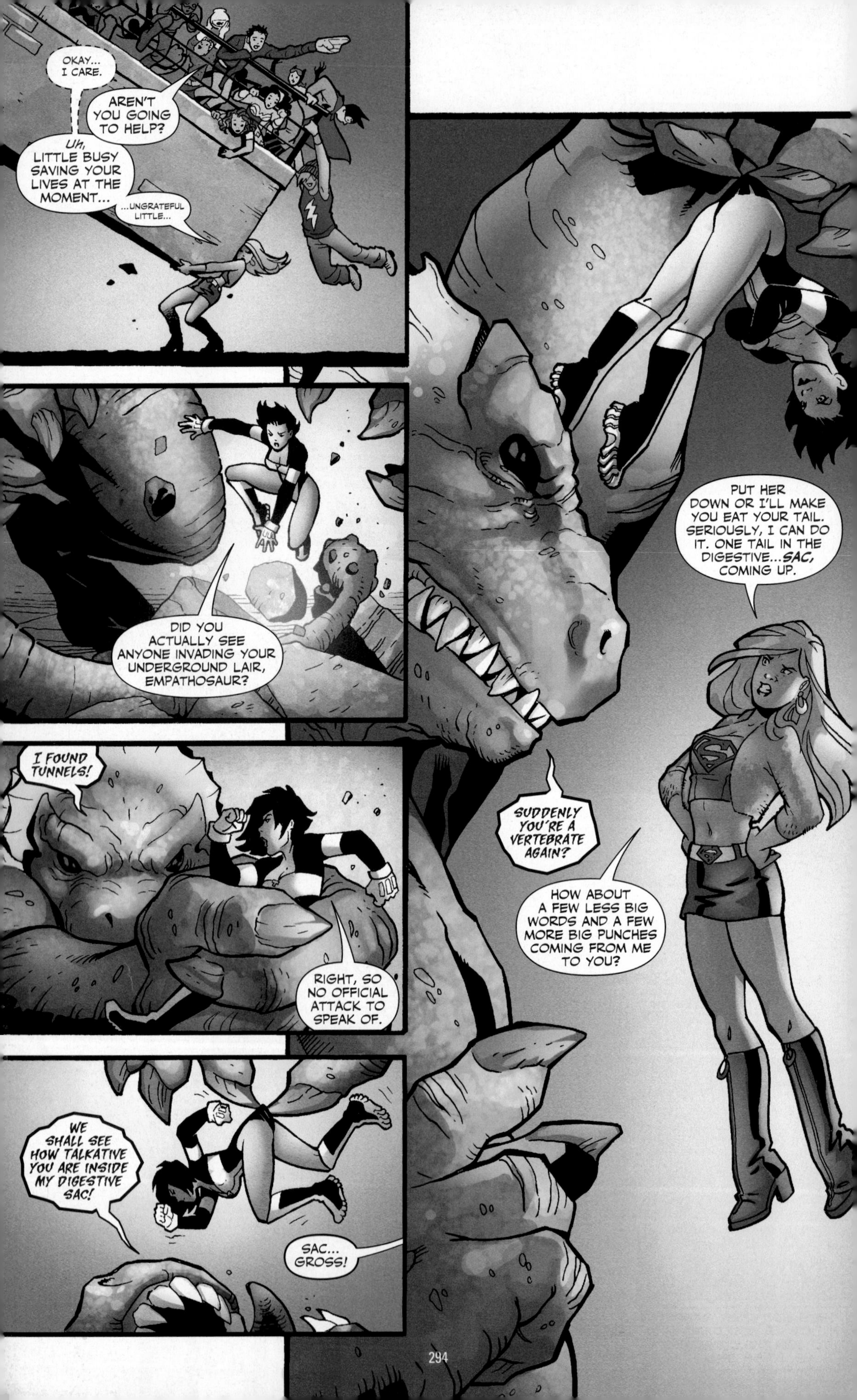
OKAY... I CARE.
AREN'T YOU GOING TO HELP?
Uh, LITTLE BUSY SAVING YOUR LIVES AT THE MOMENT...
...UNGRATEFUL LITTLE...
DID YOU ACTUALLY SEE ANYONE INVADING YOUR UNDERGROUND LAIR, EMPATHOSAUR?
I FOUND TUNNELS!
RIGHT, SO NO OFFICIAL ATTACK TO SPEAK OF.
WE SHALL SEE HOW TALKATIVE YOU ARE INSIDE MY DIGESTIVE SAC!
SAC... GROSS!
PUT HER DOWN OR I'LL MAKE YOU EAT YOUR TAIL. SERIOUSLY, I CAN DO IT. ONE TAIL IN THE DIGESTIVE...SAC, COMING UP.
SUDDENLY YOU'RE A VERTEBRATE AGAIN?
HOW ABOUT A FEW LESS BIG WORDS AND A FEW MORE BIG PUNCHES COMING FROM ME TO YOU?

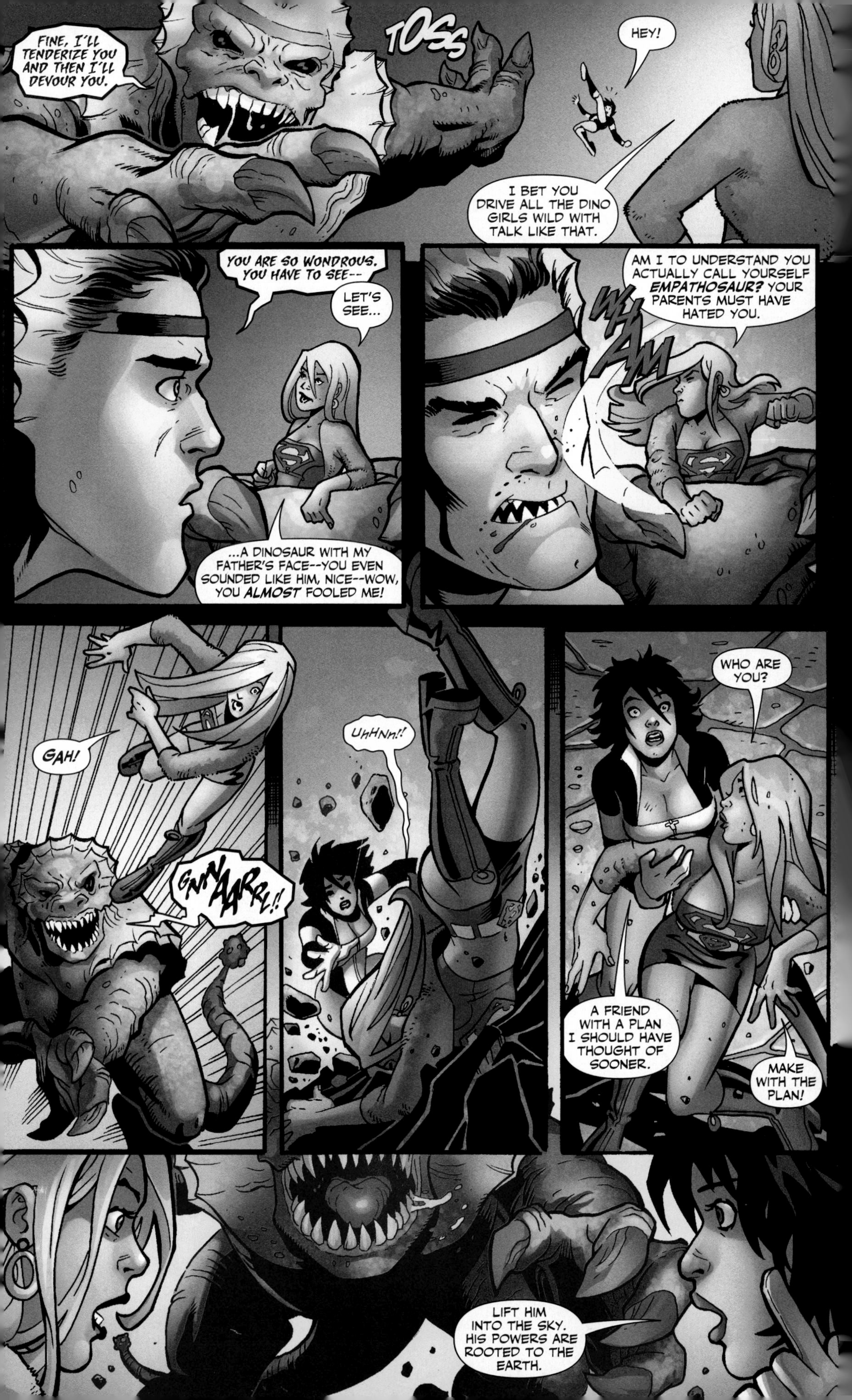
FINE, I'LL TENDERIZE YOU AND THEN I'LL DEVOUR YOU.
TOSS
HEY!
I BET YOU DRIVE ALL THE DINO GIRLS WILD WITH TALK LIKE THAT.
YOU ARE SO WONDROUS. YOU HAVE TO SEE--
LET'S SEE...
...A DINOSAUR WITH MY FATHER'S FACE--YOU EVEN SOUNDED LIKE HIM, NICE--WOW, YOU ALMOST FOOLED ME!
AM I TO UNDERSTAND YOU ACTUALLY CALL YOURSELF EMPATHOSAUR? YOUR PARENTS MUST HAVE HATED YOU.
WHAM
GAH!
GNNAARRL!!
UhHNn!!
WHO ARE YOU?
A FRIEND WITH A PLAN I SHOULD HAVE THOUGHT OF SOONER.
MAKE WITH THE PLAN!
LIFT HIM INTO THE SKY. HIS POWERS ARE ROOTED TO THE EARTH.

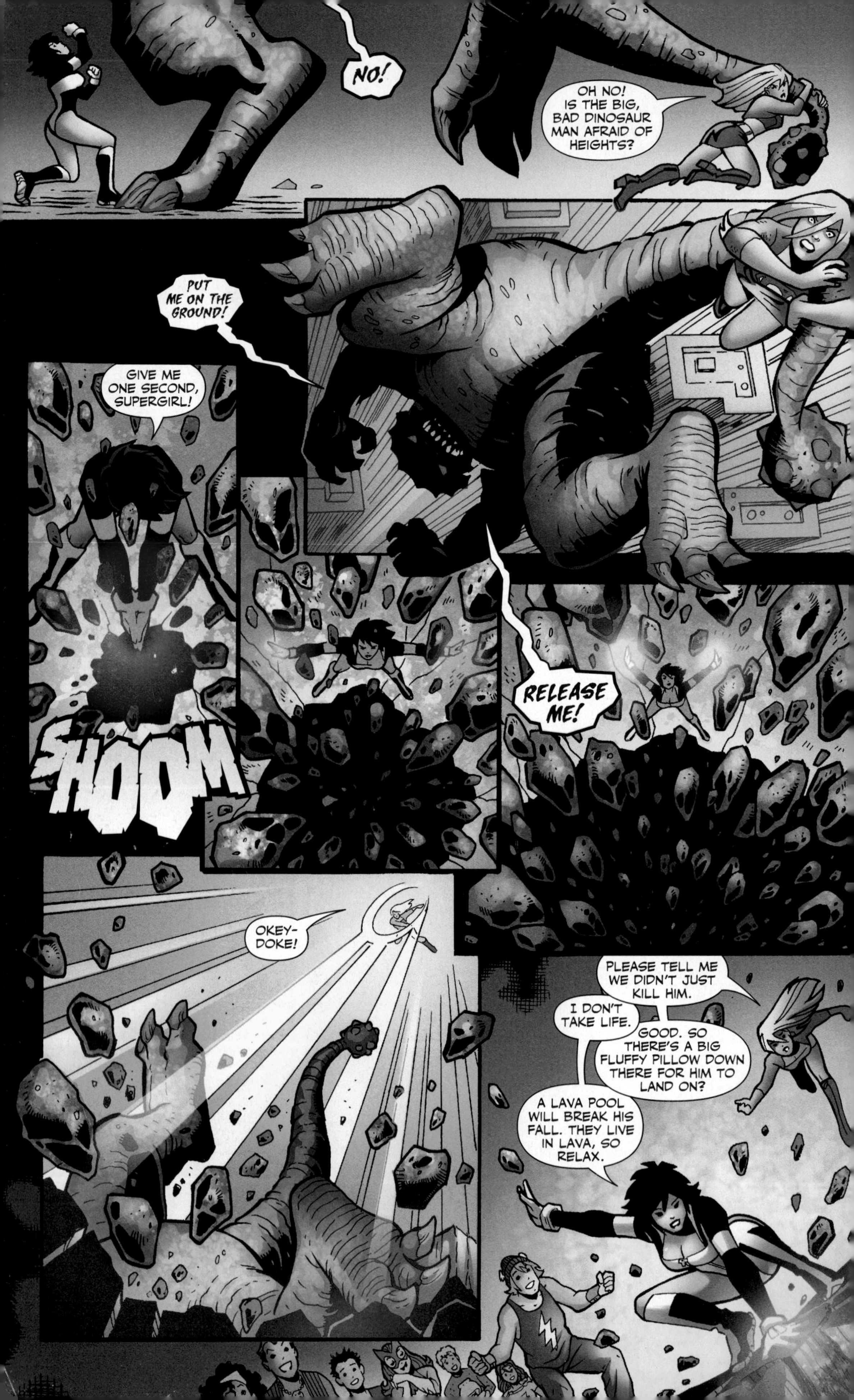
NO!
OH NO! IS THE BIG, BAD DINOSAUR MAN AFRAID OF HEIGHTS?
PUT ME ON THE GROUND!
GIVE ME ONE SECOND, SUPERGIRL!
SHOOM
RELEASE ME!
OKEY-DOKE!
PLEASE TELL ME WE DIDN'T JUST KILL HIM.
I DON'T TAKE LIFE.
GOOD. SO THERE'S A BIG FLUFFY PILLOW DOWN THERE FOR HIM TO LAND ON?
A LAVA POOL WILL BREAK HIS FALL. THEY LIVE IN LAVA, SO RELAX.

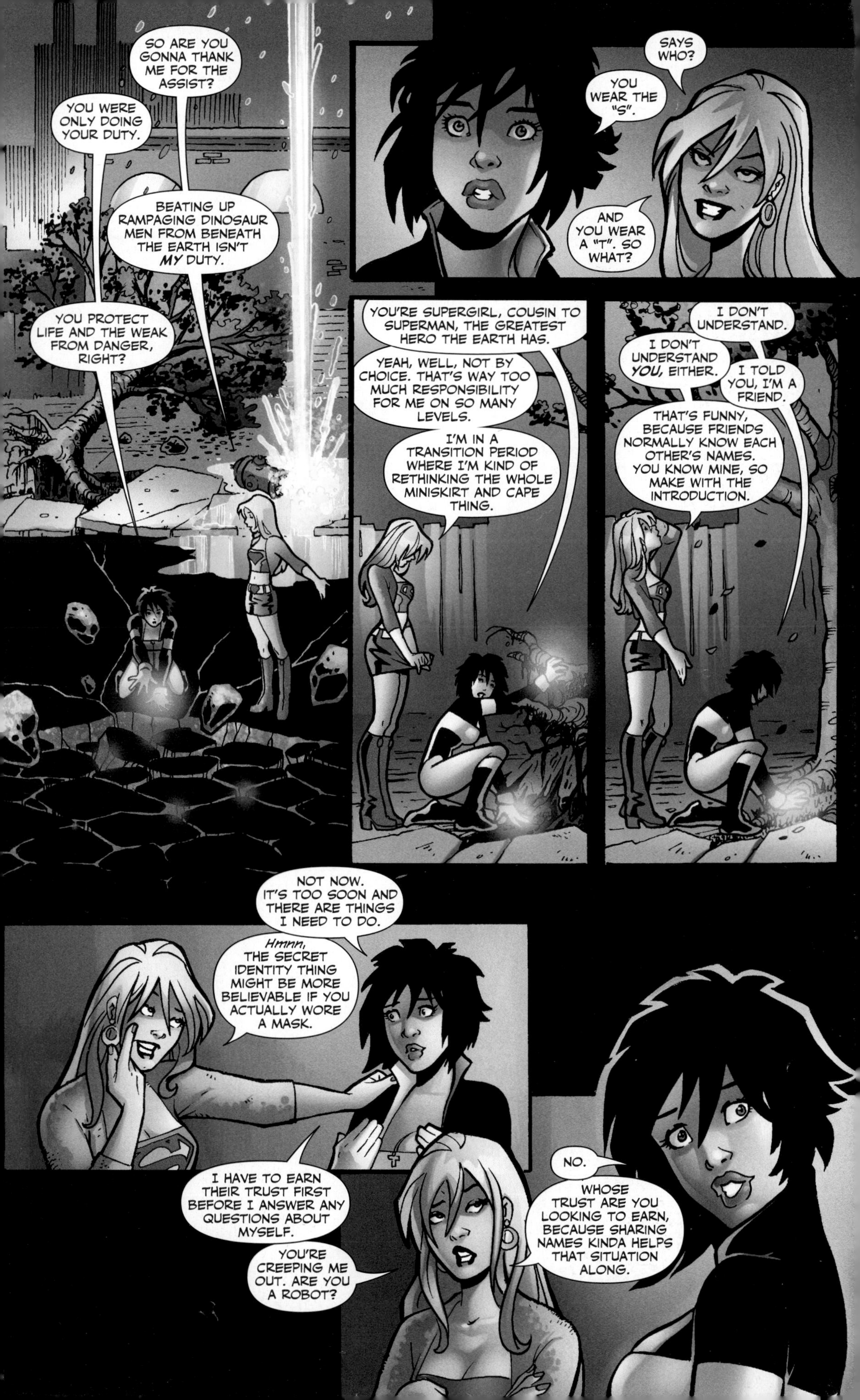

SO ARE YOU GONNA THANK ME FOR THE ASSIST?
YOU WERE ONLY DOING YOUR DUTY.
BEATING UP RAMPAGING DINOSAUR MEN FROM BENEATH THE EARTH ISN'T *MY* DUTY.
YOU PROTECT LIFE AND THE WEAK FROM DANGER, RIGHT?
SAYS WHO?
YOU WEAR THE "S".
AND YOU WEAR A "T". SO WHAT?
YOU'RE SUPERGIRL, COUSIN TO SUPERMAN, THE GREATEST HERO THE EARTH HAS.
YEAH, WELL, NOT BY CHOICE. THAT'S WAY TOO MUCH RESPONSIBILITY FOR ME ON SO MANY LEVELS.
I'M IN A TRANSITION PERIOD WHERE I'M KIND OF RETHINKING THE WHOLE MINISKIRT AND CAPE THING.
I DON'T UNDERSTAND.
I DON'T UNDERSTAND *YOU,* EITHER.
I TOLD YOU, I'M A FRIEND.
THAT'S FUNNY, BECAUSE FRIENDS NORMALLY KNOW EACH OTHER'S NAMES. YOU KNOW MINE, SO MAKE WITH THE INTRODUCTION.
NOT NOW. IT'S TOO SOON AND THERE ARE THINGS I NEED TO DO.
Hmnn, THE SECRET IDENTITY THING MIGHT BE MORE BELIEVABLE IF YOU ACTUALLY WORE A MASK.
I HAVE TO EARN THEIR TRUST FIRST BEFORE I ANSWER ANY QUESTIONS ABOUT MYSELF.
YOU'RE CREEPING ME OUT. ARE YOU A ROBOT?
NO.
WHOSE TRUST ARE YOU LOOKING TO EARN, BECAUSE SHARING NAMES KINDA HELPS THAT SITUATION ALONG.

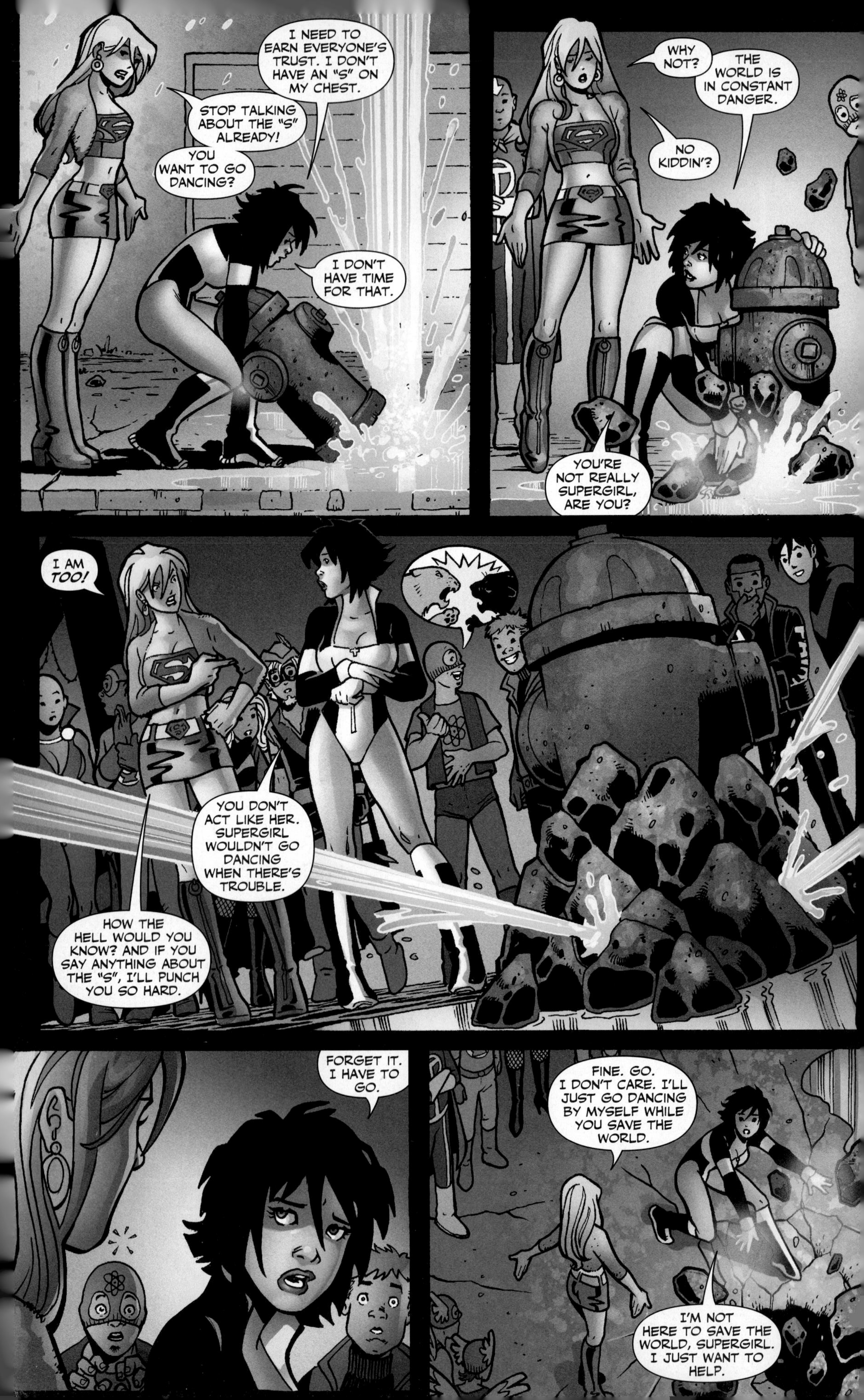
I NEED TO EARN EVERYONE'S TRUST. I DON'T HAVE AN "S" ON MY CHEST.
STOP TALKING ABOUT THE "S" ALREADY!
YOU WANT TO GO DANCING?
I DON'T HAVE TIME FOR THAT.
WHY NOT?
THE WORLD IS IN CONSTANT DANGER.
NO KIDDIN'?
YOU'RE NOT REALLY SUPERGIRL, ARE YOU?
I AM TOO!
YOU DON'T ACT LIKE HER. SUPERGIRL WOULDN'T GO DANCING WHEN THERE'S TROUBLE.
HOW THE HELL WOULD YOU KNOW? AND IF YOU SAY ANYTHING ABOUT THE "S", I'LL PUNCH YOU SO HARD.
FORGET IT. I HAVE TO GO.
FINE. GO. I DON'T CARE. I'LL JUST GO DANCING BY MYSELF WHILE YOU SAVE THE WORLD.
I'M NOT HERE TO SAVE THE WORLD, SUPERGIRL. I JUST WANT TO HELP.

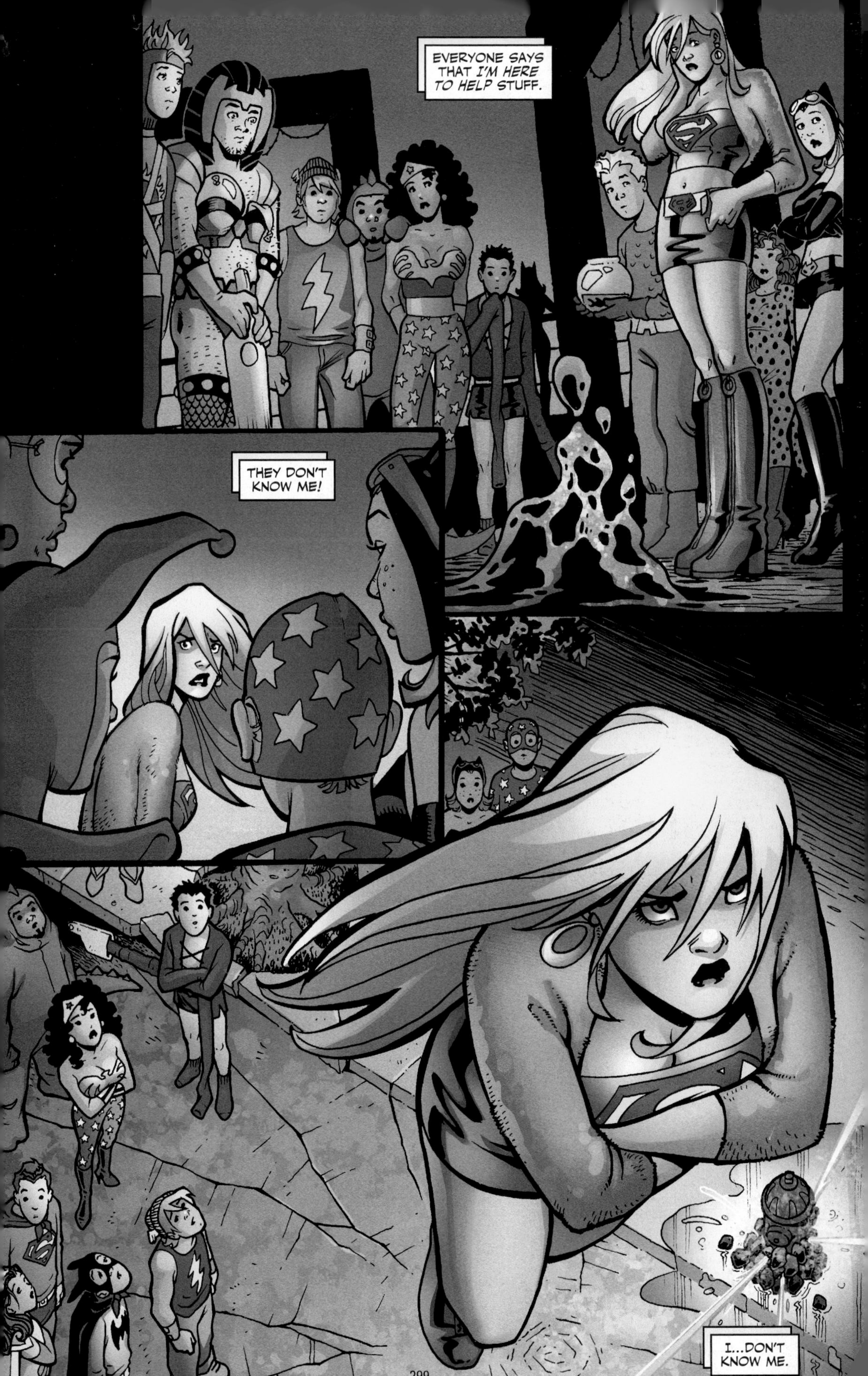
EVERYONE SAYS THAT I'M HERE TO HELP STUFF.
THEY DON'T KNOW ME!
I...DON'T KNOW ME.

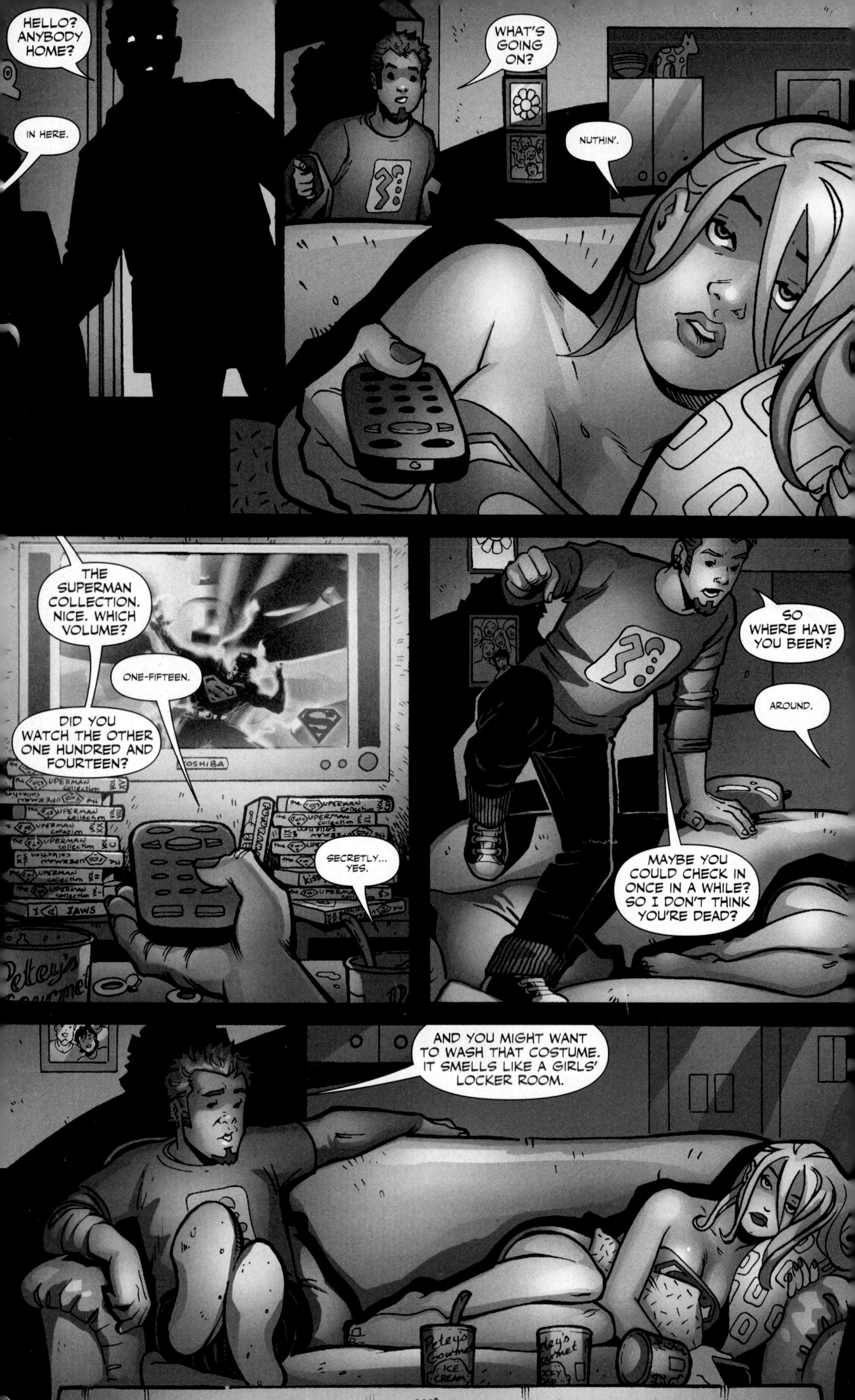
HELLO? ANYBODY HOME?
IN HERE.
WHAT'S GOING ON?
NUTHIN'.
THE SUPERMAN COLLECTION. NICE. WHICH VOLUME?
ONE-FIFTEEN.
DID YOU WATCH THE OTHER ONE HUNDRED AND FOURTEEN?
SECRETLY... YES.
SO WHERE HAVE YOU BEEN?
AROUND.
MAYBE YOU COULD CHECK IN ONCE IN A WHILE? SO I DON'T THINK YOU'RE DEAD?
AND YOU MIGHT WANT TO WASH THAT COSTUME. IT SMELLS LIKE A GIRLS' LOCKER ROOM.

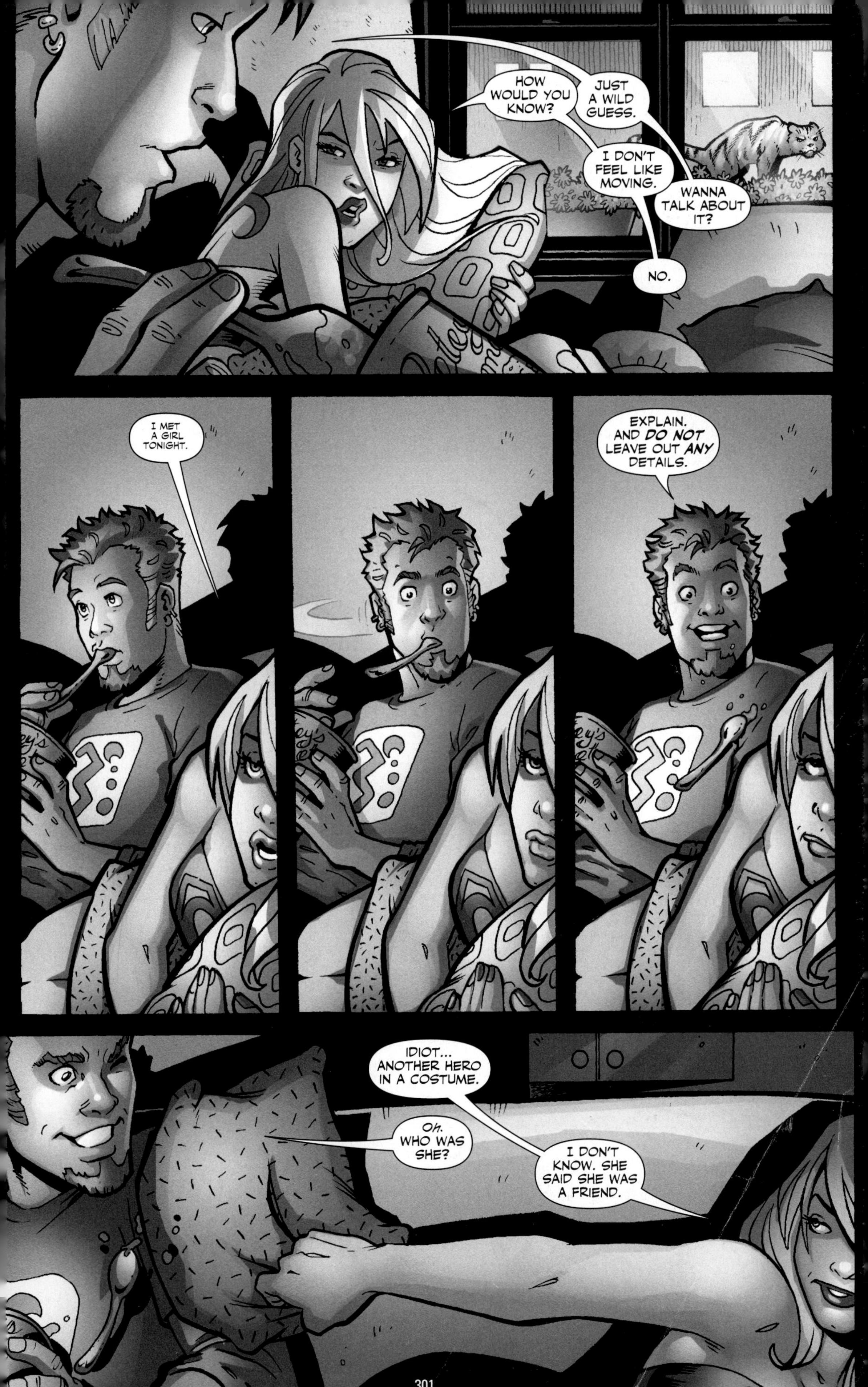
HOW WOULD YOU KNOW?
JUST A WILD GUESS.
I DON'T FEEL LIKE MOVING.
WANNA TALK ABOUT IT?
NO.
I MET A GIRL TONIGHT.
EXPLAIN. AND DO NOT LEAVE OUT ANY DETAILS.
IDIOT... ANOTHER HERO IN A COSTUME.
OH. WHO WAS SHE?
I DON'T KNOW. SHE SAID SHE WAS A FRIEND.

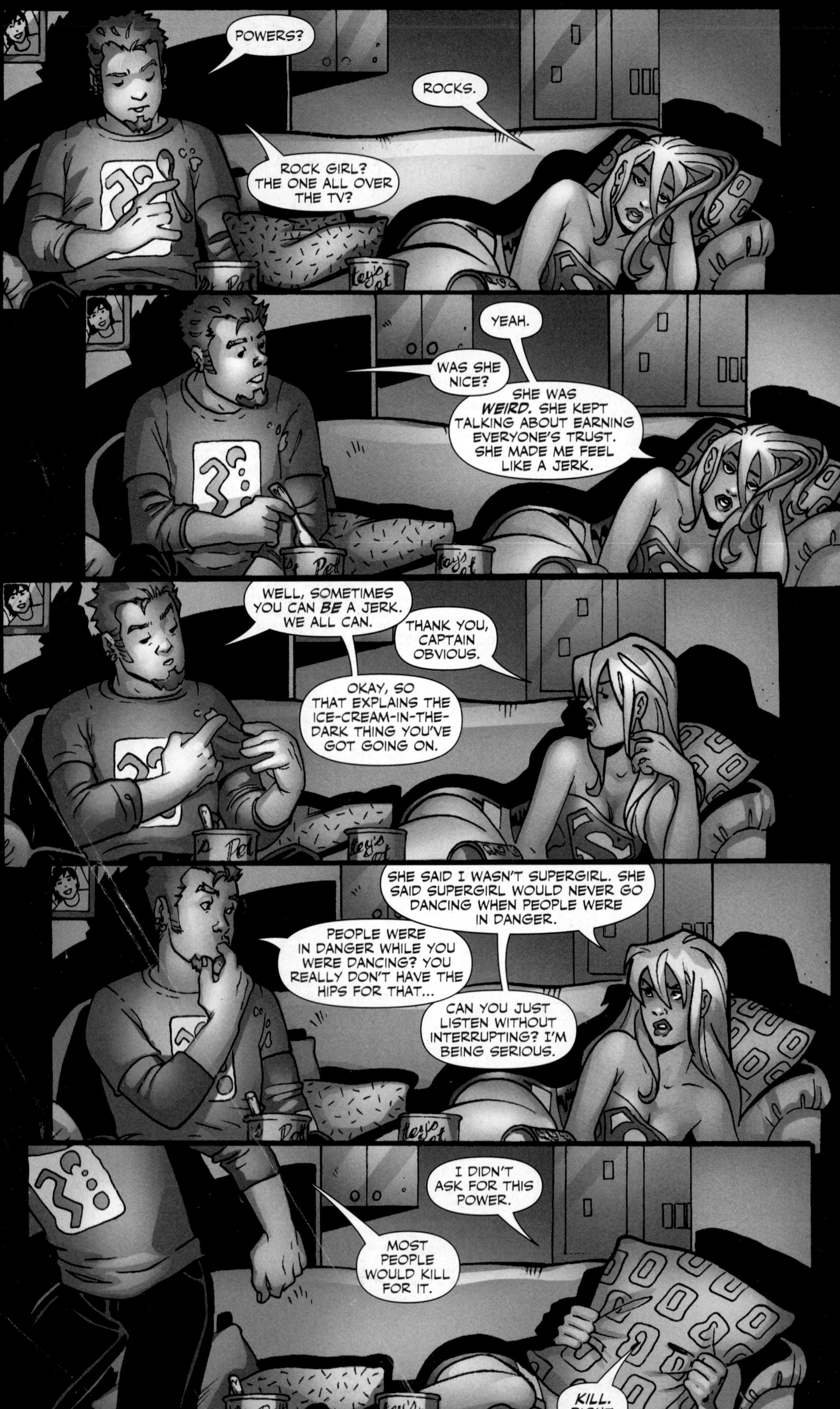
POWERS?
ROCKS.
ROCK GIRL? THE ONE ALL OVER THE TV?
YEAH.
WAS SHE NICE?
SHE WAS *WEIRD.* SHE KEPT TALKING ABOUT EARNING EVERYONE'S TRUST. SHE MADE ME FEEL LIKE A JERK.
WELL, SOMETIMES YOU CAN *BE* A JERK. WE ALL CAN.
THANK YOU, CAPTAIN OBVIOUS.
OKAY, SO THAT EXPLAINS THE ICE-CREAM-IN-THE-DARK THING YOU'VE GOT GOING ON.
SHE SAID I WASN'T SUPERGIRL. SHE SAID SUPERGIRL WOULD NEVER GO DANCING WHEN PEOPLE WERE IN DANGER.
PEOPLE WERE IN DANGER WHILE YOU WERE DANCING? YOU REALLY DON'T HAVE THE HIPS FOR THAT...
CAN YOU JUST LISTEN WITHOUT INTERRUPTING? I'M BEING SERIOUS.
I DIDN'T ASK FOR THIS POWER.
MOST PEOPLE WOULD KILL FOR IT.
KILL. RIGHT.

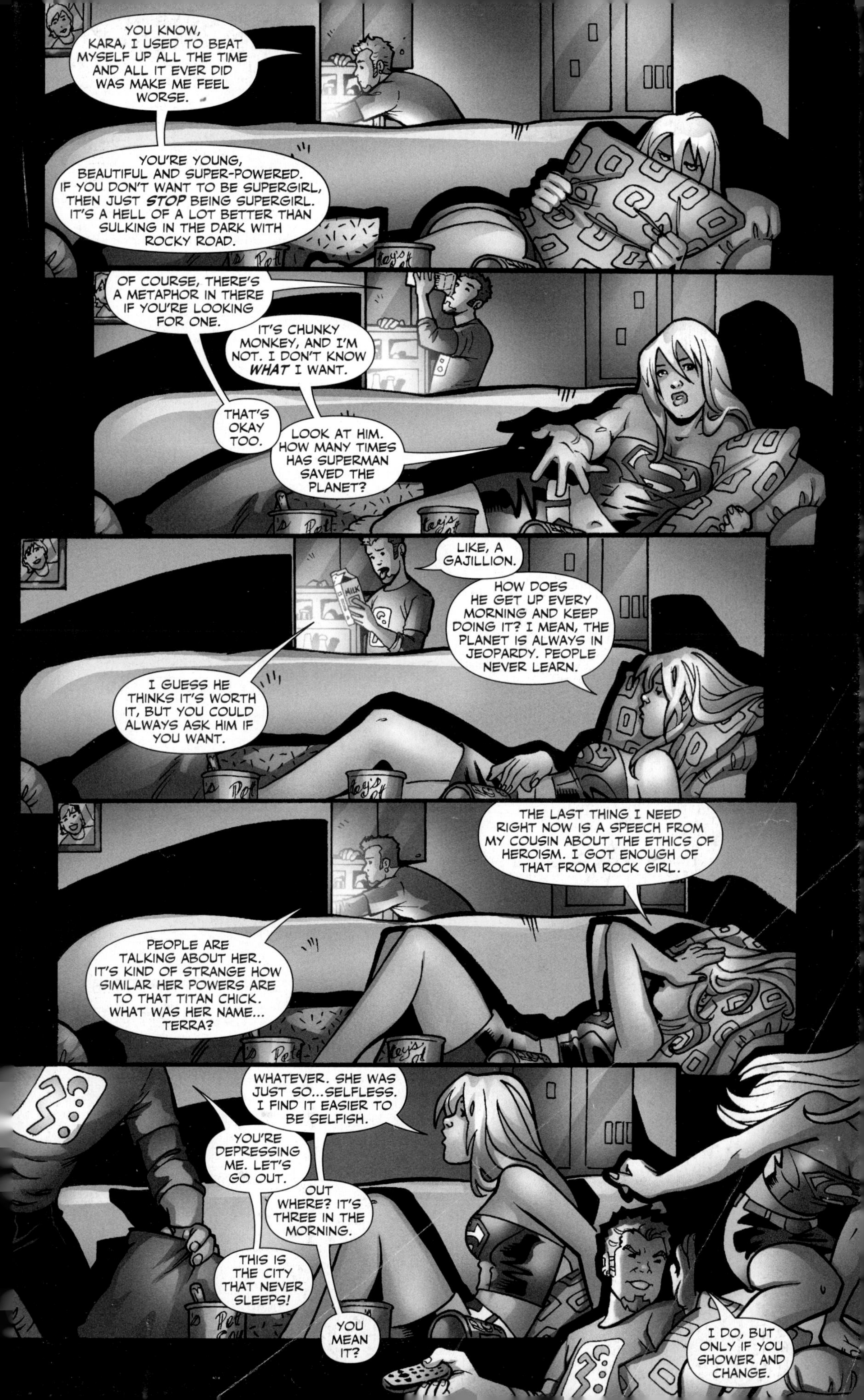
YOU KNOW, KARA, I USED TO BEAT MYSELF UP ALL THE TIME AND ALL IT EVER DID WAS MAKE ME FEEL WORSE.
YOU'RE YOUNG, BEAUTIFUL AND SUPER-POWERED. IF YOU DON'T WANT TO BE SUPERGIRL, THEN JUST STOP BEING SUPERGIRL. IT'S A HELL OF A LOT BETTER THAN SULKING IN THE DARK WITH ROCKY ROAD.
OF COURSE, THERE'S A METAPHOR IN THERE IF YOU'RE LOOKING FOR ONE.
IT'S CHUNKY MONKEY, AND I'M NOT. I DON'T KNOW WHAT I WANT.
THAT'S OKAY TOO.
LOOK AT HIM. HOW MANY TIMES HAS SUPERMAN SAVED THE PLANET?
LIKE, A GAJILLION.
HOW DOES HE GET UP EVERY MORNING AND KEEP DOING IT? I MEAN, THE PLANET IS ALWAYS IN JEOPARDY. PEOPLE NEVER LEARN.
I GUESS HE THINKS IT'S WORTH IT, BUT YOU COULD ALWAYS ASK HIM IF YOU WANT.
THE LAST THING I NEED RIGHT NOW IS A SPEECH FROM MY COUSIN ABOUT THE ETHICS OF HEROISM. I GOT ENOUGH OF THAT FROM ROCK GIRL.
PEOPLE ARE TALKING ABOUT HER. IT'S KIND OF STRANGE HOW SIMILAR HER POWERS ARE TO THAT TITAN CHICK. WHAT WAS HER NAME... TERRA?
WHATEVER. SHE WAS JUST SO...SELFLESS. I FIND IT EASIER TO BE SELFISH.
YOU'RE DEPRESSING ME. LET'S GO OUT.
OUT WHERE? IT'S THREE IN THE MORNING.
THIS IS THE CITY THAT NEVER SLEEPS!
YOU MEAN IT?
I DO, BUT ONLY IF YOU SHOWER AND CHANGE.

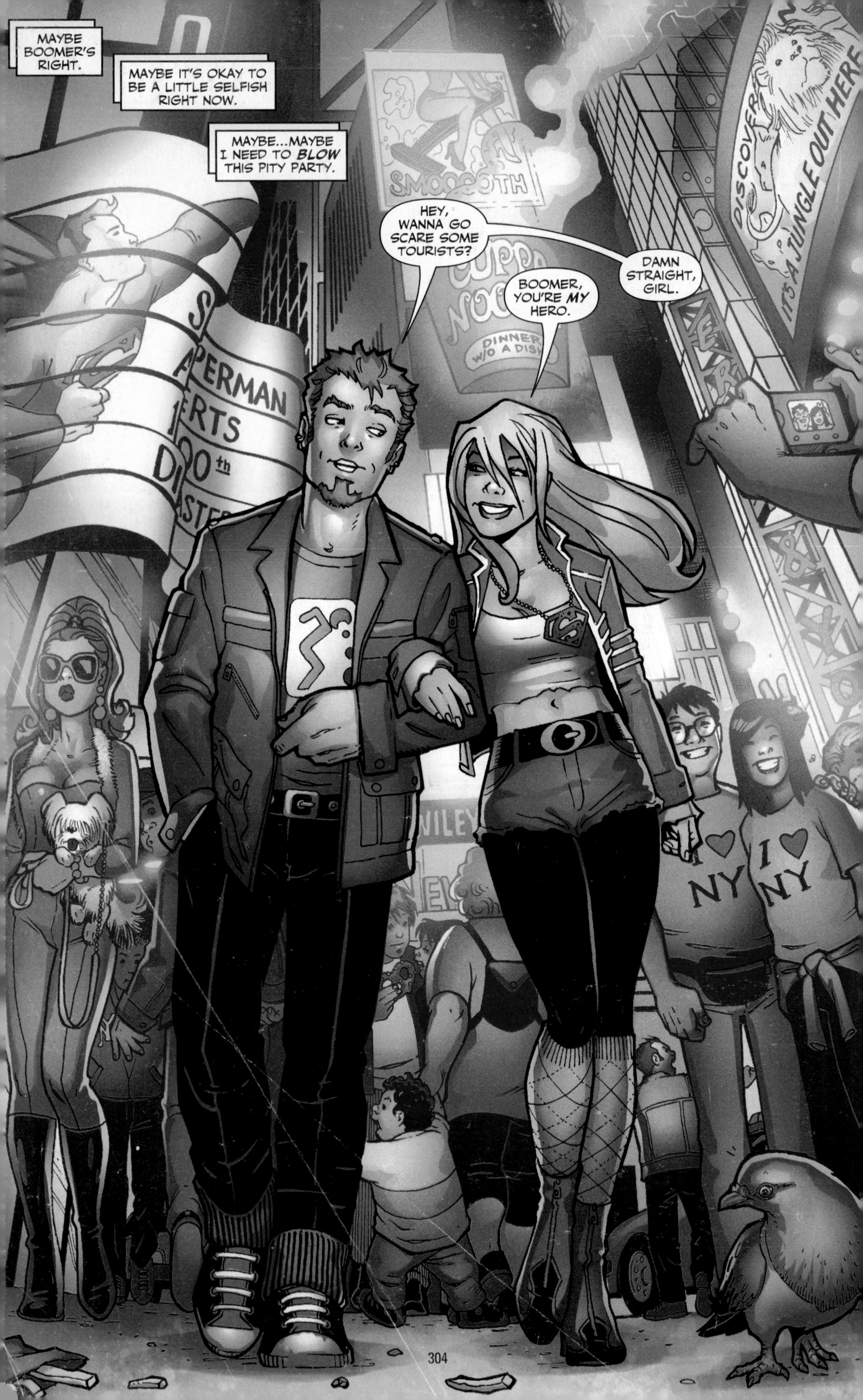
MAYBE BOOMER'S RIGHT.
MAYBE IT'S OKAY TO BE A LITTLE SELFISH RIGHT NOW.
MAYBE...MAYBE I NEED TO *BLOW* THIS PITY PARTY.
HEY, WANNA GO SCARE SOME TOURISTS?
BOOMER, YOU'RE *MY* HERO.
DAMN STRAIGHT, GIRL.
SMOOOOTH
DINNER W/O A DISH
DISCOVER
IT'S A JUNGLE OUT HERE
PERMAN
RTS
00th
I NY
I NY